PERSPECTIVES ON MENTAL REPRESENTATION

Experimental and Theoretical Studies of Cognitive Processes and Capacities

PERSPECTIVES ON MENTAL REPRESENTATION
Experimental and Theoretical Studies of Cognitive Processes and Capacities

Edited by

Jacques Mehler
Ecole Des Hautes Etudes En Sciences Sociales

Edward C. T. Walker
Merrill Garrett
Massachusetts Institute of Technology

LEA LAWRENCE ERLBAUM ASSOCIATES, PUBLISHERS
1982   Hillsdale, New Jersey   London

Lawrence Erlbaum Associates, Inc., Publishers
365 Broadway
Hillsdale, New Jersey 07642

Library of Congress Cataloging in Publication Data

Perspectives on mental representation.

Bibliography: p.
Includes indexes.
1. Cognition. 2. Human information processing.
3. Psycholinguistics. 4. Neuropsychology. I. Mehler,
Jacques. II. Walker, Edward C. T. III. Garrett,
Merrill F. [DNLM: 1. Cognition. 2. Speech perception.
3. Language development. BF 311 P467]
BF311.P374 1982   153   82-7275
ISBN 0-89859-194-5   AACR2

Printed in the United States of America
10 9 8 7 6 5 4 3 2 1

Contents

Preface

The domain of interest normally going under the heading of Cognition is one that has greatly developed in the past decade. To a large extent the precursors of this boom can be located with relative ease. After the important paper of Lashley entitled the problems of serial order in behavior, and the impact of Chomsky's mentalistic position in linguistics and psychology, many developments took place in the sixties. On the one hand, we can focus on the impact that computer science had in psychology. Indeed, computers not only entered the psychological laboratories as experimental tools but also as models of human mental activity. The theories and explanations of behavior took the form of simulations or of information processing accounts of the interaction of individuals and the context in which they were operating. On the other hand, we must also stress the great importance that some formal branches had in promoting new conceptions of behavior. Throughout the past two decades Chomsky and his coworkers presented grammars conceived of as theoretical accounts of the underlying capacity an organism must embody in order for it to be capable of acquiring natural languages. The stress thus shifted from the study of corpora of actual language behavior to the analysis of grammatical competence at least insofar as linguistics was concerned. If we also add that, for many formal linguists, the study of grammars is part of theoretical cognitive psychology, we can grasp the major effect that the progress in linguistics has had upon our field.

To these influences we may add a third. The neurosciences have thrived greatly in the past ten years and their effect upon cognitive psychology has been felt more intensely in these times. Furthermore, the kinds of inductions that can be made about the mental abilities required in order to acquire competencies in domains as distinct as language performance, logical thought, and perception, require us to dwell upon the specificity of the human mind that make these possible.

Once such specificities are postulated, the exploration of possible relations of the human mind to the nervous system are immediately part of the most exciting problem that can be raised within the domain.

It is not, of course, that the problem is a new one in the history of ideas. It is, rather, that we are facing an old problem with new tools and conceptions. And if the issues are fascinating, the dangers are also great. Indeed, pressure exists both from the neurosciences on the one hand and the formal disciplines on the other to neglect the functional accounts that are the proper domain of cognitive psychology. Only by making an adequate account of the functional capacities and properties of the device can the link between behavioral capacities and the physical structure responsible for performance be understood. If a structure is discovered in the cortex but no idea is to be had as to its function, it is most obvious that the account of the way in which that structure works cannot help us understand the relations among functional systems or their outputs. Thus, it is of interest to the neuroscientist and the formalist as well as the psychologist to work with some coordinated understanding of the relationship obtaining between these different ways of describing human behavior.

Nowhere is the need for this theoretical, neuroscientific, and psychological approach more evident than in the domain of child psychology. Decades of almost exclusive dedication to the study of acquisition and development failed to yield a clear indication as to the way in which an organism acquires novel conceptual knowledge, and a sort of morosity seems to have overcome practitioners in those areas. An exception, however, of the past decade has been the field of infant psychology. It has experienced incredible growth. This reflects a shift in theoretical stance among infant psychologists. The beliefs of behavioristically oriented theoreticians led to years of research based on the premise that general purpose learning devices could cope with the acquisition of novel behavior. The modification or abandonment of that presumption has led to wide ranging efforts to understand the special properties of infant capacities in different behavioral domains. One of the reasons the situation in cognitive psychology is so exciting today is that there has been so much suggestive progress in our appreciation of the invariant properties of the human mind and its underlying neural specification, yet so little development of our ability to apply that to accounts of how the growth of encyclopaedic knowledge results in changes in the flexibility and power of the invariant properties of mind.

That problem challenges us not only for individual human development but also for broader achievements of the human mind. Although some views are available to explain some of the ways in which the organism can and does gain information and stores it for future use, we have no ideas how it can be that major changes in the history of intellectual disciplines embody not only an encyclopaedic increase but also some major conceptual growth as well. A case in point is the history of mathematics and logic, even if we are reluctant to include some such domains as relativity and quantum physics. Obviously, the kinds of conceptual tools that go into these domains are not the kind available, except in the most precursor-like fashion, to the primitive inhabitant of the planet a few millenia back. Thus, the history of ideas shows growth in conceptual terms, but we have no more certain understanding of it than we do of its apparent existence within a single individual. It is one of the many riddles that cognitive psychology will have to solve in the future.

Other riddles have to do with the relative status of analogical and propositional representations in the mind. Indeed, in the past few years the data gathered in several laboratories has convinced many of us of the great capacity for analogical thought. Images and imagery in general have come back as a main chapter in cognitive psychology, but though the phenomena are apparent, the explanatory status of imagery is poor. We cannot recapitulate the debates in the domain but the conundrum confronting the theoretician should be pointed out. Even though images are necessary postulates to account for such processes as mental rotation or responding to questions about geography, the notion of image is descriptive. The aim of psychology is to give an explanatory account of how the mind works, not to merely describe the possible functions. Specifying how images are generated as well as what their structural properties are is required. Something is known about the latter domain but relatively little in the first domain seems established.

Our field is clearly in need of explanatory accounts for many different areas. This volume presents statements of the status of research in several areas by scholars at the forefront of our discipline. It tries at the same time to juxtapose theoretical and experimental perspectives in order to display some of the major lines of tension in the field.

Some comment is called for to explain to the reader the origin, if not the justification, for many of the papers included in this volume. Two years ago one of us was asked by the CNRS to organize a conference in France to disseminate information as to the state of the art in Cognitive psychology. It is of some interest that this was a necessary thing to do since the domain of the field seems so obviously to transcend disciplinary boundaries. However, the particular status of Cognitive psychology, as an intermediary between humanistic disciplines and natural science, has tended to increase the provincial reflexes of the practitioners in the different areas of the world. Of course, not all is bad in such a state of affairs. But, perhaps it is time for systematic dialogue to begin. The conference from which the present book evolved is part of that dialogue.

Jacques Mehler
Edward Walker
Merrill Garrett

PERSPECTIVES ON MENTAL REPRESENTATION

Experimental and Theoretical Studies
of Cognitive Processes and Capacities

THEORETICAL PERSPECTIVES

1 On the Representation of Form and Function

Noam Chomsky
Massachusetts Institute of Technology

I have departed from the title assigned me, though not really from the topic. It has repeatedly been suggested that there is a rationalist flavor to much recent work in cognitive psychology, specifically, in the study of language. I think this is correct, and not uninteresting. There are, I think, certain leading ideas in what we might reasonably call "rationalist psychology" that can and should be adapted as part of a framework for contemporary study of language and cognition more generally. Among these are the concern for intrinsic determinants of knowledge and perception: innate structures of mind that take a specific form under the effect of experience, and modes of cognition that play a central role in determining what and how we perceive and think. A related notion, emphasized by Descartes and perhaps his most lasting contribution to psychology, is that our interpretation of the world is based in part on representational systems that derive from the structure of the mind itself and do not mirror in any direct way the form of things in the external world. Descartes offers the account of how a blind man comes to know the character of things he touches with a stick; the "resistance and movement of these bodies which is the only cause of the sensations he has of them" is "in no way similar to the ideas that he conceives of them," the latter forming part of an abstract system of representation. Similarly, in normal vision a sequence of visual sensations evokes in the mind the idea of an object that is "in no way similar" to these sensations or their organization, but rather is based on abstract systems of coding in terms of intrinsic systems of mental representation. We see a triangle, though the mind has been presented with a sequence of curves and angles that are parts of a (distorted) geometrical figure. To take a contemporary example, presented with a sequence of 2-dimensional images the mind might construct the "idea" of a 3-dimensional rigid body that could have given rise to them under motion, perhaps using Shimon Ullman's rigidity principle for determining structure from motion. The "blind man with a stick" model of perception is a central component in Descartes's doctrine of innate ideas. Related notions have arisen in contemporary work, and in my view at least, point to some of the directions that should be followed as we try to assimilate the study of cognition to the natural sciences.

I would like to discuss some of the ways in which ideas of this sort have entered research on language in the past several decades. The study of generative grammar in the modern sense—there are, of course, various antecedents, which I will not discuss—was marked by a significant shift in focus in the study of language. To put it briefly, the focus of attention was shifted from "language" to "grammar." In earlier work, and much contemporary work as well, the object of inquiry is taken to be a particular language, or perhaps general properties of many or all languages. From this point of view, we might think of language, following Aristotle's familiar phrase, as sound with a meaning. The English language, then, would be regarded as a set of pairs (s,m) where s is a certain real world object, a physical sound, and m is its meaning. The linguist's theoretical notions are based on these objects. If, for example, the sound s is regarded as a sequence of phonemes, then the phonemes are taken to be bundles of features that literally inhere in successive segments of the physical event, or sets of such segments constructed on the basis of principles of classification. Other linguistic units are constructed by means of various principles of segmentation and classification of parts of s. Morphemes are sequences of phonemes, phrases are classes of sequences of morphemes or words, and so on. The grammar of a language is a description of these elements and their relations, which might be associated with intensional objects (representing meanings) by some sort of compositional rules. (Here and below, I will often ignore obvious type-token distinctions.)

An obvious problem to be faced is that the language, the set of pairs (s,m), is infinite. This is not a logician's quibble. The set of sentences from which we draw in normal conversation or writing, or that we understand with no difficulty, is so vast that for all practical (let alone theoretical) purposes, we might as well take it to be infinite. And as irrelevant constraints of time and attention are removed, we see at once that there are no bounds to our knowledge of the sound-meaning pairing. Without any change in what we know, we can understand new and more complex linguistic expressions, in principle without limit, as constraints on time, attention, and "computing space" are relaxed. It must be true, then, that our knowledge of language is somehow represented as a finite system of rules (a grammar) that determine the properties of the infinite number of sentences of the language. Furthermore, each person who knows a human language has constructed this finite system of rules with infinite scope on the basis of a finite exposure to data which enormously underdetermines its form. It is obvious in principle, and not difficult to show in practice, that we know many things about sound, meaning, and their interrelation for which we have no adequate inductive evidence or confirmation from experience, in any general sense of these notions; and this knowledge is largely shared within a speech community. What is the nature of this knowledge and how does it develop in the mind? If we are concerned with these questions, we enter into the study of generative grammar.

Pursuing these questions, we shift our focus from the language to the grammar represented in the mind/brain. The language now becomes an epiphenomenon; it is whatever is characterized by the rules of the grammar (perhaps, in conjunction with other systems of mind, or even other factors, depending on how we choose to conceive of the notion "language"). The grammar in a person's mind/brain is real; it is one of the real things in the world. The language (whatever that may be) is not. From the point of view I am taking, there is no need to suppose that the notion "language" is well-defined at all. One can define it as one likes—as a social phenomenon of some sort, a system of conventions and shared practices, a pairing of linguistic objects and truth conditions, an ideal object of some sort, or whatever. But the grammar, a real object, is what it is: a system of rules that is in fact represented somehow in the mind/brain, more or less in the same way among individuals whom we may choose (from some other point of view) to think of as "speakers of a given language." We may perfectly well think of the grammar of, say, English, as assigning a structural description to every possible sound. Some will be characterized simply as noise, others as sounds of perhaps some language (but not mine), others as expressions of my language with some figurative interpretation, others as paired with strict "literal interpretations," and so on. The question "what is the language generated by the grammar? is not well-defined, and it does not seem very important to try to sharpen it. What is important is to determine the rules and principles of the grammars and the kinds of structures they assign to expressions; and further, to discover how these systems arise in the mind and how they interact with other systems in thought, expression, action, and interpretation.

Pursuing this course, we need no longer think of the linguist's theoretical notions as constructed in some way out of the phonetic or semantic materials. Rather, the linguist is studying mentally-represented rules and the representations they generate. Phonemic representation, for example, is one mode of mental representation, with its specific properties and relations to other modes of representation. It is mapped into sound in some fashion that must be made precise, but there is no reason to suppose that its basic elements will correspond to physically isolable segments of sound or their features. The same is true of other levels of mental representation. At certain levels—syllables or words, for example—elements of mental representation may correspond in a simple way to isolable physical events. At other levels, this appears not to be true in general. This point of view is developed, for example, in my *Logical Structure of Linguistic Theory* (1955). We are, in short, studying the systems of mental representation that provide our modes of cognition in the case of language, and more deeply, innate principles that select a specific grammar with its highly articulated system of rules and principles, given some interaction with the environment. The rationalist flavor, in the sense of my earlier remarks, is fairly evident, as is the analogy to recent work in other areas of cognitive psychology.

The basic cognitive notion, then, is "knowledge of grammar," not "knowledge of language"; and if we decompose it in relational terms, the basic cognitive relation holds between a person and a grammar. Knowledge of grammar, like knowledge of mathematics, of biology, of the behavior of objects in the physical world, of one's place in a social system, etc., is not expressible as some variety of true belief, as in one standard view. Knowledge of language, so understood, involves or perhaps entails particular instances of *knowledge-that* and *belief-that*—e.g., knowledge that some expression *s* means *m*. But knowledge is not constituted of such elements and no atomistic, element-by-element account of the character or growth of knowledge of this sort is possible. A system of knowledge, in this sense, is an integrated complex represented in the mind, developed in the mind on the basis of some interaction with the environment, but shaped by innate principles of structure and organization and perhaps containing specific innate constituents. There is little reason to believe that all such systems arise in the same way; knowledge of physics and knowledge of language or the behavior of objects appear to arise in radically different ways, for example. We might say that each such cognitive system pertains (in a way that must be made precise) to a specific domain of potential fact, a kind of mentally-constructed world. If there is a domain of actual fact that is not too dissimilar, the cognitive system can be effectively used. The case of language is unusual in that, there being no external standard, the domains of potential and actual fact are identical; *X*'s grammar is just what *X*'s mind constructs. But other cognitive systems can be viewed in much the same way. There is some preliminary discussion of these questions, which I think merit much more careful study, in my *Reflections on Language* (1975) and *Rules and Representations* (1980).

The study of generative grammar has often been criticized as a departure from the canons of the natural sciences in that it is avowedly "mentalistic"—that is, concerned with the rules and representations of the mind/brain—and does not base itself firmly, so it is argued, on the actual events that are observed, such as particular sounds, speech acts, or whatever. To me it seems that exactly the reverse is true. The shift of focus from language (an obscure and I believe ultimately unimportant notion) to grammar is essential if we are to proceed towards assimilating the study of language to the natural sciences. It is a move from data-collection and organization to the study of the real systems that actually exist (in the mind/brain), and that enter into an explanation of the phenomena we observe. Contrary to what is widely assumed, the notion "language" (however characterized) is at a higher order of abstraction and idealization than grammar, and correspondingly, the study of "language" introduces new and more difficult problems. One may ask whether there is any reason to try to clarify or define such a notion and whether any purpose is served in doing so. Perhaps so, but I am skeptical.

I will continue to use the term "language" in something like the usual way, but with the qualifications noted in mind.

Shifting focus from language to grammar, we may think of the grammar attained by an individual as a relatively stable component of transitory mental states. Development of the grammar in the mind involves fairly radical transitions in an early stage of life, but it is reasonably clear that a steady state is attained after which modifications are marginal, and may, for our purposes, be ignored. It also seems clear that little distortion is introduced if we abstract away from such individual differences as may exist and assume that there is a fixed initial state of mind, call it S_0, which constitutes the human language faculty, one component of our common biological endowment, on a par with the factors that determine that we will have a human rather than an insect visual system, or will grow arms rather than wings. In the early years of life, under normal conditions, S_0 is progressively modified and elaborated until it reaches a steady state. The grammar is a characterization of the steady state; the term "universal grammar" is now often used as a characterization of the initial state S_0. With systematic ambiguity, the same terms are used for the steady state and initial state themselves.

Both terms—"grammar" and "universal grammar"—are modified from traditional usage, in accordance with the shift of focus from language to grammar. Universal grammar may be thought of as some system of principles, common to the species and available to each individual prior to experience. It determines the basic character of this experience and of the particular grammars that develop at the steady state; that is, it determines the basic properties of the state of knowledge attained. The principles of universal grammar may be thought of in part as a system that enters into the construction of experience and in part as a function that maps experience into grammar. Endowed with these principles, a system provided with adequate experience will develop a grammar of the peculiar and specific sort characteristic of human language, just as a human visual system develops to a relatively steady state given early interactions with the environment. Lacking these principles, a system will develop no grammar or some different system. The telephone exchange, for example, has "heard" much more English than any of us, but lacking the principles of universal grammar (inter alia), it develops no grammar of English as part of its internal structure.

Qualitative considerations give us some idea of the kind of system we should expect to find in investigating universal grammar. It is, in the first place, obvious that the transition to the steady state is vastly underdetermined by the evidence available. Many simple inductive generalizations are never made. Specific systems develop as part of the attained grammar on the basis of evidence that provides no inductive basis for them, and this is done uniformly and without conscious awareness or effort by all normal speakers. Correspondingly, much of the knowledge attained—knowledge that certain forms have certain meanings, for example—must be regarded as knowledge without (adequate) grounds, warrant, or justification, in any sense of these terms that will bear the burdens required in the tradition of epistemology. It seems, then, that the principles of universal grammar must be highly restrictive. In fact, if some current theories are near the mark, then it seems that only a finite set of grammars is available in principle, for a basic and substantial core of language.

At the same time, languages appear to be highly diverse. Thus, universal grammar must be sufficiently rich in structure to effect the transition from S_0 to a highly specific steady state that is not modeled on experience in any simple way, and yet sufficiently open in structure so as to permit the range of possible human languages. It is natural to assume, then, that universal grammar consists of a system of principles with a certain degree of intricacy and deductive structure, with parameters that can be fixed in one or another way, given a relatively small amount of experience. Small changes in the values assigned to parameters in a rich system may lead to what appear to be radically different grammars, though at a deeper level, they are all cast in the same mold. Something of the sort seems to be what we should expect to discover in the study of universal grammar. It is hardly necessary to emphasize that we are very far from having principles of universal grammar of any depth that appear valid for more than a fraction of existing languages, or more than partially so even for these, not a very surprising state of affairs.

In the work of the past few years, various systems have been studied that begin to exhibit the right properties, I think. This seems to me something new and exciting in the long and productive history of the study of language, something that points the way to a linguistic theory of a new and promising kind. As these systems function and interact, small shifts in parameters do lead to significant differences in the "languages" generated, in some well-studied and nontrivial cases. Luigi Rizzi's work on parameters for subjacency is one example. The ideal is to reach the point where we can literally deduce a particular human grammar by setting parameters of universal grammar in one or another of the permissible ways. The process of so-called "language learning" can then naturally be regarded in part as a process of fixing these values; when they are fixed the "learner" knows the language generated by the grammar that is determined by universal grammar, specified in this way. Such knowledge will far transcend experience if universal grammar is a system with a rich intrinsic structure, and will not be inductively grounded in experience, though without experience there will be no knowledge, and the knowledge attained is a function of experience. Whether such a process should be considered "learning" is an open question; it seems more akin to what we normally call "growth," and perhaps should be understood as the growth of a particular system, a "mental organ," under the triggering and partially shaping effect of experience. I think that many other crucial aspects of cognitive development and attainment of systems of knowledge and belief should be approached in more or less the same manner.

Let us now turn to some more specific questions. What kinds of mental representation should we expect a grammar to generate? Suppose that we begin with the Aristotelian conception of language as sound with a meaning. Then the grammar will generate representations of sound and representations of meaning. Actually, what we want is something a bit more abstract. The representation of sound in the grammar will not determine the physical event corresponding to the linguistic expression with this representation. Different utterances of a single speaker, or of different speakers, will differ in their physical properties though we consider them instances of the same sentence. The representation of sound given by the grammar interacts with other systems to yield a physical event. The representation of sound is the contribution of the grammar, of the speaker's knowledge of language, to the physical event, and is thus more abstract than a characterization of the physical properties of a specific utterance.

Much the same is true of representations of meaning. For example, one aspect of meaning involves truth conditions, but in general sentences do not have truth conditions; rather, sentences (at least, some sentences) can be used to make statements which have truth conditions. To take an example of the sort discussed by John Austin, the sentence

(1)   Boston is 200 miles from New York

is neither true nor false in itself. For one thing, there may be several cities named "Boston" and what is said using this sentence may be true for one choice but not for another. Furthermore, even if the reference is fixed (a matter that raises many problems), truth value is still indeterminate. Suppose that an instance of (1) is produced in answer to a query motivated by uncertainty as to whether to fly or walk from Boston to New York. Then the statement would be judged to be true. Suppose, on the other hand, that I have exactly 10 gallons of gasoline in my car, which goes exactly 20 miles to the gallon, and I want to get from Boston to New York without stopping to refuel, all of this known to my interlocutor. Then if the actual distance is 220 miles, I might well judge an utterance of (1), in response to my query, to be false. It seems reasonable to think of truth value, in this and many other cases, to be assigned to statements rather than sentences (quite apart from the question of indexicals such as demonstratives, tense, etc.). It will depend in complex ways on intention, circumstances of utterance, etc., as do other aspects of meaning. Furthermore, use of language is possible only against a certain background of belief and expectations, which also may enter into formulation of truth conditions; unless these are more or less satisfied, semantic notions become indeterminate and their values cannot be fixed. Similar conclusions follow from Quine's "holistic" approach to the meaning of sentences in natural language. Like the representation of sound, the representation of meaning given by the grammar appears to be only one factor that enters into the semantic characterization of a particular utterance, in general.

Assuming still that the grammar, representing knowledge of language, is a real object, something represented in the mind/brain in some fashion, then it is a question of fact, not decision, whether the abstract representations of sound and meaning given by the grammar have this or that property, even if a rather subtle and often perplexing question of fact. Putting aside many important questions, let us refer to the representation of sound given by the grammar as the "surface structure" of a sentence, namely, a representation of it in terms of syllable structure, abstract phonetic segments, groupings of these into wordlike elements, further groupings of these into phrases, and so on. And let us refer to the representation of meaning assigned by the grammar to an expression as its "LF"—a term intended to suggest "logical form." Even this minimal description of linguistic representations begs interesting questions; perhaps representations of sound enter in a crucial way into determination of meaning. But in this account, I will overlook many plausible, and perhaps correct alternatives to the course I will sketch.

The term "LF" in the sense of this discussion is not to be identified, conceptually at least, with the term "logical form" in other familiar uses. The investigation of the so-called "logical form" of sentences of natural language may be motivated by an interest in formalizing inference, or in determining ontological commitment. These concerns might, incidentally, lead to different notions of "logical form." For example, from the sentences (2) we can infer the corresponding sentences of (3) (I will, henceforth, ignore important distinctions between sentences and statements):

(2)(a) he found a fly in the cup
  (b) he found a flaw in the argument
(3)(a) there is a fly in the cup
  (b) there is a flaw in the argument

If our concern is formalization of inference, we might then assign essentially the same logical form to (2a) and (2b). But no one uses (2b) or (3b) with the understanding that among the things in the world—including abstract entities—there are flaws, some of which are in arguments. This is true even though we use "referential" terms such as pronouns to "refer" (in some sense) to flaws, e.g., adding "but it is unimportant" to (3b), or speaking of "the same flaw" in several arguments.

One sometimes hears the term "real semantics" used to refer to the study of the relation between language and the world. Adopting this usage, in "real semantics" we will assign to (2b) a very differe it "logical form" from that assigned to (2a), even though the distinctior. may play no role in natural-language inference or in the use of "referential" expressions such as pronouns or *same*. This is in general true in the case of what Ryle called "systematically misleading expressions," and is a familiar observation in modern philosophy of language, and indeed, since at least the 18th century, when du Marsais argued that the "logical form" of the sentence *I have an idea* is something like *I think* (as distinct from *I have a book*), an observation employed by Thomas Reid as part of his critique of the theory of ideas. If practitioners of model-theoretic semantics for natural language intend to do "real semantics," they will be concerned with "logical form" in a sense relevant to ontological commitment. But it is, again, a question of fact, not decision, whether notions of "logical form" that derive from concern with ontological commitment or formalization of inference correspond to the representations of meaning, what I have been calling "LF," generated by a particular system of the mind/brain. The term "LF" (which I will read "logical form," assuming the provisos just given) seems to me appropriate, since there is empirical evidence that LF has some interesting properties of what is called "logical form" from other points of view, but there is also evidence, which I will not review here, that it differs from systems of representation motivated by other concerns.

Focusing attention now on LF, what are some of the crucial elements that enter into it? In work on descriptive semantics there is a fair consensus—though terminologies differ—that LF should include a characterization of "thematic relations": that is, such notions as "agent of action," "goal," "patient" or "theme," etc. The lexicon of a language will specify, for each lexical element, the complement structure associated with it and the thematic roles played by elements that fill this complement structure. For example, the verb *persuade* takes two complements, a noun phrase and a clause, assigning to each a particular thematic role—henceforth, "θ-role."

As is well-known, surface structure may not indicate θ-role representation. There appears to be no relevant difference in surface structure between *he persuaded John to leave* and *he expected John to leave,* but at the level of θ-role representation they are quite different. Similarly, consider the sentence (4):

(4)   John was believed to have been killed

In the θ-role representation, *John* is assigned the same θ-role as in (5), but its surface structure position is entirely different:

(5)   they killed John

The grammar must contain rules determining surface structure, θ-role assignment, and the relation between them. In pursuing the further question of what these rules are, we enter into specific, theory-laden assumptions about the form and nature of grammar and mental representations. From the earliest work in generative grammar, as in traditional grammar, it has been assumed that what I am now calling "θ-role" is determined in part by a representation in terms of grammatical functions such as subject-of, object-of, and so on. In (5), for example, *they* is the subject of the sentence and *John* is the object of the verb phrase *killed John.* Following one familiar practice (see, for example my *Aspects of the Theory of Syntax,* 1965, or in a more general setting, *Logical Structure of Linguistic Theory*), let us use the notation "[NP,S]" to express the relational notion "subject" and the notation "[NP,VP]" to express "object." Thus *they* in (5) bears the grammatical relation [NP,S] to the sentence (5) and has the grammatical function: [NP,S] of (5). Particular lexical properties of the verb *kill* assign to its object a specific θ-role. Analogously, properties of the verb phrase assign a θ-role to the subject of (5).

In more complex structures, such as (4), representations at various levels may include more than one occurrence of a particular category, for example clauses (S). We may distinguish these by indexing: S_1, S_2, . . . I will use the notation "[NP,S_1]" to express the grammatical function [NP,S] of S_1, i.e., subject-of-S_1, and so on.

This way of describing the relation between grammatical functions and θ-roles assumes a certain asymmetry between object and subject. The object is assigned its θ-role by the verb within VP, the traditional "predicate." The subject is assigned its θ-role by the VP within S, the traditional "clause" or "proposition." There does, in fact, seem to be a significant asymmetry. Idioms apart, every element in the complement of VP is assigned a θ-role (though there remain some problematic cases), but this is not true of subjects. In (4), for example, the noun phrase that bears the relation [NP,S] to the complete sentence has no θ-role apart from its θ-role as [NP,VP] (i.e., object) of the VP *kill John.* Similarly, in (6) every element of the VP has a particular θ -role, but the subject has none; nor does the embedded subject:

(6)   it [$_{VP}$ seems to me [that it will rain]]

In Edwin William's terminology, the subject is an external argument of the verb, its complements, internal arguments.

It is perhaps not unreasonable to suppose that the θ -role of the subject (where it exists) is determined compositionally by the VP in general, as may also be the case within VP in quasi-idiomatic constructions such as *take him seriously*. Consider (7):

(7)(a)   John broke the window
   (b)   John broke his arm

In (7a), John is understood to be the agent of the action, though there is another interpretation in which he is taken to be the instrument, as in *the hammer broke the window,* where we think of the hammer (or John) as being wielded by someone who is the agent. Sentence (7b) has these interpretations, but its more normal interpretation takes John to be something like "patient." Thus (7b), but not (7a), might be the response to: *What happened to John?*

Whether a verb assigns (or better, perhaps, participates in assigning) a θ -role to a subject depends on the syntactic structure in which it appears. In (4), *believe* assigns a θ -role in the normal way to an abstract clause of the form "someone killed John," but no other θ -role is assigned to *John*; and the verb *believe*, as (4) shows, need assign no θ -role to a subject at all, even if one is present, as in this case—though one might take *John* to be the subject of the copula rather than the verb, in the derived sense of the notion "subject of verb." Similarly, in (8a) the same θ -role is assigned to *Bill* as in (8b), but in (9a), *belief*, which is simply the nominalized form of *believe*, need assign no θ -role to the subject (missing in this case), as in (4):

(8)(a)   Bill believes that John will leave
   (b)   Bill's belief that John will leave
(9)   the belief that John will leave

It seems to me, then, that there is merit to the traditional view that there is a distinction between the notions [NP,S] and [NP,VP] in that the former is related to the verb only indirectly, while the latter is related directly to the verb that is the head of the predicate VP. Similar remarks apply to adjectival and nominal phrases (like (8b), (9)).

We are now assuming that two factors enter into the determination of θ -role: intrinsic lexical properties of lexical items that are heads of phrase categories (as the verb is the head of VP), and grammatical functions such as subject, object, clausal complement, head, etc. To assign θ -roles properly in the sentence (7a), for example, we must know that *John* is [NP,S], *window* [NP,VP], and *break* [V,VP] (a special case of the more general notion "head"). Let us assume that there is a level of representation at which such grammatical functions are directly specified, calling it "D-structure" ("deep structure"). Suppose that the grammar contains rules generating D-structure—henceforth, "base rules." These assign to (7a) something like the representation (10) at this level:

(10)   [$_S$[$_{NP}$ John][$_{VP}$[$_V$ broke][$_{NP}$ the window]]]

Then in familiar and obvious ways (see the references cited), the grammatical relations are directly represented in the D-structure.

Note that it is unnecessary for a grammar expressing knowledge of English to include base rules generating the structure (10) in full detail, since much of the information expressed in (10) is, in effect, determined by the lexicon. Thus, *break* must be specified in the lexicon as an item that assigns a certain θ-role to its object and that (given an object) assigns a certain θ-role to its subject. If *break* were inserted into a D-structure in which these θ-roles could not be assigned, then the result would not be a grammatical expression. Therefore, the base rules need only express the idiosyncratic properties of English—that subjects precede VPs, that the heads of major categories precede their complements, and so on. Apart from these, we may think of the base rules as generating arbitrary structures satisfying certain very general properties of the base, specifically, the principles of X-bar theory. Where improper structures are generated, they will be excluded by properties of the lexicon. Exactly how much structure must be specified by the base rules is an interesting question. Consideration of other subsystems of grammar, such as Case theory in the sense of Vergnaud, suggests that the base rules are in fact quite restricted in the information they provide. Note that this is in effect the question of parametric variation at the level of base structure.

A reasonable condition on D-structures, implicit in the foregoing, is that every θ-role determined ultimately by the lexical entries in the D-structure must be filled by some lexical expression, and that each lexical expression must fill exactly one θ-role, where we take a "lexical expression" to be a major category (NP, S, etc.) that contains lexical elements and is not an "idiom chunk," that is, a proper part of an expression assigned a unique role by an idiom rule; e.g., *advantage* in *they took advantage of Bill*. Thus in (10), each NP fills exactly one θ-role and each θ-role is properly filled. Let us call this condition, which can be made precise relatively easily, the "θ-criterion." The θ-criterion is a generalization of Robert Freidin's conditions of functional uniqueness and functional relatedness. Notice that while reasonable, it is not obviously correct; Ray Jackendoff, in his pioneering work on this topic, explicitly rejects it, for example (see his

Semantic Interpretation in Generative Grammar, 1972). Whether it is tenable or not in this strong form depends on the still obscure question of the nature of θ-roles and the positions in which they are assigned (e.g., what about topics, heads of relatives, predicate nominals, etc?). I will tentatively assume it, putting aside many pertinent questions.

The assumption that D-structures meet the θ-criterion plays a role in eliminating the need for base rules, apart from language-specific idiosyncracies, and has a number of other empirical consequences when embedded in further theory. Thus, consider such sentences as (11):

(11)(a) John persuaded Bill to leave
  (b) John preferred to do it himself
  (c) John believed Bill to be incompetent
  (d) John tried to do it himself
  (e) John wondered who to visit

Clearly, the lexical entry for *persuade* must specify that it takes an object and a clausal complement, assigning to each a θ-role, as in (12):

(12)   John persuaded—Bill—that he should leave

Since the same θ-roles are assigned in (11a), by the θ-criterion we must assume that the D-structure underlying (11a), in which grammatical relations are represented, is (13a); and by a similar argument, that the D-structures corresponding to (11b-e) are (13b-e), respectively:

(13)(a) $[_S[_{NP}$ John$][_{VP}[_V$ persuaded$][_{NP}$ Bill$][_S$ NP* to leave$]]]$
  (b) $[_S[_{NP}$ John$][_{VP}[_V$ preferred$][_S$ NP* to do it himself$]]]$
  (c) $[_S[_{NP}$ John$][_{VP}[_V$ believed$][_S$ Bill to be incompetent$]]]$
  (d) $[_S[_{NP}$ John$][_{VP}[_V$ tried$][_S$ NP* to do it himself$]]]$
  (e) $[_S[_{NP}$ John$][_{VP}[_V$ wondered$][_S$ who NP* to visit$]]]$

Details aside, such representations as (13) assign the grammatical functions required for determination of θ-role. Given lexical properties, these characteristics of the D-structures need not be specified by base rules, for reasons already mentioned.

The item represented as NP* in (13) lacks phonetic features but fills a θ-role. Let us consider it to be in effect a pronoun with the features person, number, and gender but no phonetic content: henceforth PRO. Three kinds of questions immediately arise concerning PRO:

(14) (i) where may PRO appear?
  (ii) where must PRO appear?
  (iii) how is the reference of PRO determined?

In response to (i), PRO may appear (in particular) as the subject of an infinitive, as in (13), but not as the subject of a finite clause, replacing *he* in

(12), or as the object of a VP—thus (11e) cannot mean *John wondered who is to visit him,* as it would if PRO were the object of *visit.* Similarly, *John knew who left* cannot mean *John knew who left him,* with PRO object of *leave* referring to John. In response to (ii), we note that PRO must appear in the positions of NP* in (13), where no lexical item may replace it. In response to (iii), we see that PRO in (13a), for example, may refer to Bill but not to John—it is "controlled" by the object of *persuade,* not by the subject of the sentence, and it must be controlled; it cannot be indefinite in reference, as in *it is unclear who to visit (it is unclear [who PRO to visit]).*

The assumptions we are considering will be supported to the extent that there are reasonable general answers to the questions (14), answers that to the maximum possible extent derive from independent considerations, so that properties of PRO are explained rather than merely stipulated. Recent work suggests that the answers to (14) derive from three central subtheories of grammar:

(15) (i)   the theory of binding
     (ii) the theory of Case
     (iii) the theory of control

Theory (iii) appears to be in part at least specific to PRO, irreducible to other assumptions. The theories of binding and Case, however, are independently motivated, and provide satisfactory answers to questions (i) and (ii) of (14) over quite an interesting range. In particular, the positions in which PRO appears are essentially those in which overt anaphoric expressions such as *each other* can appear and in which overt pronouns have the property of disjoint reference, though the situation is more complex in interesting ways. The fact that the questions (14i,ii) are answered on independently motivated grounds provides evidence in support of the θ -criterion and the D–structure representations (13) that it implies. If we were to abandon the θ -criterion as stated and were to assume, e.g., that *to leave* in (11a) is represented simply as a VP rather than a clause, as in surface structure, or as a clause lacking a subject in D–structure (or whatever structure we suppose to underlie LF), then we would have to stipulate that finite and infinitival clauses differ as they do with regard to "missing elements," rather than explaining these facts in terms of properties of overt elements such as reciprocals and (overt) pronouns. The assumptions we are now considering imply that there is a principled reason why "missing elements," which function in effect as pronominal anaphors, have properties analogous to those of overt anaphors and pronouns. There is no space here to make these observations precise, but at least the relevant considerations should be clear.

Let us consider more closely the examples (11c), (11d). By the θ -criterion, we are led to assign them the D–structures (13c), (13d), respectively, as representations of the grammatical relations that enter into determining θ -role. But then the question arises why we have a lexical subject *Bill* in the embedded clause of (11c) but an embedded subject PRO in the corresponding position of (11d). Investigation of a range of cases in English and other languages indicates that (11c) is the exception to the rule illustrated in (11d); it is a "marked property" of English that (11c) is grammatical. Note that in French or German, for example, the corresponding sentences would have the form of (11d) with PRO, rather than (11c) with an overt lexical item. Correspondingly, the theory of Case predicts (11d), but not (11c). It seems, then, that (11c) reflects some modification or relaxation of conditions of universal grammar; we would predict that unless presented with explicit examples such as (11c), a child learning English would assume that the structures should be as in French or German, with PRO as subject of the embedded infinitival, rather than adopting a marked option.

What is this marked property of English? The theory of Case requires that every overt lexical NP receive Case, and predicts that subjects of infinitives will not receive Case unless the language has some marked principle assigning Case in this position. In fact, English is unusual in that subjects of infinitives appear as lexical items. It is interesting that this exceptional appearance of lexical subjects is restricted to the positions in which Case might be assigned: namely, following verbs and prepositions, the two Case-assigning categories in English. Thus we have (11c), but not, say, "Bill to be incompetent is what John believed," and we have such structures as "John would prefer for you to do it yourself," which relates to (11b) as (12) relates to (11a). It is reasonable, then, to suppose that (11c) results from a property of "exceptional Case-marking" that allows certain verbs such as *believe* (but not *try*) to assign objective Case across a clause boundary, a marked property. On this assumption, the θ -criterion is not violated.

Kayne has suggested (forthcoming) that the two cases of exceptional Case assignment reduce to one, namely, assignment of Case by a preposition, either *for* or a null preposition, and has shown that a number of differences between French/Italian and English can be readily explained on this assumption.

One might approach the exceptional character of (11c) in other ways. For example, suppose one were to argue that the D-structure of (11c) is (16), analogous to (13a) for (11a):

(16) $[_S[_{NP}$ John]$[_{VP}[_V$ believed]$[_{NP}$ Bill]$
         $[_S$ PRO to be incompetent]]]

Then (11c) would be a control structure, with *Bill* controlling PRO. The exceptionality of (11c), then, is that it violates the θ -criterion, since the object *Bill* of *believe* receives no θ -role, as distinct from (11a) = (13a) where it does. An approach along these lines differs slightly in empirical consequences from an approach in terms of exceptional Case-marking. For example, consider such structures as (17), with the D–structure (18):

(17)   John pleaded with Bill to leave

(18) $[_S[_{NP}$ John$][_{VP}[_V$ pleaded$][_{PP}$ with Bill$][_S$ PRO to leave$]]]$

Evidently, this is a control structure; *Bill* is in a position that permits control of PRO. Assuming then that the θ –criterion permits marked violations, as in (16), there might be a verb *PLEAD* such that *PLEAD with* (like *plead with*) means (roughly) "exhort," so that (19) would mean (roughly) that John exhorted that Bill leave:

(19)   John PLEADED with Bill to leave

If we take the contrary position, assuming that the θ –criterion is inviolable and that (11c) is therefore accounted for by exceptional Case-marking, no such verb *PLEAD* can exist, since the D–structure of (19) would have to be (20), and prepositions do not take clausal complements (this a consequence of lexical properties and the θ –criterion):

(20) $[_S[_{NP}$ John$][_{VP}[_V$ PLEADED$][_{PP}$ with $[_S$ Bill to leave$]]]]$

There seem to be no such exceptional structures as (19), analogous to (11c). Assuming that this is a fact and not an accidental one—that there are principled reasons for the fact—it follows that (11c) should be interpreted as a case of exceptional Case-marking, the θ –criterion being inviolable. There are other considerations that lead to the same conclusion.

Note that an underlying assumption throughout is that base rules are limited to specification of language-specific idiosyncracies, and that the D–structures are determined in their essential properties as a kind of "projection" from lexical structure. This is the optimal assumption, reducing language-specific features of the grammar to a minimum; and its empirical consequences seem valid over an interesting range. Note also that the same assumptions also lead to appropriate conclusions in the case of such structures as (11e). Clearly, the embedded phrase is clausal. On our assumptions, all *wh*-clauses are of the form (21), again clearly the simplest assumption:

(21)   *wh*-phrase – S, where S is a clause of the form NP–VP

The investigation of properties of "missing elements" is of particular interest for the study of mental representations. Their properties presumably are not derived by the language learner from actual expressions, since the elements in question are not physically present. Rather, they derive from properties of the system of grammar, and thus give unique insight into the nature of the principles of grammar; i.e., they derive from the mind, rather than from experience. If our interest is the mind, not the organization of events in the external world, these elements are thus of unique interest. It is important, then, that many of their fundamental properties follow from general principles of much greater generality: binding and Case theory, which hold for anaphors and overt pronouns as well as "missing" pronominal anaphors, and the θ -criterion.

So far, we have been considering the level of D-structure in which the grammatical relations relevant to determining θ -role are directly represented. But it is clear that other grammatical functions are also relevant to LF. Consider again the sentences (4) and (5):

(4)   John was believed to have been killed
(5)   they killed John

In the sentence (4), *John* bears the relation [NP,VP] to the abstract predicate *kill John* exactly as it does in (5). But it also bears the relation [NP,S] to the sentence (4) itself. Each of these grammatical relations plays a role in determining properties of LF. The former determines the θ -role of *John,* as patient or theme. To illustrate the contribution of the latter to LF, consider the sentences (22):

(22) (i)   it seems to each other that they are happy
       (ii)   they seem to each other to be happy

The lexical properties of *seem* indicate that it takes a *to*-phrase and a clausal complement, so by the θ -criterion the D-structure of both sentences of (22) is (23):

(23) $[_{S_1}$ NP* $[_{VP}[_V$ seem]$[_{PP}$ to each other]
          $[_{S_2}$ they INFL be happy]]]

where INFL (inflection) is finite in (22i) and infinitival in (22ii) (we disregard the number agreement of *seem*), and NP* is an empty phrase assigned no θ -role and ultimately filled by pleonastic *it* or by the subject of the embedded clause. In both sentences, the θ -role of *they* is subject of the predicate *be-happy*. That is, this θ -role is determined by the grammatical function of *they* as [NP,S$_2$]. But in (22ii), *they* can serve as the antecedent for the reciprocal *each other,* whereas in (22i) it cannot, so that the latter sentence is ungrammatical, with an anaphor lacking an antecedent. The reason is that in (22ii), but not (22i), *they* takes on a secondary grammatical function: [NP,S$_1$] alongside of [NP,S$_2$]. Each of these grammatical functions thus contributes to LF. There are many other examples of the contribution of such secondary, non-thematic grammatical functions to LF; for example, in Japanese and many other languages, subjects (whether thematic or not) and only subjects can be antecedents for the reflexive element.

It seems, then, that we have two notions of "grammatical function" that are relevant to LF; call them GF-θ and GF-$\overline{\theta}$, where the former is the notion relevant to assigning θ -role and the latter is relevant to LF (if at all) only in other ways. The representation that determines GF-θ is what we have been calling "D-structure." Let us refer to the representation that determines GF-$\bar\theta$ as "S-structure." As is evident from the examples, S–structure is more or less similar to surface structure; in fact, it is reasonable to suppose that surface structure is derived from S–structure by mechanical rules of morphology and phonology, and can be regarded as in essence an "impoverished" form of S–structure in which some of the abstract structure of the latter is not represented (though this characterization is oversimplified in certain respects). Assuming so, the question of how form and meaning are related now resolves to the question of how S–structure is related to D–structure, and how these two levels are related to LF. In substantial part, this is the question of how GF-θ representations are related to GF-$\bar\theta$ representations.

The theory of transformational generative grammar (one variety of generative grammar) offers one answer to these questions, an answer that I think is correct in essence though insufficiently general. The answer is that D–structure, determining GF-θ, is mapped onto S–structure by a certain class of rules, grammatical transformations, which perform quite independent functions in the grammar apart from expressing this relation. For example, rules of this type relate the quasi-quantifier *who* in (24) to the abstract variable that it binds (assuming the LF–representation (25)), and express the fact that in (26) the subject of the predicate *is here* is the abstract phrase *a man whom you know,* along with much else:

(24)   who did you think would win
(25)   for which $x,$ x a person, you thought [that x would win]
(26)   a man is here whom you know

Thus one basic assumption of transformational generative grammar is that the rules assigning GF-θ, the thematically relevant grammatical functions, to elements of surface form are rules of the same kind that serve many other functions in grammar, rather than being rules of some new and distinct type.

Early work in this framework attempted to develop some notion of "grammatical transformation" rich enough to capture a wide range of properties of surface form and its relation to GF-θ. The notion that was developed (e.g., in the references cited above and much related work) was rich in descriptive power, and correspondingly weak (though not empty) in explanatory power. Since the early 1960s, and particularly in the past 10 years, much effort has been devoted to showing that the class of possible transformations can be substantially reduced without loss of descriptive power through the discovery of quite general conditions that all such rules and the representations they operate on and form must meet. Given such conditions, detailed properties of the rules for particular cases need not be stipulated, so that the variety of possible rules can be reduced and explanatory power correspondingly enhanced. Among the ideas that have been explored are, e.g., the A-over-A condition, the condition of recoverability of deletion, Ross's island conditions, Emonds's analysis of rule types, the principle of subjacency (which incorporates several island conditions), and the theory of binding and Case, which incidentally constrain transformational rules, though motivated by other concerns. The limit to which this investigation tends is the thesis that transformational rules, at least for a substantial core grammar, can be reduced to the single rule "Move α," where α is an arbitrary category: i.e., move any category anywhere. If something like this is true, or near true, then there must be very restrictive general conditions in universal grammar on the nature of linguistic representations and the applicability of rules. Investigation of these conditions and their parameters is, in fact, the recent phase of linguistic work that I described at the outset as very promising, in my opinion. The strongest thesis we can formulate, in this framework, is that a single rule—the rule "Move α," which is in effect a rule arbitrarily associating two positions in a structure—plays the role of assigning GF-θ to surface form as well as other roles, such as those illustrated in (24-6), with differences among languages determined by variation in parameters of the principles within which this rule is embedded. I will return to a generalization of this thesis.

I will consider here only one aspect of the attempt to reduce the descriptive power and variety of transformations, one that is particularly relevant to the questions I have been discussing. Consider the sentences (27), (28):

(27)   three men from England arrived last night

(28)   there arrived last night three men from England

Presumably, the common D-structure of these sentences, representing GF-θ, is something like (29):

(29)   [$_S$[$_{NP}$ three men from England][$_{VP}$ arrived last night]]

Then *three men from England* bears the grammatical function [NP,S], and gains its appropriate θ -role by virtue of filling this grammatical function in the sentence. The S-structure corresponding to (28) is formed by application of a transformational rule, call it T. In the earliest versions of transformational grammar, it was assumed that transformations can be constructed by compounding of elementary operations. In this case, T would be formed by compounding of a movement rule that places the subject to the right of the VP, and a rule of *there*-insertion that fills the gap vacated by the moved subject. Implicit in this view, and explicit in the formalizations of it, was the assumption that the abstract position of the moved subject remains to be filled by *there* in the second stage of the transformation, *there* being a noun phrase by virtue of the fact that it fills the vacated NP position. Let us call this abstract position left behind by the moved element its "trace." Thus the basic assumption was that if a movement rule is part of a more complex transformation, then it leaves a trace, namely, an empty category of the same type as that of the moved element; in this case, NP. Using the symbol *e* for the empty element, the trace left by the first phase of the transformation T is [$_{NP}$ *e*], in the subject position of (29).

One major step towards reducing the class of possible transformations is to eliminate the possibility of compounding elementary operations. Thus the role relating (27) and (28) (actually, the structures associated with them) is decomposed into two entirely distinct and separate rules: (i) Move NP, and (ii) insert *there*. Pursuing the goal of reducing the variety of transformational systems further, let us assume that (i) is simply a special case of the general rule "Move α" and that (ii) is a rule that allows *there* to be inserted in any position (by virtue of the principle of recoverability of deletion, only in an empty position), and that these two rules are entirely independent of one another, dependencies among rules being excluded in principle in this more stringent theory. A major problem will now be to discover general principles that exclude unwanted applications of these rules, not an insignificant challenge. Suppose that it can be met. Notice that the earlier assumption that movement leaves a trace when it is a component of a more complex transformation now becomes the principle that the rule "Move α" always leaves a trace, namely, an empty category of the type α. This assumption is at the heart of what is called "trace theory," which, as we see, derives in a natural way from the process of reducing the potential descriptive power of grammar, and correspondingly enhancing the explanatory power of linguistic theory.

Two obvious questions arise at once, when trace theory is made explicit. First, how do the properties of S–structure, including trace, relate to determination of LF; second, how does the empty category trace relate to the empty category PRO that we have already discussed. Let us consider these in turn.

Consider again the representations of sentence (4), under trace-theoretic assumptions. The D-structure is along the lines of (30) and the S–structure along the lines of (31), where I assume here, as is natural, that the rule "Move α" coindexes the moved element and its trace uniquely, so that D- and S-structure can be properly related if "Move α" is applied to several elements:

(4)   John was believed to have been killed

(30)   [$_{S_1}$ NP* [$_{VP_1}$ was believed [$_{S_2}$ NP* [$_{VP_2}$ to have been killed [$_{NP}$ John]]]]]

(31)   [$_{S_1}$[$_{NP_i}$ John][$_{VP_1}$ was believed[$_{S_2}$[$_{NP_i}$ *e*]
[$_{VP_2}$ to have been killed[$_{NP_i}$ *e*]]]]]

We might take NP*, the empty element of the D–structure, to be [$_{NP}$ e], i.e., identical to trace, apart from index.

To obtain the representation (31) from (30), we assume that the rule "Move α" applies twice, first moving *John* to the subject position of the embedded sentence (where it might have remained, e.g., in the sentence "we believed John to have been killed"), and a second time to the subject position of the full sentence. There are good reasons for the assumption that movement is "successive cyclic" in this sense. In the first place, there is strong evidence that the rule "Move α" is governed by a condition that prevents an element from being moved "too far" (the subjacency condition), and a one-step movement from (30) to (31) would be "too far" in the relevant sense, when it is made precise. Secondly, the intermediate traces often function in much the same way that GF-$\bar{\theta}$ does in the examples (22). Consider, e.g., the sentence (32), analogous to (23), where the medial trace serves in effect as the antecedent of *each other*, which requires an antecedent in the same clause in such cases for other reasons:

(32)   they$_i$ are likely [[$_{NP_i}$ e] to appear to each other [[$_{NP_i}$ e]
        to be happy]]

To put it differently, *they* in (32) serves as antecedent of *each other,* via its trace, thought it is neither the D–structure nor the S–structure subject of the clause in which *each other* appears, and thus is not in a position to serve as antecedent in either of these structures.

Note that there is now a good sense in which the S–structure (31) represents both GF-θ and GF-$\bar{\theta}$; namely, *John* bears the grammatical relation [NP,S$_1$] by virtue of its actual position in (31), and bears the relations [NP,S$_2$] and [NP,VP$_2$] by virtue of the positions of its traces. Suppose we associated with each lexical NP in S–structure a sequence $(p_1, \ldots, p_n)$ which, in an obvious sense, represents the derivational history of this NP by application of "Move α"; thus, p_1 is the position of the lexical NP itself; p_2 is the position (filled by a trace) from which it was moved to its final position; etc., p_n being the position (filled by a trace) occupied by the NP in D–structure. Correspondingly, let us associate with each lexical NP in S–structure the sequence of grammatical functions $(GF_1, \ldots, GF_n)$, where GF_i is the grammatical function of the element filling position p_i (the lexical NP itself for $i = 1$, a trace in each other case), as determined by the S–structure configuration. Then GF_n is the grammatical function of the NP at D–structure, which, by the θ –criterion, is assigned a θ –role in LF. We can easily generalize these notions to idiom chunks, which differ only in that GF_n is assigned no θ –role. Let us call $(GF_1, \ldots, GF_n)$ the *function-chain* of the NP filling GF_1.

I have defined the function chain in terms of successive applications of "Move α," but it can in fact be recovered from S–structure itself, given other properties of representations. Thus, when we improve the theory of transformations by eliminating the possibility of compounding elementary operations and of stipulating dependencies among rules, yielding trace theory as an immediate consequence, we see that S-structure becomes an enriched D-structure, incorporating the contribution of D-structure to LF. We may think of D-structure and the rule "Move α" as the two components that interact to yield the full S-structure.

Returning to (31), *John* is assigned the function chain (GF_1, GF_2, GF_3), where GF_1 is $[NP, S_1]$ and GF_3 is $[NP, VP_2]$. Thus *John* acquires the θ-role assigned by *kill* to its object, and is the S-structure subject of the whole sentence, no θ-role being being assigned to this position, which can therefore be filled by idiom chunks, as in (33), or by other expressions with no referential function, as in (34):

(33)   advantage was believed to have been taken of John
(34)   it was believed that John was killed

The θ-criterion was formulated above as applying at D-structure. Plainly, when properly stated, it must apply at LF, requiring in particular that each expression of an appropriate sort drawn from the lexicon (e.g., names, but not idiom chunks) must have one and only one θ-role, and that each θ-role determined ultimately by the lexical entries must be filled by some appropriate expression. Suppose that *John* has the function chain $(GF_1, \ldots . , GF_n)$ in some S-structure. Then GF_n must be determined in a position that receives a θ-role (namely, the θ-role assigned to *John*), and furthermore, no GF_i other than GF_n may have this property. For if some GF_i $(i \neq n)$ is determined in such a position, then the corresponding θ-role will not be assigned and the θ-criterion will be violated. It follows that movement must always be to a position to which no θ-role is assigned, and (apart from idiom chunks or other expressions that are not "referential" in the appropriate sense) it must be initially from a position in D-structure to which a θ-role is assigned. For example, since a θ-role is assigned obligatorily in VP (apart from idiom chunks), there can be movement from object to subject or from subject to subject, but not to a position within VP or to the position of a subject assigned a θ-role by its predicate VP.

Given that both GF-θ and GF-$\bar{\theta}$ can be recovered directly from S-structure, we may assume that LF is determined by rules that apply to S-structure alone. It seems that other aspects of syntactic form that enter into LF are also determined at S-structure. We may assume, then, that the general structure of a grammar is as in (35):

(35)

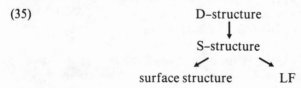

Recall that we have, in effect, "factored" S-structure into two components: D-structure and the rule "Move α."

Consider now the second of the two questions raised above in connection with trace theory: how does the trace relate to PRO? Suppose that the NP-trace relation could be reduced to the NP-PRO relation. Then there would be strong reason to suppose that S-structure is generated directly by base rules and that both NP-PRO relations and NP-trace relations (now identified) fall under the theory of control. But the two kinds of relations differ in fundamental ways.

One crucial difference is that the function chain of an NP is associated with only one θ-role, as just noted; furthermore, the S-structure position of an NP with a function chain of two or more elements is assigned no θ-role. In the case of the set containing NP and a controlled PRO, however, each has an independent θ-role (which may, in fact, be determined by an associated trace, in each case). There are a number of other properties that correlate with this difference. Consider, for example, (36):

(36) (i)   they thought that to help each other would be difficult
     (ii) they seem that to help each other would be difficult

In case (i), the subject of *help each other* is PRO, with an antecedent that has an independent θ-role. In case (ii), the subject of *help each other* is trace, since its antecedent has no independent θ-role; (36ii) must have been formed by "Move α" applied to *they* in the D-structure position of subject of *help each other*. But sentence (ii) is ungrammatical. It is impossible to apply "Move α" in such a case, since this would violate subjacency, a property of all movement rules, including those that associate S-structure and GF-θ.

There are other examples that illustrate the fact that the theory of control, relating an NP with a θ-role and a PRO with an independent θ-role, is different in its properties from the theory relating an NP and its trace. To illustrate with a different kind of case, consider the following examples (noted by Luigi Burzio):

(37) (i)   they assigned one interpreter each to the visiting diplomats
     (ii)   one interpreter each was assigned t to the visiting diplomats
     (iii) one interpreter each seems [t to have been assigned t to the visiting diplomats]
(38)   one interpreter each tried [PRO to be assigned t to the visiting diplomats]

Throughout, *t* stands for the trace of a moved element; *one interpreter each* in (37), PRO in (38). Evidently, (38) is ungrammatical though it differs from (37iii), which is grammatical, only in replacement of trace by PRO. The distinction corresponds again in the expected way to θ-role assignment. Without attempting to formulate precise mechanisms, we might say, roughly that the D–structure position of *one interpreter each* must be "close enough" to the phrase *the visiting diplomats* for *each* to be interpreted appropriately as a quantifier related to the latter phrase; we might think of the association as being established prior to movement of *one interpreter each,* perhaps by a rule of *each*–movement, also leaving trace. But whatever the mechanism, clearly PRO and trace differ in fundamental respects.

The α–trace relation, for any category α, may be thought of abstractly in terms of certain general properties associated with it. One such property is subjacency; another, that α must be in a position to which no θ –role is assigned. These two properties correlate. We might think of them as defining the rule "Move α." Note that these properties hold of the cases of "Move α" mentioned above: (i) "Move NP," which associates an NP in S–structure with a GF-θ; (ii) "Move *wh*-phrase," which relates the quasi-quantifier *what* to the abstract variable that it binds; (iii) extraposition, which associates an extraposed phrase to a position within a larger phrase that receives a θ –role. In all of these cases, subjacency is observed and the antecedent is in a position that lacks a θ –role. Other relations that "connect" two elements do not observe these two conditions: e.g., antecedent–anaphor relations where the anaphor is not a trace, antecedent–PRO relations, the relation of an NP to a pronoun disjoint in reference from it, the relation of a quantifier to a pronoun interpreted as a variable bound by it.

The trace of a noun phrase and PRO differ in other respects as well. Trace must have an antecedent; PRO need not, as in "it is unclear [what PRO to do]." The trace of an NP is always governed (in the sense of the theory of government, which underlies both Case and binding theory), while PRO never is. Kayne has suggested that this property and subjacency may be reduced to the same principle (viz., ECP, which I cannot discuss here, a principle that holds of trace but not PRO). But the trace of NP and PRO are alike in certain crucial respects. For example, like overt anaphors, each can appear as subject of an infinitive but not of a tensed clause. The trace of a *wh*-phrase has somewhat different properties. It satisfies the two conditions defining "Move α," but the trace left behind must satisfy ECP and cannot appear as the subject of an infinitive (apart from exceptional Case-marking of one of the two subvarieties mentioned above), and it may appear as subject of a tensed clause, though there are interesting constraints on this possibility (again, related to ECP). The theory of grammar must explain why empty elements of various kinds have these specific properties and how languages may vary in these respects; interesting clusters of properties have been discovered that appear to be reducible to ECP. The theories of binding, Case and other related notions seem to account for a fair number of these properties in a principled way, though numerous problems remain open and the choice among alternative approaches is far from resolved. See my *Lectures on Binding and Government* (1981), Kayne's "ECP Extensions," and many other current publications.

The differences between trace and PRO eliminate one motivation for recasting the theory outlined in (35) with S-structure generated directly by the base rules. But they do not show that it is incorrect to do so. In fact, it is not clear that when these apparent alternatives are made precise, there is an empirical distinction between them. They may simply be two alternative formulations of the same fundamental theory. This possibility was noted in early work on trace theory and despite much progress since, the issue (if there is one) remains open. If the two formulations are empirically distinct, it seems that the distinctions must be fairly subtle. The more important point is that various clusters of properties of empty elements and antecedent-anaphor relations exist, posing significant empirical conditions that a theory of grammar must satisfy. The theory outlined above approaches these collections of properties in one particular way. It isolates two properties defining "Move α," and correspondingly separates two components of S-structure and the function chains it determines: D-structure determination of GF-θ and "Move α." Other properties of empty elements and of antecedent-anaphor relations follow from the theories of government, binding and Case. It is a matter of secondary importance (perhaps, ultimately, of null importance) whether this particular approach is adopted or a superficially different one that distinguishes several types of "interpretive rules," including "Move α" with its properties as one particular type. Perhaps there is more to the issue, but if so, it has not been made clear what more may be at stake, though there are some suggestions in the literature. It goes without saying that these two approaches (which may or may not be distinct) do not exhaust the possibilities for the study of this network of problems.

Continuing to adopt the framework so far outlined, recall that we have mentioned several kinds of applications of "Move α," as illustrated in (39):

(39) (i)   [a man t] was here [whom you know]
    (ii) John wondered [what PRO to do t]
    (iii) John seems [t to be sad]
    (iv) John was killed t
    (v)   John is believed [t to be sad]

Each type of example has the two defining properties of "Move α" just discussed. Case (i) is an example of extraposition; (ii) of *wh*-movement; (iii) of raising; (iv) of passive. What about case (v)? Is it an example of raising or of passive? From our point of view, the question is meaningless. All of these are simply examples of "Move α." True, they have different properties, apart from those that they share, but these follow from the interaction of the various subsystems of the theory of grammar.

Of these various constructions, it is the so-called "passive" that seems to have the most interesting properties with respect to the questions that we have been considering. Passive constructions such as (39iv,v) fall naturally into the category of "Move α" phenomena in English and similar languages. As in the case of elements moved by *wh*-movement, extraposition and raising, the subject of the passive sentence is in a position to which no θ -role is assigned, and it receives its θ -role from the final element in the associated function chain. The position of this final element, as in the case of raising, is one to which no Case is assigned; movement is obligatory in both cases for this reason. For both raising and passive, the D–structure position need be assigned no θ -role, as in the case of idiom chunks. If a θ -role is assigned in this position, it may be assigned by the passivized verb itself, as in (39iv), or by some other element, as in (39iii,v) or in (40), where the θ -role of the trace (hence of its antecedent) is assigned by a different element of the VP (its adjective phrase in cases (i), (ii); a preposition—in part at least—in case (iii)):

(40) (i)   John was considered t stupid
      (ii) he was pronounced t dead on arrival
      (iii) the bed was slept in t

In case (i), as in (39v), there is no reason to suppose that there is any θ -role assigned to the position of the trace by the verb *consider;* the same is true of (ii). Whatever the proper treatment of pseudo-passives such as (40iii) may be (perhaps, grammatical restructuring, with *sleep-in* restructured as a verb), the θ -roles seem to be assigned exactly as in corresponding active sentences, including those that do not permit passivization. For example, there seems to be no difference in θ -role assignment in the examples of (41), though (i) can be passivized as (iii) (like 40iii) while (ii) cannot be passivized as (iv):

(41) (i)   they spoke to John
      (ii) they spoke angrily to John
      (iii) John was spoken to
      (iv) John was spoken angrily to

In these respects too, passive is no different from raising.

But passive is a more general phenomenon, both in English and in other languages, so it may be useful to approach it from a point of view slightly more general than what has just been outlined, as a preliminary to a more abstract and general treatment of the entire complex of questions that I have been considering. What is usually called "passive" seems to have two crucial properties:

(42) (i) [NP,S] does not receive a θ -role

    (ii) [NP,VP] does not receive Case within VP, for some choice of NP in VP

In the structure (43), underlying (39iv), the subject position is assigned no θ -role (and so can be filled by idiom chunks and other expressions that bear no θ -role) and the object is assigned no Case:

(43)   [$_{NP}$ e] was killed John

Assuming that the participle *killed* assigns no Case (property (42ii), *John* must be moved or the Case filter will be violated. It can only move to subject position, as already noted, where it receives Case and is assigned a θ -role by virtue of the position of its trace. But a similar configuration of phenomena is found in languages with no evidence for movement.

It seems doubtful that properties (i) and (ii) of (42) are independent. Therefore, it is reasonable to inquire into the assumptions necessary to derive one from the other. There seems no way to derive (ii) from (i), but the example just reviewed, involving "Move α," suggests how we might derive (i) in general from (ii). Suppose then that the unique property of the passive morphology is that in effect it "absorbs" Case: one NP in the VP is not assigned Case under government by the head V of VP. Call this NP "NP*." By the Case filter, NP* must receive Case. By assumption (42ii), taken now as the defining property of passive, NP* must receive Case on the basis of some GF it assumes outside of the VP. This can only be [NP,S]. Therefore, NP* must assume the GF [NP,S] in addition to its D-structure GF as [NP,VP]. But if this GF [NP,S] is one to which a θ -role is assigned, then the θ -criterion will be violated since this θ -role will not be assigned (NP* receives its θ -role from its D-structure GF just as if it had not assumed [NP,S], whether by "Move α" or by some other rule). Therefore, passive morphology must satisfy property (i) of (42).

This is only the outline of an argument, and must be extended. I have omitted the case of idiom chunks and other expressions that lack θ -role, but it is easy to accommodate this case. I will omit this and other refinements here.

Suppose that passive morphology is assigned to a verb that has no NP in its complement, for example, *believe* or *reason* (which, as Edwin Williams notes, never takes an object or clausal subject in passive) in (44):

(44) (i) [$_{NP}$ e] was believed [$_{S}$ that John was a fool]

    (ii) [$_{NP}$ e] was reasoned [$_{S}$ that the conclusion was false]

The verbs *believe* and *reason* take clausal complements, so that the D-structure, projected in the usual way from lexical structure, is as in (44). Since there is no NP in the VP lacking Case, no movement has to apply; more generally, no NP must assume the secondary GF [NP,S]. In fact, (44) is converted to an S-structure simply by the rule that inserts pleonastic *it* in the non-θ-position of the subject. Thus passive morphology is not necessarily associated with movement and interchange of grammatical function. The traditional characterization of passive as involving a change of object to subject is correct, then, but only as a special case. The same will be true in languages in which intransitives can be passivized (e.g., German, Dutch, Arabic, Hebrew).

We may also find properties of passive without passive morphology, as, e.g., in nominals. Thus, *X*-bar theory would lead us to assign essentially the same structure to the verb *destroy* and its complements as to the noun *destruction* and its complements. Underlying (45), then, we have the D-structure (46):

(45) (i)   the destruction of Rome
      (ii) Rome's destruction
(46)   [$_{NP}$ Determiner [$_{\overline{N}}$[$_N$[$_V$ destroy] nom][$_{NP}$ Rome]]]

As it stands, (46) violates the Case filter, since *Rome* receives no Case. English has a device to overcome the fact that NP-complements of nouns and adjectives receive no Case; namely, insertion of the semantically empty preposition *of* in the context [+ N]—NP (prenominally after a noun or adjective), acting as a kind of Case-marker, since prepositions assign Case. This device yields (45i). Alternatively, "Move α" can apply, yielding (45ii), where *Rome* is assigned genitive Case by regular processes, giving a form that is passive-like but without passive morphology. French causatives provide another example, Richard Kayne has shown that properties of passive hold of the embedded phrase in (47) (see his *French Syntax,* 1975):

(47)   faire [manger la pomme par Pierre]

As Osvaldo Jaeggli has observed, there is no need for NP-movement to "save" the construction, as in a morphological passive, since the verb *manger* still assigns Case to its object.

Some auxiliary assumptions are necessary for these arguments to go through, but they appear plausible. Let us assume so. Then the basic (and perhaps the only) property of passive morphology will be that it absorbs Case, as in (42ii). In English, French and other languages of similar type, this property follows directly from the copular structure of the passive construction, with the participle being quasi-adjectival (presumably [+ V]), a complement of the copula. In other languages (e.g., Arabic), it is simply a property of the passive element.

Note that the trace left by movement to form passive serves several distinct functions. In the case of movement of an NP that requires a θ-role (e.g., *John* in (39iv)), the trace of the moved NP "transmits" the θ-role—which, as noted, may or may not be assigned by the passivized verb. But if the moved element is one that lacks a θ -role (e.g., the idiom chunk *advantage* in (48)), then the trace plays a different role; namely, it allows the idiomatic interpretation to be constructed:

(48)   advantage was taken of John

Putting it differently, idiom interpretation applies (in effect) at the D-structure level, "idiom rules" being analogous to lexical insertion rules of the base. Development of an appropriate formalism is straightforward, with interesting consequences regarding properties of idioms that I will not pursue here.

I have been assuming so far that grammatical functions are determined directly by the structural configurations of D-structure and transformationally-derived S-structures. But there are languages in which this is not so. In these "nonconfigurational languages" there seems little if any reason to believe that the rule "Move α" applies at all; one might argue, in fact, that in principle it cannot apply. Kenneth Hale has argued that languages fall into two major typological categories: configurational languages, which are of the type we have been considering, and nonconfigurational languages (his W^*-languages) lacking the full range of syntactic configurations in various degrees. He has suggested also that Japanese is essentially of the nonconfigurational type; in fact, as has often been noted, there is little if any reason to believe that rules of the form "Move α," or any transformational rules, apply in Japanese. Let us assume that these suggestions are correct, and ask how the framework I have been outlining can be generalized to accommodate a language of this type. Here I adapt some recent work of Ann Farmer (*On the Interaction of Morphology and Syntax,* 1980).

Suppose that the central base rule of Japanese is (49):

(49) $\overline{X} \longrightarrow W^* X$

*where W^* stands for a sequence of zero or more categories that are "maximal projections" (let us say, NP or S), and X is the head of the maximal projection $\overline{X}$. In particular, the base will generate such structures as (50), where we take S to be $\overline{V}$:

(50) $[_S NP_1 NP_2 \dots NP_n V]$

Let us assume further that the lexicon of Japanese is essentially the same as that of English; for example, the verb *tabe (eat)* takes an NP complement, assigning it the θ -role patient and forming with it a VP that assigns the θ -role agent to the subject; *atae (award)* takes double NP-complement assigning θ -role accordingly; etc. Japanese also has a word-forming element *sase* (causative), which takes a clausal complement as a lexical property, assigning to it the appropriate θ -role and assigning the θ -role agent to the subject of the verb V-*sase*. It also has a word-forming element *rare*, which serves as passive morphology. Assume further that grammatical functions are represented exactly as in English: [NP,S] for subject, [NP,VP] for object, [S,VP] for clausal complement in VP, etc. Suppose further that we distinguish the GFs [NP,VP] (direct object) and [NP′,VP] (indirect object). The basic difference between Japanese and English, then, is that the con-figurations that determine grammatical function (whether GF-θ or GF-$\bar{\theta}$) are not represented in the syntax in the X-bar system in D- or S-structure. Let us now compare D- and S-structures and the rules that relate them in the two languages.

For the verbs *eat-tabe,* English will have the D-structure (51a) and Japanese the D-structure (51b):

(51)(a)   [$_S$ NP$_1$ [$_{VP}$ eat NP$_2$]]
   (b)   [$_S$ NP$_i$ NP$_j$ tabe] ($i = 1$ and $j = 2$, or $i = 2$ and $j = 1$)

The D-structure assigns GF-θ. For English, the assignment is direct, given the configurations, along the lines sketched above. For Japanese, we may take the assignment to be random, which is to say that order is irrelevant. In each case, NP$_1$ = [NP,S] and NP$_2$ = [NP,VP]. Assuming essentially the same Case-assigning rules in the two languages, NP$_1$ receives nominative Case and NP$_2$ objective Case (GA and O, respectively, in Japanese). In both languages, θ -roles are assigned on the basis of GF-θ, in the obvious way. Note that if random GF assignment had proceeded differently in Japanese, the θ -criterion would have been violated.

Consider next the passive D-structures (52), generated by the base rules:

(52)(a)   [$_S$[$_{NP}$ e][$_{VP}$ was [$_{[+\bar{V}]}$ eaten NP]]]
   (b)   [$_S$ NP tabe-rare] (an instance of NP* V, with NP* = NP and V = *tabe-rare*)

The general property of passive is that the passive element absorbs Case (namely, (42ii)). Therefore, as we have seen, the construction assigns no θ -role to [NP,S] (property (42i)). In English, "move α" applies, giving the S-structure (53):

(53)   [$_S$ NP [$_{VP}$ was [$_{[+\bar{V}]}$ eaten t]]]

Along the lines already discussed, NP is assigned the function chain ([NP,S], [NP,VP]). The second element determines the θ -role in LF, and the first might play a role elsewhere in LF, as noted. Nominative Case is assigned to NP with the S-structure grammatical function [NP,S], the in-itial element of the function chain.

In Japanese, the D-structure (52b) must be converted to an appropriate S-structure in which NP can receive Case, since the passive element *rare* absorbs Case, by assumption. This cannot be done by an application of "move α," as in English, since GF is not configurationally defined. The obvious analogue of the rule "move α" for Japanese is the rule (54):

(54)   Assume a grammatical function

We understand (54) as assigning to an NP the function chain (GF$_1$, GF$_2$), where GF$_2$ is the grammatical function it already has, and GF$_1$ is an arbitrary grammatical function. Applying (54) to (52b), we form an S-structure identical in form with the D-structure but with NP assigned the function chain (55):

(55)   (GF$_1$, [NP,VP])

What is GF$_1$? It must be a grammatical function that will permit Case to be assigned to NP, or the Case filter will be violated. By assumption, NP cannot be assigned Case within VP, so GF$_1$ must be [NP,S], just as "move α" must always move α to the subject position. Therefore, NP is assigned the function chain ([NP,S], [NP,VP]) in S-structure, exactly as in English, and θ-role as well as Case are assigned exactly as in English, with the nominative GA and the θ-role patient assigned to NP.

Consider next *atae = award*. In English, we have (56a); in Japanese, (56b), the only choice of D-structure that will not violate the θ-criterion:

(56)(a)   [$_S$ NP$_1$ [$_{VP}$ give NP$_2$ NP$_3$]]
    (b)   [$_S$ NP$_i$ NP$_j$ NP$_k$ atae] (where (i,j,k) is some permutation of (1,2,3))

In each case, NP$_1$ = [NP,S], NP$_2$ = [NP$'$,VP], NP$_3$ = [NP,VP]. S-structure is identical with D-structure, and assignment of θ-role and Case (in Japanese: NP$_1$ = GA, NP$_2$ = NI, NP$_3$ = O) is straightforward.

Consider next the corresponding passives. In English, the passive morphology absorbs the Case assigned to NP$_2$, so that NP$_2$ must move to subject position, with θ-role and Case assigned in the familiar way. In Japanese, passive absorbs either the Case of NP$_2$ or NP$_3$ (as in English dialects that permit both "a book was given Bill" and "Bill was given a book"). Then rule (54) assigns the GF [NP,S] to whichever NP does not receive Case, giving either a GA-O or GA-NI form for passive.

Consider finally the causative forms in Japanese, namely, (57), (58):

(57)   NP$_1$ NP$_2$ NP$_3$ [$_V$ tabe-sase] (NP$_1$ causes NP$_2$ to eat NP$_3$)
(58)   NP$_2$ NP$_3$ [$_V$ tabe-sase-rare] (NP$_2$ is caused to eat NP$_3$)
For convenience, I pick a particular ordering.

The lexical properties of *tabe* require that it bear the grammatical relation [V,VP$_1$], where VP$_1$ has an object [NP,VP$_1$] and VP$_1$ assigns a θ-role to [NP,S$_1$]. By random GF assignment, following the (arbitrary) numerical conventions adopted in (57), we take NP_3 = $[NP,VP_1]$ and NP_2 = $[NP,S_1]$. Thus the lexical structure of (57) will include (59), which is simply a convenient shorthand for a list of the GFs associated with elements of (57):

(59) $[_{S_1}$ NP_2, $[_{VP_1}$ NP_3, $[_{V_1}$ tabe]]]

Lexical properties of *sase* require that it bear the grammatical relation $[V,VP_2]$ to a verb phrase VP_2 with a clausal complement $[S,VP_2]$, where VP_2 assigns a θ -role to the $[NP,S_2]$ of a sentence S_2 containing VP_2 as its VP. Thus the lexical structure of (57) must contain the GFs represented in (60), including (59), if the θ -criterion is to be met at LF:

(60) $[_{S_2}$ NP_1, $[_{VP_2}$ (59), $[_{V_2}$ sase]]]

S-structure is identical in form with D-structure. θ -role assignment is straightforward, given (60), which was derived by random assignment of GF to the D-structure (57). Case assignment is also straightforward. On the assumptions so far discussed, we expect NP_1 = GA, NP_3 = GA. For reasons that we may disregard, the form of NP_2, the subject of *tabe,* is actually NI.

Consider next the passive (58). As noted, passive morphology precludes assignment of θ -role to the subject; therefore the D-structure (58) necessarily lacks an NP which takes on the GF [NP,S] in the full sentence, i.e., $[NP,S_2]$. Random assignment of GF to (58) in such a way as to satisfy the θ -criterion therefore gives a structure that we may represent as (61), keeping to the notational conventions used above:

(61) $[_{S_2}$ $[_{VP_2}$ $[_{S_1}$ NP_2, $[_{VP_1}$ NP_3, $[_{V_1}$ tabe]]]$[_{V_2}$ sase-rare]]]

Since *sase* is passivized as *sase-rare,* one NP in its complement will not receive Case. But there is no NP in its complement; rather only an S. Therefore, this condition is vacuous. Thus there is no reason to apply the rule (52); S-structure is identical in form to D-structure. NP_2, having the GF [NP,S], receives the nominative Case GA; NP_3, with the GF [NP,VP], receives the objective Case O. θ -roles are assigned exactly as in the active counterpart.

Note that we might have approached the matter slightly differently. Suppose, as has sometimes been argued, a general property of causative is to assign the GF indirect object (i.e., [NP´,VP]) to the subject of clausal complement. This would account for the fact that we have GA–NI–O rather than GA–GA–O in (57), and perhaps the principle might be extended to languages that have a rather different way of forming causatives, e.g., the Romance languages. If so, then what we would say at this point is that this property of assigning NI (dative) to [NP´,VP] is absorbed by the passive morphology under principle (42ii), giving the same result as in the foregoing account.

Compare now the passive of a double-object verb (namely, (62)), with the passive of the causative of a single-object verb (namely, (63)):

(62)   NP NP atae-rare
(63)   NP NP tabe-sase-rare

In (62), we have the Case structure GA–O or GA–NI, depending on whether the direct or indirect object of the verb is passivized. In (63), we have only the Case structure GA–O, where the GA form is the subject of the embedded verb in the corresponding active. But no special rules are required to achieve these results, which simply fall out as the only ones possible. Since Japanese allows either object to lose Case under passive, we derive either GA–O or GA–NI for (62). Since *sase* has no NP–complement, no Case is absorbed by the passive *sase-rare* (apart from the consideration of the preceding paragraph, not relevant here), so that the Case structure of the corresponding active is preserved.

Note that the passive of the causative is closely analogous to the English examples such as (44) in which the rule "Move α" did not have to apply to yield the S-structure of a grammatical sentence:

(44)   it was believed (reasoned) that John was a fool

Similarly, in the case of the passive of the causative in Japanese, the corresponding rule "Assume GF" did not have to apply. The reason, in each case, is that there was no NP in the complement of the passivized verb to lose Case under passive morphology.

Summarizing, Japanese is nonconfigurational, English configurational. Thus GFs are not represented in D– and S–structures in Japanese in terms of the formal structures, but are assigned (randomly) to D– and S–structures. Given that GFs are represented configurationally in formal structures in English, English uses the rule "Move α" to permit an NP to assume a new GF, extending its function chain. Lacking this formal representation of GFs, Japanese uses the analogous rule "Assume GF." The lexicons are essentially identical, as are the grammatical relations and functions. The common property of passive, its only stipulated property, is that it "absorbs" Case. In both languages, the base rules are minimal, stipulating only such idiosyncracies as order. In other respects, D-structures are "projected" from lexical structure, by virtue of the θ –criterion. While nothing quite as simple as this can be expected to work out without further problems, this seems a reasonable start towards generalizing the theory sketched earlier to what appear superficially to be radically different language types. If this reasoning is correct, the differences lie essentially along the parameter that Hale identifies as configurational vs.

W^*-language. Evidently, there are subtypes of each category, not dealt with here, and it may turn out that these are not two "language types" but rather more abstract properties that subsystems of a language may instantiate in one or another manner.

The discussion so far has been quasi-historical. I have discussed the ways in which a certain approach to linguistic structure has been developed, guided by the fundamental methodological principle of restricting the category of attainable grammars so that the explanatory adequacy of the theory can be enhanced. Thus, trace theory is the immediate consequence of eliminating the possibility of compounding elementary operations to form more complex transformational rules. At each stage, certain questions arise in a natural way: e.g., What are the properties of empty elements such as trace and PRO? How can principles derived from the study of one type of language be generalized to other types?

Suppose we now put aside the historical approach, and consider from a more abstract point of view the system that has emerged. The basic level of grammatical representation is S–structure. In S–structure, each lexical NP and embedded clause (where "lexical NP" includes PRO, a kind of pronoun, lacking phonetic features) is assigned a function chain $(GF_1, \ldots, GF_n)$. GF_n determines the θ –role (if any) of the element with this function chain; the GF_i's may play other roles in determining LF representation, as may other properties of S–structure. We have decomposed S–structure into two factors: D–structure, which is a representation of GF-θ, i.e., GF_n of the function chain; and a rule adding GF's to a function chain, either "Move α" (for configurational languages, in which GFs are determined by formal configurations) or "Assume GF" (for nonconfigurational languages). S–structure is converted to surface structure, which is in effect an impoverished form of S–structure; and independently, it is converted to LF. For configurational languages, the rule "Move α," now regarded as a special case of the principle for constructing a function chain, has several fundamental properties: (i) subjacency; (ii) ECP; (iii) lack of θ –role assignment in the position of every antecedent. The third property is more general, holding as well in the case of "Assume GF" in nonconfigurational languages. Furthermore, "Move α" with these properties, serves other roles in the grammar, e.g., relating wh-phrases to abstract variables, and extraposition. "Move α" permits the construction of function chains with $n > 2$, which may be impossible in the case of the rule "Assume GF." The Case filter determines applicability of the paired rules "Move α" and "Assume GF" for constructing function chains, though as noted, "Move α" plays other roles as well, so that there might be languages that use "Move α" for, say, wh-movement, while using its counterpart "Assume GF" for constructing function chains. The theory of government and its subtheories (Case theory and binding theory), the theory of control, and no doubt other systems interact to determine permissible grammatical structures consisting of representations at each level. A crucial role is played by the θ –criterion. Given this criterion and the principle that θ –role (if any) is assigned by the final element in the function chain, D–structures are narrowly restricted as a "projection" of lexical structure. Correspondingly, S–structures are limited in variety, given the way they are formed by their two-components: D–structure and the principle for constructing function chains. X–bar theory imposes other constraints on D–structures (hence on S–structures). Apart from these conditions derived from the lexicon (via the θ –criterion) and X–bar theory, base rules will stipulate idiosyncrasies of D–structures (hence S–structures), e.g., ordering properties.

The principles of grammar admit of a certain degree of parametric variation (e.g., choice of bounding nodes for subjacency, exceptional Case-marking, configurational vs. nonconfigurational). It is no doubt necessary to embed the various systems of grammar within a markedness theory. Certain options will be selected as "unmarked" in the absence of evidence to the contrary by the person acquiring knowledge of the language (i.e., acquiring a grammar). Evidence may be direct—e.g., examples of exceptional Case-marking. Or it may be indirect—e.g., a not unreasonable acquisition system can be devised with the operative principle that if certain structures or rules are not exemplified in relatively simple expressions, where they would be expected to be found, then a marked option is selected excluding them in the grammar. In this way, so-called "negative evidence" might be available to the "language-learner," though there is reason to believe that direct negative evidence—e.g., corrections by the speech community—is not a necessary element in acquisition of grammar. It is also possible that "functional considerations"—e.g., compatibility of grammar with analytic principles for parsing, assumed given—might play a role in determining choice of grammar. These and many other questions must be considered in the development of a comprehensive theory of universal grammar, as a characterization of the initial state of the language faculty.

It is obvious without comment that the examples discussed of possible principles, options and alternatives, and other relevant factors barely scratch the surface. Further questions arise when we ask how the language faculty in its initial or steady state interacts with other cognitive systems, such as the systems of conceptual structure and organization, which have their own properties. Obviously the lexicon is one point of contact, but not necessarily the only one. It also goes without saying that the approach I have outlined is not the only one that should be seriously considered, either in its specific details or in its general organization and principles.

I have been assuming implicitly a "modular" approach to problems of cognition, isolating the language faculty as a specific system with its perhaps distinctive properties, and assuming further that this faculty embraces separate though interacting subsystems. It seems to me that this is a reasonable approach to the general problems of cognitive psychology. When a number of systems come to be better understood, it will be possible to raise further questions: Are there principles and properties that hold of many or all such systems?; How do systems interact in cognitive development and in thought and behavior. Obviously many other questions can be raised in principle: How are these systems neurally represented? Can anything substantive be said about the social dimensions of cognition in growth and development or thought and action? Furthermore, I have not mentioned many other avenues of approach to these questions, for example, the study of pathology. What I have been attempting to illustrate is one kind of approach to questions of cognitive psychology that has proven quite fruitful and seems to offer a great deal of promise, and to indicate how one system that is surely basic in human thought and action has begun to yield at least some of its secrets.

2 On Recent Developments in the Theory of Phonology

Morris Halle
Massachusetts Institute of Technology

INTRODUCTION

Phonology is concerned with the physical actualization of sentences, with the sounds of language and with the way these are produced. From a purely physical point of view, the utterances that we produce and perceive are quasi-continuous signals; yet to normal speakers, utterances appear as sequences of words that in turn are sequences of sounds. A basic task of phonology is to provide a proper account for this perceptual "illusion." That it is appropriate to regard it as an illusion, i.e., as something in the speaker's and hearer's mind rather than as something directly present in the signal, becomes clearer when one considers the fact that our ability to recognize words and sounds in utterances is drastically impaired when instead of utterances in a language we know, we are presented with utterances in languages we do not know. Since the fidelity of the signal is not impaired, the drop in our ability to recognize words and sounds must be attributed to our lack of knowledge of the language in which the utterance is produced; i.e., to something within us rather than to a property of the signal. This "something within us" is the proper subject matter of phonology, just as it is the proper subject matter of syntax, semantics, and all the other subdisciplines concerned with the nature of language.

For most of its history the scientific study of the sounds of language—phonology, for short—has made do with simple common sense concepts and operations. For instance, the commonly accepted frameworks for characterizing different speech sounds, all of which ultimately derive from that proposed by Alexander Melville Bell in Visible Speech (1867), develop (somewhat unsymstematically) the obvious observation that a certain small number of basic articulatory configurations and gestures are involved in (the production of) different sounds of speech. Thus, for example, the consonants [p b m] are produced by creating a closure of the vocal tract with the lips, the consonants [k g η] are produced by creating a closure with the body of the tongue, whereas in [t d n] the closure is created by the blade of the tongue. Of the nine consonants just cited, three [m n η] are produced with a lowered velum, which results in the resonances of the nasal cavity being acoustically excited, while the remaining six are produced without lowering of the velum and, hence, without such nasal resonances. Finally, [p t k] are produced without simultaneous vibration of the vocal cords, whereas vocal cord vibration is present in [b d g m n η].

It was only in the 1930's that these common-sense observations were further developed into a theory with some integral structure of its own. R. Jakobson (1939) proposed that the basic gestures and configurations such as those illustrated in the preceding paragraph ARE the elementary phonic constituents of language. He termed these gestures and configurations "distinctive features" and stated that each speech sound is not a further unanalyzable entity, but is rather (nothing but) a complex of distinctive features. Moreover, he proposed that all features are of a binary character, that their number is strictly limited—of the order of twenty or less—and that there are various restrictions of what features can be combined to make up a particular sound. These proposals have provided explanations for many facts recorded in the literature and have led to the discovery of previously unsuspected regularities (see Chomsky & Halle, 1968).

Students of language have long been familiar with the fact that the sounds of a language are subject to various rules. Thus, for instance in English the sounds [p t k] are pronounced differently in such words as *pill, till, kill,* than in *spill, still, skill.* Some of the greatest achievements of nineteenth century linguistics involved the discovery of the effects of such phonological rules or "sound laws" in the evolution of the Indo-European languages; e.g., Grimm's and Verner's Laws in Germanic, Grassmann's Law in Sanskrit and Greek, and Saussure's Law in Lithuanian, etc., are phonological rules that function (or once functioned) in the different sub-branches of Indo-European. Although the discovery of "sound laws" was extensively pursued by linguists for well over a century, relatively little attention was paid to the form of the "laws." This changed radically in the 1950's when, largely as a result of Chomsky's work on syntax, it became clear that a central component of every speaker's knowledge of his language must be made up of rules, including phonological rules. Since that time, the study of rules has been a major topic in phonology.

MAIN TOPICS OF PHONOLOGICAL RESEARCH

Natural Classes

Phonological rules typically involve not single sounds but classes of sounds. The classes of sounds that figure in the phonological rules that have been studied by scholars are not just arbitrary collections of sounds, but almost always are sets of sounds that share a small set of distinctive features. Thus, we frequently find such sets as [p t k] or [b d g] or [m n ŋ], whereas sets such as [p n g] or [m n k] are practically never encountered. What distinguishes the two types of sets is that the former can be uniquely specified by mentioning one or two distinctive features, while such simple specification is not possible in the case of the latter type of set. The classes of sounds that figure in rules thus provide some support for Jakobson's suggestion that speech sounds are (nothing but) complexes of distinctive features. Moreover, the suggestion exemplifies a result of phonology that is somewhat beyond common-sense considerations.

Interactions among Rules

Formally a phonological rule may be thought of as having the effect of rewriting part of the distinctive feature complexes of specific sounds in particular contexts, thereby replacing these sounds by others. Thus, for instance, part 1 of Grimm's Law replaces [p t k] by [f θ x] respectively. Similarly, part 2 of Grimm's Law replaces [b d g] by [p t k]. The question of interest here is whether or not the [p t k] resulting from part 2 of Grimm's Law are also subject to part 1 of the law. To answer this question, an elaborate theory of rule ordering was developed that has led to important results of a nature that goes far beyond the initial common-sense assumptions of the theory. In particular, work by Kiparsky (1979), Mascaro (1978), Rubach (1980), and others has shown that it is necessary to recognize at least two classes of rules in phonology—those that apply in a cyclic order to each nested constituent in turn and those that apply after the cyclic rules—and that different restrictions apply to the two types of rules.

Three Dimensional Representations

A third topic of interest has been the form of the abstract representation of sound sequences to which phonological rules apply. As noted above, sounds are complexes of binary features. Thus, a word is represented by a two-dimensional matrix where each sound is represented by a column of distinctive feature specifications. The matrix may be subdivided into various sub-sequences of distinctive feature columns to reflect the fact that the word in question is composed of a number of morphemes, i.e., prefixes, stems, suffixes, etc. It has, however, been known almost from the very beginning of scientific concern with language that words are also organized simultaneously into sequential sub-strings of another kind, namely syllables. What was particularly disturbing is that the syllabic organization is totally independent of the organization of a word into constituent morphemes. This dual organization of the words *originality* and *interment* is illustrated in (1), where for typographical convenience each distinctive feature column is represented by a letter:

$$
\begin{array}{ccccccc}
m_1 & & m_2 & m_3 & m_1 & m_2 & m_3 \\
\end{array}
$$

This dual organization of words has been explored less than is warranted because until quite recently the only means for delimiting subsequences in the phonetic string that linguists have seriously entertained have been boundary markers or junctures that can be intercalated at appropriate points in the string. The problem with this device is that it introduces into the phonological representation all sorts of symbols that, if taken seriously, tend to make the statement of various phonological regularities impenetrably complex as illustrated in (2), where # represents word boundaries, / syllable boundaries, and + morpheme boundaries:

$$
\#+/o/ri/gi/n+a/l+i/ty\#+/ \qquad \#+/in+/ter+/ment\#+/ \qquad (2)
$$

The opacity of the representation in (2) is a direct consequence of the fact that phonological representations have been regarded as unilinear sequences of entities. As a result of work by Williams (1976), Goldsmith (1975), Leben (1973), and others, it has become clear that tonal phenomena in many languages cannot be adequately treated by means of unilinear phonological representations and require at least two parallel sequences of units: tones and phonemes. Thus, Leben (1973) points out that in Mende there are five contrasting melodies on monosyllabic words: Low, High, Rising, Falling, Rising-Falling. On bisyllabic words, however, we don't find $5^2 = 25$ melodies, but only 5: HH, LL. LH, HL, L-Rising. On trisyllabic words, we find again only 5 melodies: HHH, LLL, LHH, HLL, LHL, not 5^3. These facts follow at once if dynamic tones such as Rising and Falling are represented as sequences—i.e., High-Low and Low-High—and if, moreover, tones and phones are represented as sequences on separate (autosegmental) tiers which are linked to each other, as shown in (3):

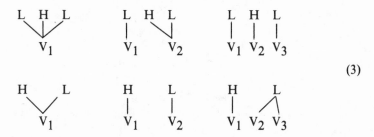

(3)

It was suggested by D. Kahn (1976) that syllables could be set up as a separate autosegmental tier, like the tones in (3), and it is all but self-evident that the same is true of morphemes. But this is, in effect, what was already done in (1), which we modify graphically as in (4) to bring out this point more clearly:

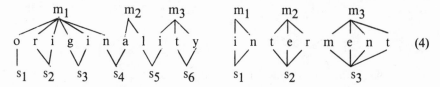

(4)

We have captured the fact that the syllabic and morphological organizations of words are independent of one another by representing the syllables $(s_1, \ldots, s_N)$ and morphemes $(m_1, \ldots, m_N)$ on separate planes or *autosegmental tiers*. There is, of course, no reason to limit the number of separate autosegmental tiers to two. From what has been said above, it is to be expected that the intonation of words would be represented on a separate tier that is orthogonal to both the morphemic and the syllabic tiers, as illustrated in (5):

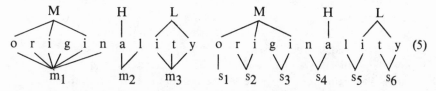

(5)

Phonological features other than tone may also appear on separate autosegmental tiers. In fact, it has been argued (convincingly to my mind) by John McCarthy (1979) that the phonemes which constitute the core of the representations above should be further analyzed into a sequence of slots which are spcified only as C(onsonant) or V(owel) and whose phonetic content (distinctive feature composition) is given on a separate autosegmental tier. We illustrate this kind of representation in (6) where we have shown on one autosegmental tier the phonetic content of the slots and on a separate tier the syllabic organization of the string.

$$
\begin{array}{cccccc}
s_1 & s_2 & s_3 & s_4 & s_5 & s_6 \\
\mid & \wedge & \wedge & \wedge & \wedge & \wedge \\
V\ C & V\ C & V\ C & V\ C & V\ C & V
\end{array} \tag{6}
$$

| | | | | | | | | | |
o r i g i n a l i t y

In sum, the phonological representation that emerges from the above considerations is that of a three-dimensional object whose core is made up of a linear sequence of C and V slots. This core, which Vergnaud and I have called the *skeleton,* is surrounded by a number of tiers, each of which consists of a linear sequence of entities: distinctive feature complexes (both phones and tones) or higher level entities such as morphemes, syllables, etc. The units in these satellite strings are linked to the slots of the skeleton in accordance with a variety of principles, of which a few are briefly reviewed below.

The Structure of Syllables

All languages have restrictions on what phonemes can combine into sequences, and speakers of a language can readily tell whether or not a given sequence would constitute a well-formed word in their language. It has been suggested by Haugen (1956) that the syllable is the domain over which the sequential constraints of the language hold. When this essentially correct insight is explored further and sequential constraints *within* syllables are examined in detail it becomes clear that different subparts of the syllable are subject to different constraints. Moreover, these subparts play also quite different roles in the phonological rule system of different languages. The central constituent of the syllable—the one that may not be missing in any syllable in any language—is the *Rime*. The rime is made up of one syllabic segment (vowel or other syllabic unit) to which may be optionally adjoined—usually on its right—one or more additional segments. The Rime may be preceded by the *Onset,* a sequence of consonants, and it may be followed by the *Appendix,* usually a highly restricted sequence of consonants. The canonical structure of the syllable is as illustrated in (7).

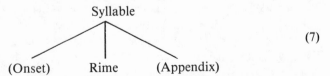

Syllable

(Onset)   Rime   (Appendix)

(7)

All languages have syllables composed of Onset + Rime. Many languages lack syllables containing Appendixes or limit severely the occurrence of such syllables. Syllables without Onset, specifically syllables consisting of a rime exclusively, are disallowed in some languages. In addition to these restrictions, each language has limitations on the number and kinds of sounds that may make up the three constituents of the syllable. Onsets and Appendixes may be composed only of consonants whereas the Rime contains a vowel which may be followed by another vowel and/or some consonants. Finally, there are restrictions on the particular consonants and vowels that appear in the different positions. Speakers of all languages are quite aware of these restrictions and take immediate notice of any violations.

While the occurrence of the syllable is not restricted in any special way, its components—the Onset, Rime, and Appendix—play rather different roles in the phonology of many languages. In most languages words are not simply linear concatenations of syllables. Rather, words have their characteristic stress contours where some syllables are subordinate in stress to others. These contours are, of course, the result of specific rules. It is an interesting fact that these stress rules take into account only the rime structure of the different syllables, but totally disregard the onset (and the appendix). This fact constitutes an additional reason (additional to the distributional constraints mentioned above) for treating the Rime, the Onset, and the Appendix as separate constituents of the syllable.

Feet

In many languages, the stress contour of a word is made up of sub-strings of rimes, called *feet*. Feet are made up of one or more binary branching nodes of which either the left or right is *dominant*. What distinguishes dominant from nondominant nodes is that only the former, but not the latter, may branch (or under special conditions, must branch). It follows from this fact that the trees constituting the feet in a language will all be left- or right-branching, whereas mixed structures of the kind illustrated in (8) are excluded as feet:

(8)

It follows from the preceding that if the terminal elements of feet are rimes, a distinction will be made between rimes that branch and those that do not. Whereas a sequence of nonbranching rimes will be gathered into a single foot, each branching rime will initiate its own foot.

A further property of metrical feet is that their nodes are labeled in accordance with one of two conventions:

(9) a. Label a node strong (and its sister weak) if and only if it is dominant.

  b. Label a node strong (and its sister weak) if and only if it is dominant *and* branching.

There are special conventions for interpreting the labels *strong* and *weak*. In some instances these labels express the relative strengths of a particular phonetic property, in other instances *strong* is interpreted as possessing a particular feature, e.g., [+ stress] and *weak* as lacking the feature; i.e., [− stress]. We illustrate in (10) with an English example:

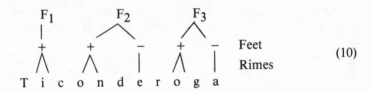

(10)

English stress feet are left-dominant and their labels are interpreted not as relative but as absolute specifications of the feature values. The feet, moreover, are gathered into a single word tree, which in English happens to be right-dominant and labeled by convention (9a), the labels of this tree being interpreted in relative rather than absolute terms, as shown in (11):

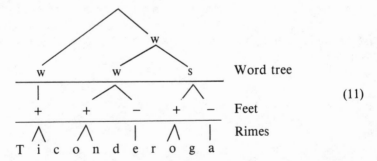

(11)

As a consequence, main stress in a word such as *Ticonderoga* is on the last foot and lesser stress on the other feet, the degree of stress being inversely proportional to the depth of embedding of the foot.

The theoretical framework sketched above provides a restricted number of choices in terms of which accentual patterns must be described. A partial list of these choices is given below:

(12) a. Does the language construct feet?
 b. Are the feet left- or right-dominant?
 c. Are the feet labeled by convention (9a) or (9b)?
 d. Is the relative or absolute interpretation to be attributed to the labeling?
 e. Is the word tree left- or right-dominant etc.?

The total number of choices is quite limited. In the light of our present knowledge, it would appear to be of the order of ten (see Hayes, 1980). There are thus about one thousand (2^{10}) possible accentual systems and one task of future research is to establish the definitive list of choices and to document the existence of the different stress systems among the languages of the world.

A different line of research opened up by the theoretical framework sketched above is the development of a realistic acquisition model. If the theory sketched above is correct, the task of learning the stress system of a particular language reduces to finding answers to the questions listed in (12). It is a reasonably straightforward matter to specify what sort of information would be required to answer the questions. For example, if a language had both primary and secondary stresses in its words, that would be an indication that the language organized the syllables (rimes) of the word into feet. The location of the primary stress in a word toward the beginning or toward the end of the word would provide an answer to the question (12e) whether the word tree is left- or right-dominant. The task of research in this domain would be to show how the requisite information is acquired by children in the course of acquiring their mother tongue and if possible how stages in this process are reflected in the phonetic form of the words produced by the learners.

ACKNOWLEDGMENTS

This word was supported by National Institutes of Health Grant #5 PO1 MH13990–15.

REFERENCES

Bell, A. M. *Visible speech*. London & New York: Funk & Wagnalls, 1867.
Chomsky, N., & Halle, M. *The sound pattern of English*. New York: Harper & Row, 1968.
Goldsmith, J. *Autosegmental phonology*. PhD dissertation, MIT, Department of Linguistics, 1975.
Haugen, E. The syllable in linguistic description. In: *For Roman Jakobson*, M. Halle, H. G. Lunt, H. McLean (Eds.), The Hague: Mouton, 1956.

Hayes, B. *A metrical theory of stress rules*. PhD dissertation, MIT Department of Linguistics, 1980.

Jakobson, R. Observations sur le classement phonologique des consonnes. In: *Proceedings of the Third International Congress of Phonetics Sciences,* Ghent, 1939.

Kahn, D. *Syllable based generalizations in English phonology*. PhD dissertation, MIT, Department of Linguistics, 1976.

Kiparsky, P. Metrical structure assignment is cyclic. *Linguistic Inquiry,* 1979, *10*, 421–441.

Leben, W. *Suprasegmental phonology*. PhD dissertation, MIT, Department of Linguistics, 1973.

Mascaro, J. *Catalan phonology and the phonological cycle*. PhD dissertation, MIT, Department of Linguistics, 1978.

McCarthy, J. *Formal problems in Semitic phonology and morphology*. PhD dissertation, MIT, Department of Linguistics, 1979.

Rubach, J. *Palatalization, cyclic phonology and borrowings into Polish and English*. Unpublished paper, MIT, Department of Linguistics, 1980.

Williams, E. Underlying Tone in Margi and Ibo. *Linguistic Inquiry,* 1976, *7*:3.

3 Perceptual and Analogical Bases of Cognition

Roger N. Shepard
Stanford University

I have been heartened by indications of two general shifts in psychological theorizing. The first, which was already underway by the time of Chomsky's (1959) review of Skinner's (1957) book *Verbal Behavior,* is, I think, now securely established. It is the shift from an exclusive preoccupation with learning and hence with environmental influences during the life of a single individual, implicity regarded as a kind of structureless tabula rasa, and toward concern for the highly developed structure that each organism brings with it into the world by virtue of its evolutionarily conferred biological endowment and through which environmental events have their particular effects and internal interpretations. The second shift, though related to the first, is more recent and perhaps less widely accepted. It is a shift from a preoccupation with discrete sequential *processes* presumed to mediate observed behavior to a concern with structurally dense parallel or analogical *representations* that are operated upon by those processes and that, in turn, guide and constrain those processes (Shepard, 1975, 1981; Shepard & Cooper, 1982).

There are two things that I particularly want to bring out in this paper: first, the possibly important role in the perceptual system of structure that has, over the eons of vertebrate evolution, internalized the most important invariants and constraints in the external world, and second, the intimate connection that I believe to exist between the perception of objects and the internal representation of their possible transformations.

EVOLUTIONARY CONSIDERATIONS

Many different kinds of indications, including empirical evidence and theoretical considerations, converge in supporting the notion that our

49

perception of the world is mediated by a complex system with a structure that is as much prewired as it is acquired. There are the obvious innate differences between individuals and, especially, between species. There is the highly specific functional cytoarchitecture evident in the sensory and motor neural systems of the newborn (Hubel & Wiesel, 1963) and the gross anatomical localization of such higher cognitive functions as language and spatial relations (Geshwind, 1978; Lenneberg, 1967). There is the ability of young children to generalize beyond an extremely limited set of experiences (e.g., to extrapolate the use of the word "doggie" after having been exposed to only a few instances and perhaps, as claimed by Chomsky, to induce a grammar on the basis of a degenerate sample of the language). There is the quite different evidence, which I have previously noted in the field of artifical intelligence (Shepard, 1964), that in order to enable a machine to begin to imitate any significant human perceptual or cognitive performance, a great deal of very specific structure must be built or programmed into that machine. And there is, finally, the simple fact of the enormous ratio between the hundreds of millions of years that our species as a whole has had to achieve a gross adaptation to this world and the ten to twenty years that each individual member of the species then has to achieve whatever additional fine tuning is necessitated by its particular, local circumstances.

In view of the extended time base of biological evolution, I suppose that it would have been the most pervasive and enduring features, invariants, or constraints of the world in which we have evolved that would have become most deeply and thoroughly entrenched in our innate perceptual machinery. Prominent among these are such enduring facts as the following: Space is three-dimensional, locally Euclidean, homogeneous, and isotropic except for a unique upright direction conferred by the local gravitational field. Time is one-dimensional and homogeneous but possesses a unique forward direction conferred by the local thermodynamic disequilibrium—which, according to one view, also has its ultimate origin in gravitation (Davies, 1977). The most significant objects tend, over time, to conserve structural identity, including semirigid structure or even rigid structure. As a result, the relative positions and motions of such objects are constrained to six principal degrees of freedom: three of relative location (or translation), and three of relative orientation (or rotation).

Ubiquitous, also, is the fact that higher organisms are themselves objects possessing a well-defined three-dimensional structure with a grossly bilateral symmetry, and possessing a canonical reference orientation with respect to gravity, and a canonical forward-directed orientation in which the sensory surfaces face the object sensed so that, in the standard mode of locomotion, they approach that object (cf., Clark 1973). Finally, being three-dimensional, the body is necessarily bounded by a two-dimensional surface through which all sensory commerce with the external world must take place. Hence, I suppose that among the rules that have been internalized in the perceptual system, are those that approximate the inverses of the rules of projection of external objects onto the two-dimensional surface (the retina, in the case of vision). In this way the organism is afforded a basis for factoring the information available at the two-dimensional sensory array into two parts: one of which then takes the form of a representation of the invariant structure of the external object; and the other of which then takes the form of a representation of the six-degrees of freedom of the spatial relation of the subject to that object (Shepard, 1979, 1981).

With a few notable exceptions, such as Gibson (1966, 1977) and Johansson (1950, 1976), students of visual perception seem to have assumed that the perception of a stationary form is less complex than the perception of such a form in motion and, therefore, that we should achieve a thorough understanding of the static case before attempting a study of the more complex dynamic one. Possibly, however, this assumption is wrong. If, as I have been suggesting, the simplest and most pervasive features of the world are the ones that have become most deeply incorporated into the nervous system, then it may well be that the general constraints entailed by the six degrees of freedom of rigid objects in space have a more basic and prior representation in the perceptual (and motor) system than do the more complex constraints entailed by the vastly greater numbers of degrees of freedom needed to specify the shapes of the different particular objects that have been of concern to us and to our remote ancestors.

Moreover, as I have recently argued in greater detail (Shepard, in press), the representation of form cannot be disassociated from the representation of rotational orientation. For, if we attempt a parametric variation of the shape of some object (for example, the two degrees of freedom of the shape of a triangle), we inevitably find that certain regions of the parameter space yield the same intrinsic shape, but rigidly rotated into a different orientation. Hence the problem of factoring the total representation into the two components having to do with the shape of the object itself and with its orientation relative to the subject is by no means trivial.

I am in fact going to suggest that the representation of the possible transformations of an object is basic to the representation of the object itself. Although this suggestion may appear somewhat radical, I believe it to be consonant with Cassirer's (1944) early insights into the role of transformational groups in perception; Garner's (1974) definition of the goodness of a figure in terms of the size of the class of figures that are equivalent to it under rigid spatial transformations; and Gibson's (1966, 1977) emphasis on the free mobility of the perceiver and on the correlated transformations induced in the optic array.

Indeed, having come to this position on the basis of these theoretical considerations and certain experimental results to be described shortly, I now find that an essential part of the experience of any object in space is a clear, if unarticulated, recognition of the possible spatial perturbations of that object—precisely the three degrees of freedom of location (movements left or right, up or down, nearer or farther) and three of orientation (attitude, pitch, and yaw). Moreover, these are immediately and fully given as part of the experience of an object in space, even when the identity of the object and the representation of its shape are not fully established. I know how to grasp the object, to save it from tipping over, or to brush it aside before I even know what the object is.

Note, incidentally, that the problem of perception far transcends the specific classical problem of the recognition of objects. For the purpose of managing in the world, the ability merely to recognize and to classify a previously experienced object is not in itself sufficient. We must also have a clear perception of our spatial relationship to that object and, often, we must be able to generate motor programs for grasping and manipulating or, alternatively, for avoiding or climbing over that object. Moreover, we must and do have a similarly clear perception of objects, surfaces, and other spatial structures and of our spatial relationships to them even when these are quite strange and encountered for the first time.

As an example, the rotation of a random three-dimensional configuration of points is perceived as rigid on the basis of its merely two-dimensional, nonrigid projection (Green, 1961). Likewise, a perceptual illusion of apparent rigid rotation is induced simply by presenting, in alternation, two differently oriented configurations (Farrell & Shepard, 1981; Shepard & Judd, 1976; Shepard, 1981). But, as a reflection of the fact that the world in which we have evolved is only three-dimensional, a two- or three-dimensional projection of a similarly rigid rotation in four-dimensional space is never perceived as rigid.

STUDIES OF THE INTERNAL REPRESENTATION
OF SPATIAL TRANSFORMATIONS

Now, by definition, a rigid object does not change in intrinsic size. Changes in the size of the image that it projects on the retina are associated, rather, with the distance of the object from the observer and hence, by an appropriate choice of (egocentric) coordinates, with one of the three coordinates (x_3, say) of spatial location. However, these three dimensions of translational position are less dependent on the degrees of freedom of shape and can more readily be factored out of the problem of representing three-dimensional form. We must, however, confront the problem of the proper representation of the set possible orientations of a rigid object in three-dimensional space, because this is more closely tied to the problem of the representation of its form.

Since there are just three degrees of freedom of rotation, the space of possible orientations of an inherently asymmetric object must be three dimensional. It is, in fact, topologically equivalent to projective space and can be modeled by the three-dimensional interior and surface of a sphere with diametrically opposite points on the surface identified. Corresponding to the fact that rotation is cyclical, bringing the object back to its original orientation after 360°, the space is finite though unbounded. Metrically, the space is a manifold in which rotation of the object about any fixed axis corresponds to the motion of a point around a closed geodesic curve or shortest path within the manifold, or in terms of the model, to the traversal of a kind of great circle between identified endpoints.

Proceeding from the conviction that the internal representation of the possible orientations of a rigid object is basic to our representation both of the spatial transformations of objects and of the objects themselves, my own research has, during the last ten years, focused primarily on the experimental study of phenomena of apparent and mental rotation. The most pertinent empirical findings that have so far emerged from the work of this type, completed by my students and me, can be briefly summarized as follows:

In mentally comparing two different simultaneously presented views of the same three-dimensional object (Shepard & Metzler, 1971), or in perceptually integrating two successively presented views (Shepard & Judd, 1976), a person internally constructs what amounts, in the manifold of possible orientations, to a locally shortest or geodesic path between the points corresponding to the two views. Thus, for pairs of computer-generated perspective views of asymmetric three-dimensional objects such as the pairs reproduced in Fig. 1, a variety of different kinds of evidence has provided converging support for the idea that the representational process actually passes through a series of internal states corresponding one-to-one to an ordered series of intermediate orientations of the external object.

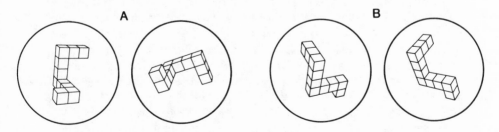

FIG. 1   Pairs of perspective views of the three-dimensional objects, illustrating an angular difference of 60° in the picture plane (A) and in depth (B).

1. As shown in Fig. 2A, the time required to determine that two such views are of objects of identical shape (rather than being enantiamorphic or mirror-image objects) increases linearly with the angular difference between the two orientations portrayed (Metzler & Shepard, 1974; Shepard & Metzler, 1971; also see Cooper, 1975, 1976). Likewise, as shown in Fig. 2B, the minimum onset-to-onset time for a good illusion of rigid apparent rotational motion, when the two views are alternately presented in the same spatial location, increases linearly with the angular different (Shepard & Judd, 1976; also see Farrell & Shepard, 1981).

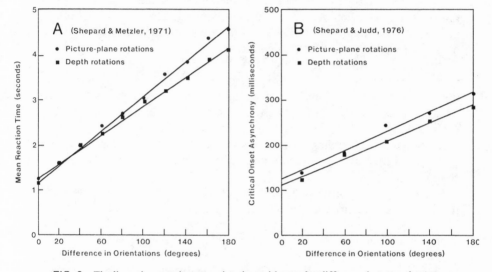

FIG. 2   The linear increase in processing time with angular difference between the two objects. (A) Time required to compare two objects presented simultaneously. (B) Minimum stimulus-onset asynchrony for rigid apparent motion between two objects presented in successive alternation.

2. The rates of apparent or mental rotation implied by the slopes of these linear functions are essentially independent of the orientation in three-dimensional space of the axis of the rotational difference between the two objects (although rotations about a vertical axis appear to have a slight advantage and rotations about a natural axis of the object itself are appreciably easier and faster). Indeed, as can be seen in Figs. 2 rotations about the line of sight, which correspond to rigid rotations of the retinal image, are no faster than rotations in depth, which correspond to nonrigid and even discontinuous transformations of the retinal projection (Metzler & Shepard, 1974; Shepard & Judd, 1976; Shepard & Metzler, 1974).

3. Particularly for pairs differing by large angles (close to 180°), subjects can unknowingly be influenced to carry out the apparent or mental rotation either the long or the short way around the circle. Accordingly, the obtained function relating time to angular differences either continues to increase as

a linear extrapolation beyond 180° or else reverses and decreases with a negative slope of equal magnitude beyond 180° (Metzler & Shepard, 1974; Shepard, 1981; also see Cooper, 1975).

4. During the course of apparent or mental rotation, subjects respond most rapidly and accurately to test probes that are in successively more and more rotated orientations, demonstrating that the internal process does indeed pass through a path corresponding one-to-one to a rotation in external three-dimensional space (Cooper, 1976; Cooper & Shepard, 1973; Metzler & Shepard, 1974; Robins & Shepard, 1977).

On the basis of these and related findings (more fully presented in Shepard & Cooper, 1982), I draw the following conclusions: (a) Our internal representation of a three-dimensional object captures something of the three-dimensional structure of that object as it exists in isotropic three-dimensional space, and is relatively unrelated to its two-dimensional retinal projection. (b) The representation is not, however, of the inherent three-dimensional shape of the object considered purely in itself; it is always of that object as viewed in a particular orientation. (c) In successfully interpreting two such views as being of the same object, the brain constructs a representational path of rigid transformation between them. (d) If the two views are sufficiently similar, this interpolated path is generally a shortest path in the (curved) manifold of possible orientations though, for views differing by nearly 180°, a geodesic path may sometimes be traversed the long way around the manifold.

Since we have evolved in a three-dimensional world populated with enduring, movable, and often animated semirigid objects, it is perhaps remarkable but not entirely incomprehensible that the brain should have acquired the tendency to interpret the superficially different figural units in two successive glimpses as representing the same enduring object, or that it should try to construct, as the more probable concrete representation of the intervening existence of that object, the most direct or minimum possible rigid transformation between the two successive views. However, such a process of mental impletion, like any mental process, must take time; and the larger the gap—that is, the larger the discrepancy between the two orientations—the greater will be the time required to construct an appropriate bridge. Thus I believe that subjectively continuous impletion that is experienced as bridging the discontinuity between two objectively discrete and isolated presentations reveals with special clarity the autonomous, synthetic tendencies of the underlying perceptual machinery of the human brain.

INVESTIGATIONS OF THE ROLE OF SYMMETRIES AND OF FORM

The three-dimensional closed manifold of possible orientations of an object can be thought of as a constraint surface in a higher-dimensional embedding space with the properties (a) that motion of a point within that three-dimensional surface represents the abstract essence of a transformation of the object that preserves its rigid structure, and (b) that motion along a geodesic path within that surface represents the minimum such transformation. Accordingly, when two orientations of an object are displayed in slow alternation, the brain is assumed to find in effect a shortest path between the two corresponding points within the constraint surface—possibly by some process of spreading activation. And, having found such a path, the alternation need no longer be represented, at this abstract level, by the appearance and disappearance of each of the two separated points. In accordance with fundamental principles of object conservation and least action, the same alternation can now be represented by a single, enduring point moving back and forth over the shortest connecting path.

However, when the rate of alternation is sufficiently increased, the brain will not have time to complete the connecting path during each cycle. (The required rate of completion exceeds, say, the rate of propagation of spreading activation within the constraint surface.) In this case, the identity of the two successively displayed objects can no longer be concretely instantiated in the strongest and therefore most preferred form of an identity of rigid structure. Instead, reflecting the fact about our world that most objects that do not conserve strictly rigid structure at least conserve semirigid structure, that most objects that do not conserve even semirigid structure at least conserve number (or volume), and so on, the brain takes recourse to successively weaker stations in a hierarchy of criteria of object identity. It relinquishes only in extremity the root hypothesis that the two objects, however transmogrified, are nevertheless at basis the same object.

By definition of the constraint surface, the breakdown in perceived rigid rotation is abstractly represented by a motion of the point outside that surface. Just as an object that has rotational symmetry must map into itself with some rotation short of 360°, an object that is not strictly symmetric but, like most real objects, possesses some at least approximate symmetries, must, under certain rotations, become, though not identical, at least more similar to itself than under other, lesser rotations. Thus, approximations to symmetry in the structure of the object, which are characteristic of most natural objects and which, indeed, can be regarded as defining their shapes via a generalized type of autocorrelation function (Shepard, 1979, 1981), can be regarded as inducing convolutions in which otherwise remote regions of the constraint surface are brought into closer proximity with each other in the embedding space. Accordingly, break-downs or short circuits (produced, say, by a weaker spreading activation outside the constraint surface) are more likely to occur via a shorter path through the embedding space. A transformation of the object is still seen, but it is experienced as nonrigid.

Joyce Farrell and I have recently investigated a special case in which (a) we reduced the dimensionality of the manifold of possible orientations from three to one by using random polygons that differed only by rotations in the picture plane, and which (b) we varied the approximation to just one specific sort of symmetry; namely, symmetry under 180° rotation (Farrell & Shepard, 1981). We generated other polygons with intermediate degrees of symmetry by a linear interpolation between each of the original random polygons and the derived, rotationally symmetric polygons (Fig. 3). On a given trial the computer-driven graphical display alternately presented two different orientations of one such polygon and, by tapping a right- or left-hand key, the subject increased or decreased the rate of alternation until the point of breakdown of apparent rigid rotation in the picture plane had been determined.

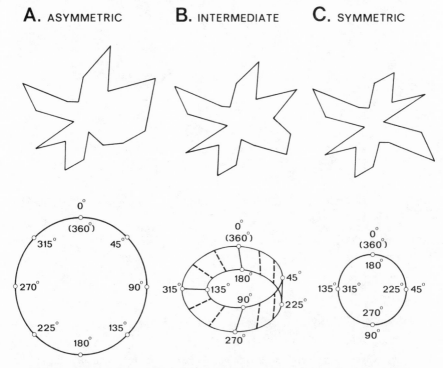

A. ASYMMETRIC   **B.** INTERMEDIATE   **C.** SYMMETRIC

FIG. 3 Example of an asymmetric random polygon (A), a derived polygon that has complete symmetry under 180° rotation (C), and a linearly interpolated polygon having an intermediate degree of symmetry (B). The curves portrayed below indicated the loci of all possible orientations of such a polygon in a four-dimensional embedding space in which perceptual similarity is represented by spatial proximity.

We found that for asymmetric polygons, the critical onset-to-onset time increased approximately linearly with angular disparity, as it did in the earlier experiment of Shepard & Judd (1976), and as it should if the motions were perceived as conserving rigid structure. For completely symmetric polygons, the critical time increased in a similar manner to 90° but then decreased with apparently the same slope towards 180° (where, of course, no motion was seen). For symmetric polygons differing by an angle, ϕ, exceeding 90°, the motion was perceived in the opposite direction, through a smaller angle, 180° − ϕ. (See Fig. 4.)

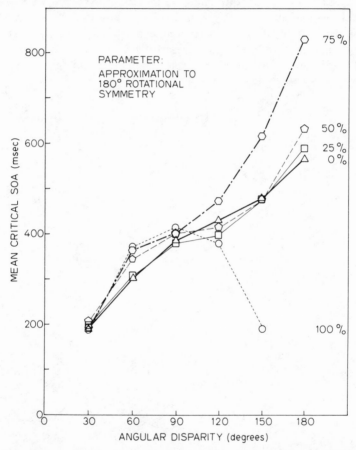

FIG. 4   Minimum stimulus-onset asynchrony for rigid apparent motion between two alternately presented orientations of a planar polygon having some percentage approximation to complete 180° rotational symmetry.

For polygons that were linearly interpolated between the asymmetric and completely symmetric polygons, the critical times beyond 90° became more variable and increased more rapidly than for the asymmetric polygons. Usually at 180° and sometimes at 150° subjects were not able to see a rigid motion no matter how much the alternation was slowed. Apparently, the pull toward the similarly shaped and similarly oriented alternative was too strong to permit the completion of the path connecting to the identically shaped but very dissimilarly oriented alternative. The trajectory then tended to "short circuit" through the embedding space rather than following the constraint surface (See Fig. 5). Stated in general terms, the fact that constructive processes necessarily take time forces a trading relation between the level in the hierarchy of criteria of object identity at which two successive sensory events can be connected, on the one hand, and the extent of the mental transformation required for the achievement of that connection, on the other.

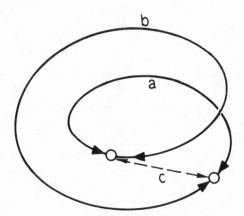

FIG. 5 Schematic representation of the alternative paths between two widely different orientations of an approximately symmetric object. (Paths a and b preserve rigid structure; the "short-circuit" path c does not.)

In a second experiment we obtained empirical data supporting the posited structure of the constraint manifold. We measured the times subjects required to determine whether two pictures of the same polygon were in the same or different orientations in the picture plane. If we assume that the discrimination times from this second experiment represent the self-similarities of the polygons in different orientations (independent of absolute orientation), the model indicates that application of Carroll's IND-SCAL scheme of "three-way" multidimensional scaling (Carroll & Chang, 1970) should yield the underlying curved manifold. The obtained four-dimensional solution was in fact almost exactly as predicted. Dimensions 3 and 4, which were most heavily weighted for the more asymmetric conditions, contained the single 360° circle of orientations (essentially as shown in the lower left of Fig. 3). While Dimensions 1 and 2, which were most heavily weighted for the more symmetric conditions, contained the double-wound circle with orientations differing by 180° identified (essentially as shown in the lower right of Fig. 3). As the degree of symmetry varies, the curve corresponding to intermediate degrees of symmetry sweeps out the curved constraint manifold in the four-dimensional embedding space.

POSSIBLE CONNECTIONS WITH NEUROPHYSIOLOGY

In this work on the representation of the transformations of complex objects in space, my students and I have been trying to establish a bridge between relatively abstract characterizations of the internal representation and external observables such as latencies of overt discriminative responses. We have not as yet mounted a serious attempt to construct a bridge, also, to the concrete neurophysiological events that must underlie the observed behavior. Indeed, the phenomena that we have been studying appear to depend on processes at a level of the nervous system that is very different from the neurophysiologically much more accessible and better understood sensory and motor processes.

Nevertheless, we can perhaps begin to discern at least one possible connection between the theoretical ideas that I have briefly sketched out here and the Fourier-analytic mechanisms that have been proposed for sensory processing in the perceptual domains of audition (since the time of Helmholtz, 1885/1954) and vision (more recently). In particular, the Fourier transform to the spatial frequency domain (in which, also, there is a kind of factoring into the representation of objects, via frequency spectra, and of their locations, via phase) seems to have much in common with the computation of autocorrelation functions, which I (like Uttal, 1975) have suggested may underlie the perception of objects. Moreover, neurophysiological mechanisms that compute cross correlations are already thought to underlie such varied perceptual functions as binocular stereopsis, pitch perception, and auditory localization (including highly developed echo location in bats and dolphins).

If, then, we take the possible spatial transformations of an object as a basis for the representation of its shape, we are led to the notion that the shape is characterized by the function giving the similarity of the object to itself under every possible rigid transformation in three-dimensional space. In addition to explaining more complex and later appearing capabilities in terms of simpler, prior ones, such a theory could provide a ready explanation for certain peculiarities of visual perception. The fact that a reflectional symmetry is more likely to be noticed if the axis of the symmetry coincides with the axis of elongation of the object, or even if it is vertical rather than oblique (Palmer & Hemenway, 1978), for example, could be accounted for in terms of the tendency for rotations around such axes to be somewhat more easily imagined. The preference for rotations about a vertical axis could, moreover, find its evolutionary explanation in terms of the fact that the only unique direction in our three-dimensional environment is the gravitationally conferred up-down direction.

Geometrical manifolds of the sort I have described here are not, of course, the only way to represent the structures of the set of possible shapes, the set of their possible positions, and the relations between these two sets. However, any attempt to deal with the complexities of the representation of form and its dependence on orientation must, I believe, deal with these same structures and, ultimately, be isomorphic to these spatial manifolds.

These manifolds do offer one way of conceptualizing the factoring of the degrees of freedom of objects (a) into those of position and orientation, which because of their relative simplicity and pervasiveness may be more deeply entrenched in the perceptual system, and (b) into those of inherent shape, which are usually more complex and specific to particular objects and stages of evolution.

Finally, though, we must remember that it is not the inherent shape of the object that is perceived, but only its three-dimensional shape as viewed in a particular orientation. Possibly, therefore, the autocorrelation function is effectively computed only over local perturbations in the three-dimensional space of orientations in the neighborhood of the currently presented orientation (see Shepard, 1979, 1981).

POSSIBLE CONNECTIONS WITH COGNITIVE SCIENCE GENERALLY

The evolutionary viewpoint adopted here suggests that higher cognitive processes of thinking and language cannot have sprung fully developed out of nothing, but most likely were built upon a previously existing system that was already effectively dealing with the external world—probably the perceptual (or perceptual-motor) system. Indeed, I would align myself with those, including Einstein, Galton, Hadamard (see Hadamard, 1945; Shepard, 1978a, 1978b), who have quite explicitly emphasized that their thinking was not so much a matter of talking to themselves as a matter (in Einstein's words) of "visualizing . . . effects, consequence, and possibilities" (Holton, 1972, p. 110).

In the parlance of the workers in artificial intelligence, as the "top-down" as well as the "bottom-up" mechanisms of perceptual organization became sufficiently highly developed, it may well have come to be that the constraints built into the perceptual system over the course of biological evolution were increasingly bent to the service of creative thought. In this way, having established an abstract goal at a higher level, the perceptual system might provide for the internal simulation of possible courses of action in the external world or, by the geometrical metaphor used here, for the impletion of a suitably direct path in the manifold corresponding to the satisfaction of the constraints imposed by the external world.

According to this viewpoint, the purely linguistic apparatus, though in some ways more abstract and versatile, if forced to operate without the benefit of the powerful rules incorporated in the perceptual system, would fail to deal effectively with the concrete exigencies of physical reality. The linguistic system is not of course without its value—particularly in the present context, for the establishment of the abstract goals and for translating the results of the analog simulation into an externalizable and communicable form. However, the conceptual-linguistic system itself, if it has (as I suggest) evolved out of a spatial-perceptual system, may at some deep level reveal the perceptual-spatial character of its own origin (see Clark, 1973; Miller & Johnson-Laird, 1976; Shepard, 1981). In the words of the linguist Jackendoff (1976, p. 149), "contrary to current fashion" insight into the semantics of natural language is to be found "in the study of the innate conceptions of the physical world and in the way in which conceptual structures generalize to ever wider, more abstract domains."

So, some consideration should perhaps be devoted to the psycholinguistic ramifications of the notion that the mental construction of connecting paths may play a fundamental role in thinking and comprehension, as well as in perception (Shepard, 1981). The linguists Bennett (1974), Gruber (1967), and Jackendoff (1978) have explicitly suggested that the comprehension of sentences may sometimes require the implicit impletion of a mental path. Thus, in an illuminating comparison of just the two verbs "look" and "see," Gruber found compelling linguistic reasons to take "a sentence such as 'John sees a cat' to be a metaphorical extension of 'John goes to a cat'." And Bennett explicitly argued that a mental path must be constructed in order to understand such a sentence as "The post office is over the hill." For, here, the preposition "over" is not understood as a relation in which one of the two objects mentioned is literally above the other in a physical space (as it might be in "The helicopter is over the hill"); it is strictly only the implied connecting path between the interlocutors and the post office that has a spatially superior relationship to the hill.

Close in spirit to the linguistic observations of Bennett, Gruber, and Jackendoff are experiments in which the comprehension of sentences appears to require an implicit spatial transformation. The following example is taken from Black, Turner, and Bower's (1979) study of spatial reference points in comprehension. For each of the initial statements labeled A, the continuation B1 is given from a spatially consistent point of view and, so, is more easily and accurately comprehended or remembered than the continuation B2, which is given from a spatially shifted point of view:

A.   Terry finished working in the yard
B1. and *went* into the house.
B2. and *came* into the house.

A.   Fred was just sitting down
B1. when his dog *brought* him his slippers.
B2. when his dog *took* him his slippers.

We are exploring the extension of this sort of paradigm to cases involving other spatial transformations and hope that we will be able to show that comprehension time, as well as accuracy, reflects the extent or complexity of the implicit transformations. For illustrations, consider sequences A–B constructed from the following sentences:

A1. The dog chased the goat.
A2. The dog faced the goat.

B1. The goat kicked the dog.
B2. The goat butted the dog.

The sequences A1–B1 and A2–B2 are consistent and do not require a spatial transformation for comprehension, while the sequences A1–B2 and A2–B1 appear to require a 180° rotation.

Mental rotation may also play a role in the comprehension of other types of sentences. To elaborate on an example suggested by Herbert Clark (1973), the statement "There is a fly above her knee" can be ambiguous if the person referred to is not in the canonical upright position but, say, is lying flat upon the beach. The fly can then be interpreted as hovering in the air "above" the knee with respect to the global coordinate framework of the external world (as in the example of the helicopter above the hill), or it can be interpreted as crawling on the leg "above" the knee with respect to the very different local coordinate framework of the recumbent person or even of her possibly upraised leg. The latter interpretation may, however, require a mental rotation between the canonical and the currently appropriate coordinate systems.

APPENDIX

Some Specific Comments on the Metaphorically Extended Spatial Uses of English Prepositions

I myself first came to appreciate the extent to which spatial intuitions permeate language use in connection with my work on multidimensional scaling (see, for example, the relevant remarks in Cunningham & Shepard, 1974). Specifically, I was struck by the fact that in talking about relations of similarity among seemingly nonspatial objects such as colors, tones, faces, voices, and the like, people quite automatically employ an unmistakably spatial metaphor. Thus they speak of one color as being "close to" or "far from" another, or of one color being "between" two others, and so on. This is not I think, an insignificant observation. The precision with which ordinal judgment of similarity relations conform to the metric constraints of distance relation in a low dimensional Euclidian space points to the implicit carryover of powerful spatial intuitions. True, it is only in the psychological laboratories that we engage in systematic elicitation of judgments of similarity. Still, since we are in everyday life rarely confronted twice with exactly the same stimulus, the implicit recognition of just such relations of similarity must govern virtually every response we make (Shepard & Chipman, 1970).

In English, prepositions, which serve as the primary vehicle for conveying spatial relationships, quite automatically carry their locative meanings over to purely metaphorical spaces (Shepard, 1981). Just as we say "The members of the band were playing something *between* Third and Four Streets," we say they were playing something "*between* two and four in the afternoon," or even "*between* jazz and folk music." Likewise, just as we say they were playing something "*at* the end of the road," we say they were playing something "*at* a barely audible level," or "*at* the president's request." Just as we say they were playing something "*on* the opposite hillside," we say they were playing something "*on* a variety of instruments," or "*on* a theme by Handel." And just as we say they were playing something "*in* the nearby woods," we say they were playing something "*in* the key of F," or "*in* very poor taste." Notice, moreoever, that in the metaphorical extensions, as much in the examples referring to concrete physical space, we do not generally accept interchange between what have been referred to as the "simple locative" *at*, the "surface locative" *on*, or the "interior locative" *in* (Bennett, 1974; Fillmore, 1971).

I agree with the spirit of Bennett's and Fillmore's characterizations of the dimensional restrictions of the locatives *at, on,* and *in,* as implied by their reference to two dimensions with "surface" or three with "interior." For, typically, we say "*at* the door," "*on* the rug," and "*in* the room." However, with Bennett himself, I would add that the choice of the locative preposition is determined by the spatial interpretation accompanying the noun phrase more than by the noun phrase itself. And perhaps, as Bennett at several points suggests, this spatial interpretation is in the form of some sort of "image." For, as he instructively notes, we speak of individuals stopping "*at*" Coventry, dropping bombs "*on*" Coventry, or living "*in*" Coventry, in accordance with our momentary spatial conception of that very same town as a point on a map, as a horizontal surface, or as an enclosed region. On further consideration, however, I have come to think that these widely accepted dimensional restrictions are not quite correct, and I would propose to amend them along the lines summarized in Table 1.

ACKNOWLEDGMENTS

Most of the research described in this chapter was supported by the National Science Foundation (Research Grants GS-2283 and BNS 75-02806). For their major contributions to this work, I wish also to thank my students and collaborators—particularly, in this case, Lynn Cooper, Joyce Farrell, Sherryl Judd, and Jacqueline Metzler.

TABLE 1
Summary of Proposed Revision of the Dimensional
Restrictions for the Locatives AT, ON, and IN.

Previously stated dimensional rectrictions (e.g., by Bennett, 1975; and by Fillmore, 1971, p. 2).	Proposed revisions of the dimensional restrictions (Shepard, October 1978)

AT

| "simple locative" (Bennett), "said to ascribe no particular dimensionality to the referent of its associated noun" (Fillmore). | A definite restriction is placed on the dimensionality of that referent; namely, that it be less than the dimensionality of an implied "medium." |

"The cattle gathered AT the river."
   (where the one-dimensional river is of lower dimensionality than the implied
   two-dimensional surface on which the cattle are free to move)

Not: "The cattle gathered AT the plain."
   (where, since "plain" has the same dimensionality as that implied surface,
   it cannot specify a properly restrictive locus within the two-dimensional
   plane of free movement)

"The light is refracted AT the surface of the water."

ON

| "surface locative" (Bennett), "said to ascribe to the referent of its head noun the property of being a line or surface" (Fillmore). | No clear dimensional restriction. What *is* ascribed to that referent is, rather, the property of supporting the referent of the logical subject. |

"The waiter balanced the tray ON the tip of one finger."
   (where the finger supports the tray and is conceived as a zero-dimensional
   point, not as a line or a surface)

"There's a fish ON the line."
"There's a coat of paint ON the wall."
"He had a shoe ON one foot."
"The smoke was carried away ON the breeze."
"We're all depending ON you."

IN

| "interior locative" (Bennett), "said to ascribe to the referent of its head noun the notion of a bounded two-dimensional or three-dimensional space" (Fillmore). | The ascribed dimensionality cannot be specified absolutely—only relatively as not less than that of the referent of the logical subject. Moreover, there need be no ascription of boundedness, since "in" often has the sense of immersion rather than containment. |

"She speared a fish IN the water."
"The astronauts were lost IN space."
"There is a strange scent IN the air."
} (without any implication of a boundary)

"The mercury rose IN the thermometer."
"Motion of the magnetic field causes
   electrons to flow IN the wire."
} (where, moreover, the dimensionality of the referent is one, not two or three)

REFERENCES

Bennett, D. C. *Spatial and temporal uses of English prepositions.* New York: Longmans, 1974.

Black, J. B., Turner, T. J., & Bower, G. H. Point of view in narrative comprehension, memory, and production. *Journal of Verbal Learning and Verbal Behavior,* 1979, *18,* 187-199.

Carroll, J. D., & Chang, J.-J. Analysis of individual differences in multidimensional scaling via an N-way generalization of "Eckart-Young" decomposition. *Psychometrika,* 1970, *35,* 283-319.

Cassirer, E. The concept of group and the theory of perception. *Philosophy & Phenomenological Research,* 1944, *5,* 1-35.

Chomsky, N. Review of B. F. Skinner, *Verbal behavior. Language,* 1959, *35,* 26-58.

Clark, H. H. Space, time, semantics, and the child. In T. E. Moore (Ed.), *Cognitive development and the acquisition of language.* New York: Academic Press, 1973.

Cooper, L. A. Mental rotation of random two-dimensional shapes. *Cognitive Psychology,* 1975, *7,* 20-43.

Cooper, L. A. Demonstration of a mental analog of an external rotation. *Perception & Psychophysics,* 1976, *19,* 296-302.

Cooper, L. A., & Shepard, R. N. Chronometric studies of the rotation of mental images. In W. G. Chase (Ed.), *Visual information processing.* New York: Academic Press, 1973.

Cunningham, J. P., & Shepard, R. N. Monotone mapping of similarities into a general metric space. *Journal of Mathematical Psychology,* 1974, *11,* 335-363.

Davies, P. C. W. *The physics of time asymmetry.* Berkeley, Calif.: University of California Press, 1977.

Farrell, J. E., & Shepard, R. N. Shape, orientation, and apparent rotational motion. *Journal of Experimental Psychology: Human Perception and Performance,* 1981, *7,* 477-486.

Fillmore, C. Deixis. Unpublished manuscript. University of California, Berkeley, 1971.

Garner, W. R. *The processing of information and structure.* Hillsdale, N.J.: Lawrence Erlbaum Associates, 1974.

Geshwind, N. Anatomical asymmetry as a basis for cerebral dominance. *Federation Proceedings,* 1978, *37,* 2263-2266.

Gibson, J. J. *The senses considered as perceptual systems.* Boston: Houghton-Mifflin, 1966.

Gibson, J. J. The theory of affordances. In R. E. Shaw & J. Bransford (Eds.), *Perceiving, acting, and knowing.* Hillsdale, N.J.: Lawrence Erlbaum Associates, 1977.

Green, B. F., Jr. Figure coherence in the kinetic depth effect. *Journal of Experimental Psychology,* 1961, *62,* 272-282.

Gruber, J. S. Look and see. *Language,* 1967, *43,* 937-947.

Hadamard, J. *The psychology of invention in the mathematical field.* Princeton, N.J.: Princeton University Press, 1945.

Helmholtz, H. von. *The sensations of tone.* New York: Dover, 1954. (Original Publication in German, 1885).

Holton, G. On trying to understand scientific genius. *American Scholar,* 1972, *41,* 95-110.

Hubel, D. H., & Wiesel, T. N. Receptive fields of cells in striate cortex of very young, visually inexperienced kittens. *Journal of Neurophysiology,* 1963, *26,* 994-1001.

Jackendoff, R. Toward an explanatory semantic representation. *Linguistic Inquiry,* 1976, *1,* 89-150.

Jackendoff, R. Grammar as evidence for conceptual structure. In M. Halle, J. Bresnan & G. Miller (Eds.), *Linguistic competence and psychological reality.* Cambridge, Mass.: MIT Press, 1978.

Johansson, G. *Configuration in event perception.* Uppsala, Sweden: Almqvist & Wiksell, 1950.

Johansson, G. Spatio-temporal differentiation and integration in visual motion perception. *Psychological Research,* 1976, *38,* 379-393.

Lenneberg, E. H. *Biological foundations of language.* New York: Wiley, 1967.

Metzler, J., & Shepard, R. N. Transformational studies of the internal representation of three-dimensional objects. In R. Solso (Ed.), *Theories in cognitive psychology: The Loyola Symposium.* Potomac, Md.: Lawrence Erlbaum Associates, 1974.

Miller, G. A., & Johnson-Laird, P. N. *Language and perception.* Cambridge, Mass.: Harvard University Press, 1976.

Palmer, S. E., & Hemenway, K. Orientation and symmetry: Effects of multiple, rotational, and near symmetries. *Journal of Experimental Psychology: Human Perception and Performance,* 1978, *4,* 691–702.

Robins, C., & Shepard, R. N. Spatio-temporal probing of apparent rotational movement. *Perception & Psychophysics,* 1977, *22,* 12–18.

Shepard, R. N. Review of E. Feigenbaum & J. Feldman's *Computers and thought. Behavioral Science,* 1964, *9,* 57–65.

Shepard, R. N. Form, formation, and transformation of internal representations. In R. Solso (Ed.), *Information processing and cognition: The Loyola Symposium.* Hillsdale, N.J.: Lawrence Erlbaum Associates, 1975.

Shepard, R. N. Externalization of mental images and the act of creation. In B. S. Randhawa & W. E. Coffman (Eds.), *Visual learning, thinking, and communication.* New York: Academic Press, 1978. (a)

Shepard, R. N. The mental image. *American Psychologist,* 1978, *33,* 125–137. (b)

Shepard, R. N. Psychophysical complementarity. In M. Kubovy & J. Pomerantz (Eds.), *Perceptual organization.* Hillsdale, N.J.: Lawrence Erlbaum Associates, 1981.

Shepard, R. N. Connections between the representations of shapes and of their spatial transformations. In R. Bajesy & N. Badler (Eds.), *Representation of three-dimensional objects.* New York: Springer-Verlag, in press.

Shepard, R. N. & Chipman, S. Second-order isomorphism of internal representations: Shapes of states. *Cognitive Psychology,* 1970, *1,* 1–17.

Shepard, R. N., & Cooper, L. A. *Mental images and their transformations.* Cambridge, Mass.: MIT Press/Bradford Books, 1982.

Shepard, R. N., & Judd, S. A. Perceptual illusion of rotation of three-dimensional objects. *Science,* 1976, *191,* 952–954.

Shepard, R. N., & Metzler, J. Mental rotation of three-dimensional objects. *Science,* 1971, *171,* 701–703.

Skinner, B. F. *Verbal behavior.* New York: Appleton-Century-Crofts, 1957.

Uttal, W. R. *An autocorrelation theory of form detection.* Hillsdale, N.J.: Lawrence Erlbaum Associates, 1975.

4 A Computer Simulation Approach to Studying Mental Imagery

Steven P. Shwartz
Yale University

Stephen M. Kosslyn
Harvard University

Most cognitive psychologists agree that they are trying to characterize how the brain *functions* is the course of processing information. The "cognitive" level of analysis, then, is at a sufficiently abstract level that it allows one to compare the mind to computer programs. Both mental states in the brain and program states in a computer can be described using a functional vocabulary. This vocabulary specifies the nature of structures and processes and specifies how sequences of processes can be coordinated to accomplish some goal. It is natural, then, that many cognitive psychologists have begun to use the computer as a way of constructing models of mental processes. The usual goal is to program the computer in such a way that its behavior emulates that of the human, presumably because both the mind and the program have the same functional states (see Anderson & Bower, 1979/1973; Newell & Simon, 1972). In this paper we describe a somewhat different use of computer models of cognitive processes, one aimed at guiding an empirical research program rather than simply providing the bases for plausible accounts of data.

We began our research program by conducting a series of experiments to delimit the class of acceptable theories. The products of this research program have been summarized in a number of places (e.g., Kosslyn, 1980; Kosslyn & Shwartz, 1978; Kosslyn, Pinker, Smith, & Shwartz, 1979), and we see no need to reiterate this summary here. Rather, in this paper we wish to show how the product of our initial research program continues to guide empirical research. The theory at the present stage is anything but complete, and is embodied in a computer simulation program that makes this clear: In implementing the theory, we realized that numerous issues had not yet been touched upon, that numerous choices about how to program the computer should be guided by the results of additional experiments. In this paper we will describe our model (and provide references to the results that motivated us to implement it as we did), and we will describe at least some of the issues left outstanding. The beauty of this method of raising issues for further empirical work is that it almost guarantees that one will collect data that complement each other, that cohere to paint an increasingly detailed picture of the phenomena under study. This methodology, centered around collecting data to motivate building a model, seems to ensure that one will pursue an integrated research program rather than merely conduct series of disconnected experiments—as is so common in cognitive psychology today (e.g., see Lachman, Lachman, & Butterfield, 1979).

The Domain

Please answer the following question: How many windows are there in your living room? Most people report that in order to answer this question they "mentally picture" the walls of the room and then scan across them, counting the windows. Our model is intended to provide accounts of what it means to "mentally picture" something, how one inspects an image, transforms images, and how images are generated in active memory from information stored in long-term memory.

As we will use the term, visual images are temporary data-structures that exist in a permanent medium (see Kosslyn, 1980, 1981). This medium is called the visual buffer. The image data-structures underlie the experience of "seeing in the absence of the appropriate sensory stimulation" that characterizes "having a mental image." When discussing our simulation model, we will refer to the implementation of the image as the "surface image" and our implementation of the visual buffer as the "surface matrix." The temporary surface images are constructed from more permanent "deep representations" in long-term memory.

Virtually all cognitive theorists find it useful to draw a distinction between structures and processes, and in the following discussion we will describe our model in terms of the structures and processes it employs. The following description of the model centers on claims that have led us to raise new issues. Thus, this description is rather sketchy at places and occasionally omits mention of entire components of the theory (especially of image transformations). For a complete treatment see Kosslyn (1980); for a more detailed brief treatment see Kosslyn (1981).

STRUCTURES

There are two kinds of structures, media and data-structures. Media carry no information on their own right, but rather support the information-conveying data-structures. Properties of the medium place constraints on what kinds of data-structures can be supported by that medium, as is discussed below.

Active Memory Structures

In this section we will discuss the structures in active memory that are recruited or created by the imagery system.

The Medium

It is useful to consider media in terms of two kinds of properties, *format ting* and *accessibility*. Formatting places constraints on what kind of data can be stored in a medium just as the formatting of a tax form constrains what can be written on it. Accessibility constrains how the medium can be accessed; a magnetic tape, for example, must be accessed serially (see Kosslyn, 1980, 1981, for more detailed discussion of these concepts).

Formatting. The visual buffer is represented in our model as a two-dimensional array (see Pinker, 1980, for empirical evidence supporting a two-dimensional rather than a three-dimensional format). Each cell of this surface matrix can support only brightness information. Images are depicted within this spatial medium by selectively filling in cells of the array on the basis of information stored in long-term memory. While we don't claim that the actual visual buffer in the human brain is a physical array, we do want to argue that it must have many of the functional properties of an array (see Kosslyn, 1981). In particular, it must support image data structures (see next section) and have a limited size (see Kosslyn, 1978, for empirical evidence) and grain (see Kosslyn, 1975, for empirical evidence). In our simulation model the property of limited size is due to the finite size of the array and the limited grain is due to the finite number of cells used to compose the array. Finally, we theorize that the visual buffer is most sharply resolved at the center, with decreasing resolution toward the periphery of the visual buffer. We model this property by having progressively larger cells toward the periphery of the surface matrix (which is implemented by averaging cells into progressively larger blocks toward the periphery, only one location in which is used to display a dot used in depicting some imaged object).

Accessibility. Due to the limited grain size of the surface matrix, contours tend to be obscured more in smaller images than in larger images, making smaller images more difficult to inspect. This property was motivated by Kosslyn's (1975, 1976) empirical results showing that smaller images *are* more difficult to discern.

In addition to grain constraints, the visual buffer has only a limited extent. This extent has been measured by Finke and Kosslyn (1980) and Kosslyn (1978). The visual buffer does not have sharp edges, however; rather, images gradually overflow, becoming progressively more blurred toward the periphery.

Finally, it is a common introspection that images fade with time. This introspection receives empirical support from Kosslyn's (1975) finding that images of objects in complex scenes were more degraded than images of objects in simple scenes. We posit that as soon as an image is constructed, it begins to decay. To counteract this decay, we suggest that a process continually works to refresh the information in the visual buffer, but that this process operates at a fixed rate (subject of course to the availability of processing resources). Thus, when an image is complex, the refresh procedure will take more time for a single refresh of the image than when an image is simple. If the image is too complex, portions will fade before the refresh cycle is complete, and will no longer be accessible. It should be noted that this decay property of the visual buffer is almost a logical necessity; if it were not true images would be maintained indefinitely unless they were explicitly "erased," which runs counter not only to the data and to people's introspections, but to the possibility that the visual buffer is shared in imagery and perception (see Kosslyn, Pinker, Smith, & Shwartz, 1979).

The Data-Structures

Data-structures can be specified with respect to their *format, content,* and *organization.* The format is the formal structure of the code, which indicates what kinds of symbols are used and how they are interpreted. The format is distinct from the content, which is the information being stored. The same content, such as that contained in the previous sentence, can be represented in numerous different formats (e.g., fluxes on a magnetic tape, dots and dashes etched in mud, etc.). The organization is the way elementary representations can be combined.

Format. The image data-structure depicts information. Spatial information is preserved under homomorphism with the real-world counterpart(s) of the imaged object(s). That is, parts of the image correspond to parts of the object (or scene) such that the relative interpoint distances among parts on the object (or between objects in a scene) are preserved in the image. The evidence that such spatial properties are preserved in images is numerous and has been reviewed elsewhere (see especially Kosslyn, 1980, for a detailed review).

Content. Images depict objects as they appear from a particular point of view. Images may be used to represent the objects actually being depicted (as in the window-counting example given above), or can be used to symbolize something else (e.g., an image of scales can be used to stand for the concept "justice"). In this latter case, however, it is important to note that the content of the image depends crucially on other parts of the cognitive system that interface with imagery. That is, in this case the image is an input to an inference or association device and derives its content only in conjunction with how that device operates.

Organization. Individual images may be composed to form a scene or a very detailed depiction of a single object. However, because we posit that encodings are activated sequentially, and activated units begin to decay immediately, images will retain an internal organization: The individual parts (generated on the basis of activating separate encodings) will be at different levels of activation, and hence will maintain distinct identities according to the Gestalt Law of Common Fate.

Problems and Issues

A major issue today, as is evident in Pylyshyn's (1981) paper, is simply whether or not there is a structure like our visual buffer. Although we have collected much data that is explained in a perspicuous way by positing such a medium (see Kosslyn, 1980), the issue is far from settled. In addition, we have not studied how three-dimensional information is actually represented in the medium. Other issues concern how color and shape are represented in the medium and the relationship between this putative medium used in imagery and one used in perception at rather early stages of visual processing (see Marr & Nishihara, 1978).

In addition, we have yet to study how images are maintained in active memory; what is the role of scanning an image in maintaining it, for example? Further, is it possible to reorganize images into increasingly larger chunks, allowing one to hold increasing amounts of material in an image?

LONG-TERM MEMORY STRUCTURES

The Medium

Formatting. Virtually nothing is known about the medium in which long-term memory encodings of images reside. The medium must be formatted such that encodings can be addressed by name, however, and is not likely to be a spatial array-like structure (see Kosslyn, 1980).

Accessibility. Our major claim here is that encodings containing lists of facts are searched serially.

The Data Structures

Format.   The long-term memory data-structures represent two kinds of information, "factual" information and "literal" information, which captures the appearance of the object (see Kosslyn, 1980, for a summary of the empirical evidence motivating these two types of data structures). The format of the factual information is the same as the format of other factual data (not necessarily related to imaginal data structures) in long-term memory. The format of the literal information is an open question; there are no data indicating that the format of the literal information in long-term memory differs from that of the factual information; it is possible that the formats of both factual and literal information can be classified as "propositional." However a distinct non-discursive format for the literal information is also a logical possibility. In our model the factual information files are ordered lists of propositions about the object, and the literal information files are lists of pairs of polar coordinates.

Content.   Let us first consider in more detail the contents of the factual encodings. There are two types of information necessary for locating parts or objects within an image: First, the absolute size of each object is stored. From this size tag, the resolution (indexed by filled cell density) necessary to "see" the part or object can be computed. Second, information about how to find a part or object in an image is given in the form of a list of library procedures that test for various spatial configurations and which, if successfully completed, will result in locating the part or object. Additionally, the factual information files contain information regarding where and how parts should be attached to an object (e.g., the location of the front tire is "UNDER FRONTWHEELBASE").

The literal information files contain lists of polar coordinates. Each r, θ pair specifies a location that should be activated in the surface matrix in order to depict an object or scene.

Organization.   The long-term memory data structures in our model are hierarchically organized. The name of a to-be-imaged object (e.g., a car) is used to access a file containing factual information about the object. In this file is a proposition that is essentially a pointer to a file containing an encoding of the literal appearance of the object. The literal information file for the object contains the global shape or skeletal outline of the appearance of the object. This is information that is presumably stored during initial inspection of the real-world object. There are also pointers to files of factual information for specific parts of the object (e.g., the tires of the car) as well as pointers to files of factual information about regional details of the objects. The part and regional detail literal information files are posited to contain information encoded during more careful inspection of the real-world object. These pointers are stored in the factual information file in order of association strength with the object, with more highly associated parts at the beginning of the file. The factual files for parts are just like those for objects, each containing a pointer to a file of literal information as well as pointers to files of factual information for their own subparts. In addition, the factual information files contain pointers to superordinate files (e.g., vehicle).

Problems and Issues

Our only claim regarding the representation of the long-term memory literal information is that the data-structures have a format that can be mapped into the surface matrix. The format of image deep representations is in fact an open issue. We represent the long-term memory literal appearance of an object as a list of polar coordinates because they allow easy placement of an image at any specified size, orientation, or location within the surface matrix. It seems most unlikely that the brain stores coordinates of points of an image. A "generalized cone" format (see Marr & Nishihara, 1978) seems more plausible at first glance, but this format encodes information about shape—and images depict information about the appearance of *surfaces*. Further, people can encode information about moving objects, such as a running horse. How this sort of data is encoded is at present a total mystery.

A second problem is that we have implemented only a two-dimensional long-term memory representation. There is ample data that three-dimensional information must exist in long-term memory (e.g., see Pinker, 1980; Shepard & Metzler, 1971). We will implement the three-dimensional representation only after we have better data about its properties.

Another issue concerns the nature of the size information stored about each object. Clearly, the processing system can either *access* absolute size information or *compute* this information. For example, when asked to imagine a rabbit standing next to an elephant, people typically image the rabbit and the elephant at their appropriate relative sizes (cf. Kosslyn, 1975). One way to model this phenomenon would be to store objects at their canonical size. Here, size information would be represented implicitly rather than with an explicit tag. However, when asked to imagine just a rabbit, in the absence of any other instructions, people will typically imagine it at about the same size as when asked to imagine just an elephant (see Kosslyn, 1978). Either objects are stored at the same size, but imaged at different sizes depending on the absolute size tag, or objects are stored at different sizes (preserving actual differences), but can be imaged such that they subtend the same angle.

Yet another issue concerns the nature of the skeletal image: Is it a degraded version of the entire object, or just the central shape?

Further issues concern the principles governing when an image data-structure will be encoded in the first place.

An entire additional set of issues is raised when one considers the possible role image deep representations may play in perception. Are these encodings used in "top down" comparisons with parts encoded from the senses (as Kosslyn & Shwartz, 1978, suggest)?

IMAGERY PROCESSES

In addition to specifying image structures, our model specifies the processes that operate on these structures. There are three main processes we have explored, image generation, inspection, and transformation.

Image Generation

Our principal theoretical claims regarding image generation are derived from the nature of the short-term and long-term memory data-structures postulated above. Image generation is a constructive process in which factual information stored in long-term memory is used to generate an image from the separately stored encodings of literal appearances of the parts or objects that make up an image.

The image generation procedures in our model are coordinated by the IMAGE procedure. IMAGE takes as input the name of the object to be imaged, whether a detailed or skeletal (without details) image should be generated, and parameters specifying the size, orientation, and location at which the object should be placed within the surface matrix. The IMAGE routine first looks up (in the factual information file for the object) the name of the file containing the literal appearance of the global shape of the object. IMAGE then invokes the PICTURE procedure to map the long-term memory literal information into the short-term surface matrix. The PICTURE procedure takes as input a literal appearance file plus size, orientation, and location parameters. For each pair of polar coordinates in the long-term memory literal appearance file, a cell in the surface matrix is activated at the maximum brightness level. The size, orientation, and location parameters allow placement of the part or object at the specified size, orientation and location.

If a detailed image is specified, IMAGE checks the factual information files for names of parts. For each part name found, IMAGE invokes the PUT procedure to integrate the part into the image. PUT takes as input the name of the part to be added to the image. PUT first looks up a location in the part's factual information file specifying where in the image the part should be placed. The location information consists of a relation plus a foundation part. For example, the factual information file for a tire specifies that the appropriate location for the tire is UNDER FRONT-WHEELBASE.

PUT invokes the FIND procedure to locate the foundation part. FIND takes as input the name of the part to be located and searches the image for the part, returning the location (in Cartesian coordinates) if successful. FIND determines how to search by looking up a description of the specified part in the part's factual information file. The description consists of a list of procedures that if executed successfully, will result in locating the part. PUT then looks up the specified relation in a file containing definitions of relations. Each relation is defined by a set of parameters that specify how to place one object in a given relation to another object. PUT then calls PIC-TURE to map the part into the surface matrix in the appropriate relation to the specified foundation part. Often, the foundation part will not be found because the image is generated at a default size and the resolution is inadequate to locate the foundation part. In this case, the part will not be integrated into the image.

Problems and Issues

A major problem that needs to be addressed is the question of when a detailed image is generated. That is, what is the default when people are asked to generate an image. One common introspection is that a part is not visible on an image until that part is "looked at." This suggests that the default is to generate a skeletal image. This issue is intimately tied to the issue of whether or not details automatically become "visible" as an image is expanded (see discussion below). Another issue concerns specifying the principles that determine the order in which parts will be placed on an image. In addition, it is possible that some parts are imaged simultaneously and some sequentially; if so, a principled distinction between the two classes would be necessary. Further issues concern the role of "visual prompts" from imaged objects as input to generate additional images and the relationship between image generation and "analysis by synthesis" (see Neisser, 1967) processes in perception.

Image Inspection

Image inspection procedures are coordinated by the LOOKFOR procedure, which takes as input the name of the part that is to be searched for and the name of the object in the image. LOOKFOR first looks up (in the part's information file) the optimal resolution (as indexed by dot density) necessary to "see" the part. The RESOLUTION procedure is then called to compute the resolution of the image currently in the surface matrix.

LOOKFOR compares the optimal and current resolutions and, if necessary, calls ZOOM or PAN (see the section on transformations) to adjust the size of the image. LOOKFOR then looks up the description of the part in the part's factual information file and from this determines the direction in the surface matrix in which the part is located. LOOKFOR then checks to make sure that the image has not overflowed the surface matrix in that direction (by checking to see if there is evidence of the image in the poorly resolved portion of the surface matrix in that direction). If overflow is detected, LOOKFOR calls SCAN to bring that portion of the image into the more highly resolved region (i.e., the center) of the surface matrix. LOOKFOR then calls FIND, which executes the procedures indexed by the description of the part to try to locate the part.

If the FIND procedure fails to locate the sought part, LOOKFOR checks the object's factual information file for notations indicating that there exists in long-term memory information (i.e., factual and literal information) about regions of an object. Implicit in encodings of general regions can be depictions of particular parts. For example, the "front region" of a car might include a hood ornament, whereas the global shape of the car did not. If regional information is found, LOOKFOR integrates the region into the image by means of the PUT procedure and then calls FIND to search again. LOOKFOR fails when the part has not been found and there are no regions left to be integrated.

Problems and Issues

The actual procedures used in the simulation for locating spatial configurations of points are sufficient for the identification of only a small number of spatial patterns. We make no claim that the procedures we have implemented have any psychological validity. In fact, we have no idea what the correct set of procedures are. It would be easy to simply state that the solution to this problem lies in research on visual pattern recognition, but careful analysis reveals that this is probably not the case. The mental image analysis problem is actually much simpler because (a) one knows what one is imaging, and (b) the image is already parsed. Not only are images segmented, but there often is no need to search the image for a part. Specifically, if the part was stored in long-term memory by itself, and integrated into the image during the generation process, then it is known exactly where the part is in the visual buffer! Only for details that are not explicitly stored, but were merely included as regional detail, is it ever necessary to search the visual buffer, and even then the location of the region in the visual buffer is known. The main issues here, then, concern when one must generate new material in an image in order to "see" particular kinds of parts, when scanning is necessary, and how one actually "recognizes" imaged patterns.

Image Transformations

In our simulation, we model three types of transformation: Size scaling is performed by the PAN and ZOOM procedures, which simulate panning back from an image (by reducing its size) and zooming in on an image (by increasing its size). Image scanning is performed by the SCAN procedure. Although scanning is technically not an imagery transformation, we treat it as one in our model. On our view, scanning involves altering the contents of the surface matrix by shifting the image data structure across the surface matrix so that a different portion is in the most highly resolved region. (Pinker, 1980, presents data indicating that this may not be all there is to scanning. However; we have yet to extend the theory to account for all of his data.) Finally, image rotation is performed by the ROTATE procedure.

The PAN procedure takes as input a target resolution for the image in the surface matrix. PAN operates by treating the image as a series of rings around the center of the surface matrix. On each iteration, PAN starts with the innermost ring, moving the contents of the cells in the inner ring closer to the center of the surface matrix by a fixed proportion. PAN then successively applies this operation to the remaining rings in order of distance from the center. In this way, PAN simulates a continuous transformation with larger size changes requiring more iterations and therefore taking longer (as occurs in human imagery; see chapter 8, Kosslyn, 1980).

The ZOOM procedure is basically the same as the PAN procedure, except that it starts with the outermost ring and moves the contents of the cells of each ring a fixed proportion away from the center. Visibility is enhanced because the contours become sharper when the image is expanded. Recall that due to the limited resolution of the surface matrix, contours are obscured in smaller images. When several pairs of coordinates in long-term memory have been mapped into a single cell of the surface matrix, that cell is activated with a multiple density marker (the implementation is to use a capital letter instead of a lower case letter). When the expansion operator is applied to such a cell, the pairs of coordinates that were mapped into this cell are retrieved and their position in the surface matrix recomputed (see below for a discussion of this implementation). In addition, the ZOOM procedure also models the emergent visibility of detail in an image as the image is expanded. In our current implementation, we maintain a missing-parts list of parts for which IMAGE failed to integrate the part into the image. Then as ZOOM expands the size of the image, ZOOM calls RESOLUTION to check the current resolution in order to determine whether the current resolution is sufficient for placement of a part on the missing-parts list. When this condition is satisfied, ZOOM calls PUT to integrate the part into the image.

The SCAN procedure takes as input a direction and distance. SCAN first determines the leading edge of the image (according to the direction of scan). On each iteration, SCAN starts with the cells at the leading edge and translates their contents to new cells a small fixed distance along the vector specified by the direction of scan. SCAN then fills the gap just created with cells behind the leading edge and continues until the contents of all cells have been moved. Because each cell is moved only a small fixed amount, longer scan distances will require more iterations and take longer (as is true in human imagery; see Kosslyn, Ball, & Reiser, 1978). The problem here, however, is how SCAN brings in new information from past the trailing edge of the surface matrix, as is discussed below.

The ROTATE procedure takes as input an angle of rotation. ROTATE works similarly to the other procedures with the contents of each cell being moved a small fixed amount on each iteration along an imaginary circle defined by the distance of the cell from the center of the surface matrix and the direction of rotation. Again, greater angles of rotation will require more iterations and take longer (see, for example, Cooper & Shepard, 1973). One problem here, however is hidden parts come into view during three-dimensional rotation, as is discussed below.

Problems and Issues

As mentioned earlier, when an object or scene is imaged at a small size, contours are obscured by the limited resolution of the visual buffer and details are hard to "see." However, when one zooms in on the images, contours become sharper and details visible. Similarly, when rotating three-dimensional objects, previously hidden surfaces become visible in the perspective view. And when scanning an image, new information must be filled in at the trailing edge of the data-structure when the trailing edge is outside of the visual buffer (i.e., when the image is "overflowed" in that direction). The problem is to explain where this new information comes from. We have described two solutions to this problem in earlier papers (Kosslyn & Shwartz, 1977; 1978) and will discuss these solutions, our current implementation, and other possible solutions below.

In Kosslyn & Shwartz (1977) we described a system designed to simulate "spatial summation," where information was present but obscured by lateral-inhibitory processes or the like. This system had two arrays, one a two-dimensional fine-grained array that contained all the information but was "invisible" to the inspection procedures of the system, and a second array with a sparser grain that was the structure available to the inspection routines for processing. The process of image generation involved filling in the fine-grained matrix from long-term memory, then updating the surface display (i.e., the array visible to the interpretive procedures). Transformation procedures operated on the fine-grained matrix with the surface display being constantly updated. The mapping function (a 4–cell to 1–cell map) from the fine-grained matrix to the surface display enabled simulation of limited resolution (i.e., contours were obscured in the surface display due to the many-to-one mapping function). The dual matrix system also simulated the emergent visibility of details when the system zoomed in on the image (i.e., when the visible image expanded in size).

The dual matrix system could also have solved the three-dimensional rotation problem if we had added a third dimension to the fine-grained array. The rotation procedure would operate on the fine-grained array, with the mapping function to the surface display producing a two-dimensional perspective view in the surface display. However, this was not implemented.

The dual matrix system was not an adequate solution to the scanning problem. That is, this system provided no way of filling in parts of images at the trailing edge of the scan as the image was shifted through the surface matrix. Similarly, if an image was expanded to a large size, such that it "overflowed" the fine-grained matrix, then was shrunk down to size, the overflowed portion would be lost.

Other problems with this representation include the large computational cost of processing two matrices and the fact that the fine-grained matrix did *not* have an infinite grain. Additionally, allowing the interpretive procedures access to one array (i.e., the surface display), but not another, was rather ad hoc.

Our second implementation (Kosslyn & Shwartz, 1978) was not much better. We now decided to eliminate the two matrices, and use an "inverse mapping function" from each cell of the surface matrix to the coordinates of the points residing in it. We did not actually implement a function, however, rather we simulated such a function by using a copy (in a linked list format) of the long-term memory perceptual information (i.e., pairs of R, θ coordinates). The surface display was filled in by marching down the list and filling in a cell in the surface display for each R, θ pair. Whenever a cell in the surface display was filled in, a pointer from the cell back to the location of the R, θ pair on the linked list was activated. When a cell was filled in by more than one R, θ pair, the surface display pointed back to the first R, θ pair which in turn pointed back to the second, and so on. This implementation had the following advantages: It reduced computational cost considerably and it allowed transformation procedures to operate directly on the surface display by virtue of the inverse-mapping function. Thus, when an image was expanded (i.e., ZOOMed in on), the R, θ pairs that previously had been mapped into a single cell could each be mapped into a different cell.

Neither of these solutions is adequate because they do not handle the problems of new information coming in at the leading edge during image scanning or the problem of loss of information when image expansion is followed by image shrinkage. Worse, both implementations postulate an additional data structure (the fine-grained array in the first solution and the linked list in the second for which there is no empirical evidence. The linked list implementation could be extended to handle these problems by mapping polar coordinate pairs that fall outside of the surface display into an "invisible" outer boundary around the surface matrix, but this would be even more ad hoc.

One of the virtues of computer simulation is that aspects of a theory that are either poorly specified or just plain wrong often present glaring problems for implementation of the simulation model. This is probably the case here. In each of the first two implementations we included an extra, ad hoc structure that was problematic. In our current implementation, we decided to eliminate this additional structure, but this left us with a dilemma: The available experimental evidence suggests that transformations (at least two-dimensional transformations) are performed directly on the surface display (see Shwartz, 1979). However, some of these transformation processes need to access three-dimensional long-term memory when new information is needed. Clearly, some type of inverse-mapping function (from image to long-term memory) is required.

In our current implementation we map the long-term memory polar coordinates directly into the surface display. In addition, we keep track of a mapping function for each part or object that is generated. That is, we store the current size, offset, and orientation for each part or object relative to the canonical values of these parameters. When images are transformed, these parameters are updated. In order for new information to be placed in an image during scanning, for example, the inverse of the mapping function is computed in the following way: For each cell in the surface display that is left blank at the trailing edge, the range of values of r, θ coordinates that would fill that cell (given the current values of the mapping function parameters) are computed, and the r, θ pairs that fall within this range are activated, filling the surface matrix appropriately.

Unfortunately, this procedure is computationally inefficient when implemented on a digital computer. Using this procedure it is often the case that the entire list of polar coordinates must be searched each time a transformation operator is applied to the contents of a cell in the surface display. Clearly, it would be more efficient to simply perform the entire transformation at the deep structure level.

In spite of this, we feel that this implementation is justified. One of the pitfalls of computer simulation on a digital computer is the inherently serial nature of the machine. The computational properties of procedures such as the one described above would be very likely to change radically when implemented on a machine with a different architecture (e.g., Hayes-Roth, 1979). The search procedure just described that is computationally inefficient when implemented on a digital machine might be quite efficient when implemented on a parallel machine or on the human brain.

The available data do not rule out yet another implementation, which seems increasingly plausible. There may be two different types of transformation: surface driven transformations and deep-structure driven transformations. Surface driven transformations access only the surface display, while deep-structure driven transformations access the long-term memory polar coordinates. Surface driven transformations have the disadvantage that new information cannot be incorporated into the image during transformation, but have the advantage of not having to access long-term memory and should therefore be much faster. Thus, transformations that can be performed entirely within the (two-dimensional) picture plane should be faster than transformations that take place in three dimensions. And Pinker (1980) found that scanning in the two-dimensional picture plane was faster than scanning in depth.

In addition to the foregoing problems there is an issue that reaches to the most basic property of image transformations, namely that they procede in small increments rather than in a single operation (see chapter 8 of Kossyln, 1980a). There is no obvious prima facie reason why this need be the case. Images are not actual objects and hence the laws of physics do not dictate that they must pass through a trajectory in the course of being manipulated. There are a number of possible theories of why people may prefer to transform images gradually (see Kosslyn & Shwartz, 1981), but there are virtually no data that bear on the issue.

The puzzle of how to model image transformations, especially those involving information about 3–D appearances, is anything but solved. We feel, however, that the issues and problems are thrown into sharp relief when one considers how to implement these procedures in an explicit way.

CONCLUSIONS

In this paper we have attempted to show how building a concrete computer model of mental processing can serve to raise interesting research questions. In addition to the questions asked thus far, however, there is an entirely different class: Namely, we can ask whether the assumptions we have made are correct. Not only can the assumptions be tested directly, such as the claim that the active memory medium functions as an array, but predictions can be generated by examining interactions among components. In fact, it is the complexity of the sorts of interactions that arise in computational systems that leads one to actually implement the system on a computer. There are simply too many things to keep track of at once to derive predictions without implementing it. In this case, then, the program serves the same role as does a scratch pad used when one is doing arithmetic.

In conclusion, let us leave the reader with a caveat: One must take care to distinguish between the uninteresting problems that arise from the nature of digital computers and common programming languages and the interesting problems that arise from the nature of the structures and processed themselves, as defined at the abstract "functional" level common to man and machine. This sometimes is easier said than done, however. We have found that as long as we focus on issues that have direct empirical consequences we will not be wasting our time. Even if the present theory is completely wrong (which seems unlikely at this point—see Kosslyn, 1980, 1981), it will at least have served a useful role in leading us to collect a body of data that cohere and have some measure of intrinsic interest as well.

REFERENCES

Anderson, J. R., & Bower, G. H. *Human associative memory*. Hillsdale, N.J.: Lawrence Erlbaum Associates, 1980. Originally published 1973.

Cooper, L. A., & Shepard, R. N. Chronometric studies of the rotation of mental images. In W. G. Chase (Ed.), *Visual information processing*. New York: Academic Press, 1973.

Finke, R. A., & Kosslyn, S. M. Mental imagery acuity in the peripheral visual field. *Journal of Experimental Psychology: Human Perception and Performance*, 1980, *6*, 126-239.

Hayes-Roth, F. Distinguishing theories of representation: A critique of Anderson's "Arguments concerning mental imagery." *Psychological Review*, 1979, *86*, 376-392.

Kosslyn, S. M. Information representation in visual images. *Cognitive Psychology*, 1975, *7*, 341-370.

Kosslyn, S. M. Can imagery be distinguished from other forms of internal representation? evidence from studies of information retrieval time. *Memory and Cognition*, 1976, *4*, 291-297.

Kosslyn, S. M. Measuring the visual angle of the mind's eye. *Cognitive Psychology*, 1978, *10*, 356-389.

Kosslyn, S. M. *Image and mind*. Cambridge, MA: Harvard University Press, 1980.

Kosslyn, S. M. The medium and the message in mental imagery: a theory. *Psychological Review*, 1981, *88*, 46-66.

Kosslyn, S. M., Ball, T. M., & Reiser, B. J. Visual images preserve metric spatial information: evidence from studies of image scanning. *Journal of Experimental Psychology: Human Perception and Performance*, 1978, *4*, 47-60.

Kosslyn, S. M., Pinker, S., Smith, G. E., & Shwartz, S. P. On the demystification of mental imagery. *The Behavioral and Brain Sciences*, 1979, *2*, 535-581.

Kosslyn, S. M., & Shwartz, S. P. A simulation of visual imagery. *Cognitive Science*, 1977, *1*, 265-295.

Kosslyn, S. M., & Shwartz, S. P. Visual images as spatial representations in active memory. In E. M. Riseman & A. R. Hanson (Eds.), *Computer vision systems*. New York: Academic Press, 1978.

Kosslyn, S. M., & Shwartz, S. P. Empirical constraints on theories of visual mental imagery. In J. Long & A. Baddeley (Eds.), *Attention and Performance IX*. Hillsdale, N.J.: Lawrence Erlbaum Associates, 1981.

Lachman, R., Lachman, J. L., & Butterfield, E. C. *Cognitive psychology and information processing: An introduction*. Hillsdale, N.J.: Lawrence Erlbaum Associates, 1979.

Marr, D., & NIshihara, H. K. Representation and recognition of the spatial organization of three-dimensional shapes. *Proceedings of the Royal Society*, 1978, *200*, 269-294.

Neisser, U. *Cognitive psychology.* New York: Appleton-Century-Crofts, 1967.

Newell, A., & SImon, H. A. *Human problem solving.* Englewood Cliffs, N.J.: Prentice-Hall, 1972.

Pinker, S. Mental imagery and the third dimension, *Journal of Experimental Psychology: General,* 1980, *109,* 354–371.

Pylyshyn, Z. W. The imagery debate: Analogue media versus tacit knowledge. *Psychological Review,* 1981, *87,* 16–45.

Shepard, R. N., & Metzler, J. Mental rotation of three-dimensional objects. *Science,* 1971, *171,* 701–703.

Shwartz, S. P. *Studies of mental image rotation: Implications for a computer simulation of visual imagery.* Ph.D. Dissertation, The Johns Hopkins University, 1979.

EXPERIMENTAL STUDIES IN PROCESSING

5 Disintegrating the Lexicon: An Information Processing Approach

John Morton
M.R.C. Applied Psychology Unit
Cambridge, England

INTRODUCTION

In this chapter, my intention is to give the reader a particular view of an information processing approach to cognitive psychology. First of all I will outline how I see the relation between psychology and other disciplines. This is just my own version of the anti-reductionist argument that many others have expressed.

Then I will trace the development of the model that I use to talk about a number of phenomena arising from the way we process words. I will show how the first model I proposed turned out to be incorrect and indicate how it was changed in response to a number of experimental findings. The resulting model is modular in form, with the primary assumption being that the individual processes that are indicated are substantially independent from one another. I will show that by experiment one can test assumptions about the detailed functioning of one of the processes, and will indicate how a model of this kind can be adapted to account for data from experimental paradigms other than those for which the model was constructed. In addition, I will show the relation between this model and other models.

In the final section I demonstrate how the model has been refined by use of data from brain damaged patients, and how it can be used in describing particular kinds of aphasic and dyslexic syndromes.

Paper delivered at CNRS Conference on Cognitive Psychology at l'Abbeye de Royaumont, 15 June 1980.

GENERAL CONSIDERATIONS

Let me begin with a firm statement of belief. For some it will be so obviously true as to be not worth the saying. For others it will be so obviously wrong that it be not worth discussion by rational beings.

There are two (perhaps more), enterprises that psychologists engage in. One is that of finding cause; and the other has to do with representation; representation of the processes and structures that determine our behavior. It is with the latter that I occupy myself. Insofar as we are concerned with representation, then, I believe that psychology is independent. Its independence derives from the level of observation with which it is concerned. It is independent from anatomy and physiology on the one hand and from sociology on the other hand since these disciplines are concerned with observations at other levels.

Thus it seems to me that there is no physiological or anatomical fact that could in principle falsify or verify a purely psychological theory. Any possible counterexamples—and those of the Gestalt psychologists, Hull and Hebb come immediately to mind—will serve to illustrate what constitutes a purely psychological theory. The relevant error in those enterprises was to try to tie a psychological model to supposed physiological facts, perhaps in the belief that it would lend it support. The consequence was that the inadequacy of the physiology caused the demise of the psychology. However, investigation of brain processes and investigation of mental processes have only a slight relation. Once we establish the former and establish the latter we can go on to establish the mapping relationships between them. This is a perfectly respectable scientific enterprise, but must not be mistaken for the other two. Of course there is the temptation to try to make the link before it is known what is being linked, but, apart from the extreme of sensory and motor considerations, success is low. It is low because there appears to be no convenient mapping, at least at the cortical level, from structures and processes that interest cognitive psychologists, to other than the most gross localizations.

This position does not prevent me from using data from neuropsychology. Towards the end of the paper I will describe data from one or two brain damaged patients. However, I will only look at their behavior: the site and cause of their lesions is of no relevance to what I am doing though it is, of course, of great interest in its own right. In passing, we can observe that the terms *neuropsychology* and *neurolinguistics* are often used in two senses. In one sense they refer to the study of brain damaged patients; in the other sense they refer to the study of the mapping of mental functions onto brain functions. The two uses, I am claiming, are quite distinct although some authors, such as Arbib and Caplan (1979), switch from one use to the other as if they were indistinguishable.

Equally, I would not feel constrained to ignore results of experiments that involved "physiological" responses such as measures of electrical or other activity in the brain or galvanic skin responses. In as much as such experiments involved stimuli that were the concern of my model, the data would be usable. But note that I would be totally unconcerned as to the purely physiological mechanisms leading to the responses and that the nature of the model would be unchanged by the use of such data. Its form would be subject to change in exactly the same way as that forced upon it by experiments involving verbal responses.

My second preliminary concerns the nature of the representation that I use. A convenient label would be that of "information processing." The notation I employ is usually that of boxes joined together with directed lines. The boxes, in general, represent either a process that converts information from one code to another or a store of information of some kind. The model gives us a way of handling complexity by allowing us to partition the processes into functionally independent units of manageable proportion. It enables us to relate together a wide variety of experimental findings and everyday observations, and to make predictions about new findings. The method has flexibility and extensibility built into it. That is, the framework itself cannot be *wrong* though it is possible to be wrong *within* the framework, as we shall see.

To illustrate the non-triviality of the enterprise as I see it at the moment, we can see in Fig. 1 the extent of the systems that I am currently concerned with. The labels have been left off the individual boxes to avoid you trying to understand the model here and now. What I have represented here seems to be the minimum required to talk about word recognition in two modalities, object recognition, speaking and writing single words, together with a little concern for larger units of language and some concern for phenomena of memory for language materials over short time intervals. Virtually every one of these boxes and connections is supported by a number of observations. Lest you feel apprehensive, let me reassure you that I will be going to talk about only a subset of these boxes.

I would like to make a couple more comments about the nature of the model. Firstly, not all the lines mean the same thing. In some cases a process must finish completely before it can output anything. In other cases a process can pass on partial results. In further cases we want to indicate that one process just accesses another process or a store of information. Unfortunately we haven't yet worked out a notation or even the typology on which such a notation might be based. Secondly, do not become confused between form and content. There are other ways of expressing the same facts that would result in models isomorphic with this diagram. The form I use happens to help me to answer some of the questions I ask. The particular form predisposes one in particular ways. This form of model

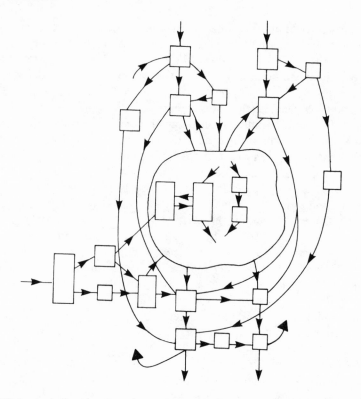

FIG. 1 An indication of the degree of elaboration necessary to express the relationships among the processes involved in word recognition, picture recognition, and naming and writing. All boxes and connections have empirical justification.

predisposes one to think in terms of the separability of processes rather than the way in which they interact. This might be a problem. However it is not a part of the theory.

Let me say again that the form I use is not a part of the theory. The same relationships could be expressed in rewrite rules or in prose. They could be implemented in any number of ways—in augmented transition networks or in production systems, for example. I chose these two examples since there are those among the users of both these systems who seem to claim that the form has content (Wanner & Maratsos, 1978; Anderson, 1976; Newell, 1980). This seems to be in error. Any notation that is rich enough will be able to represent the things we are interested in. What is crucial in the choice of a particular form is whether the generalizations are interesting ones, whether the ideas are communicable; whether the model is extendable in novel ways so as to predict novel findings.

The full model, even if properly labeled, will only serve as a means of communication for a certain range of questions. And, in general, at any one time we will only want to consider segments of the model. Thus, since we are not, at the moment, interested in object recognition, in writing, or in segments larger than the word, we will be left with the much more manageable structure shown in Fig. 2. This will enable us to look at questions of the organization of the internal lexicon. Note that even now we are faced with a problem of selection. What will be represented are what seem to be the most important processes and interconnections. Such an evaluation will, of course, be subject to modification.

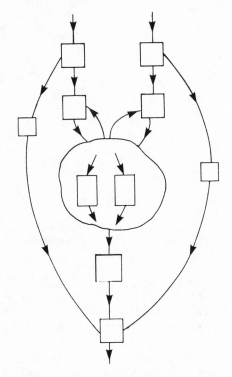

FIG. 2   A subset of the model in Fig. 1. This is required to account for data on word recognition. The origins and nature of this part of the overall model will be described in the following text.

As a final preliminary, we will see that the boxes themselves may be more or less specified. The intention is that the way in which a particular process functions does not affect the operation of the rest of the system. Inasmuch as this modularity fails, then the model will be in need of modification and the form may be unsuitable.

THE NATURE OF THE INTERNAL LEXICON

One extreme view of the internal lexicon is that all information about an individual word; its acoustic, visual, semantic, articulatory, graphic, and other descriptions, is to be found in the same "place"—where place is to be defined in terms of whatever model form is used. My own work has found itself concerned with the progressive separation of individual elements of what might otherwise be seen as a unified lexicon.

The first separation was that of the Logogen System from the Cognitive System as in Fig. 3. Each logogen was associated with a word or morpheme.

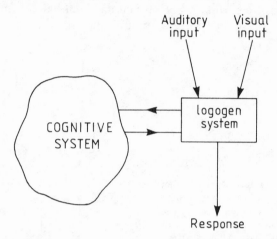

FIG. 3   The initial division of the lexicon. The logogen system is a device for categoriz-ing verbal stimuli. It is the site of the facilitation effects described in the text. It gives outputs that can be interpreted either by the speech output processes or by the Cognitive System. The latter includes all syntactic and semantic processing.

Given an input from the visual or auditory analysers, the logogens collect evidence that a particular word has occurred. When the decision is made, then the phonological code is made available to the response system and some code is sent to the Cognitive System, where computations relevant to the meaning or reference of the word could be made. Most of the interesting work went on in the Cognitive System, which was, and still is, relatively unspecified (but see Morton, 1968; Morton & Patterson, 1980a). The logogen was also the means whereby words were produced in spontaneous speech and object naming, for example. The Cognitive System produces an appropriate code—let us loosely call it semantic—and the logogens collect evidence from it in just the same way. For the recognition of words in con-text, there would be both sensory information and information derived from the context. The logogens would regard all this information as equivalent and simply access the evidence.

One other feature of the logogens was that there were after-effects of their having been active. The crucial experimental paradigm is one where subjects have some pretraining task followed by the main task in which words are presented in a tachistoscope for identification. The duration of exposure required for a correct response is found to be influenced by the pretraining task. Perhaps the first experiment using this paradigm was Neisser (1954) who showed that if subjects had seen the word PHRASE in the pretraining, then their visual duration threshold for that word was lower than for subjects who had not seen it. Prior experience with the homophone FRAYS, however, had no effect on the subsequent recognition of PHRASE.

One variation on this paradigm served to better define the nature of the unit concerned. Murrell and Morton (1974) showed that so far as recognition of the word SEES was concerned, prior experience with SEEN was almost as effective as SEES itself. Having read SEED in the pretraining, however, had no effect on the subsequent recognition of SEES. Thus it seemed to be the morphology and not the physical resemblance that was crucial. Note that the time interval we are concerned with is anything from 15 to 45 minutes, and may, indeed, be orders of magnitude longer. In this respect, as we shall see later, these experiments are very different from those showing facilitation over time intervals of a few seconds.

By themselves such experimental findings would be subject to a number of possible interpretations. In the model, however, and thus in the context of all the experimental findings that had served to form the model, the only account was that the effect was to be located in the logogens, the effect of prior exposure serving to reduce the amount of sensory information required for subsequent identification.

This account, as found in Morton (1969, 1970), led to certain predictions. The only event that could have such consequences was the firing of a logogen. But it was a part of the model that the firing of a logogen would have the same consequences regardless of the cause of the firing. The model thus predicted that if one named a picture in the pretraining, then there would be consequences in the subsequent identification task. This turned out not to be the case. Winnick and Daniel (1970) showed that naming the picture of a butterfly or saying the word in answer to a definition had no detectable consequences on the subsequent visual duration threshold for the printed word BUTTERFLY. These data were replicated by Clark and Morton (unpublished) who also found that there was good transfer from reading a word written in a casual cursive script to the subsequent recognition of the printed word (see Morton, 1979).

Thus the model as it stood was incorrect. The site of the facilitation and the source of the phonological code could not be the same. Thus the original single Logogen System was split into two, one for input and one for output. The Input system maintained all the properties required for word recognition. It would remain unaffected when a picture was named or a word produced spontaneously. The new form of the model is shown in Fig. 4.

Note that there are alternative solutions such as supposing separate

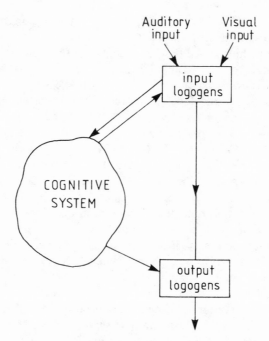

FIG. 4   The second division of the lexicon. This differs from Fig. 2 in that the logogen system has been divided into two parts. The input logogen system serves to categorize verbal stimuli and is the site of facilitation. The output logogen system is a store of phonological codes. This model permits an account of the lack of effect of picture naming on the subsequent visual recognition of the name.

sources for the phonological code following reading and naming. However, there appear to be a number of objections to such alternatives.

The next stage was that the input modalities had to be separated. Clark and Morton had also found very little transfer from hearing a word in the pretraining to the subsequent visual recognition of the word. Next, Jackson and Morton (unpublished) found that there was relatively little effect of having made a semantic judgment on the visually presented word on the subjects ability to recognize the word when it was spoken in a background of noise (see Morton, 1979). This compared with strong effects when the words were presented auditorily either in the same or in a different voice. The latter experiment has been repeated in unpublished experiments by Peter Gipson and Andrew Ellis, in different laboratories, and with tighter controls and under the right conditions, it turns out that there is no cross modal transfer whatsoever. The resulting model is shown in Fig. 5 with auditory and visual categorization systems (input logogens) kept separate. The facilitation effects referred to above take place in these systems.

Let us next consider briefly a couple of additions to the model that will come in useful later. In the first place nothing has been said about the nature of the information fed into the input logogen systems. We can finesse this problem for the moment by adding a couple of processes to symbolize the transformation of sensory information into a suitable form. We can simply label these as analysis systems, for convenience of reference. The important point here is that so far as the functioning of the rest of the model is concerned it doesn't matter how these devices work nor what is the nature of the information they pass on to the categorization systems. Thus the information from the visual analysis could be in the form of letters. There are a number of models of word recognition that suppose this step as necessary (Massaro, 1975). I happen to think there is good evidence against this, not least of which is our ability to read carelessly written script. But the assembly of this evidence and the subsequent decision have no consequence as far as the rest of the model is concerned. Equally, the output from the auditory analysis system could be syllables, or phonemes, or simple acoustic features. This decision, too, is separate.

One addition that is necessary later is a way of reading and of repeating

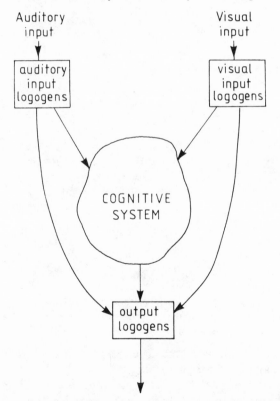

FIG. 5 The third division of the lexicon. The lack of cross-modal facilitation necessitates separate input logogen systems. The direct connection between input and output logogen systems is speculative.

nonwords. This I indicate by the addition of grapheme-phoneme and auditory-phonemic routes. The boxes symbolize the processes, and while they are diagrammed as being separate from the lexical routes, the model is not discomforted by the possibility that we read nonwords by analogy with real words; it is merely complicated. These processes feed into the Response Buffer, which is the process responsible for converting all phonological code into speech output. The resulting model is shown in Fig. 6.

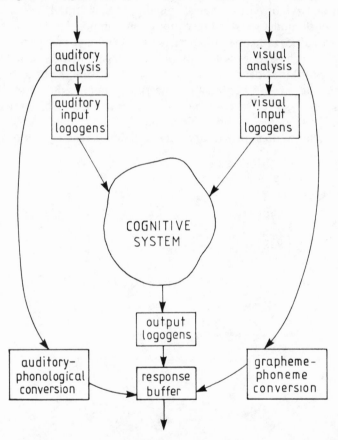

FIG. 6   An elaborated version of the model showing the sensory analysis systems, a response buffer, and routes connecting the two that bypass the lexical processes. These latter are necessitated by our ability to read or repeat nonwords.

Next we can consider the kind of decision we have to make about the detailed functioning of the processes. In the original formulation of the logogen model I supposed that each logogen collected evidence relevant to itself from the context and from the current stimulus. It was supposed that the first logogen to accumulate an amount of evidence greater than a particular threshold would then fire. The effect of this would be to stop any other logogen from firing. I took the simplest assumption for the interaction of stimulus and context information; that the two added together. It was then possible to test the assumptions by comparing three situations: recognizing a word presented in isolation; recognizing a word presented in context; and producing a response to the context in the absence of any stimulus information. It is clear that the underlying processes are not deterministic with respect to a particular task. Even the same subject does not always make the same response to complete an open-ended sentence. A usual assumption is that the system is noisy with respect to the current task—that is, that there is concurrent processing unconnected with what the experimenter is interested in. With this assumption I was able to use Luce's Choice Axiom in order to derive predictions about performance in the three situations. The resulting equation was:

$$\text{Logit } P_{SC} = \text{Logit } P_S + \text{Logit } P_C + K$$

where logit P is given by $\log(p/(1 - p))$, and P_C, P_S and P_{SC} are the probabilities of being correct with context alone, with stimulus alone, and with both stimulus and context. I took data from Tulving, Mandler, and Baumal (1964) who had looked at the effect of context on the visual recognition of words. The equation, then, and the processing assumptions behind it, would apply to the visual input logogen system. I found the relationship as in Fig. 7. The straight lines have a slope of unity, predicted by the equation, and were fitted by eye (Morton, 1969). The fit seems to be good, and still strikes me that way.

The point about this demonstration is that it illustrates how one can make precise predictions about the operation of the model when one element is specified in detail. The experiments then allow us to accept or reject particular assumptions about the way the processes operate. Note, however, that if the predictions had failed, it would not affect the overall structure of the model, just the assumption about visual categorization. In addition, if it turns out that the data I used was peculiar in some way and that, after all, the equations do not predict what happens in a series of replications, all that will happen is that the specification of the way in which the visual input logogen system functions will have to be changed. Again, nothing else need be affected.

Let me add to this that there are likely to be differences in the mode of operation when the stimulus is clear compared with when there is stimulus impoverishment, as when the words are presented in a tachistoscope. In particular, with clear stimuli, the influence of context on the categorization process is likely to be minimized. In addition, it is certain that inhibitory processes operate from the stimulus, but not from the context. Thus, seeing the sentence,

She was wearing a bright red xacket

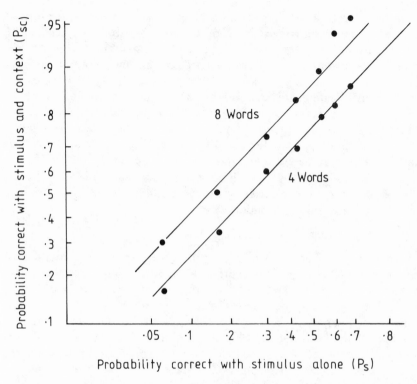

FIG. 7   A graph showing the relationship between the probability of recognizing a word with and without a context. The straight lines of slope = 1 were predicted by the model and were fitted by eye (from Morton, 1969).

the final word is not going to be read as "jacket" when it is presented clearly and read with caution. The reader may be able to work out that the word ought to have been *jacket* but would not think it *was* jacket.

The new form of the model has had an unexpected advantage. The separation of the auditory and the visual input logogen systems carries with it the consequence that the two may well operate in different ways. Thus, in the last few years, Marslen-Wilson and his collaborators have proposed a different model for auditory word recognition, which has been called the "cohort model" (Marslen-Wilson & Welch, 1978; Marslen-Wilson & Tyle, 1980). By this account the recognition process has two stages. After the first two or three phonemes have been analyzed, a set of possible candidates is isolated. Thereafter, subsequent inputs serve to eliminate members of this "cohort" set until only one candidate remains. He had produced some persuasive evidence in favor of such an idea, but it remains to be seen whether this model can also account for all the other data that has gone into the logogen model, as it remains to be seen whether an evidence-collecting system, like the old logogen system, can be modified to account for his data. If it turns out that the cohort model wins, then the consequences are clear. The logogen system would have to be modified such that the auditory input categorization system operates on cohort principles and would thus be different from the visual system in this respect. Again, the modularity of the approach prevents the consequences from being more severe than this.

LEXICAL DECISION

A number of other models of the lexicon have been proposed over the past few years. A number of these have started from a different set of data, the most usual being the lexical decision task. In this task the subject is presented with a string of letters and has to decide whether or not they constitute a word in the language. There are, perhaps, a hundred or two such studies published in the last ten years. In a number of them the logogen model has been rejected on the grounds that it made the wrong predictions. Unfortunately, in every case, this conclusion has been drawn in the belief that a lexical decision would have to be made on the basis of the operation of the logogen system, or, in the case of the revised model, as a result of the operation of the visual input logogen system. Logically speaking, this would be a possibility, since nonwords do not have a representation in the input system. Thus, if the letter string is successfully categorized it must, indeed, be a word. There are a number of problems with this account of what happens. In particular it would be impossible to account satisfactorily for responses to nonwords. The first difficult finding was that nonwords that were homophones of real words, such as BRANE, took longer to reject than nonwords having no real word equivalents, such as BLANE (Rubenstein, Lewis, & Rubenstein, 1971; Coltheart, Davelaar, Jonasson, & Besner, 1977). This effect could only arise if the letter strings are converted into the appropriate phonological codes and it would be difficult to involve the input systems in any subsequent decision.

A second problem relates to the strong word frequency effect in the lexical decision task. If the word frequency effect in this task is to be assigned to the logogen system then there should be an interaction of this effect with the effects of stimulus degradation. In fact, there are at least three experiments showing that word frequency and degradation are *additive* factors indicating that they act at different places (Stanners, Jastrzembski & Westbrook, 1975; Becker & Killian, 1977, expts. 3 and 4). Thirdly, Becker (1976) has shown that response times in the lexical decision task are subject to the attentional demands of a secondary task. This could not be the case if the logogen system was involved, since it is designed as a passive, non-attention demanding system.

These, and some other objections, lose their force, however, if we assume that lexical decisions are based primarily on the operation of the processes in the cognitive system. The reason why the logogen system cannot be so used can be answered in a number of ways, the simplest being that we simply have no means of monitoring the system at the appropriate point. With the lexical decision based on the cognitive system we have a number of degrees of freedom that enable an account to be given of the problem results. These involve some elaboration of the available mechanisms, but the result is not noticeably more complicated than other accounts. Thus, the effect of the nonword homophones is accounted for by supposing that the phonological code is automatically produced and then used to access semantic information. This would succeed, but subsequent checks on the spelling would prevent an error response. While such checks are not a property of the logogen system, we have no reason to exclude them from the cognitive system. We would, however, hope to find evidence for them in other tasks. Secondly we can attribute the word frequency effect in the lexical decision task to the structure of the semantic and associative components of the cognitive system. In fact, I prefer to think of word frequency as being an index of some other property rather than having direct representation in the cognitive system. Thus, we could imagine that, in general, more frequent words have stronger or richer associations. The account one would give here would depend upon what processes were thought to be necessary for other reasons at this stage in the processing. In any case, given that the word frequency effect in this task is located in the cognitive system, we would then expect no interaction of frequency with stimulus degradation, since the latter variable must have its effect at the input logogen level or earlier. Finally, we now have no prior reason for supposing that the lexical decision should not be subject to attentional demands. Becker's result, referred to above, serves then to tell us something about the nature of the operations involved in finding information in the cognitive system. Again, we would demand that any other task whose explanation involved the relevant parts of the cognitive system would also show the same attentional effects. Such a task has not yet made itself known, but it surely will. There are degrees of freeedom remaining in our ability to account for data, but we have to expect that every new postulate is capable of a number of applications.

At this point I should acknowledge that Forster (1976, 1978) has put forward a model of lexical access that is superficially very different from the logogen model. The most striking difference is that the system uses *search* as the means of access, rather than automatic content addressing, which is the characteristic of the logogen model. A detailed comparison of the two approaches is in preparation. Two points might be made here. Firstly, the account given of some data is considerably more elegant in Forster's model than in mine. For some other data, however, he has to elaborate his system well beyond the original intention, while the logogen model handles this data with ease. Such facts simply reflect the starting points of the two theories. The second point is that as the models become more elaborated, they begin to resemble each other. Thus, while I would reject search principles as a property of the input systems, there is no reason to exclude them from the cognitive system.

READING IN JAPANESE

The question has been posed in discussion as to the predictions that would be made from the Logogen Model as to results in certain experiments when using Japanese script. In Japanese there are two writing systems, *Kana,* which is a syllabic script, and *Kanji,* which is an ideographic script. It is clear that the model has nothing to say about how these scripts are processed by native readers of the language. However, the methodology used in establishing the information processing account for alphabetic scripts should be usable for Japanese. How it will look is an empirical question.

A FINAL CAUTION

As I have indicated, the model has been elaborated to account mainly for experiments involving single words. It remains open the extent to which the same processes will operate in the same way in continuous performance. Naturally, I would hope that only minimal changes would have to be made, but it remains possible that in continuous tasks some of the categorization decisions are made further into the system. One possibility is that in rapid speech, the segmentation problem cannot be satisfactorily solved without taking into account the kind of pragmatic constraint that it would be unreasonable to suppose could be fed back to the input systems. The operation of the overall system then might more resemble the HEARSAY program. It might be noted, however, that recent work by Marcus (in press) indicates that the segmentation problem may be soluble without the need of such added complexity.

In any case, a model that accurately represents the mental operations involved in the processing of individual words promises to have its uses. In particular the logogen model is currently being both tried and extended in neuropsychology. It turns out that a lot of the standard tests given to brain damaged patients involve the use of the single words. Patients are typically required to read them, categorize them, repeat them, write them to dictation, and use them to name objects that are seen, touched,or heard. In the final section of this paper I will outline some of the results of this endeavor.

SOME NEUROLINGUISTIC CONNECTIONS

Recently, the logogen model or variants on the form have been used as a means of describing aphasic symptoms (Dérouesné & Beauvois, 1979; Goldblum, 1980; Morton & Patterson, 1980a, b; Patterson, 1980; Shallice, 1980; Schwartz, Saffran, & Marin, 1980). In addition, data from patients has been used to extend the model. One example is due to the patient P.W. studied by Morton and Patterson (1980a, b). This patient is known as a deep dyslexic (the relevant symptoms will be described later). In addition he is agrammatic. The agrammatism emerges in a number of ways. To start with, he finds function words much more difficult to read out loud than other words. Of a sample of 406 function words (taking the broadest definition of the class) he read correctly only 23%. This compares with 50% correct with a set of nouns. He also had a seeming inability to comprehend function words or use them. Since the patient is totally incapable of reading nonwords, and so, in terms of the model, must lack the grapheme-phoneme route, we originally entertained the hypothesis that function words were not represented in the logogen system but rather were read via the grapheme-phoneme route. This theory was abandoned when Patterson (1978) showed that P.W. was virtually perfect on a lexical decision task involving function words together with nonwords which closely resembled function words (e.g. THISE, THORE, WHAR, WETH). Next we discovered that he had access to the meaning of function words. We tested this by means of word triplets; the patient having to point to one word of a pair when "went with" a third word. Examples are

(over/under   up)   (every/few   all)   (except/with   but);

these three representing space, frequency, and logical number. He performed well above chance on all these and others, but failed on judgments that were vaguely syntactic. Thus he could not judge the case of pronouns (he/him   her), or relative pronouns (that/this   these) though he could judge the number of these words (those/that   many). We established his comprehension of prepositions in a number of ways. Then we tried him on sentences such as:

Put the cup on the saucer.

In one session he got 11 wrong out of twelve, making errors of the type of putting the saucer on the cup. We presumed that he was treating the preposition as if it was an adjective, and so attaching it to the following noun. Our conclusion was that while the semantic aspects of the function words were relatively unaffected, their structural aspects were missing (Morton & Patterson, 1980b). Overall, then, we came to the conclusion that function words normally had two representations in the central part of the lexicon, one of which, the structural, was not operational for P.W. (Morton & Patterson, 1980a).

We can now think about the lexical decision task again. For normal subjects we know that there is a strong word frequence effect, which is almost always tested with content words. In the one exception, Bradley (1978) found that there was no word frequency effect for lexical decision times using function words. The simplest conclusion, in terms of the model we have elaborated, is that function word lexical decisions can be based on the structural component of the lexicon. The rationale of this is that the number of structural possibilities (usually only one) of function words will not be affected by how common it is in the language. We would also deduce from the data that access to the structural output was in general faster than access to the semantic component, though this would not be a necessary conclusion. If the structural component was lost, however, lexical decisions would have to be based on the semantic component in which, as we have seen, there is a word frequency effect. Indeed, Bradley showed that this was the case. Needless to say, we didn't actually predict these data before we saw Bradley's thesis, but we might have done so if we had been really smart.

Let me now say a little more about P.W. who is a typical deep dyslexic. His problem with reading may be summarized as follows:

1. He is completely incapable of reading any nonword, and, indeed, appears to be unable even to get single phonemes except via a real word, which may be a part. At the same time he can repeat nonwords without much trouble.

2. In reading words he makes about 50% errors. All his responses are real words. The errors may be classified into three main types:

semantic: e.g. paddock is read as 'kennel'
derivational: e.g. edition is read as 'editor'
visual: e.g. narrow is read as 'marrow.'

In general he is aware of the semantic errors but not aware of errors of the other two classes. This is a simplification of the data, and a full account is given in Patterson (1978, 1979).

3. He makes more errors on function words than on other types of words. In this respect he resembles a typical agrammatic. Thus he can read *inn* but not *in,* bee but *be* and he can only read the word *over* when he is reminded that the word is also a term in the game of cricket (see also Gardner & Zurif, 1975).

Karalyn Patterson and I have given a detailed analysis of this and other data (Morton & Patterson, 1980a). What we have done is locate the 'lesions'

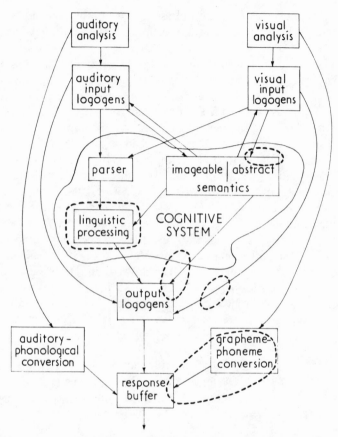

FIG. 8   An expansion of the logogen model indicating the location of the functional deficits in a deep dyslexic patient (from Morton & Patterson, 1980a).

in the model. This is illustrated in Fig. 8. Basically we attribute the problem with nonwords to a breakdown of that system which effects conversion from graphic to phonological forms. From the modeling principles outlined above, it should be clear that such an attribution is independent of the nature of this system. The semantic errors are due to a problem with the connection between the cognitive system and the output logogen system together with an absence of the direct input-output route. The visual errors are due to a problem with the connection between the input system and the cognitive system. Note that the visual errors cannot be attributed to a problem with visual analysis since the patient does not produce word responses to nonwords that very closely resemble words. Thus he would not read *narket* as "market" but, rather, would say that it was not a word. Awareness of the semantic errors arises from the fact that he has a representation of the target in the cognitive system that can be compared with his response. The same would not be true for the visual errors. The derivational errors we would associate with his problems with function words and with syntactic function in general. This we represent as a problem with the module labeled "linguistic processing."

This patient contrasts readily with a number of others. Thus, the *phonological alexic* patients studied by Beauvois and Dérouesné (1979) had reading problems only with nonwords. The problem here would be solely with the grapheme-phoneme route. Then the class of patients termed *surface dyslexics* have equivalent problems with words and nonwords (Marshall & Newcombe, 1973). In such cases, we would say that the visual input logogen system was not functioning correctly. There is then a class of patient who has problems with repetition of spoken words, but who has unimpaired reading (Morton, 1980), or reading problems of an unrelated kind (Goldblum, 1980). Such patients reinforce the belief in the fractionation of the lexicon.

More detailed comparisons of these and other patients are made by Patterson (1981). From all these patients, we get a feel for the suitability of a model that stresses the modularity of the compenent processes. Within the model we can readily form contrasts between the patients.

It should be noted that the model does not permit us to state why there is a tendency for loss of the grapheme-phoneme route to be accompanied by agrammatism, or a number of other correlations. Such facts I take as being the province of activity I separated out at the beginning of this chapter—that of the mapping of psychological function onto brain function. This task becomes much simpler when we begin to get an adequate description of the component processes and the way in which they interrelate. The question might have occurred to you that the use of aphasic patients in forming the model presupposes localization of function. In fact this is not the case. A number of the critical patients have massive lesions, and it would not be safe to say any more than that most of the functions in question use a particular region of the left hemisphere. Beyond that we have the problem of not knowing whether the loss of function has to do with the destruction of the process or its disconnection. Such distinctions may well become important in the near future, but at the moment we get the feeling of progress in our work without worrying too much about this. Finally we have no guarantee that the identical lesions in the brains of identical twins will give the same result.

I hope that I have shown how an information processing approach to cognition and language has the properties one demands of a scientific-pursuit.

We can relate together a wide variety of facts.
We can predict new facts.
We can ask new questions and apply new descriptions in an applied area.
We can falsify individual elements of the structure of the model (though not the form).

I think that all this can only be done in an *interesting* way, if we tackle the evident complexity of the mental processes. I hope that the model I have described is sufficiently complex to be interesting and that the form is congenial enough to be intelligible.

REFERENCES

Anderson, J. R. *Language, memory and thought.* Hillsdale, N.J.: Lawrence Erlbaum Associates, 1976.

Arbib, M. A., & Caplan, D. Neurolinguistics must be computational. *The Behavioural and Brain Sciences,* 1979, *2,* 449–483.

Becker, C. A. Allocation of attention during visual word recognition. *Journal of Experimental Psychology: Human Perception and Performance,* 1976, *2,* 556–566.

Becker, C. A., & Killian, T. H. Interaction of visual and cognitive effects in word recognition. *Journal of Experimental Psychology: Human Perception and Performance,* 1977, *3,* 389–401.

Beauvois, M-F, & Dérouesné, J. Phonological alexia; three dissociations. *Journal of Neurology, Neurosurgery and Psychiatry,* 1979, *42,* 1115–1124.

Bradley, D. C. *Computational distinctions of vocabulary type.* Ph.D. Thesis, MIT, 1978.

Coltheart, M., Davelaar, E., Jonasson, J. T., & Besner, D. Access to the internal lexicon. In S. Dornic (Ed.), *Attention and performance VI.* Potomac, Md.: Lawrence Erlbaum Associates, 1977.

Dérouesné, J., & Beauvois, M-F. Phonlogical processing in reading: Data from alexia. *Journal of Neurology, Neurosurgery and Psychiatry,* 1979, *42,* 1125–1132.

Forster, K. I. Accessing the mental lexicon. In E. C. T. Walker & R. J. Wales (Eds.), *New approaches to language mechanisms.* Amsterdam: North Holland, 1976.

Forster, K. I. Accessing the mental lexicon. In E. Walker (Ed.), *Explorations in the biology of language.* Hassocks: Harvester Press. (The M.I.T. work group on the biology of language), 1978.

Gardner, H., & Zurif, E. BEE but not BE: Oral reading of single words in aphasia and alexia. *Neuropsychologia,* 1975, *13,* 181–190.

Goldblum, M. C. *Auditory equivalents to deep dyslexia.* Paper delivered to the meeting of the European Psycholinguistics Association on Information processing models in aphasia, Paris, 1980.

Marcus, S. M. ERIS—context sensitive coding in speech perception. *Journal of Phonetics,* in press.

Marshall, J. C., & Newcombe, F. Patterns of paralexia: A psycholinguistic approach. *Journal of Psycholinguistic Research,* 1973, *2,* 175–199.

Marslen-Wilson, W. D., & Tyler, L. K. The temporal structure of spoken language understanding. *Cognition,* 1980, *8,* 1, 1–71.

Marslen-Wilson, W. D., & Welch, A. Processing interactions and lexical access during word recognition in continuous speech. *Cognitive Psychology,* 1978, *10,* 29–63.

Massaro, D. W. Primary and secondary recognition in reading. In D. W. Massaro (Ed.), *Understanding language: An information processing analysis of speech perception, reading and psycholinguistics.* New York: Academic Press, 1975.

Morton, J. Considerations of grammar and computation in language behaviur. In J. C. Catford (Ed.), *Studies in language and language behaviour.* C.R.L.L.B. Progress Report No. VI, University of Michigan, 1968.

Morton, J. The interaction of information in word recognition. *Psychological Review,* 1969, *76,* 165–178.

Morton, J. A functional model for memory. In D. A. Norman (Ed.), *Models of human memory.* New York: Academic Press, 1970.

Morton, J. Some experiments on facilitation in word and picture recognition and their relevance for the evolution of a theoretical position. In P. A. Kolers, M. E. Wrolstad, & H. Bouma (Eds.), *The processing of visual language 1.* New York: Plenum Press, 1979.

Morton, J. Two auditory parallels to deep dyslexia. In M. Coltheart, K. Patterson, & J. C. Marshall (Eds.), *Deep Dyslexia.* London: Routledge & Kegan Paul, 1980.

Morton, J., & Patterson, K. E. A new attempt at an interpretation, or an attempt at a new interpretation. In M. Coltheart, K. Patterson, & J. C. Marshall (Eds.), *Deep dyslexia.* London: Routledge & Kegan Paul, 1980. (a)

Morton, J., & Patterson, K. E. "Little words—No." In M. Coltheart, K. Patterson, & J. C. Marshall (Eds.), *Deep dyslexia.* London: Routledge & Kegan Paul, 1980. (b)

Murrell, G. A., & Morton, J. Word recognition and morphemic structure. *Journal of Experimental Psychology,* 1974, *102,* 963–968.

Neisser, U. An experimental distinction between perceptual process and verbal response. *Journal of Experimental Psychology,* 1954, *47,* 399–402.

Newell, A. HARPY: Production systems and human cognition. In R. Cole (Ed.), *Perception and production of fluent speech.* Hillsdale, N.J.: Lawrence Erlbaum Associates, 1980.

Patterson, K. E. Phonemic dyslexia: errors of meaning and the meaning of errors. *Quarterly Journal of Experimental Psychology,* 1978, *30,* 587–601.

Patterson, K. E. What is right with 'deep' dyslexic patients? *Brain and Language,* 1979, *8,* 111–129.

Patterson, K. E. Derivational errors. In M. Coltheart, K. Patterson, & J. C. Marshall (Eds.), *Deep dyslexia.* London: Routledge & Kegan Paul, 1980.

Patterson, K. E. Neuropsychological approaches to the study of reading. *British Journal of Psychology,* 1981, *72,* 151–174.

Rubenstein, H., Lewis, S. S., & Rubenstein, M. A. Evidence for phonemic recoding in visual word recognition. *Journal of Verbal Learning and Verbal Behavior,* 1971, *10,* 645–657.

Schwartz, M. F., Saffran, E. M., & Marin, O. S. M. Fractionating the reading process in dementia: Evidence for word-specific print-to-sound associations. In M. Coltheart, K. Patterson, & J. C. Marshall (Eds.), *Deep dyslexia.* London: Routledge & Kegan Paul, 1980.

Shallice, T. Case study approach in neuropsychological research. *Journal of Clinical Neuropsychology,* 1980, *1,* 183–211.

Stanners, R. F., Jastrzembski, J. E., & Westbrook, A. Frequency and visual quality classification. *Journal of Verbal Learning and Verbal Behavior,* 1975, *14,* 259–264.

Tulving, E., Mandler, G., & Baumal, R. Interaction of two sources of information in tachistoscopic recognition. *Canadian Journal of Psychology,* 1964, *18,* 62–71.

Wanner, E., & Maratsos, M. An ATN approach to comprehension. In M. Halle, J. Bresnan, & G. A. Miller (Eds.), *Linguistic theory and psychological reality.* Cambridge, Mass.: MIT Press, 1978.

Winnick, W. A., & Daniel, S. A. Two kinds of response priming in tachistoscopic recognition. *Journal of Experimental Psychology,* 1970, *84,* 74–81.

6 Propositional Representations, Procedural Semantics, and Mental Models

P. N. Johnson-Laird
University of Sussex

There is one incontrovertible fact on which this paper is based: there are mental processes, largely outside conscious awareness, that underlie speaking and understanding a natural language. A generation ago this assertion might have been considered a dangerous speculation; today, behaviorists and phenomenologists apart, it seems like a truism. Several of its implications, however, are controversial, and I shall deal with some of them that concern what is known as "procedural semantics"—an approach to the psychology of meaning based originally on computer programming, and which accordingly emphasizes the *process* of interpretation.

There has been a certain amount of misunderstanding about the nature of procedural semantics, which has in part been fostered by the fact that there is no central consensus of views about it. Rather than attempt to delineate the different versions of it, my aim is to try to clarify its main virtues as a basis for psychological theorizing.

Let me begin with a very common misunderstanding. Many people suppose that the central procedural doctrine is that the mental representation of the meaning of a word is a procedure which, if executed, determines the extension of the word; that is, it determines for any arbitrary entity whether or not that entity is appropriately named by the word. There are many words that do not designate objects, but that is not at issue. Even if we restrict ourselves to words such as "cat," "red," "table," which can be used to designate objects and properties, the doctrine that the meanings are procedures for deciding whether or not something is a cat, or red, or a table, is one with little to recommend it. The reason should be clear. If I tell you that in the next room there is a cat sitting on a red table, then your understanding of my utterance does not require you to verify that indeed there is a cat there, and a table that is red. Nor, of course, in uttering such a sentence am I required to carry out such a process of verification. Plainly, the idea that the meaning of a word is represented by a procedure that checks out its applicability to arbitrary objects fails to square with these elementary observations. It is analogous to that old behaviorist blunder of identifying a word with a conditioned stimulus. You may salivate when someone describes a gorgeous concoction from haute cuisine, but your salivation is contingent upon your understanding of the description; it is *not* part of the understanding itself.

Another, though less serious, misunderstanding is to assume that procedural semantics is necessarily committed to a particular position in the "procedural-declarative" controversy that flourished a few years ago among the artificial intelligenzia. This argument was really about whether quantificational assertions such as, "all black cats are invisible on a dark night," should be stored in the data base of some computational system in the form of assertions in some formal language resembling, say, the predicate calculus, or in the form of procedures, such as those provided by the programming language PLANNER. The answer to this question is: it all depends . . . on what the system is supposed to do. Although it was sometimes argued that the difference is related to Ryle's (1949) celebrated distinction between *knowing that* and *knowing how,* this claim is somewhat dubious. Certainly, there appears to be no strong empirical consequences in claiming that a certain piece of information is stored in memory procedurally as opposed to declaratively.

What, then *is* procedural semantics from a psychological standpoint? I propose to answer this question in a series of stages.

THE MEANINGS OF WORDS

There is a very old phenomenon associated with the meaning of words. Everyone is familiar with it, but it seldom draws comment from psychologists or linguists. The phenomenon is this: when you are taking part in normal conversation, you readily choose words appropriate to your communicative purposes, and you readily grasp the meanings of the words in other people's utterances provided that their vocabulary is not too erudite. I ask you, for example, "Have you ever spent any time in Sussex?" You understand me without difficulty. However, if I extract one of my words from its customary setting and ask you what it means, then you may be extremely perplexed. What exactly is the meaning of the word "time," which occurred in my utterance? Children have the happy knack of stumping us with just such questions. Indeed, we think we understand the meanings of words—we must understand a good part of them—yet we have considerable difficulty in bringing to mind a suitable semantic analysis of them. It is perhaps significant that one of the few thinkers to comment on the phenomenon was a poet, Paul Valéry (1939). In a telling image, he likened it to a man crossing an abyss on a narrow plank: it's fine if he keeps moving—the plank will just support him, but if he should stop to think then it will break beneath him.

An obvious consequence of the difficulty of semantic analysis is the existence of lexicologists. Likewise, our inability to recover syntactic rules by mere introspection gives rise to the existence of grammarians. But, is it not odd that these individuals should exist—that the mind is so organized that it regularly makes use of knowledge that passes its own understanding? The reason for such an organization is, I believe, speed. As I have argued elsewhere, it appears to be an intrinsic part of the mental processes that underlie linguistic performance that much is computed in parallel. The bugbears of parallel computation such as "deadly embraces" are avoided by promoting one processor to a superordinate and supervisory role, and consequently many of the other processes, including those governing lexical meaning, are outside conscious awareness. We gain speed from parallel computation at the cost of insight into how we perform (see Johnson-Laird, 1979).

A more immediate moral from "the plank across the abyss" is that psychologists should enquire into the role that the meaning of a word plays in normal use rather than try, like philosophers, to cut up its meaning on the logic-chopping board. What we discover from considering ordinary usage is, as we have seen, that a word can be used in many different sorts of sentences—questions, requests, assertions, and the full panoply of illocutions. It follows that its semantic representation—perhaps, even within a sentence in which it occurs—must fit into a whole range of different mental processes that can be characterized globally as asking and answering a question, making and understanding a request, and so on and on. In the past, considerable confusion about procedural semantics has arisen simply because theorists have discussed examples that concern the verification of assertions. Philosophers of language are especially attuned to the doctrine of verificationism, i.e., the notion that the meaning of a sentence is the means whereby its truth or falsity is established, and have advanced apparently invincible arguments against this doctrine. Some proceduralists, notably Bill Woods, are prepared to fight a rearguard action on behalf of verificationism. But, in order to avoid this vexatious issue I propose to make the following minimal assumption. Some people on some occasions are able to determine whether or not some utterances are true or false. As a simple example consider the assertion:

The letter "A" is on the right of the letter "B."

This sentence is true of the following arrangement of letters:

B   A

and the reader should have no difficulty in determining that the sentence is true of the display. There are many other ways, of course, in which you might make use of your understanding of the sentence. For example, you could merely imagine an array that would satisfy its description; alternatively, given the array, you might formulate the sentence as a description of it; given the location of the letter B in a complicated array of letters, you could use your grasp of the sentence's meaning to search in the appropriate direction to see whether or not there is indeed a letter A there. All of these various processes depend on your ability to understand the meaning of the expression, "on the right of." None of these various abilities should be identified with that process of understanding—they are, as I have already emphasized, contingent upon it.

It seems then that the ordinary understanding of a word—the understanding that occurs as we cross the delicately poised plank between utterance and idea—is one that requires us to postulate that the semantic representation of a word must be able to enter into a variety of different mental processes. In the particular example of spatial relations, it is relatively simple to specify a procedural semantics with the required flexibility. But, as a preliminary to expounding this theory, it is necessary to consider first the technical notion of "freezing in" the value of a variable in a function so as to produce a new function—a notion that is made use of in the high-level programming language, POP-2.

A simple arithmetic function such as addition, takes two variables, x and y, and when it is called during the execution of a program by an instruction such as:

$$ADD\ (x,y)$$

the current values of x and y are sought and then added together. A new function can be obtained from ADD by freezing in the value of a variable. Thus, we could freeze in 5 as the value of the second variable and then assign the name, ADD5, to this new function. Let us suppose that we have a programming language such as POP-2 that allows us to perform this operation using the following expression:

$$ADD(\%5\%)\ \longrightarrow\ ADD5;$$

What we have done is to partially apply the function ADD so as to yield the new function, ADD5. The function ADD5 takes just a single variable and adds 5 to whatever its value is. We could make the same step again and freeze in a specific value for that variable, say, 8. The result would be a function that does not take any variables, and that merely adds 8 and 5 together whenever it is called.

This simple computational machinery has a natural extension that can be exploited in many ways. Instead of freezing in numerical values for variables, we can freeze in functions as the values of variables. We will presently see the role that this idea plays within a procedural semantics.

Our aim is to develop a procedural semantics for spatial relations, which we will implement in a computer program. The program is neither a demonstration in the computer simulation of human performance nor an exercise in artificial intelligence. The intention is rather to devise a small-scale model of the theory of procedural semantics that will enable us to explore the theory much as a molecular biologist can explore conjectures about the structure of molecules by constructing models of them. A molecular model captures only certain aspects of the substance under investigation—it would be foolish to criticize it on the grounds that its color and taste were wrong. Likewise, the program is intended to capture only certain aspects of comprehension; it is deliberately kept as small and as simple as possible so that essential principles can be readily distinguished from ad hoc patches.

Let us suppose that we wish to type in assertions of the following sort:

A is on the right of B
C is in front of B
D is on the left of C

from which the program is to construct a spatial array that satisfies the description, and display the entities as though they were laid out on a table top:

B   A

D   C

We also will want the program to respond to sentences that are incompatible with its current array, pointing out that they are inconsistent with the previous sentences, and to respond to sentences that can be inferred from the previous input by pointing out that they are redundant. Such a program clearly requires a number of general procedures. It will need a procedure (1) that will begin the construction of the spatial array, when it is presented with the initial sentence, by forming an array and inserting the items referred to in the initial sentence. For the subsequent sentences of a description, it will need a general procedure (2) that looks to see if it can locate any of the items referred to in a sentence, and, having found one of them, inserts the other at an appropriate position in the array. Should it find both of the items referred to in a sentence, then it will require another general procedure (3) for verifying whether or not the current relation holds between them. If a description appears to be true of the current array, then a general procedure (4) will be required in order to determine whether or not the entities in the array can be rearranged so as to render false the current sentence; conversely, if the description appears to be inconsistent with the current array, then there will have to be a further general procedure (5) that attempts to rearrange it so as to render the description true. In short, the program contains a number of very general procedures for responding to sentences by constructing, manipulating, or interrogating, spatial arrays. The details of most of these procedures are straightforward and can be left to the intuition of the reader. But, the procedures for manipulating an array are more complicated. When you attempt to move one item there may be others whose positions are defined in terms of it, and hence, before you can move the first item, you must see whether you can move these other items, but they, too, may have still further items related to them, and so you must first check whether they can be moved . . . and so on. The only way to cope with the general problem is to use what computer scientists call a "recursive" procedure. It is worth dwelling a moment on recursion since psychologists, if they have encountered it at all, tend to know it only in the context of recursive rules of the sort proposed by linguists, and tend to assume that it is relevant only to syntactic theory. There is, of course, a fairly direct correspondence between the two notions. A recursive rule in linguistic theory is one in which the same symbol occurs on both the left and the right-hand side, such as:

$$A \longrightarrow a + (A)$$

A crucial sort of recursive rule gives rise to self-embedding structures:

$$A \longrightarrow a + (A) + b$$

and these rules are most closely related to the computational notion of recursion. Recursion in a procedure contrasts with iteration. An interative procedure is one that is just applied over and over again until it produces the right result. Let us suppose that you wish to formulate a procedure that will compute the factorial of any integer, e.g., the factorial of 3, which is symbolized 3!, is $3 \times 2 \times 1 = 6$, and the factorial of 0 is stipulated to be 1. A simple iterative procedure would multiply the number, n, by $n - 1$, then multiply the product by $(n - 1) - 1$, and so on, until the repeated subtractions reduce n to 1. In an iteration, the procedure loops round and round, carrying out the same computation until a given criterion is reached to complete the process. A recursive procedure for computing the factorial function is shown here:

Factorial n;
If $n = 0$ then 1;
Else $n \times$ Factorial $(n - 1)$.

The first line names the function, "Factorial," and specifies that it takes a single argument, n. The second line stipulates that the factorial of 0 equals 1.

The third line is required if n is not equal to 0, and here something interesting happens: the procedure calls itself by name. If you follow this procedure as it computes the factorial of 3, then it goes through the following steps:

3! = 3 × (Factorial(2) which equals:
    2 × (Factorial(1) which equals:
        1 × (Factorial(0) which equals:
            (1))))

Only when it gets to the last step of recovering the factorial of 0 does it carry out the actual multiplication. Although factorials can be computed iteratively or recursively, some functions have to be used recursively. The way to *parse* self-embedded structures, for example, is by a recursive use of the same procedure, and this fact establishes the connection between a particular sort of recursive rule in linguistics and a recursive procedure. However, as we have seen, there are also general cognitive procedures such as the rearrangement of mental models that also require recursion—it is not peculiar to linguistic processing.

To return to the question of the meanings of words and how they may be modeled in the program for spatial inference, what we need is a system in which a given utterance can elicit the appropriate general procedure depending on both the meaning of the utterance and the context in which it occurs. It is important to emphasize that although the program deals only with assertions, there are a variety of different general procedures that it has to contain in order to cope with them. For the simple world of the program, context is merely the present state of the array. Hence, if you type in:

C is in front of D

then the general procedure that will be called depends solely on the present state of the array. If both C and D are already in the array, then the program checks whether the assertion is true. If neither C nor D is in the array, then the utterance is, as it were, starting a new topic—it is about a new array, though it may ultimately be integrated into the old one should there occur an assertion that interrelates items in both of them. If only one of the items, C or D, is in the array, then the program inserts the other item into the array in an appropriate position. The particular procedure that is ultimately executed depends on the referents of the referring expressions in the assertion. In this respect, the program reflects a principle that applies outside its limited domain and propensities, though obviously there are other factors that also determine how listeners actually react, if at all, to an utterance.

Once a general procedure has been selected on the basis of reference and context, the meaning of the assertion has to be used in running the procedure appropriately. It is here that the business of "freezing in" the value of a variable plays its part. Suppose that in coping with the assertion, "C is in front of D,'' the general procedure that has been selected is one for inserting C into the array, i.e., D is already sitting in the current array. It is necessary to ensure that the procedure for inserting one item, which we will call: IN-SERT1, is modified so that it inserts the new item *in front of* the old item. There are many ways in which this modification could be done, but one neat way that exemplifies the general thesis that I am trying to establish is by freezing in the values of variables. The program is contrived so that every general procedure, including INSERT1, contains a mechanism for scanning in any arbitrary direction. Basically, the scanning mechanism works iteratively by incrementing the x and y dimensions of the current location. The actual increments depend on the values of two variables, DX and DY, which accordingly specify the direction. Hence, given that the position of D in the array is the one illustrated below:

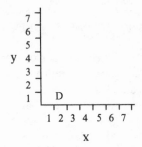

then if DX and DY are both set to the value 1, then the scanning mechanism will look at the sequence of locations obtained by progressively incrementing the x and y coordinates of D's location, i.e., the sequence of locations will be: (2,1), (3,2), (4,3), and so on. Since a scanning mechanism is embodied in *all* the general procedures, then the meaning of *in front of* can be specified in the following simple way: in front of: (%0, − 1%). What this instruction does is freeze in values for DX and DY that ensure that the scanning mechanism holds its x-coordinate constant and increments the y coordinate by − 1. In other words, if the matrix were laid in front of you, then the scan is in a downward direction; INSERT1 will accordingly insert C in front of D. There is no danger of falling off the edge of the "known universe": an array can always be expanded to accommodate a new item.

The program for spatial inference is not intended as anything other than a simplified model of a theory of how the meanings of words are mentally represented. One of its most blatant oversimplifications is that we do not normally require that one object lie directly in the line of sight for it to count as being in front or behind another object (in the deictic sense of these expressions). Human beings tolerate a certain amount of vagueness, but how it is best accommodated within the truth conditions of sentences is problematical.

There have been one or two ventures in model-theoretic semantics to cope with vagueness, but it remains an almost untouched problem in psychology. Some aspects of the program, however, are intended to be psychologically realistic.

Consider the nature of the lexical entry given above for *in front of.* Is it procedural or declarative? The answer is, in fact, that it is a very special sort of procedure—almost midway between a conventional procedure and a piece of declarative information. It is a procedure that cannot be executed on its own: it takes other procedures and produces from them new procedures. Its effect is really to represent the *truth conditions* of the predicate, because what the new procedures do is to construct models that satisfy those truth conditions, to examine existing models and to see whether they satisfy those truth conditions, and so on. It is difficult to resist the assumption that the mental lexicon similarly represents truth conditions, which can be employed in many different mental processes.

Once one has a mental representation of truth conditions, then there is no need to specify the logical properties of the term. This is an extremely important aspect of the present species of procedural semantics. The entailments of sentences are captured not by rules of inference or meaning postulates that explicitly lay out the logical properties of terms, but rather these properties emerge directly from the bald formulation of truth conditions. The point can be illustrated by considering the logical property of transitivity. Many relations are transitive in that they support inferences of the following form, where R designates an appropriate relation:

$$x \text{ R } y$$
$$y \text{ R } z$$
$$\overline{\therefore x \text{ R } z}$$

One way in which to ensure the validity of such an inference is to posit the existence of an appropriate meaning postulate, e.g., for any x, y, and z, if x is on the right of y, and y is on the right of z, then x is on the right of z. Theories that seek to capture logical properties in this way have been advocated by Kintsch (1974), Fodor, Fodor, and Garrett (1975). Meaning postulates, ever since they were first introduced by Carnap (1956), are indeed a commonly employed method of capturing logical properties within model-theoretic semantics. However, given an explicit representation of the truth conditions of a predicate, there is no need to add such meaning postulates to the system.

The fact that meaning postulates are redundant in psychological semantics does not, of course, establish that they are never embodied in the mind; but, there are some rather telling arguments against their general existence. The point has been made before (see Johnson-Laird, 1980) and so I will be brief here. The logical properties of many spatial expressions are singularly flexible. If you are talking about people seated round a table, then there is a limit to the extent to which expressions of the (non-deictic) form, "x is on y's right," function transitively. But, if people are seated along one side of a straight table, then the same expression designates a wholly transitive relation. These various usages can be accommodated in a single semantics of the procedural sort exemplified above: the term establishes a dimension by reference to the frontal plane of an individual sitting at the table, and a mental model built up from such a semantics yields transitive inferences in just those cases where they are warranted. (Transitivity is *not* built into the machinery of arrays; otherwise it would be impossible to allow it to break down in the case of circular tables.) A logic of the required flexibility can be accommodated within the meaning postulate account only at a cost of considerable complexity. Moreover, such an account in itself does not specify the truth conditions of a term. Hence, even if the meaning postulate system were modified so as to cope with the complexities of transitivity, it would still be necessary to specify some additional machinery for dealing with the truth conditions of the relation. What we have seen, however, is that once one adds such a representation of truth conditions, then the meaning postulates are no longer necessary. Perhaps the key psychological datum in favor of the present theory is the mere existence of the vagaries in the logical properties of many terms. If their semantics were truly embodied in mental meaning postulates, it is extremely difficult to see how such vagaries could arise. However, if their semantic representation is essentially a specification of truth conditions, then these truth conditions will naturally give rise to a logic of considerable flexibility.

When Miller and I became interested in procedural semantics, our primary goal was to explore the nature of the mental lexicon that made possible efficient interpretation (see Miller & Johnson-Laird, 1976). What was not at first apparent was the importance of the *outcome* of the mental processes underlying comprehension. The spatial inference program, for example, works in the way that it does only by relying on an internal representation of spatial relations that corresponds to a *model* of them. What is of crucial psychological importance is not the ultimate nature of such a representation—everything can in principle be reduced to a propositional representation, i.e., a structured sequence of symbols, just as every computational device can be reduced to a Turing machine—but rather the functional significance of the representation. This significance depends on the level of description of the representation. In a high-level programming language such as POP-2, programmers can work directly with spatial arrays, that is, they can write code that directly inserts items into specified positions in arrays, tests the values of specified positions, and so on. The programmers need not concern themselves with how such arrays are represented at the level of machine code, and the machine code corresponding to the spatial inference program would be singularly unrevealing. If one asks why it is that there are programming languages with such high-level facilities, the answer is plain: they have evolved, not because they allow computations to be carried out that would be otherwise impossible, but because they make the business of writing and developing programs easier for the programmer. In my view, this moral applies equally well to mental software. New programs will be easier to develop in mental languages that admit high-level representations. Psychologists should recognize that a major appeal of mentalism is that it allows one to postulate different levels of representation within the mind. It is in this spirit that I make a sharp distinction between mental models and propositional representations (in a narrow sense of the term).

Propositional representations are best exemplified by those theories of psychological meaning, such as Kintsch's (1974) and Fodor, Fodor, and Garrett's (1975) which make use of meaning postulates in order to capture entailments. What do meaning postulates operate on? The answer is, psychologically speaking, that they operate on representations of utterances that correspond closely to their linguistic form. The reason for this constraint arises directly from the nature of meaning postulates. A meaning postulate semantically interrelates different items in the vocabulary of a language. Hence, a psychological theory that makes use of meaning postulates must postulate a representation that corresponds "virtually one-to-one," to use Fodor et al.'s phrase, with the lexical items in the language. Kintsch takes very much the same point of view, and proposes that a sentence such as, "The old man smiled and left the room," has the following propositional representation:

(OLD, MAN) & (SMILE, MAN) & (LEAVE, MAN, ROOM)

The important factor here is not the syntax of the expression and its conjunctive form, which give rise to problems, but rather the direct correspondence between the lexical items in the sentence and the words in capitals, which designate mental tokens.

The advantage of such propositional representations is the ease with which they can be constructed. Comprehension is a rapid process that takes place in real time, and this rapidity is consistent with a theory that involves essentially little more than translating utterances into corresponding mental tokens. Moreover, there is no overwhelmingly convincing evidence that the semantic complexity of lexical items has any detectable effects on comprehension speed. This is a rather striking negative finding, but I believe it to be true—if only because my colleagues and I have wasted a considerable amount of time over the years searching for such effects. It is important to emphasize that there *are* effects of semantic complexity to be obtained, but customarily they occur in tasks that demand more than mere comprehension (whatever that may be).

The disadvantage of propositional representations is that the only inferential machinery that can work directly with them is a system based on meaning postulates or rules of inference. Since I have already argued against such a system, I must now try to resolve this difficulty. In fact, the resolution is easy. The initial stage of comprehension is indeed a process by which utterances are translated into a mental language that contains tokens corresponding to lexical items. This process appears to be automatic, rapid, and involuntary, for a native speaker. However, the resulting propositional representation is by no means the end of comprehension. The great virtue of the processes of comprehension is that they can vary in their depth of operation, from barely registering the words through to a concentrated effort to capture every nuance and implication. The major distinction in level of understanding depends on whether or not an individual attempts to go beyond the initial propositional representation. Thus, the propositional representation can be treated as the input for the procedural semantics, which, operating in the manner illustrated by the spatial inference program, constructs an appropriate mental model.

A decade ago, I suggested that a reader or listener implicitly sets up a non-linguistic model of discourse, similar to one that would be constructed from actually perceiving (or imagining) events instead of merely reading or hearing about them—a process that may well involve the introduction of additional material in order to render the model more meaningful (see Johnson-Laird, 1970). Subsequent work has confirmed this conjecture, and made it possible to propose the present theory. Before the argument can be advanced any further, however, some evidence for the existence of two sorts of representation for language must be considered. The essence of the empirical case can be illustrated by one of a series of experiments that Kannan Mani and I have designed and conducted. The subjects were read a series of descriptions of the spatial layouts of sets of objects. After each description, such as:

The spoon is to the left of the knife
The cup is to the right of the knife
The fork is in front of the spoon
The plate is in front of the knife

the subjects were shown a simple diagram containing the names of the appropriate objects in a spatial arrangement:

Spoon   Knife   Cup
Fork   Plate

The subjects' task was to decide whether or not the description tallied with the diagram. Half the descriptions were, in fact, consistent and half were inconsistent with the diagrams. The major variable of interest was whether the description was determinate, like the one above, or grossly indeterminate and thus consistent with at least two different spatial layouts. The following description, which differs in only a single noun phrase from the previous one, is grossly indeterminate:

The spoon is to the left of the knife
The cup is to the right of the spoon
The fork is in front of the spoon
The plate is in front of the knife

and consistent with either of the following two layouts:

| Spoon | Knife | Cup | | Spoon | Cup | Knife |
| Fork | Plate | | | Fork | | Plate |

After the subjects had classified each description-diagram pair, there was an unexpected recognition test of memory for the descriptions.

We predicted that subjects would construct a mental mode of the spatial layout characterized by a determinate description, but that they would abandon the attempt to do so in interpreting an indeterminate description as soon as they encountered the indeterminacy, and instead try to hold on to a propositional representation of the sentences. The advantage of the propositional representation is that it would obviate the need to construct two alternative mental models, which would otherwise be necessary in order to ensure a correct classification of the subsequent diagram. We knew that the greater the *amount* of processing the better an item is recalled—a finding that we have established both for memory for words (Johnson-Laird, Gibbs, & de Mowbray, 1978) and for memory for sentences (Johnson-Laird & Bethell-Fox, 1978). Hence, we predicted that the subjects' memory for the layout would be better for the determinate than for the indeterminate descriptions, since the construction of a mental model necessarily requires more processing than merely constructing the propositional representation on which it is based. We further predicted that subjects would confuse the original description with a description that could be inferred from the layout in the case of determinate descriptions, but that their relative ability to make a *verbatim* recall would be better for indeterminate descriptions than for determinate descriptions since a propositional representation is close to the linguistic input.

These predictions were confirmed. Every subject carried out the recognition test better for determinate than for indeterminate descriptions. The subjects readily confused a description that could be inferred from the layout with the original determinate descriptions, but even though their overall performance was poor for indeterminate descriptions, their *verbatim* recall was better for them than determinate descriptions. This pattern of results corroborates the idea that the subjects were using two different sorts of representation as a function of the determinacy of the descriptions (see Mani and Johnson-Laird, in press).

This experiment also provides the beginning of an answer as to why two different sorts of representation may be a desirable feature in the use of language. A system that could represent discourse only in the form of structural models would get into very considerable trouble with the indeterminacies of everyday discourse. On the one hand, it could attempt to keep track of all the different possible models consistent with the linguistic input, but this strategy would soon succumb to a combinatorial explosion. On the other hand, it could opt for just a single mental model—its best guess, perhaps, but then it would run into trouble in those cases where its best guess was wrong. There is accordingly a clear advantage for a system that allows discourse to be represented propositionally, i.e., in a form that is close to language and that therefore copes equally readily with determinate and indeterminate sentences. Granted this facility, the reader may wonder what advantage accrues to a system that also allows mental models. For an answer to this question, we must consider the psychology of reasoning.

THE PSYCHOLOGY OF REASONING

How is it possible to make a valid inference? Psychologists without exception, if they have cared to answer the question, have argued that there is a mental logic that underlies this skill. There are many difficulties with this proposal—how is the logic acquired, for example?—but its severest problem is that it lacks any empirical content. You might suppose that the fact that people commit fallacies establishes that the doctrine of mental logic is false, but as Mary Henle (1962, 1978) has pointed out, these errors may arise because of misinterpretations of the premises, faulty memories for them, or failures to stick to the required exercise of "pure" logic. One suspects, in fact, that the nature and frequency of errors, particularly in the case of syllogistic inferences, suffices to refute the doctrine of mental logic. But it must be admitted that there are no criteria independent of the controversy by which the matter can be adjudicated, and it is for this reason that one must ultimately take the view that the doctrine lacks empirical content. Doubtless, a specific hypothesis within its general framework may well be refutable. However, rather than attempt to examine such hypotheses, I intend to propose a wholly different approach to reasoning—an approach that derives from the procedural representation of meaning.

There are three main sorts of deductive inference that we need to consider: reasoning with relational terms, such as "taller than," "relation of," "in front of," reasoning with propositional connectives, such as "and," "or," "not," and reasoning with quantifiers, such as "all," "none," "most." I shall deal briefly with each of these domains in turn.

One way in which to make the following sort of inference that hinges on a relation:

> Alice is taller than Bertha
> Carol is shorter than Bertha
> ∴ Alice is taller than Carol

is to construct a mental model that directly represents the relative heights of the three individuals. Such a construction depends, first, on possessing the appropriate procedural semantics for the relation "taller than," second, on being able to form a unitary model from two premises in virtue of the fact that they both make reference to the same individual, and third, on being able to examine the mental model so as to determine the relation between those individuals that have not been explicitly related in a premise. There are obvious problems about the direct encoding of real numbers, since the continuum is infinitely and uncountably dense, and could not be embodied in a finitary device such as the human brain. However, it is plausible to suppose that lengths are mentally represented by a digital approximation. In other words, the inference can be made simply by imagining three individuals of heights that satisfy the truth conditions of the premises, and there is no need to make recourse to a mental logic containing a principle of transitivity and information to the effect that "taller than" is a transitive relation. One virtue of this analysis is that it becomes very much easier to understand why children do not master transitivity in an all-or-nothing way: they gradually master the various relational terms over a period of some time—a phenomenon that has caused Piaget to talk of a horizontal décalage. What is happening, according to the present account, is that children simply take time to acquire the meaning of the various relational terms that give rise to transitivity. Another incidental virtue, pointed out to me by my colleague, Josef Perner, is illustrated by the fact that children appear to master those relations, such as length, which are visible, faster than they master those relations, such as weight, which are not immediately visible. It seems that it is easier to build a mental model of the visible world than of the invisible world.

Inferences based on propositional connectives tend to be rather harder to make, as witness the Piagetian claim that the underlying mental logic—the propositional calculus—is not mastered completely until the stage of formal operations (which is attained at about the age of 12). Most of the controversy about whether it is the propositional calculus that is mentally embodied has hinged on the proper interpretation of the conditional. Although there is no doubt that the word "if" does give rise to interesting and important problems, the controversy about it has deflected interest from the more important issue—whether or not *any* calculus is mentally embodied. It may seem necessary to have rules of inference in order to make valid inferences, but what I shall now establish is the illusory nature of the necessity, and once again, my argument will proceed by examining a computer program (written in POP-2) that is a small-scale model of a general theory of inference.

The program takes as input the following sort of formulas:

$$p \text{ and } q$$
$$p \text{ or } q, \text{ and } r$$
$$\text{if } p \text{ or } q \text{ then } r$$

where the variables are taken to stand for simple atomic propositions such as, "The plane is late," "There is a fog," "The airport is closed." The program's output is a valid conclusion that follows from the premises. Of course, there are always an infinite number of possible valid conclusions that can be drawn from any set of premises. Even granted premises of the form:

$$p$$
$$q$$

one can infer such conclusions as:

$$p \text{ and } q$$
$$p \text{ or } q$$
$$p \text{ and, } p \text{ or } q$$
$$q \text{ or } p, \text{ and } p \text{ or } q$$

and so on. These conclusions are obviously wholly trivial and no one in their right mind would ever bother to draw them. What this negative phenomenon establishes is that there must be an inferential heuristic, wholly outside logic, that determines which particular valid inference, if any, an individual makes from a given set of premises. A heuristic, which I believe to have considerable psychological validity, can be based on the notion of semantic information. Psychologists are familiar with the statistical concept of information that derives from the work of Shannon, but that has nothing whatsoever to do with the meaning of messages. However, it is possible to develop a measure of semantic content, on the basis of the plausible assumption that the greater the amount of such information contained in a proposition the more states of affairs the proposition rules out. A conjunction, *p* and *q*, clearly contains more semantic information than the categorical premise, *p*, which in turn contains more semantic information than the disjunction, *p* or *q*. It is a relatively straightforward matter to devise a measure of semantic information that works for propositional inferences. In essence, the metric simply reflects the proportion of contingencies in a truth table that the premise rules out (see Johnson-Laird, forthcoming).

No valid inference can yield a conclusion with a greater amount of semantic information than is contained in its premises. A heuristic that governs the inferences that people spontaneously draw can now be stated: *No conclusion should contain less semantic information than the premises on which it is based or fail to express that information more parsimoniously.* In other words, propositional inference is essentially the business of expressing the same semantic content as the premises with greater linguistic economy. For example, a set of premises of the following form:

p or q or r
if p and not-r then q
either r and q, or else not-r and not-q
if r then p

validly imply:

p and q and r.

This conclusion contains the same semantic information as the premises (it eliminates a proportion of .875 of the contingencies in a truth table) but it obviously expresses it with maximum economy—just three atomic assertions combined by two connectives. The heuristic explains why people do not make inferences of the form:

p
therefore, p or q

The conclusion contains less information than the premises. Likewise, the heuristic explains why, given premises of the form:

p
q

subjects claim that nothing of interest follows. They refrain from drawing such valid conclusions as:

p and q

because such a conclusion is no more economical linguistically than the premises on which it is based.

There is one important related heuristic principle to be stated. Given premises of the form:

p
not-p or q

one can validly infer:

p and q.

However, it is not normally necessary to repeat a simple categorical premise in a conclusion—the reasoner does not need to state something that can be taken for granted (Grice, 1975)—and hence, the conclusion is usually stated in the simple form:

therefore, q

Only if this conclusion is considered together with the unrepeated categorical premise is the heuristic of not losing information observed. It is important to bear in mind this interplay between the Gricean principle and the inferential heuristic.

The heuristic is merely a constraint that is intended to govern inferences, but now we must turn to the mechanism that the program uses to make the inferences. We will see that in fact it automatically fulfills both the inferential heuristic and the Gricean maxim without having explicitly to incorporate them. The mechanism assumes a knowledge of the truth conditions of the propositional connectives. It makes no claim about how this information is mentally represented; it seems that people cannot mentally inspect a complete truth table, but rather that they do know, for example, that if there is an inclusive disjunction between two propositions:

John will meet you or Mary will telephone (or both)

and that one of these propositions is true, then the disjunction as a whole is true. And, likewise, if one of these propositions is false, then the only way in which the disjunction as a whole could be true, is if the other proposition is true. In other words, they possess the ability to build up the truth value of a complex proposition from a knowledge of the truth values of its constituents: they are capable of building up such meanings compositionally.

The program can accordingly make use of a simple procedure for making any inference based on a categorical premise. This procedure relies neither on inferential schemata nor on rules of inference, but on a knowledge of the meanings of connectives and the ability to carry out compositional semantic interpretation. The simplest way to convey the way in which the program works is by example. Let us suppose that it is given premises of the form:

p
if p or q then r

since p is asserted categorically, then it can be taken as true, and the program accordingly substitutes the value true, for its occurrence in the complex premise:

if true or q then r

The truth conditions for *or* (in its inclusive sense) are such that, as we have seen, whenever one disjunct is true the disjunction as a whole is true. The program accordingly carries out this piece of compositional semantics, which yields a simplified antecedent to the conditional:

if true then r

On the assumption that the truth conditions for the ordinary conditional are such that whenever the antecedent is true and the conditional as a whole is true, then the consequent is true, the final compositional step is to reduce the conditional to the categorical conclusion:

$$r$$

It will be noted that the premises are actually equivalent in their semantic content to:

$$p \text{ and } r.$$

However, by carrying out its compositional semantics directly on the complex premise, the program automatically delivers a conclusion in accordance with the Gricean principle: it does not repeat the categorical premise that is the basis of the inference. Moreover, only if it is able to effect a compositional simplification does it bother to draw any conclusion at all, and in this way it automatically performs in accordance with the inferential heuristic.

Not all propositional inferences, of course, derive from treating premises as categorical assertions. A paradigm case is perhaps an argument in the form of a dilemma:

$$p \text{ or } q$$
$$\text{if } p \text{ then } r$$
$$\text{if } q \text{ then } r$$

therefore, r

Once more, however, it is unnecessary to propose rules of inference in order to capture such inferences. All that is required is a mechanism that, when categorical inferences have failed to produce anything of interest, combines the conclusions from separate constituents of a premise according to the connective that it contains. Compositional semantics will do the rest. The same principle will also accommodate hypothetical inferences. Hence, there is no major sort of propositional inference that cannot be carried out by the program.

Turning finally, to inferences based on quantified assertions, I can be brief since I have elsewhere argued for a theory based on mental models (Johnson-Laird, 1975, Johnson-Laird & Steedman, 1978, Johnson-Laird, 1980). The theory assumes, first, that quantified assertions such as

All the artists are beekeepers

are mentally represented by mental models containing individual tokens, here corresponding to artists and beekeepers; second, that representations of separate premises are combined according to an inferential heuristic that seeks to establish as many identities on as few individual tokens as possible; and, third, such integrated models are then submitted to a test in which a search is made for an interpretation of the premises that is inconsistent with the model. The theory, which has also been implemented in a program, is compatible both with the sorts of errors that subjects make and with the possibility of valid deduction provided that the test process is carried out completely. Hence, there appears to be no branch of deductive inference that requires us to assume the existence of a mental logic in order to do justice to the psychological phenomena. To be logical, an individual requires, not formal rules of inference, but a tacit knowledge of the fundamental semantic principle governing any inference: a deduction is valid provided that there is no way of interpreting the premises correctly that is inconsistent with the conclusion. Logic provides a systematic method for searching for such counterexamples. The empirical evidence suggests that ordinary individuals possess no such methods.

CONCLUSIONS

This paper has outlined a theory of psychological semantics that postulates two stages in the interpretation of sentences, an initial and rather superficial propositional representation and a more articulated and integrated mental model. A procedural semantics is employed to construct the mental model from the propositional representation, though this process is also likely to involve inferences based on general and specific knowledge. Now, at last, the reader should have understood why the title of this paper refers to propositional representations, procedural semantics, and mental models. It summarizes the central claim: Apply procedural semantics to a propositional representation in order to obtain a mental model.

The advantage of using propositional representations is that they provide an economical way of retaining grossly indeterminate information. The advantage of mental models is still greater. They enable us to make inferences without a knowledge of rules of logic. We put together the information from separate assertions into a single integrated model. In the case of simple relational inferences and propositional inferences, an error-free process of integration guarantees us a valid conclusion provided that we have not forgotten or misinterpreted any of the premises. In the case of quantified assertions, however, the process of integration is under the control of an inferential heuristic that cannot deliver any such guarantee, and it is accordingly necessary to submit the model to a series of tests. This qualitative difference is, of course, reflected in the very much greater difficulty of quantified inference over inference with propositions and simple relations. The point to be emphasized is that it is only because we can construct mental models that we are able to make inferences based solely on the meanings of expressions and without recourse to any system of mental logic.

REFERENCES

Carnap, R. *Meaning and necessity: A study in semantics and modal logic* 2nd ed. Chicago: University of Chicago Press, 1956.

Fodor, J. D., Fodor, J. A., & Garrett, M. F. The psychological unreality of semantic representations. *Linguistic Inquiry,* 1975, *4,* 515–531.

Grice, H. P. Logic and conversation. In D. Davidson & G. Harman (Eds.) *The Logic of grammar* Encino, Calif.: Dickenson, 1975.

Henle, M. On the relation between logic and thinking. *Psychological Review,* 1962, *69,* 366–378.

Henle, M. Forward to R. Revlin and R. E. Mayer (Eds.), *Human reasoning* Washington, D.C.: Winston, 1978.

Johnson-Laird, P. N. The perception and memory of sentences. In J. Lyons (Ed.) *New horizons in linguistics* Harmonsworth, Middx.: Penguin, 1970.

Johnson-Laird, P. N. Models of deduction. In R. Falmagne (Ed.) *Reasoning: Representation and process in children and adults* Hillsdale, N.J.: Lawrence Erlbaum Associates, 1975.

Johnson-Laird, P. N. Language and human mentality. In K. Connolly (Ed.) *Psychology Survey No. 2* London: Allen and Unwin, 1979.

Johnson-Laird, P. N. Mental models in cognitive science. *Cognitive Science,* 1980, *4,* 71–115.

Johnson-Laird, P. N. *Mental models* Cambridge: Cambridge University Press. Cambridge, Mass.: Harvard University Press, (forthcoming).

Johnson-Laird, P. N., & Bethell-Fox, C. E. Memory for questions and amount of processing. *Memory and Cognition,* 1978, *6,* 496–501.

Johnson-Laird, P. N., Gibbs, G., & de Mowbray, J. Meaning, amount of processing, and memory for words. *Memory and Cognition,* 1978, *6,* 372–375.

Johnson-Laird, P. N., & Steedman, M. J. The psychology of syllogisms. *Cognitive Psychology,* 1978, *10,* 64–99.

Kintsch, W. *The representation of meaning in memory.* Hillsdale, N.J.: Lawrence Erlbaum Associates, 1974.

Mani, K., & Johnson-Laird, P. N. The mental representation of spatial descriptions. *Memory and Cognition,* in press.

Miller, G. A., & Johnson-Laird, P. N. *Language and Perception* Cambridge: Cambridge University Press, 1976.

Ryle, G. *The concept of mind* London: Hutchinson, 1949.

Valéry, P. Poetry and abstract thought. Oxford: Clarendon, 1939. (Rep. in *The Art of poetry, Vol. 7: The collected works of Paul Valéry.* London: Routledge & Kegan Paul.)

7 Two Mechanisms of Lexical Ambiguity

Joan Ryder
Edward Walker
M.I.T. Center for Cognitive Science

To understand an isolated word, its phonological or orthographic properties must be used to locate some internal representation from which the word's meanings and usages can be retrieved. Although some words have only one sense, a great many words have more than one distinct meaning or can serve more than one function in a sentence. For example, in the sentence, "The artist began to draw a picture," the word "draw" means "to sketch" rather than "to pull" or "a tie." The extent of lexical ambiguity in natural language is often underestimated, but the difficulty of writing machine translation programs (Kelly & Stone, 1975; Kuno & Oettinger, 1963; Yngve, 1964) attests to the problem of ambiguity resolution in recovering meaning from a string of orthographic or phonological symbols.

Gaining an understanding of how ambiguity is avoided or resolved and how grammatical function is assigned bears on a number of important theoretical questions about human language use. Among these are: What information is represented in the mental lexicon and how is it organized? What is the procedure for accessing that lexical information? How and when is the syntactic function of each item in the sentence determined? How and when is the meaning of each item determined?

At a minimum, the representation of each lexical item in the mental lexicon must include its phonological, syntactic, and semantic properties, stored in a form that supports language comprehension and production. For literate language users, the relevant orthographic properties of the item must also be represented. Further specificity than this becomes controversial. For example, are ambiguous words represented once or separately for each usage?

One proposal (Katz & Fodor, 1963) is that each different word constitutes a single lexical item, with all possible meanings and uses of the item represented distinctly. Ambiguous items are first subcategorized by grammatical function, then by distinct senses within each function.

McCawley (1968), following Weinreich (1966), questions the assumption that form alone should individuate lexical items. Instead, he proposes that differences in semantic and syntactic characteristics as well as orthographic or phonological form should separate lexical items. Thus, his position is that each usage of an ambiguous word constitutes a separate lexical entry.

A third proposal (Rubenstein, Lewis, & Rubenstein, 1971) differentiates lexical items by meaning and form but not by syntactic function. According to this view, a word such as "paint," which can be used as either a noun or a verb, has a systematic relationship between the two uses and, thus, would be represented as one lexical item. This view could be extended to include similarity in the uninflected stem. Thus, morphologically related word pairs such as "destroy" and "destruction" would also be part of one lexical entry.

Still another proposal is that lexical items are distinguished by form and syntactic function but not by meaning (Lyons, 1977). Syntactic equivalence could be interpreted weakly to include only the same major syntactic categories (i.e., noun or verb), or strongly to include subclasses of each syntactic category (i.e., mass vs. count nouns or transitive vs. intransitive verbs). The weak interpretation would yield separate noun and verb entries for "paint" but would include the readings of "bank" as "side of a river" and "financial institution" within a single entry.

A careful examination of lexical processing involving ambiguous words might help resolve such questions about the form of lexical entries, in addition to providing insights into the process of lexical retrieval itself. Moreover, studying ambiguous words might help clarify our understanding of the autonomy and interaction of processing levels within the comprehension system.

One strong position holds that lexical, syntactic, and semantic processing are hierarchically arranged autonomous subsystems (Forster, 1979; Garrett, 1978). Proponents of this position argue that interaction between levels is restricted to passing the output of lower levels of processing to the next higher level. In other words, higher level processing does not interact with processing at lower levels. A lexical processor recognizes words based on the output it receives from lower-level phonological processing and from knowledge of words represented in long-term memory. This lexical information is then made available to the syntactic processor, which computes a structural description for the sentence. Semantic processing of this output results in an interpretation for the sentence, based on individual words' meanings and their structural configuration.

The extreme opposing viewpoint is that the comprehension system is completely interactive, with processing in one subsystem directly affecting the internal operations of others (Marslen-Wilson, 1975; Marslen-Wilson & Tyler, 1980; Marslen-Wilson & Welsh, 1978; Rumelhart, 1977). This view allows for "top-down" interactions as well as the usual "bottom-up" flow of information. Thus, knowledge that "gift" is a word, while "kift" is not, may directly affect whether "g" or "k" is perceived at the beginning of a phonologically ambiguous utterance (see Ganong, 1980). By similar arguments, the contributions of a variety of "higher level" knowledge are thought to contribute to the operation of "lower level" processes.

It is important to emphasize here that the debate is not whether higher and lower level processes interact, but when and how the interaction proceeds. On the one hand, the so-called autonomy position does not preclude higher level considerations from influencing post-processing decisions or error-recovery routines or, indeed, from such global effects of prior context as associative spread. Thus, syntactic or semantic analysis might contribute to the selection of a set of lexical entries or influence decisions among entries once multiple candidates have been accessed (Garrett, 1978). On the other hand, the on-line interactive position obviously must provide for processing to proceed when higher order information is absent and cannot constrain lower level processing.

The way in which lexical ambiguity is resolved provides an interesting test of these two positions. If lexical processing is strictly autonomous, then ambiguous words should be processed identically in neutral contexts and in contexts biased toward one usage. If context does influence lexical processing involving ambiguous words (or unambiguous words, for that matter), then the time course of that interaction should provide clues to its nature. There are three general hypotheses about the role context plays in the interpretation of ambiguous lexical items. One holds that all readings of ambiguous words are accessed whenever the word is encountered, whether in isolation, in a neutral context, or in a context biased toward one reading. According to this view, context can aid only in the selection of an appropriate reading after all readings have been accessed. For the sentence above, the readings of "draw" as "to sketch," "to pull," and "a tie" would all be accessed and context used to determine that "to sketch" was appropriate.

Alternatively, it has been suggested that while all usages of an ambiguous word might be accessed in a neutral context, contextually appropriate usages are facilitated in a biasing context. In the example sentence, only the "to sketch" reading of "draw" would be accessed, since that usage is more contextually correct.

The third hypothesis is that readings of ambiguous words are accessed sequentially in order of their relative frequency of usage in the language. This hypothesis implies that context itself has no effect on the order with which the usages are accessed, but may serve to terminate lexical search when a contextually acceptable reading is found. Referring again to the example above, "to pull," the most frequent usage of "draw," would be accessed and eventually found inappropriate.[1] Then "to sketch" would be accessed and found fitting, precluding access of "a tie."

While these three general positions are distinct enough, past research on the influence of context on lexical processing has not produced clear-cut results. Evidence from a number of tasks has shown that the processing complexity of a sentence is greater if it contains a semantically ambiguous word than if it contains an unambiguous word matched in frequency and length. The increased processing load presumably arises from considering the multiple interpretations of the ambiguous word. In these studies the difficulty associated with processing ambiguous words does not decrease when prior semantic context is biased toward one reading of the ambiguous word (Chodorow, 1979; Cutler & Foss, 1974; Foss & Jenkins, 1973; Holmes, Arwas, & Garrett, 1977). These findings suggest that lexical access is independent of on-going semantic processing. Moreover, additional evidence that all readings of ambiguous words must be accessed has been obtained. This evidence is based on the phenomenon of automatic activation of word meaning (Collins & Loftus, 1975; Meyer & Schvaneveldt, 1971) in testing which reading or readings of an ambiguous word have been accessed. Again, the evidence supports the position that lexical access is independent of semantic context (Conrad, 1974; Lackner & Garrett, 1972; Oden & Spira, 1978; Swinney, 1979).

However, other studies have shown a reduction or elimination of ambiguity effects by semantic context (Hogaboam & Perfetti, 1975; Schvaneveldt, Meyer, & Becker, 1976). One of these experiments involved a post-sentence decision and the other used isolated words as contexts, whereas the former research used more or less on-line tasks such as understanding time compressed speech, rapid serial visual presentations, or phoneme-monitor tasks. It may be that in making judgments about individual words, no semantic or syntactic processing at the sentence level is ongoing. Similarly, post-sentence decision tasks may not measure momentary processing difficulties because an interpretation for the sentence may have already been completed. In fact, there is evidence that ambiguity effects have disappeared as soon as three syllables after the end of the ambiguous word (Cairns & Kamerman, 1975; Swinney, 1979). Thus, the conflicting evidence may reflect quite different aspects of lexical processing.[2]

---

[1]The "to pull" usage of "draw" cannot be eliminated since the artist may have drawn the picture across the room with a piece of clothesline. The extent to which context may be widened in search of clues to interpretation is a general problem for the interactive position, but that problem is beyond the scope of the present discussion.

[2]A further complication is that the phoneme-monitoring task, which has been widely used as a measure of processing complexity, is sensitive to such properties as length, frequency, and initial phoneme of the word containing the monitored phoneme and the word processing it (Mehler, Segui, & Carey, 1978; Newman & Dell, 1978). These properties have been confounded with the ambiguity manipulation in many studies (Cutler & Foss, 1976; Foss & Jenkins, 1973). Furthermore, it may be that phoneme-monitoring latencies reflect post-access processes rather than access itself (Cairns & Hsu, 1979; Swinney, 1979).

A further problem with previous research turns on the characteristics of ambiguous words themselves. Words can be ambiguous not only with regard to meaning (e.g., *duty* as a tax or a responsibility) but also ambivalent with regard to their function (e.g., *defeat* as a noun or a verb). Despite the potentially important consequences of these distinctions for lexical processing, many earlier studies have failed to distinguish syntactic from semantic ambiguity and have not taken note of frequency of usage for meaning or function in question. Consequently, most have not investigated whether lexical processing is independent of syntactic, as well as semantic, context.

One distinction that has been made in the literature is that between systematic and unsystematic homographs (Forster & Bednall, 1976; Rubenstein, Lewis, & Rubenstein, 1971). Systematic homographs are ambivalent but not ambiguous (e.g., cart); that is, they have one meaning but can serve different syntactic functions. Unsystematic homographs have multiple meanings with no regular relationship (e.g., club). However, the meanings can occur in different syntactic categories. Therefore, the distinction between systematic and unsystematic homographs is not sufficient.

Furthermore, Hogaboam and Perfetti (1975) have found that the relative frequency of each reading of an ambiguous word may be an important variable when subjects must decide if the last word in a sentence was ambiguous. When the word was presented in its primary (most frequent) sense as opposed to its secondary sense, subjects took longer to decide that the word was in fact ambiguous (provided there was a large difference in relative frequency between the two usages). Forster and Bednall (1976) also found that more frequent readings of ambivalent homographs are accessed more quickly than less frequent readings. Their subjects had to decide if a word was a noun or a verb. If the word could serve both functions but one was more commonly used, the decision could be made more quickly for the more frequent usage.

One examination of the effect of syntactic context on grammatically ambivalent words (Oden & Spira, 1978) found that syntactic context did not increase activation of the appropriate reading of the word but did inhibit activation of the inappropriate reading. In contrast, Tanenhaus, Leiman, & Seidenberg (1979) found that both readings of noun-verb ambivalent words were activated momentarily in sentences biased toward one usage of the word, a finding that suggests that the syntactic context does not direct lexical access. It should be noted, however, that the test sentences of the latter experiment followed a standard format and provided minimal contextual information (e.g., "She held the _____." or "They all _____."). Thus, subjects may have adopted a strategy which minimized the role of the context.

Nevertheless, there are reasons to believe that syntactic processing might affect lexical access in ways that semantic processing does not. Even though a large proportion of English words are ambivalent with regard to grammatical category (One estimate [Carroll, 1970] is that 43% of all words and 72% of the 1000 most frequent words can serve multiple grammatical functions.), local syntactic cues based on function words and on sequences of categories may largely fix the function of a potentially syntactically ambiguous word (Bahl & Mercer, 1976; Milne, 1978; Muckstein, 1979). Since many of the locally permissible combinations of ambivalent words do not yield grammatical sentences, eliminating inappropriate category assignments from consideration or assigning grammatical function independently would improve the efficiency of a language recognizing system. In fact, many parsing systems simply assume that input strings will contain lexical items unambiguously assigned to one category. (See Marcus, 1977, Frazier & Fodor, 1978, or Church, 1980, for recent examples.)

Psycholinguistic evidence also indicates that syntactic processing is ongoing *during* sentence comprehension (see, for example, Bever, 1970; Garrett, Bever, & Fodor, 1966; Holmes & Forster, 1972; or Marslen-Wilson & Tyler, 1980). Since structural relations are being computed during sentence processing, such information is available to interact predictively with lexical access. Furthermore, Bradley and Garrett (see Bradley, Garrett, & Zurif, 1979) argue from evidence that closed-class vocabulary items (function words such as determiners, conjunctions, etc.) are accessed differently than open-class vocabulary items (content words such as nouns, verbs, and adjectives) that the closed-class items play a crucial role in guiding structural analysis. It has also been argued that grammatical affixes may be processed distinctly from content morphemes (Taft & Forster, 1975, 1976) in lexical access.

Two types of indirect evidence also suggest that an ongoing syntactic analysis may be available to guide lexical access. First, a structural analysis can readily be assigned to strings of nonsense words with grammatical morphemes (e.g., " 'Twas brillig and the slithely toves did gyre and gymbal in the wabe."). In such cases lexical representations cannot provide the basis for assigning function for these items. Similarly, parsing programs (e.g., Thorne, Bratley, & Dewar, 1968) that use a dictionary look-up only for closed-class words and inflections (and a small number of verbs) can be remarkably successful in analyzing the structure of a wide variety of English sentences.

Finally, if, as recent linguistic research indicates (Bresnan, 1978, forthcoming), important details of grammatical structure are encoded in lexical representations and lexical rules, then the early assignment of grammatical function to words would seem economical, if not essential, to the comprehension process.

To these arguments may be added the results of an experiment we conducted in order to examine whether the syntactic category and the relative frequencies of the usages of ambiguous and/or ambivalent words affect performance on a synonym verification task. The task asked simply that subjects decide as quickly as possible whether two words were synonyms. The first word of each synonym pair was either unambiguous, ambiguous, ambivalent, or both ambiguous and ambivalent. The second word could be a synonym of any usage of the first.

Thus, subjects were asked to make synonym judgments involving the three types of ambiguous words (and a set of unambiguous control words) shown below:

1. Semantic ambiguity—noun *or* verb usage; more than one reading
2. Syntactic ambivalence—both noun *and* verb usages; systematically related readings
3. Mixed ambiguity—*both* noun and verb usages; more than one reading

The following are examples of each type, together with a synonym of a primary and a secondary meaning or usage of each.

1. Semantic	DUTY	RESPONSIBILITY
		TAX
2. Syntactic	CART	WAGON
		CARRY
3. Mixed	BOOK	TEXT
		RESERVE

To respond correctly subjects must have accessed and compared internal representations of the two words. Since each response was based on a specific usage of the ambiguous word, the task allowed us to assess the availability of the usage involved and compare the availability of different usages of each ambiguous or ambivalent word. Our immediate purpose was to clarify some of the confusion among the studies referred to earlier. The data to be presented here are not in themselves sufficient to distinguish models of contextual disambiguation in sentences; however, our general purpose in conducting the experiment was to provide preliminary data for detailed studies of the contribution of context in sentence processing. A full report of the work discussed here appears in Ryder and Walker (forthcoming). For the present purposes a brief description of the stimulus materials will suffice.

The stimuli used were pairs of English content words. In all, four types of synonymous pairs of words were tested. In Type I the first member of the pair was an *Unambiguous* noun or verb. In Type II, *Semantically Ambiguous* words having either two or more noun readings or two or more verb readings were used as the first member. The first member of Type III pairs was *Syntactically Ambivalent*. Each had systematically related noun and verb usages. Type IV pairs had first members that were *Both Semantically Ambiguous and Syntactically Ambivalent*. The noun and verb readings tested were not systematically related. The relative frequency of the various readings of each word was taken from a compilation by West (1964).

For the unambiguous (Type I) and semantically ambiguous pairs (Type II) half the first members were nouns and half were verbs. For each ambiguous or ambivalent pair (Types II, III, and IV) one-third had two equally probable usages and two-thirds had one primary usage and at least one less frequent usage. Usages were considered equally probable if their frequencies differed by less than 20% of the total frequency. In other words, the primary usage occurred at least 20% more often than the infrequent usage. Half of the syntactically ambivalent probes with unequal usage frequencies (Types III and IV) had dominant noun usages, and half had dominant verb usages. The syntactically ambivalent words provided neither morphological nor stress cues to their category of usage in order to insure that acoustic recoding would not disambiguate these words.

For each first member, two synonyms and two nonsynonym distractors were chosen as the second member of the pair. For the ambiguous or ambivalent word pairs, a separate synonym was chosen for each of two usages.

To be able to examine the effect of the printed frequency of the second word (synonym) on verification latency, we paired one high-frequency synonym and one low-frequency synonym with each unambiguous word (with the cutoff at 25 occurrences per million according to Kucera & Francis, 1967). Nonsynonym distractors for each pair were matched with synonyms in frequency, length, and syntactic category.

Three control factors were taken into consideration in choosing synonyms: the closeness of the synonymy relation between members of the pair, printed word frequency, and word length. Prior to the experiment, a large pool of possible synonym pairs were rated for degree of synonymity by nine judges (graduate students in psychology in Brandeis University). Only those pairs which had a median rating of "Fairly Close," "Very Close," or "Exact" (3 or higher on a 7–point scale) were used. The frequency constraint was observed as follows. Both synonyms of the first word had to be in the high-frequency range (25 or more occurrences per million) or the low-frequency range (less than 25 occurrences per million). Furthermore, no low-frequency words were rare—all of them had at least two occurrences per million. The length constraint was observed if more than one synonym satisfied the synonymity and frequency criteria. A fully developed example of the synonym pairs, as well as a complete list of the stimulus materials appears as an appendix to this chapter. Finding fairly close synonyms of each reading so strongly constrained the set of stimulus materials that it was not possible to match the characteristics of the two synonyms of each ambiguous or ambivalent word more closely. Nor was it possible to match characteristics among Types II–IV.

Each trial began with a one-second adapting field that provided a fixation point and served as a warning signal. The first word was then presented for one second, followed immediately by the second word, also presented for one second. Reaction times were measured from the onset of the second word to the subjects' voice response of "Yes" or "No," indicating whether the two words were synonymous.

The general results of the experiment are given in Table 1. To summarize briefly, pairs with both ambiguous and ambivalent words did require more

TABLE 1
Mean Reaction Time (msec) and Percent Errors for "Yes" and "No" Responses for Each Ambiguity Type

AMBIGUITY TYPE	YES				NO			
	RT MEAN	SE	% ERRORS MEAN	SE	RT MEAN	SE	% ERRORS MEAN	SE
I. UNAMBIGUOUS CONTROLS	1356	69	5.3	1.6	1918	59	3.6	1.1
II. SEMANTICALLY AMBIGUOUS	1619**	64	16.9**	3.7	2054	68	5.0	1.0
III. SYNTACTICALLY AMBIVALENT	1531*	76	10.3	3.4	1931	51	2.8	0.9
IV. MIXED	1690**	125	17.8**	4.4	2104**	52	5.6	1.7
MEAN	1549		12.6		2002		4.2	

*Greater than Unambiguous controls ($p < .05$).
**Greater than Unambiguous controls ($p < .01$).

time to verify and produce more errors than pairs with unambiguous words. However, when the results are broken down according to the frequency of the usage tested (see Table 2), semantic ambiguity and syntactic ambivalence produced markedly different patterns of effects.

While there seems to be a fairly uniform increase in reaction time and error rate for both primary and infrequent meanings of an ambiguous word, only the infrequent usage of syntactically ambivalent words produced a higher reaction time and error rate. Synonyms of the primary usage were verified as rapidly and accurately as those of unambiguous words.

These preliminary results indicate that the assignment of grammatical function to a syntactically ambivalent word may differ from determining the meaning of a semantically ambiguous word. Although there is some indication that frequency of usage might affect results within semantically ambiguous pairs, reaction time and frequency were not correlated. Rather, the number of possible readings for a word was correlated with reaction time to verify its synonyms. Given the strong effect of usage frequency on syntactically ambivalent pairs, it is not surprising that frequency and reac-

TABLE 2
Mean Reaction Time (msec) and Percent Errors for "Yes" Responses in
Each Ambiguity Subcategory

AMBIGUITY-TYPE	RT		%ERRORS	
	MEAN	SE	MEAN	SE
I. UNAMBIGUOUS CONTROLS	1356		5.3	
II. SEMANTICALLY AMBIGUOUS	1619		16.9	
Unequal-Dominant	1555	106	10.8	3.1
Unequal-Infrequent	1671*	124	15.0*	4.7
Equal	1630*	113	25.0**	9.3
III. SYNTACTICALLY AMBIVALENT	1531		10.3	
Unequal-Dominant	1382	88	0.8	0.8
Unequal-Infrequent	1780**	162	20.8**	8.3
Equal	1430	90	9.2	4.2
IV. MIXED	1690		17.8	
Unequal-Dominant	1516	108	10.0	2.2
Unequal-Infrequent	1853**	256	23.3**	9.8
Equal	1702*	263	20.0**	8.7

*Greater than Unambiguous controls ($p < .05$).
**Greater than Unambiguous controls ($p < .01$).

tion time were correlated for these pairs. However, it is somewhat more interesting that the difference in frequency between primary and infrequent usages was not correlated with reaction time.

Taken together these results make it seem likely that in accessing a semantically ambiguous word, all meanings are activated; whereas, in accessing a syntactically ambivalent word, only the primary usage is activated, even though the latter words have more or less the same meaning in both uses.

The critical case then becomes the mixed ambiguous and ambivalent words, for which we tested unrelated meanings in two categories of usage. For these words, frequency of usage of the function being tested correlated with reaction time and accounted for about three times as much variance as the frequency of the meaning being tested. We would expect to find a correlation between number of meanings and reaction time, but unfortunately there were insufficient examples within this experiment on which to base the comparison.

To conclude briefly, the weight of the literature and the results of our research argue that semantic ambiguity and syntactic ambivalence are profoundly different phenomena. The former appears to have a more or less uniform effect on lexical access for all meanings of the word in question, an effect that apparently is not mitigated by contextual constraint. The latter seems to produce an all-or-none effect limited to the less frequent usage. To anticipate our future research somewhat, we expect—from studies indicating that few words in a sentence are more than locally ambivalent—that the determination of syntactic function will be strongly influenced by contextual factors. We are presently attempting to demonstrate such contextual effects.

REFERENCES

Bahl, L. R., & Mercer, R. L. Part of speech assignment by a statistical decision algorithm. Paper delivered at the 1976 International Symposium on Information Theory, Ronneby, Sweden, June 23 (abstract in IEEE Catalog No. 76CH1095-9IT, pp. 88–89).

Bever, T. G. The Cognitive Basis for Linguistic Structures. In J. R. Hayes (Ed.), *Cognition and the Development of Language.* New York, Wiley, 1976.

Bradley, D., Garrett, M. F., & Zurif, E. B. Syntactic deficits in Broca's aphasia. In D. Caplan (Ed.), *Biological studies of mental processes.* Cambridge, Mass.: MIT Press, 1980.

Bresnan, J. W. A realistic transformational grammar. In M. Halle, J. Bresnan, & G. Miller (Eds.), *Linguistic Theory and Psychological Reality,* Cambridge, Mass.: The MIT Press, 1978.

Bresnan, J. W. (Ed.), *The Mental Representation of Grammatical Relations.* Forthcoming.

Cairns, H. S., & Hsu, J. R. Effects of prior context upon lexical access during sentence comprehension: A replication and reinterpretation. *Journal of Psycholinguistic Research,* 1979.

Cairns, H. S., & Kamerman, J. Lexical information processing during sentence comprehension. *Journal of Verbal Learning and Verbal Behavior,* 1975, *14,* 170–179.

Carroll, J. B. Comprehension by 3rd, 6th and 9th graders of words having multiple grammatical functions. Final Report, ETS, Princeton, N.J., December, 1970. Project No. 9-0439, Grant No. OEG-2-9-400439-1059, US Office of Education (ERIC Document Reproduction Service, Doc. ED 04831).

Chodorow, M. S. Time-compressed speech and the study of lexical and syntactic processing. In W. E. Cooper, & E. C. T. Walker (Eds.), *Sentence processing: Psycholinguistic studies presented to Merrill Garrett.* Hillsdale, N.J.: Lawrence Erlbaum Associates, 1979.

Church, K. W. On memory limitations in natural language processing. Unpublished M.S. Thesis, M.I.T., 1980.

Collins, A. M., & Loftus, E. F. A spreading activation theory of semantic processing. *Psychological Review,* 1975, *82,* 407–428.

Conrad, C. Context effects in sentence comprehension: A study of the subjective lexicon. *Memory and Cognition,* 1974, *2,* 130–138.

Cutler, A., & Foss, D. J. Comprehension of ambiguous sentences: The locus of context effects. Paper presented to the 46th annual meeting of the Midwestern Psychological Association, Chicago, May, 1974.

Forster, K. Levels of processing and the structure of the language processor. In W. E. Cooper, & E.C. T. Walker (Eds.), *Sentence processing: Psycholinguistic studies presented to Merrill Garrett.* Hillsdale, N.J.: Lawrence Erlbaum Associates, 1979.

Forster, K. I., & Bednall, E. Terminating and exhaustive search in lexical access. *Memory & Cognition,* 1976, *4,* 53–61.

Foss, D. J., & Jenkins, C. M. Some effects of context on the comprehension of ambiguous sentences. *Journal of Verbal Learning and Verbal Behavior,* 1973, *12,* 577–589.

Frazier, L., & Fodor, J. D. The sausage machine: A new two-stage parsing model. *Cognition,* 1978, *6,* 291–325.

Ganong, W. F. Phonetic categorization in auditory word perception. *Journal of Experimental*

Psychology: Human Perception and Performance, 1980, *6,* 110-125.

Garrett, M. F. Word and sentence perception. In R. Held, H. W. Leibowitz, & H.-L. Teuber (Eds.), *Handbook of sensory physiology, Vol. 6: Perception.* Berlin: Springer Verlag, 1978.

Garrett, M. F., Bever, T. G., & Fodor, J. A. The active use of grammar in speech perception. *Perception and Psychophysics,* 1970, *1,* 30-32.

Hogaboam, T. W., & Perfetti, C. A. Lexical ambiguity and sentence comprehension. *Journal of Verbal Learning and Verbal Behavior,* 1975, *14,* 265-274.

Holmes, V. M., Arwas, R., & Garrett, M. F. Prior context and the perception of lexically ambiguous sentences. *Memory and Cognition,* 1977, *5,* 103-110.

Holmes, V. M., & Forster, K. I. Perceptual complexity and underlying sentence structure. *Journal of Verbal Learning and Verbal Behavior,* 1972, *11,* 148-156.

Katz, J. J., & Fodor, J. A. The structure of semantic theory. *Language,* 1963, *39,* 170-210.

Kelly, E., & Stone, P. *Computer recognition of English word senses.* Amsterdam: North-Holland, 1975.

Kucera, H., & Francis, W. N. *Computational analysis of present-day American English.* Providence, R.I.: Brown University Press, 1967.

Kuno, S., & Oettinger, A. G. Multiple path syntactic analyzer for English. In *Proceedings 1962,* C. N. Popplewell (Ed.). Amsterdam: North-Holland Press, 1963.

Lackner, J. R., & Garrett, M. F. Resolving ambiguity: Effects of biasing context in the unattended ear. *Cognition,* 1972, *1,* 359-372.

Lyons, J. *Semantics,* Volume 2. Cambridge: Cambridge University Press, 1977.

Marcus, M. P. *A theory of syntactic recognition for natural language.* Unpublished doctoral dissertation, MIT, 1977.

Marslen-Wilson, W. D. Sentence perception as an interactive parallel process. *Science,* 1975, *189,* 226-228.

Marslen-Wilson, W. D., & Tyler, L. K. The temporal structure of spoken language understanding. *Cognition,* 1980, *8,* 1-71.

Marslen-Wilson, W. D., & Welsh, A. Processing interactions and lexical access during word recognition in continuous speech. *Cognitive Psychology,* 1978, *10,* 29-63.

McCawley, J. D. The role of semantics in a grammar. In E. Bach, & R. T. Harms (Eds.), *Universals in linguistic theory.* New York: Holt, Rinehart & Winston, 1968.

Mehler, J., Segui, J., & Carey, P. Tails of words: Monitoring ambiguity. *Journal of Verbal Learning and Verbal Behavior,* 1978, *17,* 29-37.

Meyer, D. E., & Schvaneveldt, R. W. Facilitation in recognizing pairs of words: Evidence of a dependence between retrieval operations. *Journal of Experimental Psychology,* 1971, *90,* 227-234.

Milne, R. W. Handling lexical ambiguity in a deterministic parsing environment. Unpublished B.Sc. Thesis, MIT, 1978.

Muckstein, E. M. M. A natural language parser with statistical applications. IBM Computer Science Research Report RC 7516 (#32506), 1979.

Newman, J., & Dell, G. The phonological nature of phoneme monitoring: A critique of some ambiguity studies. *Journal of Verbal Learning and Verbal Behavior,* 1978, *17,* 359-374.

Oden, G. C., & Spira, J. L. Influence of context on the activation and selection of ambiguous word senses. Wisconsin Human Information Processing Report #6, August, 1978.

Rubenstein, H., Lewis, S. S., & Rubenstein, M. A. Homographic entries in the internal lexicon: Effects of systematicity and relative frequency of meanings. *Journal of Verbal Learning and Verbal Behavior,* 1971, *10,* 57-62.

Rumelhart, D. E. Towards an interactive model of reading. In S. Dornic (Ed.), *Attention and performance VI.* Hillsdale, N.J.: Lawrence Erlbaum Associates, 1977.

Ryder, J. M., & Walker, E. C. T. Two kinds of ambiguity. Forthcoming.

Schvaneveldt, R. W., Meyer, D. E., & Becker, C. A. Lexical ambiguity, semantic context, and visual word recognition. *Journal of Experimental Psychology: Human Perception and Performance*, 1976, *2*, 243–256.

Simpson, G. B. Meaning dominance and semantic context in the processing of lexical ambiguity. *Journal of Verbal Learning and Verbal Behavior*, 1981, *20*, 120–136.

Swinney, D. A. Lexical access during sentence comprehension: (Re)Consideration of context effects. *Journal of Verbal Learning and Verbal Behavior*, 1979, *18*, 645–659.

Taft, M., & Forster, K. I. Lexical storage and retrieval of prefixed words. *Journal of Verbal Learning and Verbal Behavior*, 1975, *14*, 638–647.

Taft, M., & Forster, K. I. Lexical storage and retrieval of polymorphic and polysyllabic words. *Journal of Verbal Learning and Verbal Behavior*, 1976, *15*, 607–620.

Tanenhaus, M. K., Leiman, J. M., & Seidenberg, M. S. Evidence for multiple stages in the processing of ambiguous words in syntactic contexts. *Journal of Verbal Learning and Verbal Behavior*, 1979, *18*, 427–440.

Thorne, J., Bratley, P., & Dewar, H. The syntactic analysis of English by machine. In D. Mitchie (Ed.), *Machine Intelligence 3*, New York: American Elsevier, 1968.

Weinreich, U. Exploration in semantic theory. In T. A. Sebeok (Ed.), *Current trends in linguistics III*. The Hague: Mouton, 1966.

West, M. *A general service list of English words*. London: Longmans, Green, 1964.

Yngve, V. Implications of mechanical translation research. *Proceedings of the American Philosophical Society*, 1964, *108*, 275–281.

APPENDIX

AMBIGUITY TYPE	PROBABILITY OF READINGS	SYNTACTIC CATEGORY	EXAMPLES	
			PROBE	TARGET
I. UNAMBIGUOUS PROBES		Noun	ABILITY	SKILL
		Verb	PROTECT	GUARD
II. SEMANTICALLY AMBIGUOUS PROBES	Equal	Noun	WAY	ROUTE
				METHOD
		Verb	SUCCEED	ACHIEVE
				FOLLOW
	Unequal	Noun	DUTY	RESPONSIBILITY (dominant reading)
				TAX (infrequent reading)
		Verb	GIVE	GRANT (dominant reading)
				YIELD (infrequent reading)

III. SYNTACTICALLY AMBIVALENT PROBES			DEFEAT	DOWNFALL CONQUER
	Equal			
	Unequal	Noun Reading dominant	CART	WAGON (dominant reading) CARRY (infrequent reading)
		Verb reading dominant	OFFER	PROPOSE (dominant reading) INVITATION (infrequent reading)
IV. BOTH SEMANTICALLY AMBIGUOUS AND SYNTACTICALLY AMBIVALENT	Equal		BAR	SALOON RESTRICT
	Unequal	Noun Reading dominant	BOOK	TEXT (dominant reading) RESERVE (infrequent reading)
		Verb reading dominant	HELP	ASSISTANT (dominant reading) STAFF (infrequent reading)

APPENDIX
Synonym And Nonsynonym Pairs Used As Stimuli

I. Unambiguous

Probe	Synonym 1	Nonsynonym 1	Synonym 2	Nonsynonym 2
Ability	Skill	Pride	Aptitude	Audition
Anxiety	Worry	Wheel	Dread	Glove
Boat	Ship	Neck	Vessel	Flavor
City	Town	Girl	Metropolis	Microscope
Joy	Pleasure	Struggle	Bliss	Blink
Success	Achievement	Imagination	Accomplishment	Accompaniment
Astonish	Surprise	Conflict	Amaze	Carve
Begin	Start	Stand	Commence	Conserve
Deceive	Fool	Push	Delude	Recite
Include	Contain	Promise	Comprise	Complain
Protect	Guard	Award	Shield	Preach
Recommend	Suggest	Conduct	Advise	Detect

II. Semantically Ambiguous

A. Equally Probable Readings

Probe	Synonym 1	Nonsynonym 1	Synonym 2	Nonsynonym 2
Post	Position	Question	Mail	Luck
Way	Route	Porch	Method	Member
Observe	Remark	Extend	Keep	Miss
Succeed	Achieve	Destroy	Follow	Supply

B. Unequally Probable Readings

Probe	Dominant Synonym	Nonsynonym 1	Infrequent Synonym	Nonsynonym 2
Application	Use	Day	Request	Passage
Duty	Responsibility	Interpretation	Tax	Top
Action	Deed	Dock	Skirmish	Juncture
Case	Illustration	Announcement	Crate	Craze
Give	Grant	Curve	Yield	Waste
Realize	Understand	Influence	Achieve	Mention
Reflect	Mirror	Prefer	Contemplate	Penetrate
Swear	Pledge	Thwart	Curse	Crawl

III. Syntactically Ambivalent

A. Equally Probable Readings

Probe	Synonym 1	Nonsynonym 1	Synonym 2	Nonsynonym 2
Delight	Pleasure	Struggle	Please	Reduce
Hope	Faith	Price	Long	Work
Decay	Decomposition	Encouragement	Spoil	Swarm
Defeat	Downfall	Blackout	Conquer	Inherit

B.   Unequally Probable Readings

Probe	Dominant Synonym	Nonsynonym 1	Infrequent Synonym	Nonsynonym 2
Cart	Wagon	Grass	Carry	Cover
Heat	Warmth	Bullet	Warm	Flow
Result	Aftermath	Affluence	Ensue	Endow
Risk	Peril	Alley	Venture	Attract
Finish	Complete	Increase	Completion	Dictionary
Rescue	Free	Tell	Recovery	Morality
Hurry	Hasten	Punish	Haste	Wrath
Offer	Propose	Relieve	Invitation	Tournament

IV.   Both Syntactically Ambivalent and Semantically Ambiguous

A.   Equally Probable Readings

Probe	Synonym 1	Nonsynonym 1	Synonym 2	Nonsynonym 2
Act	Bill	Hair	Perform	Furnish
Point	Moment	Office	Direct	Appear
Bar	Saloon	Sermon	Restrict	Consult
Draw	Tie	Cat	Sketch	Stride

B.   Unequally Probable Readings

Probe	Dominant Synonym	Nonsynonym 1	Infrequent Synonym	Nonsynonym 2
Book	Text	Goal	Reserve	Release
Store	Shop	Fund	Save	Grow
Order	Classification	Rehabilitation	Dictate	Deprive
Rock	Boulder	Balloon	Sway	Scan
Help	Assist	Insist	Staff	Doubt
Deal	Handle	Attend	Contract	Judgment
Fall	Descend	Discern	Autumn	Savage
Watch	Inspect	Convert	Clock	Crash

The Structure and Time-Course of Information Interaction During Speech Comprehension: Lexical Segmentation, Access, and Interpretation

David A. Swinney
Tufts University

The comprehension of speech is clearly an integrative process. In fact, such a statement seems so self-evident as to be nearly tautologous; to understand an utterance we must, in some fashion, retrieve information about the words in that utterance, discover the structural relationship and semantic properties of those words, and interpret these in the light of the various pragmatic and discourse constraints operating at the time. Further, all of this takes place at a remarkably rapid pace, a fact (among several others) that has led a number of theorists to characterize the comprehension system *in general* as being a contextually determined or "top down" process, a system that allows all temporally previous information to affect the analysis of new information at any point in its procesing, thus providing maximally rapid processing and interpretation of new sensory information. Some impressive empirical work demonstrating the very rapid effects of certain "higher" order information sources upon the processing of "lower" order information has recently provided some important substantiation for this position (see, in particular, Marslen-Wilson & Tyler, 1980).

To a great extent, such interactionist points of view have developed in response to the limitations of a particular model of speech understanding, one derived from a rigid mapping of Transformational Generative Grammar onto a putative comprehension system. Under this particular system, comprehension is viewed as being composed of a series of serially encountered, hierarchically organized autonomous processing modules (see Marslen-Wilson, 1976, and Tyler, 1982, for excellent detailed discussions of these approaches).

The goal of this paper is to examine both the interactionist and modularist positions from an empirical perspective. In this, emphasis will be placed on detailing the structure and temporal course of information processing that takes place during speech understanding, with particular focus on the lexical recognition process. In general, the data will be seen to support a modular characterization of the comprehension system.

BASIC CONSIDERATIONS

There are a number of critical problems that confront those involved in the enterprise of developing a model of comprehension, problems that underly several aspects of the distinction embodied in the interactionist/modularist differentiation. The first, and perhaps most basic, of these is the fact that we do not presently have an adequate account of what types (sources) of information are functionally involved in speech understanding. While systematic observation in linguistics has allowed for the characterization of a number of general informational types (phonetic, syntactic, semantic, etc.), such descriptions are based on the rules and constraints of linguistic description and observation and may thus only have an indirect or indeterminant relationship to the character of information actually involved in the process of comprehension (as, similarly, the systematic divisions devised for the color spectrum bear little necessary resemblance to the relevant informational sources involved in our perception of color). The development of psychologically relevant characterizations of functional information sources is a fundamental necessity in the enterprise of understanding speech comprehension, and it is clear that the problem is an empirical one, one to be resolved only through examination of the microstructure of the process itself.

A corresponding problem relates to the need for establishing the details of the nature and time-course of interaction among those relevant information sources. Together, the goals of detailing the structures and their interactions circumscribe a major area of endeavor in psycholinguistics, and there is at least one consideration concerning this domain that should be noted because it has important consequences for the form that a solution to the problem will take. This is simply the point that the representational characterization of these information types, the processes involved in their interaction, and the processes by which we attempt to examine these interactions are intimately related. They must all be modeled simultaneously, both in the sense that the choice of a particular information type places constraints on the form that the processing interactions with that source may take (see Garrett, 1978, for an eloquent discussion of this interface problem), and also in the sense that assumptions about underlying representations and processes depend critically on assumptions made about the operation of the empirical task used to reveal them. Each of these, then, constrains the other; there is, unfortunately, no simple window which allows examination of a mental representation or process without affecting that process in some fashion (see Forster, 1979; Swinney, 1982, for further discussion).

A second problem related both to the modeling of comprehension and to the interactionist/modularist distinction has to do with claims of the general form that the comprehension device must be a "top down" system, or else it would not be capable of handling underdetermined or ambiguous sensory information (see, e.g., Cole & Jakimik, 1979; Marslen-Wilson, 1980). Such a claim is often accompanied by the suggestion that allowing "higher order" contextual information to interact freely with ambiguous sensory information solves the difficulty. There is no denying that ambiguity poses an important problem for any model of comprehension. However, the top down argument, while perhaps seeming plausible at first, is really not a tenable one. A modular, bottom-up system can handle ambiguity at one level of analysis by allowing resolution to take place at a higher level of processing (in fact, this is one of the strengths of a hierarchical system). It is, in principle, no more difficult for resolution to take place in this fashion than it is for it to take place under a highly interactional system in which higher order information forces resolution at an "early" stage of processing. In short, the question of exactly when and how higher order information is used in resolving ambiguity or indeterminacy is simply an empirical one and not one to be decided by arguments of this type.

A similar point relates to evidence showing that words are more accurately reported when they are heard in context and that this effect is enhanced under noisy conditions. Such results are often given as example of the interactive effects of higher order context upon word processing (see, e.g., Cole, 1973; Cole & Jakimik, 1979). However, this is an example of what might be called an interpretation/perception confusion. There can be little doubt that an interpretation will be found for any stimulus if it can be computed, and that the system will incorporate whatever information is available in discovering such an interpretation. However, what is in question is the nature of the process by which this occurs—whether the effects of context take place during the primary perceptual (automatic) analysis of the word or only after this analysis. The distinction is a critical one. Unfortunately, tasks that simply require conscious report of a final *interpretation* for a word are simply not sensitive to distinctions relating to the *perception* (or, unconscious recognition) of a word, because the latter occurs logically prior to any consciously available response. In general, most report or recognition tasks that are involved in studies of effects of contextual enhancement reflect only post-perceptual phenomena, and thus have no force with respect to claims about perceptual processing (except to place an upper limit on the type of maximal interaction that might take place). Once again, it is left to further empirical work, employing more sensitive tasks, to detail the time course of processing in a manner that will convincingly demonstrate the order and nature of the interaction of context with sensory information.[1]

Finally, in their radical forms neither the modularist nor the interactionist hypothesis withstands careful scrutiny. The radical serial modularist account fails simply because the empirical data do not support it. Marslen-Wilson (1980) and Tyler (1982) have demonstrated, for example, that "higher" level knowledge does affect processing at lower levels in a manner not compatible with a strictly serial account, an account in which one level of processing (e.g., syntactic clause analysis) must be totally completed before processing of the next level (e.g., semantic) begins. Thus comprehension does not involve a strictly serial processing of traditional linguistic informational sources. The radical interactionist account also fares poorly upon closer analysis. Most important among the criticisms is the point that models that allow for completely unconstrained interaction among information sources constitute empty *processing* theories; unprincipled interaction and lacks of detail about the sources of interaction allows a position to "explain" any possible outcome but to predict none. In addition, it might be noted that the radical interactionist model provides no internal justification for maintaining the distinction among information types. Unconstrained information interaction can best be represented at a level compatible to all the information involved (on the least common denominator principle) and there is no external justification in the theory itself for maintaining the distinction of informational types, a distinction that is none the less usually maintained.

While there appears to be good reason to not maintain either a radical modular or a radical interactionist approach, the more moderate form that an appropriate alternative might take is presently undetermined. As has been argued, above, the matter is largely one for resolution by empirical

---

[1]In general, any claim about such processes that relies on intuitional facts is subject to the same argument. When we feel that we can predict what is going to be said from the context or that we are only aware of the contextually relevant meaning of words, we are relying on data that are notoriously poor reflections of underlying processes. The insensitivity of report or intuitional data to the unconscious substructure of mental events has been shown time and again (see, e.g., Foss & Swinney, 1973). By and large, such techniques tend to reflect either the end result of unconscious processing (the final interpretation assigned to the information) or are confabulations based on reconstruction-by-rule or other learned processes (see, e.g., Nisbett & Wilson, 1977). In addition, a number of predeterministic claims have been refuted by experimental work. Gilford, 1980, for example, has shown that the maximum predictability of any word in text, even if that text is highly constraining and if there is no time limit on task performance, is less than 37% correct. This failure success ratio is sufficiently low as to make such prediction a major liability to a comprehension device.

data, and thus the remainder of this paper is devoted to presenting evidence relevant to the critical questions.

The data presented focus on the time-distributed details of information interaction as it occurs during sentence comprehension. In particular, the work examines the nature of the effects of a number of different sources of contextual information upon the processing of words in sentences. Word recognition forms a focal point for this work for several reasons, the most salient being that words are acknowledged to play an important role in most psychological and linguistic accounts of language comprehension. In addition, as word recogntion is typically considered to be a major point of intersection for syntactic, semantic, and acoustic-phonetic information, it is a logical realm in which to investigate the nature of information interaction.

The basic question that will be examined concerns whether or not there is any evidence that some aspect of lexical processing forms an isolable, autonomous (modular) subsystem in the comprehension processes. Following from work studying this question, details of the time-course of lexical segmentation, access, and interpretation will be sketched.

EVIDENCE ABOUT THE REAL-TIME
PROCESSING OF WORDS

With respect to word recognition, the interactionist/modularist distinction comes down to being a claim about exactly where and how contextual information exerts its influence on lexical interpretation. In its most simple form, this corresponds to a distinction between what have been labeled Contextually Predictive and Contextually Independent models of lexical processing (see, e.g., Swinney, 1979). Under the Contextually Predictive theory, contextual information constrains and directs all of the various stages of lexical processing, whereas under the Contextually Independent model, higher order contexts will only act on the output of the lexical access process. Thus, the problem can be characterized as one concerning whether or not lexical *access* is independent of contextual constraint.

Lexical ambiguities (typically, unsystematic lexical homophones and homographs) form a useful vehicle for examining questions concerning the autonomy of lexical access. Not only are they arguably as common as unambiguous words in language use, but, because nearly all words exhibit some type of indeterminacy in characterization of their meaning, ambiguity processing can be seen to be reflective of language processing in general. Furthermore, they provide an easily discernable basis for examining the effects of various types of contextual information upon lexical access; because the independent meanings of lexical ambiguities can be differentiated rather easily, the selective effects of higher order contextual constraints upon the functional activation of each of these meanings is readily available to empirical examination.

Finally, as was suggested previously, the examination of on-line (or, real-time) perceptual events such as lexical access requires the use of experimental techniques sensitive to the various and brief perceptual states that constitute the unconscious processing of words in sentences. Tasks that only reflect post-perceptual processing will simply not provide the critical data. In addition, such examination requires use of techniques that impart as little as possible of their own characteristics to the natural, real-time, process (for the reason, mentioned above, that conclusions drawn about mental representations or processes rest critically on assumptions made about how the experimental technique interacts with, and perhaps changes, their state or operation). For these reasons, a Cross Modal Lexical Priming technique was used in most of the studies to be reported here.

This technique utilizes the facts of automatic semantic priming (response facilitation) to detect the activation of word meanings during sentence comprehension. Its use in this function stems from the demonstration that lexical decisions (word/nonword judgments) for a word are facilitated when the word is semantically related to a previously presented word (see, e.g., Meyer, Schvaneveldt, & Ruddy, 1975; Neeley, 1977). This effect has been demonstrated to hold cross-modally, where the lexical decision is made to a visually presented letter string and the related word is presented auditorily— either in isolation or as one of the words in a sentence (Swinney, Onifer, Prather, & Hirshkowitz, 1978). It is, of course, the fact that priming can be driven from words in sentences that makes the task of interest here. Not only is the task flexible (the primed visual word can be presented at any point while a subject is listening to a sentence), but it has been demonstrated to reflect the relative degree of activation of the target word in a sentence as a function of the amount of facilitation obtained for the lexical decision. (The amount of priming for an experimental word is determined by comparison to the lexical decision reaction time for an unrelated, but otherwise equivalent, control word presented at the same point in the sentence.) There are three additional points about this task that are worth noting. First, occurrence of the visual word (for the lexical decision) only takes place at some point *after* subjects hear the experimental word that is being examined in the sentence. Thus, processing of the sentence, up to that point at least, is relatively natural. Secondly, the task does *not* require subjects to try to manipulate the sentence or relate the visual material to the sentence in any way, and thus the task is considerably less intrusive into the natural comprehension process than several other on-line tasks seem to be. Finally, when the ratio of materials in which the visually presented word relates to some word in the sentence (compared to filler trials in which there is no such relationship) is kept sufficiently low, subjects rarely report noting this critical relationship and, in fact, apparently do not even try to do so after the first few practice trials.

Thus, given a task that is an index of the degree of activation of word meanings in sentences, the rationale of its use in the examination of the effects of context upon the access of ambiguous words is no doubt apparent. If prior contexts constrain or predetermine lexical access, then one should only find priming for visual words related to the contextually relevant meaning of an ambiguity; because context prevents the inappropriate meaning from being accessed and activated there is no basis for a priming response from that meaning. On the other hand, if access is an autonomous process one would expect that all meanings related to a particular acoustic/phonetic word form would be accessed, and thus words related to all meanings, contextually appropriate or not, would be primed at least momentarily.

EFFECTS OF SEMANTIC CONTEXTS ON
LEXICAL ACCESS

The initial experiments (Swinney, 1979) examine the effects of local lexical-semantic contexts upon the access of meanings for equibiased unsystematic ambiguities, utilizing a set of materials from which subjects listened to sentence pairs such as the following (where the material in parentheses constitutes the context manipulation):

> Rumor had it that, for years, the government building had been plagued with problems. The man was not surprised when he found several (spider, roaches, and other) bugs in the corner of his room.
>   1   2

Visual lexical decisions were required for words related to the contextually appropriate meaning of the ambiguity [ANT], for words related to the contextually inappropriate meaning of the ambiguity [SPY], and for unrelated control words [SEW]. These materials were presented both at a point immediately following occurrence of the ambiguity [1] and at a point three syllables later [2]. The results given in Table 1 clearly support the Contextual Independence model of lexical access; significant facilitation occurred for lexical decisions to visual words related to each meaning of the ambiguity, even in the presence of a strong constraining lexical-semantic context, when tested immediately following the ambiguity [1]. Importantly, at the delayed test point [2], significant facilitation was obtained only for lexical decisions made to words related to the contextually relevant meaning and *not* the contextually inappropriate meaning. This result strongly support the concept that a post-access decision process takes place that utilizes context

TABLE 1
Amount of Priming for Each Meaning of an Ambiguity (in msec)

TEST POINT	$\overset{\triangle}{1}$		$\overset{\triangle}{2}$	
Meaning:	appropriate	inappropriate	appropriate	inappropriate
Biasing context	70	50	53	−1 N.S.
No biasing context	58	49	45	−1 N.S.

All values are significant at Min F' p < .05, unless otherwise noted. Note that comparisons of degree of facilitation between appropriate and inappropriate cells is not valid because the materials were not equated for degree of relationship to each sense of the ambiguity.

to determine the appropriate meaning for the word. The result of this process is that activation is maintained for the appropriate meaning but the other, inappropriate, meanings of a word are allowed to rapidly decay (or, perhaps, be suppressed). These results also provide strong support for the assumption that this task is sensitive to the roles of words throughout the time-course of sentence comprehension; the effect of context on the interpretation of ambiguities is reflected clearly in these data.

A second, related, set of experiments was run using this identical paradigm, but with a different set of ambiguous materials. In this, strongly polarized lexical ambiguities—words having one very frequent meaning (89% frequency-of-use) and one very infrequent meaning (11% frequency-of-use) were examined in strongly biasing contexts. Thus, an examination of the time-course and tradeoff of frequency-of-meaning and contextual bias was possible (see, Onifer & Swinney, 1981, for details). In these studies, subjects heard sentences such as:

The postal clerk put the package on the scale to see if there was sufficient postage.
$\overset{\triangle}{1}$ $\overset{\triangle}{2}$

or

The dinner guest enjoyed the specially prepared river bass, although one guest did get a scale caught in his throat.
$\overset{\triangle}{1}$ $\overset{\triangle}{2}$

The examination for activation of each meaning of the polarized ambiguity [WEIGHT/FISH] took place at the indicated points, [1] and [2] (which were separated by 1.5 sec). The results of this study (see Table 2) are identical in form to those in the previous set of experiments. That is, *all* meanings for the ambiguity are activated immediately after the ambiguity is heard [1], including the very infrequent meaning. Further, this occurs even when the context requires just the more frequent meaning. However, by 1.5 sec later [2], only the contextually appropriate meaning for the ambiguity—be it the most or the least frequent meaning—is still active. Thus, even when both frequency and semantic context dictate that one meaning is

TABLE 2
Amount of Facilitation (in msecs) for Meanings
of Polarized Ambiguities

TEST POINT		$\overset{\triangle}{1}$		$\overset{\triangle}{2}$	
Meaning:		most frequent	least frequent	most frequent	least frequent
biasing sentence context	Toward primary meaning	34	34	29	−3 N.S.
	Toward secondary meaning	25	72	−1 N.S.	52

both unlikely and inappropriate, that meaning is still momentarily activated by the lexical access system. These data provide a strong case in support of there being an autonomous, form-driven lexical access subsystem (module) in the comprehension process, and they support the argument that context does not behave in a predictive or totally interactive fashion with respect to lexical access.

Further, these data argue that lexical access is an exhaustive process, not a terminating ordered search as has been argued throughout much of the literature (see, e.g., Forster, 1976; Hogaboam & Perfetti, 1975). (In a terminating ordered search, candidate word forms are compared against internal representations in order of their frequency-of-use in a search that ends once some context-compatible entry is encountered. This fact, while not bearing directly on the interactionist/modularist controversy, is an important one for theories of lexical processing). It is worth noting that Oden and Spira (1980) have recently reported results very similar to these using a stroop color-naming interference task to examine activation of meanings for ambiguities.

Finally, in a study carried out by Bill Onifer directed toward discovering the status of the posited autonomous access and post-access decision modules, the polarized ambiguity materials from this last set of studies were used with a different population of subjects: chronic schizophrenics. Persons with chronic schizophrenia have a well documented symptom that involves their interpreting ambiguous words (almost solely) in terms of the inherently most frequent meaning of those words. Further, they often appear to completely ignore the context of the situation in choosing this interpretation (Chapman, Chapman, & Miller, 1964). It was reasoned that chronic schizophrenics might provide a critical diagnostic test case for the hypothesized independence of the access and contextually-involved decision-process modules. If access is independent of (and prior to) the effects of higher order context, and if the schizophrenic condition affects only the use of context, then it can be hypothesized that data from schizophrenic patients on polarized ambiguity materials examined at the immediate test point [1] would be identical to those obtained for the normal population. However, at the delayed test point [2], a point following the decision-process incorporating contextual information, it would be expected that the schizophrenic's data would depart from the pattern found for normal listeners (reflecting a disruption of post-accession decision process module in these subjects). And, this is precisely the pattern of results that was found. Both the high and low frequency meanings of polarized ambiguities were activated immediately [1] upon occurrence of the ambiguity under all conditions of context. However, unlike the data for normal subjects (see Table 2), only the *most* frequent meaning for the ambiguity was still activated at the delay test point [2] in the condition containing a context dictating the *less* frequent interpretation (this meaning was also the only one activated, for both normal and schizophrenic subjects, when context favored the most frequent interpretation, as was to be expected). Thus, while the interpretation given a word is ultimately dictated by the use of context in a post-access decision process for normal listeners, the operation of this process for schizophrenics appears to be impaired, and schizophrenics appear to maintain activation for only the most frequent meaning of a word.

This result provides strong functional evidence for the autonomy of the access process and for the existence of a separate (and temporally subsequent) decision process that uses context to determine the eventual interpretation of words; in the case of differential damage to this process, as appears to be the case in schizophrenia, word interpretation is determined solely on the basis of frequency-of-meaning.

EFFECTS OF NON-SEMANTIC SOURCES OF
CONTEXT UPON LEXICAL ACCESS

While it appears that lexical access is independent of constraints generated by semantic contexts, this represents only one step in evaluating the Contextual Independence model. In fact, it may be reasonable to hypothesize that syntactic information is far more likely to constrain access to the lexicon than is semantic information; it has been argued that local syntactic cues (particularly sequences involving closed-class words) largely determine the permissible grammatical roles for syntactically ambiguous words (Garrett, 1978). And, as it has been determined that syntactic processing takes place during the course of sentence comprehension (see, e.g., Marslen-Wilson & Tyler, 1980) it is reasonable to suggest that any higher order information able to predict the grammatical (syntactic) class of subsequent words may be used to constrain the access process for these words. Just such a role has been assigned to the closed class vocabulary (the words in the minor grammatical categories, the so-called "function words"). It has been argued that these words are actively employed in the development of the structural description of a sentence, largely by virtue of facilitating the assignment of appropriate grammatical classifications to open class vocabulary (see, e.g., Bradley, 1978; Garrett, 1976). For example, a context consisting of "the" or "the large" can clearly aid the disambiguation of words with multiple grammatical class entries, such as "watch." These facts were utilized (Prather & Swinney, 1977; Swinney & Prather, 1982) in a set of experiments designed to determine whether such local grammatical information could constrain lexical access. Sentences that contained unsystematic categorical lexical ambiguities (e.g., "watch," "cross"), which were themselves preceded in the sentence by different degrees of local syntactic cues (always incorporating a closed-class word), were presented to subjects. For example, subjects heard one of the following (where the word in parentheses constituted a second context condition):

The seasoned old woodsman told the young boy the (battered) cross the indian gave
him was made of silver.
$\triangle$

or

The seasoned old woodsman told the young boy to (quickly) cross the stream above
the beaver pond.
$\triangle$

Again, employing the cross modal lexical priming technique, access and activation of the noun meaning and the verb meaning for the ambiguity were examined in each of these biasing context conditions (compared to a matching noun control and verb control, as appropriate). Under *all* context conditions the evidence indicated that *both* meanings of the ambiguity were immediately accessed, even when the grammatical class of one of the accessed meanings was inappropriate. Tanenhaus, Leiman, & Seidenberg (1979) have found similar results—that both syntactically relevant and syntactically irrelevant meanings are momentarily accessed for a word even when syntactic cues provided by sentence contexts allow only entries from a single grammatical category. Tanenhaus et. al. used a naming latency task similar to the cross modal lexical priming task.

   In sum, while the inventory of possible higher order constraints on the access process has certainly not been exhausted, the available research strongly suggests that the access of lexical information is unconstrained by higher order information during sentence comprehension. Lexical access appears to be a contextually independent subprocess operating on a bottom-up principle in the sentence comprehension routine (a fact not recognized in many current theories of lexical processing (e.g., the logogen model of Morton, 1969, simply has no principled way to distinguish access from final interpretation). Further, the final interpretation given a word appears to be the result of an independent decision process that occurs temporally posterior to access. In this, the relative weights of frequency-of-meaning and the various sources of contextual information are rapidly utilized to determine an interpretation for a word. Apparently this decision process takes no longer than 1 sec, and, in fact the present data most likely underestimates the speed of the post-access decision process; it may have been completed well before the point at which it was tested [2]; (see, e.g., Tanenhaus et. al., 1979; Marslen-Wilson, 1980). While these data do not allow us to determine the manner in which the contextually irrelevant meanings for a word are suppressed or discarded, they do support the conclusion that a post-access decision process occurs immediately following lexical access for each word, and does not wait for the conclusion of clausal processing. Further, it seems reasonable to suggest that this post-access decision mechanism may be a general process; only a subset of all the information stored and accessed for any word (whether it comprises a single "sense" of an unambiguous word or a single "meaning" of an ambiguity) will be selected by this process for integration into ongoing sentential analysis.

SEGMENTATION OF WORD CANDIDATES AND THE ROLE OF CONTEXT

Finally, some recent and influential work by Marslen-Wilson and Tyler (1980; this volume) has argued that while lexical access does incorporate a bottom-up (data-driven) priority in analysis of the speech signal, selection of a particular candidate occurs "optimally"—as early as the context can conceivably allow, given the bottom-up information.[2] This general proposal constitutes what they call a cohort model of lexical processing, in which the initial acoustic/phonetic string for a word activates a "cohort" of potential candidates, all beginning with that same initial acoustic/phonetic sequence. The role of prior higher order context in the model is to augment the bottom-up analysis so that selection of a single appropriate meaning from the activated cohort occurs as early as possible. Thus, if a context is present that fits only a single of the activated members of the cohort, then *that* meaning will be immediately selected, even before the word has been fully heard by the listener. If context is not sufficient to uniquely distinguish an appropriate candidate from the cohort, a final interpretation is only as-

---

[2]It should be noted that Marslen-Wilson and Tyler characterize their work as support for an interactionist rather than a modular position, despite specifying a modular-type obligatory bottom-up priority as the first stage of word recognition. The reasons for this labeling distinction are historical in nature and the model, whatever its label, is extremely compatible with the modified autonomous modular processing system that has been argued for in this paper.

signed when the word has been uniquely distinguished from all other words on the basis of its serially analyzed acoustic/phonetic characteristics. This model is of particular interest because its authors have presented a considerable amount of support for it from various on-line tasks—including phoneme monitoring, word monitoring, and rapid shadowing.

What is in question here, then, is not whether the initial access of material is autonomous and bottom-up, but details about how and when context may begin to have its effect on selection of a single interpretation for a word (i.e., details of the post-access decision process). There is evidence from the processing of certain complex lexical items—idioms—that bears on this question.

It has been demonstrated that idioms are represented in the lexicon as words (albeit large words; Swinney & Cutler, 1979). As such, idioms provide an excellent tool for examining the activation and segmentation of words in language, both because they are quite long (thus providing a reasonable temporal interval for examining processing effects) and because many of them are ambiguous (e.g., "kick the bucket" has both a literal and an idiomatic interpretation). A series of experiments incorporating these "grammatical" idioms was performed with the goal of discovering the relative time-course of activation of the idiomatic and literal meanings (and, simultaneously, with the goal of discovering something about the order of priority involved in segmenting word candidates from the speech stream). In these studies, subjects heard sentences such as the following (where the first sentence contains a neutral context and the other two contain contexts which bias the interpretation toward the idiomatic and the literal meaning, respectively):

It was hoped that the young man would see the light and come home safely.
1   2

The psychologist hoped that the confused young man would see the light and come
1   2

back to live with his parents.

The optomotrist hoped that the young man would see the light and thus not be blind
1   2

as was once thought.

Lexical decisions were obtained for visually presented words which were related to the literal meanings of the major words in the idioms string ('see' & 'light') and to the idiomatic meaning of the entire string, at each of the two indicated test points.

The results are easily summarized. In the neutral context, only the literal meaning ('see,' in the example) was facilitated at test point [1]; a word related to the idiomatic meaning was *not* primed at this point. However, at test point [2], priming was obtained for words related both to the literal word ('light,' in the example) and to the idiom string as a whole. Important-

ly, current research (which has been run in collaboration with Robin Hel-
fand, Susan Wish, and Shelly Rosenfeld) suggests that the very same pattern of results holds for the conditions containing biasing contexts. In short,
in spite of the presence of 'higher order' contexts, it appears as though *only*
the first potential word that is encountered in the speech stream is accessed
from the initial acoustic/phonetic-sequence. There is no evidence of access
of the entire idiom, which should be a member of the hypothesized cohort
(although it is at least possible that the priming task is not sensitive to the
activation of cohort members). Further, any and all other potential word
candidates which are encountered in the speech stream, even those incorporating the initially accessed candidate (as does the idiom) are themselves
accessed, at least momentarily. (This fact of multiple access of word meanings within the idiom strings, even in the presence of biasing context, has
been recently supported with the results of a phoneme monitoring task; see
Swinney, 1982, for more details about these sets of studies). More to the
point, these data argue against an "optimally early" use of context in determining the appropriate interpretation from among a series of candidates;
despite the presence or absence of biasing context, the comprehension
routine appears to segment and access word candidates in a consistent, exhaustive autonomous manner.[3]

CONCLUSIONS

The argument has been made that the determination of a theoretically relevant characterization of nature of sentence processing is basically an empirical matter, one requiring sensitive data about the time-course of information interactions. The data presented here support the hypothesis that
sentence comprehension (or at least that portion of it concerned with word
recognition) is composed of a set of isolable, autonomous substages, where
these substages constitute domain specific processing modules (see, Forster,
1976; Garrett, 1978, for further details of such a system). The concept of a
system that operates based on isolable processors that routinely and consistently evaluate informatin in terms of highly practiced, automatic, internally consistent rules, and that is independent of constraint by information

---

[3]It can at least be tentatively suggested that Marslen-Wilson and Tyler's on-line results,
which support "early" effects of context, may be the result of situations in which the task itself
introduced changes in the underlying process. When, for example, the task (or, query) given to
the system requires that words in a sentence be interrogated (as occurs in the word monitoring
task, for example), it may be the case that a search for a "match" to the query interrupts the
automatic processing exactly at that level being searched for a match (word recognition) and
thus allows different, non-automatic, processing routines to take place, some of which may
utilize context in their slower, less automatic operation.

from other domains, obviously characterizes a somewhat brute-force device. However, given facts about the rapidity and non-interruptability with which automatized mental structures can efficiently process information (see, e.g., Posner & Snyder, 1975), the hypothesis seems quite tenable. (Note that such models are not at all restricted to a strictly serial organization). Further, and most importantly, this hypothesis is supported by the data.

Beyond arguing that the appropriate form of the model appears to be a modular, contextually independent one, it should again be stressed that the answers to the important remaining questions are empirical in nature. The details of information interaction discussed here merely scratch the surface of the complexity of both theory and fact that must yet be discovered to provide a sufficient characterization of the comprehension system. It is, however, instructive to examine the form that details of one part of that system—that of lexical processing—take, as these are likely to be representative of the nature of the device in general.

ACKNOWLEDGMENT

This paper was written while the author was a visiting Fellow at the Max-Planck-Institut für Psycholinguistik in Nijmegen, Holland. The support of the institute in this enterprise is gratefully acknowledged and greatly appreciated, as is the help of Marion Klaver in the preparation of this manuscript.

REFERENCES

Bradley, D. C. 1978. *Computational distinction of vocabulary type.* Unpublished Ph.D. dissertation, Boston, MA. Psychology Department, Massachusetts Institute of Technology.

Cairns, H. S., & Hsu, J. R. Effects of prior context upon lexical access during sentence comprehension: A replication and reinterpretation. *Journal of Psycholinguistic Research,* 1980, *9,* 1–8.

Chapman, L. J., Chapman, J. P., & Miller, G. A. A theory of verbal behavior in schizophrenia. In Maher (Ed.), *Progress in experimental personality research.* New York: Academic Press, 1964.

Cole, R. A. Listening for mispronunciations: A measure of what we hear during speech. *Perception & Psychophysics,* 1973, *1,* 153–156.

Cole, R. A., & Jakimik, J. A model of speech perception. In R. A. Cole (Ed.), *Perception and production of fluent speech.* Hillsdale, N.J.: Lawrence Erlbaum Associates, 1979.

Forster, K. I. Accessing the mental lexicon. In R. J. Wales, & E. Walker (Eds.), *New approaches to language mechanisms,* Amsterdam: North-Holland, 1976.

Forster, K. I. Levels of Processing and the Structure of the Language Processor. In W. E. Cooper, & E. Walker (Eds.), *Sentence Processing: Psycholinguistic.* Studies presented to Merrill Garrett. Hillsdale, N.J.: Lawrence Erlbaum Associates, 1979.

Foss, D. J., & Swinney, D. On the psychological reality of the phoneme: Perception, identification and consciousness. *Journal of Verbal Learning and Verbal Behavior,* 1973, *12,* 246-257.

Garrett, M. F. Word and sentence perception. In R. Held, H. W. Liebowitz, & H. L. Teuber (Eds.), *Handbook of sensory physiology,* Vol. VIII: *Perception.* Berlin: Springer-Verlag, 1978.

Garrett, M. F. 1976. Syntactic processes in sentence production. In R. J. Wales, & F. Walker (Eds.), *New approaches to language mechanisms.* Amsterdam: North-Holland. Pp. 231-256.

Garrett, M. F. Does ambiguity complicate the perception of sentences? In G. B. Flores D'Arcais, & W. J. M. Levelt (Eds.), *Advances in psycholinguistics.* Amsterdam: North-Holland, 1970.

Hogaboam, T. W., & Perfetti, C. A. Lexical Ambiguity and Sentence Comprehension. *Journal of Verbal Learning and Verbal Behavior,* 1975, *14,* 265-274.

Marslen-Wilson, W. D. Speech Understanding as a psychological process. In J. C. Simon (Ed.), *Spoken language generation and understanding.* Dordrecht: Reidel, 1980.

Marslen-Wilson, W. D. Linguistic descriptins and psychological assumptions in the study of Sentence Perception. In R. J. Wales, & E. Walker (Eds.), *New approaches to language mechanisms.* North-Holland: Amsterdam, 1976.

Marslen-Wilson, W. D., & Tyler, L. K. The temporal structure of spoken language understanding. *Cognition,* 1980, *8,*1-71.

Meyer, D. E., Schvaneveldt, R. W., & Ruddy, M. G. Loci of contextual effects on visual word recognition. In P. M. A. Rabbit, & S. Dornic (Eds.), *Attention and performance V.* London/New York: Academic Press, 1975.

Morton, J. The interaction of information in word recognition. *Psychological Review,* 1969, *60,* 329-346.

Neeley, J. Semantic priming and retrieval from lexical memory; Roles of inhibitionless spreading activation and limited capacity attention. *Journal of Experimental Psychology: General,* 1977, *106,* 226-254.

Nisbett, R. E., & Wilson, T. Telling more than we can know! Verbal reports on mental processes. *Psychological Review,* 1977, *84*(3), 231-259.

Oden, G., & Spira, J. L. *Influence of context on the activation and selection of ambiguous word senses.* Paper presented at Psychonomic Society, St. Louis, 1980.

Onifer, W., & Swinney, D. Accessing logical ambiguities during sentence comprehension: Effects of frequence-of-meaning and contextual bias, *Memory & Cognition,* 1981, *9,* 225-236.

Prather, P., & Swinney, D. *Some effects of syntactic context upon lexical access.* Presented at a meeting of the American Psychological Association, San Francisco, California, August 26, 1977.

Posner, M. I., & Snyder, C. R. Attention and cognitive control. In R. Solso (Ed.), *Information processing and cognition.* Hillsdale, N.J.: Lawrence Erlbaum Associates, 1975.

Swinney, D. Lexical processing during sentence comprehension: Effects of higher order constraints and implications for representation. In T. Myers, J. Laver, & J. Anderson (Eds.), *The cognitive representation of speech.* Amsterdam: North-Holland, in press, 1982.

Swinney, D. Lexical Access during Sentence Comprehension: (Re)Consideration of context effects. *Journal of Verbal Learning and Verbal Behavior,* 1979, *18,* 645-659.

Swinney, D., & Cutler, A. The access and processing of idiomatic expressions. *Journal of Verbal Learning and Verbal Behavior,* 1979, *18,* 523-534.

Swinney, D., Onifer, W., Prather, P., & Hirshkowitz, M. Semantic facilitation across sensory modalities in the processing of individual words and sentences. *Memory & Cognition,* 1978, *7,* (3), 165-195.

Tanenhaus, M. K., Leiman, J. M., & Seidenberg, M. S. Evidence for multiple stages in the processing of ambiguous words on syntactic contexts. *Journal of Verbal Learning and Verbal Behavior,* 1979, *18,* 427–440.

Tyler, L. K. Serial and interactive theories of sentence processing. *Theoretical Linguistics.* (in press) 1982.

9 Speech Comprehension Processes

Lorraine Komisarjevsky Tyler
William D. Marslen-Wilson
Max-Planck Institute for Psycholinguistics
Nijmegen, The Netherlands

INTRODUCTION

The aim of the research reported here is to characterize the basic properties of human spoken language understanding; of the mental events that take place as the listener hears an utterance. The research is carried out within the framework of the claim that speech understanding is mediated by a set of central on-line processes, and that the primary goal of psychological research into speech understanding is to determine the properties of these processes.

We should stress at the outset that we are concerned here only with spoken language, and that our research very much depends on the special temporal properties of speech as a communication medium. The speech waveform is intrinsically ordered in time, and the listener typically hears a stimulus distributed over relatively long periods—from a few hundred milliseconds to several seconds. Over these relatively long time-periods, the listener develops some form of mental representation of the speech input, and our goal is to determine *what* forms of analysis develop *when*. Given an experimental response tapping the listener's representation of the input at some particular point in time, we can then try to determine what kind of representation the listener has developed, given the input available to him at the point the response occurs. In particular, we can determine whether, and to what extent, his internal representation can be accounted for strictly on the basis of information carried by the available signal, and to what extent it is determined by internally generated knowledge.

This focus on processing events in time has led to our methodological emphasis on fast reaction-time tasks. The closer in time the response is to the relevant stretches of the signal, the more closely we can specify the properties of the internal mapping processes involved. We do not, of course, mean to claim that these types of fast response task—which we call "on-line" tasks—are the *only* adequate ways of studying speech understanding. But we do want to claim that they provide uniquely powerful data about certain aspects of speech understanding. Much of the theoretical structure we have started to develop is in fact highly dependent on certain straightforward temporal facts about the relationship between the speech signal and its interpretation—facts, that is, about the central processes mediating on-line speech understanding.

We characterize the central processes as those that carry out the basic mapping from the signal to the message in normal speech understanding; that is, in normal successful communication between normal human adults. What we will do here is to define, and then motivate with respect to a variety of experimental results, what we take to be the important general properties of these processes.

CENTRAL PROCESSES IN SPEECH UNDERSTANDING

The first two properties we want to claim for speech understanding are that the processes underlying it are *optimal* and are *interactive*. Both of these rather slippery terms need to be defined for the speech understanding context.

What we mean by "optimal" is the following strong claim: The human speech understanding system is organized in such a way that it can assign an analysis to the speech input at the *theoretically earliest* point at which the type of analysis in question can be *securely* assigned.

This is a claim, then, about optimality in terms of processing efficiency *in time*; that the system can assign the appropriate readings to the input as soon as the processing information, accumulating over time, allows this reading to be assigned. The definition of "theoretically earliest point" depends itself, of course, on a definition of the space of possibilities within which the correct reading can be assigned. This can be done least problematically in the word-recognition domain, and we will later describe experiments that appear to demonstrate optimal processing efficiency in this domain.

The second property here, of interaction, is closely related to the claim for optimality. The notion of interaction is normally contrasted with the notion of autonomy, and concerns the possible directions in which information can flow through the processing system. The autonomy hypothesis, stated in processing terms, claims that information flows through the processing system in one direction only—from the *bottom-up:* that is, through some sequence of processing components that mediate the serial processing of the input over successive levels of analysis—from acoustic-phonetic analyses onwards. What this autonomy claim is generally taken to mean is that analyses within any one processing component cannot be affected by information deriving from processes any higher in the system. Thus, for example, word-recognition processes cannot be directly affected by the syntactic or interpretative context in which the word is occurring, and syntactic analysis processes cannot themselves be affected by considerations of semantic plausibility (c.f., Forster, 1979; Garrett, 1978; Marslen-Wilson & Tyler, 1980).

We reject the autonomy hypothesis, in so far as it leads to this type of serial ordering of processes at different levels; we reject it both because there is experimental data against it (which we will come to later), and because it is inconsistent with the assumption of optimality. Clearly, if a processing system is to function optimally with respect to the information potentially available in time, then it cannot permit this sequential separation of the contribution of different forms of analysis. Word-recognition in normal utterances, for example, takes place in a syntactic and interpretive context that places constraints on the words that are able to, or are likely to, occur at a given point in that utterance. Our claim is that speech understanding is interactive in the sense that it permits the integration, during processing, of all available sources of information, so that, for example, the recognition of a word depends on the interaction of the set of constraints simultaneously provided by the sensory input and by the word's utterance and discourse context.

However, to say that processing is fully interactive will get one into terrible theoretical trouble if one takes "interaction" to mean direct top-down control of lower-level processes. In particular, we then not only run the risk of hallucinating what we hear—rather then creatively synthesizing it—but also the system has no intrinsic control structure. There is nothing in a fully interactive system to determine the flow of processing events through the system from signal to message. To avoid these and other problems, we assume two further properties for the system: The central processes are *obligatory,* and they operate on the principle of *bottom-up priority.* These two properties are very closely related, and we will treat them together.

What is meant by bottom-up priority is that processes within any one knowledge source are initially determined by the bottom-up input to that source. Taking, again, the case of word-recognition, this means that the set of possible word-candidates is defined in the first instance by the sensory input to the word-recognition system. Top-down constraints are not permitted to restrict the set of possible candidates in advance of the relevant sensory input (c.f., Oden & Spira, 1978; Swinney, 1979).

The term obligatory here means that given that a knowledge source receives the input appropriate to it, then it *must* run through its characteristic operations on this input. If a speaker utters a string of speech sounds that form a word in a language that the listener knows, then he must hear the input as constituting that word, and similarly for strings of words structured as grammatical and meaningful sentences. These joint properties —of obligatory bottom-up priority—give the system an intrinsic control structure, and require that the analysis of the input propagates as far through the system as it can, as it is being heard, while at the same time ensuring that this analysis remains in contact with the sensory input.

The way we attempt to resolve the apparent inconsistency between these properties, and the property of interaction, is to allow a parallel processing system. To explain the evidence for optimal interactive processing in time, and to accommodate the constraints of obligatory and bottom-up priority processing, we have to assume a distributed processing system, in which multiple analysis paths can be followed in parallel. The properties of on-line speech processing seem fundamentally inconsistent with the basic computational metaphor of a serial machine in which there is a central processing unit that can only do one thing at a time.

We turn now to some of the evidence for the view of speech understanding we have been developing, and for the general properties we assign to it.

CONTEXTUAL INTERACTIONS WITH WORD-RECOGNTION PROCESSES

We begin with word-recognition processes, which, we believe, not only play a central role in speech understanding, but also provide our best experimental window on the range of processes involved.

The critical point about word-recognition in normal utterance contexts is that it is not only very fast, but also very early, relative to the total durations of the words involved. Using a variety of reaction-time tasks, one finds that words in utterance contexts can be recognized, on average, within about 200 msec of their onset. The important point here is not so much the absolute speed of recognition as its earliness. In one experiment, for example, where we obtained reaction-times of about 275 msec, the average duration of the words was almost 400 msec (Marslen-Wilson & Tyler, 1975; 1980). That is, the words were being recognized well before all of them could have been heard; in fact, when only about half of the acoustic-phonetic input corresponding to the word had become available.

This means, in particular, that words in context can be recognized *before* sufficient acoustic-phonetic input could have accumulated to uniquely specify what the word was. The argument for this depends, first, on the basic temporal facts of the matter. The first 200 msec of a word corresponds on average, to the first two phonemes of the word (e.g. Sorenson, Cooper, & Paccia, 1978). If one goes to a phonetic dictionary, and determines the sizes of the sets of words compatible with any given two-phoneme initial sequence, then the median size of this set is around 65 members. This implies that there will on average be many words compatible with the available input at the point that recognition apparently occurs.

A second type of evidence derives from a quite different sort of experiment, using the "gating" paradigm developed by Grosjean (1980). This is a situation in which the listener is given successively longer fragments of a word—starting with the first 30 msec, and increasing the amount by 30 msec on successive presentations until all of the word has been heard. At each presentation point the subject is asked to say what he thinks the word is or is going to be. This is not a reaction-time task, but it does enable one to estimate the minimum amount of input that the listener needs to hear to correctly determine what the word is. For words in isolation, Grosjean obtained an average discrimination point of about 330 msec; the listeners needed to hear 330 msec of the words, on average, before they could correctly identify them.

This is to be contrasted with the results for the same words—the same acoustic tokens in fact—heard in sentential contexts. For these cases Grosjean obtained accurate identification, on average, after the subjects had heard less than 200 msec worth of the words. This estimate is very close to the average recognition time we estimate for words in context in reaction-time tasks—and suggests, by extension, that the words in our experiments are also being recognized before sufficient acoustic-phonetic information could have accumulated to allow the word's recognition on that basis alone.

But if this is the case, then word-recognition must in some way be an interactive process; contextual information *must* participate in the analysis process to provide the missing information. We can see this reflected, first of all, in the reliable finding that reaction-times increase when words are presented in situations where different types of contextual constraint are not available.

In one experiment, for example, we used stimuli of the following sort:

Normal Prose: (The church was broken into last night.)
                   Some thieves stole most of the *lead* off the roof.
Anomalous Prose: (The power was located in great water.)
                   No buns puzzle some in the *lead* off the text.
Scrambled Prose: (In was power water the great located.)
                   Some the no puzzle buns in *lead* text the off.

These stimuli provide very general contrasts: Normal Prose allows all normal forms of analysis to be developed; in Anomalous Prose only some form of syntactic analysis can be developed; and Scrambled material is just a string of unrelated words.

These materials were presented auditorily and the subject's task was to press a response key as soon as he recognized the prespecified target word. Monitoring reaction-times increased from 275 msec in Normal Prose to 336 msec in Anomalous Prose to 360 msec in Scrambled Prose. Subtracting from these responses the time the subject takes to actually make the key-pressing response—which on a reasonable estimate would be between 50–75 msec— then we are left with recognition times of about 200 msec in Normal Prose, 260 msec in Anomalous Prose, and 285 msec in Scrambled Prose (The average durations of the target words in the three contexts were, respectively, 369, 384, and 394 msec).

These results, then, provide us with two critical facts about word-recognition in context:

a. That it occurs before sufficient acoustic-phonetic information to make the recognition decision could have accumulated.
b. That contextual influences intervene early in this recognition process.

To account for these facts we have to assume that contextual variables interact with word-recognition processes at a point when many words may be compatible with the available input, and that the joint contributions of contextual and sensory inputs determine when the correct word can be separated from this initial set of possibilities. Note, of course, that the principle of bottom-up priority requires that this initial set is determined by the sensory input, and not by top-down contextual pre-selection.

It is worth stressing that what we are getting here can also be viewed as a rapid real-time solution to a very complex set-intersection problem. The word that surfaces—the word-sense that is selected—is that candidate, from among all the candidates compatible with the acoustic-phonetic input early in the word, that best matches the correct structural and discourse context. It is almost certain that this could not be done, within the observed temporal constraints, by a serial machine—let alone one made of slow elements like neurons (c.f., Fahlman, 1979). We have to assume instead a parallel analysis system, in which all word-candidates are assessed in parallel for their contextual suitability. Only some form of parallel machine could show the required insensitivity to the size of the search space within which the on-line set-intersection problem has to be solved.

We have, elsewhere, proposed a specific parallel word-recognition model, with the appropriate properties, which fully accounts for the phenomena we have just described, and which has the general properties we have assigned here to the operations of the speech understanding system in general (c.f., Marslen-Wilson & Welsh, 1978; Marslen-Wilson & Tyler, 1980; Marslen-

Wilson, 1980). There is not the space here to discuss this model; instead we will briefly outline an experiment this model encouraged us to do that seems to demonstrate optimal efficiency in speech processing.

OPTIMAL WORD-RECOGNITION PROCESSES

The claim we made earlier was that the human speech understanding system is organized in such a way that it can assign an analysis to the speech input at the theoretically earliest point at which the type of analysis in question can be securely assigned. What is meant by the term "securely" here is that the system does not, within limits, make guesses about the correct analysis of the input.

This general claim can be translated as follows into the word-recognition domain: A word is recognized at that point, starting from the beginning of the word, at which the word in question becomes *uniquely distinguishable* from all of the other words in the language *beginning with the same sound sequence.* What is meant here can be illustrated by looking at an example—that is, at the relationship of a given word to the set of words in the language that begin with the same sound sequence.

Table 1 lists the words in British English (Gimson & Jones, 1977) that begin with the sound sequence /tre/. We will refer to this list as *the word-initial*

TABLE 1

Word-initial Cohort for /tre/

treacherous	tremolo
treachery	tremor
tread	tremulous
treadle	trench
treadmill	trenchant
treasure	trend
treasury	trepidation
treble	trespass
trek	tress
trellis	trestle
tremble	

cohort for /tre/. Assume, for example, that the word to be recognized is "trespass" /trespəs/. We can determine (see Table 1) the point at which /trespəs/ becomes uniquely distinguishable from all of the other words beginning with /tre/. The word is not discriminable at the /tre/, nor at the /tres/, since there are two other words in the language that share this initial sequence (tress, trestle). But immediately following the /s/ these two can be excluded, so that the /p/ in /trespəs/ is the theoretically earliest point at which the word could be recognized.

It is at this point, therefore, that an optimal recognition system should be able to recognize the word. It cannot do so earlier, since there are other words that cannot be excluded. But if it does so any later—if the word is not discriminated until the /ə/ or the final /s/—then the system would not be optimally efficient. It would be using more sensory information to make the recognition decision than was strictly necessary.

This level of performance requires a word-recognition system that can continuously assess the sensory input against the sets of possible word-candidates that are compatible with this input at different points in time. It is only by simultaneously considering all possible lexical interpretations of the accumulating sensory input that the system can be sure, on the one hand, of not prematurely selecting an incorrect candidate, and, on the other, of being able to select the single correct candidate as soon as it becomes uniquely discriminable—that is, at the point where all other candidates become excluded by the sensory input. The experiment we will now describe shows that listeners have access, in real time, to information about the input that could only have derived from an analysis of this type.

The experiment used an auditory lexical decision paradigm, in which the subjects heard isolated sound sequences, and made non-word decisions (pressed a response key) whenever they thought they heard a sound sequence that did not form a word in English. The important variable here was the point in each non-word sequence at which it became a non-word, and the way in which these "non-word points" were determined. The non-word points varied in position from the second to the fifth phoneme in a sequence, in sequences that were one, two, or three syllables in length.

The calculation of the non-word point for each stimulus was based on the cohort structure of the language (General British English). For example, one of the non-words was "stadite." This becomes a non-word at the /d/, since there are no words in the word-initial cohort for /stæ/ that have the continuation /d/. Another example would be the non-word /trenkər/. This becomes a non-word at the /k/, since there are no words in English beginning with /tren/ that continue with /k/ (see Table 1). A total of 218 non-word sequences were constructed, and were presented to the subjects in isolation, mixed in with an equal number of real English words.

If processing is indeed optimal, then the subjects should have been able to begin to make the non-word decision, in each non-word sequence, at precisely that point where the sequence diverged from the existing possibilities for words in English. The results clearly confirmed this hypothesis. Decision-times were constant, averaging around 450 msec, when measured from the onset of the non-word point in a sequence. This held true independently of where in the sequence the non-word point occurred, and independently of the total length of the sequence. For example, in the non-word "sthoidik" (/sθɔidik/), which becomes a non-word at the /θ/, the mean decision-time was 449 msec from the onset of this phoneme. In the non-word "feathorn" (/feθɔ:n/), which becomes a non-word at the /ɔ:/, decision-time was 450 msec measured from this point.

These results indicate that spoken word-recognition is founded upon an optimally efficient real-time analysis of the speech signal. In the non-word detection task, this allows a non-word to be discriminated as soon as it diverges from the existing possibilities in the language. In the normal recognition of real words, this allows a word to be discriminated as soon as it diverges from other possible words in the language. And in the case of real-word recognition, the word's compatibility with its context may interact with this discrimination process to further optimize the use of the available input.

STRUCTURAL AND INTERPRETATIVE ASPECTS OF SPEECH-UNDERSTANDING

In the two preceding sections we have supported our claims about the properties of the central processes underlying speech understanding by concentrating on spoken word-recognition (in and out of context). For the remainder of the chapter, we will examine the implications of our research for the further, structural and interpretative aspects of the system.

The system's optimally efficient use of processing information as it becomes available in time, and the possibility for cooperative interactions between different forms of analysis, appears to lead to a processing system in which the analysis of an utterance is always conducted with immediate reference to the discourse context in which it occurs.

From the first word of an utterance the listener is constructing what we can call an interpretative representation of this utterance. This interpretative representation is the outcome of an on-line integration of linguistic and nonlinguistic analyses. That is, listeners are integrating together constraints derived from the specific discourse context and from their general knowledge of the world, with their analysis of the linguistic properties of the utterance itself. As each word is heard and recognized, its semantic and syntactic properties become immediately available and are mapped onto this developing interpretative representation. This means that the syntactic and semantic properties of utterances, as linguistically defined, do not correspond during processing to computationally distinct syntactic and semantic "levels of analysis." Leaving aside the question of whether or not one assumes that the listener's syntactic knowledge constitutes a separate knowledge type (or "knowledge source") within the processing system, we assume here that this syntactic knowledge is not realized during processing as a computationally distinct level of syntactic analysis of the input. Rather, syntactic knowledge functions during processing to guide the assignment of structural relations within the developing interpretative representation.

The model does not assume that, moreover, there is a semantic interpretation process of the classical type—that is, a processor that operates on word-meanings and syntactic relations to produce a semantic representation which is then, and only then, integrated with pragmatic variables and the discourse context (c.f., Fodor, Bever, & Garrett, 1974; Kintsch, 1974; Clark, 1976). This is because there is assumed to be no stage of processing during which the semantic properties of words are being analyzed independently of their interpretation in some "context of use." This is not to say that no formal distinction can be drawn between the semantic and pragmatic aspects of meaning, but that this distinction is not one that corresponds to functional subdivisions in the processing system. Given the lexical semantic information made available when words are being recognized, this information is directly pragmatically interpreted in its discourse context, subject to the available syntactic constraints (for further discussion see Marslen-Wilson & Tyler, 1980).

This general view of language understanding does not just depend on the application of processing principles observed in word-recognition experiments, but derives as well from a series of experiments examining the properties of structural and interpretative processes. One such experiment was the monitoring study mentioned earlier (Marslen-Wilson & Tyler, 1975; 1980), which contained manipulations designed to measure the effect of discourse (interpretative) context upon on-line processing.

In this experiment, apart from the variation of prose type (Normal, Anomalous and Scrambled Prose), we also manipulated the serial position of the word the subject had to listen for. The target words were evenly distributed across the test-sentences, which allowed us to track the availability of syntactic and interpretative constraints as they developed across the sentence. In addition, each test sentence was presented either in isolation or was preceded by a lead-in sentence that provided a discourse context in terms of which the test sentence could be interpreted. It is this contrast which provides evidence for the type of on-line effects we are concerned with here.

The critical finding was that word-recognition decisions in Normal Prose were facilitated right at the beginning of a test sentence—but *only* when the sentence was preceded by a lead-in sentence. Thus, Normal Prose sentences with a prior discourse context showed a significant advantage of 50–60 msec over Anomalous Prose at the beginning of a sentence, and this advantage stayed constant across word positions. When the lead-in sentence of each sentence-pair was omitted, however, this early advantage of Normal over Anomalous Prose disappeared, and a Normal Prose advantage only developed later in the sentence. This established, then, that the early advantage of Normal Prose derived from the first sentence of each sentence-pair, which provided an interpretative context onto which each incoming word of the test sentence could be mapped. Note that this result provides two sorts of information. On the one hand it reflects the sensitivity of word-recognition processes to their discourse context, and, on the other, it implies that a discourse-level representation is constantly being developed.

The claims for interactions between different knowledge sources are illustrated more directly in a second experiment, which demonstrates the on-line integration of lexical, structural, and interpretative sources of information (Tyler and Marslen-Wilson, 1977; Tyler, 1980). In this experiment we used structurally ambiguous fragments, such as "shaking hands," and "landing planes." These fragments were preceded by a context clause which biased the fragment towards one of its two readings. For example:

2a. As a traditional way of gaining votes, *shaking hands* . . .
2b. If you're trying to thread a needle, *shaking hands* . . .
3a. If you've been trained as a pilot, *landing planes* . . .
3b. If you walk too near the runway, *landing planes* . . .

Written pre-tests had established that each context clause biased one reading or the other of the fragment, and the purpose of the experiment was to determine whether these biasing effects operate on-line. That is, whether by the time the listener has heard the ambiguous fragment preceded by a context clause, he has already established a preference for one reading rather than another.

To determine this, we presented the context clause and the ambiguous fragments auditorily, over headphones. Immediately at the offset of the last word in the fragment (e.g., "hands") we presented *visually* a continuation word, which was compatible with one of the readings of the fragment. Thus, following the context clause and the ambiguous fragment in, for example, sequence (2a), the subject would immediately see either the word "IS" or the word "ARE." His task was simply to say the word as rapidly as possible. Our assumption was that naming latency would be slower when the continuation word was inconsistent with the preferred analysis of the fragment—but only if the subject had already computed this preferred analysis by the time he saw the continuation word.

This assumption was confirmed by the results. Naming latency to inappropriate continuations was significantly slower than to appropriate continuations. Thus the latency to name "IS" was slower in contexts (2b) and (3b) than in contexts (2a) and (3a), while latency to name "ARE" was slower in the (2a) and (3a) contexts than in the (2b) and (3b) contexts. The speed of the subjects' responses (500–600 msec) meant that they had little time available for post-stimulus analyses. The effects of context could only have derived from analyses that were already available to them when the fragment ended.

This result illustrates the cooperation during on-line speech understanding between at least three different sources of processing information—lexical, structural, and interpretive. No single one of these could, by itself, have been sufficient to produce the on-line preferences observed in this experiment. Take, for example, the context clause "If you walk too near the runway . . . ." This context leads to a preferred reading for "landing planes," but it is not by itself the only source of the preference. If the fragment had been "avoiding planes," for example, then the alternate structural reading would have been adopted, even though the context stayed the same. The preferences obtained in this experiment must involve the on-line analysis of the meanings of the words and their structural properties, relative to the most plausible interpretation of this information given the scenario set up by the context clause.

The descriptions of this and the previous experiment give the general flavor of the approach we have been developing to the problem of speech understanding. We emphasize here the finding that the fundamental goal of the speech understanding process—the interpretation of the message—is not only in progress immediately an utterance begins, but it is also intimately connected to analysis processes throughout the system. Furthermore, our research indicates that all speech processing involves an immediate attempt at a mapping onto a mental representation of the previous and current discourse interpretation. This means then, that no lexical item is ever analyzed in isolation from the consequences it should have for its interpretative context.

We now turn to a final experiment, which again looks at the relationship between the processing of an utterance and its discourse context, but in which the nature of the devices linking the utterance to its context have been explicitly varied (Tyler & Marslen-Wilson, 1981).

The major contrasts are reflected in the following sample stimulus set:

1. As Philip was walking back from the shop, he saw an old woman trip and fall flat on her face.
2a. He only hesitated for a moment
2b. She seemed unable to get up again
3a. Philip ran towards . . .
3b. He ran towards . . .
3c. Running towards . . .

This stimulus set is made up of a context, or scene-setting sentence, followed by six possible continuations; sentence (1) can be followed either by

(2a) or by (2b), and each of these in turn can be followed by either (3a), or (3b), or (3c). Each of these sequences was presented auditorily (to different subjects). Immediately at the offset of the continuation fragment (3a, 3b, or 3c), a visual probe was presented to the subject, whose task was to name this probe word as quickly as possible, and then to write down whether or not the probe was an appropriate continuation of the fragment. For the examples given above, the probe word would be either "HIM" or "HER," and in each case "HIM" would be the inappropriate continuation. Just as in the "shaking hands" experiment described earlier, we expected naming latencies to be slower to inappropriate probes.

The major variable here was the means by which the continuation fragments were linked to the preceding discourse. The devices we used were various types of anaphoric elements. In (3a) the device is simply the repetition of the name of the antecedent individual; in (3b) it is an (unambiguous) personal pronoun; while in (3c) there are no explicit linguistic cues at all. It is clear that rather different procedures need to be invoked to cope with these three cases. In (3a) a simple matching of the name could be sufficient. To resolve (3b), a straightforward heuristic could be used to match the pronoun against the set of possible antecedents, and find the one that is male, animate, and singular. To resolve (3c), however, pragmatic inference has to be invoked. It is necessary to infer, given the scenario set up by the preceding context sentences, who is most likely to be running towards whom.

The critical point for our present argument is the contrast between (3c) and the other two types. If it is indeed the case that discourse links that depend entirely on inference are necessarily more difficult and more time-consuming for the processor, then one should predict a smaller difference between the appropriate and inappropriate probes in (3c) than in (3a) or (3b). We note that there is a clear assumption in much of the AI and psychological literature on discourse-utterance links that inference should be brought into the process as late as possible, because inferencing is expensive in time and resources (e.g., Haviland & Clark, 1974).

We also included two other variables in the experiment. The first involved the length of the continuation fragment, which varied from one to four words in length. Thus, for example, the fragment ranged from a single word, such as "Opening," to an adverb followed by a verb plus a preposition and particle such as "Carefully getting out of." The motivation for this variation was that if the discourse linkage is indeed more time-consuming in (3c), then one might only find a difference between appropriate and inappropriate probes when the listener has more processing time—that is, in the longer fragments.

The other variable was a manipulation of the structure of the discourse— namely, whether or not the antecedent for the anaphor in each fragment had been "foregrounded" in the intervening sentence (2a or 2b). Again, one might expect an interaction between this variable and the type of anaphoric linkage. The assignment of Philip as the agent in (3c) might be easier when it was preceded by (2a)—"He only hesitated for a moment"—than when it was preceded by (2b)—"She seemed unable to get up again."

The results support a view of speech comprehension stressing a major role for pragmatic inference with respect to a discourse model. The results (Table 2) show an equally large difference between appropriate and inappropriate probes in all conditions. In an analysis of variance, the only significant effect was a large main effect for probe type. Whether the probe came after a more or less explicit anaphor, and independent of the foregrounding manipulation and of the length of the continuation fragment, the subjects had an equally strong preference for one rather than the other of the two probes. The experiment was in fact run two times, on two very different populations of native English speakers, and we found exactly the same results in both cases.

TABLE 2
Mean Naming Latencies (msec)

	Foreground Sentence					
		2a			*2b*	
Probe Type	*App.*	*Inapp.*	*Diff.*	*App.*	*Inapp.*	*Diff.*
Continuation Type						
3a. Full NP	379	427	48	378	431	53
3b. Pronoun	382	432	50	388	436	48
3c. Zero	381	417	36	388	423	35

There are two conclusions we want to draw from this experiment. Firstly, just as in the "landing planes" experiment, mentioned earlier, we see evidence of the on-line cooperation of lexical, syntactic, and interpretive information. But the most important point we want to make here is that the results show that purely inference-based textual linkages do not necessarily cost the listener more in terms of time or success.

CONCLUDING REMARKS

Taking a wider perspective on these properties of on-line speech understanding, we suggest that they can best be understood as an optimal solution to the problems posed by a communicative system based on speech. Natural biological systems, once one begins to understand how they work, usually turn out to be very well adapted to the problem in whose context they evolved. There is no reason to suppose that human speech processing should be an exception to this regularity.

The particular problem that the speech channel poses is that it is intrinsically *slow*. The speech production device—the vocal tract—can only do one thing at a time, and is limited in the speed with which series of articulatory gestures can follow each other. The response of the recognition system to these limitations is to have optimized the efficiency with which the speech input is utilized, and, therefore, the speed with which the message can be both produced and interpreted. We assume, of course, that the main pressure on the system is indeed to maximize the speed with which complex messages can be transmitted, and the earliness with which their interpretation can begin.

The principal strategy the processing system employs in optimising the use it makes of its input, is to move the analysis of the sensory input as rapidly as possible into a domain where all available sources of information can be brought to bear on its further analysis and interpretation. The essential link here is the word-recognition system. It is only when the signal has been brought into contact with the word-recogntion system that its analysis can begin to be integrated with the structural and interpretative context in which it is occurring.

This not only facilitates the word-recognition process, but also means that the interpretation of the message can begin immediately. At the same time the constraints imposed by the principles of bottom-up priority and obligatory processing keep these interactions under control. The domain of possible readings is always being defined from the bottom-up: deriving ultimately from the properties of the sensory signal itself.

This, then, is the outline of a processing system that allows for optimally early and optimally accurate real-time interpretation of the speech signal—and we feel that this is the way it ought to be: Life is so short, and otherwise the spaces between words would be so long!

REFERENCES

Clark, H. H. *Semantics and Comprehension*. Janua Linguarium, The Hague: Mouton, 1976.

Fahlman, S. E. *NETL: A system for representing and using real-word knowledge*. Cambridge, Mass.: MIT Press, 1979.

Fodor, J. A., Bever, T., & Garrett, M. *The psychology of language*. New York: McGraw-Hill, 1974.

Forster, K. Levels of processing and the structure of the language processor. In: W. E. Cooper & E. C. T. Walker (Eds.), *Sentence processing: Psycholinguistic studies presented to Merrill Garrett*. Hillsdale, N.J.: Lawrence Erlbaum Associates, 1979.

Garrett, M. F. Word and sentence perception. In: R. Held, H. W. Leibowitz, & H-L. Teuber (Eds.), *Handbook of sensory physiology, Vol. VIII, Perception*. Berlin, Springer Verlag, 1978.

Gimson, A. C., & Jones, D. *Everyman's English pronouncing dictionary.* London: J. M. Dent, 1977.

Grosjean, F. Spoken word recognition and the gating paradigm. *Perception and Psychophysics,* 1980, *24,* 267–283.

Haviland, S. E., & Clark, H. H. What's new? Acquiring new information as a process of comprehension. *Journal of Verbal Learning and Verbal Behaviour,* 1974, *13,* 512–521.

Kintsch, W. *The representation of meaning in memory.* Hillsdale, N.J.: Lawrence Erlbaum Associates, 1974.

Marslen-Wilson, W. D. Speech understanding as a psychological process. In: J. C. Simon (Ed.), *Spoken language generation and understanding.* Dordrecht: Reidel, 1980.

Marslen-Wilson, W. D., & Tyler, L. K. Processing structure of sentence perception. *Nature,* 1975, *257,* 784–786.

Marslen-Wilson, W. D., & Tyler, L. K. The temporal structure of spoken language understanding. *Cognition,* 1980, *8,* 1–71.

Marslen-Wilson, W. D., & Welsh, A. Processing interactions and lexical access during word recognition in continuous speech. *Cognitive Psychology,* 1978, *10,* 29–63.

Oden, G. C., & Spira, J. L. *Influence of context on the activation and selection of ambiguous word senses.* W.H.I.P.P. No. 6, Dept. of Psychology, University of Wisconsin, Madison, 1978.

Sorenson, J. M., Cooper, W. E., & Paccia, J. E. Speech timing of grammatical categories. *Cognition,* 1978, *6,* 135–153.

Swinney, D. A. Lexical access during sentence comprehension: (Re)consideration of context effects. *Journal of Verbal Learning and Verbal Behaviour,* 1979, *18,* 645–659.

Tyler, L. K. Serial and interactive-parallel theories of sentence processing. *Theoretical Linguistics,* 1980, *8.*

Tyler, L. K., & Marslen-Wilson, W. D. The on-line effects of semantic context on syntactic processing. *Journal of Verbal Learning and Verbal Behaviour,* 1977, *16,* 683–692.

Tyler, L. K., & Marslen-Wilson, W. D. *Processing utterances in discourse contexts: On-line resolution of anaphors.* Manuscript. Max-Planck Institute for Psycholinguistics, Nijmegen, 1981.

10 A Perspective on Research in Language Production

M. F. Garrett
Massachusetts Institute of Technology

INTRODUCTION

My intention is two-fold. First, it is to characterize the general theoretical orientation that directs research in our laboratory at MIT, and second, to discuss that orientation in terms of research (our own and that of others) in the area of language production. In fact, of course, our investigation of language production processes is quite closely tied to work on comprehension processes. I will comment on that connection and its implication for theories of the relation between formal grammatical theory and processing theory.

ORIENTATION OF RESEARCH

To begin the first point simply: Our basic goal is to develop models of human language communication. Human beings communicate in a variety of ways; our focus is on the linguistically mediated ways. Indeed, it is a primary issue in our research to ascertain the relation between linguistically mediated communication and that effected by other means. Put more broadly, this is the question of what relation holds between language and other cognitive systems. Is the exercise of language merely a particular instance of the exercise of more general cognitive capacities, or is it the exercise of a system, perhaps species specific and heavily determined by endogenously fixed mechanisms, whose character is peculiar to language? Is there, in short, a *language faculty* distinct from other cognitive capacities in its computational instantiation and/or its organizational principles? I will explore the background of this question in more detail momentarily. First, let me simply enumerate the research questions that emerge when one seeks an experimentally certifiable characterization of the language faculty. In each case, I note the working hypothesis in terms of which we approach the question.

1. Is there a principled distinction between the mental processes involved in comprehending or producing a sentence and those involved in determining the consequences, inductive or deductive, of the information it expresses? Hypothesis: Sentence recognition and production processes are distinct from inferential processes.

2. How are the representations computed by speakers and hearers related to formal linguistic levels of representation? Hypothesis: Each linguistic level of representation corresponds to a level of mental representation normally computed during linguistic communication.

3. How are the levels of representation that are computed for sentences during linguistic communication related to each other for the on-line information processing purposes of comprehension and production? Hypothesis: Each level of representation corresponds to an autonomous subcomponent of the language processor; interaction among these subcomponents is fixed in its character and time course.

I note in passing that the notion of *autonomy* is not identifiable with *seriality* in the development of representations. Indeed, the notions of "bottom-up" and "obligatory" processing (see remarks by Marslen-Wilson and Tyler, this volume) entail the principle of autonomy, though the character of the particular subsystems required is left open, of course. Such serial consequences as there may be will depend upon what structural limits there are on the accessibility of information among components. If, for example, in the case of syntax, that limit proved to be full sentences or surface clauses, something like the strong seriality condition would hold; if accessibility is possible for lexical or phrasal outputs, the seriality condition for interaction between, e.g., syntactic and semantic processes is correspondingly weakened. But, so long as internal processes of the syntactic analyzer are not modulated by the consequences of "higher order" interpretations of its partial products (i.e., so long as its processes are bottom up and obligatory), the subcomponent is autonomous.

I state these views briefly and baldly, not supposing that they will seem surprising, but wishing to be clear about the working hypotheses at the outset. I do not pretend that they are now fully established: However, they do determine our specific approach to experimental and observational enquiry. They are, moreover, closely related hypotheses: 2 and 3 are possible answers to the query: What *is* it (as 1 suggests) that is hypothesized to be distinct from cognitive processes at large and from inferential processes in particular? The hypotheses of 2 and 3 assert that there are autonomous, language specific processors whose outputs are the representations of sentences specified by grammars.

Why do we find this a useful formulation? There are several reasons, chief among them that we garner thereby a processing account of the regularities of sentence form, and that we provide a strong and potentially extendible claim about the relation between grammars and processors—namely, that the gross architecture of the processor reflects that of the grammar. Such a formulation is crude enough to be currently researchable, and precise enough to provide strong empirical claims. Moreover, if it proves correct, even in its initial form, it may provide a lever for evaluating alternative grammatical proposals. Given this principle for the computational decomposition of the language faculty and strong experimental evidence for a *particular* organization of language processing, the grammar which best comports with that organization would be preferred.

You might at this point wonder why or whether this approach differs from one that seeks to find direct correspondences between mental operations and specific grammatical operations (e.g. "DTC"; Fodor, Bever, & Garrett, 1974). Such a consequence is one possible culmination of the research approach I've characterized; but, it is not a necessary one. It is entirely possible that, at the level of rule systems, a strong organizational constraint could exist, while at the level of the formulation of specific rules for specific languages, it would not.

Let me turn now to the problem of studying language production, and comment on what I think are some findings and observations that comport with the general approach I've outlined.

SOME OBSERVATIONS ABOUT LANGUAGE PRODUCTION

What is language production? It is—obviously, though not very helpfully— bringing about a correspondence between instructions to the articulators and some communicative intention. What is required, on any reasonable view, is that the representation produced permit a listener who shares the speaker's language conventions to reconstruct that intention unambiguously.

What would it be for such a system to be modular? or non-modular? It would require that a given system subcomponent not be "penetrated" at just any level or point by other language components or other aspects of cognitive function. So, in the ideal case, the intention to emit a particular speech act of given content once set in train, would run itself off without modification because of subsequently determined logical or pragmatic consequences. Again, this is not to say that such inferential processes do not affect production—it is rather to assume that these effects are introducable only at specific, structurlaly determined points in the constructive process. Finding out what those points are, and the points of interaction among the putatively language specific components of the process is a large part of the study of language production.

How do we study language production? Well, linguistics is certainly one way. But here we wish to focus on the real time constructive process; there are a number of avenues open for this enquiry. One of them is to model the process in the way that workers in artificial intelligence seek to—by providing a procedural specification of the process. Though I think this is a valuable approach, I will have little to say of it, since I wish to concentrate on some processing evidence from human performance that would dictate *which* of many procedural approaches one might take.

The evidence most persuasively related to on-line processes of sentence construction is that from various observations of spontaneous speech—observations of the type and loci of a variety of errors in that process, ranging from nonfluencies of the sort induced by jet lag, to smoothly articulated disasters like "it makes the warm breather to air," (for: "it makes the air warmer to breathe"). Hesitation phenomena and speech errors form an important part of the data base for examining production processes. To these one may add the study of various language disorders, and finally, the products of direct attempts at experimental intervention in the process.

My own work on production processes relies primarily on the study of speech errors, and, as my introductory remarks would suggest, to me it indicates a processing system organized in levels of differing internal organization, which, moreover, reflect the distinctions among major structural types in grammars rather closely. I am far from the first to make such an observation. Others, (e.g., Fromkin, 1971) have previously reached a similar conclusion, though phrased somewhat differently.

I will run quickly through some observations about such production data to suggest the flavor of the outcome to date. These observations indicate aspects of syntactic planning and lexical retrieval for language production; they are based on the distributional features of a corpus of spontaneous speech errors. The remarks here summarize work reported elsewhere (see Garrett, 1980, and references therein).

There are many different kinds of speech errors, and they have been studied by a variety of investigators. The sorts of errors that I have focused on are those which seem to have a rather clear involvement of phrasal structure in their mechanism. These are errors that indicate movement of some segment of the intended output. In such cases, one can determine from the error output the intended site of the erroneously placed elements. So, for example, in *exchanges* of sounds or morphemes or words (e.g., "Why was that *horn* blowing his *train*?" or "My *tar* was *cowed* away."), one can determine two error loci, those of the two misplaced elements. Similarly, in *shift* errors, one can also determine two error loci; the locus of the erroneously placed element and the site from which it was moved (e.g., "mermaid – moves their legs together").

The analysis of such errors indicates an interaction between the nature of the error mechanism (e.g., exchange or shift) and the nature of the error elements (word classes or morpheme classes). Further, we find an interaction between phrasal structure and the nature of the error elements that are involved—words, morphemes, or sounds. These two interactions (which I will describe in a moment), indicate the existence of two levels of sentence planning, each of which is involved in phrasal construction in different ways.

Put most simply, the interaction between error element type and phrasal structure is as follows: If the two elements involved in an exchange error are words—not bound morphemes or sound elements—they will be words from distinct phrases; word exchange errors are predominantly between-phrase errors. If the interacting elements in an exchange error are sound segments, they will be internal to a simple phrase; sound exchanges are phrase-internal errors. Morpheme-exchange errors appear to be of both types. There is a further constraint one observes in exchange errors that permits us to assign a given morpheme-exchange error to one or the other of the two categories —either that characteristic of word exchanges or that characteristic of sound exchanges—with some confidence. That constraint involves a correspondence of grammatical category for the interacting words (in the case of sound exchanges, of the words that contribute the interacting sounds): Whenever there is an exchange error involving elements of different phrases, the elements are not only almost always words, but those words are also almost always of the same grammatical category; nouns exchange with nouns, verbs with verbs, adjectives with adjectives, and prepositions with prepositions. When there is a morpheme exchange between two phrases, they obey this additional constraint—the exchanged morphemes come from words of corresponding category. When the morpheme exchange occurs internal to a phrase, of course, this constraint is rarely observed. The salient point is that when an exchange occurs *between* phrases, morpheme exchanges obey the same constraint as the word exchanges. This is not the case for sound exchanges. When sounds do exchange between phrases—though this happens only rather infrequently—there is no indication of such a grammatical category constraint. These and other related observations have led me to characterize the planning operations that give rise to such errors in terms of two levels of sentence planning activity. The first of these deals in multiphrasal representations for which the functional roles of words are at computational issue: The second of these is a single-phrase planning level in which the sound structure and serial ordering of the elements in the string are at issue.

There is, in addition to the observations I have just made, some indication of clausal structure constraints on these errors. I will not explore the matter here beyond noting that at the first hypothesized level of phrasal planning—the multiphrasal level—it may be argued that the planning operations are constrained to the domain of two, surface adjacent, syntactic clauses as a maximum, while at the second hypothesized planning level—the single phrase integration level—there is reason to argue that the domain of planning is not specifically syntactic, though it is clearly syntactically constrained. It is perhaps for this latter process that the notion of phonemic clause or phonological phrase is relevant (I will comment further on this below). At all events, aspects of clausal structure are implicated in these two planning levels, and there is some indication that the relation of the two levels to such structure differs (see Garrett, in press, for discussion).

Let me turn now to the second interaction between errors and language structure: that is, the interaction between error mechanism (i.e., exchange vs. shift errors) and vocabulary type (i.e., word or morpheme categories). There is strong evidence of a restriction of exchange errors of the sort discussed above to major grammatical types. That is, exchange errors, whether of words, morphemes, or sounds, arise principally for the major grammatical categories—nouns, verbs, and adjectives. Shift errors on the other hand are, by and large, restricted to minor grammatical categories— pronouns, conjunctions, quantifiers and qualifiers, and so forth. Note that these observations for free forms are paralleled for bound forms. If one examines the elements of exchange errors in which morphemes exchange positions, one finds that the morphemes that move are stem morphemes rather than derivational or inflectional morphemes. By contrast, if one examines the morphemes that move in shift errors, one finds that they are predominantly inflectional morphemes, not stem morphemes.

There is, in fact, a persuasive case to be made that the difference between the two planning levels characterized above—one a multiphrasal planning level in which the functional role of elements seems to be at issue, and the other a single phrasal level in which the sound structure and serial order of elements seems to be at issue—may be construed in terms of a difference in *computational vocabulary*. The first level of phrasal planning primarily involves decisions over major grammatical category items. The second level of planning consists in the integration of these functionally characterized major category items with detailed phrasal configurations that are expressed partly in terms of a vocabulary of minor category elements. Exchange errors may be understood to arise either as a consequence of the elaboration of the initial functional level of organization or in terms of the second level of phrasal organization in which there is integration of the two vocabulary types.

The computational distinction between major and minor grammatical categories that seems to be manifest in the distributional properties of the speech errors is one that I and a number of my colleagues have begun to refer to as a distinction between *open* and *closed* class vocabularies (see e.g., Bradley & Garrett, 1980). One reason for this terminological convention is to clearly label the distinction as having a computational motivation rather than a formal grammatical motivation. The distinction between open and closed class vocabularies in the description of speech errors should be thought of as a claim about a particular computational function hypothesized to hold between the phrasal planning levels characterized above. Whether this contrast of computational vocabularies may be formally characterized more precisely than the description I presented, namely that of major versus minor grammatical categories, remains to be determined. It is possible that some other formal characterization in terms of semantic constructs or in terms of phonological and non-phonological structures should be adopted instead; I will return to this latter possibility shortly.

Before doing so, we must observe that this difference in the apparent properties of various classes of speech errors, as construed in terms of open and closed classes, is clearly related to characteristic failures in aphasia. In particular, the elements typically omitted from the agrammatic speech of Broca's aphasics are those of the closed class—they are the elements that, in normal speech, are prominent in shift errors and that are not directly involved in exchange processes. In complementary fashion, it appears that the closed class is that part of the vocabulary preserved in canonical cases of fluent aphasias—i.e., Wernicke's aphasia and anomia. This is, of course, not a new observation. It is one oft made in summary characterizations of two major classes of aphasic disorders—those associated with anterior and posterior lesion sites—under the rubric of grammatical and nongrammatical words, or "content" and "function" words. (See Saffran, Schwartz, & Marin, 1980, for a recent discussion.)

Given the level of our current understanding of aphasic deficits and of the nature of speech error phenomena, one cannot say how detailed the correspondence between normal error patterns and patterns in language disorders may prove to be. One would hope, of course, that careful comparisons of disordered speech with the patterns of normal error processes would reveal more precise and illuminating characterizations of these and related phenomena. As an example, consider again the question whether the computational contrast between open and closed class vocabularies should be cast in terms of the shift from syntactic to phonological structures. It has, in fact, been argued (see Kean, 1977) that the aphasic syndrome of agrammatism is best described formally in terms of an impairment of phonological structures. Thus, her construal of agrammatism suggests that, if it is to be properly described as the impairment of a computational capacity associated with closed class vocabulary, that vocabulary should be given a phonological characterization. And, indeed, there is some specific evidence for this conclusion in the speech error data: Prepositions appear in word exchange errors, but do not contribute to sound exchanges. This pattern seems best understood in light of the change in the role of prepositions from syntactic to phonological rule systems (see Garrett & Kean, 1980).

We cannot pursue these matters further here; however, it is enough for present purposes to note that the general character of the contrast in processing vocabularies appropriate for the description of speech errors in normal populations may turn out to be very similar to that required for description of production failures in language disordered populations. Both of these areas of observation indicate similar conclusions via a vis the gross organizational features of the language production system.

From this cursory examination of phrasal planning in production, we turn now to another feature of language production processes, that of word selection. Again, we draw upon observations from speech errors, but this time on those of single word substitutions rather than of movement errors. There are two features of such errors that I wish to call to your attention. One has to do with the dissociation of word substitutions into two types, and the other with the role of morphological structure in such errors.

It is a striking feature of the observed errors of word substitution that they fall into two broad classes: those in which there is a clear relation between the form of the intruding word and the form of the target word, and those in which there is a relation between the meaning of the intruding word and the meaning of the target word. The latter class of errors is readily understandable in terms of our intuitive notion of what transpires when we seek to talk: We search for some form of words expressing the meanings that we wish to communicate; errors in which the substitution is between lexical items that are meaning related make straightforward good sense in that picture. However, the occurrence of form-based errors (e.g., substitution of "sympathy" for "symphony" or substitution of "menu" for "memo") must be counted as mildly surprising. One might expect mishearings on the basis of form but not misspeaking—unless, of course, one's model of production processes incorporates (a meaning independent) access to a word inventory organized by form. Just such a proposal has been made by Fay and Cutler (1977). They suggest that the inventory of word forms relevant to perceptual performance is used in production as well, a suggestion to which we will return momentarily. The parameter of form that Fay and Cutler find most prominent is segmental similarity, with those segments in initial word position being most significant: Target and intrusion correspond segment by segment, with decreasing probability from early to late segments. Stress and word length are also implicated, though it is difficult to establish the precise description that determines their role in access processes.

To these observations, we may add another that concerns one further structural feature of word substitutions in production, namely, an effect of morphological structure. For morphologically simple cases, a straightforward access account as segment by segment, biased to initial positions, seems adequate; for prefixed items, however, the situation is more complex. Exceptions to the principle that initial segments correspond arise with more than chance frequency when prefixed words are involved. Fay (1979) has recently argued for a view of such errors that presumes storage of word stems, with prefixes as "addenda." Note that the relevant morphological decomposition is fundamentally a form-based phenomenon, since very many of the morphological structures are not semantically regular.

In brief summary: The picture that emerges from the word substitution error data is one of separate meaning and form-based retrieval systems, with both segmental structure and morphological structure providing organizational principles guiding retrieval operations. The error data from exchanges and shifts reviewed earlier indicated a multilevel planning process in which the detailed surface phrasal organization of sentences is integrated separately from underlying functional organization of the sentence. In this latter contrast, we implicated a vocabulary contrast between, roughly, content and function words that we have referred to as the open and closed class vocabularies in order to emphasize its more general character (both bound and free forms are implicated) and its computational basis.

I want to turn now to a brief examination of some comprehension performance factors that parallel the ones I have called to your attention from production processes. The reason for this should be clear given my introductory remarks. If the organization of processing systems truly reflects the decomposition of the language faculty suggested by the organization of grammars, it should show up in both places—in production and in comprehension. But if the organization of language processors is primarily dependent upon modality-specific and task-specific demands, we might expect sharp divergences. The facts as I see them support the first of these two possibilities: Though there surely are differences one might note, the correspondences between production and comprehension seem to me impressive.

For example, let me first recall the features of word retrieval in production that are indicated by regularities of word substitution errors. Briefly, they were: (1) a sensitivity to morphological structure, and (2) a "left-to-right" or temporal bias in the analysis of input sentences. As already noted, those regularities are strikingly like those which seem to guide word recognition processes. Recent work by Marslen-Wilson (1979) has shown effects in auditory word recognition that indicate a segment by segment analysis of the input signal; reaction times for the determination of lexical identity seem, from about the first syllabic nucleus onward, to be a linear function of the serial position of the sound segment that uniquely (perhaps to a family of derivational variants) determines the lexical status of the presented string. Earlier work by Taft and Forster (1975, 1976) with visually presented words indicates a similar (i.e., left-to-right, segment by segment) analsysis scheme. Moreover, the work of Taft and Forster reveals as well as strong effect of prefix structure, the upshot of which is a claim that the entry to the stored form of prefixed words is via their stem form. The experiments I have mentioned are perhaps the clearest, though by no means the only, indicants that the organizational parameters that are effective in production are effective in comprehension as well.

To these positive evidences, we might at this time also add a "negative" convergence, namely the separation of meaning and form-based systems in retrieval for both production and comprehension. Recall that the word substitution errors indicate the operation of two independent retrieval systems, the one based upon form just commented on, and one based on meaning relations. Just as the form related substitutions show no meaning similarities, so too the meaning related substitutions show no contributions from form. Evidence for a similar dissociation in recognition performance comes from a variety of sources. See, for example, Forster (1979) and Garrett (1978). Swinney has reported (see Swinney, this volume) the results of recent experiments designed to test contextual (semantic/pragmatic) influences on recognition processes for ambiguous words. That work seems to indicate that though semantic relations do certainly play a fundamental role in our recognition of words, they do so independently of the operation of form-based retrieval systems.

Finally, I would like to return your attention to the distinction I have drawn between open and closed class vocabularies in production processes. Speech error regularities implicate that distinction in the production processes for phrasal construction. There are several indications of a similar contrast in comprehension processes. For example, Thorne and his colleagues (Thorne, Bratley, & Dewar, 1968; Bratley & Dakin, 1968) have emphasized the role of function words and some inflections in fixing the syntactic analysis of sentences, and their parsing proposals used an open class/ closed class dictionary concept in their design. Of course, there are also some well known behavioral indications of the salience of this vocabulary distinction for recognition processes. For example, syntactically organized nonsense strings (strings constructed by substituting nonsense forms for *open* class vocabulary (e.g., "a vapy koobs desaked the citar molently") can be assimilated more quickly and recalled better than nonsense strings not so organized (see, e.g., Epstein, 1961; Forster, 1966). Further, it seems clear that our conscious sensitivity to details of the form of elements of the two classes differs—the closed class is in some way less readily available for report (e.g., repetitions or inversions of closed class items are more likely to be overlooked in proofreading than are repetitions of open class items). Possibly related to this is recent evidence we have that children (about 3.5 to 4 years) differ in their metalinguistic judgments about words from the two classes—"word status" is more readily assigned to open class than to closed class items in a word-nonword classification task (Egido, Carey, & Garrett, 1981). To these observations which attest a difference in the processing of these vocabulary classes, we may add others that implicate lexical access procedures.

That work explores the thesis that the organization of lexical retrieval systems is tailored to the demands of parsing processes. In particular, it tests for the possibility that there are distinct lexical recognition routines for closed and open classes on the grounds that the former play a special role in the comprehension procedures that assign phrasal structure to sentences. The similarity of this to my earlier claims about the role of closed class items in production processes should be evident.

I will not summarize these results in detail but will simply note some of the initial experimental indications of divergent recognition processes. One such finding indicates a different effect of frequency variables in the two classes. The normally observed pattern is for a correlation between frequency of occurrence and recognition performance; in lexical decision tasks, more frequent items are responded to faster. Our results for visual lexical decision tests show no such effect in the closed class (Bradley & Garrett, 1980). If, as seems plausible on grounds of many experimental results, a frequency ordered access is characteristic of open class retrieval, it may not prove so for the closed class. I should note by way of caution that this result has not been observed in recent experiments by investigators of French (Frauenfelder, personal communication) and Dutch (Kolk, personal communication), though we have observed results similar to those for English in a Spanish test (Garcia-Albea, Bradley, & Garrett, 1979, unpublished).

A second finding showing a recognition contrast depends upon the earlier mentioned left-to-right scan in recognition analysis. A partial analysis that uses the initial elements of the stimulus array seems to guide selection of candidate items from the stored mental lexicon. A striking example of this occurs when a *non*-word presented for decision has a real word embedded left-to-right (e.g., as in "setitude" or "thinage"). The decision times to reject such items as non-words are elevated as compared to decision times for non-words with no such embedding (e.g., as in "dititude" or "thonage"). Note: No such effect arises when a real word is embedded at the end of a non-word (as in "prithin" or "thaset"); see Taft & Forster (1976) for a discussion. Again, however, our results (Bradley & Garrett, 1980) indicate that this effect is specific to the open class retrieval process. Comparable items beginning with the closed class elements (as, "fewlet" or "thanage") show no evidence of such interference effects—their response times are not different from the non-word controls.

A third indication, albeit of a somewhat different character, is one of an apparent hemifield difference for recognition of the two vocabulary types. Recognition accuracy for closed class items is inferior to that for open class items in right hemifield presentation but *not* in left hemifield presentation; performance levels are equal for the two classes in the latter condition, though left hemifield performance levels for both classes are, of course, inferior to both right hemifield levels (Bradley, 1978). We may hypothesize that this circumstance arises because of a (left) hemisphere-specific recognition process for the closed class; that specific process is disabled by the stimulus degradation inherent in the non-foveal presentation required to insure hemifield stimulation. This admittedly speculative account of the hemifield differences would be strengthened by a clear demonstration that the operation of the closed class retrieval system depends on high stimulus quality. We have some indication of such a circumstance in a preliminary finding that stimulus degradation induces a frequency effect in the closed class—i.e., renders its processing characteristic of open class organization.

To this we may also add evidence from tests of an aphasic group—these are findings from only a single study, but the results are quite interesting both from the perspective of a possible hemispheric specialization and from the perspective of relations between production and comprehension performances. I earlier noted the possible connection between a characteristic impairment of Broca's aphasics, that of agrammatism, and certain speech error patterns implicating the open and closed class vocabulary distinction. And, here again for *recognition* tests with a group of such patients, we have evidence for an impairment of the class specific access mechanisms indicated by the frequency, inference, and hemifield experiments noted above. A group of Broca's aphasics tested with the materials for the frequency and interference experiments did not show the contrast in performance for the two vocabularies. Rather, both word classes showed the same performance factors—those typical of the open class (see Bradley, Garrett, & Zurif, 1980). If one were to identify the locus of the specialized closed class retrieval processes as the language-involved tissue of the left hemisphere, the results of the experiments with language disordered patients and those of the hemifield experiments with normals could be linked.

Perhaps it is worth reiterating at this point the reasons for our interest in this vocabulary distinction. It is not just that one is interested in establishing the generality of the performance parameters for word recognition, and perhaps seeing what relation they may bear to those of word retrieval for production. It is rather that the open-closed class vocabulary distinction constitutes part of an hypothesis about what an autonomous syntactic processor might dispose in a lexical recognition or production device. If, e.g., basic parsing mechanisms are not dependent upon the idiosyncracies of association or inference for major lexical classes, then such an abstraction in lexical retrieval mechanisms is a plausible consequence. If the contrary (i.e., that situation specific inferential patterns determine parsing decisions) were true, however, then little premium might be placed upon the early identification or recruitment of the closed class elements. They might instead by relegated to some confirmatory role for those configurational hypotheses based on the situationally relevant lexical descriptions. Thus, it is a conviction about the centrality of the autonomy thesis to language investigation, coupled with observations that suggest a context-free role for syntactic and phonological categorizations for vocabulary that impels the focus on these particular experimental variables.

SUMMARY STATEMENT

In overview, it seems to me that there are strong preliminary indications that the major organizational features of formal grammars appear in both comprehension and production systems, and, moreover, that the computational manifestations of that organization are remarkably similar. There is enough evidence to warrent systematic investigation of the hypothesis that grammars establish the modularity of processors. We need, therefore, to determine just how detailed the correspondence is between the organization of grammars and that of processing systems. We need to know how modality-specific effects modulate the organization of language processors. Perhaps it is far less than we might have imagined.

Most certainly, not all the relevant issues of areas of enquiry that bear on the thesis advanced here have been touched upon. Indeed, there is one area of great promise that I have not mentioned at all and cannot forbear a parting comment on. That is the study of the structure and processing of sign languages. In the areas thus far investigated, the properties of sign languages are amenable to formal treatments similar to those for spoken language (see Bellugi & Klima, 1979). Moreover, some tests of processing structures for sign show interesting similarities to those for processing of spoken and written language (see, e.g., Grosjean, 1980, 1981). We are far from a firm conclusion on the matter, of course, but the possible implications are striking. If, in an exercise of language so distinct from the usual vocal/auditory one, we were to find relations between grammars and processing systems that are like those indicated for speech and writing, it would be compelling evidence against modality-specific bases for the organization of language processors. Assuming such an outcome and the correctness of my earlier interpretation of the processing evidence, an organizational principle stated in terms of informational structure is indicated, namely: Every linguistic rule system requires an autonomous processing type, the parameters of whose computational activity reflect only the structural distinctions in the representations of its corresponding rule system. Such a specific construal of the grammar/processor relation seems eminently worth pursuit so long as the experimental evidence does not absolutely prohibit it.

ACKNOWLEDGMENTS

Some of the work discussed in this chapter was partially supported by NIMH grant HD 05168 to J. A. Fodor and M. F. Garrett and by a grant from the Alfred P. Sloan Foundation to the MIT Center for Cognitive Science. The general research program characterized here is one whose responsibility I share with J. A. Fodor and E. C. T. Walker, though they, of course, are absolved of any error I may make in the expression of its goals.

REFERENCES

Bellugi, U., & Klima, E. *The signs of language.* Cambridge, Mass.: Harvard University Press, 1979.

Bradley, D. C. *Computational effects of vocabulary type.* Ph.D. dissertation, M.I.T., Cambridge, Mass., 1978.

Bradley, D. C., & Garrett, M. *Computational distinctions in vocabulary type,* Occasional paper no. 12, Cognitive Science Center, M.I.T., Cambridge, Ma., 1980.

Bradley, D. C., Garrett, M., & Zurif, E. Syntactic deficits in Broca's aphasia. In D. Caplan (Ed.), *Biological studies of mental processes,* Cambridge, Mass.: M.I.T. Press, 1980.

Bratley, P., & Dakin, J. A limited dictionary for syntactic analysis. In E. Dale & D. Michie (Eds.), *Machine intelligence,* 2, Edinburgh, Oliver, & Boyd, 1968.

Egido, C., Carey, S., & Garrett, M. *Invisibility of closed class words in children's word judgments.* Unpublished research report, Psychology Dept., M.I.T., Cambridge, Mass., 1981.

Epstein, W. The influence of syntactical structure on learning. *American Journal of Psychology,* 1961, *74,* 80–85.

Fay, D. Prefix errors. Paper presented at the fourth Salzburg International Linguistics Meeting. Salzburg, Austria, Aug. 15-27, 1979.

Fay, D., & Cutler, A. Malapropisms and the structure of the mental lexicon. *Linguistic Inquiry,* 1977, *8,* 505–520.

Fodor, J. A., Garrett, M. F., & Bever, T. G. *The Psychology of Language.* New York: McGraw Hill, 1974.

Forster, K. I. The effect of syntactic structure on nonordered recall. *Journal of Verbal Learning & Verbal Behavior,* 1966, *5,* 292–297.

Forster, K. I. Levels of processing in sentence comprehension. In W. Cooper & E. Walker (Eds.), *Sentence processing.* Hillsdale, N.J.: Lawrence Erlbaum Associates, 1979.

Fromkin, V. The non-anomalous nature of anomalous utterances. *Language,* 1971, *47,* 27–52.

Garrett, M. Word and sentence perception. In R. Held, H. Leibowity, & H-L Teuber (Eds.), *Handbook of sensory physiology, vol. 7 Perception,* Berlin, Springer-Verlag, 1978.

Garrett, M. Levels of processing in sentence production. In B. Butterworth (Ed.), *Language production,* vol. 1. London; Academic Press, 1980.

Garrett, M. Language production: Observations from normal and pathological speech. In A. Ellis (Ed.), *Normal and Pathological Language Performance.* London: Academic Press, in press.

Garrett, M., & Kean, M-L. Levels of representation and the analysis of speech errors. In M. Aronoff & M-L Kean (Eds.), *On juncture,* San Francisco, AMNI Libri, 1980.

Grosjean, F. (1981) Sign and word recognition: A first comparison. *Sign Language Studies,* in press.

Grosjean, F. Psycholinguistics of sign language. In H. Lane & F. Grosjean (Eds.), *Recent perspectives on american sign language,* Hillsdale, N.J.: Lawrence Erlbaum Associates, 1980.

Kean, M-L. The linguistic interpretation of aphasic syndromes. *Cognition,* 1977, *5,* 9–46.

Marslen-Wilson, W. Speech understanding as a psychological process. In J. C. Simon (Ed.), *Spoken language generation and understanding.* Dordrecht, Holland: D. Reidel, 1979.

Saffran, E., Schwartz, M., & Marin, O. Evidence from aphasia: Isolating the components of a production model. In B. Butterworth (Ed.), *Language Production,* vol. 1 London: Academic Press, 1980.

Taft, M., & Forster, K. I. Lexical storage and retrieval of prefixed words. *Journal of Verbal Learning and Verbal Behavior,* 1975, *14,* 638–647.

Taft, M., & Forster, K. I. Lexical storage and retrieval of polymorphemic and polysyllabic words. *Journal of Verbal Learning and Verbal Behavior,* 1976, *15,* 607–620.

Thorne, J., Bratley, P., & Dewar, H. The syntactic analysis of English by machine. In D. Michie (Ed.), *Machine Intelligence,* 3, Edinburgh, Edinburgh University Press, 1968.

11 Prosody and Sentence Perception in English

Anne Cutler
Centre for Research on Perception and Cognition
University of Sussex

Spoken sentences are strings of segments that vary not only in spectral quality but in pitch, amplitude, and relative length. To understand what a speaker has communicated, a listener must identify the segments composing the utterance, and the order in which they occur; but a good deal of information is also encoded in the pitch, amplitude, and timing variations, i.e., the prosody of the utterance, and listeners make good use of it. Prosodic processing can be so efficient that listeners will attend to prosodic continuity at the expense of semantic continuity (Darwin, 1975). This paper addresses the question of the extent to which listeners make use of available prosodic cues, and the types of information they extract from them. All of the experimental studies cited in the three main sections below deal with the processing of English only.

A central topic of my own research has been the processing of sentence accent, or primary sentence stress, and the first section of this paper describes a series of experiments that addresses this issue. In sections 2 and 3 these studies are integrated with other work on the processing of prosody, in particular on the use of prosodic information to locate syntactic boundaries and to ascertain lexical stress patterns.

1. THE PERCEPTION OF SENTENCE ACCENT

All the studies to be reported below used the phoneme-monitoring task, a technique for studying sentence comprehension processes devised by D. J. Foss (1969). In a phoneme-monitoring experiment, subjects listen to sentences and press a button as soon as they hear a word beginning with a specified sound. Reaction time to the target sound is significantly faster when the target-bearing word bears sentence accent—as it does for instance in (1a) and (2a) below—than when it does not (1b, 2b), and this is true both when the target-bearing word is an open class word such as a noun, verb or adjective (2) and when it is a closed class word such as a conjunction or preposition (1).

(1) target: /b/ a. I'm not sure Shakespeare's plays are even BY Shakespeare.[1]

  b. I'm not sure Shakespeare's plays are EVEN by SHAKESPEARE.

(2) target: /k/ a. Does John really want to KEEP that old van?

  b. Does John really WANT to keep that old van?

These findings were reported by Cutler and Foss (1977). Similarly, if the target sound begins a nonsense word, response time is faster if the initial (target-bearing) syllable of the nonsense word is stressed than if it is unstressed (Shields, McHugh, & Martin, 1974).

In a subsequent experiment, it was demonstrated that the reaction time advantage of accented target bearing words is not solely due to the heightened acoustic clarity that without doubt prevails in stressed syllables in comparison with unstressed syllables. Cutler (1976) recorded sentences in two prosodic versions, one in which the target-bearing word received primary sentence accent (e.g., 3a) and one in which it did not (3b):

(3) target: /b/ a. The couple had quarreled over a BOOK they had read.

  b. The couple had quarreled over a book they hadn't even READ.

The target-bearing word itself was then spliced out of each version and replaced by acoustically identical copies of the same word taken from a third recording of the same sentence in which the stress level of the target word was intermediate, falling between the other two versions. This resulted in two versions of each experimental sentence, with acoustically identical target-bearing words but markedly different prosodic contour on the words preceding the target: In one case the prosody was consistent with sentence accent occurring at the location of the target, in the other case it was consistent with reduced stress at that point.

Under these circumstances the target in the "accented" position is still responded to significantly faster than the target in the "unaccented" posi-

---

[1]The words in upper case bear sentence accent.

tion. Since there were no acoustic differences between the target words themselves that could account for this result, and the only difference in the preceding context lay in the prosody, it was concluded that listeners had been making use of prosodic cues that indicated where accent would occur.

The way in which the acoustically identical target words were spliced into the differing prosodic contexts in this experiment, however, allowed the interpretation that the effective component of the preceding prosody was in the tenth of a second or so immediately preceding the splice. The word-initial splices were made as close as possible to the release of the stop consonant burst (all target words began with /b/, /d/ or /k/). The closure before the burst of a stop consonant, however, tends to be longer in stops preceding stressed vowels than in stops preceding unstressed vowels, and in fact in the Cutler (1976) materials the stop closures were consistently longer before targets in "accented" contexts than before those in "unaccented" contexts. This could have allowed subjects more proces<ing time in the "accented" case, which in turn could have produced faster response times. (This argument is directly analogous to the explanation given by Mehler, Segui, & Carey, 1978, for the fact that reaction time to phoneme targets is faster when the word before the target is polysyllabic rather than monosyllabic.)[2]

In order to investigate this possibility, the preceding experiment was replicated with position of the word-initial splice and hence duration of the stop closure explicitly manipulated: Splicing at the stop burst was compared with splicing at the onset of the pre-burst closure (Cutler & Darwin, 1981). The conditions of the previous experiment were repeated except that each experimental sentence occurred in four versions, resulting from the comparison of the two accent conditions ("accented" and "unaccented") and the two splicing position conditions (splicing at the burst and splicing at the closure onset). In the burst-splice condition the closure duration of the target stop was longer in the "accented" than in the "unaccented" versions of the sentences, whereas in the closure-splice condition both versions had stop closure durations of equal length. Again, the targets in "accented" position were responded to significantly faster than the targets in "unaccented" position, but the splicing manipulation had no effect: The reaction time advantage for targets in accented positions was equally strong in both the burst-splice and closure-splice conditions. In other words, the duration of closure of the target stop consonant does not have an effect on response time. This result allows us to reaffirm that the reaction time difference found in the earlier study was indeed due to differences in the prosodic contour preceding the target word. Listeners were using cues in the preceding

---

[2]I am grateful to R. Diehl for suggesting this possibility.

prosody that pointed to the locations of primary sentence stress; in effect, they were actively looking for accented words.

Why should listeners want to do this? A suggested answer was provided by Cutler and Fodor (1979), who pointed out that the location of primary sentence stress usually corresponds to the most informative part of a sentence, or the semantic focus. Thus when a listener determines where the primary sentence accent will fall, he has found out which part of the sentence will be semantically most central. Cutler and Fodor provided support for this interpretation by demonstrating that focused words enjoy a phoneme-monitoring response time advantage analogous to that of accented words. They presented listeners with sentences like (4):

(4) target: /k/ (or /d/)   The house with the carport must belong to the doctor's widow.

The sentence's focus was determined by preceding it with a question about some aspect of the content. Each sentence had two alternative target positions—in (4), the /k/ on "carport" and the /d/ on "doctor's"—and two alternative questions, one of which focused on the part of the sentence in which the first target occurred, while the other focused on the part where the second target occurred. For (4), the two questions were (5a) and (5b):

(5) a.   Which house must belong to the widow?
    b.   Which widow must the house belong to?

Although the sentences remained acoustically invariant—i.e., all subjects heard exactly the same recording of each sentence irrespective of which preceding question they heard or which target they were listening for—targets in earlier position produced faster responses if the preceding question had focused on the early part of the sentence, whereas targets in later position produced faster responses when the preceding question had focused on the later part of the sentence. That is, varying the position of semantic focus affects response time in much the same way as varying the position of sentence accent.

It is not clear, however, that using prosody to locate sentence accent and using semantic information within the sentence to locate sentence focus are merely two alternative procedures for accomplishing exactly the same end, one or other (but not both) to be pursued according to the information available in the utterance. Some relevant evidence was provided by a further experiment in which semantic focus and sentence accent were varied independently. In this study, carried out at the University of Sussex as an undergraduate project by Louise Lee Seng, sentences like (6) were prepared in two prosodic versions, one in which sentence accent fell on the target-bearing word and one in which it fell elsewhere. The sentences were preceded by one of two alternative questions, one of which focused on the part of the sentence where the target occurred, while the other focused on some other part of the sentence.

(6) target: /b/   – Where did he drive yesterday?
                 – Who did he meet yesterday?
        a. Yesterday he drove to the BEACH and met his friend there.
        b. Yesterday he drove the the beach and met his FRIEND there.

The effects of semantic focus and sentence accent in this experiment turned out to be significant, equally strong, and additive, in that when the target-bearing word was both accented and focused, its reaction time advantage in comparison with the unaccented unfocused case was twice as large as when it was either accented, or focused, but not both. Note that in this experiment the sentences were not spliced; the acoustic advantages of accented over unaccented words were present and available to the listener. In the Cutler (1976) experiment the unspliced original sentences showed an accent effect more than twice as large as the effect in the spliced sentences; i.e., the effect due to prediction of accent location from preceding prosody was overlaid by a further effect due to the heightened acoustic clarity of the accented words. This may also have been the case in this experiment. Nevertheless, the RT advantage of the accented but unfocused condition—in which cues to accent were present both in the preceding prosody and in the acoustic form of the target word itself—in comparison with the unaccented unfocused condition was only half as large (46 msec) as that of the condition in which the target was both accented and focused (105 msec; focus alone produced a 50 msec RT advantage). Thus it does appear that the focus effect is separable from any accent effect.

Clearly, the case in which accent and focus coincide is the norm in English utterances; so that it is possible that when the target-bearing word was accented but not focused, or focused but not accented, the sentences were perceived to be abnormal and an inhibitory effect thus reduced the reaction time advantage. Of course it is also possible that the reaction time advantage of accented and focused words respectively represent entirely independent phenomena that just happens to coincide in most utterances. This, though, makes no capital of the fact that the effects of focus and accent on phoneme-monitoring response time are identical in kind and remarkably similar in magnitude. Perhaps an appropriate interpretation is that search for primary sentence stress on the basis of prosodic information and search for semantic focus on the basis of non-prosodic information are separate strategies proceeding in parallel but directed at the same end. In normal sentence understanding both strategies are invoked in order that the semantically most central portions of the incoming message may be located as rapidly as possible.

So far, by using the general term "prosody," we have begged the question of exactly what information in the acoustic signal is sufficient, or necessary, to indicate the location of sentence accent. An attempt to investigate this question more closely was undertaken by Cutler and Darwin (1981). Of the three major dimensions of prosodic variation, pitch, amplitude, and timing, the one that seemed an obvious candidate for initial study was pitch. Lea (1974), for example, has claimed that fundamental frequency variation is the most useful cue for the automatic location of sentence accent; Faure, Hirst, and Chafcouloff (1980) have reported that judgments of compound stress (e.g., "blackbird" versus "black bird") cannot be reliably made in the absence of pitch information. Thus it appeared that if any prosodic dimension were to prove a necessary source of information from which to locate sentence accent, it would most likely be pitch. Moreover, pitch is the only prosodic dimension that lends itself readily to simple test—its contribution can be gauged by eliminating pitch variation entirely, i.e., by monotonizing the sentences. Manipulation of duration and amplitude is far more difficult, and cannot simply be achieved by eliminating variation along the dimension in question, since amplitude variations are vital for many segmental distinctions, whereas uniform timing requires an a priori decision as to the relevant units of speech (phonemes? syllables? inter-stress intervals?) that should be rendered uniform in length.

Accordingly, Cutler and Darwin tested whether the absence of pitch information would alter the effectiveness of preceding prosodic cues to sentence accent location. The experiment consisted essentially of a replication of the Cutler (1976) study, with the added variable of presence or absence of pitch information. The spoken sentences were coded into LPC parameters and two versions were synthesized, one with the original pitch contour and one with a monotone pitch; the amplitude envelope of the speech was the same in each version. Thus each experimental sentence occurred in four versions, resulting from the comparison of the two accent conditions ("accented" versus "unaccented") and the two pitch conditions (intact versus monotonized). The target-bearing word was acoustically identical (monotone, neutral-stress) in all four versions of each sentence. Once again the targets in the "accented" position were responded to more rapidly than the targets in "unaccented" position, but surprisingly, the absence of pitch information made absolutely no difference to the magnitude of the accent effect. Thus it would appear that pitch variation is *not* a necessary component of the prosodic variation that enables listeners to determine in advance the location of sentence accent.

The question remains open whether either durational or amplitude variation is necessary, or whether any prosodic information is sufficient. There is a certain amount of evidence that the information contained in durational variation may be particularly important. Phoneme-monitoring RT is extremely sensitive to manipulations of sentence rhythm. Meltzer et al. (1976) showed that minor temporal displacements of phoneme targets from their originally uttered positions (by as little as 50 msec) resulted in an increase in response time. An analogous conclusion may be drawn from an experiment of my own in which a short interval of silence was spliced into a sentence to alter the rhythm. This experiment was based on an earlier study by Martin (1970), who reported that splicing a silent interval into a sentence led to a shift in the locations at which subjects reported perceiving stress. To test whether this effect carried over into the phoneme-monitoring response advantage for sentence stress, sentences were constructed with two alternative target-bearing words, one immediately after the other, and spoken rhythmically and in such a way that stress fell on the second of the two possible target words. Thus in (7) the target could be the /d/ of "dead" or the /k/ of "cat," but stress in the original utterance fell on "cat" and not on "dead":

(7)   My friend was upset by the sight of a dead cat on the road.

A second version of each sentence was prepared in which a silent interval, equivalent to half of the rhythmic inter-stress interval, was spliced into the sentence immediately before the first of the two potential target words. This should have the effect of moving the *subjective* location of stress, i.e., the rhythmically determined point at which stress ought to occur, back to the first target word even though the second target word was the objective location of stress. For each sentence half the subjects listened for one target, and half for the other, and within each group, half heard the sentence with the silent interval and half the version without. Targets in the second position—/k/ in (7)—which were stressed in the original utterance, produced faster RTs in the original version than in the version with the rhythm-altering interval of silence. Targets in the first position—/d/ in (7)—which became the subjective location of stress once the silent interval had been added, produced faster responses in the version with the silent interval than in the version without. In other words, manipulation of the timing relationships within a sentence can have a strong effect on phoneme-monitoring response time; by implication, this effect is mediated by the effect of durational manipulations on the location of perceived stress.

It would appear, therefore, that durational variations may contain sufficient information to indicate where stressed syllables will occur. Note, however, that not all stressed syllables are accented syllables. Accent gives prominence to one word or phrase at the expense of the rest of the sentence, and only occurs once or at most a very few times in each sentence. But in English, which is a so-called stress-timed language, there is a clear difference between stressed and unstressed syllables in general. Polysyllabic words always have one syllable marked for higher stress than the others. Within an utterance there is a rhythmic arrangement of the syllables by which, ceteris paribus, only those syllables marked for stress receive their full durational value, while unstressed syllables tend to be shortened. Sentence accent is applied only to syllables which are already marked for stress, and is in a sense overlaid on the rhythmic stress value, so that accented stressed syllables may actually be assigned even greater durational weight than non-accented stressed syllables. Thus following cues to the location of rhythmic stress beats would not be a very effective strategy for locating sentence accent, since many words are rhythmically stressed but not accented. Moreover, the recordings of the sentences used in the series of splicing experiments which began with Cutler (1976) were submitted to a panel of judges experienced in the analysis of English sentence rhythm, who marked the locations of rhythmic stress beats and of sentence accent in each sentence. The judges were in agreement that the target-bearing words were rhythmically stressed even when they were not in accented position. That is to say, rhythmic stress beats fell on both "accented" and "unaccented" target words; so if anticipation of rhythmic stress beats alone were responsible for the facilitation of response time, there should have been no difference between the two versions of each sentence. There was a difference, however; thus discussion of durational cues to the location of sentence accent must invoke not the rhythmic arrangement of stressed and unstressed syllables alone, but additional cues to the location of sentence accent.

The experiment by Shields et al. cited previously provides some further relevant evidence because it included a control condition in which the nonsense word targets from the experimental sentences were embedded in lists of other nonsense words. Under these conditions, with all the lexical stress information present but accentual variation absent, the phoneme-monitoring response time advantage for stressed-syllable over unstressed-syllable targets disappeared.

These findings make it appear likely that durational information should be of use in the location of sentence accent. Nevertheless, we are still left with the earlier report by Lea (1974) that pitch variation provides a sufficient cue to accent position. Furthermore, Huss (1975) found that fundamental frequency was a powerful cue to stressed syllable location in *accented* (but not in unaccented) words. Thus, although pitch is not a necessary source of information about the position of accent, it may well be a sufficient cue. The question of necessary versus sufficient information is also the theme of the next two sections, which consider the usefulness of the various sources of prosodic variation for making syntactic and lexical decisions during sentence processing.

2. PROSODIC CUES TO THE LOCATION OF
SYNTACTIC BOUNDARIES

There has been a very large amount of work on this topic in recent years, and among the findings are two suggesting that some caution should be exercised before results from this work are generalized to the perception of natural speech. The natural way to study perception of syntactic boundaries is to use syntactically ambiguous sentences, whether simple bracketing ambiguities such as (8) and (9) or more complex ambiguities such as (10) or (11):

(8)   Add sage and thyme or oregano for flavor.
(9)   He sells used Peugeots, Motobecanes, and Raleighs.
(10) These days few people know how good bread tastes.
(11) Smoking cigarettes can be offensive.

But the presence of disambiguating prosodic cues to syntax in natural speech may depend crucially on whether the speaker is aware of the ambiguity. Lehiste (1973) recorded speakers reading ambiguous sentences and then played the recordings to listeners who were asked to pick the interpretation intended by the speaker. They were fairly successful at doing so when the speaker had been consciously trying to disambiguate the sentence, but much less successful when the speaker had been unaware of the ambiguity. Exactly the same result is found with strings that are ambiguous between an idiomatic and a literal reading, such as (12) (van Lancker & Canter, 1981):

(12) They have all gone on the wagon.

Moreover, prosodic cues often do not suffice to disambiguate when there exists a strong frequency bias in favor of one or other reading of an ambiguous sentence (Wales & Toner, 1979); again, the same is true of idiom-literal ambiguities in which there exists a general bias towards idiomatic readings (van Lancker & Canter, 1981).

These reservations should be borne in mind when considering the studies of prosodic cues to syntactic boundaries; most of these studies, however, have dealt with simple bracketing ambiguities like (8) and (9), which Lehiste (1973) found to be the most easily disambiguated kind of syntactic ambiguity and the most likely to be disambiguated even when the speaker was not consciously trying.

On the one hand, we find that durational variation forms a very effective cue to syntactic boundary location. Lehiste, Olive, and Streeter (1976) reported that lengthening the foot (inter-stress interval) containing a syntactic boundary was a sufficient indicator of the presence of the boundary. To a certain extent boundary information may be retrieved from pause duration alone (O'Malley, Kloker, & Dara-Abrams 1973). But investigation of the exact nature of the lengthening cue by Scott (1982) has shown that the effects both of pause and of phrase-final lengthening are primarily a reflection of their effect in lengthening the foot containing the boundary, relative to the lengths of other feet in the utterance. Compare this result with that of Huggins (1972), who found that listeners' perceptions of segment length depended crucially on the effect that variations in segment duration had on relative foot duration. Klatt and Cooper (1975) found further evidence that listeners' expectations of segment length depend on a segment's position in the syntactic structure of the utterance.

Thus we see that durational information can be a sufficient cue to phrase boundary location. But on the other hand so can pitch. The location of a fall in fundamental frequency is a highly efficient way of automatically detecting a syntactic boundary (Lea, 1973); Collier and 't Hart (1975) also found that listeners judge non-final falls in fundamental frequency to indicate the presence of a boundary.

When listeners have the option of using a number of cues—as they presumably do in natural speech—then the effects of pitch and duration sum rather than interact; both of these cues are more informative than cues provided by amplitude variations, however (Streeter, 1978). Nakatani and Schaffer (1978), on the other hand, found duration to be a stronger cue to *word* boundary location than either pitch or amplitude.

Therefore it must be concluded that listeners are very versatile in their use of prosodic cues to syntactic structure. Either pitch or durational information will suffice. Scholes (1971) has claimed that amplitude information may also be relied upon. There is no indication in any of the syntactic studies, however, that any particular prosodic cue is *necessary*.

3. PROSODIC CUES TO LEXICAL STRESS

In languages, like English, that have variable lexical stress, this information is also carried by the prosody. Lexical stress patterns strongly influence word perception in English—when words are misheard, stress pattern is maintained (Garnes & Bond, 1975), and erroneously stressed words may be perceived as other words with the (erroneous) stress pattern, in defiance of segmental information (Bansal, 1966, cited in Huggins, 1972). False recognition of nonsense syllables can be precipitated by stress pattern similarity (Robinson, 1977).

Again, a great deal of research effort has been expended on investigation of prosodic cues to lexical stress, and again, all kinds of prosodic information have been found to be effective. Fry (1955, 1958) investigated the perception of lexical stress in synthesized isolated words and found that both duration (1955) and pitch movement (1958) were strong and effective cues, whereas amplitude information was less useful. Similarly, Nakatani and Aston (1978) reported that duration was the best cue to perceived stress in nonsense disyllables, with fundamental frequency a less effective cue, and intensity information almost useless. Morton and Jassem (1965), however, found that while pitch movement was a better cue than either duration or intensity, the latter were about equally effective. Lieberman (1960) found effects of both fundamental frequency and intensity.

More recent work has concentrated on combinations of cues. Lea (1977) found the best algorithm for automatic location of lexical stress to be one based on a combination of pitch and intensity information. Cheung, Holden, and Minifie (1977), however, found their listeners' judgments of lexical stress to be based mainly on fundamental frequency variation. Huss (1975) found that both duration and fundamental frequency could act as indicators of syllable stress; Gaitenby (1975) found that a method of detecting stressed syllables that used all three sources of information—pitch, amplitude, and duration—was highly effective. Similarly, Isenberg and Gay (1978) found that all three parameters were sufficient cues for the perception of syllable stress; Gay (1978) has since argued that stress perception in natural speech most likely involves the use of multiple cues. Indeed, M. Smith (personal communication) has determined that listeners' perception of stress in nonsense disyllables is not fully accounted for by appealing to any first-order physical information alone, but appears to involve the use of very complex interactions of information.

It appears that for the detection of lexical stress, whatever may be the optimal combination of cues, just about any prosodic information is *sufficient*.

4. CONCLUSION

Given the findings of studies on prosodic cues to lexical stress and to syntactic structure, it does not appear surprising that pitch contour information turns out not to be a necessary cue to the location of sentence accent. The weight of the evidence indicates that with respect to prosodic processing the English speaker's sentence perception device is extremely flexible; it does not, for example, insist on durational cues to phrase boundaries and pitch cues to accent, or vice versa, but accepts and makes use of whatever information is available. Indeed, the fact that in some cases a particular prosodic dimension A has been reported to be more informative than another dimension B may reflect the fact that with certain materials or under certain experimental conditions A may have more scope for variability than B—i.e., there may be objectively more information available in the signal of A than of B, rather than a listener preference for A information over B.

Of course, it is also entirely possible that under natural sentence perception conditions it may be a useful strategy to use different dimensions of the prosody as sources of different information. All the experimental studies tell us is that no single prosodic cue appears to be necessary for any of the three tasks we have considered; identification of lexical stress pattern, location of accent, and location of syntactic boundaries. (Note that these are not the only uses of prosody—cues to meaning, for instance, can be extracted from particular pitch movements: Studdert-Kennedy & Hadding 1973; Mulac & Nash 1977.)

But versatility in prosodic processing should not be unexpected if one considers that a prosodic component is likely to be integral to the human language processor. Languages differ widely in the type of information they encode in the prosody (tone languages and lexical stress languages encode lexical information that other languages don't, for instance) and in the prosodic dimensions they employ (English and other "stress-timed" languages make more varied use of durational information than do French and other "syllable-timed" languages, for example). Thus if any of the work cited had proven amplitude, timing, or pitch contour to be a *necessary* cue to detection of syllable stress, sentence accent or syntactic boundaries, we would have to reckon with the possibility that it would be a necessary cue only in the perception of English, i.e., a language-specific criterion.

There is a good deal of evidence that the nature of prosodic processing differs with the language being processed (although we have only dealt with English here, Lehiste, 1970, is a source of data from languages other than English). For example, the same speakers can be shown to be making use of different cues to the same information in English and Spanish (Hutchinson, 1974). Similarly, when the same nonsense syllable stimuli were presented to English (Morton & Jassem, 1965) and Polish listeners (Jassem, Morton, & Steffen-Batog, 1968), the relative effectiveness of cues to lexical stress, in particular of durational variation, differed across the two groups. A recent parallel investigation by Berinstein (1979) compared the effect of durational variation on the perception of stress in nonsense syllable strings presented to speakers of English and of K'ekchi (a Mayan language with fixed final stress). Berinstein found that whereas duration was an effective cue to stress for the English speakers, the K'ekchi speakers tended to perceive final stress irrespective of the durational pattern of the strings. It was shown, however, that this lack of durational effect for the K'ekchi speakers was not simply due to the presence of fixed stress patterns in their language, but was of more complex origin; speakers of Cakchiquel, another Mayan language that also has fixed final stress, but differs from K'ekchi in that K'ekchi has phonemic vowel length whereas Cakchiquel does not, do find durational variation an effective cue to lexical stress. Thus durational information is not used as a cue to stress by K'ekchi speakers because, it seems, they are already using it as a cue to vowel length. However only pre-emption of this kind appears to rule out use of a particular kind of prosodic variation as a possible source of information on which to base stress, accent or syntactic grouping decisions in any language for which such decisions have to be made.

This is not to say that prosodic characteristics of a given language do not predispose its speakers' prosodic perception. It is not surprising to find that Berinstein's Cakchiquel speakers, though they could make judgments of non-final stress on the basis of durational information, required more durational difference between stressed and unstressed syllables to make this judgment than did English speakers; Cakchiquel has final stress whereas English has variable stress (with a slight bias towards initial stress). Similarly, when duration was equal, K'ekchi speakers judged the strings to have final stress whereas English speakers judged them to have initial stress.

Interestingly, it is not clear that this language-specific effect carries over into the perception of the grouping and relative salience of non-speech sounds. Jakobson, Fant, and Halle (1952) claimed that sequences of knocks are grouped differently by Czech, Polish, and French speakers on the basis of word stress regularities in their respective languages, but Bell (1977) reports an experiment in which the perceived grouping and relative prominence of a sequence of tones heard by speakers of English, Bengali, French, and Polish showed no correspondence with the stress patterns characteristic of the languages in question. Similarly, one cannot invoke differences between English and German, which are accentually similar, to account for the fact that an identical vehicle siren sequence is perceived by English-speaking children as a high-low alternation (doo-dah, doo-dah) but by German-speaking children as a sequence of low-high tones (ta-tü, ta-tü). The predisposing effects of linguistic structure on prosodic perception may be confined to the pitch, amplitude, and duration of *speech*.

The conclusion that we draw from the available evidence, then, is that the human language processor embodies a very versatile capacity to process prosodic information. Characteristics of individual languages may determine that only a subset of the prosodic information available is normally used; but where there are multiple prosodic cues to stress, to accent or to syntax, we are *capable* of using them all.

ACKNOWLEDGMENTS

Preparation of this chapter was supported by a grant from the Science Research Council. I am grateful to my prosodic colleagues at Sussex, Chris

Darwin, Steve Isard, Christopher Longuet-Higgins, and Donia Scott, for many fruitful discussions of the issues involved in the perception of prosody, and to the first two in particular for helpful criticism of the present paper. They are of course not responsible for its defects.

REFERENCES

Bansal, R. K. *The intelligibility of Indian English: Measurements of the intelligibility of connected speech, and sentence and word material, presented to listeners of different nationalities.* Ph.D. thesis, London University, 1966.

Bell, A. Accent placement and perception of prominence in rhythmic structures. In L. M. Hyman (Ed.), *Studies in stress and accent.* Southern California Occasional Papers in Linguistics 4, 1977.

Berinstein, A. *A cross-linguistic study on the perception and production of stress.* UCLA Working Papers in Phonetics 47, 1979.

Cheung, J. Y., Holden, A. D. C., & Minifie, F. D. Computer recognition of linguistic stress patterns in connected speech. *IEEE Transactions on Acoustics, Speech & Signal Processing,* 1977, ASSP-25, 252-256.

Collier, R., & 't Hart, J. The role of intonation in speech perception. In A. Cohen & S. Nooteboom (Eds.), *Structure and process in speech perception.* Heidelberg: Springer, 1975.

Cutler, A. Phoneme-monitoring reaction time as a function of preceding intonation contour. *Perception & Psychophysics,* 1976, *20,* 55-60.

Cutler, A., & Darwin, C. J. Phoneme-monitoring reaction time and preceding prosody: Effects of stop closure duration and of fundamental frequency. *Perception & Psychophysics,* 1981, *29,* 217-224.

Cutler, A., & Fodor, J. A. Semantic focus and sentence comprehension, *Cognition,* 1979, *7,* 49-59.

Cutler, A., & Foss, D. J. On the role of sentence stress in sentence processing. *Language & Speech,* 1977, *20,* 1-10.

Darwin, C. J. On the dynamic use of prosody in speech perception. In A. Cohen & S. Nooteboom (Eds.), *Structure and process in speech perception.* Heidelberg: Springer, 1975.

Faure, G., Hirst, D., & Chafcouloff, M. Rhythm in English: Isochronism, pitch and perceived stress. In L. Waugh & C. H. van Schooneveld (Eds.), *The melody of language.* Baltimore: University Park Press, 1980.

Foss, D. J. Decision processes during sentence comprehension: Effects of lexical item difficulty and position on decision times. *Journal of Verbal Learning & Verbal Behavior,* 1969, *8,* 457-462.

Fry, D. B. Duration & intensity as physical correlates of linguistic stress. *Journal of the Acoustical Society of America,* 1955, *35,* 765-769.

Fry, D. B. Experiments in the perception of stress. *Language & Speech,* 1958, *1,* 120-152.

Gaitenby, J. H. Stress and the elastic syllable: An acoustic method for delineating lexical stress patterns in connected speech. *Haskins Laboratories: Status Report on Speech Research,* 1975, SR-41, 137-152.

Garnes, S., & Bond, Z. S. Slips of the ear: Errors in perception of casual speech. *Papers from the Eleventh Regional Meeting, Chicago Linguistic Society,* 1975.

Gay, T. Physiological and acoustic correlates of perceived stress. *Language & Speech,* 1978, *21,* 347-353.

Huggins, A. W. F. On the perception of temporal phenomena in speech. *Journal of the Acoustical Society of America,* 1972, *51,* 1279-1290.

Huss, V. Neutralisierung englischer Akzentunterschiede in der Nachkontur. *Phonetica,* 1975, *32,* 278-291.

Hutchinson, S. J. P. *The learning of English suprasegmental rules for stress and final syllables by Spanish speakers.* M.A. Thesis, University of Texas, 1974.

Isenberg, D., & Gay, T. Acoustic correlates of perceived stress in an isolated synthetic disyllable. *Journal of the Acoustical Society of America,* 1978, *64,* S21.

Jakobson, R., Fant, G., & Halle, M. *Preliminaries to speech analysis.* Cambridge, MA: MIT Press, 1952.

Jassem, W., Morton, J., & Steffen-Batog, M. The perception of stress in synthetic speech-like stimuli by Polish listeners. *Speech Analysis and Synthesis,* 1968, *1,* 289-308.

Klatt, D. H., & Cooper, W. E. Perception of segment duration in sentence context. In A. Cohen & S. Nooteboom (Eds.), *Structure and process in speech perception.* Heidelberg: Springer, 1975.

Lea, W. A. *Prosodic aids to speech recognition: II. Syntactic segmentation & stressed syllable location.* Sperry Univac Technical Report No. PX 10232, 1973.

Lea, W. A. *Prosodic aids to speech recognition: V. A summary of results to date.* Sperry Univac Technical Report No. PX 11087, 1974.

Lea, W. A. Acoustic correlates of stress & juncture. In L. M. Hyman (Eds.), *Studies in stress and accent.* Southern California Occasional Papers in Linguistics 4, 1977.

Lehiste, I. *Suprasegmentals.* Cambridge, MA: MIT Press, 1970.

Lehiste, I. Phonetic disambiguation of syntactic ambiguity. *Glossa,* 1973, *7,* 107-122.

Lehiste, I., Olive, J., & Streeter, L. A. The role of duration in disambiguating syntactically ambiguous sentences. *Journal of the Acoustical Society of America,* 1976, *60,* 1199-1202.

Lieberman, P. Some acoustic correlates of word stress in American English. *Journal of the Acoustical Society of America, 1960, 32,* 451-454.

Martin, J. G. Rhythm-induced judgments of word stress in sentences. *Journal of Verbal Learning & Verbal Behavior,* 1970, *9,* 627-633.

Mehler, J., Segui, J., & Carey, P. Tails of words: Monitoring ambiguity. *Journal of Verbal Learning & Verbal Behavior,* 1978, *17,* 29-35.

Meltzer, D. H., Martin, J. G., Mills, C. B., Imhoff, D. L., & Zohar, D. Reaction time to temporally-displaced phoneme targets in continuous speech. *Journal of Experimental Psychology: Human Perception & Performance,* 1976, *2,* 277-290.

Morton, J., & Jassem, W. Acoustic correlates of stress. *Language & Speech,* 1965, *8,* 159-181.

Mulac, A., & Nash, R. Effects of intonation pattern of synthesized and natural speech upon listener resolution of semantic ambiguity. *Language & Speech,* 1977, *20,* 274-279.

Nakatani, L. H., & Aston, C. H. Perceiving stress patterns of words in sentences. *Journal of the Acoustical Society of America,* 1978, *63,* S55.

Nakatani, L. H., & Schaffer, J. A. Hearing "words" without words—prosodic cues for word perception. *Journal of the Acoustical Society of America,* 1978, *63,* 234-245.

O'Malley, M. H., Kloker, D. R., & Dara-Abrams, B. Recovering parentheses from spoken algebraic expressions. *IEEE Transactions on Audio & Electroacoustics,* 1973, AU-21, 217-220.

Robinson, G. M. Rhythmic organization in speech processing. *Journal of Experimental Psychology: Human Perception & Performance,* 1977, *3,* 83-91.

Scholes, R. J. On the spoken disambiguation of superficially ambiguous sentences. *Language & Speech,* 1971, *14,* 1-11.

Scott, D. R. Duration as a cue to the perception of a phrase boundary. *Journal of the Acoustical Society of America,* 1982, *71* (in press).

Shields, J. L., McHugh, A., & Martin, J. G. Reaction time to phoneme targets as a function of rhythmic cues in continuous speech. *Journal of Experimental Psychology,* 1974, *102,* 250-255.

Streeter, L. A. Acoustic determinants of phrase boundary perception. *Journal of the Acoustical Society of America,* 1978, *64,* 1582–1592.

Studdert-Kennedy, M., & Hadding, K. Auditory and linguistic processes in the perception of intonation contours. *Language & Speech,* 1973, *16,* 293–313.

van Lancker, D., & Canter, G. J. Idiomatic versus literal interpretations of ditropically ambiguous sentences. *Journal of Speech and Hearing Research,* 1981, *24,* 64–69.

Wales, R. J., & Toner, H. Intonation and ambiguity. In W. E. Cooper & E. C. T. Walker (Eds.), *Sentence processing: Psycholinguistic studies presented to Merrill Garrett.* Hillsdale, N.J.: Lawrence Erlbaum Associates, 1979.

12 On Neologisms

André Roch Lecours
Laboratoire Théophile Alajouanine
Centre de Recherches du Centre Hospitalier
Côte-des-Neiges
Centre de Recherches en Sciences Neurologiques
Université de Montréal

1. INTRODUCTION (A LINGUISTIC DEFINITION OF NEOLOGISMS)

Eberhard Bay (1964), of the *Neurologischen Klinik der Medizinischen Akademie* of Düsseldorf, used to teach (a) that there exists only one type of "pure aphasia," which he called "genuine" aphasia although it is generally known as "amnestic" aphasia, and (b) that a particular difficulty in the evocation of certain classes of words, which he called "determined words," is the single fundamental perturbation to be observed in genuine aphasia. Although this is a typical example of both clear teaching and bold dogmatism, aphasics of all types do experience word finding difficulties. According to Albert Pitres (1898), this particular "amnesia" for words involves mostly grammatical words in certain aphasics, the agrammatics, and it involves only lexical words in others. Although this is a typical example of oversimplification, which I have taken care not to quote until this day, it can be taken as accounting for a most important observation: in a way, at least when it is disorganized by certain focal lesions, the human brain honors the distinction that linguists have made between closed and open class words. I shall illustrate this with various data at a later point.

A large proportion of aphasics thus experience particular difficulties in accessing or retrieving lexical words. In their conversational behavior, this can be manifested by a lack of production: The phrase is then interrupted, at the point where a lexical word is missing, and another attempt can be made through the formulation of another phrase or sentence, or else the speaker abandons. Replacement of the missing word is another manifestation of aphasic difficulties in lexical access: Whether the speaker takes or does not take conscience of this, that is, whether or not he is anosognosic, which varies with types of aphasia, the replacing element can then be a circumlocution, often quite inadequate, and it can also be another word (a *verbal paraphasia*), or else it is a *neologism.*

This communication bears on neologisms, more precisely on the spoken neologisms, which are observed to occur in the discourse of jargonaphasics, on the one hand, and of schizophasics, on the other hand. Word substitutions also occur in such discourses, to which I may have to refer: I will then talk of *semantic verbal paraphasias* when a conceptual relationship exists between target and uttered words, and I will talk of *formal verbal paraphasias* when the relationship between the two is one in phonemic content rather than meaning. The acception of the word *neologism,* as I will be using it here, therefore excludes the unconventional use of existing words. The following four characteristics might be taken, more or less, as an empirical definition:

- Neologisms are word-like entities, which are not there to be found in (appropriate) dictionaries.
- Considered one by one, the phonemes that constitute neologisms are conventionally pronounced, that is, each corresponds to a regular cotemporal combination of features.
- In unilinguals, the choice and serial integration of the phonemes and syllables that constitute neologisms usually abide by conventions inherent to the speaker's mother tongue. This suffers very few exceptions.
- As a rule, the verbal context in which a neologism occurs is such that the listener perceives it as belonging with a particular class of words (such as nouns, adjectives, verbs, and so forth), and as playing a particular syntactic function (such as subject, direct or indirect object, attribute, and so forth).[1]

Although this is a purely linguistic definition, which has at least the advantage of delineating my subject matter with some precision, my discussion about neologisms will encompass clinical and psycholinguistic as well as linguistic aspects of neologistic production. By this, I mean that, besides attempting to characterize various types of neologisms within the semiology of various symptom-complexes and to raise the possibility that it is sometimes related to an acquired anomaly in lexical access or retrieval.

I have chosen, given my current argument, to classify neologisms under

---

[1]One might add that the very existence of neologisms tells us that it does make sense, at least in aphasiology, to consider speech production at word level (among other levels).

three separate headings: (a) *phonemic paraphasias* and related entities, (b) *morphemic deviations,* and (c) *abstruse neologisms.* I will discuss each in turn, after which I will also comment, briefly, on a somewhat bizarre discursive behavior known as *glossolalia.*

2. PHONEMIC DEVIATIONS IN CONDUCTION APHASIA

Phonemic deviations—that is, phonemic paraphasias and related entities—are not uncommon in the discourse of standard speakers and of certain schizophasics, and they are characteristically common in several types of aphasia. On the whole, their structure is more intricated in the latter.

In Broca's aphasia, the production of phonemic deviations is quantitatively restricted in direct proportion to the reduction of speech production as a whole. Moreover, a large proportion of Broca's aphasic's phonemic deviations are further distorted by a more fundamental executive disturbance known as *phonetic disintegration* (Alajouanine, Ombredane, & Durand, 1939): Feature realization itself is impaired by anomalies such as weakness and dystonia in articulatory muscles contraction. In Wernicke's aphasia proper and in glossomaniac schizophasia, the production of phonemic deviations intermingles with that of several other types of deviant entities (Lecours & Vanier-Clément, 1976). Conduction aphasia, on the other hand, comprises a more abundant and much purer production of phonemic deviations, without phonetic distortions. I shall therefore concentrate on this particular condition—conduction aphasia—with regard to my argument about phonemic paraphasias and related entities.

In right-handed adult literates, and in its archetypical form, conduction aphasia is believed to be the result of a focal lesion of the left supramarginal gyrus and underlying arcuate fasciculus (Geschwind, 1974). Such a lesion apparently disturbs neuronal nets which are somehow involved in the selection of phonemes within the context of units of a higher order of complexity (Lecours, Deloche, & Lhermitte, 1973); serial integration of phonemes is also involved, in a secondary manner, that is, phonemes are often uttered out of turn, for instance in metatheses and assimilations, but the production remains phonologically rule-governed (Lecours & Rouillon, 1976). With regard to spoken discourse, the two cardinal manifestations of conduction aphasia are a word-finding difficulty and a production of phonemic deviations. Although they can be dissociated clinically, both of these bear on the same verbal classes and it is not infrequent for one to observe, in relation to the same word, delayed evocation followed by production of phonemic deviations. As a result of this, one has the overall impression that the word-finding difficulty of conduction aphasics and their particular perturbation in encoding are but two aspects of a same dysfunction specifically involving open class words and, therefore, one finds it difficult to establish a clear-cut distinction, in conduction aphasia, between disorder in lexical access and disorder in lexical production.

Conduction aphasia interferes with all forms of spoken expression (conversational speech, naming, repetition, and, often to a lesser degree and for a shorter period, reading aloud). The speech of conduction aphasics comprises several types of phonemic deviations; the main ones are *phonemic paraphasias, phonemic télescopages,* and *formal verbal paraphasias (Cf. supra)*. Phonemic paraphasias constitute the basic type, of which the others can be considered as variants.

2.1. Phonemic Paraphasias

Phonemic paraphasias are neologisms that can be described, by reference to a positively identified target, in terms of deletions, additions, and/or displacements of phonemes, much less frequently of syllables, or in terms of various combinations between these three elementary operations (Lecours & Lhermitte, 1969). Such combinations end up in one or several interphonemic substitutions. Examples (1) to (7), all of which were produced by the same conduction aphasic in the course of repetition test (single words presented isolatedly), illustrate the notion of phonemic paraphasia:

1. *descendant* (offspring): /dɛsãdã/ → /dɛsdã/;
2. *poulailler* (hen-house): /pulaje/ → /apulje/;
3. *déambulant* (sauntering): /deãbylã/ → /debãbylã/;
4. *sécurité* (security): /sekyRite/ → /sykRite/;
5. *solidarité* (solidarity): /sɔlidaRite/ → /sɔledaRite/;
6. *aviculteur* (poultry-farmer): /avikyltœR/ → /vatikyltœR/;
7. *abominable* (abominable): /abɔminabl/ → /amɔninabl/.

Examples (1) to (3) respectively illustrate elementary operations, i.e., simple deletion, simple addition, and simple metathesis; examples (4) to (6) illustrate simple substitution resulting from the co-occurrent application of two elementary operations; example (7) illustrates double substitution resulting from the co-occurrent application of three elementary operations. (And so forth.) Quite often, several deviations of this sort can thus transform a single target. This is the case in examples (8) to (10):

8. *grand-oncle* (great-uncle): /gRãtɔ̃kl/ → /gRɔ̃tãgl/;
9. *malhabile* (clumsy): /malabil/ → /amalabim/;
10. *agent de police* (police agent): /aʒãdœpɔlis/ → /aplaʒãdœplɔtis/.

Example (8) comprises a reciprocal metathesis and a simple substitution by anterograde assimilation; example (9) comprises an addition by anticipation as well as an anterograde assimilation combined to an anterograde dissimilation; and let us leave example (10) for the computer to decode.[2]

As a manifestation of the word finding difficulties of conduction aphasics, the production of phonemic paraphasias is interesting in several manners. One of the most striking is that it bears near exclusively on open class words. This has been substantiated by a study that Renée Willems (1979) has made of a conversation I had had with a patient presenting archetypical conduction aphasia (Table 1). The patient uttered 1923 words in the course of this conversation. It should be noted that, in the discourse of this patient, the predilection of the disorder for lexical words is, roughly, twice as manifest for names as it is for adjectives, twice as manifest for adjectives as it is for nouns, and twice as manifest for nouns as it is for verbs: These figures indicate—but this could be an artefact—progressively greater fragility with decrease in frequency of word class. Be that as it may, the greater involvement of names constitutes another illustration of a long known fact: For a large majority of (non-agrammatic) aphasics—and for standard speakers as well—names are likely to give rise to difficulties in word retrieval more than any other types of words.

TABLE 1

	A	B		C	
NAMES	11	40	(2.1%)	27	(67.5%)
ADJECTIVES	54	72	(3.7%)	22	(30.6%)
NOUNS	104	266	(13.8%)	42	(15.8%)
VERBS	54	325	(16.9%)	25	(7.7%)
ARTICLES	8	201	(10.5%)	1	(0.5%)
PRONOUNS	25	378	(19.7%)	1	(0.3%)
PREPOSITIONS	13	210	(10.9%)	0	
CONJUNCTIONS	10	99	(5.2%)	0	

TABLE 1   Distribution of phonemic deviations, in open and in closed class words, in the discourse of a patient with archetypical conduction aphasia. Total production: 1923 words. (A) number of different words in class. (B) number of words in class and percentage by reference to total production. (C) number of words in class that led to phonemic deviations and percentage of phonemic deviations by reference to number of words in class.

Another fact deserving mention (as well as systematic confirmation) has to do with lexical words comprising both lexemic and morphological components: It is my very definite impression that phonemic deviations, as a

---

[2]Given current arguments concerning phonemes *versus* syllables as fundamental units in speech perception, one might suggest that the very existence of phonemic—rather than syllabic—paraphasias in the discourse of literate conduction aphasics pleads in favor of phonemes as fundamental units in speech production. Of course, one still has to find out about illiterate conduction aphasics.

nearly absolute rule, bear primarily or exclusively on the lexemic rather than on the morphological components of lexical words; in the few instances of affix or verb ending involvement, the lexeme is also involved, as a rule, and interdependency between lexemic and morphological involvement is usually manifest. The latter is illustrated by example (11):

11. *Il finissait* (He was finishing): *Il* /finisɛ/ → *Il* /fisinɛ/,

in which there occurs a reciprocal metathesis involving one phoneme from the lexeme and one from the verb ending.

Thus, from this first set of observations on phonemic paraphasias, one can conclude not only that there are circumstances in which the brain honors a distinction between closed and open class words, but also that there are circumstances in which it honors a distinction between closed and open class morphemes. One might of course add that the brain also honors, when disturbed by conduction aphasia, a distinction between shorter and longer words, or perhaps between more frequent and less frequent words. This was clear, for example, in the single word repetition data obtained by Poncet, Degos, Deloche, & Lecours (1972) (Table 2).

TABLE 2

	1 SYLLABLE	2 SYLLABLES	3-4 SYLLABLES
% Pm.P.	13.7%	25.5%	38.3%

TABLE 2 Conduction aphasia (8 patients). Single word repetition (150 monosyllabics; 50 bisyllabics; 100 tri- and quadrisyllabics). Percentage of stimuli leading to at least one phonemic deviation.

At first sight, the data in Table 2 seem to indicate, at least for monosyllabics and bisyllabics, that the probability for the production of phonemic deviations in a given word is directly proportional to the number of syllables in this word. This, however, is only part of the story since the presence of consonantic clusters in the words to be retrieved and produced is also a factor linked to an increase in the number of phonemic deviations.

I shall not turn to a second set of observations pertaining to the neologistic productions of conduction aphasics and to their difficulties in lexical access. The leading clue, this time, is that conduction aphasics are aware, on the whole, of the unconventional nature of their phonemic deviations and often try to correct them. Their successive attempts at correction then result in what Joanette, Keller, & Lecours (1980a) have called *sequences of phonemic approximations*. Examples (12) and (13) illustrate this notion:

12. *J'ai été ensuite chargé . . . . d'interroger des prisonniers allemands.*
    (I was then charged . . . . to question German prisoners.)
12. *d'interroger* (to question): *d'*/ɛ̃teR ʒe/ → *d'*/ɛ̃tɛg/↓ deↆ

d'/ɛ̃teʀɔg/↓ .... d'/ɛ̃teʀɔ/↓ oui, d'/ɛ̃teʀɔge/;

13. *. . . sous de grands sacs de jute qui sentaient le cadavre.* (. . . under large gunny bags which smelled of cadaver.)

13. *cadavre* (cadaver): *le* /kadavʀ/ → *le* /tavaʀ/↓ *le* /tʀava/↓ . . . . *le* /ka/↓ *le* /kava/↓ *le* /kadʀav/↓ *le* /kadavʀ/.

On the whole,—and patients often comment that speaking slower helps a lot in this respect,—such sequences end up in the conduction aphasic getting closer to his target, as in (12), or even realizing a complete correction, as in (13). This can be demonstrated by considering interphonemic substitutions only and by measuring, in terms of common features and phoneme by phoneme, the similarity between each of the successive approximations, on the one hand, and the target, on the other hand. The data presented here in this respect (Fig. 1) bear on 140 sequences of approximations—such as (12)

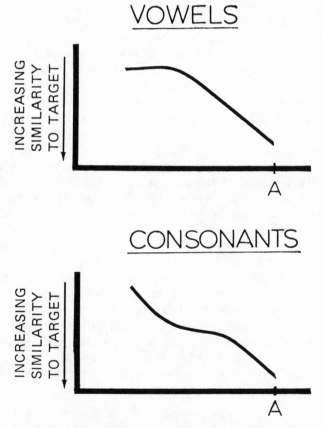

FIG. 1   Conduction aphasia (8 patients). Tape recorded conversations; 140 sequences of phonemic approximations; similarity between each of the last four approximations and the target (see text). "A" corresponds to the last approximation.

and (13)—excerpted from tape recorded conversations with conduction aphasics. Only the last four approximations were taken into account whenever a sequence comprised more than four.

The story behind these data is rather clear: On the one hand, the difficulty of conduction aphasics with regard to lexical words does not involve semantics and, on the other hand, conduction aphasics do retain, in some manner, an internal phonemic representation of the lexical words that they cannot access and/or produce conventionally. The latter is demonstrated both by the progressive improvement usually observed in sequences of phonemic approximations, which can only be attained through successive comparisons to some internal model, and by the fact that conduction aphasics do recognize target words—and neologisms—as such when they are proposed by an interlocutor. Moreover, when conduction aphasics abandon a sequence of phonemic approximations at a point where the target word has been more or less closely approached without being entirely correct, and thereafter go on with the rest of their sentence, they often behave as if they considered their production good enough, given the context, for the listener to have reconstituted the target, that is, as if they considered their production adequate for their message to have been entirely understood. Since conduction aphasics are not at all anosognosic, this means that they do make hypotheses as to the amount of information that their listeners should have derived from syntactic context as well as from imperfect production of certain lexical words.

Now, the sequences of phonemic approximations uttered by conduction aphasics are frequently interrupted by various events that have their origin either in the discourse of the patients or in that of their interlocutors. Joanette, Keller, Viau, & Lecours (1980b) have studied these events. They have found, for instance, in conversational speech, that an explicit slowing of the production significantly increase the chances for the speaker to get closer to his target or to reach it, which probably indicates that time— remember Jacques Lordat's (1843) comments about his own aphasia?—is an important factor in the course of successive comparisons to internal models. A positive effect has also been found, in conversational language, when the interlocutor provides either a phonemic or a verbal induction to the missing form[3], which shows that conduction aphasics are capable of paliating their difficulty in lexical access and/or production by taking various clues into account, including syntactic and semantic ones. On the other hand, interruption of a sequence of phonemic approximations by an

---

[3]Verbal induction occurs when the interlocutor tries to facilitate conventional production by uttering an incomplete sentence that provides a strongly determinant context for the involved word. Phonemic induction occurs when the interlocutor tries to facilitate by uttering the first phoneme or syllable of the involved word.

emotional reaction, such as a swear, has been shown to exert an adversive effect, which shows that conduction aphasics are human too.

If context, as we have just seen, can be a factor in the rectifications made by conduction aphasics on the lexical components of their discourse, it can also be a factor in their errors. This becomes obvious when a word—usually a lexical one—that has already been uttered or one that is shortly forthcoming determines in part the structure of a phonemic deviation. This notion is illustrated by example (14):

14. . . . *avec de la vraie glaise grise.* (. . . with true gray clay.): *de la* /vRɛ glɛz gRiz/ → *de la* /gRɛ/ ǀ *de la* /vRɛ glɛz gRiz/,

in which the transformation of /vRɛ/ into /gRɛ/, in the forthcoming context of /glɛz/ and of /gRiz/, no doubt represents intermorphemic retrograde assimilation, a phenomenon that has been well documented by Sheila Blumstein (1973). The existence of such contaminations shows that the difficulty experienced by conduction aphasics in lexical access and/or production should be studied, at least when one considers conversational production, both by reference to specific targets and by reference to contextual events.

2.2. Synonymy and Phonemic Télescopages

I have said earlier that semantics are not involved in conduction aphasia. Further evidence in this respect is provided when patients, being incapable of conventional production of given lexical targets, formulate definitions of the intractable words. As in example (15), where the target word is {(antiques): *antiquités*}, this may in turn exert a facilitating influence:

15. /ɑ̃tikite/ → /ativite/ ǀ /ak/ ǀ /a/ ǀ An /akti/ ǀ Something that is old. Something ancient. Something ancient. /ɑ̃ti/ ǀ /ɑ̃tikite/.

A similar—and somewhat spectacular—behavior is observed when a conduction aphasic suddenly abandons a sequence of approximations that has gone astray and produces, without hesitation, an acceptable synonym. This behavior, which one might qualify as synonymy, is not infrequent. It is illustrated by the following two examples:

16. *J'étais encore au FRONT . . . . dans la BATAILLE.* (I was still on the BATTLE FRONT . . . . in the FIGHT.): *J'étais encore au* /fRɔ̃/ . . . → *J'étais encore au* /fɔ̃/ ǀ *sur le* /fɔ̃/ ǀ . . . . *sur le* /flɔ̃/ ǀ *le* /fa/ ǀ *le*ǀ *la*ǀ *dans*ǀ *dans la BATAILLE.*

17. *J'avais FINI . . . . Je venais de TERMINER mon droit.* (I had FINISHED . . . . I had just COMPLETED my studies in law.): *J'avais* /fini/ . . . → *J'avais* /fiji/ ǀ *Je venais de* /f/ ǀ *euh* /fi/ ǀ *TERMINER mon droit.*

Note, in (16), that the production of the synonym is prepared by an appropriate change in the gender of the article (see *le* and *la*). This is not uncommon and it shows that anticipatory syntactic constraints keep playing their role in the discourse of conduction aphasics (but see Hécaen, 1972).

The very fact that conduction aphasics remain capable of considering several possibilities when syntactic constraints require the production of a single lexical word occasionally—perhaps not more often than it does in the discourse of standard speakers—leads to the production of a particular type of neologism known as phonemic *télescopage* (which corresponds to the second of the three types of phonemic deviations I enumerated earlier). Phonemic *télescopages* are neologisms in which the listener can positively identify phonemic components borrowed from at least two potential targets. In the context of a sentence partially quoted in (13) *(Cf. supra)*, a patient thus hesitated between the words {(bag): *sac* /sak/} and {(±satchel): *sacoche* /sakɔʃ/}, which became explicit through further comments, and thereafter produced the neologism comprised in (18), /saʃk/:

18. . . . *sous de grands* {*sacs* or *sacoches*} *qui* . . . (. . . under large {bags *vs.* ±satchel} which . . .): *sous de grands* /sak/ + /sakɔʃ/ → *sous de grands* /saʃk/.

Obviously, the formal structure of phonemic *télescopages* is very much akin to that of the intermorphemic contaminations illustrated in (14): Indeed, the only difference is that the game is played, here, along the paradigmatic rather than the syntagmatic axis.

2.3. Formal Verbal Paraphasias

Formal verbal paraphasias, that is, replacement of a dictionary word by another dictionary word on the basis of formal kindship, constitute the third type of phonemic deviations. There was one formal verbal paraphasia in example (16) where, at one point, {(battle front): *front* /fʀɔ̃/} was replaced by {(bottom): *fond* /fɔ̃/}. Deviations of this type can be fairly frequent in the discourse of conduction aphasics. Obviously, they do not answer the definition I gave of *neologism*. Their kinship to phonemic paraphasias have nonetheless been demonstrated: A computer programmed to simulate the production of phonemic paraphasias also produced, without any instruction in this respect, a proportion of outputs that are assimilable to formal verbal paraphasias (Lecours et al., 1973). One can therefore suggest, with regard to the physiopathology of conduction aphasia, that a single disturbance might be at the origin of the production of both phonemic paraphasias and formal verbal paraphasias (Lecours, 1974).

3.   MORPHEMIC DEVIATIONS

Morphemic deviations occasionally occur in the discourse of standard speakers (see Anne Cutler's chapter in this volume). The same can be said of the discourse of patients with classical Wernicke's aphasia although the clinical picture, in this condition, usually does not comprise an abundant production of this particular type of neologism; I shall however report, in a moment, on a remarkable exception to this rule. Finally, the production of morphemic deviations—although not under this label—has long been known to belong with the clinical picture of glossomaniac schizophasia (Bobon, 1952).

3.1.   Derived Morphemic Deviations

There exist several types of morphemic deviations. The first one I will discuss is known as *derived morphemic deviation.* These are word-like entities made of at least one bona fide lexical morpheme and at least one bona fide affixial morpheme; although these entities answer the definition I gave of *neologism,* their constitutive morphemes are conventionally associated. One can therefore assert that the production of these particular neologisms is both phonologically and morphologically rule-governed. The notion of derived morphemic deviation is illustrated by example (19):

19. *Mon* /sɔld-aʒ/ — *si vous voulez* — *s'emploie différement.* (My /sɔld-aʒ/ — if you want — is employing itself differently.),

in which the neologism is made of a lexical element, /sɔld/, as in {(soldier): *soldat* /sɔld-a/}, and of a common French suffix, /aʒ/, the two being combined following a derivation rule that is very common in French.

My discussion of derived morphemic deviations will first bear on the discourse of a most exceptional patient with Wernicke's jargonaphasia (Lecours & Lhermitte, 1972), and then on a form of discourse that is characteristic of glossomaniac schizophasia (Lecours, Navet, & Ross-Chouinard, 1981).

3.1.1.   *Derived Morphemic Deviations in Wernicke's Jargonaphasia.* As observed in Western Europe and North America, the clinical picture of Wernicke's aphasia proper has been shown to result, in right-handed adults, of a focal lesion of the caudal half of the first temporal convolution in the left cerebral hemisphere. The jargon that characterizes the earlier phases of Wernicke's aphasia proper comprises an abundant production of phonemic paraphasias, formal verbal paraphasias, semantic verbal paraphasias, abstruse neologisms, and other forms of deviant entities. The speaker is anosognosic, that is, he apparently remains unaware of the unconventional nature of his utterances.

In the case I will now discuss, the jargon comprised relatively few abstruse neologisms and, again most exceptionally, it comprised a lot of derived morphemic deviations. Example (19), which I just quoted, was one of them.

The lexical components of the derived morphemic paraphasias, in this particular case, were sometimes borrowed from a word in the immediate context. This is illustrated by examples (20) and (21):

20. *On remballait à l'arrière. C'était un* /bal-aʒ/ *assez dur.* (We were packing behind the lines. It was a rather tough /bal-aʒ/.);
21. *C'est très* /fʀɑ̃s-jɛl/ *des Français, ça.* (This is very /fʀɑ̃s-jɛl/ of the French.).

In (20), the lexical component of /bal-aʒ/ is obviously borrowed from a prepositioned word, {(were packing): *remballait* /ʀɑ̃-bal-ɛ/}; in (21), the lexical component of /fʀɑ̃s-jɛl/ is obviously borrowed from a post-positioned word, {(French): *Français* /fʀɑ̃-ɛ/}. As to their lexical components, the structure of these neologisms thus corresponds to anterograde and retrograde assimilations, which shows that contextual interferences of this sort can bear on morphemes as well as on phonemes; Nespoulous and Lecours (1980) have shown that they can also bear on discursive entities of a level of complexity greater than that of the morpheme.

In the great majority of cases, it was not possible for the listener of this patient's discourse to make reasonable hypotheses as to the speaker's targets nor, indeed, to be at all sure that there were in fact conventional targets behind the patient's derived morphemic deviations. In a few cases, however, such hypotheses could be made from strong contextual clues. As a rule, the lexical components of the neologisms were then apparently chosen in a manner very much akin to that observed in the semantic verbal paraphasias (*Cf. supra*) of Wernicke's aphasics. This is illustrated by example (22), where the obvious target word is {(spare time): *loisirs*}. The patient had just been asked if he practiced sports:

22. *Dès que j'aurai des LOISIRS, je m'y remettrai.* (As soon as I have SPARE TIME, I will start again.) → *Dès que j'aurai des* /pʀɔmn-aʒ/, *je* etc. (As soon as I have /pʀɔmn-aʒ/, I etc.).

The lexical component in this neologism, /pʀɔmn/, is obviously the same as in {(walking): *promenade* /pʀɔmn-ad/}: as in semantic verbal paraphasias, therefore, it shares semic elements with the (presumed) target word. Another easily detected example of this occurred when the patient, explicitly aiming at {(America): *Amérique* /ameʀ-ik/} after having spoken of {(Algeria): *Algérie* /alʒeʀ-i/}, transformed his target in the following manner:

23. *En Amérique? Non.* (In America? No.) → *En* /alʒeʀ-ik/? *Non.* (In /alʒeʀ-ik/? No.).

With regard to choice of lexical components, the neologisms for which a one-to-one contextual (20; 21) and/or paradigmatic (22; 23) semantic influence could be unraveled were thus relatively few. On the other hand, concerning a fair number of those in which such an influence could not be detected, it was striking that their lexical components belonged with the military-paramilitary paradigm (an interesting fact given that the patient was a general of the French army). Quotations (24) to (27) exemplify this point:

24. *Ce n'est pas le⎮ le* /fɔʀs-jal/ *habituel—si vous voulez—qui⎮* (It is not the⎮ the usual /fɔʀs-jal/—if you want—which⎮);
25. *Ca n'intéresse personne les⎮ les⎮ les* /blɑ̃ʃ-aʒ/ *avec les gens du sud.* (Nobody is interested by the⎮ the⎮ the /blɑ̃ʃ-aʒ/ with the people from the South.);
26. *Mais⎮ Mais c'est⎮ c'est pas des* /fɔʀm-œtyʀ/ *brillantes.* (But⎮ But these are⎮ these are not brilliant /fɔʀm-œtyʀ/.);
27. *Ca sera difficile comme⎮ comme* /flɑ̃b-yʒ/, *ça.* (This will be difficult as a⎮ as a /flɑ̃b-yʒ/.).

Besides 49 phonemic paraphasias, which were distributed more or less as in the case of conduction aphasia described previously (Table 1), the long conversation I had with General X comprised 250 other neologisms, most of them derived morphemic deviations. Like his phonemic paraphasias, the latter occurred within a very fluent conventional syntactic framework, i.e., they occurred in place of lexical words, nouns in particular, with a predilection for direct objects among nouns (Table 3). This production therefore provided further validation for a fundamental distinction between close and open class words, i.e., it testified to the existence of a particular difficulty in lexical access or retrieval or something. Nonetheless, this difficulty differed from that linked to the production of phonemic paraphasias. On the one hand, there existed a major difference in that the listener very seldom had evidence that the General's neologisms replaced particular target words: Indeed, the specific message, if any, was near totally lost (at best, one perceived that the General was talking about military things—see examples 24 to 27). On the other hand, in the very few cases when there was reasonable evidence as to the existence of a particular target word, this was because of exceptionally rich contextual clues (see examples 22 and 23), never because of formal similarity between target and actual utterance; moreover, no sequences of approximations ever occurred in this case that might have shown that the speaker had retained a capacity to compare his deviant productions to some internal models of his presumed targets.

Further evidence of the General's difficulty with the retrieval of lexical words was provided by the fact that the production of his morphemic devia-

TABLE 3

			203 NOUNS:		
NOUNS:	203	(81.2%)	DIRECT OBJECTS:	100	(49.3%)
ADJECTIVES:	25	(10.0%)	INDERECT OBJECTS:	53	(26.1%)
VERBS:	11	(4.4%)	COMPLEMENTS OF NOUNS:	35	(17.2%)
NAMES:	6	(2.4%)	SUBJECTS:	12	(5.9%)
LEXICAL ADVERBS:	1	(0.4%)	ATTRIBUTES:	3	(1.5%)
ARTICLES:	0		11 VERBS:		
PRONOUNS:	0		AUXILIARIES:	0	
PREPOSITIONS:	0		INFINITIVES:	0	
CONJUNCTIONS:	0		PARTICIPLES:	10	
RELATIVES:	0		DECLINED VERBS:	1	
UNDIFFERENTIATED:	4	(1.6%)			

TABLE 3 Distribution of 250 derived morphemic deviations (and abstruse neologisms) in the context of the conversational discourse of a patient with Wernicke's aphasia proper. All of the neologisms occur in place of lexical words, particularly of nouns.

tions (and abstruse neologisms) disrupted the flow of his discourse more often than did the production of conventional lexical words, whether the latter were adequately chosen or not (Table 4). In order to substantiate this,

TABLE 4

	NEOLOGISMS (101)	CONTROL WORDS (182)
WITHOUT DISRUPTIONS:	29.7% (30)	55.5% (101)
WITH DISRUPTIONS:	70.3% (71)	44.5% (81)
HESITATIONS:	45.5% (46)	25.8% (47)
REPETITIONS:	61.4% (62)	31.9% (58)
COMMENTS:	16.8% (17)	6.0% (11)
before item:	5.9% (6)	2.7% (5)
after item:	10.9% (11)	3.3% (6)

TABLE 4   Wernicke's aphasia proper (jargon comprising a production of derived morphemic paraphasias). Distribution of disruptive events (HESITATIONS, REPETITIONS, COMMENTS) in relation to the production of 101 noun-like and adjective-like neologisms as opposed to 282 nouns and adjectives (verbal paraphasias included).

Lecours, Travis, and Nespoulous (1980b) have studied these disruptions as they occurred, within the first 15 minutes of an interview with the patient, in relation to 101 noun-like and adjective-like neologisms, on the one hand, and, on the other hand, in relation to 182 nouns and adjectives (verbal paraphasias included). Three types of disruptions were considered: HESITATIONS (i.e., filled and empty pauses) related to a neologism or control word, REPETITIONS of an article, preposition, etc., related to a neologism or control word, and COMMENTS related to the production of a neologism or control word. The notion of repetition is illustrated by examples (24) to (27). Comments were *a parte* utterances such as *"Si vous voulez"* (If you want) and *"Comment dirais-je?"* (How could I say?): This is exemplified in examples (19) and (24). These disruptive events, comments in particular, could occur after as well as before the considered item. As in (24), where both repetition and comment took place, more than one type of disruption could occur in relation to a single item.

Like other Wernicke's aphasics, the General had retained a capacity to abide by phonetic and phonological conventions, and he experienced a pathological tendency to keep talking and talking, a phenomenon known as *logorrhea* (or ±*pressure of speech*). On the other hand, he showed evidence of a tremendous reduction in access to lexical stocks. He thus had to solve the paradox facing one who has good reasons to talk and good reasons to shut up: Apparently, given his preserved capacity to build as many morphosyntactic infrastructures as needed, he could only adapt to his functional deficit—under the pressure of syntactic constraints (if I can once more resort to simplistic terms)—by filling the lexical gaps with neologistic (and paraphasic) entities.

Be that as it may, the General also showed, as Wernicke's jargonaphasics do, *anosognosia* for his language disorder, that is, he acted as if he was unaware of the anomalous nature of his neologistic productions. But was he really? Or, rather, how total is the anosognosia of Wernicke's jargon-aphasics? Does not the distribution of disruptive events, especially those following neologisms, comments in particular, indicate that momentary awareness of some sort occurs at some level just after or just before neologistic production? I will come back to this in the context of my discussion of abstruse neologisms.

3.1.2. *Derived Morphemic Deviations in Glossomaniac Schizophasia.* As noted earlier, a predominant production of derived morphemic deviations represents a most exceptional fact in Wernicke's aphasia (and it never occurs in other forms of aphasia). On the other hand, it constitutes as far as I know a necessary element of a particular discursive behavior known as glossomaniac schizophasia (Lecours et al., 1981). Although the terminology is not the same, this is apparent in the numerous quotations found in the dissertation of Michel Cénac (1925) and in that of Jean Bobon (1952), as well as in a case study published long ago by Lévy-Valensi, Migault, and Lacan (1931). Glossomaniac schizophasia is an episodical discursive behavior that is sometimes—indeed very seldom, nowadays—observed in schizophrenia and probably in mania as well. This discursive behavior comprises several forms of unconventional entities, including phonemic, morphemic, and verbal deviations, as well as abstruse neologisms. The schizophasic speaker is perfectly aware of the unconventional nature of his discursive behavior: Upon request, he will comment, for instance, on the signification of a particular neologism he has uttered. In my opinion, there is no evidence—in spite of a number of intriguing articles that have been recently published in psychiatric books and journals (Abrams & Taylor, 1979; DiSimoni, Darley, & Aronson, 1977; Flor-Henry, 1973, 1976; Gur, 1978, 1979; Rieder, Donnelly, Herdt, & Waldman, 1979; Wexler & Heninger, 1979)—indicating that schizophrenia and mania, with or without schizophasia, might be related to lesion or structural anomaly of the brain.

The following quotation, excerpted from the transcript of a tape-recorded conversation between Gil Assal and one of his schizophrenic patients, beautifully illustrates the use of derived morphemic deviations in glossomaniac schizophasia. It comprises three derived morphemic deviations, /a-paʒ-e/, /a-paʒ-mã/, and /a-paʒ-ã/, as well as one composed morphemic deviation, *"page-commis" (Cf. infra),* and one abstruse neologism, /kʀwado/ *(Cf. infra):*

28. *Et on a, à ce classement, un* /kʀwado/, *qui est le premier* /apaʒe/, *ou premier PAGE-COMMIS de bureau. Mais un clerc d'*/apaʒmã/ *du métier! C'est-à-dire qu'un* /apaʒã/ *lui met l'abécédaire dans les*

mains. Et il commencera. (And one has, with this classification, a /kʀwado/, who is the first /apaʒe/, or else the first PAGE-CLERK of the office. But an /apaʒmã/ cleric of the trade┃ I mean to say that an /apaʒã/ puts the abecedary in his hands. And he will start.).

As obvious from this quotation, the main difference between the derived morphemic deviations in schizophasic speech as opposed to those in the jargon of General X pertains not to morphology but to semantics: Their signification is readily apprehended in the former, but not in the latter. It is immediately manifest, in (18), that an /apaʒe/ is one who has been made a page-boy, that /apaʒmã/ means the fact of becoming a page-boy, and that an /apaʒã/ is one who makes someone else a page-boy. This is so much so that one might easily accept "appaged", "appagement" or "appaging", and "appageant" or "appageator", as likely English translations of these French neologisms. I might add that the listener understands not only because of the contextual richness, which in itself constitutes a most unaphasic feature, but mainly because of the qualities inherent to the morphemic deviations themselves. (The same could be said of the entities discussed by Cutler, in this volume.)

I do not yet have quantitative data on the discourse of glossomaniac schizophasics. Nonetheless, I have very closely examined several transcripts, some of them rather long, thus observing that derived morphemic deviations, in this type of discourse, occur exclusively in place of lexical words, with an overwhelming predilection for nouns and predicative adjectives. I have also observed that disruptive events also occur, in glossomaniac schizophasia, in relation to the production of derived morphemic deviations. The latter is illustrated by the REPETITION in (29) and by the COMMENT in (30):

29. *Il est à porte de communale┃ de communale┃ de┃ de* /duanʀi/ /akapital/. (He is at the door of the Commune┃ of the Commune┃ of the┃ of the /duanʀi/ /akapital/.)[4];
30. *Il sent les* /pʀɛsyʀ/ *d'autour—n'est-ce pas?—et là* . . . (He perceives the surrounding /pʀɛsyʀ/—is it not?—and then . . .)[4].

Glossomaniac schizophasics thus have difficulties of their own in lexical choices, and the overt manifestations of these difficulties are not—in certain respects—unlike those observed in Wernicke's jargonaphasia. The schizophasic's problem, however, is not that he lacks standard words to account for standard thought, as does the aphasic, but rather that he regularly creates new words in an attempt to account for his very particular—and

---

[4]/duan-ʀi/: noun-like, ± border line, institutions related to customs duties. /a-kapit-al/: adjective-like, ± a geographical entity without a chief town. /pʀɛs-yʀ/: noun-like, ± external constraints.

often paradoxical *(Cf. infra)*—ideational preoccupations. As a matter of fact, the less docile of us, standard speakers, do just that when we wish—once in a while and parsimoniously, as a rule following HESITATION or REPETITION and with COMMENT—to give linguistic form to a not so conventional notion for which an appropriate bona fide word is not immediately accessible (or does not exist). By the way, this behavior is also very much—how could I say?—unaphasic. (For some reason, this kind of game is easier in English than it is in French. Or is it just easier in any language you happen to have learned relatively late in life?)

3.2. Composed Morphemic Deviations

The second type of morphemic deviation I will discuss is known as *composed morphemic deviation*. Composed morphemic deviations are (composed) word-like entities made of at least—and usually—two lexical morphemes. Although their constitutive morphemes are associated following conventional rules, these entities answer the definition I gave of *neologism* since they are not listed in dictionaries.

Composed morphemic deviations occasionally occur in the discourse of particularly indocile standard speakers; they very seldom if ever occur in the discourse of speakers with Wernicke's jargonaphasia; and, to the best of my knowledge, they constitute a necessary component of glossomaniac schizophasia. Quotation (31), which is excerpted from a conversation that Gil Assal had with his patient, illustrates the notion of composed morphemic deviation:

31. *Et alors, le vrai calendrier est différent du faux. Et le calendrier géorgien a été ainsi céé: ils l'ont fait d'un premier à un trente-et-un, et à plusieurs jours de⊢ de mois—n'est-ce pas?—de /ʒ/⊢ de nuit et jour et de JOUR-NUIT. Et le quinze avril est au quinze octobre, pour l'ÉTÉ-HIVER, et le quinze octobre est au quinze AVRIL-RÉ-AVRIL pour l'HIVER-ÉTÉ, de telle sorte qu'on passe un ÉTÉ-HIVER et un HIVER-ÉTÉ, de FROID-CHAUD ou de CHAUD-FROID.* (And then, the true calendar is different of the false one. And the Georgian calendar was thus created: They made it from a first to a thirty-first, and to a number of days of⊢ of months—is it not?—of /d/⊢ of night and day and of DAY-NIGHT. And the fifteenth of April corresponds to the fifteenth of October, for the SUMMER-WINTER, and the fifteenth of October corresponds to the fifteenth of APRIL-RE-APRIL for the WINTER-SUMMER, so that one goes through a SUMMER-WINTER and a WINTER-SUMMER, with COLD-HOT or with HOT-COLD.).

As far as I know, and although one could imagine a few interesting compositions of grammatical words (such as ''before-after,'' ''above-below,'' and so forth), composed morphemic deviations only occur as open class entities. As a matter of fact, they are used as nouns in nearly all cases. Although this remains to be documented quantitatively, it is my impression that the production of composed morphemic deviations does not disrupt the flow of discourse more than does the production of standard lexical words, which might indicate that schizophasics, for some reason, master composition more easily than derivation.

A striking fact about the composed morphemic deviations of schizophasic speakers is that there nearly always exists a strong semantic relationship between their lexical components; moreover, this relationship is nearly always—as far as I know—one linking the components along the paradigmatic rather than the syntagmatic axis. This is illustrated by *"page-commis"* (page-clerk) in quotation (28), as well as by all of the eight neologisms in quotation (31). As in seven of the latter {*"jour-nuit"* (day-night), *"été-hiver"* (summer-winter), *"chaud-froid"* (hot-cold), etc.}, the semantic relationship if often one of antonymy: These particular neologisms thus represent the simplest form of a long known feature of schizophasic discourse that several authors have identified as *opposite speech* (Andreasen, 1979; Laffal, 1965); more complex forms of this behavior have been discussed elsewhere (Lecours et al., 1981).

In my opinion, the production of composed morphemic deviations, whether it be by schizophasics or by other categories of speakers, such as punners and poets, for instance, constitutes a particularly clear demonstration of the possibility of an adaptation of linguistic mechanisms—in the present case, those related to the semantic aspects of lexical retrieval—to an unconventional mode of ideation. To the best of my knowledge, this does not apply to aphasia and, indeed, composed morhemic deviations are the only type of neologisms that I have never observed as a significant component of jargonaphasic discourse.

4. ABSTRUSE NEOLOGISMS IN WERNICKE'S APHASIA

Within the domain of speech pathology, *abstruse neologisms* are observed to occur in the discourse of aphasics and in that of schizophasics. These neologisms constitute a composite group. In fact, I use this label to designate any word-like entity that cannot be positively identified as a phonemic paraphasia (or related entity), nor as a morphemic deviation; which underlines the fact that the attribution of these labels is a matter often determined not only by the speaker's (in)competence as an encoder but also by listener's (in)competence as a decoder. Having observed jargonaphasics whose discourse, during the earlier phases of their disease, comprised an abundant production of abstruse neologisms and, in later phases, turned out to be full of identifiable phonemic paraphasias, I am quite sure that my use of the label *abstruse neologism* covers my own in-capacities as much as my patient's, that is, I am quite sure that a number of entities that I consider to be abstruse neologisms are in fact phonemic paraphasias that I cannot recognize as such. I have also observed, in the written productions of Wernicke's aphasics, a similar evolution from jargonagraphia to dysorthographia. In brief, it is probable that a number of abstruse neologisms do represent the transformation of specific target words. Whether or not these are conventionally selected is a different matter.

There are sometimes favorable circumstances in which one can further study the structure of abstruse neologisms. Consider, for instance, quotation (32):

32. *C'est une* /kyklyʀ/. (It is a /kyklyʀ/.).

When the patient—a Wernicke's aphasic—produced this utterance, I could only identify /kyklyʀ/ as an abstruse neologism, but then he corrected to {(fence): *clôture* /klotyʀ/}, which was not yet quite correct since his target finally turned out to be {(window): *fenêtre*}. Therefore, this not so abstruse neologism was in fact a compounded semantic and phonemic paraphasia, i.e., the patient's difficulty involved both semantic and phonemic aspects of lexical retrieval and/or production:

32. {(window): *fenêtre*} → {(fence): *clôture* /klotyʀ/} → /kyklyʀ/.

It takes few of these to make one's conversation rather difficult to follow. I suspect that this is not infrequent in Wernicke's jargonaphasia.

Besides the fact that it is phonologically rule-governed, another interesting point concerning the linear structure of abstruse neologisms (in Wernicke's aphasia) is that a number of them—and the proportion no doubt varies with patients—begin and/or finish on an element that the listener perceives as a bona fide affix of the speaker's mother tongue. This is illustrated by quotation (33):

33. *Elle prenait* . . . *le* /namyt-yʀ/, *la* /tɔkt-œʀ/, *et l'*/ɑ̃-bœt-jɛʀ/, *pour qu'elle sache tous ces*↓ *ces choses, pour qu'elle sache*[5] *à bien s'*/ɛ̃-skʀym-e/↓ *à bien*↓ *bien s'*/ɛ̃/↓ *bien s'*/ɛ̃-kym-e/. (She took . . . the /namyt-yʀ/, the /tɔkt-œʀ/, and the /ɑ̃-bœt-jɛʀ/, in order to learn all these↓ these things, in order to learn[5] at correctly /ɛ̃-skʀym-e/ herself↓ at correctly↓ correctly /ɛ̃/↓ /ɛ̃-kym-e/ herself.).

Incidentally, Andrew Kertesz (1980) recently told me that neologisms occurring in place of participles and finishing with an "ed" morpheme are frequent in the discourse of English speaking Wernicke's jargonaphasics. My suggestion, with regard to this particular subgroup of abstruse neologisms,

---

[5] A verbal paraphasia by anterograde assimilation.

is that some of them might well represent the result of compounded opera-tions in which the lexical components of derived morphemic deviations are further transformed by phonemic paraphasias. Well, I'm guessing.

A fourth point, about abstruse neologisms, is that there are cases in which a large proportion of them borrow their phonemic components to (lexical) words of the immediate context (Buckingham & Kertesz, 1976). Consider, for instance, quotation (34) in which an abstruse neologism, /asɑ̃Rwe/, used as an infinitive, borrows most of its phonemic components to an infinitive in the immediate context {(to get better): *arranger* /aRɑ̃ʒe/}:

> 34. *Attendez de vous {arranger* /aRɑ̃ʒe/}, *de vous* /asɑ̃Rwe/. (Wait till you get better, till you /asɑ̃Rwe/.).

In entities such as (34), there is no way for the listener to find out for sure if the production is targetted or utterly asemantic. Of course, one might sus-pect that, without being conventionally targetted on a particular word, these neologisms could borrow semic as well as formal components from the context. This might be the case in (34) where /asɑ̃Rwe/, given the re-petition in syntactic context, would then become, more or less, a deviant synonym of its generator, /aRɑ̃ʒe/; and one could therefore consider these deviations as just another form of phonemic paraphasias. As a rule, how-ever, the syntactic context is such that the above interpretation does not come to mind as easily (although kinship to phonemic deviations remains quite possible). Consider (35), for instance, in which an abstruse neologism, /pale/, again an infinitive-like entity, shares its formal components not with an infinitive but with both a prepositioned name, {(Paris): *Paris* /paRi/}, and a postpositioned noun, or rather verbal paraphasia, {(palace): *palais* /palɛ/}:

> 35. *Tous les jours, elle venait à {Paris* /paRi/} *pour* /pale/ *dans les* /kɔsig/ *parce qu'elle prenait . . . . le {palais* /palɛ/} etc. (Every day, she came to Paris in order to /pale/ in the /kɔsig/ because she took . . . . the palace etc.).

If abstruse neologisms such as /pale/ are not asemantic, their eventual mean-ing would become sharable only if the speaker provided explanations. Wer-nicke's jargonaphasics never do that. Glossomaniac schizophasics, on the other hand, occasionally produce similar neologisms, and if asked to do so, will comment about their signification. This is illustrated in the following quotation of Assal's patient, in which an abstruse neologism, /gRosjomiʒ/, is uttered in the context of {(invectives): *grossièretés* /gRosjɛRte/} and defined as a kind of disease or as a kind of beast:

> 36. *. . . en allant dire des {grossièretés* /gRosjɛRte/}. *. . . . C'este une espèce de maladie, de* /gRosjomiʒ/.
>
> ASSAL: What is a /gRosjomiʒ/?
>
> *C'est une espèce de bête. Voilà. C'est un terme que j'ai créé, que*

j'ai fait, comme ça, pour⌐ pour donner une petite base personnelle, privée. Voilà.

(. . . by uttering invectives. . . . . It is a kind of disease, of /gʀosjomiʒ/.

ASSAL: What is a /gʀosjomiʒ/?

It is a kind of beast. That's that. It is a term that I created, that I made, like that, in order to⌐ to provide a little personal and private basis. That's that.).

The situation is thus quite clear in (36): On the one hand, theneologism borrows parts of its formal components from the context and there is no evidence that the speaker is aware of this and, on the other hand, the neologism is semantically targetted but not in line with a sharable convention. Schizophasics will be schizophasics; and I doubt that jargonaphasics, with their brain lesions, are at all capable of playing this kind of game.

In fact, there are cases of Wernicke's jargonaphasia in which the very structure of neologisms suggests that their semantic load, if any, might indeed be very thin. In such cases, abstruse neologisms are numerous and a majority of them seem to be formal variants of a single entity. A patient of François Lhermitte thus kept using, in place of lexical words, a preferential entity (Lhermitte, Lecours, Ducarne, & Escourolle, 1973):

37. /tʀefwɛlg/,

as well as several variants of it, such as:

37. /fʀɛlg/,
/ɛnfɛlg/,
/fɛfɛlg/,
/defɛld/, etc.

I have also observed a behavior of this sort in an epileptic patient whose spells took the form of a temporary aphasia (Lecours & Joanette, 1980). From one spell to another, this patient's neologism of predilection remained more or less the same:

38. /tuwaʀe/,
/twaʀe/,
/tuwaʀi/,
/tuʀuaʀi/, etc.

Given that this patient's linguistic capacities are normal between spells, his comments concerning his repeated experience of aphasia are indeed of particular interest: Although he remains globally aware—throughout his aphasic spells—of a difficulty in speech production and speech comprehension, and although he has invented tricks to hide his handicap and even to assess its regression, he remains totally unaware of the neologistic or paraphasic nature of his utterances; however, during the last phases of his episodes of paroxysmal aphasia, when neologistic production has disappeared, he becomes aware of a particular difficulty in lexical retrieval, and he states that any word that is accessible for inner formulation is also available for overt utterance.

Now, it should be clear from the above that abstruse neologisms, whatever the subtype, also occur in place of open class and not of closed class words. Let us consider, in this respect, the 447 abstruse neologisms that occurred in the context of a tape–recorded conversation I had with a Wernicke's aphasic displaying archetypical neologistic jargon (Table 5). As in the General's interview (Table 3), a majority of the neologisms occurred in place of nouns but this patient used verb-like neologisms four times more often than the General did; moreover, she did produce declined verb-like entities on 28 occasions. As in examples (39) to (41), most of these were perceived as declined verb-like entities without a particular ending (present tense, singular):

39. *Je m'/ɑ̃tid/ tous les jours* etc. (I /ɑ̃tid/ myself everyday etc.);
40. *Je /vɛstoʀmil/ mais* etc. (I /vɛstoʀmil/ but etc.);
41. *On me /depif/ toujours* etc. (People always /depif/ me etc.).

In a way, such neologisms provide particularly clear evidence of the specificity of neologistic production for lexical components of discourse (in the classical form of Wernicke's aphasia).

As in the case of the General (Table 4), further evidence of the patient's particular difficulty with the retrieval of lexical words was provided by the fact that the production of her abstruse neologisms disrupted the flow of her discourse more often than did the production of conventional lexical words, whether the latter were adequately chosen or corresponded to verbal paraphasias (Table 6). As in the General's corpus, this was documented by counting HESITATIONS, REPETITIONS, and COMMENTS as they occurred, during the first 15 minutes of the interview, in relation to 101 noun-like and adjective-like abstruse neologisms, on the one hand, and, on the other hand, in relation to 112 nouns and adjectives taken as control words. Given this patient's logorrhea, these results indicate that she faced, again like General X, the semeiological paradox inflicted upon one who has to deal, at the same time, with pressure of speech and with a major difficulty in lexical word retrieval.

Brian Butterworth (1979) recently analyzed the pauses in the discourse of a Wernicke's aphasic with neologistic jargon and documented a relative increase in the duration of pauses preceding the production of neologisms. He attributed this to a word-finding difficulty that he further characterized, in boxological terms, as "a failure in the mechanism which associates word-

TABLE 5

NOUNS:	284	(63.5%)	**284 NOUNS:**		
ADJECTIVES:	27	(6.0%)	DIRECT OBJECTS:	103	(36.3%)
VERBS:	74	(16.6%)	INDERECT OBJECTS:	39	(13.8%)
NAMES:	32	(7.2%)	COMPLEMENTS OF NOUNS:	107	(37.7%)
LEXICAL ADVERBS:	5	(1.1%)	SUBJECTS:	15	(5.3%)
			ATTRIBUTES:	20	(7.0%)
ARTICLES:	0				
PRONOUNS:	0		**74 VERBS:**		
PREPOSITIONS:	0		AUXILIARIES:	0	
CONJUNCTIONS:	0		INFINITIVES:	12	(16.2%)
RELATIVES:	0		PARTICIPLES:	34	(45.9%)
			DECLINED VERBS:	28	(37.8%)
UNDIFFERENTIATED:	25	(5.6%)			

TABLE 5 Distribution of 447 abstruse neologisms in the context of the conversational discourse of a patient with Wernicke's aphasia proper and archetypical neologistic jargon. All of the neologisms occur in place of lexical words, particularly of nouns.

TABLE 6

	NEOLOGISMS (101)	CONTROL WORDS (112)
WITHOUT DISRUPTIONS:	28.7% (29)	58.0% (65)
WITH DISRUPTIONS:	71.3% (72)	42.0% (47)
HESITATIONS:	57.4% (58)	36.6% (41)
REPETITIONS:	40.6% (41)	17.9% (20)
COMMENTS:	23.8% (24)	2.7% (3)
before item:	9.9% (10)	(0)
after item:	13.9% (14)	2.7% (3)

TABLE 6   Wernicke's aphasia proper (archetypical neologistic jargon). Distribution of disruptive events (HESITATIONS, REPETITIONS, COMMENTS) in relation to the production of 101 (sic) noun-like and adjective-like abstruse neologisms as opposed to 112 nouns and adjectives (verbal paraphasias included).

sounds with word-meanings," and added that "The patient strategically adapts to this functional impairment by substituting a neologism when lexical search fails." I guess that the above data on disruptions (Table 6) might be taken as a confirmation of Butterworth's interpretation in the case of disruptions preceding abstruse neologisms. Disruptions following abstruse neologisms, on the other hand, might indicate—as in the case of the General (Cf. supra)—that, in spite of overall anosognosia, momentary awareness of some sort can occur at the moment of neologistic production. In fact, some of the 14 comments that my patient made after uttering an abstruse neologism leave little doubt in this respect. Consider, for instance, quotations (42) and (43):

42. . . . mon /Rɑ̃po/ était parti . . . . à /laʒ/↓ /salɛmɔn/↓ oui /salmɔn/↓ /salɛmɔn/↓: je ne sais plus! (. . . my /Rɑ̃po/ had left . . . . for /laʒ/↓ /salɛmɔn/↓ yes: /salmɔn/↓ /salɛmɔn/↓: I do not know any longer!);
43. Il y a↓ Il y a des /ʃastRy/: ça↓ ça n'existe pas! (There are↓ There are some /ʃastRy/: This↓ this does not exist!).

In both quotations, it is quite clear that the speaker entertains doubts as to the adequacy of her utterances.

5.   GLOSSOLALIA IN APHASIA AND SCHIZOPHASIA

I will now turn, briefly, to another form of neologistic production known as glossolalia. Glossolalia is a fluent discourse-like behavior that a qualified listener will perceive as being entirely neologistic or nearly so. Such a behavior is sometimes—in fact, very seldom—observed in Wernicke's aphasia (glossolalic jargonaphasia), always in elderly patients, and it is sometimes observed in schizophrenia (*glossolalic schizophasia*). Moreover, it is common among pentecostal believers, who consider it to be a God-given charism, and there are non-aphasic-non-schizophasic-non-believer individuals who are quite good at it. Quotation (44) is excerpted from the production of an aphasic, quotation (45) from the production of a schizophrenic, quotation (46) from the production of a charismatic, and quotation (47) from the production of a rather normal friend:

44. /sε̃ dikte di tʀ⁵ k⁵deʀe dʀik⁵dedeʀe digœʀe dis tis tilave kl⊃ʀe œ le d∅ tʀ⁵ke ditibεdœʀe disœ te kotegoʀe dil k⁵deteʀe/ /a wi dœ vilε̃bʀiʃ ʒe la lã̃bet⊃ʀi de dεl lã̃tetεʀœeme di kateg⊃ʀe/ /e œ e εlzekute εlmœepuʀimak⁵te tã̃ tutse dœgʀedœegʀe dis gy lateʀe digeloteʀe/;

45. /la ʀœk⁵fj⊃ʀanis ε̃tʀ⊃beʀ⊃gad bʀakal dœ ʀœk⁵fjεʀjanis ε̃tʀœbeʀ⊃gad bʀakal dœ ʀœk⁵fj⊃ʀjasj⁵ mã̃bʀal yn bʀibεʀgasj⁵ pineʀo peʀikal bʀabal dœ ʀœk⁵fjεʀjanis ε̃tʀ∅beʀ⊃gad bʀabal la ʀœk⊃mfj⊃ʀasj⁵ lastʀ∅ bœnalfjε̃ pineʀo peʀika bʀabal dœ ʀœk⊃mfjœʀjanis ε̃tʀ∅beʀœgal bʀakal ʀjanik/;

46. /putʃta jato amadea se atʃtu hoʀa o maʀia ʃtuja talasul e maʀja atunda asuja inʃtigoso jεtʃteni/ /o maʀja tuskundea deseu in dios kuna majʃte/ /o njanatʃe maʀjana idonjaʃte koskena ε no nj⊃nεskena/ /o niʃtεne maʀja tosε no no sw⊃ʃtεnei ε no εʃeʀo sw⊃ndinu udaʃse/;

47. /i evistimi tanto elevεnte bεste vanto elevεsti bika anevεnti mitistan elevεnti liministaʀe inivindi me dast⊃nte elekεsti kue tikanto eliminimista batεnto elevanta tεstamεnto alavinto e anvekemistan elividimistan elibidimistaj kede vete anto ivaj emindisti/.

Obviously, I do not claim that the segmentation I made of the above quotations is the only one possible.

The results of studies made in my laboratory about the structure of glossolalic discourse have been reported elsewhere (Lecours, Travis, & Osborn, 1980a). The following are some of the conclusions reached through these studies:

• The main difference between the aphasic glossolalic and other glossolalic speakers is that the aphasic cannot talk otherwise whereas the others can also talk conventionally. In several other respects, the glossolalia of Wernicke's aphasics shares more with the glossolalia of speakers without brain lesions than it shares with other forms of aphasic discourse.

• Glossolalia is not a form of cryptophasia but rather a learned game—and a rather simple one at that—founded on a capacity to maintain standard prosodical models (usually not those of ordinary conversation) and standard phonetics, while fluently uttering in line with simplified phonological and greatly impoverished morphosyntactical conventions. In unilinguals, the latter are usually borrowed from mother tongue.

• The distribution of phoneme-like and word-like entities in glossolalic discourse is very much unlike the distribution of phonemes and words in natural tongues. In fact, I suspect that a similar distribution of phoneme-like entities could be achieved through a simple Markovian process. The differences between glossolalia and natural tongues in this respect lead one to suggest that glossolalic discourse is asemantic. This behavior might thus provide evidence as to the possibility of dissociated functioning in the nerve nets responsible for speech production.

• As far as I know,—and this assertion is based on the study of more than twenty samples,—glossolalic discourse always comprises the repetitive use of families of isomorphic word-like entities such as:

48. /manakala/,
     /manakolo/,
     /monokolo/,
     /manaʃkala/,
     /manaʃkolo/, etc.

Obviously, these are mere variants of a single basic form and the rules through which they are generated are quite simple.

• As far as I know, glossolalic discourse always comprises the repetitive use of a few units that belong with a level of complexity greater than that of the phoneme and syllable, i.e., it comprises the production of a few morpheme-like entities. These are recognizable as such, as a rule, because they are borrowed from the speaker's mother tongue (or else, they correspond to hackneyed foreign prototypes). An overwhelming majority—or indeed all—of these loans are from closed class categories, such as articles, prepositions, conjunctions, affixes and so forth. This means that glossolalic behavior, although less clearly than other types of neologistic production, also supports the validity of a fundamental distinction between closed and open class entities. It might also mean that the basic trick behind glossolalic simulation is the replacement of lexical words by asemantic neologisms; the source of the latter could be a dissociated device applying a limited number of (learned) phonotactic rules more or less at random.

6. SUMMARY AND CONCLUSION

In this chapter, I attempted to deal simultaneously with three different issues, all of them related to the notion of neologism: [a] the characterization and classification of neologisms along linguistic lines; [b] the characterization of neologisms along psycholinguistic lines; and [c] the characterization of certain aphasic and schizophasic symptom-complexes by reference to neologistic production.

With regard to the latter, it should be clear from my discussion that the material I have observed, or rather the analysis I have made of it, has shown no qualitative difference between various types of aphasia and schizophasia as far as the linguistic characteristics of neologisms are concerned. Considered from a qualitative point of view, the linguistic characteristics of phonemic paraphasias are, for instance, the same in Broca's aphasia and in conduction aphasia. Or again, the abstruse neologisms of Wernicke's aphasics and those of glossomaniac schizophasics are qualitatively the same. As a matter of fact, providing one does not take articulatory disorders into account (dysarthrias, phonetic disintegration), the deviation sometimes observed in samples of ordinary, nonpathological discourse are also qualitatively similar, in their linguistic structures, to those in various aphasic and schizophasic discourses.

In most cases, however, one identifies schizophasic and jargonaphasic behaviors rather confidently when witnessing one or the other; and—outside of the meeting rooms at Royaumont—one seldom experiences major difficulties in distinguishing either from ordinary, nonpathological language behavior. Why this is so is obviously due, in part, to the attribution of diagnostic labels based on anamnestic data and on the observation of events and behaviors having little to do with language production proper. As a rule, nonetheless, a differential diagnosis between ordinary discourse, aphasia and schizophasia remains feasible on the sole basis of tape-recorded samples of sufficient length; this is the case even if one is not given pathognomonic information about the longitudinal evolution of the language disorder, such as mode of onset and changes in language behavior with time passing. In my opinion, a differential diagnosis established in these conditions resorts mainly to considerations of two orders: The first are linguistic in nature and pertain to quantitative appraisals of various types of neologisms and paraphasias; the second are psycholinguistic in nature and pertain to interpretations of the listener as to the speaker's intention and modes of ideation. Unless I am being deliberately misled by the productions of a qualified punner (or by those of a computer), I can recognize the discourse of a conduction aphasic because it comprises an abundant and nearly exclusive production of phonemic deviations, which is a quantitative linguistic appraisal, and because I can see evidence that the speaker is aware of his deviations, that he retains internal models of the lexical targets he cannot conventionally utter, and that he experiences no particular difficulty with semantics, which illustrate the type of psycholinguistic interpretations that a listener can resort to at the time of attributing labels. Likewise, I can distinguish Wernicke's jargonaphasia from glossomaniac schizophasia, even if both can comprise a rather abundant production of abstruse neologisms, because the latter but not the former also comprises a marked production of morphemic deviations, including composed ones, and because there is evidence that the jargonaphasic but not the schizophasic remains at least partly unaware of the unconventional nature of his neologistic productions and, a fortiori, does not create them deliberately.

It should also be obvious from my discussion that the linguistic definitions I gave of various types of deviations are not to be taken to imply that each type results from a unique dysfunction. In this respect, I have for instance underlined the fact that the production of both phonemic paraphasias and formal verbal paraphasias, which are distinct entities from a purely linguistic point of view, could be subserved by a single dysfunction. And I have also shown that the production of abstruse neologisms, for which I could only propose a single label given my linguistic criteria, could be subserved by various dysfunctions and combinations of dysfunctions.

Another linguistic characteristic of neologisms on which I insisted is that their productions is always governed by phonetic and phonological rules and sometimes, as in the case of morphemic deviations, by morphological rules as well.

Various linguistic distinctions that the human brain apparently honors in the presence of focal pathology have also been mentioned, such as a distinction between open and closed class words and even between open and closed class morphemes, a distinction between "shorter" and "longer" words or else between "more frequent" and "less frequent" words, and so forth.

Finally, my characterization of neologisms along psycholinguistic lines has dealt with oppositions such as awareness *versus* anosognosia and completeness *versus* uncompleteness of unawareness in the latter cases, absence *versus* presence of a semantic load and conventionality *versus* unconventionality of this load in the latter case, absence *versus* presence of a conventional phonemically structured target and/or of an internal representation of this target, and so forth.

In fact, I do not really know if (and to what extent) the study of pathological discourses might tell us something about lexical access, retrieval and production in the normal nor, for that matter, about normal language production and comprehension as a whole. Well, my own guess is that yes it might.

ACKNOWLEDGMENTS

Centre de Recherches en Sciences Neurologiques, Université de Montréal. Research funded by Grant MT-4210 of the *Conseil de la Recherche Médicale du Canada.*

REFERENCES

Abrams, R., & Taylor, M. A. Differential EEG patterns in affective disorder and schizophrenia. *Archives of General Psychiatry, 36,* 1355–1358, 1979.

Alajouanine, Th., Ombredane, A., & Durand, M. *Le syndrome de désintégration phonétique dans l'aphasie.* Masson, Paris, 1939.

Andreasen, N. J. C. Thought, language and communication disorders: 1. Clinical assessment, definition of terms, and evaluation of their reliability. *Archives of General Psychiatry, 36,* 1315–1321, 1979.

Bay, E. Principles of classification and their influence on our concepts of aphasia. In, A. V. S. de Reuck & M. O'Connor, eds., *Disorders of Language,* 122–142, Churchill, London, 1964.

Blumstein, S. E. *A Phonological Investigation of Aphasic Speech,* Mounton, the Hague, 1973.

Bobon, J. *Introduction historique à l'étude des néologismes et des glossolalies en psychopathologie,* Vaillant-Germanne, Liège, 1952.

Buckingham, H. W., & Kertesz, A. *Neologistic Jargonaphasia,* Swets & Zeitlinger, Amsterdam, 1976.

Butterworth, B. Hesitation and the production of verbal paraphasias and neologisms in jargonaphasia. *Brain and Language, 8,* 133–161, 1979.

Cénac, M. *De certains langages créés par les aliénés: contribution à l'étude des glossolalies,* dissertation, Faculté de Médecine, Paris, 1925.

DiSimoni, F. G., Darley, F. L., & Aronson, A. E. Patterns of dysfunction in schizophrenic patients on an aphasia test battery. *Journal of Speech and Hearing Disorders, 42,* 498–513, 1977.

Flor-Henry, P. Psychiatric syndromes considered as manifestations of lateralized temporal-limbic dysfunction. In, L. V. Laitimen & K. E. Livingstone, eds., *Surgical Approaches in Psychiatry,* M.T.P., Lancaster, 1973.

Flor-Henry, P. Lateralized temporal-limbic dysfunction and psychopathology. *Annals of the New York Academy of Sciences, 280,* 777–795, 1976.

Geschwind, N. *Selected Papers on Language and the Brain,* Reidel, Dordrecht and Bosotn, 1974.

Gur, R. E. Left hemisphere dysfunction and left hemisphere overactivation in schizophrenia. *Journal of Abnormal Psychology, 87,* 226–238, 1978.

Gur, R. E. Cognitive concomitants of hemispheric dysfunction in schizophrenia. *Archives of General Psychiatry, 36,* 269–274, 1979.

Hécaen, H. *Introduction à la neuropsychologie,* Larousse, Paris, 1972.

Joanette, Y., Keller, E., & Lecours, A. R. Sequences of phonemic approximations in aphasia. *Brain and Language, 11,* 30–44, 1980a.

Joanette, Y., Keller, E., Viau, A., & Lecours, A. R. Une approche dynamique à l'étude des séquences d'approximations phonémiques dans l'aphasie. *Grammatica VII, 1,* 217–237, 1980b.

Kertesz, A. Personal Communication.

Laffal, J. *Pathological and Normal Language,* Atherton Press, New York, 1965.

Lecours, A. R. Linguistic analysis of paraphasias. *Neurosciences Research Program Bulletin, 12,* 555–564, 1974.

Lecours, A. R., Deloche, G., & Lhermitte, F. Paraphasies phonémiques: description et simulation sur ordinateur. In, *Colloques I.R.I.A.—Informatique Médicale (Vol. I),* 311–350, Institut de Recherche d'Informatique et d'Automatique, Rocquencourt, 1973.

Lecours, A. R., & Joanette, Y. Linguistic and other psychological aspects of paroxysmal aphasia. *Brain and Language, 10,* 1–23, 1980.

Lecours, A. R., & Lhermitte, F. Phonemic paraphasias: linguistic structures and tentative hypotheses. *Cortex, 5,* 193–228, 1969.

Lecours, A. R., & Lhermitte, F. Recherches sur le langage des aphasiques: 4. Analyse d'un corpus de néologismes; notion de paraphasie monémique. *Encéphale, 61,* 295–315, 1972.

Lecours, A. R., Navet, M., & Ross-Chouinard, A. Langage et pensée du schizophase. *Confrontations Psychiatriques, 19,* 109–144, 1981.

Lecours, A. R., & Rouillon, F. Neurolinguistic analysis of jargonaphasia and jargon-agraphia. In, H. Whitaker & H. Whitaker, eds., *Studies in Neurolinguistics (Vol. II),* 95–144, Academic Press, New York, 1976.

Lecours, A. R., Travis, L., & Osborn, E. Glossolalia as a manifestation of Wernicke's aphasia: a comparison to glossolalia in schizophasia and in possession. In, O. Höök & M. Taylor-Sarno, eds., *Aphasia: Concepts of Analysis and Management,* 212–230, Almquist & Wiksell, Stockholm, 1980a.

Lecours, A. R., Travis, L., & Nespoulous, J.-L. Néologismes et anosognosie. *Grammatica VII, 1,* 101–114, 1980b.

Lecours, A. R., & Vanier-Clément, M. Schizophasia and jargonaphasia: a comparative description with comments on Chaika's and Fromkin's respective looks at 'schizophrenic' language. *Brain and Language, 3,* 516–565, 1976.

Lévy-Valensi, J., Migault, P., & Lacan, J. Ecrits 'inspirés': schizographie. *Annales médico-psychologiques, 89,* 1–26, 1931.

Lhermitte, F., Lecours, A. R., Ducarne, B., & Escourolle, R. Unexpected anatomical findings in a case of fluent jargonaphasia. *Cortex, 9,* 433–446, 1973.

Lordat, J. Analyse de la parole pour servir à la théorie de divers cas d'alalie et de paralalie (de mutisme et d'imperfection du parler) que les nosologistes ont mal connus. *Journal de la Société de Médecine Pratique de Montpellier, 7,* 333–353, *7,* 417–433, *8,* 1–17, 1843.

Nespoulous, J.-L., & Lecours, A. R. Du trait au discours, *Grammatica VII, 1,* 1–36, 1980.

Pitres, A. L'aphasie amnésique et ses variétés cliniques. *Le Progrès Médical, 7,* 321–324, *7,* 337–340, *7,* 369–371, *7,* 401–404, *8,* 17–23, *8,* 65–70, 1898.

Poncet, M., Degos, C., Deloche, G., & Lecours, A. R. Phonetic and phonemic transformations in aphasia. *International Journal of Mental Health, 1(3),* 46–54, 1972.

Rieder, R. O., Donnelly, E. F., Herdt, J. R., & Waldman, I. N. Sulcal prominence in young chronic schizophrenic patients: CT scan findings associated with impairment of neuropsychological tests. *Psychiatry Research, 1,* 1–8, 1979.

Wexler, B. E., & Heninger, G. R. Alternations in cerebral laterality during acute psychotic illness. *Archives of General Psychiatry, 36,* 278–284, 1979.

Willems, R. Etude linguistique d'un jargon aphasique, dissertation, Universitaire Instelling Antwerpen Romaanse Filologie, Antwerpen, 1979.

III NEUROPSYCHOLOGICAL STUDIES IN PROCESSING

13 Cognitive-Neuroscience: Developments Toward a Science of Synthesis

Michael I. Posner
University of Oregon

Roy Pea
Clark University

Bruce Volpe
Cornell Medical College

INTRODUCTION

Almost from the inception of the effort to develop information processing models of cognition investigators have argued that at some point there would be important links between the study of elementary mental operations crucial to the performance of complex tasks (Chase, 1978) and the brain systems that support such operations. This view is clearly outlined by Herbert Simon in his important Compton Lectures (Simon, 1981) as follows:

> The main reason for this disembodiment of mind, is, of course, the thesis that I have just been discussing. The difference between the hardware of a computer and the hardware of the brain has not prevented computers from simulating a wide spectrum of kinds of human thinking . . . . It would be unfortunate if this conclusion were altered to read that neurophysiology has nothing to contribute to explanations of human behavior. This would be a ridiculous doctrine. It is to physiology that we must turn for an explanation of the limits of adaptation . . . . As our knowledge increases, the relation between physiological and information processing explanation will become just like that relation between quantum mechanical and physiological explanations in biology . . . . They constitute two linked levels of explanation . . . the limiting properties of the inner system showing up at the interface between them. (page 97).

It is the theme of this chapter that the time has arrived for the development of the detailed analysis of the physiology of human cognition. For the last 15 years, a number of separate biological fields have coalesced under the name of "neuroscience." Neuroscience is concerned with the basic principles of organization of nervous systems. Although the field has, from its start, included studies of normal and pathological human brains, the bulk of the work has concerned animal models, and in particular, synaptic and intracellular phenomena. Except for occasional interest in language and its pathology, neuroscientists rarely choose human organisms as the object of study. In part, this arises because of the complexity of human functioning and also because of the difficulty, until recent methodological developments, in doing experimental physiology with human beings.

Within the last few years, a number of sciences related to the study of cognition in human beings have been coming into contact under the name "cognitive science." Many of the problems of concern to cognitive science arise from the great complexity of information stored in human semantic memory, and the cultural matrix in which the programming of this information develops. In the terms Simon uses in the previous quote, they are problems of software to which a science of the artificial is properly addressed. The study of semantic memory, problem solving, language and social cognition are issues of human concern that fall within the domain of cognitive science.

Although in principle any aspect of cognitive science might be illuminated by principles of neuroscience, and vice versa, it seems most fruitful to begin with the study of elementary mental operations (Chase, 1978) performed by human beings in the execution of complex behavior. These would seem to be an appropriate level of analysis for efforts to understand the relationship between mind and brain processes. Just as neuroscientists develop model systems of sufficient simplicity to work out the detailed wiring diagrams underlying animal behavior and learning, cognitive scientists interested in the interface with neuroscience need to seek model cognitive systems where appropriate experimentation may yield close contact with related neurophysiology. In many cases, the choice of such cognitive systems is dictated by the ease of time locking the occurrence of mental events to physical stimuli. What is not widely recognized by many neuroscientists is the impressive evidence that has been adduced during the last dozen years that purely mental events, such as ideas and images, can be time locked to critical environmental events (see Posner, 1978 for review). Occurrence of neuropathological syndromes and the breakdown of component mental functions provide natural sources of stimulation for the cognitive-neuroscience interface. Because of the biological bias obviously present in the study of cognitive processes from a neuroscience viewpoint, both evolutionary and developmental considerations are extremely important in the choice of cognitive systems and in their interpretation.

We will define cognitive neuroscience as the interface of neuroscience and cognitive science with the relationship between mental events and the brain as its foremost empirical question. In our view, it is useful to divide cognitive neuroscience into subproblems based on candidate cognitive systems. The term "cognitive system"[1] is defined in terms of its relation to the idea of organ systems. Organ systems are "differentiated structures in animals and plants made up of various cells and tissues and adapted for the performance of some specific function and grouped with other substructures into a system" (Webster, *New American Dictionary*). Clearly then, cognitive systems must also depend upon differentiated brain structures even though they may be widely distributed within the brain. Thus the question of localization of function becomes one important issue within cognitive neuroscience.

Any cognitive system may be described in terms of the brain functions that support it, in terms of the subjective experiences or processing operations to which it gives rise, or in terms of the pathologies created by breakdowns of components of cognitive systems. These three approaches correspond to the disciplines of neuroscience, cognitive science, and neurology. It is these three constituent disciplines that provide historical background and a methodological base out of which cognitive neuroscience as a discipline must grow.

Our emphasis on the development of a "science" contrasts rather markedly to the usual analysis of mind-brain relationships. This is a field that has had considerable work, but much of it has been highly theoretical and philosophical. Perhaps stemming from the long tradition of philosophical speculation about the relationship between mind and brain, most of the literature involves a priori solutions to the mind-brain relationship rather than accumulation of the methods and findings that normally accompany the development of a scientific area. In this chapter, we will not stress philosophical or theoretical solutions. We do not suggest that such solutions are at hand or may ever be possible. Rather, we believe that new methods and accumulating findings have made an exciting discipline of cognitive neuroscience even should no solutions to the vexed philosophical problems of mind-brain relationships emerge.

In addition to the common influence from general philosophical questions about the relationship between brain and mind, the disciplines of neurophysiology, neurology, and psychology have had a great deal of contact over the last hundred years. In particular, all three disciplines have been concerned and influenced by general assumptions about the ability to localize particular cognitive functions within the human brain. So dominant has been the question of localization of function that it caused Miller (1978) to remark as follows:

---

[1] We thank George A. Miller for bringing to our attention the concept and term cognitive system.

Psychologists sometimes wonder why their neurological colleagues place so much store by the localization of functions in different parts of the brain, since it is not obvious that knowing where something happens tells us much about what is going on there. But localization is merely one aspect of the traditional neurological approach to brain science; a more comprehensive view of the neurological approach would have to include the general assumptions that (1) complex brain functions can be decomposed into simpler, more general processes; (2) these component processes can be localized anatomically and studied in relative isolation; (3) complex behavior can be decomposed into simpler, more general processes; and (4) the simpler brain processes can be correlated directly with their simpler behavioral processes. (Miller & Lenneberg, 1978, page 6)

Until recent times, the effort to make component analysis of complex mental skills (e.g., reading or chess) has not been available and, thus historically, the disciplines of neurology, neuroscience, and psychology have concentrated heavily upon localization of function. All three constituent fields of cognitive neuroscience went through periods of extreme localization prior to the turn of the century, followed by a movement toward more wholistic views strengthened by Gestalt arguments and supported by Gestalt-influenced neurologists. Through the influence primarily of modern neuroscience, all have tended to return to ideas of localization of brain processes (see Uttal, 1978 for a review). This similar waxing and waning of enthusiasm about localization of function indicates that cross-fertilization has occurred across the three disciplines, providing at least implicit recognition of the relevance of research in each of the fields for the others.

Although in a rough sense ideas of brain localization have come full circle from the nineteenth century, there are still differences between current ideas and past ones. Recognition of complex central systems have replaced undue emphasis upon strict reflexive control (Edelman & Mountcastle, 1978; Hebb, 1949). Cybernetic concepts have provided ideas about the logical principles underlying central control of input and output pathways (Wiener, 1948). These have influenced both concepts of neural organization and concepts of the complex networks that organize the flow of information in models of cognitive psychology.

The flavor of the common language of neural and cognitive scientists interested in the basis of mental processes can be seen by a comparison of the two recent quotes, one from a prominent neuroscientist (Mountcastle, 1978) and the other by a cognitive researcher (McClelland, 1978).

It is well known from classical neural anatomy that many of the large entities of the brain are interconnected by extrinsic pathways into complex systems, including massively reentrant circuits.—These modules are local neurocircuits of hundreds of thousands of cells linked together by a complex intramodular connectivity. The modules of any one entity are more or less similar throughout, but those at different entities may differ strikingly.— (Page 39)

Distributed systems are thus composed of large numbers of modular elements linked together in eschelon, parallel and serial arrangements. Information flows through such a system may follow a number of different pathways, and the dominance of one path or another is a dynamic and changing property of the system. Such a system has many entries and exits and has access to outflow systems of the brain at many levels. A distributed system displays the redundancy of potential loci of command, and the command function may from time to time reside in different loci of the system, in particular, and in that part processing the most urgent and necessary information.

An important feature of such distributed systems, particularly those central to primary sensory and motor systems, is that the complex function controlled or executed by the system is not localized in any one of its parts. The function is a property of the dynamic activity within the system: it resides in the system as such. This may explain why local lesions of the distributed system scarcely ever destroy system function completely, but degrade it to an extent determined by lesion size and the critical role of the locus destroyed for system function. (Page 40)

The spirit of order within great complexity is also reflected in current cognitive science models and ideas. Consider, for example, a recent description of cascading processes determined from studies of the time relation of mental processing in human performance (McClelland, 1979).

1. The system is composed of several subprocesses or processing levels.
2. Each subprocess is continuously active, working to let its output reflect the best conclusions that can be reached on the basis of its inputs.
3. The output of each process is a set of continuous quantities that are always available for processing at the next level.
4. Processing at each level is based on the results of processing at the preceding level only. Outputs are passed in only one direction through the system of processes, with no skipping or bypassing of subprocesses. (Page 290)

This convergence on similar views of localization of function provides the needed conceptual basis for the organization of a cognitive neuroscience. However, the most important change that makes cognitive neuroscience a possibility is the availability of new methods for the examination of hypotheses relating brain function to psychological processes. As Mountcastle (1976) has suggested.

It has been clear for a long time—at least since the time of Lashley—that the quantitative study of behavior, traditionally the domain of the Psychologist, and of neural events in the brain, called "Neurophysiology," are conceptually different approaches to what are generically the same set of problems, an identity long emphasized by Jung (1972). What is new is that it is now possible to combine in one experiment the methods and concepts of each to yield a deeper insight into the brain mechanisms that govern behavior than is possible with either alone. In this "combined experiment," one controls and measures behavior and records simultaneously the signs of cerebral events through relevant. [p. 1].

METHODS OF STUDY

Methods play a particularly important role in every scientific endeavor. This is certainly true with respect to the hope of producing a physiological analysis of human mental activity. Although theories of localization of mental function have been present all through the history of the constituent disciplines, the methods for examination of the correlation between cognitive function and brain activity have been indirect. Much of the classical work has involved examination of brain sections following death. Those damaged areas of the brain could then be related to the behavior of the organism. *In vivo* examinations of the human brain by measurement of electrical activity have only been possible for 20 years and the use of non-invasive neurologic imaging techniques are even more recent.

Neuroscience approaches have emphasized spatial methods that give hope of a means of studying localization. Cognitive science approaches have tended to place emphasis upon temporal organization of information flow within the nervous system.

Spatial Methods

During the last few years, clinical neurology has been greatly aided by the presence of computerized tomography as a method of examination of lesions (Oldendorf, 1978; Osborn, 1979). In this technique, a series of narrowly collimated x-rays exposures is made from a number of different angles, and the data thus acquired are then used to reconstruct sectional images by computer. The spatial representation of the cortex thus achieved allows accurate location of lesions (Swets, Pickett, Whitehead, Getty, Schnur, Swets, & Freeman, 1979). In a few minutes, sufficient data can be collected to produce an accurate brain scan. Such scans provide a static picture of the health of the brain by an analysis of tissue density. Dyes may be used to enhance the differences between normal and damaged areas. The ability to obtain an accurate localization of the damaged area while the patient lives obviously provides increased opportunity for studying the relationship of human brain lesions to mental state and performance. In addition the size and location of a lesion can be traced over time as, for example, in the case of tumor growth or where radioactive treatment might produce a reduction in tumor tissue. The size and extent of lesions can be known while the subject is tested for associated cognitive deficit. This allows the possibility of quantitative analysis of the relation of brain tissue to detailed cognitive processes, such as might be involved in reading.

Radioactive tracer methods of measuring cerebral blood flow or metabolic activity may provide a more dynamic method of tracing cerebral activity during sustained cognitive tasks (Lassen, Ingvar, & Skinhøj, 1978).

One method involves the use of a radioactive xenon source, the concentration of which may be measured during sustained cognitive activity. For example, the rates of blood flow have been measured during silent reading and other cognitive tasks relative to a resting condition. The task of reading silently shows concentrated blood flow activity in the areas of the frontal cortex associated with eye movements, in visual association areas, supplementary motor area, and Broca's speech area as well. A lower level of activity is present in the posterior association area (Wernicke's area). The potential of this method for articulating the spatial localization of brain areas during cognitive activity is obvious and has already begun to be widely exploited (Risberg, 1980).

Another approach to the study of brain activity during cognition involves the use of positron emission tomography (Raichle, 1979). A glucose molecule is labeled with a radioactive tracer. The distribution of the labeled substance is monitored by annihilation radiation generated when positrons are absorbed. This radiation is sensed by an array of detectors. The limits of spatial resolution of this method may be within 1–6mm. The method has been applied as quickly as within four minutes after injection although longer times are most often employed. This method can be used to measure blood flow and may have the potential of examining dynamically the metabolism in different areas of the brain if certain assumptions are made. Ultimately one would hope to be able to compare metabolic activity in neural systems involving different transmitters as well as in spatially separate brain areas.

One disadvantage of the spatial examination methods of CT scan and cerebral blood flow is the lack of fine temporal resolution of these methods. Although methods under current development such as positron emission tomography could improve the temporal resolution to within the range of seconds (Raichle, 1979), it may always be necessary to supplement them with methods that are temporally more refined.

Temporal Dynamics

The various imaging methods described do not give the kind of dynamic picture of information flow required by the analysis of many cognitive tasks where differences of 20–100 msec are frequently found between processing codes (Posner, 1978) or successive stages (Sternberg, 1969).

The simplest chronometric method is to measure the time between two events. When the first event is a stimulus and the second the response to it, the measure is called reaction time. A very closely related technique is to provide an informative event or cue and measure the length of time it takes before the reaction to a following imperative event has reached its minimum. This technique can be used to measure the time required to encode the cue event in an optimal way.

Some investigators prefer to control the time subjects have available to interact with the stimulus and observe errors they make with a given exposure duration. One such technique is to follow a brief exposure of a target with a second masking event. The assumption is made that the mask serves to restrict the time that is available for dealing with the target. An alternative method to masking is to train subjects to respond at different rates of speed and then to observe the errors they make at each rate of processing. This technique makes use of the fact that the people can obtain greater accuracy by going more slowly. Measurements of the accuracy of performance following different durations of stimulus exposure are based on an implicit notion that quality of information builds up over time and that subjects can access that information at different places in its build-up. Faster access means lower information quality and thus greater errors until asymptote is reached.

In simple cognitive tasks like reading of letters and words these techniques have and are being used to trace the time course of buildup and decay of visual, phonetic, and semantic codes. For highly-familiar and overlearned items, these translations are automatic in the sense that they occur even when we attempt to prevent them from taking place. But even though they are automatic, they are not immediate. Estimates of the time course of activation of these codes suggest that the phonetic code follows activation of physical codes by 80 to 100 msec and that semantic codes require in excess of another hundred msec for their development. These time estimates arise from experiments involving various aspects of mental chronometry. Though the use of time-dependent measures is an old one in experimental psychology, in recent years there has been a proliferation and integration of methods and theory in an effort to trace the time course of activity in the nervous system.

SPATIO-TEMPORAL METHODS

Event related electrical activity recorded from the scalp of humans or other animals provides a method that involves both spatial and temporal information. Although it is often difficult to determine the exact location of the generators of such potentials, different components do give rise to different scalp distributions. Components within the first 100 msec often relate closely to sensory aspects of the signal and show scalp distribution dependent upon the modality of input. Later components tend to relate more to states of the organism and task and tend to show peaks in the association areas. There have been efforts to locate the generators of these potentials either by an analysis of their scalp distributions or by use of depth electrodes (Goff,

Allison, & Vaughan, 1978; Woods, 1980). When the event related potentials are collected from two different behavioral tasks, they can be compared chronometrically. For example, attending to a visual or auditory location produces amplification in the event related potential about 90–120 msec following input; while detecting a target defined by a semantic category tends to produce differences between targets and non-targets that do not occur for about 300 or more msec after input. These differences correspond to the distinction made in performance theories between sensory and response set and reflect the complexity of the decisions and degree of conscious processing of the unselected item. The comparison of wave form for the attended and unattended input provide a very precise and complete temporal picture of influence of the attentional instruction.

In recent years it has been possible to record from single neural cells in alert organisms. This method provides precise spatial and temporal resolution. Activity that is time-locked to a stimulus can be recorded and used to construct a picture of the firing rate of the neuron millisecond by millisecond following input. This method can provide an accurate picture of how different neural systems are affected by psychological conditions. For example Goldberg and Wurtz (1972) showed that single cells in the superior colliculus (a midbrain structure related to eye movements) whose receptive fields are targets for an eye movement show enhanced firing rates well before the eye actually begins to move. This selective enhancement effect can occur within 50 msec after the cue for the eye movement. On the other hand, cells in the primary visual areas show no such selective enhancement; while parietal cells do so but at a latency usually longer than that shown for collicular units. These results can help provide a picture of the ordering of the neural systems related to attention and eye shifts. The use of post-stimulus latency histograms is limited to organisms for which electrode penetrations are possible and this of course limits their utility for the study of higher cognitive functions in humans, but for some tasks the non-human primate makes an excellent model.

Neurological Deficits

A combination of spatial and temporal methods have given us a greatly expanded capability of learning about the physical basis of cognition. The incentive for such studies has been greatly increased by study of the disconnections of cognitive function that can be revealed by cases of brain injury. The split brain syndrome has revealed the ability to make complex discriminations by the right hemisphere without availability of information to the language system (Gazzaniga, 1970). The results obtained with this disconnection syndrome have greatly increased confidence in our ability to analyze the relationship between cognitive function and brain activity. This

faith has also been bolstered by experiments, showing that subjects with occipital lesions can orient to stimuli (with their eyes) that they are unable to
bring to consciousness (Poppel, Held, & Frost, 1973; Weiskrantz, Warrington, Sanders, & Marshall, 1974). Such dissociations fit with the assumed
functions of the primary visual system in conscious recognition and of the
secondary (midbrain) system in localization, but they remain very striking
evidence of the possibility of understanding of cognition at a neural system
level. Similarly the finding in deep dyslexia (Marshall & Newcombe, 1973)
that patients may demonstrate knowledge of the meaning of a word they
cannot name has helped support the idea of different routes to the meaning
of lexical items.

COGNITIVE SYSTEMS

These methods have already had a value in increasing the belief of
psychologists in the ability to tie cognitive activity to important aspects of
the brain. The view of only a few years ago that there were no convincing
links between cognition and the activity of brain cells seems now to have
passed in favor of the firm conviction that we will come to understand mental processes in terms of brain activity within the next generation or so.

These changes in the faith of investigators in the strength of the relationships between brain and mind face two important dangers. One danger is
from a naive attempt to reduce cognition to neuroscience that may lead to
an overconcentration on the physical basis of brain activity without concomitant attention to the cognitive functions performed. Reductionism of
this sort tends to prevent interesting questions of cognition from guiding the
development of studies of brain activity. On the other hand, cognitive scientists need not claim that their field should be completely divorced from
brain activity, but there are very fundamental cognitive questions that do
lend themselves to tight links to the neurosciences. The claim that cognitive
science must be completely independent of the studies of brain activity is
one that may be appropriately advanced against naive reductionism but
should not stand in the way of the development of a genuine science at the
boundary between cognition and neuroscience that will benefit from constraints in both fields.

A second danger that may prevent the development of a genuine cognitive
neuroscience is the tendency of many in cognition to avoid questions like
those of consciousness and of emotion that do not fit well into the computer
simulations of human mentation (see Norman, 1980, for a discussion of important areas of cognitive science). No doubt the information-processing
language developed in part from studies of the computer has played an important and liberating role in the development of cognitive theory.

However, many important questions that will link the unique nature of the human brain to our mental activity are not easily handled by extant computer models.

The balance of this chapter will deal with two candidate cognitive systems in an effort to illustrate how the constituent areas of cognitive neuroscience approach common problems. These areas are among the most active ones for the joint examination of cognitive, neuroscience, and neurological approaches. The first is comprehension of lexical items. On the one hand, this area is very much at the center of problems in cognition and on the other, cases of brain injury have provided opportunities to study the neural systems involved. Second, is selective attention. In this area it is possible to link central problems in cognition with studies recording from single or small groups of cells in alert animals performing cognitive tasks. The reviews of each of these areas are necessarily highly selective and designed to illustrate the various approaches and how they might be combined rather than to establish any particular theory. We do not hope to provide a complete picture of work on the relationship of brain and mind even in the two areas chosen, but rather attempt to provide a sufficiently general picture of current efforts to give the reader a feeling of new developments and some sources that can provide a more complete background.

COMPREHENDING LANGUAGE

As is obvious from this volume, there is intrinsic interest throughout cognitive science in a theory of natural language that would explain linguistic universals and the rapid development of natural language in individual human minds (Miller & Johnson-Laird, 1976). Much of this interest in language is not reflected in this chapter. The current work that best allows connections between cognitive studies and brain processes is in the area of the storage and retrieval of individual lexical items. This is a very limited aspect of language, but the relative stereotypy of lexical items in comparison to the generative character of sentences makes analysis of lexical processing more appropriate to the methods available to the constituent fields of cognitive neuroscience.

There is a long history within neurology of deficits in language ability due to brain injury. There is much active work by neuropsychologists that examines deficits in language function with the same tools and to a large extent the same theoretical ideas as used in current studies of language function in normals (Coltheart, Patterson, & Marshall, 1980; Marshall & Newcombe, 1973; Zurif, 1980). In this section we examine two of these approaches and then compare the result with studies of normal function.

Peripheral Codes

Linguistic stimuli represent an important opportunity to a neuroscience of cognition. Language is a species-specific characteristic of the human being in which input arising from different modalities has access to highly overlearned correspondences. An individual word in a skilled reader can be contacted automatically both by auditory and visual input. The neuroscience approach to nervous systems has often been bound by sensory modalities. This in part is because of the importance of the sensory modality in the organization of brain activity. The bimodal characteristics of language makes it a natural place for the examination of the integration of modality-specific pathways at higher levels of the nervous system (Coltheart, Patterson, & Marshall, 1980).

The study of reading and its deficits has been an area of intense activity relating cognitive theory to brain injury. One disorder of reading shows the parallel nature of input of information arising from the visual modality to semantic processes. Both logic and cognitive science analysis suggest that information about words may reach semantic systems both from a translation that names the word and then uses pathways already available to speech or from visually specific information that does not rely on phonological translation. Deep dyslexics, according to some analyses (e.g., Marshall & Newcombe, 1973), have interruption of pathway leading to the word name and a sparing, or relative sparing, of semantic input from vision.

The flow of information that one infers from these studies of dyslexia (e.g., Marshall & Newcombe) is similar to diagrams developed from studies of normal human cognitive function during reading (LaBerge & Samuels, 1974). An important issue is the interpretation of such a flow diagram in terms of functional systems reflected by the neurological organization of language processing. In cognitive science, the ability to dissociate functions into separate boxes is sometimes called isolability or modularity. The argument for isolability rests upon experiments that show independent manipulation of the codes present in the component boxes. One example is the effort to show independence between visual representation of a letter or word and its phonological representation. Posner (1978) has reviewed studies showing such isolability. For example, if the two words are presented in contrasting colors, subjects are slower in determining that they are physically identical but there is no increase in times to read the word names. Similarly, if the subject has to hold other names in memory, the time for physical matches is unaffected whereas the phonetic times are affected. This ability to dissociate codes by the independent manipulability of their time courses in normal subjects has been taken as favoring isolability. Good evidence of this type exists for isolability of visual and auditory codes of words, and between each of those codes and their phonological interpretation.

The internal representation of visual and auditory words does not seem to involve isolable systems but appears to involve the same system. When subjects are performing a task requiring them to monitor auditory words for a particular phoneme its presence in a simultaneous irrelevant visual word influences their reaction times (Hanson, 1978). This suggests that the visual word produces a representation within the same system as the auditory word.

An interesting application of the common system for auditory and visual word processing has recently been proposed by Tallal (1980). She argues that difficulty in making fine phonemic discriminations in auditory tasks might predict reading deficits. This view rests upon the common code available to both visual and auditory language. Deficits in such a common code show up in reading problems. Similarly, it has been shown that long term exposure to high levels of noise that produce no discernible auditory deficit can interfere with children's learning to read (Cohen, Glass, & Singer, 1973). The main mechanism here could be a reduction in phoneme discriminiability making the grapheme to phoneme correspondence loop more difficult for these children.

Syntax

These results illustrate the convergence of neurological and cognitive analysis on common questions of isolability and suggest common results that illuminate important issues. Zurif (1979) describes an extension of this approach to show the isolability of two central components both involved in an understanding of language. These are the syntactic and semantic aspects of words. Some words in the English language are used primarily for syntactic purposes (function or closed system) and others primarily for semantic purposes (content or open system). Zurif argues that there is a separate system reserved for function words.

He further argues that it is selective impairment of the syntactic system involving the function of words that typifies the Broca's aphasic rather than an expressive inability to produce grammatical speech. Zurif rests his argument on the idea that Broca's aphasics show impairment both in the production and comprehension of speech, rather than merely in its production as had been argued by others. This suggests that the distinction between Broca's and Wernicke's aphasia lies not in the receptive-expressive distinction, but rather in dissociations of central mechanisms of language.

Zurif's argument with respect to syntactic and semantic processing is a version of the isolable-system issue. It is a particularly interesting and important one since it does not involve the separation of peripheral codes (e.g., auditory and visual from phonological) from more central language systems but a possible separation within the central language system itself. To the extent that Zurif can show isolability between semantic and syntactic processors, this will provide new tools and methods for dealing with the internal representation of the neural systems of language.

One argument (Caramazza & Zurif, 1976) is that Broca's aphasics have difficulty in the comprehension of center-embedded sentences. The idea here is that their general syntactic deficit makes it difficult for them to comprehend sentences where the syntax is crucial to an understanding of the word string. Much of this work involves showing that normals have no deficit, while Broca's are deficient in center-embedded sentences and not in other sentence forms. It is possible that normal subjects say the sentences to themselves in the process of understanding them. If such a mechanism was used, the problem found in the aphasics could be due to difficulty in generating the internal phonological string in the process of comprehending the sentence.

One effort to address this problem has examined the reaction time for normals and Broca's aphasics to decide whether a string of letters is a word or not (lexical decision) (Bradley, 1979; Zurif, 1979). The reaction times of normals show a strong dependence on word frequency for content (open class) words and not for function (closed class) words. The reaction times of Broca's aphasics are longer and show a strong dependence on word frequency both for the open class and for the closed class words. Zurif argues there may be separate stores for the two types of words. One store contains both open and closed class words to be used in the service of semantic processing. Another rapid access store contains only closed class words used for syntactic processing. Brain injury that interferes with retrieval from this second store forces use of the slower access frequency dependent store that serves for both content and function words. This account would fit with the finding that Broca's aphasics show difficulty in the production and comprehension of sentences where syntactic cues are important.

A possible alternative account for the different effects of word frequency on lexical decision time turns on the use of word frequency data. If the effect of frequency on reaction time approaches asymptote and if closed class words are really more frequent than our measures reveal, the data Zurif reports from normal on closed class and open class reaction times may come from different points on the same exponential curve. One consequence of this objection is that we are then less inclined to think of the Broca's performance as revealing a loss of processing ability for closed class words. Instead, since they use closed class items rarely, their reaction times on closed class would be slower than normal and thus the frequency effect would not be at asymptote. This interpretation does not do very well with the data showing longer reaction times on non-words that begin with words for normals but not Broca's aphasics. Although the question of isolability is still open, it is important to pursue the notion of separate semantic and syntactic processes.

Techniques are now present to examine the isolability question by studies of localization of putative separate stores. The use of simple chronometric tasks such as lexical decision allows for the time locking needed to apply such methods. For example, event related potentials might be used to localize putative components of language task (Ritter, personal communication).[2] If open and closed task words are handled in different brain locations, then scalp topography of critical endogenous components should differ between the two sets of words. Indeed, there are some hints in the literature now that different classes of words produce different scalp distributions in the evoked potential. One might expect a more anterior distribution for the closed class words than for the open ones.

This argument must be a step further advanced by looking at the scalp distribution of evoked potential for closed class words under two conditions. In one condition, subjects respond to the semantic aspect of the closed class words (for example, deciding whether it signifies a plural or singular condition). In the other condition they respond to the syntactic aspect of the closed class word. In the former condition, the retrieval processes should involve semantics, while in the latter, syntax. Again, assuming a difference in brain location, one would expect a different scalp distribution of the evoked potential. The use of regional blood flow might be another spatial method useful in the possible localization of neural system underlying language. Such experiments illustrate how neuroscience approaches could be used to test critical aspects of theories developed from brain damage or cognitive science.

Semantics

One of the most exciting areas of contact between studies of brain injury and normal language function is in the operation of the system that provides the meaning of words. Zurif (1979) argues that the semantic system of the deep dyslexic is identical to that of the normal but that the dyslexic does not have the peripheral codes necessary to stabilize the normally ambiguous operations of this system.

His argument for the ambiguity of the semantic system rests on the literature of spreading activation where essentially any word activates a range of semantic associations (Collins & Loftus, 1975). If a person is asked to say specifically what the word was, he must use codes available from

---

[2]These comments were made by Walter Ritter during the course of a discussion of the role of event related potentials in language studies.

visual, phonetic, or acoustic analysis rather than the semantics itself. This is more true for words that have large numbers of associations, such as concrete nouns. Abstract words may be more fully implied by their activation pattern.

Normal subjects may be primed to be aware of only one of the multiple activation patterns of an ambiguous word by context (Conrad, 1974; Swinney, 1979). The fact that the deep dyslexics show relatively little problem with auditory meaning suggests that auditory primes ought to drive their interpretation of visually presented words in predictable directions. By pursuing this line of research on deep dyslexics, we might at once determine the degree of similarity between the deep dyslexic and the normal and contribute to cognition by showing the operations of a pure semantic system unencumbered by the peripheral devices present in the normal.

The idea that a given visual word should activate a range of associations below the level of the subject's consciousness is a very important one in cognitive science (Conrad, 1974; Marcel & Patterson, 1978). It suggests that the reading and listening tasks are both sufficiently automatic that the full range of their activation patterns are not available to the subject. Nonetheless, such patterns affects the interpretation of words of which one is aware. These results open up to psychological analysis the study of those factors that produce disambiguation of the activation patterns of any given word to provide an overall meaning to a phrase or sentence.

Although many of these ties between the study of brain damage and normals remain speculative, encouraging developments within cognitive science provide additional faith in them. The early work on isolability of systems involved primarily single letters and words (see Posner, 1978, for a review). The lexical decision task has also generally been confined to words or small strings of items. Recently, it has been shown (Aaronson, 1976; Davidson, 1978) that many of the same principles occur during continuous reading tasks. Davidson (1978) showed that words fitting the overall meaning of the paragraph subjects were reading are classified as lexical items more rapidly than unrelated words. The faster speed in processing semantically related words does not extend to their homophones. Access to semantics during reading of simple material appears to be via a grapheme to semantic route, not via the grapheme to phoneme route. Nonetheless, Davidson was able to show the effects on homophones when subjects had to make a lexical decision about a word that had been presented in the string earlier. On the second occasion repeated words are classified more rapidly than non-repeated words. The effect also occurs to the homophones of repeated words. This indicates that the string of material carried in memory does include a phonological code. These results confirm many findings (Coltheart, Davelaar, Jonasson, & Besner, 1977; Kleiman, 1975) that have been made with small numbers of letters or words and show the role of the same principles in a more natural reading task.

Linguistic Awareness

While much of the processing involved in reading and listening goes on out-side of awareness, it is important to develop an understanding of the role of conscious processing in the understanding of language. To do so it is impor-tant to have techniques useful in separating processing of which we are unaware from processing involving awareness. In connection with object recognition we argued that it is possible to examine mental representations independent of the activation produced by stimulus input. One effort to do so involved the lexical decision task described earlier (Neely, 1977).

This method uses a priming stimulus prior to the introduction of a stimulus to which the subject must respond. The priming stimulus may either be a neutral warning signal or a word. Sometimes the prime word is the name of a category of the stimulus. For example, the prime "animal" followed by item "dog." Subjects decide whether t] e item that follows the prime is a word or a non-word (lexical decision).

Let us describe how a theory (Posner & Snyder, 1975) of automatic and unattended processing predicts various aspects of this simple task. Informa-tion in automatic pathways builds up quickly and automatically. Attention, however, takes time to shift to the represented category. If automatic is taken to mean parallel activation, then one can activate many of these pathways at the same time. This implies that the activation of the pathway will have a positive effect on reaction time (benefit) but no negative effect (cost). Thus, one would expect benefit to build up quite rapidly but cost only to be associated with the operation of a slower attentional mechanism. The results confirm this idea. Following a prime, benefit is present very rapidly, but cost builds up very much more slowly than benefit.

Neely's experiment found very systematic asymmetries in the time course of buildup of cost and benefit of the type that would be expected from the theory described above. In this condition, the priming stimulus serves both as a means of activating internal pathways and of serving as a cue for the subject's active attention.

A second condition that Neely used was to prime the subject with a category name but when it was presented the subject was supposed to think consciously of a different category. For example, if the word "animal" was presented, he was to think "furniture." Neely traced the time course of cost and benefits. According to the theory, one ought to expect symmetric build-up of costs and benefits, since there is no automatic pathway activation. This is the result. Most interesting is the case where the subject is given the word "animal" and must switch his attention to "furniture" but then is given an instance of the original category (e.g., "dog"). The theory predicts that the initial automatic benefit will switch to cost and again this is the result obtained. Some experiments have raised questions with aspects of the Neely results (Antos, 1979). Nonetheless, it remains a good demonstration of how cognitive science thinking about a "pure" mental representation can lead to methods that separate conscious and unconscious processes involved in language comprehension.

There is evidence that violation of an expected event leads to active, highly conscious processing and to a particular component of the event related potential that is positive in sign and occurs about 300 msec after input (P-300) (Donchin, Ritter, & McCallum, 1978). Recently, such unexpected events have been studied in language tasks (Kutas & Hillyard, 1980). With a physical violation such as an unexpectedly large print, there is an enlarged P-300; an unexpected semantic stimulus however, produced an enlarged negativity at about 400 msec. Hillyard suggests that semantic violation may be processed separately from physical violations.

Recent evidence provides interesting links between the P-300 latency and aspects of awareness. Duncan-Johnson (1979) has shown that the P-300 latencies are not as labile as reaction time. A highly primed stimulus produced a P-300 that occurs before the overt response, while for an unprimed stimulus P-300 occurs after the response. This result fits with the idea that P-300 represents the entry of a stimulus to processing by a system related to the awareness of the subject rather than his response. Sometimes one is conscious of an event prior to responding, sometimes after, depending on how automatic the relationship between stimulus and response is. There are questions about some aspects of the Duncan-Johnson work because she did not dissociate the priming of the stimulus from the priming of the response. The person who expected a particular event could prepare for the motoric response of that event. Methods available in cognitive psychology could be used to insure priming of the stimulus alone.

Data arising from studies using language stimuli are of particular importance because they are at the heart of the cognitive science approach and because they allow us to get beyond sensory-specific stimuli to study aspects of bimodal processing systems. The brain injury data and the event related potential methods provide important links to the brain processes. However, language is a species-specific property of the human being and does not allow easy use of the animal models that lie at the heart of neuroscience methods. In the next section we examine some putative-cognitive systems that allow further links between human and animal results.

ORIENTING OF ATTENTION

The preceding section on linguistic awareness illustrates the importance to cognition of understanding the mechanisms of awareness. However, the use of linguistic materials prevents the kind of animal studies that are central to neuroscience methods. It is possible to forge closer links between cognition and neuroscience work by using tasks that involve "detection" of non-linguistic stimuli. Many organisms have similar highly developed mechanisms for active scanning of the visual environment. There is a great deal known about parts of the visual system that are necessary for detection. Much of the neuroscience understanding of vision has involved study of anesthetized animals who are not using the cognitive mechanisms for detection available in alert organisms. In this section we will be concerned with efforts to understand the central mechanisms that give rise to detection when organisms are "cognitive" in the sense of using active strategies to scan their environment.

Recently there has been interest in the relationship between attention and movement both in neuroscience (Goldberg & Wurtz, 1972; Mountcastle, 1978) and in cognitive psychology (Posner, 1980). For visual events, the major concern has been in the relationship between orienting (overtly by eye movements, or covertly via shifts of attention) and the efficiency of detecting (making arbitrary responses, or being aware of) stimuli. Work in cognition has explored three general points:

1. Measurement of covert orienting of attention by changing in the efficiency of detecting stimulus events at different spatial positions.
2. The relationship between movements of covert attention and movements of the eyes.
3. The pathways controlling both covert and overt orienting.

A useful task to explore orienting involves selection of positions in visual space (Posner, Nissen, & Ogden, 1978). The subject is given a single key and asked to respond as quickly as possible whenever a visual flash occurs. A cue provides the subject with varying information about the likely spatial location of the stimulus. There is little doubt that subjects could perform this task without committing attention in advance. Subjects could simply wait until the visual event occurs and respond by pressing the key with very little likelihood that they would ever miss any of these suprathreshold stimuli. One might suspect that there would be no evidence of attention limits in this task. Indeed, many experiments using paradigms like this have failed to show selective effects (Grindley & Townsend, 1968; Mowrer, 1941). Recent results, however, have shown evidence for the role of selectivity in this task.

Evidence is of clear costs and benefits from knowledge about where in space a visual stimulus will occur even when eye movements are eliminated (Posner, Nissen, & Ogden, 1978). To a surprising extent, the mechanisms responsible for this effect are independent of the visual system. For example, this spatial selectivity is not related to the fine structure of the retina that distinguishes fovea from periphery. Although foveal stimulation is processed faster, the costs from an unexpected peripheral event and from an unexpected foveal event are identical (Posner, 1978). This finding applies only to detection of luminance that is clearly above threshold. It is not the case that attention can compensate for the high acuity provided by the fine structure available for foveal stimulation. When acuity is required, the equipotentiality of the retina with respect to attention no longer holds. Indeed, the behavior of subjects exquisitely reflects this difference. If left free to move their eyes in a luminance detection situation, subjects quickly suppress any tendency to move them and this conforms to the optimal behavior for this task. On the other hand, in an acuity task, the tendency to move the eyes to the stimulus is very powerful and subjects attempt to do so whenever possible (Posner, 1980).

The second sense in which attentional orienting is relatively independent of the fine structure of the visual system is the relationship between movements of attention and movements of eyes. The term "movements of attention," is used because it is possible to show that attentional shifts from one place in space to another are analogue (Shulman, Remington, & McLean, 1979). That is, probes at positions between fixation and target are facilitated at times intermediate between leaving fixation and arriving at the target. This result shows that covert changes of attention can be measured quite objectively and are as time-locked as eye movements themselves. These findings fit well with similar analogue results reported earlier for imagery experiments.

Attention movements are not slaved to the saccadic eye movement system. Attention can move while the eyes are still; a program to move the eyes does not automatically cause an attention shift (Klein, 1980); and it can be shown that attention can move in a direction opposite from where the eyes are programmed to move (Posner, 1980).

This relative independence of eye movements from attention can be compared with developing work in the single cell domain (Mountcastle, 1978; Robinson, Goldberg, & Stanton, 1978). It has been shown that at the collicular level there is a close relationship between enhancement of single cell activity and eye movement. At parietal levels the relationship between selective enhancement of single cell activity and movements is in dispute. Mountcastle (1978) has stressed the close relationship of attention to movements of the hands and eyes. He finds that the earliest input to parietal lobe is to neurons that have no foveal representation and whose input is from midbrain structures. On the other hand, Robinson, Goldberg, and Stanton (1978) argue that their data suggest that the activity of cells in area 7 is better understood as signaling the presence of a stimulus than as commanding movement.

If the simple reaction time is taken as a measure of the efficiency of detecting a stimulus and the movements of attention are thought to be related to orienting, the behavioral results indicate that orienting and detecting are separable properties of attention. This same dissociation is born out in pathological data. Occipital scotomas produce an inability to detect consciously the occurrence of the event, but may spare the ability of the subject to orient (Weiskrantz, 1977). On the other hand, parietal lobe damage seems to reduce spontaneous orientation to the opposite side in space but preserves the ability to detect stimuli should attention be forced to that position in space.

It is possible to suppose that a single underlying mechanism is responsible for both limited capacity results discussed under language and for the luminance detection results discussed in this section. This view requires that the subject be able to orient attention either to a high level semantic analysis or to commit it at a very early stage to a location in visual space. If this single mechanism view is correct, one would expect the selection of dimensions such as orientation, size, position, and color to be handled by the same mechanism but be associated with different time courses.

One reason for favoring the idea of a single neural system responsible for both types of selection is that both the single cell results on spatial selection and the scalp distribution of P–300 implicate parietal lobe sites. Another reason for postulating a single mechanism is that one would not expect subjects to be very successful in maintaining an early selection by spatial location when occupied at the same time with an attention demanding task like mental arithmetic. If peripheral selection breaks down under conditions where the subject is occupied with an irrelevant attention demanding task, one must believe that early selection draws upon the same underlying capacity as do other aspects of attention.

The event-related potential results, however, do not seem entirely consonant with the single mechanism view. Hillyard (Hillyard, Picton, & Regan, 1978) reports a dissociation between N–100 enhancement when a spatial position is selected and P–300 when a semantic target is detected. This could suggest that early selection is programmed by some sort of filter, as originally suggested by Broadbent (1958), while late selection is achieved by a different neural system. In favor of this view is the finding that target and non-target events that arrive on the attended channel seem to produce the same evoked-potential effects prior to P–300. If the same system were responsible for early and late selection, one might expect that once selected by this mechanism, targets and non-targets would be handled differently.

There are also differnces in detail between the N–100 event-related potential results and the luminance-detection reaction time results. Eason, Harter, and White (1969) and Von Voorhis and Hillyard (1977) have reported event-related potential differences (N–100) between attended and unattended positions. These studies have used blocked presentations where attention is kept fixed at one location. Under these conditions, N–100 appears to be enhanced at the attended position. The event-related potential enhancement seems also to be linked to situations in which there is rapid presentation of information from given positions in space with attention consistently directed to one position. With slow presentation and single trial cuing such as used in the luminance RT work, no N–100 effects are found. On the other hand, benefits in reaction time are smaller with blocked presentation than with trial-by-trial cuing. The reasons for these differences between event-related potential and reaction time results is not known.

A point to consider in this connection is that the paradigms that show N–100 effects also involve effective exclusion of non-targets from consciousness. In the cuing paradigm that has been described in this report for reaction time, no such exclusion occurs although the expected position has a latency advantage. Perhaps the N–100 results are indicative of filtering mechanisms used only in conditions of high overload. It would not necessarily be adaptive to prevent any information from non-attended signal sources from reaching consciousness. The difficulty of concentration that most of us have suggests that selective mechanisms are neither effortless nor completely effective. These are promising avenues for development of ideas relating different brain systems to aspects of attention.

Some work tracing the neural systems involved in spatial attention has already been carried out. It has long been believed that the superior colliculus plays a special role in programming overt movements of the eyes. Mammals tend to have stronger pathways from the retina to the contralateral superior colliculus than ipsalateral connections. It is possible to test the functional significance of this anatomical relationship by allowing subjects to view stimulus displays monocularly (Posner & Cohen, 1980). Subjects are instructed to move toward the temporal visual field in accordance with the anatomical connections cited above (Posner & Cohen, 1980). This asymmetry does not occur with eye movements to auditory commands nor does it occur strongly in conscious judgments of temporal order that do not involve movements of the eyes. There appears to be a similar bias in infants occurring even when only a single stimulus is presented (Lewis, Maurer, & Milewski, 1979).

Shulman (1979) sought to determine if a similar bias toward the temporal visual field existed in covert shifts of attention. He first determined the advantage in reaction time when attention was brought to a position in the visual field by the occurrence of a single peripheral target. He had subjects view monocularly trials in which physical targets occurred simultaneously to the left and right of fixation. A bias toward the temporal visual field should have produced a temporal field advantage of about 70 msec, but no such bias was found. This and other work leads to a rejection of the idea that covert attention is controlled via midbrain pathways alone. It should be possible to explore this result further to determine if the pathways of the second (e.g., retinal-collicular) visual system are important in the control of covert shifts of visual attention by use of patients who suffer from collicular degeneration.

Spatial attention is currently an active area where a variety of neuroscience and cognitive techniques have been applied to common questions. The work has advanced sufficiently to suggest that alert organisms use central mechanisms in the detection of visual stimuli that are distinct from the visual system as usually studied. There is promise that an understanding of these central attentional mechanisms will aid in a general approach to the physical basis of awareness.

CONCLUSIONS

This chapter delimits a unique set of problems that concern people working at the boundary between cognition and neuroscience. We expect work on this set of problems to grow during the coming years as new techniques are used to explore the neural systems activated by cognitive tasks. A major problem of the field is to develop a level of theory that allows contact between the study of normal and pathological material and between cognitive and physiological approaches. The development of such a theory has certainly been enhanced by the use of information processing concepts. The very generality of such a language does pose difficult problems. There is a tendency to use such language in a way that avoids problems that are unique to specific cognitive systems. For example, the claim that language and visual perception are not different because they can both be described in the same propositional code does not help us to understand the dissociation that occurs in brain injury. If the goal is to develop an interface between cognition and brain processes it will not be useful to speak at a level of analysis at which brain systems do not seem to be of importance. On the other hand, too strong a concentration on the problem of localization leaves the cognitive scientist with the impression either of a new phrenology or at least a lack of commitment to the dynamic interactions among neural systems that are likely to underlie much of the interesting aspect of cognition. Fortunately, as outlined in our introduction, some of neuroscience has begun to move in the direction of understanding complex interactions among neural systems that could provide a basis for cognition.

Our main goal has been to outline two cognitive systems in which specific questions have been studied by different techniques. Although no set of principles or theory has emerged from this inquiry, we feel that promising starts for combined work have begun and that enough is known to suggest that cognitive neuroscience can be developed in the coming years.

ACKNOWLEDGMENTS

This chapter is a report based on a six-month seminar at Cornell Medical College-Rockefeller University sponsored by the Alfred P. Sloan Foundation in a grant to Michael S. Gazzaniga and George A. Miller. The paper was written while the first author held a John Simon Guggenheim fellowship.

REFERENCES

Aaronson, D. Performance theories for sentence coding: Some qualitative observations. *Journal of Experimental Psychology: Human Perception and Performance,* 1976, *2,* 42–50.

Antos, S. J. Processing facilitation in a lexical decision task. *Journal of Experimental Psychology: Human Perception and Performance,* 1979, *5,* 527–545.

Bradley, D. C. Computational distinctions of vocabulary type. Unpublished doctoral dissertation. MIT, 1979.

Broadbent, D. E. Perceptions of Communication. London: Percanoni, 1958.

Caramazza, A., & Zurif, E. B. Dissociation of algorithmic and heuristic processes in language comprehension: Evidence from aphasia. *Brain & Language,* 1976, *3,* 576–582.

Chase, W. G. Elementary information processes. In W. K. Estes (Ed.), *Handbook of learning and cognitive processes,* Vol. 5, Hillsdale, N.J.: Lawrence Erlbaum Associates, 1978.

Cohen, S., Glass, D. C., & Singer, J. E. Apartment noise, auditory discrimination and reading ability in children. *Journal of Experimental Social Psychology,* 1973,*9,* 497–422.

Collins, A. M., & Loftus, E. F. Spreading-activation theory of semantic processing. *Psychological Review,* 1975, *87,* 407–428.

Coltheart, M., Davelaar, E., Jonasson, J. T., & Besner, P. Access to the internal lexicon. In Dornic, S. (Ed.), *Attention & Performance VI,* Hillsdale, N.J.: Lawrence Erlbaum Associates, 1977, 535–556.

Coltheart, M., Patterson, K. E., & Marshall, J. C. (Eds.). *Deep dyslexia,* Routledge & Kegan Paul, London: Boston & Henley, 1980.

Conrad, C. Context effect in sentence comprehension: A study of the subjective lexicon. *Memory & Cognition,* 1974, *2,* 130–138.

Davidson, B. J. Coding of individual words during reading. Unpublished doctoral dissertation, University of Oregon, Eugene, Oregon, 1978.

Donchin, E., Ritter, W., & McCallum, W. C. Cognitive psychophysiology: The endogenous components of the ERP. In Callaway, E., Tueting, P., & Koslow, S. H. (Eds.), *Event-related potentials in man.* New York: Academic Press, 1978.

Duncan-Johnson, C. *The relationship of P*-300 to reaction time as a function of expectancy. Unpublished doctoral dissertation, University of Illinois, 1979.

Eason, R. G., Harter, R., & White, C. T. Effects of attention and arousal on visually evoked cortical potentials and reaction time in man. *Physiology and Behavior,* 1969, *4,* 283–389.

Edelman, G. M., & Mountcastle, V. B. *The mindful brain.* Cambridge: MIT Press, 1978.

Gazzaniga, M. S. *The bisected brain.* New York: Appleton-Century-Crofts, 1970.

Goff, W. R., Allison, T., & Vaughan, H. C. *The functional neuroanatomy of event-related potentials.* In Callaway, E., Tueting, P., & Koslow, S. H. (Eds.), *Event-related potentials in man.* New York: Academic Press, 1978.

Goldberg, M. E., & Wurtz, R. H. Activity of superior colliculus in behaving monkeys. II. Effect of attention on neuronal responses. *Journal of Neurophysiology*, 1972, *35*, 560-574.

Grindley, C. G., & Townsend, V. Voluntary attention is peripheral vision and its effects on acuity and differential thresholds. *Quarterly Journal of Experimental Psychology*, 1968, *20*, 11-19.

Hanson, V. L. Common coding of visual and auditory words. *Memory & Cognition*. 1981, *9*, 93-100.

Hebb, D. O. *Organization of behavior*. New York: WIley, 1949.

Hillyard, S. A., Picton, T. W., & Regan, D. Sensation, perception and attention: Analysis using ERPs. In E. Callaway, P. Tueting, & S. H. Koslow (Eds.), *Event-related brain potentials in man*. New York: Academic Press, 1978.

Kleiman, G. M. Speech recoding in reading. *Journal of Verbal Learning and Verbal Behavior*, 1975, *14*, 323-339.

Klein, R. Does oculomotor readiness mediate cognitive control of visual attention? In R. Nickerson (Eds.), *Attention and performance VIII*. Hillsdale, N.J.: Lawrence Erlbaum Associates, 1980.

Kutas, M., & Hillyard, S. Reading senseless sentences: brain potential and alert semantic incongruity. *Science*, 1980, *207*, 203-205.

LaBerge, D., & Samuels, J. Toward a theorty of automatic information processing in reading. *Cognitive Psychology*, 1974, *6*, 293-323.

Lassen, N. A., Ingvar, D. H., & Skinhøj. Brain function and blood flow. *Scientific American*, 1978, *238*, 62-71.

Lewis, T. L., Maurer, D., & Milewski, A. E. *The development of nasal detection in young infants*. ARVO abstracts, May 1979, 271.

McClelland, J. L. On the time relations of mental processes: An examination of systems of processes in cascade. *Psychological Review*, 1979, *86*, 287-331.

Marcel, A. T., & Patterson, K. E. Word recognition and production: reciprocity in clinical and normal studies. In J. Requin (Ed.), *Attention and Performance VII*, Hillsdale, N.J.: Lawrence Erlbaum and Associates, 1978.

Marshall, J. C., & Newcombe, F. Patterns of paralexia: A psycholinguistic approach. *Journal of Psycholinguistic Research*, 1973, *2*, 175-198.

Miller, G. A., & Johnson-Laird, P. *Perception and language and thought*. Cambridge, Massachusetts: Harvard University Press, 1976.

Miller, G. A., & Lenneberg, E. (Eds.), *Psychology and biology of language*. New York: Academic Press, 1978.

Mountcastle, V. An organizing principle for cerebral function: The unit module and the distributed system. In Edleman, G. M., & Mountcastle, V. B. (Eds.), *The mindful brain*. Cambridge: MIT Press, 1978.

Mountcastle, V. The world around us: Neural command functions for selective attention. *Neural Sciences Research Bulletin*, 1976, *16*, #2 Supp.

Mowrer, O. H. Preparatory set (expectancy)—Further evidence of its "central" locus. *Journal of Experimental Psychology*, 1941, *28*, 116-133.

Neely, J. H. Semantic priming and retrieval from lexical memory: Roles of inhibitionless spreading activation and limited-capacity attention. *Journal of Experimental Psychology: General*, 1977, *106*, 226-254.

Norman, D. Twelve issues for cognitive science. *Cognitive Science*, 1980, *4*, 1-32.

Oldendorf, W. H. The quest for an image of brain. *Neurology*, 1978, *28*, 511-533.

Osborn, A. G. Computed tomography in neurologic diagnosis. *Annual Review of Medicine*, 1979, *30*, 189-198.

Poppel, E., Held, R., & Frost, D. Residual visual functions after brain wounds involving the central visual pathways in man. *Nature*, 1973, *243*, 295-296.

Posner, M. I. *Chronometric explorations of mind: The third Paul M. Fitts lectures.* Hillsdale, N.J.: Lawrence Erlbaum Associates, 1978.

Posner, M. I. Orienting of attention. The VIIth Sir Frederic Bartlett Lecture, *Quarterly Journal of Experimental Psychology,* 1980, *32,* 3–25.

Posner, M. I., & Cohen, Y. Attention and the control of movements. In G. E. Stelmach & J. Requin (Eds.), *Tutorials in motor behavior.* Amsterdam: North Holland, 1980.

Posner, M. I., Nissen, M. J., & Ogden, W. Attended and unattended processing modes: The role of set for spatial location. In H. L. Pick & I. J. Saltzman (Eds.), *Modes of perceiving and processing information.* Hillsdale, N.J.: Lawrence Erlbaum Associates, 1978.

Posner, M. I., & Snyder, C. R. R. Attention and cognitive control. In R. Solso (Ed.), *Information processing and cognition: The Loyola Symposium.* Hillsdale, N.J.: Lawrence Erlbaum Associates, 1975.

Raichle, M. E. Quantitative in vivo autoradiography with positron emission tomography. *Brain Research Reviews,* 1979, *1,* 47–68.

Risberg, J. Regional cerebral blood flow measurements by 133 Xe inhalations: methodology and application in neuropsychology and psychiatry. *Brain and Language,* 1980, *9,* 9–37.

Robinson, D. L., Goldberg, M. E., & Stanton, G. B. Parietal association cortex in the primate: Sensory mechanisms and behavioral modulations. *Journal of Neurophysiology,* 1978, *41,* 910–932.

Shulman, G. L. *Spatial determinants of attention allocation.* Unpublished doctoral dissertation, University of Oregon, 1979.

Shulman, G. L., Remington, R. W., & McLean, J. P. Moving attention through visual space. *Journal of Experimental Psychology: Human Perception & Performance,* 1979, *5,* 522–526.

Simon, H. A. *The sciences of the artificial.* Cambridge, Mass.: MIT Press, Revised edition, 1981.

Sternberg, S. The discovery of processing stages: Extensions of Donders' method. In W. G. Koster (Ed.), *Attention and performance II.* Amsterdam: North-Holland, 1969. (*Acta Psychologica,* 1969, *30,* 276–315).

Swets, J. A., Pickett, R. M., Whitehead, S. F., Getty, D. J., Schnur, J. A., Swets, J. B., & Freeman, B. D. Assessment of diagnostic technologies. *Science,* 1979, *205,* 753–759.

Swinney, D. A. Lexical access during sentence comprehension. *Journal of Verbal Learning and Verbal Behavior,* 1979, *18,* 645–659.

Tallal, P. Auditory temporal perception, phonics and reading disabilities in children. *Brain and Language,* 1980, *9,* 182–198.

Uttal, W. R. *The psychobiology of mind.* Hillsdale, N.J.: Lawrence Erlbaum Associates, 1978.

Von Voorhis, S., & Hillyard, S. A. Visual evoked potentials and selective attention to points in space. *Perception and Psychophysics,* 1977, *22,* 54–62.

Weiskrantz, L. Trying to bridge some neuropsychological gaps between monkey and man. *British Journal of Psychology,* 1977, *68,* 431–448.

Weiskrantz, L., Warrington, E. K., Sanders, M. D., & Marshall, J. Visual capacity in the hemianopic field following a restricted occipital ablation. *Brain,* 1974, *97,* 709–728.

Wiener, N. *Cybernetics.* New York: Wiley, 1948.

Woods, C. Depth electrode studies of P-300. Paper delivered to the 2nd Carmel Conference on Cognitive Psychophysiology, January 1980.

Zurif, E. B. Language mechanisms: a neuropsycholinguistic perspective. *American Scientist,* 1980, *68,* 305–311.

14 The Two Sides of Cognition

José Morais
Laboratoire de Psychologie expérimentale
Université libre de Bruxelles

1. INTRODUCTION

Interest in hemispheric specialization for mental functions has grown considerably in the past twenty years. It owes much to the fact that two powerful approaches became available in the early sixties. One is the possibility of assessing the capabilities of each hemisphere, independently of the other, by testing split-brain subjects; the other is the possibility of studying cerebral asymmetries in normal subjects through the occurrence, in some circumstances, of perceptual laterality effects.

The question of what the hemispheres are specialized for, and why, when, and how cerebral asymmetries emerge and develop are, undoubtedly, important questions in neuropsychology and cognitive psychology. However, many cognitive psychologists still tend to look at these matters, or at the present state of knowledge about them, with some scornfulness. Scholars who are prone to elegant models of mental life could hardly take pleasure in the distinction, so simple, between left and right sides of the brain. Reticence was certainly justified by a large part of published work on hemispheric specialization, which merely attempted to collect laterality evidence for any kind of stimulus and satisfied itself with classifications in terms of general functions, like language versus non-language. But lack of interest in cerebral asymmetries has never characterized all the scientists of cognition. Still, in the sixties, some of them tried to take advantage of laterality effects as arguing in favor of their theoretical views, for example right-ear advantage for consonants but not for vowels was thought to support the claim that a special mechanism exists for processing phonemes highly encoded in speech (Liberman, Cooper, Shankweiler, & Studdert-Kennedy, 1967). Later, other researchers were impressed by data showing that the right hemisphere has some linguistic capabilities and that the left hemisphere can be better at processing non-verbal information in some circumstances. They began to search for the common features that might be present in the lateralized abilities of one hemisphere, in terms of particular ways of processing information. It was already accepted in neuropsychology that the two hemispheres are functionally different. Cognitive psychology is now realizing that the existence of two different brains presumably implies the existence of two different forms of cognition. As Moscovitch (1979) recently stated, it is no more at issue "that two fundamentally different systems exist that are capable of processing information somewhat independently of each other" (p. 417).

The existence of these two different systems is probably a very special instance of the localization of mental activities in the brain. Consider the intra-hemispheric organization of units for analyzing information. Cells in the primary occipital cortex respond to light, not to sound, cells in the primary temporal cortex respond to sound, not to light, and cells that lie on the boundary between the occipital, temporal, and post-central cortex are multimodal. This intra-hemispheric organization does not seem to be based on cognitive distinctions. Lashley (1960) wrote that "the discrimination of qualities or "dimensions" within any sense modality does not seem to involve any processes psychologically different from those in discrimination between modalities, so that one cannot . . . appeal to discrimination to account for localization" (p. 329–330). He therefore discarded mentalistic explanations of localization, and attributed separation of functions to "some physiological necessity" (p. 341), and more substantively to "incompatibility or mutual exclusion of physiologic processes" (p. 333). It seems to me, however, that we have to consider localization in the context of the evolution of the human brain. In the late stages of this evolution, localization phenomena may have developed that, although admitting a physiological description, are determined by emergent cognitive necessities. Inter-hemispheric organization of mental activities might be the case. Levy (1969) also assumed incompatibility, but referred to two different types of cognitive processing that would tend to be mediated mainly by different halves of the brain. Recently, Kinsbourne and Hicks (1978) suggested that when the brain does two different things there may be necessity of a "barrier" between the corresponding control centers, and this barrier consumes neural capacity. They predicted that "a given cerebral control center is surrounded by more intense inhibition when an adjacent center is concurrently active than when a more distant is concurrently active" (p. 272). Whether or not inhibition in the nervous system will provide the best physiological description for incompatibility, it would seem adaptive to part two different types of mental processes in two distinct but communicating neural spaces if they are such that we permanently need both. These types of mental processes might be for Man (take this as a metaphor) like the hand that holds the nail and the hand that holds the hammer, one providing the stable frame for the strokes of the other.

If hemispheric specialization depends on some cognitive necessity, we may use it as an heuristic for developing a taxonomy of cognitive processes. We may use the hemispheric basis of human abilities to generate hypotheses about the relationships between these abilities. Of course, simply knowing *where* a particular function occurs does not tell us anything about *which* processes are occurring, *which* abilities are involved. We do not have a better understanding of, say, language just by discovering that language is mainly a function of one hemisphere. But suppose we have determined that functions a and b are (predominantly) left-hemisphere functions, and c and d (predominantly) right-hemisphere functions. We may then search for features common to functions a and b on one hand, and c and d on the other hand, and for features distinguishing the two pairs of related functions. In other words, we may look, through complex functions, for more general processes and abilities and for deeper distinctions in mental life. The direction of lateral (cerebral) asymmetry in tasks in which the weight of particular abilities is manipulated should provide a way of testing the hypothesized taxonomies. To start with, if we assume that functions a and b are left-hemisphere functions because they rely heavily on ability x, and functions c and d right-hemisphere functions because they rely heavily on ability y, then any task (whatever the function that is accomplished) that requires the predominant intervention of ability x (y) must yield superiority of the left (right) hemisphere.

The experimenter may, indeed, deceive himself in assuming that behavior in the task he designed implies one particular ability. But, insofar as he also assumes, on the basis of previous evidence, left (or right) hemisphere superiority for one particular ability, he may investigate under which conditions this ability is used by the subjects. The disappearance of asymmetry, or a change in its direction, in a given experimental situation would indicate some limit to the use of that ability. And at some point in the course of his study he may have assembled an amount of evidence on the conditions under which the ability is used (as revealed by coherent asymmetry outcomes) such that he realizes that the ability supposed to be working should be described more exactly in a different way. Each assumption is thus, alternatively, working hypothesis and hypothesis submitted to test. This might allow us not only to develop taxonomies of mental processes and abilities, but also to study the mental processes and abilities themselves in a continuous movement from one pole to the other. It should be apparent that the general purpose of research on hemispheric specialization as depicted here is not to understand mental processes in terms of brain activity, but to use an index of brain activity as a tool to understand mental processes and to describe them in cognitive terms.

It is implicit in the assumption of non-random hemispheric specialization for mental processes and abilities that some rational organization affords mind an advantage, a superior level of efficiency. The available data on the relative efficiency of the bilateral and the asymmetric brains do not support the prediction. However, we must take into account, when interpreting these data, that bilaterality has generally been assessed in terms of one particular function, more precisely as bilaterality for expressive speech. We do not know to what extent the component processes and abilities of a particular function are the same and identically arranged in the bilateral and the asymmetric brains. Unless we assume they are, we certainly need to compare bilaterality and cerebral asymmetry at the component level. And, anyway, we need to ascertain whether bilaterality, in the few cases in which it will presumably be observed, holds for all or only some of those processes and abilities for which hemispheric specialization is shown in the large majority of people.

In this chapter I wish (1) to review briefly the last twenty years evolution of conceptions on the question of *what* the hemispheres are specialized *for,* and (2) to examine and evaluate one of the distinctions—perhaps the most promising although still foggy—that have been put forward to characterize hemisphere differences at the process level.

2.   FROM STIMULUS- TO MODES OF PROCESSING-ORIENTED DICHOTOMIES

Ten years ago (and, for some people, still now), the hemispheres were supposed to be specialized for dealing with stimuli of a particular nature. The notion that the left hemisphere is better for processing verbal material and the right hemisphere non-verbal material, previously suggested by clinical data on the effects of unilateral lesions, seemed consistent with the first results observed with split-brain and normal subjects. Most influential have been Kimura's (1961, 1964) discoveries of right- and left-ear advantage in the recall of dichotic pairs of digits according to left- and right-hemisphere dominance for speech production, respectively, and of left-ear advantage for the recognition of dichotic melodies in subjects displaying right-ear advantage in the digits test.

The assumption that the direction of laterality effects is a function of the nature of the material has been dismissed by a lot of experimental results in the early seventies. For instance, when the task is to judge the pitch of a syllable (Day, Cutting, & Copeland, 1971) or to identify the emotional tone of a sentence (Haggard & Parkinson, 1971), a left-ear advantage is observed. The left hemisphere would be specialized not for dealing with any speech stimuli with any purpose, but for extracting linguistic information from speech. It must be noted that if pitch judgments generally yield left-ear advantage it is not simply because the right hemisphere would be better in processing the corresponding acoustic parameter in the stimulus. In fact, Haggard and Parkinson (1971) also tested the identification of stop consonants differing only in voicing and synthetized in such a way that voicing was conveyed only by a rising or a falling fundamental frequency, and they obtained a right-ear advantage. Similarly, the identification of pairs of consonants differing in formant transitions (the acoustic cues of place of articulation) leads to right-ear advantage while the identification of isolated formant transitions tends to be better in the left ear (cf. Liberman, 1974). The nature of the task thus appears to be a more crucial factor than the nature of the stimulus or the nature of the critical stimulus parameter.

More recently, however, another stimulus parameter-oriented hypothesis has become influential, that the perception of temporal patterns is primarily mediated by the left hemisphere. Speech would be better processed in the left hemisphere because it contains rapid temporal variations. The left hemisphere-temporal processing hypothesis has been substantiated by several results, and it might provide an attractive complement to the belief (probably too simple) that the right hemisphere is specialized for processing spatial information. It fails, however, to explain why the right hemisphere is frequently better in recognizing melodies. Of course, some musical stimuli might not be distinguished by the subjects on the basis of temporal features (Gordon, 1978), as it happens for chords, which usually yield left-ear advantage. But the fact that right-ear advantage may also be obtained for chords in some tasks (Shanon, 1980) suggests that the left hemisphere-temporal processing hypothesis is insufficient for characterizing the abilities of this hemisphere. Quite recently, Schwartz and Tallal (1980) argued for the hypothesis of left-hemisphere superiority in processing rapidly changing events on the basis of increased right-ear advantage when the duration of transitions is reduced from 80 msec to 40 msec without altering phonemic identification. It must be noted, however, that Blechner (1977) found faster reaction times for the left-ear signal than for the right-ear signal in a situation in which the subjects had to discriminate between a rising and a falling 50 msec transition, which, in speech, cue the /b–d/ distinction. A rapid temporal variation is thus not a sufficient stimulus characteristic to induce right-ear advantage. Again, the crucial factor determining the direction of laterality effects seems to be the kind of information to be extracted from the stimulus (for instance, linguistic information), not the stimulus itself or any of its characteristics.

One can imagine, however, that particular kinds of information may be extracted in more than one way, and that the property distinguishing the hemispheres is not exactly the kind of information to process, but the processing mode.

In one of my experiments (Morais, 1976), the subjects were induced to use either one processing mode or another processing mode, one lateralized in the left hemisphere, the other not, for the same speech stimuli and in the same type of task: identification of CV syllables in a choice reaction time paradigm. On each trial, one syllable was presented, among /ba, da, ta, ka/, in one ear only. In one condition, the subjects had to move a two-way switch as fast as possible in one direction if the syllable was /ba/ or /ta/, in the other direction if the syllable was /da/ or /ka/. A significant right-ear advantage has been observed (465 msec for the left ear, 450 msec for the right ear, in average). In another condition, the syllable /ba/ occurred with a .50 probability and was associated alone with one response; the other three shared evenly the remaining probability and were associated with the other response. In this condition there has been no laterality effect (349 msec for the left ear, 347 msec for the right ear), and the difference between the ear differences in the two conditions was significant. My interpretation is as follows. In the last condition (condition "1-1, 3-1") the subject would generate an image of the more frequent syllable, and he would employ a matching strategy sufficiently informative for the demands of the task. Such a matching operation would be performed as efficiently in the right as the left hemisphere. On the other hand, in condition "2-1, 2-1," the four syllables are equally frequent and even if the subject expects one of them, a negative output to the match does not permit a decision; so, phonetic analysis leading to full identification of each speech signal is needed and results in right-ear advantage.

The findings of this experiment suggest two remarks. First, a linguistic judgment does not necessarily lead to right-ear advantage. The left hemisphere would be specialized not to make linguistic judgments in general, but to make linguistic judgments in a certain way. Second, it might be convenient to distinguish mode of processing and strategy. It has become somewhat popular to say that laterality effects are a function of strategies. It should more properly be said that laterality effects are a function of processing modes, because in many situations there might be no room for strategies. The notion of strategy implies that some option between different modes of processing is available, whether consciously or unconsciously. In some tasks, only one mode of processing can probably be used, and I believe that this was the case in condition "2-1, 2-1." This mode of processing (analysis of phonetic features) would have been imposed also in most of the situations in which right-ear advantage has been observed for speech stimuli. In condition "1-1, 3-1," however, a choice was possible, and the subjects seem to have chosen the mode of processing leading to the fastest decisions. An heuristic for future research might be the following: to control for possible strategies when the aim is to determine the kind of processing modes differentiating the hemispheres; and to create experimental situations open to strategies in order to ascertain the conditions in which a given choice appears better suited when the aim is to study the processing modes themselves.

Another experiment showing that the use of different processing modes, differently lateralized in the brain, is determined more by the constraints of the task than by the nature of the task was reported by Papçun, Krashen, Terbeek, Remington, and Harshman, in 1974. Material consisted of Morse signals, presented dichotically, taken either in the full set of letters or in a subset including only signals with a small number of dots and dashes. Subjects who did not know Morse were tested, and they showed a left-ear advantage for the full set, but a right-ear advantage for the restricted one. So, the nature of the material was the same in the two conditions, as was the nature of the task, but the processing mode the subjects used for dealing with signals consisting of a small number of elements would not be useful for signals consisting of a great number of elements. Focusing on the details of the signals, which might be a mode of processing typical of the left hemisphere, would be suitable for small sequences, not for large ones.

Both the Morais' and Papçun et al's. experiments are coherent with the view that the left hemisphere is specialized for a mode of processing that can be called analytic. When decoding of phonetic features is necessary or when attention to the components of a sequence is useful, left-hemisphere superiority is apparent. When the task may apparently be performed in some non-analytic way, i.e., without decomposition of the stimulus, either no asymmetry or right-hemisphere superiority is observed. In the literature, non-analytic processing associated to right-hemisphere superiority is frequently called "holistic" (not all non-analytic processes are necessarily "holistic"). In the next pages, I will consider this "analytic-holistic" distinction.

3. THE "ANALYTIC-HOLISTIC" DICHOTOMY

3.1. Preliminary remarks

The use of the distinction between analytic and holistic modes of processing for characterizing hemispheric specialization received much of its support and popularity from the research carried out, mainly on splitbrain patients, by Bogen, some of the collaborators of Sperry (in particular, Levy, Zaidel, Nebes) and Sperry himself, in the early seventies. The latter author (Sperry, 1974), after summarizing the activities in which the left and the right hemispheres excel, concludes that they seem to be "analytic and fragmentary" and "holistic and unitary" (p. 11), respectively.

Although this view has inspired a growing number of experimental studies and interpretations of experimental data, many authors speak very unfavorably of it. Moscovitch (1979), for instance, finds the "analytic-holistic" dichotomy "vague, intuitive," and supported by "descriptive and somewhat anecdotal evidence" (p. 414). I completely agree with Moscovitch in that the analytic-holistic distinction has still to be elaborated. It is not very far beyond common sense to claim that to process a stimulus analytically is to process it in terms of its constituent parts or dimensions and to process a stimulus holistically is to process it as a unitary piece of information. It must be recognized that no substantive hypotheses have been made, at least in the neuropsychological literature, about the way analytic and holistic processors would operate on parts and wholes.

At first sight, it would be easier to understand what is meant by analytic processing (we are aware of paying attention to parts of things) than to understand how an holistic processor operates. This is probably one of the reasons why it was and is currently assumed that the processing of a stimulus begins with the processing of its parts. The roots of this belief are deep in the history of psychology. Helmholtz, quoted by James (1890, p. 520), refers to the fact that what appears to conscious perception as a simple whole (for instance a certain instrument's voice) is the fusion of many sensations (a combination of partial tones). And commenting on Helmholtz's text, James says that "synthetic perception" is "perception in which each contributory sensation is felt *in* the whole, and is a co-determinant of what the whole shall be, but does not attract the attention to its separate self" (pp. 520–521). According to this view, each impression (which is related to some part or component of the stimulus), although not being experienced by the mind, is a component, an element of the "integral impression" (pp. 488 and 503).

There are also many writers who, following the Gestalt psychologists, believe that processing of the whole is (or may be) prior to the processing of its parts. A pattern would be more than the simple sum of its elements, it would depend on organizational or structural rules. The Gestalt psychologists attempted to describe these rules, but as they postulated that brain processes mirror the intrinsic structure of the stimuli they did not afford us any real knowledge about holistic mental processes. They influenced the development of template-matching models of pattern recognition, according to which a newly encountered pattern is perceived by its coincidence or similarity with an internal canonical form or with the image of a previously perceived form. Template matching is thought of by some authors to be a holistic process, because it would deny any independence in processing to the parts or components of the stimulus. Bever (1975), for instance, says that there are "two ways of organizing our behavior in response to a stimulus: we may analyze the stimulus in terms of component parts, or we may respond to the stimulus if it triggers a holistic behavioral "template." Consider, for example, the perception of a square. It may be analyzed either as four equal-length lines at right angles enclosing a space, or it may be directly perceived by triggering a template that is set for a "□" (p. 252). However, although in template matching there is (or there might be) no decomposition of the whole, we cannot say that specific characteristics of the whole necessarily play a more important role than the parts. Perfect coincidence of the whole is obtained when coincidence holds for any of the parts. It seems to me that the notion of holistic processing should refer, instead, to processing that takes into account high-order relationships between the parts or elements of a form. I would propose that a holistic process is a process that concerns global or structural features, whilst an analytic process is a process that concerns partial or local features. Matching of a stimulus against an internal template can occur in the course of analytic processing and in the course of holistic processing depending on whether local features or structural features, respectively, are employed.

According to Garner (1978), who discusses properties of stimuli rather than modes of processing, wholistic properties include both templates, which would not be more than the sum of the parts, and configurations, which are emergent properties. The sense in which I use the expression "holistic (or wholistic) processing" would thus be better conveyed, in Garner's terminology, by the expression "configurational processing." However, and in spite of the obvious advantage of homogenizing terminology, I use here the term "holistic" for the extraction of configurations because, in the neuropsychological literature, it became a key word for the perceptual abilities of the right hemisphere, and these abilities are probably mostly concerned with the extraction of configurations.

In the last years some interesting attempts have been made to identify global or structural features. I will mention two of them here. Fox (1975) has found evidence suggesting that structural features like bilateral symmetry, colinearity, and parallelism are relevant factors of the rapidity of comparison of two unfamiliar geometric patterns, and he proposed that the holistic process may be related to the use of "structural diagnostics." Pomerantz, Sager, and Stoever (1977) have shown some configural superiority effects that seem to imply that wholes are not recognized by prior recognition of parts. They suggested that wholes may be perceived on the basis of emergent features (which stem from the interaction of parts), in particular by global features like symmetry and closedness.

I may expect that the kind of work we have just mentioned, together with other paradigms relevant to the "analytic-holistic" distinction that will be referred to later, will inspire those researchers who are engaged in studying the problem of hemisphere differences. On one hand, it might suggest some tests of the "analytic-holistic" dichotomy as a way of characterizing hemispheric specialization. On the other hand, the lateral asymmetry data that would be gathered from these tests might lead to reconsideration of present hypotheses and formulation of new ones about the use of local and global features in perception.

I will come now to the experimental evidence already available, on the basis of which we can examine the neuropsychological relevance of the "analytic-holistic" dichotomy. Some data are provided by studies on brain-damaged patients. For example, the task of seeing a figure that is hidden or embedded in a larger, more complex pattern, is well performed by the left hemisphere of split-brain subjects, but very poorly by the right hemisphere (cf. Zaidel, 1978a). On the contrary, the task of perceiving an apparently disorganized group of parts as a meaningful whole is a very right-hemisphere type of task, according to Zaidel. In the first case the subject has to see a part in the whole, in the second case a whole from the parts (or despite the parts). Other experimenters have observed similar results in apparently similar tasks. Bouma (1980) asked normal subjects to decide whether or not an embedded figure was present in the display, and he observed faster reaction times to the stimuli presented in the right visual field. He interpreted the result in terms of superiority of the left hemisphere for analytic processing. Nebes (1971, 1972) used two different tasks of perception of the relationship between the parts of a stimulus and the overall configuration (to match a given arc with a complete circle, and to match a fragmented visual shape with a solid form), and in each case he found that the left hand of split-brain subjects was very accurate while the right hand performed at chance level. The effect could not be due to specialization of the right hemisphere for dealing with haptic non-verbal information in general, since the right hand was as accurate as the left hand when complete forms were to be matched. Some structural features would be extracted in the right hemisphere both from the complete forms and the fragmented or partial stimuli in order to succeed in the part-whole matching.

Although experiments on brain damaged patients often show dramatic effects, my review will be concentrated mainly on those studies that showed auditory and visual laterality effects in normal subjects. Besides the theoretical importance of testing hypotheses about hemispheric specialization in subjects whose brain is intact, the possibility of doing that offers practical advantages for the researcher. Curiosity is impatient, and we come more often into contact with normal people than with people with the suitable lesion.

3.2. Auditory experiments

In one of the most influential studies in the literature on laterality, Bever and Chiarello (1974) found results that they interpreted in terms of the "analytic-holistic" dichotomy. The stimuli were melodies, sequences of 12 to 18 notes, presented monaurally, on which two tasks were to be performed. One was to say whether or not each melody had already been presented in previous trials. A group of non-musicians showed a left-ear advantage, but a group of musicians showed the opposite effect. The other task was to say whether or not a two-notes sequence was an extract from the melody heard just before. This seems to require an analysis of the internal structure of the melody, and as only musicians were able to perform above chance level Bever and Chiarello concluded that only musicians were analytic processors of melodies. When recognizing melodies musicians also used an analytic mode of processing, and for this reason they showed right-ear advantage. Non-musicians, on the contrary, would deal with a melody as a whole, a holistic mode of processing typical of the right hemisphere.

In an experiment recently run in Brussels (Peretz & Morais, 1980), we have found evidence for distinguishing between analytic and holistic modes of processing, the first linked to the left hemisphere, the second to the right one, while maintaining constant both the demands of the task and the degree of subject's experience with that kind of task and material. We used melodies consisting of 6 to 8 notes, and we tested only non-musicians, who never played an instrument and were unable to read a note on a stave. On each trial, a pair of dichotic melodies was presented, followed by four binaural tokens among which the subject had to recognize the dichotic melodies. In one condition, the melodies presented on each trial differed in tonal pattern only, more precisely in two notes. In a second condition, they differed in rhythm only, in two positions. In a third condition, they differed both in tonal pattern and rhythm, but again in two positions only. In neither of the three conditions was a significant laterality effect observed for the entire group of subjects. But subjects who reported the varying dimension, tried to detect positions where there was a change, and pay attention to these positions in the binaural melodies (so, subjects who apparently used an analytic strategy), tended more often to display right-ear advantage. On the contrary, subjects who reported that they tried to retain each melody as a whole and subjects who were unable to tell how they did the task more often had better performance for the left ear than for the right. And the difference in terms of laterality scores between the analytic and non-analytic subjects was significant in each of the three conditions. In the experiment, there was also a mixed condition, in which "tonal pattern" and "rhythm" trials were presented in an unpredictable order, and the expected difference in laterality scores between analytic and non-analytic subjects came out significantly for "rhythm" trials.

Non-musicians can thus analyze melodies and, hence, engage predominantly their left hemisphere if the melodies differ in precise and limited ways. In Bever and Chiarello's experiment, the analytic–nonanalytic (or holistic) distinction parelleled the musician–non-musician distinction, and the different results of the two groups of subjects may be explained by the capability of the first, but not the second, to use verbal labels. In our experiment, however, the analytic–non-analytic distinction could be drawn within a group of non-musicians and was related to their ability or inability to notice the discrimination cues.

It must be noted that the difference in laterality between analytic and non-analytic subjects was obtained for each of the two musical dimensions (tonal pattern and rhythm) manipulated in our study. Among the facts that contributed to the notion of a specialization of the left hemisphere for dealing with temporal patterns there is the usual finding of right-ear advantage in rhythm discrimination. Therefore, it is important to emphasize the fact that the analytic–non-analytic distinction holds for rhythm processing, too, and that non-analytic subjects in this condition, although less numerous than in the other conditions of our experiment, showed an apparent left-ear advantage.

It is also interesting to compare the results obtained by Peretz and Morais (1980) with those by Zatorre (1979), who found left-ear advantage for melodies in both musicians and non-musicians. From his results, he concluded that "what seems to be implicated in hemispheric processing differences is not so much cognitive strategy, but rather correspondences between a stimulus dimension and the hemisphere best equipped for processing that dimension" (p. 614). I think, however, that Zatorre's results might be expected and that they are not contradictory to ours. In fact, in his experiment, no two melodies had the same two notes in the same position. In these circumstances, it would not be practical to look selectively for differences in particular positions, since there might be confusions with notes in the adjacent positions. When overall contours are quite different, a mode of processing consisting of comparing them to each other is probably more useful. In the experiment by Peretz and Morais, however, overall contours were rather similar, and paying attention to one or two details of the internal structure of the melodies should allow some improvement in performance, as it actually did. (Analytic subjects were better than non-analytic ones only in the multiple choice paradigm, not in a same-different task in which there was no stimulation between the two melodies to be compared.) It may be predicted that if melodies differing in only one note in a constant position over trials are used, the chances of inducing analytic processing will increase. This prediction is already partially supported by available data. Gaede, Parsons, and Bertera (1978) used melodies differing in one note, and their subjects (non-musicians) showed, in average, a small right-ear advantage.

I suggested that non-analytic subjects tried to compare the melodies on the basis of overall contours. But what does this proposition exactly mean? I do not believe that these subjects could have some kind of "physical" matching, since the dichotic presentation must have prevented them from forming a clear representation of each melody. Some more abstract representation of each melody was presumably used, implying the extraction of some structural feature. This holistic mode of processing might also be involved in our ability to recognize a melody despite an octave transposition.

3.3. Visual experiments

Above, I have used the distinction between analytic and holistic processing modes to account for ear differences in the recognition of musical stimuli. It seems to me that the same distinction might also be appropriate to the understanding of visual laterality effects in normal subjects. Let me take, for instance, the case of laterality effects for nonsense shapes like Vanderplas and Garvin's random polygons. There are at least three experiments in the literature that employed these forms, exactly the same, and all the possible outcomes have been found: Fontenot, in 1973, observed a left-visual field superiority; Hannay, Rogers, and Durant, in 1976, a right-visual field superiority; and Birkett, in 1978, no lateral difference in average.

It is important to notice that in Birkett's experiment the more accurate subjects tended to display greater hemifield differences, in whatever direction, than the less accurate ones. This fact seems to imply that the task might be performed in at least two ways, one involving more specifically the left hemisphere and the other the right hemisphere. Birkett used a multiple-choice recognition task, the subject being presented with a shape and asked to select it from a display of five shapes. Fontenot also used a multiple-choice recognition task, but the subject was asked to select the stimulus from a display of 30 forms. Selecting a shape from such a number of foils does not encourage an analytic mode of processing, because too much time would be wasted in analyzing each foil and, on the other hand, finding one or two details of the stimulus in more than one foil would not permit an immediate decision. In fact, the greater the number of foils in the display, the greater the probability that the same detail will appear in a quite different configuration. Attending to the whole pattern in order to extract some global feature might allow a subject to locate the target quicker and more unequivocally. This may be the reason why Fontenot obtained right-hemisphere superiority. Hannay et al., on the contrary, obtained left-hemisphere superiority. But the task they used was a same-different classification task, in which the subject had to compare the stimulus presented to him with a shape on a card displayed subsequently by the experimenter. In this situation, attending to one or a few details might provide unambiguous information for the response.

Umiltà, Bagnara, and Simion (1978) also found right-visual field superiority, so left-hemisphere superiority, in a same-different classification task of two nonsense patterns consisting of several straight and/or curved lines and presented simultaneously in a vertical arrangement. In "different" trials the forms shared little or no detail, and in addition only eight forms were used in the entire experiment. This task might thus be performed by focusing on one or a few details.

Then, we decided in Brussels (Morais, Ben-Dror, Vanhaelen, & Bertelson, in preparation) to run an experiment also using nonsense patterns in a same-different classification task, but we presented in succession the two patterns to be compared in a trial, and we used fifteen pairs of forms. In one condition, the difference between two forms concerned one or two details, for instance a line was straight in one pattern and curved in the other. A significant left-visual field superiority was obtained, indicating right-hemisphere superiority. The subject could not know in advance which detail might be different in the two forms, so he was dissuaded from focusing on details and persuaded to rely on overall configuration. We ran a second experiment in which, in one condition, the different patterns were mirrored versions of each other, and we observed no significant lateral asymmetry in average. In this condition, an analytic mode of processing might be used, and was presumably used in some trials or by some subjects. In fact, one possible strategy was to focus on whichever detail and judge whether that detail occupied the same position in the second form, for instance on the right side of the form, or a corresponding position, on the left side. In another condition, the second form presented in each trial was rotated by 45° to the left or to the right relative to the first one, and the subject had to classify the two forms as same or different, irrespective of rotation. A clear left-hemifield superiority came out in this condition as in the previous experiment, probably because the strategy of focusing on one detail was now hindered by the spatial rotation. It should be noted that in the second experiment the hemifield by condition interaction was statistically significant.

If we compare now the experiments on melodies and on nonsense patterns, we can see that the number of differences (different notes, different segments) between the items is not the only relevant variable influencing the choice (or the efficiency) of a particular mode of processing. In the melody experiments, reducing the number of differences seemed to increase the probability of a right-ear advantage; in the nonsense pattern experiments, however, reducing the number of differences seemed to increase the probability of a left-hemifield advantage. Obviously, we must take into account other characteristics of the experimental situation. In our experiment on melodies, the subjects had the opportunity to compare the two dichotic melodies, and they had time to locate the differences, before being presented with the four probes; in our experiment on nonsense patterns, the time pressure did not encourage the subjects to try to match the two forms, first on the basis of one detail, then on the basis of another detail, and so forth.

The influence of the number of local differences on the choice (or efficiency) of a processing mode probably depends on the nature of the details and on the availability of special procedures for dealing with them. The very different nonsense patterns used by Umiltà, Bagnara, and Simion yielded a right-visual field superiority, while our very similar nonsense patterns yielded a left-visual field superiority. In the same way, Umiltà and his colleagues found a right-visual field superiority for complex geometrical figures of 5 to 8 sides, which, in "different" trials, differed by more than two sides, but a left-visual field superiority for complex geometrical figures of 9 to 12 sides, which, in "different" trials, differed by one or two sides. These results contrast, however, with hemifield data from other experiments. Using also a reaction time situation, but schematic faces of three features (eyes, nose, and mouth) as stimuli, Patterson and Bradshaw (1975) found a left-visual field superiority when the two faces to be compared (only one was presented in a trial, the other was held in memory) differed on every feature, but a right-visual field superiority when the two faces differed on a single feature. (These results have been confirmed by two recent and yet unpublished experiments by Fairweather, Brizzolara, Tabossi, & Umiltà). Virostek and Cutting (1979) measured the accuracy of signers in identifying alphabetical and numerical hand configurations from the American Sign Language, in a same-different task, and found greater right-visual field superiority in the alphabetical condition, in which the pairs of stimuli differed, on average, by only 1.3 features, than in the numerical condition in which the pairs of stimuli differed by 2.2 features. In addition, when alphabetic pairs were separated according to whether they differed by one or two features, a significant right-visual field superiority appeared only in the first case. The right-visual field superiority observed for the largest differences by Umiltà and his colleagues, and for the smallest differences by Patterson and Bradshaw, and by Virostek and Cutting, were interpreted by all these authors as revealing an analytic mode of processing. Differences in experimental procedure cannot easily explain the apparent discrepancy. But the fact that both Patterson and Bradshaw's and Virostek and Cutting's experiments used stimuli that evoke very familiar kinds of configurations (faces, and handshapes, respectively) might be of some importance.

I assumed that the right hemisphere has developed some special rules for extracting high-order relationships between elements of an object (structural features), instead of extracting, as the left hemisphere apparently does, the elements as such, independently of each other (local features). So, what we need to know first in order to specify holistic processing is what high-order relationships the right hemisphere considers in a face, a geometric figure, a nonsense shape, etc. They would not reduce to a contour or overall shape. They would presumably be related to those characteristics that better discriminate between members of a same class and are not affected by changes in viewpoint, by degraded conditions of inspection or by some changes in the object itself. A face, for instance, should be recognized whether it appears as a full face or a three-quarter face, whether it is sad or smiling, whether a moustache is added or not, whether time has produced wrinkles or not. Left-visual field advantage for faces is observed whenever the subject has to extract high-order physiognomic information; that is when, for example, in a same-different classification task some transformation is accomplished in one stimulus relative to the other, which prevents the subject from making a physical match or using particular details in the material. Bertelson, Vanhaelen, and Morais (1979) have found left-visual field superiority in same-different reaction times to pairs of photographs of the same person, or different ones, taken from different viewing angles ("facial identity" condition), but no hemifield effect for pairs of photographs taken from the same viewing angle. A further experiment run in the same laboratory and using a change in expression, rather than a change in viewing angle, yielded similar outcomes. Moscovitch, Scullion, and Christie (1976) also found no hemifield effect for "identikit" pictures that were either identical or very different, but a clear left-visual field superiority in a task involving comparison of photographs and caricatures.

Confronted with the very different schematic faces of Patterson and Bradshaw's experiment, the right hemisphere might have performed the task easily on the basis of the apprehension of the high-order relationships between the elements that the subject has developed for faces. Apprehension of these structural features might even be easier for schematic faces than for more complex stimuli such as photographs or "identikits." But, on thee other hand, faces are never distinguished by a single element. In the condition in which only one element was different between the two faces, the subject would have inspected them element by element, either serially or in parallel, and this is probably the reason why (1) left-hemisphere superiority was observed, and (2) "different" responses were much faster than "same" responses.

Another way of making it difficult to extract the structural features of faces is, apparently, to present the faces upside-down. While Patterson and Bradshaw (1975) obtained a right-hemisphere superiority for comparing upright schematic faces differing on every feature, the same authors found no hemifield effect in a further, unpublished experiment (mentioned in Bradshaw, Gates, & Patterson, 1976) that repeated the 1975 one but inverted the faces. The results observed by Yin (1970) were probably even more impressive. Yin found that faces are better recognized than houses in upright presentation, but less well with inverted presentation. This interaction was shown by normal controls and several groups of brain-damaged subjects. There was an exception, however. Right-posterior patients had better performance for faces than for houses in both upright and inverted presentations, and for the inverted faces they were even more accurate than normals. In addition, the difference in performance between upright faces and upright houses was almost null for right-posterior patients, and it was smaller for them than for any other group. It would thus seem that right posterior lesions impair the mechanism that enables a subject to extract the structural features of a face. While normals and patients in whom this mechanism has been spared would try to use it for dealing with the inverted faces, as they apparently do—in this case efficiently—with upright ones, right-posterior patients would be free to use a less specific configurational mode of processing or a mode of processing based on local features.

Yin's results suggest either that the high-order relationships between the elements of a pattern depend on the spatial orientation of the pattern to a different extent according to the type of pattern (perhaps more for a house than for a square, but certainly more for a face), or that the ability to process the structural features of a face in its usual orientation is a special one, different from the ability to process the structural features of other common objects. I wish to make clear, here, that the hypothesis that the right hemisphere is endowed with a special ability for dealing with faces would not be contradictory to the characterization of the same hemisphere as a holistic processor. Recognizing faces despite physical transformations seems to require the extraction of structural features, i.e., a holistic mode of processing. These structural features might be peculiar to faces, and the mechanism operating on them a specific one. This would simply imply that there is a holistic mechanism suitable for faces, which is different of the holistic mechanism suitable for houses, ears, or shoes. They might not be the same, but they would share at least one important property, to know that they operate on structural features. The fact that face recognition seems to imply a right-hemisphere ability strengthens, rather than weakens, the more fundamental claim of a holistic right hemisphere. It would be consistent with the principle that mental activities of the same nature tend to be

represented anatomically in the same place or near places if the two supposed special abilities, one for recognizing faces, the other for decoding
speech, were linked to a holistic and an analytic hemisphere, respectively.

3.4. General issues

Having discussed the possible basis of right-hemisphere superiority for face
recognition, it now seems necessary to consider the possible reasons for
right-hemisphere inferiority for language.

The conception that language pertains to the left hemisphere has been
moderated by evidence indicating that the right hemisphere also has some
linguistic capabilities. However, one should not look at left-hemisphere
dominance for language as a matter of degree. When a function is accomplished evenly by either hemisphere, or more efficiently by one than the
other, one must wonder whether the hemispheres are contributing to the
function in qualitatively different ways. The right hemisphere might not
simply be dealing with language at a lower level than the left hemisphere, it
might be dealing with language in a different way, or on the basis of abilities
or mental processes of a different nature. The inferiority of the right
hemisphere would thus come from the cognitive processing of the left
hemisphere being more suitable for language. Perhaps it might be said that
the specific way of knowing of the left hemisphere allowed language to
evolve as it did.

The work by Zaidel (1976; 1977; see also Zaidel, 1978 b and c) on the
linguistic capabilities of the disconnected hemispheres is especially relevant
to this issue. It suggested an unsuspected substantial amount of language in
the right hemisphere. But, as Zaidel (1978 b) pointed out, this right-hemisphere language does not correspond to "any stage in first language acquisition," nor does it quite resemble "any specific aphasic syndrome" (p. 178).
Striking differences were observed in performance level between different
abilities, namely between phonetic discrimination and auditory comprehension. Tests of comprehension of single spoken words required the subject to
point with one hand to the correct picture among four alternatives. These
tests suggested that the disconnected right hemisphere of two commissurotomized patients has access to a rich auditory lexicon, corresponding to
11 and 18 years of age, and including action verbs as well as nouns. Interestingly, all the errors in one test were confusions between semantically related
words ("table-chair"), and they usually occurred in pairs (if "dog" was
confused with "horse," then "horse" was also confused with "dog").

There is compelling evidence that perception of single spoken words by
the right hemisphere is based on some auditory, non-phonetic mechanism.
When the stimulus had to be recognized among pictures representing rhym-
ing words (a much more difficult task for the right hemisphere), adding

noise resulted for the right hemisphere in a performance decrement relative to a normal child, but for the left hemisphere it resulted in an improvement relative to a normal child. According to Zaidel, "it would seem that the Noise, lacking specific phonetic information, interferes with auditory analysis by the RH, which depends on general acoustic cues, much more than it interferes with phonetic analysis by the LH" (p. 185). It is also worth noting that, while the disconnected hemisphere can point to the picture corresponding either to the printed form or to the auditory name of a word (or even corresponding to a spoken letter, in many instances), it cannot go from print to sound and it cannot read a word that would not be understood when presented orally. This means that the right hemisphere lacks the ability to use grapheme-phoneme correspondences, an ability that is lost in a form of pathological reading, called "deep dyslexia," which follows some traumas of the left hemisphere. Lastly, the task of matching auditorily presented CV syllables (/ba, da, ga, . . . /) to the initial letters of the syllables, presented in one visual hemifield, was performed at chance level by the right hemisphere. Language comprehension by the right hemisphere would thus take place without phonetic discrimination of stop consonants. We may tend to agree with Zaidel when he says that the right hemisphere "somehow retrieves the meaning of the word by its auditory gestalt rather than by analyzing its phonetic components" (p. 183), but we have little idea if any of what the "auditory gestalt" of a word is and exactly *how* the right hemisphere does such a task (what structural features are extracted?). It should not be an impossible task, since words spoken in isolation display relatively stable auditory patterns. It is worthwhile to remember here that the right hemisphere is skilled in recognizing faces in spite of considerable physical transformations.

More complex ought to be the task of recognizing words from fluent speech. First, most of the sentences we hear each day are novel for us, so we could not have elaborated some mental pattern from previous experience. Second, variability of the acoustic characteristics is much greater for a word in a phrase or sentence context than when spoken in isolation. And, third, the hearer has to locate the word boundaries in a continuously varying signal. These may be some of the reasons why the disconnected right hemisphere, asked to point to the correct picture corresponding to a sentence, manifested great difficulty for sentences longer than three words. The right hemisphere also displayed very poor performance for those items of the Token Test that include adjectival modifying phrases such as "the large green square," although these words were well recognized when presented in isolation (Zaidel, 1977). Errors increased with position in the array, thus suggesting that segmentation may be a major obstacle (recognition of a word might be a condition for determining where the next one begins). Although the error's curve is not entirely consistent with Zaidel's interpretation that the deficit would be due to a limitation in short-term sequential verbal memory, one may agree with him in that a right hemisphere lacking a phonetic analyzer cannot produce a phonetically-based trace and entertain the trace in an internal articulatory device. Since this type of code is presumably most useful for temporary storage, its unavailability might contribute to the difficulty of the right hemisphere in understanding non-redundant sentences in a non-redundant communication context.

I wish to return to the single-word task to point out that the two commissurotomized patients tested by Zaidel showed better performance in a free-field situation in which the two hemispheres acted together than in the right-visual field–left-hemisphere situation. Although this result is insufficient to conclude that there is interaction between the hemispheres, it evokes the problem of knowing whether, how, and to what extent the right hemisphere contributes to language comprehension in the normal subject. The meaning of utterances is usually related to an environmental and emotional context. It would not be surprising if a hemisphere that seems to be highly implicated in the perception of forms, expressions, and emotions were shown to interact, in normal communication, with the hemisphere that contains an analytic linguistic processor. And interaction may require from the non-analytic hemisphere the ability to identify very quickly words that refer immediately to, say, a scene or a feeling. It seems, for example, that the right hemisphere plays an important role in imagery. In fact, it was found by Marcel and Patterson (1978), with normal subjects, that imageability affects recognition scores for left-visual field presentations, by Jones-Gotman and Milner (1978) that right-temporal lobectomy leads to a selective impairment in the recall of pairs of high-imagery words, and by Richardson (1975) that "deep" dyslexics can apparently generate images and preserve the correct reading of many imageable words. The existence of two different hemispheres might allow convergence of two ways of representing reality, thus ensuring a more meaningful interpretation of external events for the self. I can, however, only state the problem of the usefulness of interaction between analytic and non-analytic processes in language and communication: I have no answer and no acceptable speculation to offer.

One criticism that has been raised against the generality of the "analytic-holistic" dichotomy as a principle underlying hemispheric specialization concerns the fact that this dichotomy is usually invoked to describe differences in information processing or perceptual aspects of behavior, and not at all to describe differences in motor aspects. No one would deny that speech production is under the control of the left hemisphere, and it would seem that there is a more general left-hemisphere superiority for fine motor programming. However, it might be misleading to present the right hemisphere as a "mute" one. Smith (1966), testing an adult patient whose left hemisphere had been removed, found that the subject could repeat simple words, name some objects, and use expletives ("No", "Well, I . . . "); he could also sing. Gordon and Bogen (1974) found that singing was abolished and recovered before speech after inactivation of the left hemisphere by sodium amobarbital, and it was severely impaired after inactivation of the right hemisphere. This fact suggests that the right hemisphere exerts control over at least one particular kind of oral expression. Levy and Trevarthen (1977) signal that "the articulations of which the right hemisphere may be capable are probably formed as motor Gestalts, and are not constructed analytically from phoneme-elicited articulemes . . . . This would account for occasional observations that the disconnected right hemisphere may initiate appropriate speech sounds, but never maintain speech flow beyond a single syllable, or possibly, beyond an habitual multisyllabic phrase" (p. 116). The inability of the right hemisphere to produce propositional speech seems to support, rather than contradict, the relevance and generality of the "analytic-holistic" distinction. Undoubtedly, to speak is a constructive act, thus requiring analytic processes. The input to the speech production system are discrete units at different hierarchical levels (e.g., words, phonemes, vocal tract specifications), and plans and rules for the sequential assembling of the units. Lenneberg (1967) compares the "composition of discourse to the assembly of a train, where the individual coaches have to be attached while the locomotive keeps moving forward. There is an overall plan that determines the order of the cars; they are held in readiness, but at a specific time they must be released and hitched onto the moving train" (p. 219). He also states that most of the language pathology is due to "lack of availability at the right time" (p. 222). Most speech errors in normal people are also evidence of processes involving discrete units. Now, note that to speak is to recombine a finite number of components into an infinite number of sequences, in other words the activity of speaking is both an analytic and generative activity. This does not support the popular but probably erroneous belief that the right hemisphere is *the* hemisphere of creativity. A holistic processor might be more suitable for recognizing what has already been experienced and expressing what has become a motor habit than for perceiving novel stimuli or dimensions and producing new articulated sequences.

A further criticism of the notion that the left hemisphere is above all a highly competent analytic processor stems from the apparent fact that intellectual deficits do not necessarily accompany language breakdown following left-hemisphere lesions. It should be noted, however, that if language is a specific combination of analytic abilities, which developed (entirely or in part) independently of the use of analytic abilities for other functions, one may expect to observe such a specific pathology. (The notion that the left hemisphere is endowed with a host of analytic abilities, among which are those involved in language, should not be taken as implying that there exists some general analytic mechanism). The same reasoning might apply to the specific loss of the ability to recognize faces by a holistic right hemisphere. In addition, we must take into account that standardized intelligence tests might not exclusively involve analytic abilities. The contribution of the right hemisphere to the behavior of aphasic patients in these tests might not be negligible. Zaidel's work on commissurotomized patients suggested that the right hemisphere has not only a good level of auditory comprehension of single words, but also a good grasp of semantic relations such as those of class inclusion and "used for." It also seems to be particularly efficient in grasping geometrical concepts. Evidence for this comes from a study on splitbrain subjects (Franco & Sperry, 1977) as well as from laterality effects in normal subjects. Simion, Bagnara, Bisiacchi, Roncato, and Umiltà (1980) used the task of comparing pairs of geometrical figures on the basis of their names (triangle, trapezoid), irrespective of shape and size, and they found a left-visual field superiority. This type of task might be more systematically used in attempts to determine the conceptual and relational abilities of the right hemisphere. We certainly need to combine the neuropsychological exploration of hemisphere differences with hypotheses about the structural features of, say, faces, words, and geometrical forms, that might be used by the right hemisphere, in order to tap the more general issue of what holistic processing is and to what extent it contributes to human knowledge.

The possibility also exists that the "analytic-holistic" dichotomy is only one among two or more dichotomies characterizing hemispheric specialization. As was said by Moscovitch (1979), "the notion of a hemispheric system need not imply the existence of a single unifying principle; it only implies that the structures that form the system are highly interrelated . . . " (p. 417). The left hemisphere has sometimes been described as "categorial." And, in fact, there are a number of results showing left-hemisphere superiority for categorial judgments (like in name matches for letters) that do not necessarily require an interpretation in terms of analytic processing. The left-hemisphere mode of processing might thus be both analytic *and* categorial. But the advantage of seeking *one* underlying principle is that it might allow us to understand the relationships between things apparently different. An underlying principle is not a principle that is at work in any experimental situation and accounts immediately for any result. When x affects behavior in a particular way because x is itself related in some way to y, we may say that y is an underlying factor. Categorial judgments might lead to lateral asymmetry scores indicating left hemisphere superiority not because categorization always requires a local feature analysis, but because it does so in most instances and becomes consequently a current activity of the left hemisphere. Categorization (x) might thus lead to, say, right-visual field superiority, in the absencee of analytic processing (y), because categorization most of the time follows analytic processing. Or, alternatively, categorization (x) might lead to right-visual field superiority because it elicits some phonetic representation (x') of the stimulus, and phonetic representations in the course of speech are products of analytic processing. Briefly, when we are confronted with several dichotomies, each allowing us to describe in the more suitable way a different set of data, we will perhaps make good progress if we manage to relate these several dichotomies to an underlying one.

The attempt to describe hemisphere differences in terms of analytic versus holistic processing modes concerns the contemporaneous mind, and not the primitive one. Hemisphere specialization may have arisen because of some necessity or advantage in distinguishing analytic and holistic processes in the neural space, but also (as some authors have suggested) because it avoids bilateral competition in the control of the articulatory structures. Man is characterized by at least three properties that are absent or very rudimentary in the other primates: work (making and using of tools), language, and hemispheric specialization. I suspect that all three are in intimate connection. Both work and language seem to imply analytic processes. But we cannot say which ones, from fine sequential articulatory movements, fine sequential finger movements, and increase of analytic capacity, was first in triggering hemispheric specialization.

3.5. Some Difficulties in the Interpretation of Laterality Experiments

I turn again to the experimental work on perceptual lateral asymmetry in normal subjects, and I will consider now some difficulties raised in its interpretation, before contemplating some possible lines of research.

In normal subjects, the analytic and holistic processors are not physically separated as they are in the commisurotomized patients. In many experimental situations the task may be such that only one processor is competent to deal with the stimuli. But in many other situations both processors can, to a greater or smaller extent, do the task. When both processors do the task independently and simultaneously, considerable variability is introduced in the results of experiments, making it difficult to assess the contribution of each type of processor. In reaction time situations, for example, the first processor to reach a decision might not be the same for different types of trials, and it might even not be always the same for a same type of trial if the two distributions overlap. "Same" and "different" judgments on pairs of stimuli have frequently yielded opposite laterality effects. For instance, in one of the experiments reported by Patterson and Bradshaw (1975), in which two schematic faces were presented in a trial and had to be judged as same or differnt, there was a left-visual field superiority for "same" responses and a non-significant right-visual field superiority for "different" responses. Different faces differed on every feature, and the right-hemisphere processor could thus be very fast in reaching the decision "same"; on the other hand, the left-hemisphere processor might have reached the decision "different" on the basis of local-feature analysis (to compare for one feature might be sufficiently informative) before the right-hemisphere processor, in an important number of trials.

As we have to rely on intuition for estimating the relative importance of the local and structural features that can be extracted from the forms presented to the subject, and the capacity required by this extraction, it is not always clear what kind of predictions should be made on the basis of the "analytic-holistic" distinction. Intuition especially is of little help in situations in which dual processing is possible. Bradshaw, Gates, and Patterson (1976) have run an experiment in which one task was supposed a priori to be an "analytic" task and the other a "holistic" task. In the "analytic" task the subject had to judge as same or different two relevant elements (two plus or two multiplication signs, or one of each), which were presented together with three irrelevant elements (a circle, a square, and a diamond). It was assumed by the authors that locating the relevant elements requires an analytic mode of processing. However, it might rather imply a holistic process by which each element in the display would be tested for the presence of a particular structural feature. On the other hand, the task was not a simple one, since it involved both locating and comparing the two targets. Nor were the results simple. They showed a left-visual field superiority for "same" judgments, and a non-significant right-visual field superiority for "different" judgments. The other task designed by Bradshaw and his collaborators required the subject to judge whether the array of five elements was symmetrical about a vertical or a horizontal axis, and perception of symmetry was assumed to depend on a holistic process. The results showed no hemifield effect. One would say that in many circumstances, but not all, symmetry may be more easily determined by a holistic process. Apparently, it was not the case here. According to the authors, "the reaction times were generally long and some subjects claimed that they frequently were forced to look for corresponding elements across the display in order to decide" (p. 675). One of the lessons of this (and other) experiment(s) is that before considering an unexpected result as a piece of evidence against the characterization of hemisphere differences in terms of the "analytic-holistic" distinction, we have to check our intuitions about these processes and examine if the experiment can suitably tap what we want it to tap. We have to know much more about analytic and holistic processes, and unexpected results are not a refutation, but may instead be a source of knowledge.

Some authors have tried to give an operational definition of analytic and holistic processes in terms of serial and parallel processes, respectively. It seems to me, however, that the two distinctions should not be assimilated. Analytic processes might, in principle, operate simultaneously on different elements or details. And the extraction of high order relationships between the elements (holistic processing) might need successive attempts until a suitable representation is reached. In a task matching two black and white grids for identity, Gross (1972) found a left-visual field superiority independently of the degree of similarity between the grids, but reaction times increased as similarity increased. When similarity is greater, the extraction of high order relationships permitting subjects to come to the conclusion of a difference between the two grids might be harder or require additional control. An increase in reaction time in such circumstances, or as a function of the number of elements in the whole, cannot be used as an indication of analytic processing.

In the more recent literature on lateral asymmetry a prominent place is occupied by the "same-different" reaction time paradigm. Models that had been elaborated to account for rapidity differences in "same" and "different" judgments may be reached by a fast, holistic process, and "different" ones by a slow, analytic process (Bamber, 1969) seemed to imply that the first type of response should be associated with right-hemisphere superiority and the second with left-hemisphere superiority. Although this outcome has been observed in several experiments, I have also mentioned some experiments that showed either right- or left-hemisphere superiority for both "same" and "different" judgments; and in an unpublished experiment run in our laboratory it was the reverse picture that was found. Indeed, the use of either analytic or holistic processing modes for reaching decisions of identity and difference, and their relative rapidities, should depend on task variables. The task might even be such that the two processing modes would be used in different subsets of trials leading, all of them, to either a "same" or a "different" response. Suppose that in Patterson and Bradshaw (1975)'s experiment on schematic faces differing in every element the structural feature that the subject extracted from the target was easy to distinguish from the structural features of two of the three non-targets, but not from the structural feature of the third non-target. One might conceive that for "same" trials and "different" trials employing the first two non-targets the holistic processor might be faster than the analytic processor, but slower than the latter for "different" trials employing the third non-target. This was probably the reason why Fairweather, Brizzolara, Tabossi, and Umiltà in the experiment, yet unpublished, that repeated Patterson and Bradshaw's found left-visual field superiority for "same" trials and two of the three types of "different" trials, and right-visual field superiority for the remaining type of "different" trial.

The same authors, in replicating Patterson and Bradshaw's experiment using schematic faces differing in only one element, found one potentially interesting result. "Same" responses were slower, faster, and equal to "different" ones, when the difference concerned the eyes, the nose, and the mouth, respectively. As the left hemisphere was faster for both "same" and "different" responses, Fairweather and his collaborators concluded that this hemisphere can operate either analytically or holistically. But another interpretation is possible. A parallel and self-terminating analytic processing might allow the subject to respond "same" faster than "different" in some types of "different" trials. It might, in fact, be easier or quicker to chose the response "same" when three independent tests yield three positive outcomes than to chose the response "different" when they yield only one or two negative outcomes. This advantage would combine with rapidity differences in dealing with the three elements to produce the observed results. The eyes difference was presumably determined more rapidly than the other differences always or almost always, and the mouth difference before the nose difference much more often than the reverse. So, while the decision "different" for the eyes was almost never preceded by a conflicting "same" decision, the decision "different" for the mouth was frequently preceded by one, and the decision "different" for the nose by two. The absence of response conflict in trials "same" might thus compensate for awaiting the outcome of the slowest test—hence, the equal rapidity for same- and different-mouth trials—and offer them an advantage relative to the different-nose ones. The conclusion about the interactions between laterality theory and "same-different" models thus seems, for the time being, the following. It is very hazardous to infer the use of either analytic or holistic processes from apriorisms about the direction of the hemifield effect for one particular type of response, the homogeneity of hemifield effects, or the relative rapidity of "same" and "different" responses. Any interpretation must be based on a careful examination of the characteristics of the task.

A further difficulty to interpretation (but also an interesting question) arises from the possibility that dual processing is not strictly automatic (unintentional) or that readiness of processors depends on context. Depending on the particular situation, the subject might rely more on one mode of processing than on the other. For example, Simion, Bagnara, Bisiacchi, Roncato, and Umiltà (1980) used the task of classifying letters as same or different in terms of their names irrespective of case, and right-visual field superiority has been found for physical matches, name matches, and "different" responses; however, when those trials were mixed with trials requiring classification of geometrical figures as same or different in terms of their names (a task which, alone, showed left-visual field superiority), right-visual field superiority only appeared for letters in the case of name matches. It seems that a context associated with important right-hemisphere processing has reduced the tendency towards left-hemisphere processing, at least in those cases in which the last mode of processing would not be obligatory. On the other hand, it may be that right-hemisphere processing is more automatic. (Among analytic processes there might be automatic ones, but also non-automatic ones such as those used by some non-musicians in recognizing melodies). In fact, in the study carried out by Simion and her collaborators, the letter-trial context did not affect the visual field asymmetry for geometrical figures. And the same phenomenon seems to be observed in the auditory modality: the mixed presentation of trials requiring pitch judgments and linguistic judgments affects the ear difference for linguistic judgments, but not the ear difference for pitch judgments (Studdert-Kennedy, personal communication).

The balance between different processing modes, although constrained to some extent by the degree of automaticity of the processes, might undergo not only immediate contextual influences, but also the influence of subjects' past experience or idiosyncrasy. We do not know which kind of factors enabled some non-musicians to deal with melodies, in some circumstances, in an analytic way. But we may conjecture (and this is a possible line of research) that these subjects will also tend to be more analytic than the others in non-musical tasks that are open to strategies. The possibility of an idiosyncratic balance between analytic and holistic processing modes, also called "hemisphericity" (Bogen, De Zure, Ten Houten, & Marsh, 1972) or "cognitive style," requires investigators to distinguish between the cerebral laterality, i.e. the relationship between the processing modes and the hemispheres, and the use of cerebral laterality, i.e. the tendency to rely more on one processing mode than the other. Many group differences, for example between males and females, dyslexics and non-dyslexics, etc., that have been observed in laterality scores, might not (or not only) express real differences in cerebral laterality, but instead (or also) differences in its use.

3.6. Possible Lines of Research

Perhaps the most important weakness of the present description of analytic and holistic processors as pertaining to the left and the right hemisphere, respectively, is that it still ignores the necessary processor interactions. If asking about the operating modes of analytic and holistic processors is to put the question of hemispheric specialization, then to consider the interactions between these processors is to tackle the problem of hemispheric interactions. Neuropsychological research on hemispheric interactions will have to take into account (and to take advantage of) thought on processor interactions and experimental paradigms devised in this domain.

One of the most influential ideas put forward by Neisser in his book *Cognitive Psychology* (1967) was that "attentive acts are carried out in the context of the more global properties already established at the preattentive level'' (p. 90). ''The preattentive processes must be genuinely 'global' and 'wholistic.' Each figure or object must be separated from the others in its entirety, as a potential framework for the subsequent and more detailed analyses of attention'' (p. 89). The claim that some global processing precedes local processing was supported more recently by, namely, Broadbent (1977) and Navon (1977). Broadbent proposed that a passive global or low-frequency system packages information into large segments that are later examined by an active high-frequency system for more detailed information. Navon, while distinguishing between global and local processing in a similar way, proposed that the distinction was more precisely not between stages of attention, but between different stages of the perceptual analysis of what is attended to.

Navon, in a very elegant paradigm, tried to demonstrate that global processing is an early stage that cannot be skipped even under instructions to attend to local features. His experimental studies tended, however, to test a weaker version of the global precedence hypothesis: Not that local processing starts only after global processing, but that global processing is always complete before local processing. He used as stimuli single large letters (for example, H) that were composed of several small letters, either identical (H) or non-identical to the large letter (for example, S). And he found an interference effect between the two levels when the subject was instructed to process the local level of the display, but none when the decision concerned the global level. The result is compatible with the idea that some stage in global processing is necessary for local processing to start, but also with the idea that global and local levels in a form are processed in parallel and global processing invariably terminates earlier. It must be noted, on the other hand, that things in the interference paradigm are much more complex than they seemed initially. Kinchla and Wolf (1979) varied the angular size of the large letter, and correspondingly the angular size of the small letters, and they found that the global level was processed faster than the local one in the smallest displays, but slower in the largest ones. They proposed that ''forms having an optimal size in the visual field are processed first, with subsequent processing of both larger and smaller letters'' (p. 228). Martin (1979a) varied stimulus sparsity, i.e., the number of local elements in the large letter, and she found faster global processing for many-element stimuli and faster local processing for the few-element stimuli. Interference effects were observed for both levels of processing with many-element stimuli and for global processing with few-element stimuli. Hoffman (1980) introduced distortion in either the large letter, the small one, both, or none, and he found either local or global precedence depending on which level was distorted. He therefore proposed that the ''different levels of a form are encoded in parallel with the 'quality' of information at each level determining the speed of encoding'' (p. 228). Factors that could affect the quality of information, and hence level priority, would include size, retinal location, length to width ratio, number of elements, clarity, continuity of contours. The analogy between the results observed with the present paradigm and the laterality one on analytic and holistic processes is striking: The relative efficiency of analytic (local) and holistic (global) processing is affected by a host of factors related to the stimuli and to the instructions given to the subjects. There is no absolute precedence (or superiority) of a given mode (level) of processing.

We might be tempted to assign the processing of the local and global levels of a form (in Navon's situation, the small letters and the large letter) to the analytic and holistic modes of processing, respectively. Martin (1979b) using an experimental situation similar to Navon's, found laterality data that strengthen this temptation. The local level was more rapidly processed in the left hemisphere, while for the global level there was either a right-hemisphere superiority or no hemisphere difference according to the existence or not of a conflict between the two levels. Nevertheless, we should be cautious and not generalize solely on the basis of this result. There is no reason for assuming a priori a simple correspondence between levels in the stimuli and modes of processing. In Martin's experiment, each part does not play a distinctive role since all the discrete elements provide the same information, and the subject might eventually process any one of them in terms of structural features. Conversely, to deal with a whole is not necessarily to process it in terms of these features. A subject asked to make a judgment about an entire form might do that through the extraction of component features. The correspondence between levels in the stimulus and modes of processing must, indeed, be tested over a variety of situations and materials.

In psychology, trust very often has to depend on convergence of results coming from different paradigms or different types of evidence. On one hand, laterality scores may provide useful information in the context of the study of analytic and holistic processes and of their interactions. On the other hand, it is hazardous to infer the use of either analytic or holistic processes only from the direction of laterality effects in the absence of independent evidence. While such evidence, from another task or subjects' introspection, has been used in some studies (remember Bever and Chiarello's and Peretz and Morais'), the speculative interpretation I offered above for a set of experiments on nonsense patterns lacks any kind of independent empirical evidence about the nature of the processing modes. Between the neuropsychological research on hemisphere differences in processing modes and the more specifically cognitive research on analytic and holistic processes there is a gap that still awaits to be filled.

A brief and incomplete list of the kind of experimental studies that might be confronted profitably with neuropsychological investigation includes: (a)

The recent developments on the interference paradigm described above. In particular it would be worth manipulating distortion and "blurring" that could selectively affect either the global or the local levels of a stimulus. (b) "Same-different" classification tasks using patterns constructed according to presumably relevant structural features like symmetry (see Fox, 1975). (c) Demonstrations of "configural superiority" effects, which reveal interactions between global and local processing. These tasks imply, for example, the perception of lines in structured forms (Weisstein & Harris, 1974; McClelland & Miller, 1979), the discrimination of elements as a function of nearby elements (Pomerantz & Garner, 1973; Pomerantz, Sager, & Stoever, 1977), and the perception of pointing of ambiguous triangles as a function of the orientational characteristics of the configuration and the shape of the surrounding forms (Palmer, 1980). (d) Experiments with multidimensional stimuli varying on integral dimensions as evidenced by redundancy gain and orthogonal interference (see, for instance, Garner & Felfoldy, 1970; Lockhead & King, 1977; Dykes, 1979).

I conclude here by saying that the "analytic-holistic" dichotomy as corresponding to left- and right-hemisphere processing modes, respectively, does not have to be true but useful. I believe, on the basis of the material reviewed here, that it begins to be useful, and that it has promise. But it would reach the top of usefulness if it could lead those who do not agree with this to demonstrate, with new and exciting findings, that it is not true.

ACKNOWLEDGMENTS

I am grateful to Michael Studdert-Kennedy, Morris Moscovitch, and my colleagues from Brussels, Jesus Alegria, Paul Bertelson, Patrizia Bisiacchi, Daniel Holender, and Isabelle Peretz, for the valuable comments they made on earlier drafts. Some of their doubts and criticisms that were not met in the final version remain obsessing in my mind.

REFERENCES

Bamber, D. Reaction times and error rates for "same-different" judgments of multidimensional stimuli. *Perception and Psychophysics*, 1969, *6*, 169–174.

Bertelson, P., Vanhaelen, H., & Morais, J. Left hemifield superiority and the extraction of physiognomic information. In I. S. Russell, M. W. Van Hof, & G. Berlucchi (Eds.), *The structure and function of the cerebral commissures*, London: McMillan, 1979.

Bever, T. G. Cerebral asymmetries in humans are due to the differentiation of two incompatible processes: holistic and analytic. In D. Aaronson, & R. W. Rieber (Eds.), *Developmental psycholinguistics and communication disorders*. Annals of the New York Academy of Sciences, 263, New York: The New York Academy of Sciences, 1975.

Bever, T. G., & Chiarello, R. J. Cerebral dominance in musicians and non-musicians. *Science,* 1974, *185,* 537–539.

Birkett, P. Hemisphere differences in the recognition of nonsense shapes: Cerebral dominance or strategy effects? *Cortex,* 1978, *14,* 245–249.

Blechner, M. J. Left-ear advantage for sounds characterized by a rapidly varying resonance frequence. *Bulletin of Psychonomic Society,* 1977, *9,* 363–366.

Bogen, J., De Zure, R., Ten Houten, W., & Marsh, J. The other side of the brain: the A/P ratio, *Bulletin of the Los Angeles Neurological Societies,* 1972, *37,* 49–61.

Bouma, A. *Hemispheric differences in the detection of embedded figures.* Paper presented to the Annual European Conference of the International Neuropsychology Society, at Chianciano, June 1980.

Bradshaw, J. L., Gates, A., & Patterson, K. Hemispheric differences in processing visual patterns. *Quarterly Journal of Experimental Psychology,* 1976, *28,* 667–681.

Broadbent, D. E. The hidden preattentive processes. *The American Psychologist,* 1977, *32,* 109–118.

Day, R. S., Cutting, J. E., & Copeland, P. M. Perception of linguistic and non-linguistic dimensions of dichotic stimuli. Status Report on Speech Research. Haskins Laboratories, 1971, SR-27, 193–197.

Dykes, J. R. A demonstration of selection of analyzers for integral dimensions. *Journal of Experimental Psychology: Human Perception and Performance,* 1979, *5,* 734–745.

Fairweather, H., Brizzolara, D., Tabossi, P., and Umiltà, C. *Functional cerebral lateralization: dichotomy or plurality?* Unpublished manuscript.

Fontenot, D. J. Visual field differences in the recognition of verbal and non-verbal stimuli in man. *Journal of comparative Physiological Psychology,* 1973, *85,* 564–569.

Fox, J. The use of structural diagnostics in recognition. *Journal of Experimental Psychology: Human Perception and Performance,* 1975, *104,* 57–67.

Franco, L., & Sperry, R. W. Hemisphere lateralization for cognitive processing of geometry. *Neuropsychologia,* 1977, *14,* 1–7.

Gaede, S. E., Parsons, O. A., & Bertera, J. H. Hemispheric differences in music perception: aptitude vs experience. *Neuropsychologia,* 1978, *16,* 369–373.

Garner, W. R. Aspects of a stimulus: Features, dimensions, and configurations. In E. Rosch, & B. B. Lloyd (Eds.), *Cognition and Categorization.* Hillsdale, New Jersey: Lawrence Erlbaum Associates, 1978.

Garner, W. R., & Felfoldy, G. L. Integrality of stimulus dimensions in various types of information processing. *Cognitive Psychology,* 1970, *1,* 225–241.

Gordon, H. W. Left hemisphere dominance for rhythmic elements in dichotically-presented melodies. *Cortex,* 1978, *14,* 58–70.

Gordon, H. W., & Bogen, J. E. Hemispheric lateralization of singing after intracarotid sodium amobarbital. *Journal of Neurology, Neurosurgery and Psychiatry,* 1974, *37,* 727–739.

Gross, M. M. Hemispheric specialization for processing of visually presented verbal and spatial stimuli. *Perception and Psychophysics,* 1972, *12,* 357–363.

Haggard, M. P., & Parkinson, A. M. Stimulus and task factors as determinants of ear advantages. *Quarterly Journal of Experimental Psychology,* 1971, *23,* 168–177.

Hannay, H. J., Rogers, J. P., & Durant, R. F. Complexity as a determinant of visual field effects for random forms. *Acta Psychologica,* 1976, *40,* 29–34.

Hoffmann, J. E. Interaction between global and local levels of a form. *Journal of Experimental Psychology: Human Perception and Performance,* 1980, *6,* 222–234.

James, W. *The principles of psychology* (Vol. 1), Holt, 1890.

Jones-Gotman, M., & Milner, B. Right-temporal lobe contribution to image-mediated verbal learning. *Neuropsychologia,* 1978, *16,* 61–71.

Kimura, D. Cerebral dominance and the perception of verbal stimuli. *Canadian Journal of Psychology,* 1961, *15,* 166–171.

Kimura, D. Left-right differences in the perception of melodies. *Quarterly Journal of Experimental Psychology,* 1964, *16,* 355–358.

Kinchla, R. A., & Wolf, J. M. The order of visual processing: "Top-down", "bottom-up", or "middle-out". *Perception and Psychophysics,* 1979, *25,* 225–231.

Kinsbourne, M., & Hicks, R. E. Mapping cerebral functional space: competition and collaboration in human performance. In M. Kinsbourne (Ed.), *Asymmetrical function of the brain.* London: Cambridge University Press, 1978.

Lashley, K. S. Functional determinants of cerebral localization. In F. A. Beach, D. O. Hebb, C. T. Morgan, & H. W. Nissen (Eds.), *The neuropsychology of Lashley. Selected papers of K. S. Lashley.* New York: McGraw-Hill, 1960.

Lenneberg, E. H. *Biological foundations of language.* New York: John Wiley & Sons, 1967.

Levy, J. Possible basis for the evolution of lateral specialization of the human brain. *Nature,* 1969, *224,* 614–615.

Levy, J., & Trevarthen, C. Perceptual, semantic and phonetic aspects of elementary language processes in split-brain patients. *Brain,* 1977, *100,* 105–118.

Liberman, A. M. The specialization of the language hemisphere. In F. O. Schmitt, & F. G. Worden (Eds.), *The neurosciences: Third study program.* Cambridge, Massachusetts: MIT Press, 1974.

Liberman, A. M., Cooper, F. S., Shankweiler, D. S., & Studdert-Kennedy, M. Perception of the speech code. *Psychological Review,* 1967, *74,* 431–461.

Lockhead, G. R., & King, M. C. Classifying integral stimuli. *Journal of Experimental Psychology: Human Perception and Performance,* 1977, *3,* 436–443.

Marcel, A. J., & Patterson, K. Word recognition and production: Reciprocity in clinical and normal studies. In J. Requin (Ed.), *Attention and Performance VII.* Hillsdale, New Jersey: Lawrence Erlbaum Associates, 1978.

Martin, M. Local and global processing: the role of sparsity. *Memory and Cognition,* 1979, *7,* 476–484(a).

Martin, M. Hemispheric specialization for local and global processing. *Neuropsychologia,* 1979, *17,* 33–40(b).

McClelland, J. L., & Miller, J. Structural factors in figure perception. *Perception and Psychophysics,* 1979, *26,* 221–229.

Morais, J. Monaural ear differences for reaction times to speech with a many-to-one mapping paradigm. *Perception and Psychophysics,* 1976, *19,* 144–148.

Morais, J., Ben-Dror, I., Vanhaelen, H., & Bertelson, P. *Laterality effects for nonsense patterns.* In preparation.

Moscovitch, M. Information processing and the cerebral hemispheres. In M. S. Gazzaniga (Ed.), *The handbook of behavioral neurobiology: Volume on neuropsychology.* New York: Plenum Press, 1979.

Moscovitch, M., Scullion, D., & Christie, D. Early vs. late stages of processing and their relation to functional hemispheric asymmetries in face recognition. *Journal of Experimental Psychology: Human Perception and Performance,* 1976, *2,* 401–416.

Navon, D. Forest before trees: The precedence of global features in visual perception. *Cognitive Psychology,* 1977, *9,* 353–383.

Nebes, R. D. Superiority of the minor hemisphere in commissurotomized man for the perception of part-whole relationships. *Cortex,* 1971, *7,* 333–347.

Nebes, R. D. Dominance of the minor hemisphere in commissurotomized man in a test of figural unification. *Brain,* 1972, *95,* 633–638.

Neisser, U. *Cognitive Psychology.* New York: Appleton-Century-Crofts, 1967.

Palmer, S. E. What makes triangles point: local and global effects in configurations of ambiguous triangles. *Cognitive Psychology,* 1980, *12,* 285–305.

Papçun G., Krashen, S., Terbeek, D., Remington, R., & Harshman, R. Is the left hemisphere specialized for speech, language and/or something else? *Journal of the Acoustical Society of America*, 1974, *55*, 319–327.

Patterson, K., & Bradshaw, J. L. Differential hemispheric mediation of nonverbal visual stimuli. *Journal of Experimental Psychology: Human Perception and Performance*, 1975, *1*, 246–252.

Peretz, I., & Morais, J. Modes of processing melodies and ear asymmetry in non-musicians. *Neuropsychologia*, 1980, *18*, 477–489.

Pomerantz, J. R., & Garner, W. R. Stimulus configuration in selective attention tasks. *Perception and Psychophysics*, 1973, *14*, 565–569.

Pomerantz, J. R., Sager, L. C., & Stoever, R. J. Perception of wholes and of their component parts: some configural superiority effects. *Journal of Experimental Psychology: Human Perception and Performance*, 1977, *3*, 422–435.

Richardson, J. T. E. Further evidence on the effect of word imageability in dyslexia. *Quarterly Journal of Experimental Psychology*, 1975, *27*, 445–449.

Schwartz, J., & Tallal, P. Rate of acoustic change may underlie hemispheric specialization for speech perception. *Science*, 1980, *207*, 1380–1381.

Shanon, B. Lateralization effects in musical decision tasks. *Neuropsychologia*, 1980, *18*, 21–31.

Simion, F., Bagnara, S., Bisiacchi, P., Roncato, S., & Umiltà, C. Laterality effects, levels of processing, and stimulus properties. *Journal of Experimental Psychology: Human Perception and Performance*, 1980, *6*, 184–195.

Smith, A. Speech and other functions after left (dominant) hemispherectomy. *Journal of Neurology, Neurosurgery and Psychiatry*, 1966, *29*, 467–471.

Sperry, R. W. Lateral specialization in the surgically separated hemispheres. In F. O. Schmitt, & F. G. Worden (Eds.), *The neurosciences: Third study program*. Cambridge, Massachussets: MIT Press, 1974.

Umilta, C., Bagnara, S., & Simion, F. Laterality effects for simple and complex geometrical figures and nonsense patterns. *Neuropsychologia*, 1978, *16*, 43–49.

Virostek, S., & Cutting, J. E. Asymmetries for Ameslan handshapes and other forms in signers and nonsigners. *Perception and Psychophysics*, 1979, *26*, 505–508.

Weisstein, N., & Harris, C. S. Visual detection of line segments: An object superiority effect. *Science*, 1974, *186*, 752–755.

Yin, R. K. Face recognition by brain-injured patients: A dissociable ability. *Neuropsychologia*, 1970, *8*, 395–402.

Zaidel, E. Auditory vocabulary of the right hemisphere following brain bisection or hemidecortication. *Cortex*, 1976, *12*, 191–211.

Zaidel, E. Unilateral auditory language comprehension on the Token Test following cerebral commissurotomy and hemispherectomy. *Neuropsychologia*, 1977, *15*, 1–18.

Zaidel, E. Concepts of cerebral dominance in the split brain. In Buser, & Rougeul-Buser (Eds.), *Cerebral correlates of conscious experience*, INSERM Symposium n° 6. Amsterdam: Elsevier/North-Holland Biomedical Press, 1978(a).

Zaidel, E. Lexical organization in the right hemisphere. In Buser, & Rougeul-Buser (Eds.), *Cerebral correlates of conscious experience*, INSERM Symposium n° 6. Amsterdam: Elsevier/North-Holland Biomedical Press, 1978(b).

Zaidel, E. Auditory language comprehension in the right hemisphere following cerebral commissurotomy and hemispherectomy: a comparison with child language and aphasia. In A. Caramazza, & E. B. Zurif (Eds.), *Language acquisition and language breakdown*. Baltimore: Johns Hopkins University Press, 1978(c).

Zatorre, R. J. Recognition of dichotic melodies by musicians and non-musicians. *Neuropsychologia*, 1979, *17*, 607–617.

15 Language and Brain: Some Points of Connection

Edgar B. Zurif
Aphasia Research Center
Department of Neurology
Boston University School of Medicine
  and
Boston V.A. Medical Center

The research briefly described here represents an attempt to use the phenomena of aphasia—the selective language deficits consequent to variously placed lesions—to help characterize language-brain relations. Like earlier accounts of a connectionist bent (e.g., Lichtheim, 1885; Wernicke, 1874; see also Caplan, 1980 and Geschwind, 1970 for summaries of this work), the present effort is rooted in the assumption that the exercise of language reflects the workings of a set of interacting subsystems. However, in sharp contrast to the initial connectionist formulations that fractionated language in terms of distinctions among different linguistic faculties (e.g., speaking as opposed to listening) and correspondingly, categorized the aphasias largely in terms of which of these faculties were judged to be relatively spared by brain damage, and which, relatively disrupted, the current focus is on distinctions among types of linguistic information or levels of structural description that are implemented whether speaking or listening. The goal is to explain the various aphasic syndromes as the result of a disruption to one or another of the constituent processing systems (phonological, syntactic or semantic) that affect the construction of these levels. In effect, this approach seeks a functional analysis of language that is neurologically adequate—that is, one in which the distinctions among linguistic processing constituents correspond to neurologically natural separations of function as revealed by patterns of language disruption in aphasia.

Support for this approach can be seen most clearly in some recent analyses of Broca's aphasia. A summary of this work follows directly.

GRAMMATICAL LIMITATIONS IN BROCA'S APHASIA

Standard clinical descriptions of Broca's aphasia—the language disorder associated with left-anterior brain damage—have held that while there is an obvious disruption to production in the form of labored and agrammatic speech, comprehension skills remain relatively intact (e.g., Lenneberg, 1973; Locke, Caplan, & Kellar, 1973). As might be expected from my introductory remarks, however, this clinical emphasis on the dissociation of productive and receptive skills has proved somewhat misleading. Finer grained analyses of the bases of "relatively intact" comprehension have indicated that speech and comprehension are not so readily separable as clinical impression would have them be. Rather, these experimental observations suggest that not only do Broca's aphasics have comprehension limitations, but that in an interesting manner this limitation roughly parallels that so easily observed in production: Just as the patients tend, when speaking, to omit grammatical morphemes, both free and bound (i.e., the closed class of minor lexical categories—determiners, auxiliaries, and morphemes signaling tense and number, and the like), so too are they unable to make use of these items as syntactic placeholders for the purpose of comprehension (Goodglass, 1976; Scholes, 1978; Zurif, Caramazza, & Myerson, 1972; Zurif & Caramazza, 1976).

As a consequence, the Broca's aphasics' understanding of utterances rests largely on their ability to infer meaning directly from the content words or open class items of an utterance—guided by their knowledge of "what makes factual sense." Indeed, when Broca's aphasics are forced to rely on syntactically indicated relations (provided by the distribution of the closed class items) in order to understand a sentence, they are clearly unable to do so (Caramazza & Zurif, 1976; Scholes, 1978).

Therefore, even granting its obvious effects on the motor implementation of speech, left-anterior brain damage does not so much dissociate production from comprehension as it does form from meaning in a manner that is general to the language faculty.

A PROCESSING ACCOUNT OF BROCA'S APHASIA

Taking this neurologically natural separation of linguistic information types as a starting point, a number of investigators have recently attempted to account for the Broca's inability to produce and recover features of sentence structure in linguistic *processing* terms (e.g., Kellar, 1978; Swinney, Zurif, & Cutler, 1980). One such attempt is tied to Bradley and Garrett's analyses of normal comprehension processes, which focus on the role of lexical retrieval mechanisms, not as a reflection of an isolated memory system, but rather in relation to a vocabulary distinction that has grammatical consequences—namely, in relation to the open class–closed class distinction (Bradley, 1978; Bradley & Garrett, forthcoming). Making use of a number of lexical decision tasks, Bradley and Garrett have obtained evidence for the existence of separate retrieval routes for open class and closed class vocabulary elements. Access to open class, or content, words was observed to be frequency-sensitive—rapidity of identification being positively correlated with frequency of occurrence; by contrast, the closed class route was not found to be frequency-sensitive.[1]

Granting that these two vocabulary classes diverge in terms of interpretive burden—that open class items bear reference whereas closed class items support syntactic analysis—it may be hypothesized that the closed class access route normally plays a special role in the assignment of structural analysis. The notion here is that this route serves as input to a parser, permitting the on-line construction of a structural representation.

The plausibility of this notion is heightened by the fact that when given the same lexical decision tasks as the neurologically intact subjects, the Broca's aphasics did *not* differentially retrieve the open and closed vocabularies. Rather, although they recognized the closed class items as belonging to their language, they treated them as they did the open class items, showing a frequency-based organization for both classes (Bradley, Garrett, & Zurif, 1980; Bradley, Garrett, Kean, Kolk, & Zurif, forthcoming; Zurif, 1980). In light of the structure-building function attributed to the closed-class retrieval mechanism, the specific disruption to this route provides a reasonable explanation in terms of the organization of processing components for the Broca's inability to make use of these items in comprehension, and—to carry this line of reasoning further—in production also. In effect, given the convergence of agrammatic output and agrammatic comprehension, the results of the lexical decision experiments suggest some overlap between the processes subserving speech and comprehension at the point of exploiting the open-closed class distinction built into the lexical inventory.

Also of interest is the finding that even though Broca's appear to have lost access to the special closed class route, they, nonetheless, recognized the closed class forms as vocabulary items. This finding forces the notion that these items are normally doubly registered, and raises the possibility that the

---

[1]The cross-language evidence for this dissociation of vocabulary classes remains unclear at present. While a Dutch lab and a French lab have failed to replicate the findings reported here (personal communications from, respectively, H. Kolk and Frauenfelder), it has been replicated for speakers of Spanish (J. Garcia Albea, personal communication), and is consistent with the results of lexical decision experiments carried out with speakers of Serbo-Croation (A. Kostic and A. Liberman, personal communication). Further, the finding has been replicated many times at M.I.T. Thus, although further study is clearly indicated, it does not seem unreasonable for the present discussion to view the phenomenon as a reliable one.

frequency-sensitive system—claimed, now, to contain items of both vocabulary classes—provides access to lexical semantic information, in complementary fashion to the syntactic function hypothesized for the closed class system. This possibility is currently being explored.

At any rate, it is important to point out that the disruption to the closed class retrieval mechanism appears tied to the agrammatism resulting from left-anterior brain damage, as opposed to being a consequence of brain damage in general. Specifically, a number of left-posterior brain damaged patients presenting primarily with a word-finding difficulty in the context of producing grammatically well-formed utterances—i.e., anomic aphasics—have already been tested on the lexical decision tasks and have shown the normal dissociation between the two classes of vocabulary items (Bradley et al., 1980; Bradley et al., forthcoming).[2]

GRAMMATICAL LIMITATIONS IN BROCA'S APHASIA: ADDITIONAL CONSIDERATIONS

To this point, I have attempted to reconstruct the facts of agrammatism in Broca's aphasia in terms of processes that implicated only the closed class items. However, syntactic information is also clearly associated with items of the open class vocabulary (e.g., certain verbs take complements; others do not). And it is entirely possible that a disruption to the special closed class access and parsing system only partially accounts for the syntactic problem; that the problem is more pervasive, implicating the ability to gain syntactic information, whether carried by function *or content words*.

In support of this last possibility, it should be noted that the omission of closed class items is only one of several clinical features of the Broca's aphasics' output. The utterances produced by these patients are also deviant in the sense that constructions more complex than simple, active declaratives are very rarely, if ever, observed. And this restriction on output could as easily be the consequence of an inability to use the syntactic information in verbs as the result of an inability to use closed class items as a syntactic vehicle.

To address this possibility we have lately begun to re-examine whether they

---

[2]It will be noted that in our use of the fluent-non-fluent (corresponding broadly to posterior-anterior) distinction as a means of bracketting constituent linguistic processes, Wernicke's aphasics were excluded. We wanted to contrast the Broca's aphasics with patients who have reasonable grammatical facility. And it is becoming increasingly clear that the syntactic "facility" shown in the spontaneous speech of Wernicke's patients is illusory—that despite their fluency, the Wernicke's aphasics are restricted to a limited number of surface forms (e.g., Gleason, Goodglass, Green, Hyde, & Weintraub, in press).

can implement relational structures even of a very basic sort, and quite apart from the normal ability to mark the constituents of a relation via closed class items. In particular, we are focusing on the fact that Broca's aphasics typically order words appropriately in their output—albeit, telegraphically and with little departure from the simple active form; and we are seeking to determine whether this capacity to order words reflects an underlying ability to encode relations, whether in subject-predicate or in verb-argument structures; or whether it reflects nothing other than a sequential labeling capacity—that is, the capacity to apply labels to different aspects of some preverbal notion; to plan these labels *one at a time;* and to sequence them according to some such strategy as, "start with an animate element."

The evidence that bears on this issue stems from a study that was conducted to investigate speech planning capacity in aphasia via an analysis of the acoustic attribute of fundamental frequence (*Fo*) during speech production (Danly, deVilliers, & Cooper, 1979).

In normal speech, *Fo* declines over the course of major constituents, the most pronounced fall occurring typically on the last word (e.g., see Sorenson & Cooper, 1980). Surprisingly, this form of declination was also observed for Broca's aphasics. Analyzing two-word utterances—the two words in each case bearing discernable verb-argument relations—from tapes of spontaneous speech of Broca's aphasics, significantly greater *Fo* falls were found in the final word than in the first word of each segment. Further, *Fo* declination was observed over the utterances as a whole, even though the words in some cases were separated by as much as five seconds. This finding suggests that Broca's aphasic patients are not reduced to programming their intended message one word at a time. Rather, they appear capable of formulating supralexical meaning structures, at least in the sense that the messages sent to innervate the vocal apparatus appear to be comprised of semantically cohesive units encompassing several words (Danly et al., 1979; Cooper & Zurif, forthcoming). Just what these remaining mediating structures are— granting the absence of the special closed class access and parsing system— remains another issue for future research.

SUMMARY

Obviously, the experimental observations described here allow only some rudimentary connections to be established between neural and cognitive organization. Yet, the fact that functionally defensible cognitive distinctions within the domain of language seem also to be honored by the brain, augurs well for the possibility of forming a more detailed plausible neurolinguistic theory.

ACKNOWLEDGMENTS

The work reported in this paper was supported by NIH grants 11408, 06209, and 15972.

REFERENCES

Bradley, D. Computational distinctions of vocabulary type. Ph.D. Thesis, MIT, 1978.

Bradley, D., & Garrett, M. F. Lexical recognition for open and closed class aphasia. In D. Caplan (Ed.), In *Biological studies of mental processes*. Cambridge, MA: MIT Press, 1980.

Bradley, D., Garrett, M., Kean, M.-L., Kolk, H., & Zurif, E. B. *Syntactic processing in Broca's aphasia*. Manuscript in preparation.

Caplan, D. Cerebral localization and Broca's aphasia. Paper presented to Academy of Aphasia, 1980.

Caramazza, A., & Zurif, E. B. Dissociation of algorithmic and heuristic processes in language comprehension and evidence from aphasia. *Brain and Language,* 1976, *3,* 572-582.

Cooper, W. E., & Zurif, E. B. Comprehension and production in language pathology. Manuscript in preparation. To appear in B. Butterworth (Ed.), *Language production,* Vol. II. London: Academic Press.

Danley, M., deVilliers, J. G., & Cooper, W. E. The control of speech prosody in Broca's aphasia. In J. J. Wolf and D. H. Klatt (Eds.), *Speech Communication Papers Presented at the 97th. meeting of the Acoustical Society of America.* New York: Acoustical Society of America, 1979.

Geschwind, N. The organization of language and the brain. *Science,* 1970, *170,* 940-944.

Gleason, J. B., Goodglass, H., Green, E., Hyde, M., & Weintraub, S. Narrative strategies of aphasic and normal subjects. *Journal of Speech and Hearing Research,* in press.

Goodglass, H. Agrammatism. In H. Whitaker & H. A. Whitaker (Eds.), *Studies in Neurolinguistics,* Vol. I. New York: Academic Press, 1976.

Kellar, L. Stress and comprehension in aphasia. Paper presented to the Academy of Aphasia, 1978.

Lenneberg, E. The neurology of language. *Daedalus,* 1973, *102,* 115-133.

Lichtheim, L. On aphasia. *Brain,* 1885, *7,* 433-484.

Locke, S., Caplan, D., & Kellar, L. *A study in neurolinguitics.* Springfield, IL: Charles S. Thomas, 1973.

Scholes, R. J. Syntactic and lexical components of sentence comprehension. In A. Caramazza & E. B. Zurif (Eds.), *The acquisition and breakdown of language: Parallels and divergencies.* Baltimore: The Johns Hopkins Press, 1978.

Sorensen, J. M., & Cooper, W. E. Syntactic coding of fundamental frequency in speech production. In R. A. Cole (Ed.), *Perception and production of fluent speech.* Hillsdale, N.J.: Lawrence Erlbaum Associates, 1980.

Swinney, D. A., Zurif, E. B., & Cutler, A. Effects of sentential stress and word class upon comprehension in Broca's aphasics. *Brain and Language,* 1980, *10,* 132-144.

Wernicke, C. *Die aphasische symptomen-complex.* Breslau, 1874.

Zurif, E. B., & Caramazza, A. Psycholinguistic structures in aphasia: Studies in syntax and semantics. In H. Whitaker and H. A. Whitaker (Eds.), *Studies in neurolinguistics, Vol. I.* New York: Academic Press, 1976.

Zurif, E. B., Caramazza, A., & Myerson, R. Grammatical judgments of agrammatic aphasic patients. *Neuropsychologia,* 1972, *10,* 405-417.

Zurif, E. B. Language mechanisms: A Neuropsychological Perspective. *American Scientist,* 1980, *68,* 305-311.

16 On the Emergence of Cognitive Neuroscience

Mary-Louise Kean
Lynn Nadel
School of Social Sciences
University of California, Irvine

In 1807 Franz Josef Gall was proposed for membership in the French Academy; the nomination was rejected in 1808 because Gall's research assumed, implausibly in the Academy's view, that the cortex was involved in thinking. While that particular battle has died down, it is nonetheless true that research on brain systems which might conceivably be related to cognition has proceeded with scant attention to the nature of the cognitive capacities and behavior of the organisms under study and, at the same time, research on cognition has proceeded with all but token glances at investigations of the presumed neural substrates of such behavior. Suffice it to say, there is a keen and justifiable interest in bringing these lines of inquiry into meaningful contact. It is not our intention here to propose a "solution" to the mind-body problem, nor can we offer with any confidence a programmatic statement that will, given a bit of sober research following its dictums, lead us inexorably toward answers. Our goal is more limited. What we will try to do is consider certain dominant trends at work in both cognitive science and neuroscience, and suggest what we take to be the right attitude.

Throughout the history of Western experimental psychology, and North American psychology in particular, the dominant tradition concerned with "higher mental processes" has been the area known as "learning theory." Hebb (1972), for instance, suggested that "the mark of a psychologist is an interest in learning and what it can or cannot explain about behavior" (p. 5). Learning theory was developed by the "system builders" such as Pavlov, Thorndike, Skinner, Guthrie, Hull, and Tolman. These systems (and their various thrusts to the study of cognition) had a number of characteristics in common. First, they typically dealt with (relatively) simple forms of behavior. Second, corresponding to the simple behaviors, these theories assumed that mental processes were also (relatively) simple. Third, the theories did not allow for much differentiation of mental processes and abilities; most often a small number of general abilities (e.g., the formation of stimulus-response bonds) were intended to be sufficient to explain all behavior. This severe restriction of theory was not infrequently accompanied by a fairly severe restriction of methodology. In a major tradition only experimental evidence, often of a particular kind and admitting of certain types of statistical analyses, was allowed to count in the construction and evaluation of theories.

In the 1960s, the psychological study of mental processes expanded from learning theory to encompass work in perception, including such complex functions as iconic memory, visual illusions, the nature of visual space, perception in non-static viewers, speech perception and many others that had not previously been considered to be a part of the study of higher mental processes (cf. Neisser's seminal book of the mid-1960s entitled *Cognitive Psychology*). At this same time there was a liberalization of paradigms in what had been the learning area to include numerous phenomena in the areas of object recognition and psycholinguistics. Much of this new domain was fueled by a central theoretical metaphor—the mind/brain as an information processing device. Intellectual developments outside of psychology, within cybernetics, information theory, computer simulation, and artificial intelligence research, penetrated the territory staked out by learning theory, and exerted a powerful influence upon the developing cognitive psychology.

What generally went unnoticed during this apparent liberalization was that in much of psychology there was a wholesale retention of the restrictive methods and theories of traditional psychology—the emphasis upon simple systems, of a highly abstract, general nature; and the simple conceptions of mental abilities. Memory has emerged as the general system to be studied in cognitive psychology, where memory is taken to be "the complex structure that organizes all our knowledge" (Anderson, 1976, p. 2). In fact, for some the study of memory does not necessarily differ from the study of learning in content, but rather only in emphasis (Rumelhart & Norman, 1978). Not surprisingly, while data from a variety of previously excluded areas are taken into consideration, memory is, as learning once was, viewed as univocal, allowing for the promulgation of non-task specific models. For example, Anderson (1976) says of his ACT model, a memory model, that "within the domain of 'higher mental processes' this is a very general theory and is probably capable of all specifiable behaviors" (p. ix). We doubt such particular claims, and we doubt the efficacy of the general systems approach in cognitive science.

At the same time that concern with the development of a general account of memory was evolving in information processing psychology, another, quite distinct approach, was emerging. The liberalization in the range of allowable paradigms and areas of interest had as a consequence the opening up of psychology to consideration of very specific behaviors on their own terms. Instead of treating, e.g., human linguistic capacity and the capacity to recognize faces, as essentially the same (barring, perhaps, a few rather uninteresting modality-dependent variables) researchers began looking closely into the specific properties of these systems—their structure, their development/acquisition, the mechanisms of their exploitation. While imaging, facial recognition, and language do indeed have general psychological properties in common—they are characteristic of the species, they are rapidly acquired capacities, and so on (properties to which we will turn later)—they are, in their particulars, quite, and significantly, distinct. An account of the mature capacity to recognize faces requires a Gestalt representation of the percept, whereas such representations play no role in language understanding; indeed a Gestalt account has been shown to be totally inadequate in both normal work and in deficit studies (Dorman, Raphael, & Liberman, 1979; Zaidel, 1977). Development of mature linguistic capacity emerges over a course of years, while in the case of face recognition there is a marked shift from the immature state (Carey, 1978). Restricting ourselves to just these two mental systems the list could go on and on; adding consideration of systems such as mental imagery, and accounts of operations on mental images, the picture that emerges of cognitive capacity is not one of a general, all-purpose, system but rather of a set of specific cognitive systems. While it is obviously the case that these specific systems interact in everyday behavior, no account of how they interact can be developed independently of a detailed understanding of the internal structure of each such system. Methodologically this means that one is neither justified in pooling results across distinct cognitive domains nor in treating any one (sub)domain as a "model system" for others.

Allegiance to the model systems approach has been a central methodological dogma of much of neuroscience. The model systems approach takes somewhat different guises in different sciences, with the following common thread: One kind of capacity (function or process), separated from its many-fold contexts, is intensively studied as a surrogate for the more complex, richly-textured, capacities one really wished one were studying, if only they were not so difficult to get at.

The model systems approach has been applied with considerable success in the more molecular of the biological sciences. By looking at the application of this methodology in one area of neuroscience, we can come to a clearer understanding of its implications, if applied at some future time, to a developing field of cognitive neuroscience. Perhaps the best example of the model systems approach is provided by the quest for an understanding of the neural bases of learning and memory. Until quite recently, most of the detailed work in this domain was done on invertebrate preparations, very elegant to be sure, but of undetermined significance for the study of learning in higher species. Within the past decade a wide variety of "model" neural systems demonstrating "plasticity" have been studied in mammals, taking advantage of what has literally been a revolution in techniques. Two such systems are worth describing here.

Activation of specific synaptic pathways in the brain structure known as the *hippocampus* is followed by both transient and long-lasting changes in the efficacy of the pathways in question. This result has been obtained in both intact, freely-moving animals (Douglas & Goddard, 1975) and in *in vitro* preparations of ultra-thin slices of the hippocampus, maintained in an appropriate environment for the course of an experiment (Lynch & Schubert, 1980). Among the important facts gathered in the study of this system are: (1) Transient and long-term plasticity (LTP) are mediated by independent physiological mechanisms; (2) the short-term increase in synaptic efficacy recurs with every burst of adequate stimulation along the appropriate path, and appears to involve what is known as post-tetanic potentiation (PTP); (3) there is a limit to the amount of change possible within the system mediating LTP, such that any given pathway can only be facilitated, in the long-term, up to this maximum; (4) in order to achieve maximum LTP some "cooperativity" among inputs seem to be required and (5) both PTP and, more importantly, LTP, which can last several weeks at least, are elicited very rapidly in all species tested to date. Work now in progress in several laboratories seeks an understanding of the precise molecular mechanisms involved in the synaptic changes just noted, with considerable promise of providing answers in the near future.

One might take this body of work on a prominent model system as indicating that we are approaching an understanding of *the* neural bases of learning and memory. Can such a general conclusion be drawn from these data? Consider a second model system used in the study of the neural basis of learning. C. D. Woody and his colleagues have, over the past decade or so, intensively studied the neural substrate of one kind of classical conditioning, using a well-studied reflex response (the glabella tap-eyeblink reflex) as the basis of their program (cf. Woody *et al.*, 1974). Pairing an initially neutral conditioned stimulus (CS) with an unconditioned stimulus (UCS) eventuallly leads to the CS eliciting a conditioned response—in this case an eyeblink. As a function of this conditioning neurons in several areas appear to undergo lasting changes. For example, motoneurons in the facial nucleus (the area responsible for eyeblink) undergo a progressive shift in threshold such that less current is subsequently required to elicit the eyeblink response via direct stimulation. In contrast with what has been reported for the hippocampal model system, the "learning" changes seen in this classical conditioning paradigm take a considerable amount of time to develop, involving many hundreds of conditioning trials. Thus, "plasticity" within the hippocampal system is rapid while in this cortical model system it is gradual; changes in the former seem to be virtually immediate, one-trial effects, those in the latter are incremental, built up by tedious repetition. Which model system provides the correct analysis of the neural basis of learning? Clearly, the answer has to be neither—just as the sterile all-or-none vs. incremental learning argument within psychology in the 1940s and 1950s missed the point that there are many different kinds of learning, the model systems approach fails to take into account the possibility of distinct physiological mechanisms underlying these different learning systems. Perhaps the special properties of particular learning systems themselves reflect the unique characteristics of the neural systems mediating them. Indeed, the kind of learning in which the hippocampus seems critically involved is just that type typically associated with one-trial, or very rapid, acquisition (cf. O'Keefe & Nadel, 1978).

Work with model systems, of the sort just described, has two prominent consequences which rarely are mentioned when one is considering their application to a particular problem area. First, with many investigators concentrating on the same system, methods become increasingly important. This can lead to a situation where "vertuoso techniques are practiced as ends in themselves," a charge recently laid at the door of neurobiology by Jacobson (1980), a master (rather than a servant) of virtuoso techniques himself. This emphasis of the model systems approach upon methods, amply described by Jacobson, will not be further discussed here. Second, model systems methodology depends upon the underlying assumption that there are "general properties" shared amongst a variety of systems that can usefully be studied by looking in detail at only one. This notion fits rather well with Skinnerian behaviorism—where operant learning could involve *any* stimulus and *any* response, paired through the operation of general laws of association—but it does not fit so well with the view that specific cognitive systems share few general properties, nor with increasing indications that certain kinds of associations are heavily "predisposed" (cf. LoLordo, 1979; and our later discussion of instructional and selectional models of knowledge acquisition).

These disadvantages associated with the use of model systems should not be taken as invalidating all possible applications of the approach. Given considerable knowledge of the function under study, and some specific hypotheses to investigate, this highly restrictive but highly controlled method can be very useful indeed. However, given limited knowledge (surely the current state of affairs in cognitive neuroscience), few viable notions to closely test, and an unhealthy tendency to rely (and even focus) on techniques, the model systems approach could easily stifle cognitive neuroscience before it gets off the starting block.

As an alternative to the use of simple model systems we would offer a neuroethological approach. We identify several considerations as central to the pursuit of cognitive neuroscience in this manner. First, we insist that each domain of study (neuroscience, ethology, cognition) have a well worked-out ontology that specifies its partition of the universe into core and marginal concepts, what could be called the hardcore and softcore of the field (with apologies to M. Piattelli-Palmarini, 1980). Second, we feel that such concepts will be legitimized by their biological grounding—the core concerns in the study of any species, or any set of species capacities, will be those capacities typical of the species, and central to adaptive function in its ecological niche. It is a remarkable fact that the study of behavior has been allowed to proceed for so long without adequate consideration of the purposes of the behaviors arbitrarily separated from their appropriate context and "modeled" in the laboratory. It would be equally misguided to begin studying the neural bases of more interesting, cognitive, capacities without reference to their purpose in the intact animal. Third, we reject the model systems approach because it makes assumptions about general processes that are currently unwarranted. Thus, in place of an information processing orientation to cognitive neuroscience we would offer a cognitive neuroethology concerned with the real, highly specialized, species-typical capacities of intact organisms, human and nonhuman alike.

Explanation in cognitive neuroscience will then, in our view, be constituted of accounts of species-typical behaviors in terms of entities defined at the neural, ethological/ecological, and cognitive levels. In general, our position is that true reduction of one such level to another is neither desirable nor possible. There is no reason to assure a priori that the "natural kinds" of one level of description of a domain (e.g., the neural units comprising, say, the categorial system of language) will be the same as those of any other level (e.g., the linguistic units of that system). In the domains of visual and auditory perception "mismatches" of the descriptive predicates of differet levels of description are not uncommon. We note, for example, the variable role of acoustic silence in the perception of speech stimuli (Dorman, et al., 1979), and, in the domain of vision, such well-known phenomena as the perception of illusions, the constancies, and the nonperception of the blind spot. That natural kind terms of one level need not map directly onto natural kind terms of another level does not, of course, entail that there will never be relatively direct mappings within components of any core domain. Thus, for example, in the domain of color vision there is a close connection between the psychophysical theory and the neurophysiological analysis of trichromacy, the former having significantly aided in the development of the latter. We can neither prognosticate nor prejudge in any way the nature of the relations that will hold between different levels of description for various core and marginal components of a scientific cognitive neuropsychology.

Of primary interest to cognitive neuroscience—its hardcore—are those capacities and behaviors that are typical of the species under study. For humans such things as language and mental imagery would be hardcore, while optional capacities such as reading and pictorial perception would be softcore. Because of their universality in the species, the capacities to develop the behaviors of the hard core are likely to be biologically "hardwired," and hence most amenable to cognitive neuroscientific analyses.

Particular species-typical behavior patterns are distinguished by the ease, and relative speed, with which they develop, a "fact" that traditional learning theory could not easily absorb. Such development, by its speed, and relative completeness even in highly degenerate environments, betrays the presence of considerable internal structure, by virtue of which particular associations are highly *prepared,* or predisposed. Experience acts to "trigger" these developments, rather than to determine their precise nature. Thus, we lean here towards a selectional rather than instructional model (cf. Jerne, 1967).

In discussing species-typical behaviors we concentrate on those systems of knowledge spontaneously acquired by individual organisms in the course of "normal" experience. For species-typical systems, even such complex systems as human linguistic capacity, what constitutes the necessary "normal" experience of a member of the species for development of the capacity may be far more impoverished than observation of the organism's everyday experience would indicate. That blind children, in the absence of visual contextual support, undergo the same course of language acquisition at the same rate as normal children (Landau & Gleitman, 1980), or that deaf children in oralist (non-signing) homes develop relatively rich linguistic systems (Feldman, Goldin-Meadow, & Gleitman, 1978), seems inexplicable if human linguistic capacity is taken to be anything other than species-typical and largely hard-wired. Within the context of normal experience, such systems grow independently of accidental spatial-temporal conjunctions of events that the organism is exposed to. Thus, the course of acquisition of language within one language community is essentially the same as that within the context of any language community (Slobin, 1970); indeed, were there significant differences in the spontaneity of a child in acquiring language, or in the rate or course of language development, we would have strong grounds for questioning the species typicality of human linguistic capacity. We do not deny the importance, the crucial importance, of experience to the development of such knowledge systems, but would deny the suggestion that such systems are literally constructed out of experience.

Similar points can be made with respect to the domain of cognitive-spatial mapping. The capacity to form internal models of the spatial layout of the environment is certainly adaptive, and seems characteristic of all vertebrate species studied to date (cf. Beritashvili, 1971). Thus, it qualifies as one of the core domains in cognitive neuroscience. The neural mechanisms by which this mapping is achieved have been partially deciphered (cf. O'Keefe & Nadel, 1978) in studies in which individual neurons were recorded from freely-moving animals given access to relatively rich environments. Modeling the special cognitive capacity subserved by this neural system is an important concomitant of the neuroscientific experiments: Concepts developed at one level illuminate analyses at the other. The extremely rapid facilitation of synaptic efficacy within this hippocampal mapping system makes sense only when we consider the type of cognitive functions in which the hippocampus participates. While the capacity of organisms to form spatial maps, and the means by which this is accomplished, seem hard-wired and relatively unchanged from animal to animal, as with other such species-typical systems, the *precise* information in these internal models will of course vary tremendously depending on the particular experiences of the subject being studied.

We have already noted our preference for selectional, as distinct from instructional, models of knowledge acquisition. This dichotomy, raised most forcefully within genetics, where Darwinian selection has become the model of choice, has recently gained adherents in immunology (Jerne, 1967) and neuroscience (Edelman, 1978). Psychology has come a long way from the "tabula rasa." When behavior is seen to follow species-typical lines, with the acquisition of new knowledge and abilities highly prepared, one can no longer speak of "learning" in the literal sense. Within a model where the environment instructs a highly plastic nervous system it does indeed make some sense to study arbitrarily chosen model systems of unknown biological significance—the rules of environmental brain-writing should be the same regardless of the content to be imprinted. However, within a model in which the environment selects, out of already available circuitry, those most appropriate to adaptive function, one must choose one's objects of study carefully. We have argued in this chapter that a failure to pay close attention to this consideration leads to an easy acceptance of model systems as meaningfully studied surrogates of all higher mental abilities. Closer analysis of current strains in both neuroscience and cognitive psychology indicate that adherence to this model systems approach can often lead both the scientist and the science astray. Emphasis on the special, species-typical, properties of individual cognitive (core) systems seems more likely to produce meaningful interaction between neuroscientists and cognitive scientists, and to provide a basis on which a field of cognitive neuroscience might develop.

REFERENCES

Anderson, J. R. (1976). *Language, Memory, and Thought.* Lawrence Erlbaum Associates, Hillsdale, N.J.

Beritashvili, I. S. (1971). *Vertebrate Memory: Characteristics and Origins.* Plenum Press, New York.

Carey, S. (1978). A case study: Face recognition. In E. Walker (Ed.), *Explorations in the Biology of Language.* Bradford Books, Montgomery, Vt.

Dorman, M. F., L. J. Raphael, & A. M. Liberman (1979). Some experiments on the sound of silence in phonetic perception. *Status Report on Speech Research, 58* (April-June 1979), Haskins Laboratories, New Haven.

Douglas, R. M., & G. V. Goddard (1975). Long-term potentiation of perforant path—granule cell synapse in the rat hippocampus. *Brain Res., 86,* 205–215.

Edelman, G. M. (1978). Group selection and phasic reentrant signaling: A theory of higher brain function. In G. M. Edelman and V. Mountcastle, *The mindful brain: Cortical organization and the group-selective theory of higher brain function.* MIT Press, Cambridge.

Feldman, H., S. Goldin-Meadow, & L. Gleitman (1978). Beyond Heroditus: The creation of language by linguistically deprived deaf children. In A. Lock (Ed.), *Action, Gesture, and Symbol: The emergence of language.* Academic Press, London.

Hebb, D. O. (1972) *Textbook of Psychology.* W. B. Saunders, Philadelphia.

Jacobson, M. (1980). Technophilia—the new *raison d'etre* of developmental neurobiology? *TINS, 3,* xxiii.

Jerne, N. K. (1967). Antibodies and learning: Selection versus instruction. In G. C. Quarton, T. Melnechuk, & F. O. Schmitt (Eds.), *The neurosciences: A study program.* The Rockefeller University Press, New York.

Landau, B., & L. Gleitman (1980). Language learning in blind children. Unpublished ms., Department of Psychology, University of Pennsylvania, Philadelphia.

LoLordo, V. (1979). Selective associations. In A. Dickinson & R. A. Boakes (Eds.), *Mechanisms of learning and motivation: A memorial volume to Jerzy Konorski.* Lawrence Erlbaum Associates, Hillsdale, N.J.

Lynch, G., & P. Schubert (1980). The use of *in vitro* brain slices for multidisciplinary studies of synaptic function. *Ann. Rev. Neurosci., 3,* 1–22.

O'Keefe, J., & L. Nadel (1978). *The Hippocampus as a Cognitive Map.* Clarendon Press, Oxford.

Piattelli-Palmarini, M. (1980). *Language and learning: The debate between Jean Piaget and Noam Chomsky.* Harvard, Cambridge.

Rumelhart, D. E., & D. A. Norman (1978). Accretion, tuning, and restructuring: Three modes of learning. In J. W. Cotton & R. L. Klatzky (Eds.), *Semantic Factors in Cognition.* Lawrence Erlbaum Associates, Hillsdale, N.J.

Slobin, D. I. (1970). Universals of grammatical development in children. In G. B. Flores-d'Arcais & W. J. M. Levelt (Eds.), *Advances in Psycholinguistics.* American Elsevier, New York.

Woody, C. D., K. A. Brown, T. J. Crow, & J. D. Knispel (Eds.), (1974). *Cellular Mechanisms Subserving Changes in Neuronal Activity.* Brain Information Service/Brain Research Institute, UCLA, Los Angeles.

Zaidel, E. (1977). Lexical organization in the right hemisphere. In P. Buser & A. Rougel-Buser (Eds.), *Cerebral Correlates of Conscious Experience.* Elsevier, Amsterdam.

IV STUDIES IN DEVELOPMENT

17

A Note on the Biology of Speech Perception

Michael Studdert-Kennedy
Queens College and Graduate Center
City University of New York
  and
Haskins Laboratories, New Haven, CT.

The goal of a biological psychology is to undermine the autonomy of whatever it studies. For language, the goal is to derive its properties from other, presumably prior, properties of the human organism and its natural environment (cf. Lindblom, 1980). This does not mean that we should expect to reduce language to a mere collection of non-linguistic capacities, but it does mean that we should try to specify the perceptual and motor capacities out of which language has evolved. The likelihood that this endeavor will go far with syntax in the near future is low, because we still know very little about the principles of motor control that might underlie syntactic capacity —that is why current study of syntax is, from a biological point of view, descriptive rather than explanatory. But the prospects are better for phonology, because phonology is necessarily couched in terms that invite us to reflect on the perceptual and motor capacities that support it.

As we come to understand the extralinguistic origins of the sound pattern of language, we may also come upon hypotheses as to its perceptuomotor mechanisms. Those hypotheses must be compatible with (and may even derive from) our hypotheses as to phylogenetic origin. If we forget this, we risk offering tautology as explanation, because we are tempted to attribute properties of language to the organism rather than functional properties of the organism to language (cf. Turvey, 1980). I believe that this happens at several points in the discussions of infant and adult speech perception by Eimas (this volume) and of hemispheric specialization by Morais (this volume). Both authors, at some point, take a descriptive property of language, its featural structure, and attribute a matching mechanism of featural analysis to the language perceiver. This, of course, is mere tautology.

Plausible hypotheses as to the nature of the perceptual mechanism must await a deeper understanding of the functions and extralinguistic origins of linguistic structure.

Consider, in this light, the data and inference that have led to current interest in features and the perceptual mechanisms that supposedly extract them. The story begins with early studies intended to define the acoustic boundaries of phonetic categories (e.g., Cooper, Liberman, Delattre, & Gerstman, 1952). The experimental paradigm entailed synthesizing a consonant-vowel syllable, varying some property, or set of properties, along an acoustic continuum from one phonetic category to another, and then calling on listeners to identify or to discriminate between the syllables. Since the end-point syllables typically differed from each other by a single phonetic feature, such as manner or place of consonant articulation, the procedure served to specify an acoustic correlate of that feature.

As is well known, listeners typically divide such a continuum into sharply defined categories and, when asked to discriminate between syllables, do well if the syllables belong to different categories, badly if they belong to the same category, so that a peak appears in the discrimination function at the boundary between categories. This phenomenon, termed "categorical perception," was of interest for several reasons. First, it was believed to be peculiar to speech; second, it was assumed to be the laboratory counterpart of the process by which listeners categorize acoustic variants in natural speech; third, the sharp categories and poor within-category discrimination hinted at some specialized mechanism (such as analysis-by-synthesis or a feature detecting device) for transforming a physical continuum of sound into the abstract, opponent categories that are the stuff of phonetic and phonological systems.

In due course, the experiments of Eimas and his colleagues, using "high amplitude sucking" with infants and selective adaptation with adults, led to an explicit model of categorical perception, in particular, and of phonetic perception, in general. This work has already stimulated almost a decade of invaluable research from which there has emerged a preliminary taxonomy of the infant's perceptual capacities for speech. However, the model that the research inspired is weak on several counts. In its early versions, the model invoked devices for extracting abstract, phonetic features; later versions, faced with accumulating evidence of contextual dependencies in selective adaptation (e.g., Bailey, 1973), not to mention the unexpected skills of the chinchilla (Kuhl & Miller, 1978), substituted acoustic for phonetic feature detectors (Eimas & Miller, 1978).

But consider the difficulties. First, we now know that categorical perception is not peculiar to speech, nor even to audition (e.g., Pastore, Ahroon, Baffuto, Friedman, Puleo, & Fink, 1977), so that we are excused from postulating a specialized mechanism to account for it. Second, we have no grounds for supposing that the laboratory phenomenon of categorical perception has anything more important in common with the categorizing processes of normal listening than that they both involve classifying variants. The acoustic variations within categories of natural speech are either prosodic variants associated with a particular phone in a particular segmental context (e.g., [d] before [a]), spoken at different rates, with different stress, and so on, or segmental variants, intrinsic to the production of a particular phone in different contexts (e.g., [d] before [a] or [i]). These are the types of variant that the listener has to categorize in natural speech, and neither of them is known to be mimicked by the continua of synthetic speech. Indeed, acoustic variants similar to those that surround a phonetic boundary on a synthetic continuum (where all the interesting effects occur, such as discrimination peaks and adaptive shifts in identification) may not only never occur in natural speech, but may even be literally unpronounceable (as in a synthetic series from [b] to [d], for example).

The third and most serious weakness is with the presumed role of acoustic feature-detecting devices in speech perception. As we have noted, the categorical perception paradigm typically manipulates a single dimension of the signal at a time to assess its contribution to a particular phonetic contrast. However, virtually every phonetic contrast so far studied can be cued along several distinct dimensions, and the various cues then enter into trading relations. The precise position of the boundary along a synthetic continuum for a given cue varies with the value assigned to other contributing cues. The most familiar instance comes from trading relations among cues to the voicing of syllable-initial stop consonants (e.g., Lisker & Abramson, 1964; Summerfield & Haggard, 1978), to which burst energy, aspiration energy, first formant onset frequency, fundamental frequency contour, and the timing of laryngeal action all contribute. Other instances are provided by cues to the fricative-affricate distinction (Repp, Liberman, Eccardt, & Pesetsky, 1978), to stops in English fricative-stop-liquid clusters (Fitch, Halwes, Erickson, & Liberman, 1980) and in fricative-stop clusters (Bailey & Summerfield, 1980), and so on (for a preliminary review, see Liberman & Studdert-Kennedy, 1978). Are we to assign a new pair of opponent feature detectors (with contextually dependent, "tuneable" boundaries) to each new dimension that we discover? This may be difficult since, as several authors have remarked (e.g., Lisker, 1978; Bailey & Summerfield, 1980; Remez, Cutting, & Studdert-Kennedy, 1980) the number of isolable dimensions, relevant to any particular phonetic contrast, may have no limit.

We cannot escape from this reductio ad absurdum by positing fewer and higher order detectors, because the absurdity lies in the detectors, not in their proliferation. For example, the goal of Stevens' work (e.g., Stevens, 1975; Stevens & Blumstein, 1978) is to arrive at an integrated, summary description of the cue complex associated with each phonetic feature contrast. Thus, in his work on stops, Stevens describes various general properties of the whole spectrum, using the terminology of distinctive feature theory (e.g., grave-acute, diffuse-compact), and posits a matching set of acoustic "property detectors." This ensures that the number of supposed detectors will be no more than exactly twice the number of distinctive feature contrasts. However, by adopting the terminology of phonological theory, it makes plain that we are dealing with tautology, not explanation.

The error in postulating detectors does not lie therefore in the claim that the signal undergoes analysis along several channels—that might even be true. Rather, the error lies in offering to explain phonetic capacity by making a substantive physiological mechanism out of a descriptive property of language. The error is attractive, because the feature or property detector has a veneer of biological plausibility: It promises to link language with ethology, on the one hand, through the trigger features of Tinbergen (1951; Mattingly, 1972) and the bird-song templates of Marler (1970), and with physiology, on the other, through the selectively responsive cells of the bullfrog (Capranica, 1965), the cat (Whitfield & Evans, 1965), and the squirrel monkey (Wollberg & Newman, 1972). But, whatever the importance of this single-cell work to physiology, its psychological import is nil, since it merely confirms the assumption that some isolable and distinctive physiological event corrsponds to every isolable and distinctive property of the physical world to which an organism is sensitive. The notion of innate song or call templates has even less to offer for an understanding of human language ontogeny. Such devices may ensure species recognition and successful reproduction among organisms, such as the chaffinch and the bullfrog, which have brief or non-existent periods of parental care, and therefore, little or no opportunity to discover the marks of their species. But this is not the human condition. And, given the varied solutions to the problem of learning a species-specific song, even among closely related species of songbird (Kroodsma, 1981), it is implausible to suppose that we can explain language ontogeny by invoking mechanisms proper to animals with a very different ecology and for which we have no evidence in the human (for elaboration, see Studdert-Kennedy, 1981). The question we should be asking is, rather: What function does the capacity for perceptual analysis fulfill? Or, a little differently, what properties of the human organism force language into a featural structure?

Before I suggest an approach to this question, let me comment on another area of research where we run into a dead end, if we do not raise the question of biological function: hemispheric specialization. Morais (this volume) brings together an impressive body of experimental findings from laterality studies, and shows conclusively that we simplify and gloss over discrepancies, when we characterize the left hemisphere as linguistic, the right as non-linguistic. He proposes to resolve the discrepancies by superor-

dinate classification of the tasks at which the hemispheres excel, terming the left hemisphere "analytic," the right "holistic."

These descriptions certainly provide a fair partition of the data. But there are two objections to the proposal. First, it is too narrow, because it confines itself to the supposed *perceptual* modes of the two hemispheres. Yet we act no less than we perceive: Perception is controlled by, and controls, action. Therefore, it is the joint perceptuomotor processes that we should try to capture in our description of a hemispheric mode. Second, the proposal is too broad, because it does not consider the question of phylogenetic origin. Presumably, a behavioral mode (if there be such) does not evolve without a behavior to support. But Morais has no suggestions as to what that behavior might be. For my part, I am inclined to suppose that it might be language.

In any event, the linguistic capacities of the left hemisphere, in most individuals, are attested by a mass of clinical and experimental data (e.g., Milner, 1974; Zaidel, 1978; Zurif & Blumstein, 1978). These capacities call for more than mere classification with supposedly kindred skills: They call for explanation. That is, they raise the question: What property of the left hemisphere predisposed it to language? Three items of evidence converge on a possible answer. First is the dominance of the left hemisphere in the motor control of speech for some 95% of the population. Second is the dominance of the left hemisphere in manual praxis for some 90% of the population. Third is the recent demonstration that American Sign Language (ASL), the first language of some 100,000 deaf individuals in the United States, has a defining property of primary, natural languages: a dual pattern of formational structure ("phonology") and syntax (Klima & Bellugi, 1979). Presumably ASL uses the hands rather than, say, the feet, because the hand has the speed and precision to support a rapid, informationally dense signaling system of the kind that a language demands.

Taken together, these facts almost force the hypothesis that the primary specialization of the left hemisphere is motoric rather than perceptual. Language would then have been drawn to the left hemisphere because the left hemisphere already possessed the neural circuitry for control of fingers, wrists, arms and for unilateral coordination of the two hands in the making and use of tools—precisely the type of circuitry needed for control of larynx, tongue, velum, lips and of the bilaterally innervated vocal apparatus. (Perhaps it is worth remarking that the only other secure instance of cerebral lateralization is also for control of a bilaterally innervated vocal apparatus—in the canary [Nottebohm, 1977]).

The general hypothesis is not new. Semmes (1968), for example, proposed such an account of the cerebral link between speech and manual control. She argued from a study of the effects of gunshot lesions that the left hemisphere was focally organized for fine, sequential, sensorimotor control, while the right was diffusely organized for holistic perception and action. Recently, Kimura (e.g., Kimura & Archibald, 1974; Kimura, 1979) and Kinsbourne (e.g., Kinsbourne & Hicks, 1978) have carried the hypothesis further, looking for evidence of competition and facilitation between speaking and manual action. Current research is developing procedures and paradigms to increase the precision and rigor of such work (Kelso, personal communication).

What insight can this motoric view of language and hemispheric specialization lend into the origins of phonetic features? Note, first, that the signs of ASL, no less than the syllables of spoken language, can be economically described in terms of features (Klima and Bellugi, 1979). Moreover, the articulators of both vocal tract and hands are relatively few: most are engaged, even if only passively, in the production of every sign or syllable. An ample repertoire of units therefore calls for repeated use of the same gesture by the same articulator in combination with different actions of other articulators. These recurrent gestures are, we may surmise, the instantiation, alone or in combination, of phonetic features (Studdert-Kennedy and Lane, 1980). However, the features are not detachable entities; rather, they are recurrent properties or attributes of the signs and segments (Fowler, Rubin, Remez, & Turvey, 1980; Turvey, 1980; Bladon & Lindblom, 1981). This view sits comfortably with recent evidence that metathesis tends to involve unitary phonetic segments rather than features (Shattuck-Hufnagel & Klatt, 1979). And from this we may well infer that, just as they are not put in, features are not taken out. That is to say, the perceived feature is an attribute, not a constituent, of the percept, and we are absolved from positing specialized mechanisms for its extraction.

None of what I have said above should be taken to imply that speech is not the peculiar and peculiarly efficient acoustic carrier of language. On the contrary, speech is peculiar and distinctive precisely because its processes of production and perception must have evolved *pari passu* with language itself. Just how speech gives the listener access to his language is still a puzzle, and not one that will be solved by bare psychoacoustic principle.

Let me illustrate with two recent experiments. First is a study by Fitch, Halwes, Erickson, and Liberman (1980), demonstrating the perceptual equivalence, in a speech context, of two distinct cues to a voiceless stop in a fricative-stop-liquid cluster: silence and rapid spectral change. They constructed two synthetic syllables, [plIt] and [lIt], the first differing from the second only in having initial transitions appropriate to a labial stop. If a brief bandpassed noise, sufficient to cue [s], was placed immediately before these syllables, both were heard as [slIt], but if a small interval of silence (long enough to signal a stop closure) was introduced between [s] and the vocalic portion, both were heard as (splIt). What is of interest is that the silent interval necessary to induce the stop percept was shorter when the

vocalic portion carried labial transitions than when it did not. By systematically manipulating the duration of the silent interval before each of the two syllables, Fitch, et al. (1980) titrated the effect of the initial transition and found it equivalent to roughly 25 msec of silence. Moreover, they demonstrated that these two diverse cues—silence and spectral shift—were additive (or multiplicative) in the sense that discrimination between [slIt] and (splIt] was close to chance when the cues were in conflict (i.e. a short interval + [plIt], or a long interval + [lIt]), but was facilitated when they worked together (i.e., a long interval + [plIt], or a short interval + [lIt]). Presumably, the grounds of this spectral-temporal equivalence are simply that the duration of stop closure and the extent of a following formant transition covary in the articulation of a natural utterance. Certainly, there are no psychoacoustic grounds for expecting the equivalence, and we may fairly conclude that it is peculiar to speech.

In fact, Best, Morrongiello, and Robson (1981) have demonstrated this in an ingenious experiment using "sine-wave speech" (cf. Remez, Rubin, Pisoni, & Carrell, 1981). Best and her colleagues constructed a sound from three sine waves modulated to follow the path of the center frequencies of the three formants of a naturally spoken syllable, [dei], in two forms: one form had a relatively long initial F_1 transition ("strong" [deI]), one had a relatively short initial F_1 transition ("weak" [deI]). Given a perceptual set for speech, some listeners identify these sounds as [deI] and [eI], while others hear them as different non-speech chords. If a suitable patch of noise is placed immediately before these sounds, they can be heard as [seI]; if a sufficient silent interval is introduced between noise and sine waves, a "speech" listener will hear [steI], and he will hear it with a shorter interval before "strong" [deI] than before "weak" [deI].

On this basis, Best et al. constructed two continua, analogous to those of the earlier experiments, varying silent interval in combination with one or other of the [deI] syllables. To obtain identification functions without an explicit request for identification, they used an AXB procedure. In this procedure A and B are endpoints of a synthetic continuum, X a variable item from the continuum, to be judged on each trial as "more like A" or "more like B". Thus, despite the bizarre quality of their stimuli, Best and her colleagues obtained identification functions and assessed the perceptual equivalence of silence and formant transitions in a manner analogous to that of the earlier [slIt - splIt] studies. Their fifteen listeners divided themselves neatly into three groups of five. Two of these groups never heard the sounds as speech and demonstrated no perceptual equivalence between silence and spectral change: One group was sensitive to variations in silence, but not in frequency, the other to variations in frequency, but not in silence. Only the five listeners who heard the sounds as [seI] or [steI] demonstrated a trading relation between silence and spectral change.

The burden of this elegant study matches the conclusion drawn by Jusczyk (this volume) from his review of infant research and by my colleague, Donald Shankweiler, and myself some years ago from a dichotic study: " . . . the peculiarity of speech may lie not so much in its acoustic structure as in the phonological information that this structure conveys. There is therefore no reason to expect that specialization of the speech perceptual mechanisms should extend to the mechanisms by which the acoustic parameters of speech are extracted" (Studdert-Kennedy & Shankweiler, 1970, p. 590).

If this conclusion is correct, we may review the goals of those who hope to advance our understanding of the biological foundations of language by studying infants. Their proper task is not so much to establish psychoacoustic capacity as to track the process by which infants discover the communicative use and linguistic organization of the sounds they hear and the signs they see (cf. MacKain, in press). This is the species-specific epigenetic process for which we shall find no counterpart in the chinchilla.

REFERENCES

Bailey, P. J. (1973). Perceptual adaptation for acoustical features in speech. *Speech Perception*. (Department of Psychology, The Queens University of Belfast), *Series 2*, 29–34.

Bailey, P. J., & Summerfield, Q. (1980). Information in Speech: Observations on the perception of (s) + stop clusters. *Journal of Experimental Psychology: Human Perception and Performance, 6*, 536–563.

Best, C. T., Morrongiello, B., & Robson, R. (1981). The perceptual equivalence of two acoustic cues for a speech contrast is specific to phonetic perception. *Perception and Psychophysics, 29*, 191–211.

Bladon, A., & Lindblom, B. (1981). Modeling the judgment of vowel quality differences. *Journal of the Acoustical Society of America, 69*, 1414–1423.

Capranica, R. R. (1965). *The evoked response of the bullfrog.* Cambridge, Mass.: M.I.T. Press.

Cooper, F. S., Liberman, A. M., Delattre, P., & Gerstman, L. (1952). Some experiments on the perception of synthetic speech sounds. *Journal of the Acoustical Society of America 24*, 597–606.

Eimas, P. D., & Miller, J. L. (1978). Effects of selective adaptation on the perception of speech and visual patterns: Evidence for feature detectors. In R. D. Walk & H. L. Pick, Jr. (Eds.), *Perception and experience.* New York: Plenum.

Fitch, H. L., Halwes, T., Erickson, D. M., & Liberman, A. M. (1980). Perceptual equivalence of two acoustic cues for stop consonant manner. *Perception and Psychophysics, 27*, 343–350.

Fowler, C. A., Rubin, P., Remez, R. E., & Turvey, M. T. (1980). Implications for speech production of a general theory of action. In B. Butterworth (Ed.), *Language production.* New York: Academic Press, 373–420.

Kimura, D. (1979). Neuromotor mechanisms in the evolution of human communication. In Steklis, H. D. & Raleigh, M. J. *Neurobiology of social communication in primates.* New York: Academic Press, 197–219.

Kimura, D., & Archibald, Y. (1974). Motor functions of the left hemisphere. *Brain, 97,* 337–350.

Kinsbourne, M., & Hicks, R. E. (1978). Mapping cerebral functional space: Competition and collaboration in human performance. In Kinsbourne, M. (Ed.), *The asymmetrical function of the brain.* New York: Cambridge University Press, 267–273.

Klima, E., & Bellugi, U. (1979). *The Signs of language.* Cambridge: Harvard University Press.

Kroodsma, D. E. (1981). Ontogeny of bird song. In Immelman, K., Barlow, G. B., Petrino-vich, L., & Main, M. (Eds.), *Behavioral development.* New York: Cambridge University Press.

Kuhl, P. K., & Miller, J. D. (1978). Speech perception by the chinchilla: Identification functions for synthetic VOT stimuli. *Journal of the Acoustical Society of America, 63,* 905–917.

Liberman, A. M., & Studdert-Kennedy, M. (1978). Phonetic perception. In Held, R., Leibowitz, H., & Teuber, H. L. (Eds.). *Handbook of sensory physiology,* Vol. *VIII.* Heidelberg: Springer-Verlag, 143–178.

Lindblom, B. (1980). The goal of phonetics, its unification and application. *Phonetica, 37,* 7–26.

Lisker, L. (1978). Rapid vs. rabid: A catalogue of acoustic features that may cue the distinc-tion. *Haskins Laboratories Status Report on Speech Research, SR–54,* 127–132.

Lisker, L., & Abramson, A. S. (1964). A cross-language study of voicing in initial stops. *Word, 20,* 384–422.

MacKain, K. S. (In press). On assessing the role of experience in infant speech perception. *Journal of Child Language.*

Marler, P. (1970). Birdsong and speech development: Could there be parallels? *American Scientist, 58,* 669–673.

Mattingly, I. G. (1972). Speech cues and sign stimuli. *American Scientist, 60,* 327–337.

Milner, B. (1974). Hemispheric specialization: Scope and limits. In Schmitt, F. O. & Worden, F. G. (Eds.). *The neurosciences: Third study program.* Cambridge: M.I.T. Press, 75–89.

Nottebohm, F. (1977). Asymmetries in neural control of vocalization in the canary. In Harnad, S., Doty, R. W., Goldstein, L., Jaynes, J., & Krauthamer, G. (Eds.). *Lateraliza-tion in the nervous system.* New York: Academic Press, 23–44.

Pastore, R. E., Ahroon, W. A., Baffuto, K. J., Friedman, C., Puleo, J. S., & Fink, E. A. (1977). Common factor model of categorical perception. *Journal of Experimental Psychology: Human Perception and Performance, 3,* 686–696.

Remez, R. E., Rubin, P. A., Pisoni, D. B., & Carrell, T. (1981). Speech perception without traditional speech cues. *Science, 212,* 947–950.

Repp, B. H., Liberman, A. M., Eccardt, T., & Pesetsky, D. (1978). Perceptual integration of cues for stop, fricative and affricate manner. *Journal of Experimental Psychology: Human Perception and Performance, 48,* 621–637.

Semmes, J. (1968). Hemispheric specialization: A possible clue to mechanism *Neuro-psychologia, 6,* 11–26.

Shattuck-Hufnagel, S., & Klatt, D. H. (1979). The limited use of distinctive features and markedness in speech production: Evidence from speech error data. *Journal of Verbal Learning and Verbal Behavior, 18,* 41–55.

Stevens, K. N. (1975). The potential role of property detectors in the perception of conso-nants. In Fant, G. & Tatham, M. A. A. (Eds.). *Auditory analysis and perception of speech.* New York: Academic Press, 303–330.

Stevens, K. N., & Blumstein, S. E. (1978). Invariant cues for place of articulation. *Journal of Acoustical Society of America. 65,* 1358–1368.

Studdert-Kennedy, M. (1981). The Beginnings of Speech. In Immelmann, K., Barlow, G. B., Petronovich, L., & Main, M. (Eds.). *Behavioral development.* New York: Cambridge University Press.

Studdert-Kennedy, M., & Lane, H. (1980). The structuring of language: Clues from the differences between signed and spoken language. In U. Bellugi & M. Studdert-Kennedy (Eds.), *Signed language and spoken language: Biological constraints on linguistic form.* (Dahlem Konferenzen). Weinheim/Deerfield Beach, Florida/Basel: Verlag Chemie, 29–39.

Studdert-Kennedy, M., & Shankweiler, D. P. (1970). Hemispheric specialization for speech perception. *Journal of the Acoustical Society of America, 48,* 579–594.

Summerfield, Q., & Haggard, M. (1977). On the dissociation of spectral and temporal cues to the voicing distinction in initial stop consonants. *Journal of the Acoustical Society of America, 62,* 436–448.

Turvey, M. T. (1980). The Structuring of Language: Clues from the organization of motor systems. In Bellugi, U. & Studdert-Kennedy, M. (Eds.). *Signed language and spoken language: Biological constraints on linguistic form.* Dahlem Konferenzen. Weinheim/Deerfield Beach, Fl./Basel: Vertag. Chemie, 41–56.

Whitfield, I. C., & Evans, E. F. (1965). Responses of auditory cortical neurons to stimuli of changing frequency. *Journal of Neurophysiology, 28,* 655–672.

Wollberg, Z., & Newman, J. D. (1972). Auditory cortex of squirrel monkey: Response patterns of single cells to species-specific vocalizations. *Science, 175,* 212–214.

Zaidel, E. (1978). Lexical organization in the right hemisphere. In Buser, P. A. & Rougeul-Buser, A. (Eds.). *Cerebral correlates of conscious experience.* Amsterdam: Elsevier/North Holland, 177–197.

Zurif, E. B., & Blumstein, S. E. (1978). Language and the brain. In Halle, M., Bresnan, J., & Miller, G. A. (Eds.). *Linguistic theory and psychological reality.* Cambridge: M.I.T. Press, 229–245.

18 Speech Perception: A View of the Initial State and Perceptual Mechanisms

Peter D. Eimas
W. S. Hunter Laboratory of Psychology
Brown University

The study of speech perception, like the study of visual or auditory perception, is ultimately concerned with a small number of basic issues. These include discovering the critical perceptual experiences of listeners and the invariant information in the speech waveform that signals these percepts, or if the latter cannot be achieved, at least cataloging the sufficient information for each percept and determining how perceptual constancy is achieved. In addition, there is the matter of developing a theory of speech perception that can explain the transduction of an acoustic signal into the perceived experience of speech. Of particular relevance for theories of speech perception has been a determination of the extent to which the mechanisms responsible for the perception of speech are species-specific adaptations that evolved for the sole purpose of processing speech. Finally, there is the concern with the developmental course of speech perception. In the past decade this endeavor has centered almost exclusively on investigating the processing abilities of very young, prearticulate infants. The latter has undoubtedly been the result of a number of factors, for example, our inherent curiosity about the initial states of the human organism, a greater acceptance of biological determinants of human behavior in recent decades, and a belief by many that investigations of relatively simple systems may yield special insights into the nature of perception.

In this chapter, two lines of research will be considered: investigations related to the perception of speech by infants and those related to theories of speech perception based on feature detectors. Although this would seem to be rather limited coverage of a phenomenon as complex as speech perception, in actuality these domains of research are deeply involved with most of the central issues. For example, an adequate description of infant speech perception must entail consideration of the critical information in the speech signal as well as the problem of perceptual constancy. Similarly, a theory of speech perception must consider the issue of species specificity as well as the nature of the mechanisms of transduction and the nature of the critical information. The present review will attempt to show that this is indeed the case.

INFANT SPEECH PERCEPTION

One approach to a discussion of the perception of speech by infants is to consider the existing literature in terms of the perceptual abilities that are necessary to transform speech into a code or representation that will help to make the child's discovery of the rule systems of language and their means of expression a universally and remarkably rapid accomplishment. A phonetic code, or at least an auditory code that begins to represent speech in terms of phonetic-like categories, is well suited to these purposes. In the first place a code of this nature provides a parsimonious means of assembling the instructions to the mechanisms of articulation. In a similar vein, it provides a representation of incoming speech signals that vastly reduces the potentially overwhelming information in the waveform, but without loss of linguistic content. And furthermore, it is possible to represent many of the rules of human languages in terms of categories that are not far removed from phonetic categories or their auditory bases.

To achieve a transformation of the speech signal into a categorical code requires first that the listener is capable of detecting the very small acoustic differences that signal the basic linguistic distinctions. In addition, the listener must be able to categorize the inherent variation in the speech signal along those acoustic continua that are critical to the phonetic distinctions of human languages. It is also necessary that the listener appreciate the organization that is the essence of the basic units of language, for example, the organization of feature values that yields segmental units and the organization of segments that yields syllables. A most critical ability is that the listener experience perceptual constancy. The variation in the temporal and spectral properties of speech, arising from such factors as coarticulation, the rate of speech, the state of the speaker, and the occasion-to-occasion alterations in the processes of articulation must not only be treated as members of the same category or equivalence class but must ultimately be experienced as the same percept. Finally, the listener must be capable of processing the information for linguistic distinctions in a relative, context-conditioned manner. This last ability is one means of achieving perceptual constancy, at least under some circumstances. In essence, these abilities, which, as we shall see, are all present in at least rudimentary form in the young infant, will result in the formation and perception of the segments and syllables of language. Given this, I would argue that the abstraction and eventual acquisition of higher forms of linguistic information that are carried by these units are more readily accomplished than if the infant had to work, for example, from some form of neural analogue of the speech signal.

Discrimination and Categorization.   From the evidence of over a decade of research, it is strikingly clear that infants as young as one month of age are capable of discriminating the information along many, and perhaps all, of the acoustic continua relevant to the perception of speech. For example, Eimas, Siqueland, Jusczyk, and Vigorito (1971) as well as Lasky, Syrdal-Lasky, and Klein (1975) and Streeter (1976) have shown that infants from English, Spanish, and Kikuyu speaking environments are able to detect rather small differences in voice onset time (VOT), an acoustic correlate of the phonetic feature of voicing. In addition, Eimas (1974), Moffitt (1971), Morse (1972) and Williams and Bush (1978) have shown that acoustic correlates of place of articulation are discriminable as is information for manner of articulation (e.g., Eimas & Miller, 1980 a, b). Although the research just described involved the discrimination of acoustic information in syllable-initial position, the infant has been shown to be capable of discriminating a number of consonantal distinctions in other than syllable-initial position (e.g., Jusczyk & Thompson, 1978). Finally, Swoboda, Morse, and Leavitt (1976) among others have shown that variation in the steady-state formant frequencies, an acoustic correlate of vowel quality, is likewise discriminable by young infants. (For a more comprehensive review of this literature, the reader is referred to Jusczyk, 1981.)

Given that the perceptual machinery exists for discriminating the sounds of speech in infants, it is possible to assess the extent to which the infant's representation of speech is categorical. A categorical representation would mean that a range of acoustic values along a speech relevant continuum (e.g., the information for voicing) would be assigned to the same category, or equivalence class, with the result that the continuum would be divided into a small number of categories.[1] A categorical representation requires that members of different categories should be highly discriminable, whereas members of the same category should be less discriminable. In adult listeners the inference is made on the basis of identification data that these categories correspond to phonetic categories, an inference not possible with infants.

---

[1] I have assumed in the present discussion that the initial representation of speech is a set of categories of auditory features, which form the basis for phonetic feature values. Although the initial representation of speech has at times been assumed to be more holistic in nature (e.g., Repp, 1977), this type of description does not offer any advantages, as noted in the final section.

However, if the existence of categories along acoustic continua relevant to speech can be demonstrated in infants it is reasonable to assume that these early categories serve as the basis for future phonetic categories. Be that as it may, the presence of a categorical representation in either population should yield discontinuous discrimination functions, with discriminability better at the region of the boundary between categories. Functions of this nature have frequently been obtained with adult listeners (e.g., Liberman, Cooper, Shankweiler, & Studdert-Kennedy, 1967; Pisoni, 1978), although with training and some psychophysical procedures it is possible to improve the discrimination of members of the same category (e.g., Carney, Widin, & Viemeister, 1977). But more important, in listening to speech under normal conversational conditions we are virtually unaware of this form of acoustic variation; categorization is nearly complete, as the merest bit of introspection will demonstrate.

If one accepts the assumption that a process of categorization is necessary for language acquisition, then it should be in evidence prior to the systematic production of language. Moreover, the manner in which it develops has relevance for those concerned with the relative influence of genetic and experiential forces on the course of language acquisition. A number of studies have shown discontinuous discriminability functions, that is, categorical-like perception, in infants only a few months of age or less. Moreover, the extent of categorization appeared to be at least equal to that found in adult listeners. For example, Eimas et al. (1971) as well as Lasky et al. (1975) and Streeter (1976) found categorical-like perception for VOT. Similar results were obtained for acoustic correlates for place of articulation (Eimas, 1974), manner of articulation (Eimas & Miller, 1980 a, b) and the distinction between the glides [r] and [l] (Eimas, 1975a). There was even a tendency for categorical perception of brief vowels in young infants (Swoboda, Kass, Morse, & Leavitt, 1978). Relevant to the issue of the origins of this process, a number of investigators have shown that specific receptive experience is not necessary for its presence (e.g., Lasky et al., 1975; Streeter, 1976), which together with the abruptness and early age of its appearance, argues strongly for a large contribution of innate determinants.

As has been noted with adult listeners as well, the ability to categorize acoustic information is not confined to the domain of speech (Jusczyk, Rosner, Cutting, Foard, & Smith, 1977). Indeed, this mode of perceptual functioning is also not confined to the auditory modality, having been demonstrated in the perception of hue by infants (Bornstein, Kessen, & Weiskopf, 1976); nor is it restricted to human beings (Kuhl & Miller, 1978). The ability to categorize stimuli would thus seem to be a characteristic of perceptual processing and at least in the case of speech, a process that is constrained and shaped by genetic factors in a way that is well matched to the demands of linguistic processing and the acquisition of language.

Perceptual Organization.   In a recent report, Miller and Eimas (1979b) described a series of studies that addressed the problem of organization in the perception of speech by infants. In one experiment they assessed whether the perceptual system of the infant registers not only the specific consonants and vowels that form syllables, but also the particular combinations of segmental units. In two other experiments, they investigated whether information about the combination or co-occurrence of phonetic features that define a segmental unit is processed.[2]

As an aid to understanding this approach to perceptual organization, the rationale for their first experiment will be presented in some detail. This study, as noted, was concerned with the infant's ability to perceive the organization of the segmental elements, [b], [d], [ae], and [a] when combined to form the four possible consonant-vowel syllables, [ba], [bae], [da] and [dae]. In actuality, the experiment was designed to assess whether infants would detect and discriminate a recombination of consonants and vowels. Thus, during an initial period of familiarization, infants heard two syllables [ba] and [dae]. After attaining a criterion of familiarization, the remaining two syllables, [bae] and [da] were presented during the test period. It is important to note that the stimuli were presented in a manner that precluded the perception of any inherent order, and that the same four individual consonants and vowels were present during both phases of the experiment. If infants perceive only individual segments, and not the fact of their combination, then no evidence should be obtained that the change of stimuli during the test phase was detected. However, if infants are able to perceive the individual segments and their manner of combination, then the change in stimulation, i.e., the recombination of segmental elements, should be detectable. The data showed that infants between the ages of two and four months reliably perceived the recombination of phonetic segments. In the second and third experiments, evidence was obtained that the recombination of featural information was likewise discriminable, the particular features being voicing and place of articulation in the second experiment, and place and manner of articulation in the third.

---

[2]It is of course true that the organization of syllables can be described in terms of phonetic units or in terms of acoustic properties. The same is true for phonetic segments. For ease of explication I have chosen to use phonetic descriptions, although I recognize that determining the appropriate description is part of an important issue involving the nature of the level or levels of speech processing.

In a further study, Eimas and Miller (in press) found that the recombination of segmental and nonsegmental information, place of articulation and pitch, could also be perceived. However, Kuhl and Miller (in press), as part of a study not specifically designed to assess perceptual organization, failed to find evidence that infants could detect a recombination of segmental and nonsegmental information, vowel quality and pitch contour, respectively. There are a number of possible explanations for the difference between the two studies. For example, it might have been the case that in the Kuhl and Miller study one of the feature distinctions was not nearly as salient as the other and thus was not processed when presented in combination with a second feature that varied. Based on their other findings, if one feature were less salient, it is likely the case that it was pitch contour. In any event, if this hypothesis is true, then it should be possible to obtain evidence for organization in perception simply by enhancing the saliency of the pitch contour distinction. A second, and perhaps more interesting, explanation attributes the difference between studies to the difference in processing that vowels and consonants undergo (e.g., Miller, 1978). However, exactly which difference in processing might be the critical one and how it would yield the present pattern of findings cannot be specified at this time.

In summary, the evidence overall supports the contention that the processing system of infants shows considerable sensitivity to the organization on the incoming signals. Moreover, the system is able to impose this organization over stretches of acoustic information at least a syllable in duration, an ability that is nicely in accord with the syllabic structure of human languages.

Perceptual Constancy.   The issue of perceptual constancy has long been one of central concern in the study of perception. Although it has been discussed primarily within the domain of vision even in modern times, perceptual constancy is an issue of great importance in the field of speech perception. As has been well documented (e.g., Liberman, et al., 1967), the extensive variation in the speech signal has resulted in a failure to find acoustic invariants corresponding to the perceived identity of phonetic segments, at least until very recent research (e.g., Blumstein & Stevens, 1979).[3] This variation in the temporal and spectral properties of the speech signal arises from the effects of coarticulation, that is, the difference in articulation produced by variation in the surrounding segments, and from variation in the position of the segment within a syllable as well as from in-

---

[3]I have used the phonetic segment as the reference unit for the lack of acoustic invariance for reasons of convenience only and not for reasons of bestowing any special significance, theoretical or otherwise, on this unit.

dividual variation in the vocal apparatus, fluctuations in the state of the speaker, stress, and rate of speech.[4]

It is of interest to note that the acoustic variation from one instantiation of a phonetic segment to another occurs in several ways. In one case, the critical acoustic information for the particular segment remains essentially the same in form, but varies in terms of specific values for the acoustic parameters. For example, the production of labial stop consonants in syllable initial position are marked by rising formant transitions. However, the absolute center frequencies of these formants vary considerably from speaker to speaker, especially, for example, from young children to adults. They also vary as a result of changes in the state of the speaker, stress, and the like. In another case, the nature of the critical acoustic information actually differs in different linguistic environments. For example, voicing distinctions in syllable-initial stop consonants can be signaled by differences in voice onset time, whereas the same differences in syllable final position can be signaled by duration in the preceding vowel. Indeed, Lisker (1978) has counted 16 cues for voicing in medial syllabic position. In yet another case, the form of the critical information changes to some extent as does the specific acoustic values when the phonetic environment is altered. This is well exemplified by the spectral changes in the consonantal transitions signaling place of articulation that occur with changes in the following vowel, perhaps the most notable example being the spectral differences between [di] and [du]. In summary, unlike perception, which is constant, the acoustic form of speech is markedly inconstant, and this inconstancy takes a number of forms and has a number of causes.

Of course the major issue is not simply to document the variation in the speech signal but to determine how listeners achieve perceptual constancy. As has been noted often times (e.g., Miller & Eimas, 1979a), there are essentially two solutions to the problem. The first assumes, in the case of speech for example, that acoustic invariance does exist in the signal and that discovery of these invariants involves, at least in principle, simply the appropriate analysis of the relevant parameters of the signal. In that the invariants will most likely be complex, higher-order properties or relations, their discovery will not be a simple matter. Be that as it may, if this position

---

[4]Of course variation in the speech signal also exists in the form of different acoustic values along a dimension that is critical to a particular phonetic distinction. For example, speakers produce considerable variation in the values of voice onset time that are to signal a particular voicing distinction. This is true even when the linguistic environment remains constant. However, the perception of this form of variation has typically been treated within the topic of categorical perception and not within the domain of perceptual constancy, where it also belongs. The present discussion has maintained this distinction.

is correct, then perceptual constancy is simply a matter of "picking up" on the critical information; perception is direct and immediate and there is no need for higher level computational procedures, such as signal normalization. The alternative explanation of constancy assumes that the mechanisms of perception impose the experienced constancy. The manner in which this may occur takes a number of different forms. In one case there would exist computational procedures that normalize the signal to some idealized form such that the variation from speaker and contextual differences is eliminated. A second variant of this hypothesis assumes that there exists a single mechanism responsive to all of the many representations of the acoustic information for a given phonetic distinction that operates in an integrative manner (cf., Cooper, 1974). Alternatively, it is possible to assume that a different perceptual mechanism exists for each of the many different variants of acoustic information, which in combination with a higher-order interpretive mechanism would yield a single perceptual experience.

The first explanation of perceptual constancy is certainly simpler and more parsimonious, and it is encouraging that in recent years evidence favoring the existence of physical invariants for complex perceptual phenomena has been obtained both in vision (e.g., Blakemore & Campbell, 1969) and in speech (Blumstein & Stevens, 1979; Stevens & Blumstein, 1981). But regardless of the ultimate explanation, it is of interest and importance to determine the developmental course of perceptual constancy for the basic units of speech. This is especially true with respect to language acquisition where it can be argued that the acquisition of the complex rule systems of linguistics requires that the young child treat all instantiations of a phonetic category as members of a single equivalence class.[5] In addition, evidence for at least the beginnings of perceptual constancy in early infancy would effectively eliminate explanations based on receptive experience and would at the same time render models requiring higher level cognitive activity less likely.

Although investigations of perceptual constancy are extremely difficult to perform with young, prearticulate infants, several studies directed toward this problem have been reported and others are currently in progress. In the first of these studies, Fodor, Garrett, and Brill (1975) presented evidence that four- to five-month-old infants " . . . can appreciate the perceptual

---

[5]Jusczyk (this volume) has argued that the development of perceptual constancy is a relatively late acquisition and that it is not necessary for the acquisition of linguistic rule systems. While this is not the appropriate place to engage in long polemics concerning our disagreement, I believe that it is impossible in practice, if not in principle, to learn phonological rules without at least the beginnings of perceptual constancy. For example, if the child treats each possible member of the two voicing categories of English as separate entities and not as perceptually identical events or at least as members of the same equivalence class, then acquisition of the rule for pluralization will necessarily be painfully slow, if ever learned.

identity of stop consonants across vowel environments.'' In essence, they showed that it was easier for infants to form an equivalence class based on two sounds when the sounds shared an initial phonetic segment, [p] in this instance, than when they did not. Similar findings were obtained by Katz and Jusczyk (1980), although it should be noted that in both the Fodor et al. and Katz and Jusczyk studies the evidence for the formation of equivalence classes was not strong. Considerably more compelling evidence has been obtained by Kuhl (1979). She found that six-month-old infants, after learning to discriminate single exemplars of the vowel categories [a] and [i] readily transferred this training to novel representations of the categories that varied with respect to speaker and intonation contour. As Kuhl noted these data indicate `` . . . that the six-month-old infant recognizes acoustic categories that conform to the vowel categories perceived by adult speakers of English,'' an accomplishment that is certainly instrumental in shaping the course of language acquisition. It should be made explicit that the ability to form equivalence classes is not fully isomorphic with the statement that the members of an equivalence class are perceptually identical, that is, that perceptual constancy exists. However, it is the case that perceptual constancy cannot be achieved without the ability to form equivalence classes.

Given that at least the rudiments of perceptual constancy are in evidence in early infancy, it would appear that the perceptual system for speech must be further constrained by biologic factors. Whether this constraint operates by means of a system that is innately tuned to invariant characteristics of the speech signal or innately capable of imposing equivalence (and perhaps constancy) on diverse acoustic representations of a phonetic category cannot be ascertained from the present data. However, the former would be simpler to genetically program than the latter, and very nicely agrees with the recent findings of Stevens and Blumstein.

Context-Dependent Processing.   It is well known that the acoustic information for a particular phonetic segment is often distributed across the entire syllable in which the segment is embedded (Liberman, 1970) and in some cases this information may even reside in adjacent syllables (Repp, Liberman, Eccardt, & Pesetsky, 1978). This is to say that the perceived order of speech does not necessarily correspond in a one-to-one manner with the temporal pattern of acoustic elements. Thus, it is often necessary for listeners to use information that is substantially removed, in temporal terms, from the perceived locus of a phonetic segment in order to arrive at a phonetic decision. In some instances, contextual information is a result of the effects of coarticulation, whereas in other cases it arises from such factors as rate of articulation or the ``top-down'' influences of higher-order linguistic information (Ganong, 1980, for example).

The research of Miller and Liberman (1979; and see Miller, 1981a), on which our initial studies of context-dependent processing in infants are based, clearly illustrates the use of contextual information during phonetic perception. They investigated the influence of syllable duration on the locus of the phonetic boundary separating the stop consonant [b] from the semivowel [w]. The stop-semivowel distinction was signaled by the duration of the formant transitions, with shorter transitions tending to be perceived as the stop consonants and longer transitions as the semivowel, *ceteris paribus*. They found that the phonetic boundary along a continuum of transition durations increased systematically as the syllable duration was increased by lengthening the vocalic portion of the consonant-vowel syllable. For example, they found that with syllables only 80 msec in duration synthetic speech patterns with transition durations longer than 32 msec were perceived as the semivowel, whereas transitions longer than 47 msec were needed to experience the same percept when the syllables were 296 msec in duration. Thus, there are values of transition duration that are ambiguous, being perceived as either a stop consonant or as a semivowel. Resolution of the ambiguity requires, in the absence of additional information, that the listeners take into account the contextual factor of syllable duration. In other words, perception of transition duration, when serving as the information critical for the stop-semivowel distinction, must be relative and not absolute. What is particularly interesting about these findings is that by using this after-occurring contextual information, which specifies rate of articulation, listeners have an effective means for normalizing the speech signal for changes in rate and for achieving perceptual constancy for this phonetic distinction.

Eimas and Miller (1980a) have shown that the ability to use syllable duration in the categorization of transition duration is within the competence of two- to four-month-old infants. Capitalizing on the fact that infants show categorical-like perception for consonantal distinctions, they found that the locus of the boundary separating readily discriminable categories, which interestingly corresponded to adult phonetic categories, shifted, just as it did for adults, when the vocalic portion of the syllable was increased. More specifically, when the speech patterns were 80 msec in duration, infants showed evidence of discriminating transition durations that were 16 and 40 msec in duration but no evidence of discrimination when the transitions were 40 and 64 msec long. Exactly the opposite pattern of discriminability was obtained with syllables that were 296 msec in duration. These data indicate that the infant is capable of processing speech in other than an absolute and temporally determined linear fashion—an ability, which if it can be applied to the processing of other forms of acoustic information and to achieving perceptual constancy in at least some rate-dependent instances, must almost incalculably facilitate the infant's task of discovering the regularity between sound and meaning.

It is worth noting that our findings attesting to the organization of segments within a syllable and to the use of syllabic duration in the classification of transition duration fit well with those of Bertoncini and Mehler (1981), showing that infants discriminate information better when it is embedded in a syllabic structure than when it is embedded in a non-syllabic structure such as a tri-consonant cluster. It would appear that the infant's perceptual system is set by endogenous factors to process speech by means of units that are approximately syllabic in structure and duration. Given the syllabic structure of human languages, this disposition must likewise expedite the infant's acquisition of phonetic structure and consequently the acquisition of syntactic and semantic competence. In summary, the evidence from studies of infant speech perception indicates that the human infant brings to the task of language acquisition a highly sophisticated perceptual system, well suited to the complexities of speech. In the next section, the nature of this perceptual system is considered.

THEORETICAL MECHANISMS

There are two major issues that have dominated the discussion of a theory of speech perception at the level at which a phonetic representation is made available to the listener. The first pertains to the specificity of the perceptual system; that is, whether it is a product of human evolution that is especially designed for speech perception and uniquely possessed by the human species. The second issue concerns the nature of the perceptual system; that is, whether it consists of feature (or property) detectors, functional channels of analysis, or a global, effectively single-channel, holistic processor or, in contrast, whether it is a more cognitively based constructive system.

That the processing of speech at the phonetic level involves a species-specific perceptual system, especially adapted for speech, is an idea that is well articulated in the speech literature (e.g., Eimas, 1974; Liberman et al., 1967; Liberman, 1970; Liberman & Pisoni, 1977).[6] In recent years, however, this conception of the speech processing system has received considerable criticism, and the evidence traditionally adduced in support of this formulation has been shown to be equivocal at best (Eimas & Tartter, 1979; Jusczyk, this volume; Pastore, 1981).[7] Thus, for example, evidence for a special speech processor based on such phenomena as the categorical

[6]I have used the term species-specific to mean uniquely characteristic of a species, specialization with respect to function, and at least in part innately determined. Thus, a species-specific speech processor is uniquely human, devoted exclusively or primarily to the processing of speech, and partially determined by genetic forces.

[7]Of course, denial of species-specific processing systems at the initial levels of speech perception (that is, up to the level at which a phonetic code is abstracted) does not negate the possibility that such systems may exist for the extraction of syntactic and semantic information from the encoded speech signal.

perception of speech, the differential processing and lateralization of speech and nonspeech sounds, and the differential analysis of speech by human and nonhuman listeners, previously believed to be compelling, simply is not.

There is, however, in my opinion, another argument favoring the existence of a specialized speech processing system based on an examination of the processing systems involved in the perception of acoustic signals representing the communicative events of nonhuman animals. While caution must always be exercised in generalizing from one species to another, given that species specificity is virtually a characteristic of all systems designed to process the biologically significant signals of communication, extrapolation of this principle to the human species is both reasonable and justified.

Consider first the production and perception of calling songs by male and female members, respectively, of two species of crickets, *Teleogryllus commodus* and *T. oceanicus*. Both processes have been shown to be finely controlled by genetic factors as has the linkage between perception and production, which makes communication and ultimately survival of the species possible (Bentley & Hoy, 1972; Hoy, Hahn, & Paul, 1977; Hoy & Paul, 1973). With regard to the mechanism of perception, Stout and Huber (1972) have found that the major temporal characteristics of the calling song of the cricket *Gryllus campestris L.* were selectively responded to by central auditory neurons of the responsive female. More specifically, some neurons responded to the presence and duration of the chirp as a whole, whereas other neurons responded to the timing between pulses that constitute a chirp. Together, these units provide information about two forms of temporal patterning in the calling song that control, at least in part, the phonotactic response of the female. From these studies one can readily conclude that the communication of crickets is controlled by innately determined, species-specific mechanisms, which, with respect to perception, appear to take the form of property detectors.

In a similar manner, Capranica, Frishkopf, and Nevo (1973) have shown that individual neurons of the auditory system of the cricket frog are selectively and rather narrowly tuned to the species-specific features of the male call. What is particularly interesting about this species is that there are geographical dialects. These are evidenced in the acoustic variation of the male call and in the necessary corresponding alterations in the neural selectivity of the female. Whether these dialects are determined by genetic or experiential factors is not known. However, considerably more is known about analogous dialects in the song of songbirds, especially the white crown sparrow, (Marler, 1970; Marler & Mundinger, 1971). Studies of the acquisition of the normal male song in the white crowned sparrow have shown that it is necessary for the immature male to experience the adult male song during a rather narrow period of time, a developmental pattern quite different from that of the song sparrow, for example, which needs only to hear the auditory feedback from his own productions. However, species-specific biological determinants of adult song are by no means absent in the white crowned sparrow inasmuch as young birds will only acquire a conspecific song, rejecting songs of even closely related species. (The latter would presumably be true of the cricket frog as well.) In fact, the white crowned sparrow is a particularly good example of how experience may at times modify initial dispositions of animal communication systems that are innately given—a phenomenon that is not unknown in human language (Eimas & Tartter, 1979, for example).

Although the discussion of the white crowned sparrow has centered on the acquisition and production of the male song, it is obvious that a similar developmental sequence must exist to shape and constrain the perceptual system of the conspecific female. Furthermore, there is evidence that the mechanism of perception may be property detectors. Leppelsack and Vogt (1976) have found individual auditory units in starlings (a species of songbird) that were selectively tuned to features of one or more vocalizations as well as units that were tuned to an entire pattern of vocalization.

The presence of a species-specific perceptual system is also indicated by the greater ease with which Japanese macaques form equivalence classes with variants of their coo calls when the distinguishing feature is relevant to the communication system of the Japanese macaque than when the acoustic feature is not "linguistically" relevant (Zoloth, Petersen, Beecher, Green, Marler, Moody, & Stebbins, 1979). It is also the case that the Japanese macaque exhibits a right-ear advantage (i.e., left-hemisphere advantage) when engaged in processing these sounds, but again only when the basis for processing is relevant to the communication system of the Japanese macaque (Petersen, Beecher, Zoloth, Moody, & Stebbins, 1978).[8]

From this review of animal communication systems, which, while selective, is representative, it appears that the processing systems underlying the perception of communicative signals are characterized by species specificity. That is to say, they are designed especially for the perception of communicative events and as such are an integral part of a species' communication system. At issue is whether this conclusion should be extended to include the perceptual system for human speech—that is, to include the

---

[8]There is evidence, at least for the squirrel monkey, that the very early processing of primate calls is accomplished by detector-like mechanisms. Winter and Funkenstein (1973) and Wollberg and Newman (1972) have recorded from individual units in the auditory context and were able to demonstrate that, although these units vary in their degree of selectivity, they appear to be capable of extracting much of the temporal and spectral information of individual calls. It would be of great interest to learn whether species-specific detectors for communicative signals are situated in the left hemisphere of the Japanese macaque.

mechanisms that provide the initial analyses and transformations from which a phonetic representation can be abstracted. Given the extent to which species-specific determinants constrain and shape the form of nonhuman communication systems as well as the nature of such human and nonhuman systems as locomotion and cognition, it would be surprising if the perceptual system for speech was not a special adaptation of human evolution.[9] Of course, scientific conclusions are not ultimately accepted or rejected on the basis of reasonableness or logical consistency, but rather on the persuasive nature of the empirical evidence. Based on a suggestion of Liberman and Pisoni (1977), we hope shortly to provide at least the beginnings of a body of empirical evidence that will bear directly on this issue.

Whether or not the initial processing system for speech is uniquely the property of human beings, there remains the problem of determining the actual form that the mechanisms mediating perception take. In the early 1970's, a number of investigators, most notably, Abbs and Sussman (1971) and Stevens (1973) began to speculate about the possibility that speech was processed by mechanisms that were functionally similar to feature detectors that had been assumed to mediate the perception of complex auditory patterns in lower animals (Evans, 1974; and the discussion immediately preceding) and of visual patterns in humans and nonhumans (e.g., Hubel & Wiesel, 1962; Blakemore & Campbell, 1969).[10] This conception of speech processing was particularly appealing in that it was a markedly more parsimonious and explicit explanation of the perception of speech than, for example, the motor theory of Liberman and his associates (Liberman et al., 1967) or the analysis-by-synthesis model of Stevens and House (1972). Moreover, it provided a means of explaining categorical-like perception, especially in infants, that did not require greater complexity in terms of mechanisms than what might conceivably be provided by genetic programming (cf., Eimas, 1975b).

Evidence supporting a feature detector model of speech perception was first published in 1973 by Eimas and Corbit. They showed that the perception, that is, the classification and discrimination, of voice onset time could be reliably altered by a selective adaptation procedure, similar in principle to procedures used in other sensory modalities, which have yielded inferen-

---

[9]If this conclusion is true, then findings such as the categorical perception of nonspeech signals (e.g., Jusczyk, this volume) must be taken to indicate that the manner in which a particular system functions is not unique. That is, both the specialized speech processor and the more geneal auditory system may show similar operating characteristics, although they are specialized to process different clases of acoustic signals.

[10]It is worth noting that it is not necessary to assume that a detector is represented neurologically by a single cell. Rather it is most likely that the categorization of information depends on populations of neural units and that it is the pattern of activity of these populations that determines the perceptual response.

tial evidence for detector systems. Moreover, the manner in which perception was altered could be readily accommodated by a relatively simple and testable model, which assumed the existence of " . . . detectors that are differentially sensitive to a range of VOT values with greatest sensitivity (as might be measured, in principle, by the output value of the detector) occurring at the modal production value for a particular voicing distinction (Lisker & Abramson, 1964)", (Eimas & Corbit, 1973, p. 108), and that are fatigued or made less sensitive by adaptation. Additional research extended the concept of feature detectors to the perception of other forms of acoustic information that are sufficient to signal phonetic distinctions based on differences in place and manner of articulation (for reviews of this literature, see Eimas & Miller, 1978; Miller & Eimas, 1979a).

In the five years after the initial publications, research directed toward explicating the operating characteristics of these detectors increased rapidly. More recently, however, there has been a marked decrease, as the hypothesis that detectors or detector-like mechanisms (i.e., channels of analysis [Simon & Studdert-Kennedy, 1978]) mediate the perception of speech has come under severe criticism. Before considering the reasons for this rather vociferous disavowal of detector theories of speech perception, it is appropriate to consider some of the experimental findings that are particularly supportive of this form of theoretical explanation. First, as was noted, the manner in which perception is altered by selective adaptation is readily accounted for by a relatively simple theory of how detectors operate, and a number of other perceptual phenomena (e.g., discriminability functions) can likewise be explained (Eimas & Corbit, 1973). Second, there is evidence that the entire range of stimulation to which a detector is assumed to be sensitive is altered by adaptation (e.g., Miller, 1977). This lends credence to the conception of a detector as a channel that functions to reduce information, by categorizing continuous input. That is to say, a detector, by mapping many continuously varying inputs onto a single output, provides the means by which the first level of categorical information is provided, a form of information that is characteristic of human languages. Third, it is possible to obtain tuning functions that are similar to the tuning functions obtained for detectors in other modalities (Miller, 1977; Miller & Connine, 1980). From these data and others it appeared that the hypothesized detectors for speech were well supported and that their operating characteristics were well within the bounds of metatheoretical discussions of this form of explanation in perception.

With regard to the criticisms of a detector theory of speech perception, there were data almost from the time of the initial empirical studies that presented difficulties for a detector model, although the extent of the difficulties was not completely apparent until rather recently (Eimas & Miller, 1978; Miller & Eimas, 1979a). For example, a number of studies have shown that the detectors for speech, if they exist, must operate in a contextually dependent manner—a finding that demands a disturbing and quite unparsimonious proliferation in the number of detectors. This contextually dependent processing was evidenced in several ways. First, there were findings of a smaller adaptation effect when the test stimuli and adapting stimulus differed along some acoustic dimension (e.g., Cooper & Blumstein, 1974). Moreover, this lessening of the adaptation effect occurred whether or not the acoustic difference produced a phonetic difference. Second, there was the discovery of contingent adaptation effects (Cooper, 1974), wherein a consonantal feature was found to be analyzed with reference to the following vowel. And finally, there were studies showing reduced and even no adaptation effects when the characteristics of the critical information in the adapting stimulus differed from that in the test stimuli (e.g., Ades, 1974). In the absence of higher-order invariants, findings of this nature require some form of integrative detectors, a version of a detector that is quite far removed from the ideal mechanism that is sensitive to trigger features of the environment.

Up to this point, we have considered only situations where detector theorists were confronted with the necessity of explaining data that, while requiring modification of the original view of detectors, were ultimately compatible with some form of detector theory. More recently, a number of investigators have presented experimental findings that they have interpreted as challenging the very idea that speech is analyzed by detectors (Diehl, 1981; Diehl, Elman, & McCusker, 1978; Diehl, Lang, & Parker, 1980; Elman, 1979). What these data have shown, in essence, is that the selective effects of adaptation can be accounted for by the consequences of stimulus contrast and alterations in response bias as opposed to the consequences of detector systems being fatigued (cf., Simon & Studdert-Kennedy, 1978). Indeed, in several unpublished studies, we have also been unable to demonstrate qualitative differences between the effects of adaptation and sensory contrast (but see Sawusch & Jusczyk [1981] for just such a demonstration), and we have failed to find reductions in d' (i.e., sensitivity) after adaptation as the original Eimas and Corbit model would predict.

While these data are contradictory to a fatigue model of selective adaptation and to the existence of feature detectors, they are not in and of themselves contradictory to the hypothesis that speech undergoes an initial analytic process. A reasonable assumption at this point of theory construction is that this analysis is performed by functional processes, channels of analysis, which have many operating characteristics in common with detectors but which are more cognitive than sensory in nature. Thus, the construction of alternative models of speech perception based on holistic processing principles does not appear to be as necessary as some would argue (e.g., Diehl, 1981).

Furthermore it can be argued, rather successfully I believe, that holistic processing models are not capable of accommodating the present literature any better than analytic models. Although processing models in which speech is represented as a neural spectrogram (Diehl, 1981) or a multidimensional prototype (Repp, 1977; and see Bryant, 1978) have an intuitive appeal, especially given the holistic nature of our perception, they have not as yet been sufficiently developed so as to be able to explain many of the basic phenomena of speech perception in a rigorous fashion. Moreover, development of theories of speech perception without an initial stage of analysis, while perhaps not impossible, will certainly be quite difficult, particularly in light of recent findings by Miller (1981b). She demonstrated that two adapting stimuli may have different relative effects depending on the nature of the acoustic information that defines the test series. For example, the syllables [bae] and [dae] were equally effective adapting stimuli when a [bae-wae] test series was used that varied in transition duration. However, the same adapting stimuli produced unequal effects on a [bae-pae] test series that varied in VOT, with [bae] producing the greater effect. It is difficult to imagine how the relative effects of two stimuli can differ if processing is based on internal representations that are holistic. This problem is readily eliminated when the assumption is made that at least at some level the internal representation is based on feature values that are probably auditory in nature. In view of these findings and the apparent pervasiveness of analytic operations in the perception of nonhuman communication signals, my own predilection at this time is to continue to develop models of speech perception based on mechanisms like channels of analysis that, if different from the original idea of feature detectors, have many of the operating characteristics of feature detectors. It is, I believe, this form of perceptual theory that is most readily adapted to explain the very sophisticated processing of speech by infants, as well as the many ways in which linguistic experience changes the initial state of perceptual processing.

SUMMARY

Research on the infant's ability to perceive speech continues to affirm the highly sophisticated nature of the processes underlying the perception of speech during infancy, as well as to reveal the rather remarkable extent to which the infant's perceptual system and the form of human language are matched. For example, a number of studies have shown that the infant processes acoustic units approximately equivalent to syllabic units. This processing yields not only the critical information for the perception of speech but also the manner in which the information is organized. Furthermore, the mechanisms of speech perception provide the infant with an initial representation of speech that is categorical and consequently a basis for the acquisition of linguistic competence.

Although there is little disagreement concerning the assumption that the initial state of human speech perception is shaped and constrained by the infant's genetic inheritance, there is, in marked contrast, only meager support for the hypothesis that the mechanisms of speech perception are species-specific. The primary reason for this is that the evidence usually cited, as Jusczyk (this volume) has noted, is at best equivocal. Despite this, the present discussion attempts to argue in favor of species specificity with regard to the perceptual apparatus for speech. The argument draws on data different from that which is usually adduced, and in essence concludes that the species specificity that is characteristic of the means for processing communicative signals in many nonhuman species should also be considered to be characteristic of the human species. Indeed, not to do so may require a rather special evolutionary history for the preliminary processors of human speech.

It is further assumed in the theoretical discussion of the processing and representation of speech that channels of analysis, functional units similar in many respects of feature detectors, perform the initial analysis of speech that yields a featural representation. This is in marked contrast to more holistic views of the processing and representation of speech which, while having considerable appeal in recent times, do not offer greater explanatory power than analytic models. Moreover, there may well be compelling data for an analytic process, which will be difficult to accommodate within holistic models of speech perception. The final resolution of these theoretical disputes can only be guessed at, although it would seem certain that our models of perception and even cognition will be greatly constrained by future findings on the initial state of speech perception and how our early predispositions serve the acquisition of language.

ACKNOWLEDGMENT

Preparation of this chapter and the author's research reported herein were supported by Grant HD 05331 from the National Institute of Child Health and Human Development. I thank Joanne L. Miller for her critical comments on an earlier version of this paper.

REFERENCES

Abbs, J. H., & Sussman, H. M. Neurophysiological feature detectors and speech perception: A discussion of theoretical implications. *Journal of Speech and Hearing Research,* 1971, *14,* 23–36.

Ades, A. E. How phonetic is selective adaptation? Experiments on syllable position and vowel environment. *Perception & Psychophysics,* 1974, *16,* 61-67.

Bentley, D. R., & Hoy, R. R. Genetic control of cricket song patterns. *Animal Behavior,* 1972, *20,* 478-492.

Bertoncini, J., & Mehler, J. Syllables as units in infant speech perception. *Infant Behavior & Development,* 1981, *4,* 247-260.

Blakemore, C., & Campbell, F. W. On the existence of neurones in the human visual system selectively sensitive to the orientation and size of retinal images. *Journal of Physiology,* 1969, *203,* 237-260.

Blumstein, S. E., & Stevens, K. N. Acoustic invariance in speech production: Evidence from measurements of the spectral characteristics of stop consonants. *Journal of the Acoustical Society of America,* 1979, *66,* 1001-1017.

Bornstein, M., Kessen, W., & Weiskopf, S. Color vision and hue categorization in young infants. *Journal of Experimental Psychology: Human Perception and Performance,* 1976, *2,* 115-129.

Bryant, J. S. Feature detection process in speech perception. *Journal of Experimental Psychology: Human Perception and Performance,* 1978, *4,* 610-620.

Capranica, R. R., Frishkopf, L. S., & Nevo, E. Encoding of geographical dialects in the auditory system of the cricket frog. *Science,* 1973, *182,* 1272-1274.

Carney, A. E., Widin, G. P., & Viemeister, N. F. Noncategorical perception of stop consonants differing in VOT. *Journal of the Acoustical Society of America,* 1977, *62,* 961-970.

Cooper, W. E. Contingent feature analysis in speech perception. *Perception & Psychophysics,* 1974, *16,* 201-204.

Cooper, W. E., & Blumstein, S. E. A labial feature analyzer in speech perception. *Perception & Psychophysics,* 1974, *15,* 591-600.

Diehl, R. L. Feature detectors for speech: A critical reappraisal. *Psychological Bulletin,* 1981, *89,* 1-18.

Diehl, R. L., Elman, J. L., & McCusker, S. B. Contrast effects on stop consonant identification. *Journal of Experimental Psychology: Human Perception and Performance,* 1978, *4,* 599-609.

Diehl, R. L., Lang, M., & Parker, E. M. A further parallel between selective adaptation and contrast. *Journal of Experimental Psychology: Human Perception and Performance,* 1980, *6,* 24-44.

Eimas, P. D. Auditory and linguistic processing of cues for place of articulation by infants. *Perception & Psychophysics,* 1974, *16,* 513-521.

Eimas, P. D. Auditory and phonetic coding of the cues for speech: Discrimination of the [r-l] distinction by young infants. *Perception & Psychophysics,* 1975, *18,* 341-347. (a)

Eimas, P. D. Speech perception in early infancy. In L. B. Cohen & P. Salapatek (Eds.), *Infant perception,* Vol. 2. New York: Academic Press, 1975. (b)

Eimas, P. D., & Corbit, J. D. Selective adaptation of linguistic feature detectors. *Cognitive Psychology,* 1973, *4,* 99-109.

Eimas, P. D., & Miller, J. L. Effects of selective adaptation on the perception of speech and visual patterns: Evidence for feature detectors. In R. D. Walk & H. L. Pick, Jr. (Eds.), *Perception and experience.* New York: Plenum Press, 1978.

Eimas, P. D., & Miller, J. L. Contextual effects in infant speech perception. *Science,* 1980, *209,* 1140-1141. (a)

Eimas, P. D., & Miller, J. L. Discrimination of the information for manner of articulation by young infants. *Infant Behavior & Development,* 1980, *3,* 367-375. (b)

Eimas, P. D., & Miller, J. L. Organization in the perception of segmental and suprasegmental information by infants. *Infant Behavior & Development,* in press.

Eimas, P. D., Siqueland, E. R., Jusczyk, P., & Vigorito, J. Speech perception in infants. *Science,* 1971, *171,* 303-306.

Eimas, P. D., & Tartter, V. C. On the development of speech perception: Mechanisms and analogies. In H. W. Reese & L. P. Lipsitt (Eds.), *Advances in child development and behavior.* Vol. 13. New York: Academic Press, 1979.

Elman, J. L. Perceptual origins of the phoneme boundary effect and selective adaptation to speech: A signal detection theory analysis. *Journal of the Acoustical Society of America,* 1979, *65,* 190–207.

Evans, E. F. Neural responses for the detection of acoustic patterns and for sound localization. In F. O. Schmitt & F. G. Worden (Eds.), *The neurosciences: Third study program.* Cambridge, Mass.: MIT Press, 1974.

Fodor, J. A., Garrett, M. F., & Brill, S. L. Pi Ka Pu: The perception of speech sounds by prelinguistic infants. *Perception & Psychophysics,* 1975, *18,* 74–78.

Ganong, W. F. III. Phonetic categorization in auditory word perception. *Journal of Experimental Psychology: Human Perception and Performance,* 1980, *6,* 110–125.

Hoy, R. R., Hahn, J., & Paul, R. C. Hybrid cricket auditory behavior: Evidence for genetic coupling in animal communication. *Science,* 1977, *195,* 82–84.

Hoy, R. R., & Paul, R. C. Genetic control of song specificity in crickets. *Science,* 1973, *180,* 82–83.

Hubel, D. H., & Wiesel, T. N. Receptive fields, binocular interaction, and functional architecture in the cat's visual cortex. *Journal of Physiology* (London), 1962, *160,* 106–154.

Jusczyk, P. Infant speech perception. In P. D. Eimas & J. L. Miller (Eds.), *Perspectives on the study of speech.* Hillsdale, New Jersey: Lawrence Erlbaum Associates, 1981.

Jusczyk, P. W., Rosner, B. S., Cutting, J. E., Foard, C. F., & Smith, L. B. Categorical perception of nonspeech sounds by 2-month-old infants. *Perception & Psychophysics,* 1977, *21,* 50–54.

Jusczyk, P. W., & Thompson, E. Perception of a phonetic contrast in multisyllabic utterances by 2-month-old infants. *Perception & Psychophysics,* 1978, *23,* 105–109.

Katz, J., & Jusczyk, P. W. *Do six-month-olds give perceptual constancy for phonetic segments?* Paper presented at the International Conference on Infant Studies, April 11, 1980, New Haven, Connecticut.

Kuhl, P. K. Speech perception in early infancy: Perceptual constancy for spectrally dissimilar vowel categories. *Journal of the Acoustical Society of America,* 1979, *66,* 1668–1679.

Kuhl, P. K., & Miller, J. D. Speech perception by the chinchilla: Identification functions for synthetic VOT stimuli. *Journal of the Acoustical Society of America,* 1978, *63,* 905–917.

Kuhl, P. K., & Miller, J. D. Discrimination of auditory target dimensions in the presence or absence of variation in a second dimension: Implications for developmental auditory perception. *Perception & Psychophysics,* in press.

Lasky, R. E., Syrdal-Lasky, A., & Klein, R. E. VOT discrimination by four- to six-and-a-half-month-old infants from Spanish environments. *Journal of Experimental Child Psychology,* 1975, *20,* 215–225.

Leppelsack, H. J., & Vogt, M. Responses of auditory neurons in the forebrain of a songbird to stimulation with species-specific sounds. *Journal of Comparative Physiology,* 1976, *107,* 263–274.

Liberman, A. M. The grammars of speech and language. *Cognitive Psychology,* 1970, *1,* 301–323.

Liberman, A. M., Cooper, F. S., Shankweiler, D. S., & Studdert-Kennedy, M. Perception of the speech code. *Psychological Review,* 1967, *74,* 431–461.

Liberman, A. M., & Pisoni, D. P. Evidence for a special speech-perception subsystem in the human. In T. H. Bullock (Ed.), *Recognition of complex auditory signals.* Berlin: Dahlem Konferenzen, 1977.

Lisker, L. Rapid vs. Rabid: A catalogue of acoustic features that may cue the distinction. In *Status report on speech research.* SR/54. Haskins Laboratories, 1978.

Lisker, L., & Abramson, A. S. A cross-language study of voicing in initial stops: Acoustic measurements. *Word,* 1964, *20,* 384–422.

Marler, P. A comparative approach to vocal learning. *Journal of Comparative and Physiological Psychology,* 1970, *71,* 1–25.

Marler, P., & Mundinger, P. Vocal learning in birds. In H. Moltz (Ed.), *Ontogeny of vertebrate behavior.* New York: Academic Press, 1971.

Miller, J. L. Properties of feature detectors for VOT: The voiceless channel of analysis. *Journal of the Acoustical Society of America,* 1977, *62,* 641–648.

Miller, J. L. Interactions in processing segmental and suprasegmental features of speech. *Perception & Psychophysics,* 1978, *24,* 175–180.

Miller, J. L. The effects of speaking rate of segmental distinctions: Acoustic variation and perceptual compensation. In P. D. Eimas & J. L. Miller (Eds.), *Perspectives on the study of speech.* Hillsdale, New Jersey: Lawrence Erlbaum Associates, 1981. (a)

Miller, J. L. Phonetic perception: Evidence for context-dependent and context-independent processing. *Journal of the Acoustical Society of America,* 1981, *69,* 822–831. (b)

Miller, J. L., & Connine, C. M. Psychophysical tuning curves for phonetically relevant acoustic information. *Journal of the Acoustical Society of America,* 1980, *67,* S52A.

Miller, J. L., & Eimas, P.D. Feature detectors and speech perception: A critical evaluation. To be published in the *Proceedings of the Symposium on the role of feature detectors in the recognition of pattern and form,* Austin, Texas, 1979. (a)

Miller, J. L., & Eimas, P.D. Organization in infant speech perception. *Canadian Journal of Psychology,* 1979, *33,* 353–365. (b)

Miller, J. L., & Liberman, A. M. Some effects of later-occurring information on the perception of stop consonant and semivowel. *Perception & Psychophysics,* 1979, *25,* 457–465.

Moffitt, A. R. Consonant cue perception by twenty to twenty-four week old infants. *Child Development,* 1971, *42,* 717–731.

Morse, P. A. The discrimination of speech and nonspeech stimuli in early infancy. *Journal of Experimental Child Psychology,* 1972, *14,* 477–492.

Pastore, R. E. Possible psychoacoustic factors in speech perception. In P. D. Eimas & J. L. Miller (Eds.), *Perspectives on the study of speech.* Hillsdale, New Jersey: Lawrence Erlbaum Associates, 1981.

Petersen, M. R., Beecher, M. D., Zoloth, S. R., Moody, D. B., & Stebbins, W. C. Neural lateralization of species-specific vocalizations by Japanese macaques *(Macaca fuscata). Science,* 1978, *202,* 324–327.

Pisoni, D. P. Speech perception. In W. K. Estes (Ed.), *Handbook of learning and cognitive processes.* Vol. 6. Hillsdale, New Jersey: Lawrence Erlbaum Associates, 1978.

Repp, B. H. Dichotic competition of speech sounds: The role of acoustic stimulus structure. *Journal of Experimental Psychology: Human Perception and Performance,* 1977, *3,* 37–50.

Repp, B. H., Liberman, A. M., Eccardt, T., & Pesetsky, D. Perceptual integration of acoustic cues for stop, fricative, and affricate manner. *Journal of Experimental Psychology: Human Perception and Performance,* 1978, *4,* 621–637.

Sawusch, J. R., & Jusczyk, P. Adaptation and contrast in the perception of voicing. *Journal of Experimental Psychology: Human Perception and Performance,* 1981, *7,* 408–421.

Simon, H. J., & Studdert-Kennedy, M. Selective anchoring and adaptation of phonetic and nonphonetic continua. *Journal of the Acoustical Society of America,* 1978, *64,* 1338–1357.

Stevens, K. N. *The potential role of property detectors in the perception of consonants.* Paper presented at Symposium on Auditory Analysis and Perception of Speech, Leningrad, USSR, August, 1973.

Stevens, K. N., & Blumstein, S. E. The search for invariant acoustic correlates of phonetic features. In P. D. Eimas & J. L. Miller (Eds.), *Perspectives on the study of speech.*

Hillsdale, New Jersey: Lawrence Erlbaum Associates, 1981.

Stevens, K. N., & House, A. S. Speech perception. In J. Tobias (Ed.), *Foundations of modern auditory theory,* Vol. 2. New York: Academic Press, 1972.

Streeter, L. A. Language perception of 2-month-old infants show effects of both innate mechanisms and experience. *Nature,* 1976, *259,* 38–41.

Stout, J. F., & Huber, F. Responses of central auditory neurons of female crickets *(Gryllus campestris,* L.) to the calling song of the male. *Zeitschrift für Vergleichende Physiologie,* 1972, *76,* 302–313.

Swoboda, P. J., Kass, J., Morse, P. A., & Leavitt, L. A. Memory factors in vowel discrimination of normal and at-risk infants. *Child Development,* 1978, *48,* 332–339.

Swoboda, P. J., Morse, P. A., & Leavitt, L. A. Continuous vowel discrimination in normal and at-risk infants. *Child Development,* 1976, *47,* 459–465.

Williams, L., & Bush, M. Infant place discrimination of voiced stop consonants with and without release bursts. *Journal of the Acoustical Society of America,* 1978, *63,* 1223–1225.

Winter, P., & Funkenstein, H. H. The effect of species-specific vocalization on the discharge of auditory cortical cells in the awake squirrel monkey *(Saimiri sciureus). Experimental Brain Research,* 1973, *18,* 489–504.

Wollberg, Z., & Newman, J. D. Auditory cortex of squirrel monkey: Response patterns of single cells to species-specific vocalizations. *Science,* 1972, *175,* 212–214.

Zoloth, S. R., Petersen, M. R., Beecher, M. D., Green, S., Marler, P., Moody, D. B., & Stebbins, W. Species-specific perceptual processing of vocal sounds by monkeys. *Science,* 1979, *204,* 870–873.

19

Auditory versus Phonetic Coding of Speech Signals During Infancy

Peter W. Jusczyk
University of Oregon
Eugene, Oregon

Not so long ago, the prevailing view was that human infants possessed little in the way of perceptual capacities during the first few months of life. Even such an astute observer of children as Piaget (1952) credited the infant under four months with only the most primitive kinds of abilities for perceiving the world. For Piaget, the basic schemas of looking, grasping, hearing, and sucking by which the child is to build up a conception of the world, were all relatively undifferentiated in the infant under four months of age. In the interim since Piaget first made his observations, a number of technological and methodological advances have made it possible to achieve a much more precise estimate of the infant's underlying perceptual capacities. As a result, our appreciation of the nature and sophistication of the young infant's perceptual capacities has grown considerably.

Perhaps in no other area of research have our expectations changed so dramatically as in the area of infant speech perception. A little over ten years ago, researchers were still wondering how infants learned to distinguish between different speech sounds. Today, some researchers in the field (e.g., Morse, Eilers, & Gavin, 1980) have been moved to comment that the most interesting kind of result would be to discover some aspect of speech perception that infants were incapable of. In short, research conducted during the past ten years suggests that infants possess many, if not all, of the necessary prerequisites for speech perception (for a review, see Jusczyk, 1981). For example, the infant's discrimination of speech sounds appears to be categorical (Eimas, 1974; Eimas, Siqueland, Jusczyk, & Vigorito, 1971). This aspect of perception is of considerable usefulness both during the process of language acquisition and in the comprehension of speech, since it enables the infant to effectively ignore irrelevant variations in the articulation of utterances and to focus only on relevant differences. In addition, the infant's aptitude for distinguishing between speech sounds is not limited to differences along a few phonetic dimensions, but extends to even those distinctions not employed in the language in the infant's immediate environment (e.g., Trehub, 1976). Nor do the infant's perceptual capacities appear to be restricted in their applicability to analyzing just a portion of an utterance. Infants appear to be as adept at detecting phonetic contrasts in medial and final positions of utterances as they are for contrasts in utterance-initial positions (Jusczyk, 1977; Jusczyk & Thompson, 1978). Finally, although sensitive to suprasegmental information (Jusczyk & Thompson, 1978; Spring & Dale, 1977), infants are able to ignore irrelevant variations in such information and similar variations in speaker's voice and vowel quality in making phonetic discriminations (Holmberg, Morgan, & Kuhl, 1977; Katz & Jusczyk, 1980; Kuhl, 1976, 1979). The latter abilities suggest that infants are able to compensate for differences in pitch or speaker's voices. In other words, infants, like adults, appear to show some form of perceptual constancy for phonetic segments.

Given the range of abilities that infants exhibit for processing speech sounds, it is tempting to conclude that they are biologically endowed with perceptual mechanisms specialized for handling linguistic information. Indeed, such a claim would appear to fit well with reports from other studies that demonstrate a special sensitivity on the part of infants towards linguistic stimuli. For instance, Condon and Sander (1974) observed that as early as the first day of life the infant engages in rhythmic movements which are synchronous with the articulated structure of human speech. Moreover, there are indications that infants may be predisposed to attend to the human voice from an early age. For instance, Wolff (1963) found that voices elicit smiling in two-week olds with greater frequency and regularity than other stimuli. Not only are young infants attracted to voices, but it appears that they are sensitive to differences in vocal quality from an early age. There is by now evidence from a variety of sources that suggests that infants are sensitive to male/female differences in speaker's voices. For example, using an intermodal paradigm, Spelke and Owsley (1979) found that infants turned more often to look in the direction of the parent whose voice was being played over a tape recorder. Furthermore, there are several reports that infants are capable of discriminating between same-sexed voices (e.g., Boyd, 1975; Brown, 1979; DeCasper & Fifer, 1980; Mehler, Barriere, & Jasik-Gerschenfeld, 1976). The Mehler et al. result was particularly interesting because the infants they tested appeared to express a preference for hearing their own mother's voice over that of a stranger.[1] A similar finding has been

---

[1] Actually, the preference was present only when both the mother and stranger spoke in a highly inflected manner. When both mother and stranger spoke in a monotone, the infant displayed no reliable preferences.

reported for infants less than three days old by DeCasper and Fifer (1980). Thus, even young infants may have the capacity to detect regular patterns in speech that serve to distinguish one speaker's voice from another. It seems clear, then, that the human voice is a very salient stimulus for the infant.

Do the findings from infant speech perception along with those demonstrating the infant's apparent attraction to voices force us to conclude that the infant is innately endowed with specialized language processing mechanisms? Not necessarily, since there are a number of other findings that may require an alternative account of the infant's speech perception capacities. A prime example concerns the findings from studies of non-human mammals' perception of speech sounds. Chinchillas display remarkable similarities to humans with respect to the perception of sounds differing in voice onset time (Kuhl & Miller, 1975; 1978). Should consistent cross-species similarities exist in the perception of other kinds of speech sounds, it would seem more sensible to look for an explanation of human speech perception in terms of general properties of the mammalian auditory system rather than in the existence of specialized language processing mechanisms. Similarly, recent demonstrations that categorical perception also exists for certain classes of nonspeech sounds (e.g., Cutting & Rosner, 1974; Miller, Wier, Pastore, Kelly, & Dooling, 1976; Pisoni, 1977) raise further questions about the "specialness" of speech processing.

In this chapter, I examine the issue of whether infants are endowed with specialized processing mechanisms for the perception of speech signals. I begin by considering what the minimal speech perception needs are for the infant in order for him or her to acquire language. Then I discuss some recent evidence that bears upon the question of whether the infant's speech perception abilities are the result of specialized processing mechanisms. Finally, I will close with a consideration of some possible answers to this question and their ramifications for our understanding of language acquisition in general and speech perception in particular.

SOME MINIMAL SPEECH PERCEPTION REQUIREMENTS
FOR ACQUISITION OF SPOKEN LANGUAGE

It almost goes without saying that speech perception is not an absolute requirement for the acquisition of all forms of human language. The capacity of deaf persons to master sign language, and in some cases, spoken language is a testament to that fact. Yet, in the normal course of events, it seems clear that language acquisition is determined in part by the basic capacities which the language learner has for perceiving spoken language. If the language learner is to make any progress at all in acquiring the words of the language, he or she must be able to distinguish between different words. Moreover, he or she must be able to recognize or categorize the different utterances of a particular word as being the same in some respect. In basic terms, the child needs to have some proficiency for the discrimination and categorization of utterances. In this respect, the needs for acquiring linguistic knowledge are not fundamentally different from those for acquiring any other form of knowledge for the infant. Let us examine more closely the ways in which discrimination and categorization apply to the infant's processing of speech signals.

Consider first the role of discrimination. The infant must be able to discriminate between all members of the set of phonemes used in the language being learned. Some selectivity is required here since even given the set of phones that appear in the language, not all potential phonetic differences may be exploited phonologically. For example, two phones might be used interchangeably with no difference to the meaning of a word. That is, they would be allophones or members of the same abstract phonemic category.[2] Furthermore, because differences between words can be cued by differences between segments in any portion of an utterance, the infant must be able to apply his discriminative capacities to the entire word.

The role of categorization is considerably more complicated. Simply put, the infant must be able to recognize the occurrence of a particular word. This task is not straightforward for the infant because utterances can vary on so many dimensions. For instance, variations between two different utterances of the same word may arise as a result of changes in (1) speakers' voices, (2) speaking rate, (3) intonation pattern, (4) surrounding words. Moreover, further difficulties are imposed by the fact that word boundaries are often not clearly marked in fluent speech. This means that the infant must also develop some skill at segmenting the speech stream in order to achieve successful categorization. Hence, by the time the child begins to pursue language learning in earnest, he or she must have achieved a considerable measure of perceptual constancy in recognizing different tokens of the same utterance type.

At this juncture, it is worth noting one speech perception skill that might not be required for acquiring a spoken language. There would seem to be no necessity that a child be able to recognize the occurrence of the same phone in different phonetic contexts. That is, for the child to acquire a spoken vocabulary for language, there appears to be no need to recognize that the initial sound of "bag" is the same as the initial sound of "bed." The recognition of such phonetic identities is clearly important in learning to read, but would seem to be of little consequence for identifying and distinguishing words in spoken language. For this reason, there is no

---

[2]It is by no means clear that such selectivity is an early achievement for the language learning child. Indeed, it may be some time before he comes to recognize that there might be two different ways of pronouncing the same word.

necessity at this point of constraining possible models of infant speech perception by making them account for the recognition of phonetic identities.[3] Of course, should infants display an ability to recognize the same phone in different phonetic contexts, then such constraints would apply.

Hence, a consideration of the prerequisites for successful language acquisition suggests that infants should possess certain capacities for the discrimination and categorization of speech sounds. The fundamental question addressed in the remainder of the paper is whether it is necessary to postulate the existence of specialized speech processing mechanisms for these capacities. We will focus first on the capacities relating to discrimination and then on those pertaining to categorization.

THE INFANT'S DISCRIMINATION OF SPEECH SOUNDS

The vast majority of studies on infant speech perception have dealt with some apsect of discrimination. Thus, we know a great deal about the variety of contrasts that infants are capable of discriminating. Initially there seemed to be little need to inquire into the basis of the infant's discriminative abilities. The work of Eimas and his colleagues (Eimas, Siqueland, Jusczyk, & Vigorito, 1971; Eimas, 1974) indicated that the infant's discrimination of speech sounds is categorical. Because categorical perception was thought to be peculiar to speech stimuli, it was assumed that the infant's discrimination of the sounds was controlled by special speech processing mechanisms. Further support for this position came from some early comparisons of the processing of speech and nonspeech sounds by infants. In two separate studies, Eimas (1974; 1975a) attempted to present infants with same acoustic differences in speech and nonspeech contexts. He set up this comparison by isolating the portion of the speech signal that serves to differentiate two speech sounds (e.g., [ba] and [da]). These isolated segments, called "chirps," do not sound like speech even though they constitute the portion of the signal that distinguishes the speech sounds. Eimas (1974, 1975a) found that infants responded differently to contrasts involving chirps than they did to ones between speech sounds. Discrimination performance for the speech contrasts tended to be categorical such that contrasts *between* members of different phonetic categories (e.g., [ba] versus [da]) were discriminated, but contrasts of

---

[3]One possibility here is that such recognition of phonetic identities is not achieved until the child is engaged in learning how to read. In that case the child would be forced to look for similarities between phones in different contexts. It is even possible that recognition of phonetic identities in different contexts is achieved through awareness of similarities in the way in which these speech segments are articulated.

stimuli from *within* the same phonetic category (e.g., [ba₁] versus [ba₂]) were not. By comparison, discrimination for the nonspeech chirps tended to be continuous with no differences in performance evident for between-category and within-category contrasts. Because the same acoustic differences were apparently processed in different ways for the speech and nonspeech contexts, Eimas took his results to be an indication that infants possess specialized processing mechanisms for the perception of speech.

The initial studies of infant speech perception suggested interesting differences in the way in which speech and nonspeech sounds are perceived by infants. However, in the interim several developments have raised doubts about the interpretation of the early findings. For example, there is some question as to whether the chirp stimuli used by Eimas and others (e.g., Mattingly, Liberman, Syrdal, & Halwes, 1971; Morse, 1972) are appropriate nonspeech controls. These stimuli omit information about the nature of first formant cues because it was claimed that such information was redundant across the items under investigation. However, the acoustic information left out of the chirps may actually be critical for perception, especially if the acoustic analysis is conducted not upon the individual formants themselves, but on the relationships between the formants. Hence, it may be inappropriate to claim that the same acoustic differences are present in both speech and nonspeech contrasts when the latter lack first formant cues. Some support for this view comes from two recent studies with adults. In the first of these, Pisoni (1976) found that the inclusion of first formant information in chirp stimuli produced sharp discontinuities in discrimination performance in contrast to the rather even levels of performance noted for chirps lacking first formant cues. Similarly, Jusczyk, Smith, and Murphy (1981) discovered that marked differences occur in subjects' classification of chirp patterns with and without first formant information.

Perhaps more damaging to the claims for specialized speech processing mechanisms in infants, is the recent evidence concerning the perception of nonspeech sounds. By now there is evidence that categorical perception is present in adults for a variety of nonspeech dimensions (e.g., Cutting & Rosner, 1974; Miller et al., 1976; Pisoni, 1977, 1979). But more importantly, infants too, exhibit categorical discrimination for certain nonspeech dimensions (Jusczyk, Pisoni, Walley, & Murray, 1980; Jusczyk, Rosner, Cutting, Foard, & Smith, 1977; Mehler & Bertoncini, 1978).

In the first of these investigations, Jusczyk et al., (1977) examined two-month-old infants' discrimination of rise-time differences for sawtooth wave stimuli. Cutting and Rosner (1974) had employed the same stimuli in their study with adults and found that sinewave stimuli with rise times shorter than 35 msec were perceived as musical tones emanating from a plucked stringed instrument. By contrast, rise times greater than 35 msec sounded as though they were produced by a bowed stringed instrument.

Cutting and Rosner's listeners readily labeled the sawtooth wave stimuli as "plucks" and "bows." Moreover, their perception of these sounds tended to be categorical so that contrasts between plucks and bows were easily detected, but contrasts between two different bows or two different plucks were not. Jusczyk et al. (1977) found similar results when they presented pairs of sawtooth wave stimuli to infants for discrimination. Infants gave reliable evidence of detecting rise-time differences that crossed the adult pluck-bow boundary (e.g., 30 msec versus 60 msec of rise time), but no evidence of discriminating rise-time differences between stimuli chosen from within the same adult category (e.g., two plucks such as 0 msec versus 30 msec). Hence, Jusczyk et al. demonstrated that categorical discrimination performance by infants could be obtained for certain types of nonspeech stimuli. This result was of considerable importance because it suggested that specialized speech processing mechanisms were not required to account for categorical discrimination. Instead, it appears that categorical discrimination may simply be a consequence of the way in which the human auditory system processes complex acoustic signals.

Because categorical discrimination results are not limited to speech signals, it seems appropriate to determine whether there might not be a psychophysical explanation for the categorical discrimination of certain speech contrasts by infants. Actually, the rise-time dimension investigated by Jusczyk et al. (1977) also has a correlate in the speech domain as one of the cues which helps to distinguish [ba] and [wa]. Thus, it is possible that a psychophysical account framed in terms of responses to rise times could explain the discrimination of [ba] and [wa] by infants that Hillenbrand, Minifie, and Edwards (1979) observed.

A more direct attempt to provide a psychophysical account for categorical discrimination along one speech dimension was made by Jusczyk, Pisoni, Walley, and Murray (1980). These investigators sought a psychophysical explanation for infants' discrimination of voice-onset-time (VOT) differences. They drew upon observations made by Pisoni (1977) with adults. Pisoni suggested that categorical perception for VOT differences might have its origins in the way in which the human auditory system responds to the temporal ordering of acoustic events. To test his hypothesis, he prepared a set of two-tone stimuli consisting of both 500 Hz and 1500 Hz tones. The onsets of the tones were temporally ordered with respect to each other so that the onset of 500 Hz tone could be leading, lagging behind, or occurring simultaneously with the 1500 Hz tone. Thus, the temporal order differences between the onsets of the tones modeled one aspect of the relations that occur between the first and second formants in signaling VOT differences. Pisoni found that adults' perception of these tone onset time (TOT) stimuli was categorical. Furthermore, the locations of the category boundaries for the TOT stimuli at −20 msec and +20 msec corresponded nicely to those observed for VOT with speech stimuli (Lisker & Abramson, 1970). Given these results, Pisoni concluded that categorical perception of VOT may arise as a consequence of the way in which the human auditory system responds to temporally-ordered events. In the case of VOT, these events involve the relative onset or timing of laryngeal to supralaryngeal events.

Jusczyk et al. (1980) employed similar stimuli in their attempt to provide a psychophysical account for the infant's discrimination of VOT. Their results indicated that although the infant's discrimination of the nonspeech timing differences tended to be categorical, there was some discrepancy between the TOT results and earlier ones with VOT. Specifically, the infants discriminated only the − 70 msec/ − 40 msec and + 40 msec/ + 70 msec TOT contrasts (both of which were within category contrasts for adults) suggesting category boundaries at slightly higher stimulus values than those inferred for VOT which are in the region of − 40 msec/ − 20 msec and + 20 msec/ + 40 msec (e.g., Aslin, Hennessy, Pisoni, & Perey, 1979; Eimas et al., 1971; Lasky, Syrdal-Lasky, & Klein, 1975). Thus, these results would seem to indicate that infants have slightly higher thresholds for resolving temporal order differences in nonspeech sounds. Consequently, while Jusczyk et al.'s results demonstrated that infants are sensitive to temporal order differences, they raise some doubts as to whether temporal order cues alone provide a sufficient basis for explaining VOT discrimination (see Lisker, 1978). In fact, the high amplitude sucking procedure employed in these infant studies provides only a very crude estimate of the category boundaries. Moreover, there are considerable differences in the spectral composition of the TOT and VOT stimuli, e.g., rapidly changing formant transitions are present in the latter but not the former. Nevertheless, Jusczyk et al. recognized that temporal order cues might not provide the sole basis for infants' discrimination of VOT. Instead, temporal order information might constitute only one of several acoustic cues that might be used in signaling VOT differences. Other possible candidates for acoustic cues to VOT involve aspects of the first formant. In particular, Stevens and Klatt (1974) suggested that first formant cutback (i.e., the presence or absence of a first formant transition) could serve infants as a cue for VOT discrimination. More recent investigations have challenged the importance of this cue, suggesting instead that it is the first formant onset frequency that is critical (Lisker, 1975, 1978; Summerfield & Haggard, 1977). Regardless of which way this dispute is resolved, either of these first formant cues would only be functional for the voiced/voiceless boundary along the VOT continuum, other cues would be necessary to signal the prevoiced/voiced boundary. In this regard, it is worth noting that demonstrations of discrimination of VOT distinctions have been much easier to obtain in the voiced/voiceless region than in the prevoiced/voiced region (e.g., see Aslin et al., 1979; Eimas,

1975b). Perhaps voiced/voiceless distinction is more inherently salient because there are more acoustic cues to signal it.

A demonstration that there was an exact correspondence between a psychophysical dimension and a given speech dimension would implicate a source for both in general auditory processing mechanisms. A failure to find such a correspondence leaves upon the possibility that special mechanisms are employed in analyzing speech sounds. Indeed, if there are a number of potential acoustic cues for VOT and these are integrated in some way to yield a perception of VOT, then the integrator itself may be equivalent to a specialized processing mechanism for speech (if no other role can be found for it in the processing of nonspeech signals). On the other hand, since two complex sounds may be discriminated on any one of a number of bases, the demonstration that categorical discrimination occurs for nonspeech dimensions indicates that a psychophysical explanation for infant speech perception must be given serious consideration as an account of their performance.

The foregoing discussion implies a potentially useful tact to take in evaluating claims for specialized speech processing mechanisms. Namely, one might do well to examine those cases in which a variety of different cues could be used to signal a particular phonetic contrast. By varying these cues individually and then in combination, one may gain some insight into the nature of the mechanisms that process this information.

One speech contrast for which multiple cues exist is the place-of-articulation distinction for fricatives. The classic research conducted by Harris (1958) suggested two potential sources of information for signaling place-of-articulation in fricatives, viz. the formant transitions and the spectral shape of the frication noise. The effectiveness of each of these cues varied across the contrasts that Harris investigated. Thus, while the spectral characteristics of the turbulent noise source proved most important for distinctions between [sa] and [ʃa], the formant transitions appeared to be the most salient cue for the distinction between [fa] and [θa].

Recently, Carden, Levitt, Jusczyk, and Walley (1981) undertook a further investigation of the cues signaling the labiodental/interdental place distinction that occurs between [fa] and [θa]. In an effort to gain a better understanding of the role of formant transitions in signaling the place distinction, Carden et al. varied their stimuli in a number of ways. In order to assess whether the formant transition differences were in themselves sufficient to cue the place distinction, they removed the frication portions of both [fa] and [θa]. To their surprise, Carden et al. found that adult listeners perceived both the resultant sounds as [ba]. Further experimentation using synthetic speech sounds indicated that this effect could not be attributed to absence of some critical distinction carried in the frication portions of [fa] and [θa]. For example, even when the synthetic [fa] and [θa] stimuli were constructed utilizing a neutral frication noise, its removal from the stimuli caused listeners to perceive the resultant sounds as [ba]. Carden et al. also examined identification performance for two speech continua created by varying formant transition starting frequencies. The continua were identical in all respects except for the addition of the neutral frication noise to beginning of the formant transitions on one of the continua. Thus, one of these continua was perceived as ranging from [ba] to [da] and the other, which included frication, ranged from [fa] to [θa]. Subjects located the place-of-articulation boundary in different regions for the two continua. Since the formant transition differences were identical across both continua, these results suggested that the identical set of formant transitions could give rise to the perception of two different places of articulation depending on whether frication was present or not. An obvious explanation for this finding is that the frication noise has some sort of masking effect upon the formant transitions that is responsible for the shift in boundary. However, Carden et al. ruled out this possible account by demonstrating that the same effect could be obtained by merely instructing subjects to label stimuli from the fricative continuum as stops, and stimuli from the stop continuum as fricatives. The boundary shifts achieved under this change in instruction sets were of the same magnitude as the original boundary differences. Therefore, given that the place boundary differences could be induced simply by changing subjects set about manner-of-articulation in the absence of any physical cue for manner, Carden et al. concluded that the perception of place-of-articulation is dependent upon subjects' perception of manner. Thus, they interpreted their results as indicating that the identification of place-of-articulation by adults involves some form of specialized (phonetic) processing.

It is hard to conceive of a psychophysical explanation for Carden et al.'s results, yet the existence of some form of phonetic processing in adults does not necessarily entail the existence of innate mechanisms specialized for processing speech sounds. In fact, a specialized mode of perception for speech might evolve as a result of experiences in acquiring language (this option will be discussed further later; see also Jusczyk, in press). For this reason, an examination of the perception of place-of-articulation information by infants could provide critical information regarding the existence of specialized processing mechanisms for speech. In fact, Jusczyk, Murray, Murphy, Levitt, and Carden (in preparation) have conducted an investigation along these lines. In a series of experiments, they tested infants' sensitivity to both formant transition and spectral noise cues for place-of-articulation in fricatives. They began by investigating whether formant transition differences would provide a sufficient cue for the discrimination of [fa] from [θa]. One group of infants was tested using natural speech tokens of [fa] and [θa]. A second group heard truncated versions of the same syllables. The truncation consisted of removing the frication portion from each syllable. Similar to Carden et al.'s (1981) results with adults, Jusczyk et al. found that although infants discriminated the [fa] and [θa] stimuli, they did not discriminate the truncated versions of these stimuli. Thus, in the absence of the differential frication noise, the formant transition differences did not appear to be discriminable for infants.

In order to ascertain whether infants might rely primarily on spectral noise differences to distinguish the [fa]-[θa] syllables, Jusczyk et al. carried out an additional experiment. They tested one group of infants with a pair of stimuli consisting only of the spectral noise portions of [fa] and [θa] directly appended to the vowel [a]. Thus, no formant transition information was available for this contrast. By utilizing these stimuli, Jusczyk et al. sought to determine if the spectral noise differences were sufficient to cue the place-of-articulation contrast for the infants.[4] In addition to this group, Jusczyk et al. tested a second set of subjects on another contrast to determine whether the presence of a constant frication noise could provide a context in which the formant transition differences for [fa] and [θa] might be discriminated. Accordingly, they created a new pair of stimulus tokens by appending the same frication noise (from a [fa]) directly to the formant transition plus vowel portions of the [fa] and [θa] syllables. Thus, in this instance, the frication noise provided no differential information to signal the contrast for the syllables, rather it served only as a context by which the differential information available in the formant transitions might be utilized. Jusczyk et al.'s results showed that both contrasts were discriminable for infants. Hence, there is sufficient information available in the spectral noise portions of [fa] and [θa] to enable infants to distinguish these syllables. At the same time, it is also clear that there is sufficient information available in the formant transitions for infants to distinguish [fa] from [θa] as long as an appropriate context is provided.

The most intriguing aspect of Jusczyk et al.'s results is the finding that the frication noise provides infants with a suitable context for detecting formant transition differences. The parallel between this result and the one observed by Carden et al. (1981) is striking. Does the frication context work because it conveys information about manner-of-articulation to the infant, or is there an alternative psychophysical explanation for this result? Recall that Carden et al. ruled out a psychophysical account for their results because the same effect could be obtained merely by changing the instruction set regarding manner-of-articulation. Unfortunately, a similar experiment with preverbal infants is impossible. Instead, it will be necessary to

---

[4]Interestingly enough, these frication plus vowel stimuli sounded like [fa] and [θa] to adult listeners.

pursue another tack in order to get at the source of the context effect in infants.

One possible psychophysical account for the context effect is that the frication noise provides the infant with an external reference point for judging the differences in formant transitions.[5] If this is so, then perhaps one could substitute a different type of reference point for the frication noise and still obtain discrimination functions similar to those for the fricative stimuli. For example, one might employ a tone of equal duration with the same frequency value as the center frequencies of the frication noise. At present, such an experiment has not been carried out, although results from a pilot experiment by Jusczyk et al. with synthetic speech stimuli suggest that the overall spectral shape of the reference point may be critical. Obviously, if only near duplicates of the natural frication noises serve as appropriate reference points, the underlying mechanisms offered in a psychophysical explanation would have to be quite specialized. One might then question whether the degree of specialization was not sufficient to consider the underlying mechanisms as being designed for speech perception.

Thus, the context effects observed with respect to the place distinction for fricatives may be indicative of specialized processing for speech sounds by infants. Jusczyk et al.'s results suggest that the perception of place cues may be dependent upon the perception of manner information for infants as well as for adults. It remains to be seen whether it will be possible to account for these findings by appealing to general features of the auditory processing system.

A different sort of context effect that occurs in the infant's perception of speech sounds has been reported recently by Eimas and Miller (1980; see also Eimas, this volume). Observations on the phonetic distinction between the stop [ba] and the glide [wa] indicate that the duration of formant transition information is a sufficient cue for signaling this contrast (Miller & Liberman, 1979). More importantly, the critical formant transition duration for cueing this distinction was shown to vary with the total duration of

---

[5]Note that a hypothesis along these lines has been put forth as a psychophysical account for categorical perception results (Miller et al., 1976; Pastore, Ahroon, Buffuto, Friedman, Puleo, & Fink, 1977). The hypothesis states that "categorical perception will be found wherever there exists a stable source of information that is more precise than the parameter information normally employed in discriminating stimuli along the given continuum" (Pastore et al., 1976, p. 687). Nevertheless, the notion of a reference point or pedestal would appear to serve very different functions in accounting for categorical perception and for context results like those described above. Specifically, as it applies to categorical perception, the reference pedestal has been invoked as an explanation for *suppressed* within-category discrimination performance (e.g., Pastore et al., 1977). In the application suggested above, its role is to explain the *enhanced* discrimination performance that occurs when a frication context is present. Whether there is some way of reconciling these apparently disparate roles cannot be determined at this point.

the syllable. Thus, for very short syllables of 80 msec durations, the boundary value for transition duration was on the order of 32 msec, such that syllables with durations shorter than this were perceived as [ba] and those with longer durations as [wa]. On the other hand, for syllables with durations 296 msec, the boundary value was estimated to be on the order of 47 msec (Miller & Liberman, 1979). The context effect observed by Miller and Liberman could not be ascribed simply to an overall increase in the duration of the syllable. If this were so, then any increases in syllable duration should have produced similar shifts in the transition duration boundaries. However, in one experiment Miller and Liberman compared the effects of increasing duration not only by increasing the duration of the steady state portion of the syllable, but also by adding an equivalent duration of formant transitions to the ends of syllables (thereby producing CVC syllables ranging from [bad] to [wad]). The two methods of increasing the overall syllable duration had entirely different effects. Whereas the first method resulted in boundary shifts towards larger transition duration values, the second method actually produced shifts towards *shorter* values. Hence, it appears that listeners were not simply computing the stop/glide boundary by using a measure of transition duration relative to overall syllable duration. Rather, the structure of the syllable itself exerted an effect upon estimates of the phonetic boundary. For this reason, Miller and Liberman argued that subjects' estimates of the rate of articulation affected their perceptions of the location of the phonetic boundary.

Because estimates of rate of articulation are presumably dictated by phonetic rather than psychophysical considerations, Miller and Liberman's results would seem to imply that some form of specialized phonetic processing is involved in locating the stop/glide boundary. However, recent research by Carrell, Pisoni, and Gans (1980) indicates that comparable effects can be obtained for rapid spectrum changes in nonspeech sounds. Moreover, there is little psychophysical data available with respect to how adults perceive the durations of components of complex acoustic signals. Thus, increasing the overall duration of a signal by adding to a steady state portion may not have the same psychophysical consequences as adding an equivalent duration that includes a rapid spectral change. Until it can be determined whether there is a comparable psychophysical segmentation for the speech signal, it is hard to know whether subjects are responding to a speech parameter like rate of articulation or a psychophysical one like rate of acoustic change. Still, whatever their origin, the context effects observed by Miller and Liberman demonstrates the capacity that humans have for dealing with the complex interactions that occur between different speech cues.

Eimas and Miller (1980) found a close correspondence between infants' responsiveness to transition durations when syllable duration was varied and the results obtained for adults by Miller and Liberman. Infants displayed categorical discrimination for formant transition duration differences, and the region of highest discriminability for these differences varied with overall syllable duration. Thus, for syllables with durations of only 80 msec, infants discriminated a contrast between syllables with transition durations of 16 and 40 msec, but not a contrast between syllables with transition durations of 40 and 64 msec (both of which are perceived as [wa] by adults). For syllables with overall durations of 296 msec the results were just the opposite, the 40/64 pair was discriminated and the 16/40 pair (both of which were now perceived was [ba] by adults) was not.

Are infants utilizing information about rate of articulation in their discrimination of formant transition differences? If so, then the implication is that infants do engage in specialized processing of speech sounds. Unfortunately, though suggestive of a tendency towards specialized speech processing by infants, Eimas and Miller's results are not definitive on this point. One critical piece of information that they did not obtain in their inquiry was whether increasing the overall syllable duration by adding formant transitions to the end of the syllable resulted in a shift in the infant's discrimination performance towards pairs with shorter transition durations. Should such an outcome occur it would be an indication that infants are sensitive to the internal structure of the syllable. Again, whether this sensitivity is traceable to a phonetic or psychophysical analysis of the syllable would have to be resolved through further experimentation using nonspeech sounds, as is currently underway in our laboratory.

In summary, the results from studies of the discrimination of speech sounds donot provide definitive evidence about the existence of a specialized speech mode of perception for infants. There are indications that infants engage in similar processing for speech and certain nonspeech signals. At the same time, recent investigations demonstrating the existence of context effects upon the infant's discrimination of speech suggest the existence of processing abilities designed to cope with the complex interactions that can occur between speech cues. Yet, whether these abilities are of phonetic or psychophysical origin is still unknown.

EVIDENCE RELATING TO THE INFANT'S CATEGORIZATION OF SPEECH SOUNDS

One of the greatest sources of frustration to workers in the field of infant speech perception has been their inability to obtain direct measures of the infant's categorization of speech sounds. To date, most of the available data regarding categorization have been obtained rather indirectly. Categorization is inferred from the infant's performance on certain tasks involving discrimination. The evidence to be considered here has been collected in studies of perceptual constancy with infants.

The basic strategy employed by researchers in this area has been to present infants with a discrimination problem along some fixed stimulus dimension and to see whether the discrimination can be maintained in the face of irrelevant variations along other dimensions. The most widely used method for conducting such a test involves training infants to make a head turn response when they detect a change in the appropriate stimulus dimension. Successful execution of this response in the face of irrelevant stimulus variations is taken as evidence that the infant has achieved some measure of perceptual constancy for the given stimulus dimension. That is, the infant has demonstrated the ability to recognize the stimulus dimension in question despite the fact that it can occur in a variety of different physical contexts. The notion of categorization enters here by the assumption that the infant has perceived some commonality in all the varied carriers of the stimulus dimension, thus treats them as being alike in some way.

The most impressive demonstrations of perceptual constancy have been obtained when pitch contour and speakers' voices have been allowed to vary irrelevantly. Kuhl (1979) tested six-month-old infants on their ability to discriminate a contrast between the vowels /a/ and /i/ when irrelevant variations in pitch contours and speakers' voices occurred. Using a transfer of training paradigm, she first taught infants to discriminate the /a/-/i/ contrast when speaker's voice and pitch contour were held constant. The infant's task was to detect a change from a continuously repeating background stimulus (e.g., /a/) to a comparison stimulus (e.g., /i/) and to turn his or her head in the direction of a display box during the interval in which the comparison stimulus occurred. If the infant correctly turned during the interval in which the comparison stimulus was played, he or she was rewarded by having the display box light up and a mechanical toy activated. In order to control for the possibility that infants might simply spontaneously turn to the display box, Kuhl employed a series of catch trials in which no change in auditory stimulation occurred. After mastering the initial discrimination, the infants passed through a number of successive training stages in which irrelevant variations were introduced to the stimulus items. For example, in one stage, pitch contour varied irrelevantly so that the background stimuli randomly varied between a rising pitch contour and a falling contour. Similar variations in pitch contour also occurred for the comparison stimuli. Despite these variations, the important contrast remained the same—a distinction between /a/ and /i/. Ultimately, the infants were able to maintain this discrimination even when tokens were presented from three different talkers, each one of whom used two different pitch contours. As a check on whether the infants' successful performance on the final stage of testing might be explained in terms of experience gained during the training procedure, Kuhl ran a second experiment in which all stages of training except the initial training stage and final test stage were eliminated. Once again, infants were able to ignore irrelevant sources of variation in making the discrimination between /a/ and /i/. Thus, perceptual constancy for vowel quality does not require specific training, rather it appears to be immediately available to the infant. Nor is perceptual constancy limited to vowel segments. Holmberg, Morgan, and Kuhl (1977) found that infants were able to ignore irrelevant variations in speakers' voices and vowel context in discriminating the fricative contrasts [s] versus [ʃ] and [f] versus [θ].

Findings such as those described above are quite provocative because they suggest that by six months of age, the infant already possesses a capacity for perceptual normalization with regard to speech sounds. This capacity is an extremely important one for the individual trying to acquire a language for it provides the means by which two different token utterances can be recognized as belonging to the same utterance type (even when those tokens are spoken by persons with very different vocal characteristics).

There are potential constancies for speech of another sort which would seem to be of less significance in the language acquisition process. These constancies pertain to the recognition of the same phonetic segment as it occurs in different phonetic contexts. As noted earlier, it is not immediately clear why it would be useful in acquiring a language to be able to recognize that "dune" and "deep" share the same initial segment. In fact, attending to phonetic similarities between words could well prove a hindrance to successful language acquisition. This is because, as many have observed (e.g., Hockett, 1960), there is a totally arbitrary relationship between sound and meaning in language. Consider the words "cat," "rat," and "mouse." Although "cat" and "rat" sound more similar than "rat" and "mouse," the meanings of the latter pair are far more similar than those of the former. This is not to say that the capacity for recognizing phonetic identities in different contexts has little relevance to the child. Certainly, this capacity is critically important for learning how to read and for discovering the phonological regularities of spoken language. Yet, neither of these processes is likely to begin in earnest until the child has acquired a working vocabulary in the language.

Nevertheless, it is clear that children eventually do display perceptual constancy for phonetic segments in different contexts. Hence, it is interesting to know whether this sort of constancy has an innate basis, is the result of some learned equivalence, or some sort of interaction between the two (Aslin & Pisoni, 1980). There have been a number of investigations dealing with the issue of whether infants display this sort of constancy. As mentioned above, Holmberg, Morgan, and Kuhl (1977) reported some evidence for perceptual constancy using fricative stimuli. However, the acoustic cues for fricatives are more nearly invariant across different phonetic contexts. Thus, a stronger case for perceptual constancy could be made by using phonetic segments whose acoustic features appear to undergo marked changes in different contexts. In particular, it has been argued that stop consonant segments undergo just such context-conditional variation (Liberman, Cooper, Shankweiler, & Studdert-Kennedy, 1967; but see Searle, Jacobson, & Rayment, 1979; Stevens & Blumstein, 1978; 1980). There have been at least three attempts to demonstrate perceptual constancy for stop consonant segments in different phonetic contexts. All three investigations provide limited support for some form of perceptual constancy for stop consonant segments (Fodor, Garrett, & Brill, 1975; Jusczyk & Derrah, in preparation; Katz & Jusczyk, 1980).

Fodor, Garrett, and Brill (1975) sought to determine whether four-month-olds would find it easier to learn a headturning task in which reinforced items came from the same phonetic category (e.g., [pi] and [pu]) as opposed to when they came from different categories (e.g., [pi] and [ka]). Fodor et al. actually chose their stimulus pairs in such a way that the members of the nonphonetic grouping shared an important acoustic feature, viz. burst-cue frequency. By cleverly arranging their test, Fodor et al. were able to directly pit groupings based upon phonetic identities against ones based upon acoustic identities. Their results indicated that infants showed reliably better performance for the phonetic groupings than for the acoustic groupings. Unfortunately, Fodor et al.'s subjects never did attain very high levels of performance even with the phonetic groupings. In fact, they made correct anticipatory head turns on fewer than 50% of the trials, and their overall hit rates were scarcely better than their false alarm rates. Because the performance levels were so low, the results of this study must be considered cautiously. At best, it could be said that the data provide weak evidence for perceptual constancy.

Another investigation of perceptual constancy for stop consonant segments was conducted by Katz and Jusczyk (1980) using six-month-old infants. These investigators examined whether infants might display perceptual constancy for the phones [b] and [d] across four different vowel contexts. The vowel contexts they chose were selected so as to maximize the variance of the formant transition cues for [b] and [d]. To test their subjects, they utilized the same basic headturning procedure as Kuhl (1979), but with a few modifications. The major modification consisted of transferring half of the subjects to groupings of synthetic speech syllables that preserved the phonetic basis for the initial discrimination, and the other half to arbitrary groupings of the same syllables. Thus, training proceeded in the following manner. All subjects were trained to discriminate a contrast between [bi] and [di]. In Stage 2 of training, half of the subjects were transferred to a task in which they had to discriminate a pair such as [bi] and [bɛ] from [di] and [dɛ] (note that while the phonetic distinction [b] versus [d] remains the same, irrelevant vowel variation has been introduced). The other half of the subjects received training on an arbitrary grouping of the same syllables (e.g., [bi] and [dɛ] versus [di] and [bɛ]). Note that for this second group of subjects, there is no common phonetic basis on which to discriminate the contrast. Hence, the transfer task for this group could only be performed successfully if subjects learned the equivalence classes for the syllables. Any subjects who successfully completed the Stage 2 task were transferred to Stage 3. For subjects with the phonetic pairings, this task involved the discrimination of [bi], [bɛ], [bo], [bɚ] from [di], [dɛ], [do], [dɚ] For subjects with the arbitrary pairings, the discrimination pitted [bi], [dɛ], [bo], [dɚ] against [di] [bɛ], [do], [bɚ]. By including a test involving an arbitrary pairing of the syllables as well as a phonetic pairing, Katz and Jusczyk reasoned that they could determine whether successful performance on the task could be attributed to perceptual constancy or to learned equivalence. Any indication that subjects learned the phonetic groupings more readily than the arbitrary ones would favor an account based upon perceptual constancy. On the other hand, if subjects with the arbitrary groupings performed as well as those with phonetic groupings, a learned equivalence explanation would be more appropriate, since presumably the arbitrary groupings could be learned only through rote memorization of the members in a particular group.

Katz and Jusczyk found that the only transfer tasks their subjects were able to master were those involving phonetic groupings of the syllables. Not one subject succeeded in passing a transfer task based upon the arbitrary groupings. Thus, it would appear that some form of perceptual constancy rather than learned equivalence is responsible for the successful performance of those subjects who passed the transfer task involving the phonetic grouping. However, Katz and Jusczyk's finding of perceptual constancy must be qualified by the fact that no subject with the phonetic groupings ever successfully completed the Stage 3 task. Thus, while subjects gave evidence of perceptual constancy, it was only for those situations in which two varying vowel contexts were used. No subject displayed perceptual constancy for the [b]-[d] discrimination when four varying vowel contexts were present. So again, these data provide weak support for the notion that infants have perceptual constancy for stop consonant segments occurring in different contexts.

In addition to the difficulties Katz and Jusczyk had in trying to train subjects on the Stage 3 discrimination task, they also found that there were a large number of infants who were unable to learn even the simple Stage 1 distinction involving stop consonants. A check of the operating procedure used in the experiment indicated that the same infants had no difficulty with a vowel distinction similar to the one employed by Kuhl (1979). Speculating on why infants had so much difficulty with the stop consonant discrimination, Katz and Jusczyk suggested that there may be a constraint on the infant's performance imposed jointly by the task demands of the headturning procedure and the difficulty of the particular speech constrast to be discriminated. A similar view has been put forth by Shatz (1978) in her discussion of the relationship between cognitive processes and the development of communication skills in children. Starting with the assumption that children, like adults are limited capacity information processors, she notes that the display of a particular skill varies with overall cognitive workload. Thus, the demonstration of a particular skill will be most easily accomplished in settings where other cognitive demands are minimized. Tasks imposing heavy cognitive demands may tax the information-handling capacities of the child, thereby preventing the demonstration of a particular skill which, though present, is inaccessible in that task setting.

Katz and Jusczyk hypothesized that it might be easier to demonstrate perceptual constancy for stop consonants like [b] and [d] by utilizing a task that imposes less demands upon the infant's information-handling capacity. For this reason, Jusczyk and Derrah (in preparation) tried to devise a measure of perceptual constancy using the high amplitude sucking procedure. Borrowing their rationale from studies of categorization employing visual habituation measures (e.g., Bornstein, Kessen, & Weiskopf, 1976; Cohen, 1977), they hoped to show that repeated exposure to different instances of a particular category would result in less responding for a new instance of the same category than for a new instance of the same category than for a new instance of a different category. Again, the measure of perceptual constancy was an indirect one relying on the following assumptions: (1) that infants would perceive the similarity between category members, (2) that they would become satiated to the category as a whole, and (3) that the effects of satiation to the category would be enough to offset any effects of novelty that might accrue to a new category instance.

Jusczyk and Derrah arranged their test by presenting two-month-old infants with randomly ordered series of the syllables [bi], [ba], [bo] and [bɚ] during the preshift phase of their experiments. After the satiation criterion was achieved for these stimuli, infants were shifted to another set of syllables. For some of these infants, the postshift set consisted of the four preshift stimuli plus the syllable [bu]. For others, the postshift set included the four preshift syllables plus the syllable [du]. Several other postshift conditions were also included, but space limitations prevent their description here. The critical comparison, though, was between the two groups described above. The results were again mixed. Although in the predicted direction, the difference in response rates between the conditions in which a new [b] category member was introduced and those in which a [d] category member occurred was not significant.

Thus, none of the three experiments that have attempted to investigate perceptual constancy for stop consonant segments provides compelling evidence for such constancy. At the same time, there are some indications in the data of all three experiments that some limited form of perceptual constancy for stop consonants may be available to the infant. Still, there are alternatives to the view that infants possess perceptual constancy for phonetic segments. As noted earlier, possession of this ability is apt to be of limited usefulness to the child in acquiring a language. Thus, it is possible that the child might not develop perceptual constancy for phonetic segments until some time after he or she is in possession of a language. One implication of this approach is that, as Bertoncini and Mehler (1981) have suggested, the syllable serves as the basic unit of speech perception for the infant. Thus, perceptual constancy for phonetic segments may be a later development arising through the child's detection of certain regularities that exist between the various syllabic units. These regularities may lie in the acoustic or even articulatory correlates of the syllables. This notion—that the child might employ syllables in perception before he or she recognizes commonalities that exist in syllabic structure—is parallel in many respects to views taken concerning the detection of regularities at the phonological (Kiparsky & Menn, 1977) and syntactic (Bowerman, in press) levels.

Putting aside for the moment the issue of whether infants have perceptual constancy for phonetic segments, one can ask whether demonstrations of perceptual constancy across variations in pitch contour and speaker's voice require the postulation of specialized mechanisms for processing speech sounds? Not necessarily. Consider the infant's ability to ignore irrelevant variations in pitch contour and speaker's voice. Similar tendencies have been observed in both the dog (Baru, 1975) and the chinchilla (Burdick & Miller, 1975). Hence, the mechanisms that extract constancies of this nature appear to be generally available in the mammalian auditory system suggesting a basis in some measure of overall acoustic similarity rather than an analysis into speech-related component dimensions.

Whether nonhuman species might also display perceptual constancy for phonetic segments in different phonetic contexts has not been investigated at the present time. However, the available evidence from the infant speech perception studies cannot be said to favor either a phonetic or a psychophysical explanation for constancy of this sort. The basic problem here is that constancy for phonetic segments in different phonetic contexts can be accounted for in either of two ways. First, it could be the case that there are invariant properties in the acoustic waveform indicating the presence of a particular phonetic segment in all its possible contexts of occurrence. Though the early research on speech perception suggested a lack of invariant features for phonetic segments such as stop consonants (Liberman et al., 1967), recent research has been more promising (e.g., Kewley-

Port, 1979; Searle et al., 1979; Stevens & Blumstein, 1978, 1980). If there are such invariant acoustic features, it would be important to know whether these features are generally available to nonhuman mammalian species. If so, then an account based on general properties of the mammalian auditory system could suffice to explain this kind of perceptual constancy. On the other hand, if there are no invariant acoustic features or if only humans prove capable of detecting the invariant features, then it would appear that constancy arises as a result of mechanisms in the human nervous system. The implication is that such mechanisms are specialized for processing speech.

Therefore, the studies of perceptual constancy with infants have not provided an answer regarding the existence of specialized speech processing mechanisms in infants. As noted earlier, one essential difficulty with these studies is that they permit only an indirect assessment of the infant's perceptual categories. The measures used in these investigations do not allow for the delineation of the structure of the categories which the infant uses. A procedure along the lines of the two-alternative forced choice or two-alternative go/no go methods outlined by Aslin, Perey, Hennessey, and Pisoni (1977) may be better suited for assessing the infant's classification schemes. We need to know more about the infant's similarity space with respect to acoustic signals. Which sounds does the infant perceive to be similar in some respect? Only when we can successfully employ measures to tap such information will we know whether the infant's categorization of speech sounds is fundamentally different from his categorization of nonspeech sounds.

SOME IMPLICATIONS OF THE DISCRIMINATION AND CATEGORIZATION OF SPEECH SOUNDS BY INFANTS

Our survey reveals that infants' abilities for processing speech go far beyond those necessary for performing simple discrimination. Infants appear to be able to impose perceptual constancy on speech signals in a variety of ways that should benefit them as they begin acquiring language. Still, while it is clear that infants do have the means for conducting a rather sophisticated analysis of the speech signals, it is less certain that the mechanisms for this analysis are specialized for speech processing. In every instance in which specialized speech processing mechanisms might be proposed, there also remains some viable alternative couched in psychophysical terms. At the present time it must be concluded, then, that there is no hard empirical evidence that infants engage in phonetic processing for speech sounds. This is not to say that infants do not engage in phonetic processing, but only that if they do so, it has not been demonstrated unequivocally.

In the long run, whether or not specialized phonetic mechanisms underlie the infant's analysis of the speech signal is probably of less consequence to our understanding of language acquisition than the discovery that the infant has such abilities. The importance of infant speech perception research for studies of language acquisition is that it specifies the capacities the infant has for coping with the sound patterns of language. Whether these capacities are exclusively the province of speech processing or not will probably have little impact on the way in which other aspects of language acquisition are viewed.

The potential ramifications with respect to the nature of the mechanisms underlying infants' processing of speech are considerably greater for theories of speech perception. Evidence from a variety of sources suggests that adults engage in some form of specialized processing for speech sounds (e.g., Best, Morrongiello, & Robson, 1981; Carden et al., 1981; Isenberg & Liberman, 1978; Repp, Liberman, Eccardt, & Pesetsky, 1978). But it is not clear whether this specialized processing occurs because of the existence of underlying speech perception mechanisms (sensory coding) or as a result of strategies that evolve in attaching linguistic meaning to acoustic signals (phonological categorization). Any indication that young infants do engage in phonetic processing for speech sounds would imply that a special speech mode of perception has an innate basis. A finding to the contrary would suggest that the speech mode develops presumably as a result of experiences encountered in acquiring a language. Elsewhere (Jusczyk, in press), I have speculated about just how the speech mode may evolve. Since those views are relevant to the present concerns, it is worth reiterating some of the general points here. First of all, the starting assumption is that the infant's analysis of speech is based upon the way in which the human auditory system responds to certain psychophysical properties inherent in the acoustic signal. Thus, the infant's initial partitioning of speech sounds is conducted with reference to well-defined psychophysical properties. This would account for why infants from diverse language backgrounds discriminate contrasts from certain speech continua in much the same way (e.g., Aslin et al., 1979; Eimas, 1975b; Lasky et al., 1975; Streeter, 1976) despite cross-language differences in the way in which adults position their phonological boundaries along the same continua (Lisker & Abramson, 1970; Williams, 1977). The speech mode begins to evolve only at the point in which the infant starts to attach linguistic significance to speech. I am in agreement with MacKain (1979) that it is the operation of trying to assign a meaning to a given set of utterance tokens that encourages the child to attend to similarities and differences that exist in the acoustic attributes of these tokens. The child must be in a position to focus upon those acoustic variations which result in a change in the meaning of the utterance. It is the feedback the child receives with regard to the meaning of the utterance that enables him to hone in on those acoustic properties of speech which are of greatest relevance to the language he is trying to learn. Presumably, the most important acoustic properties will be reflected in the phonological constraints of the language. Hence, as the child begins to acquire the phonological structure of the language, one would expect to see him combine the various acoustic cues present in the speech signal according to their salience in marking distinctive contrasts in the language. It is at this point, when the child begins to weight the acoustic cues present in speech according to their relevance in signaling differences in meaning, that the speech mode develops. At the level of perception, the speech mode exists as an interpretive schema for the acoustic cues picked up by general auditory processing mechanisms. In other words, the difference between the speech mode of perception and a nonspeech mode of perception consists solely in the weighting given to various aspects of the acoustic signal.[6]

What the argument above illustrates is that the notion that there is a psychophysical basis for the infant's perception of speech is not incompatible with the existence of a specialized speech mode of perception. Instead, it views the speech mode of perception as a natural consequence of acquiring a language rather then the result of specialized innate mechanisms. Just how much empirical support there is for such a view remains to be determined.

In conclusion, there is nothing in our review of the existing literature that would preclude the possibility that infants engage in phonetic processing of speech. But at the same time, the available infant speech perception data appear to be explicable without positing specialized speech processing mechanisms. Rather, it seems likely that the infant begins to analyze speech in terms of well-defined psychophysical dimensions. Only when speech acquires communicative significance for the infant is it likely that speech sounds undergo specialized processing.

ACKNOWLEDGMENTS

This manuscript was prepared in part while the author was at Dalhousie University and was supported by an N.S.E.R.C. grant A-0282 to the author. I wish to thank Nancy Beattie and Colleen Snyder for the excellent job they did in typing earlier versions of the present manuscript. I am also grateful to David Pisoni for his critical reading of an earlier version of this manuscript.

---

[6]It is worth noting that the linguistic factors involved in determining the weightings for the speech mode may be quite complex, drawing upon knowledge gained not only about the phonological structure of the language, but the morphological, syntactic, and semantic structure as well.

REFERENCES

Aslin, R. N., Hennessey, B., Pisoni, D. B., & Perey, A. J. *Individual infants' discrimination of voice onset time: Evidence for three modes of vocing.* Paper presented at the biennial meeting of the Society of Research in Child Development, San Francisco, Calif., 1979.

Aslin, R. N., Perey, A. J., Hennessey, B., & Pisoni, D. B. *Perceptual analysis of speech sounds by prelinguistic infants: A first report.* Paper presented at the 94th Meeting of the Acoustical Society of America, Miami Beach, December, 1977.

Aslin, R. N., & Pisoni, D. B. Some developmental processes in speech perception. In G. H. Yeni-Komshian, J. Kavanagh, & C. A. Ferguson (Eds.), *Child Phonology: perception and production* (vol II). New York: Academic, 1980.

Baru, A. V. Discrimination of synthesized vowels [a] and [i] with varying parameters in dog. In G. Fant & M. A. A. Tatham (Eds.), *Auditory analysis and the perception of speech.* London: Academic Press, 1975.

Bertoncini, J., & Mehler, J. *Syllables are units in infant speech perception. Infant Behavior & Development,* 1981, *4,* 247-260.

Best, C. T., Morrongiello, B., & Robson, R. Perceptual aspects of two acoustic cues is specific to perception of a speech contrast. *Perception & Psychophysics,* 1981, *29,* 191-211.

Bornstein, M. H., Kessen, W., & Weiskopf, S. Color vision and hue categorization in young human infants. *Journal of Experimental Psychology: Human Perception and Performance,* 1976, *2,* 115-129.

Bornstein, M. H., Kessen, W., & Weiskopf, S. Color vision and hue categorization in young human infants. *Journal of Experimental Psychology: Human Perception and Performance,* 1976, *2,* 115-129.

Bowerman, M. Reorganizational processes in lexical and syntactic development. In L. Gleitman & E. Wanner (Eds.), *Language Acquisition: The State of the Art.* Cambridge: Cambridge University Press (in press).

Boyd, E. F. Visual fixation and voice discrimination in 2-month-old infants. In F. D. Horowitz (Ed.), *Visual attention, auditory stimulation, and Language Discrimination in Young Infants.* S.R.C.D. Monograph #39, 1975.

Brown, C. Reactions of infants their parents' voices. *Infant Behavior & Development,* 1979, *2,* 295-300.

Burdick, C. K., & Miller, J. D. Speech perception by the chinchilla: Discrimination of the sustained /a/ and /i/. *Journal of the Acoustical Society of America,* 1975, *58,* 415-427.

Carden, G., Levitt, A., Jusczyk, P. W., & Walley, A. Evidence for phonetic processing of cues to place of articulation: Perceived manner affects perceived place. *Perception & Psychophysics,* 1981, *29,* 26-36.

Carrell, T. D., Pisoni, D. B., & Gans, S. J. *Perception of rapid spectrum changes: Evidence for context effects with speech and nonspeech signals.* Paper presented at the 100th Meeting of the Acoustical Society of America, Los Angeles, November, 1980.

Cohen, L. B. *Concept acquisition in the human infant.* Paper presented at the Society for Research in Child Development meeting, New Orleans, March, 1977.

Condon, W. S., & Sander, L. W. Neonate movement is synchronized with adult speech: Interactional participation and language acquisition. *Science,* 1974, *183,* 99-101.

Cutting, J. E., & Rosner, B. S. Categories and boundaries in speech and music. *Perception & Psychophysics,* 1974, *16,* 564-571.

DeCasper, A. J., & Fifer, W. P. Of human bondings: Newborns prefer their mothers' voices. *Science,* 1980, *208,* 1174-1176.

Eimas, P. D. Auditory and linguistic processing of cues for place of articulation by infants. *Perception & Psychophysics,* 1974, *16,* 513-521.

Eimas, P. D. Auditory and phonetic coding of the cues for speech: Discrimination of the [r-l] distinction by young infants. *Perception & Psychophysics,* 1975, *18,* 341–347. (a)

Eimas, P. D. Speech perception in early infancy. In L. B. Cohen & P. Salapatek (Eds.), *Infant perception: From sensation to cognition,* Vol. II. New York: Academic Press, 1975. (b)

Eimas, P. D., & Miller, J. L. Contextual effects in infant speech perception. *Science,* 1980, *209,* 1140–1141.

Eimas, P. D., Siqueland, E. R., Jusczyk, P., & Vigorito, J. Speech perception in infants. *Science,* 1971, *171,* 303–306.

Fodor, J. A., Garrett, M. F., & Brill, S. L. Pi ka pu: The perception of speech sounds by prelinguistic infants. *Perception & Psychophysics,* 1975, *18,* 74–78.

Harris, K. S. Cues for the discrimination of American English fricatives in spoken syllables. *Language & Speech,* 1958, *1,* 1–7.

Hillenbrand, J., Minifie, F. D., & Edwards, T. J. Tempo of spectrum change as a cue in speech sound discrimination by infants. *Journal of Speech & Hearing Research,* 1979, *22,* 147–165.

Hockett, C. The origin of speech. *Scientific American,* 1960, *203,* 88–96.

Holmberg, T. L., Morgan, K. A., & Kuhl, P. K. *Speech perception in early infancy: Discrimination of fricative consonants.* Paper presented at the 94th meeting of the Acoustical Society of America, Miami Beach, December 16, 1977.

Isenberg, D., & Liberman, A. M. Speech and nonspeech percepts from the same sound. *Journal of the Acoustical Society of America,* 1978, Suppl. #1, J20.

Jusczyk, P. W. Perception of syllable-final stop consonants by two-month-old infants. *Perception & Psychophysics,* 1977, *21,* 450–454.

Jusczyk, P. W. Infant speech perception: A critical appraisal. In P. D. Eimas & J. L. Miller (Eds.), *Perspectives on the study of speech.* Hillsdale, N.J.: Lawrence Erlbaum Associates, 1981.

Jusczyk, P. W. The processing of speech and nonspeech sounds by infants: Some implications: In R. N. Aslin, J. Alberts, & M. Peterson (Eds.), *Sensory and perceptual development: Influences of genetic and experiential factors.* New York: Academic Press (in press).

Jusczyk, P. W., & Derrah, C. *Do two-month-olds categorize stop consonants?* (In preparation).

Jusczyk, P. W., Murray, J., Murphy, C., Levitt, A., & Carden, G. The perception of place of articulation in fricatives by two-month-old infants. (In preparation)

Jusczyk, P. W., Pisoni, D. B., Walley, A., & Murray, J. Discrimination of relative onset time of two-component tones by infants. *Journal of the Acoustical Society of America,* 1980, *67,* 262–270.

Jusczyk, P. W., Rosner, B. S., Cutting, J. E., Foard, C. F., & Smith, L. B. Categorical perception of nonspeech sounds by two-month-old infants. *Perception & Psychophysics,* 1977, *21,* 50–54.

Jusczyk, P. W., Smith, L. B., & Murphy, C. The perceptual classification of speech and nonspeech sounds. *Perception & Psychophysics,* 1981, *30,* 10–23.

Jusczyk, P. W., & Thompson, E. Perception of a phonetic contrast in multisyllabic utterances by two-month-old infants. *Perception & Psychophysics,* 1978, *23,* 105–109.

Katz, J., & Jusczyk, P. W. *Do six-month-olds have perceptual constancy for phonetic segments?* Paper presented at the International Conference on Infant Studies, New Haven, Ct., April, 1980.

Kewley-Port, D. Continuous spectral change as acoustic cues to place of articulation. *Research on speech perception,* 1979, Progress Report #5, Indiana University.

Kiparsky, P., & Menn, L. On the acquisition of phonology. In J. Macnamara (Ed.), *Language learning and thought.* New York: Academic Press, 1977.

Kuhl, P. K. Speech perception in early infancy: The acquisition of speech-sound categories.

In S. K. Hirsh, D. H. Eldredge, I. J. Hirsh, & S. R. Silverman (Eds.), *Hearing and Davis: Essays honoring Hallowell Davis.* St. Louis: Washington University Press, 1976.

Kuhl, P. K. Speech perception in early infancy: Perceptual constancy for spectrally dissimilar vowel categories. *Journal of the Acoustical Society of America,* 1979, *66,* 1668-1679.

Kuhl, P. K., & Miller, J. D. Speech perception by the chinchilla: Voiced-voiceless distinction in alveolar-plosive consonants. *Science,* 1975, *190,* 69-72.

Kuhl, P. K., & Miller, J. D. Speech perception by the chinchilla: Identification functions for synthetic VOT stimuli. *Journal of the Acoustical Society of America,* 1978, *63,* 905-917.

Lasky, R. E., Syrdal-Lasky, A., & Klein, R. E. VOT discrimination by four and six-and-a-half-month-old infants from Spanish environments. *Journal of Experimental Child Psychology,* 1975, *20,* 215-225.

Liberman, A. M., Cooper, F. S., Shankweiler, D. P., & Studdert-Kennedy, M. Perception of the speech code. *Psychological Review,* 1967, *74,* 431-461.

Lisker, L. Is it VOT or a first-formant transition detector? *Journal of the Acoustical Society of America,* 1975, *57,* 1547-1551.

Lisker, L. In qualified defense of VOT. *Language and Speech,* 1978, *21,* 375-383.

Lisker, L., & Abramson, A. S. The voicing dimension: Some experiments in comparative phonetics. In *Proceedings of the Sixth International Congress of Phonetic Sciences,* Prague, 1967, Prague: Academia, 1970.

MacKain, K. S. *On assessing the role of experience in infant speech discrimination.* Unpublished manuscript (Haskins Laboratories), 1979.

Mattingly, I. G., Liberman, A. M., Syrdal, A. K., & Halwes, T. Discrimination in speech and nonspeech modes. *Cognitive Psychology,* 1971, *2,* 131-157.

Mehler, J., Barriere, M., & Jasik-Gerschenfeld, D. La reconnaisance de la voix maternelle par le nourrisson. *La Recherche,* 1976, *70,* 787-788.

Mehler, J., & Bertoncini, J. Infants' perception of speech and other acoustic stimuli. In J. Morton & J. Marshall (Eds.), *Psycholinguistic series II.* London: Elek Science Books, 1978.

Miller, J. D., Wier, L., Pastore, R., Kelly, W., & Dooling, R. Discrimination and labeling of noise-buzz sequences with varying noise-lead times. *Journal of the Acoustical Society of America,* 1976, *60,* 410-417.

Miller, J. L., & Liberman, A. M. Some effects of later-occurring information on the perception of stop consonant and semivowel. *Perception & Psychophysics,* 1979, *25,* 457-465.

Morse, P. A. The discrimination of speech and nonspeech stimuli in early infancy. *Journal of Experimental Child Psychology,* 1972, *14,* 477-492.

Morse, P. A., Eilers, R. E., & Gavin, W. J. *Exploring the perception of the "Sound of Silence" in early infancy.* Paper presented at the International Conference on Infant Studies, New Haven, Ct., April, 1980.

Pastore, R. E., Ahroon, W. A., Buffuto, K. J., Friedman, C. J., Puleo, J. S., & Fink, E. A. Common factor model of categorical perception. *Journal of Experimental Psychology: Human Perception and Performance,* 1977, *4,* 686-696.

Piaget, J. *The origins of intelligence.* Trans. by Margaret Cook. New York: International Universities, 1952.

Pisoni, D. B. Discrimination of brief frequency glissandos. *Research on speech perception,* 1976, Progress Report #3, Indiana University.

Pisoni, D. B. Identification and discrimination of the relative onset time of two-component tones: Implications for voicing perception in stops. *Journal of the Acoustical Society of America,* 1977, *61,* 1352-1361.

Pisoni, D. B. Some remarks on the perception of speech and nonspeech signals. Paper presented at the *Ninth International Congress of Phonetic Sciences.* Copenhagen, August, 1979.

Repp, B. H., Liberman, A. M., Eccardt, T., & Pesetsky, D. Perceptual integration of acoustic cues for stop, fricative and affricate manner. *Journal of Experimental Psychology: Human Perception and Performance,* 1978, *4,* 621-637.

Searle, C. L., Jacobson, J. E., & Rayment, S. G. Phoneme recognition based on human audition. *Journal of the Acoustical Society of America,* 1979, *65,* 799-809.

Shatz, M. The relationship between cognitive processes and the development of communication skills. In C. B. Keasey (Ed.), *Nebraska symposium on motivation, 1977,* Lincoln: University of Nebraska Press, 1978.

Spelke, E., & Owsley, C. Intermodal exploration and knowledge in infancy. *Infant Behavior & Development,* 1979, *2,* 13-27.

Spring, D., & Dale, P. The discrimination of linguistic stress in early infancy. *Journal of Speech and Hearing Research,* 1977, *20,* 224-231.

Stevens, K. N., & Blumstein, S. E. Invariant cues for place of articulation in stop consonants. *Journal of the Acoustical Society of America,* 1978, *64,* 1358-1368.

Stevens, K. N., & Blumstein, S. E. The search for invariant acoustic correlates of phonetic features. In P. D. Eimas & J. L. Miller (Eds.), *Perspectives on the study of speech.* Hillsdale, N.J.: Lawrence Erlbaum Associates, 1980.

Stevens, K. N., & Klatt, D. H. Role of formant transitions in the voiced-voiceless distinction for stops. *Journal of the Acoustical Society of America,* 1974, *55,* 653-659.

Streeter, L. A. Language perception of two-month-old infants shows effects of both innate mechanisms and experience. *Nature,* 1976, *259,* 39-41.

Summerfield, Q. S., & Haggard, M. On the dissociation of spectral and temporal cues to the voicing distinction in initial stop consonants. *Journal of the Acoustical Society of America,* 1977, *62,* 435-448.

Trehub, S. E. The discrimination of foreign speech contrasts by infants and adults. *Child Development,* 1976, *47,* 466-472.

Williams, L. The perception of stop consonant by Spanish-English bilinguals. *Perception & Psychophysics,* 1977, *21,* 289-297.

Wolff, P. Observations on the early development of smiling. In B. M. Foss (Eds.), *Determinants of infant behavior,* Vol. 2. London: Methuen, 1963.

20 Oriented Mouthing Activity in Neonates: Early Development of Differences Related to Feeding Experiences

J. Alegria
E. Noirot
Université libre de Bruxelles, Belgium

In this chapter we discuss some data from studies dealing with early development of spatial skills. The procedure chosen for approaching the problem consists of presenting babies with an invisible source of sound and to observe several aspects of their behavior in this situation. We were particularly interested in spatially oriented activities displayed by the babies, head- or eye-turning, for example. The reason is that when this type of behavior shows a systematic relation to some of the spatial properties of the sound, it becomes possible to speculate about the baby's spatial skills. For instance, to turn the head systematically in the direction of the sound source (or in the opposite direction) it is necessary to translate the stimulus' spatial properties into a motor program that is also spatially organized. Therefore, the baby is able to localize sounds in the distal space. This conclusion is not guaranteed if the baby's behavior is not spatially oriented. Let us suppose an experiment showing that babies cry considerably more when a sound is presented at their left side than when it is presented at their right side. Such a result would certainly indicate that the infants distinguish between sound coming from the left and the right hemifield, but it does not allow the conclusion that the discrimination was based upon spatial location of the stimulus. Another plausible alternative supposing that the infants discriminate at the level of sensory or proximal information, can not be ruled-out. If however an infants' response translates the place occupied by the stimulus in space, we must necessarily postulate that there has been decoding of proximal sensory input in terms of distal properties of the stimulus.

Interest in the study of spatial competence in newborns is aroused by the idea that space does not have a position equivalent to that of the object within it. Rather it plays the role of a framework where objects are and events happen. Thus, studying spatial competence in babies consists of examining their ability to relate objects to each other. From a developmental point of view it is extremely important to understand the nature of framework initially and how it develops. For example, S. Millar (1974) has used the operant conditioning paradigm to examine the spatial relations between actions and their results necessary for the baby to become aware of the existence of contingencies. When the baby manipulates an object, a sound comes either from the object itself, $5°$, or $60°$ away to the right or to the left of it. Six-month-old babies accept the $5°$ separation but not the $60°$, one while 12-month-old babies accept both. These kinds of developmental changes in spatial constraints are important because they play a role in integrating intersensory and sensory motor experiencies and thus, in generating coherence.

One way to put the question of the newborn spatial competencies in empirical terms might be to ask from which age it is possible to observe *oriented responses,* i.e., responses whose spatial properties are systematically related to those of the stimuli. Evidence coming from a number of experiments shows that even the younger infants tested have at least an elementary spatial framework. The work of Wertheimer (1961) and Turkewitz, Birch, and Cooper (1972) concerning the eyes' *oriented responses* and those of Alegria and Noirot (1978) and Muir and Field (1979) on head orientation show that babies aged a few days, a few hours, or even a few minutes (in Wertheimer's experiment) perceive sounds, in a space that is at least divided into a right and a left side. More data are necessary to know whether newborns are able to discriminate between auditory events coming from the same hemifield on the bases of their spatial location. Bower's (1974) theory concerning the development of spatial competence in infancy postulates that newborns are able to discriminate in distal terms only between stimuli coming from the right, the left, and straight ahead. These directions are the only ones to be specified by proximal stimulation, the binaural disparity, in an invariant way during growth. Finer localization in right and left hemifields depends on the head dimension and are supposed to develop during infancy by relating binaural disparity values to the motor activity necessary to cancel it. This theory shares with others (more strongly supported by empirical evidence) the idea that the motor activity plays an important role in the calibration of the intersensory and sensory-motor organization (see, for example Held, 1968). Pertinent data concerning this problem in the infants' case are missing at present.

In our search for *oriented responses* in the behavioral repertoire of very young babies we have been lucky enough to observe that, when presented with a voice, they frequently respond by twisting their mouths into a completely asymmetrical posture. The subjective impression is that they tend the upper lip to the left or to the right (see Fig. 1). The first question concerning this behavior was to know whether it was *oriented* or not with respect to the sound source. Previously (Alegria & Noirot, 1978), we have studied the babies' asymmetrical mouthing (AM) as a function of the absence- versus -presence of a human voice and as a function of the voice's spatial location. Babies, aged between 1 and 6 days were seated individually in a small chair surrounded by a uniform white curtain. A male voice was transmitted successively through three loudspeakers placed at the left, the right, or in front of the chair. Two observers recorded head orientation, eye opening, mouth activity, and crying during the voice presentation. A different group of babies, serving as controls, was observed in exactly the same conditions but without any voice.[1] The first finding concerning the effects of the voice on mouthing was that an important increase of AM appeared when the voice was presented: Only 17% of the control babies (2/12) showed at least one episode of AM during the experiment, whereas, the percentage reached 89% (32/36) in the experimental group. More recent data allow us to say that this particular mouthing response could be a response specific to human sound production. C. Genevrois and J. Taylor from our laboratory did an experiment, identical to the one just outlined but using non-vocal sounds recorded in the babies' neighborhood instead of a human voice. The results concerning AM are similar to those obtained by the previous control group: Only 21% of the babies (5/24) show at least one episode of AM. It is worth noting that the analysis of some items other than AM shows that the babies presented with sounds behave similarly to babies presented with a human voice in our previous experiment. This fact eliminates an explanation of Genevrois and Taylor's data in terms of some general lack of interest for the sounds used in their experiment.

Our main question was whether this voice-related AM was *oriented* or not. The definition or *oriented* responses brings one to look at the relationships between spatial location of loudspeakers, at the right or at the left of the baby,[2] and the orientation of the AM, also right or left. The analysis of the data produced unclear results until the population was split into breast- and bottle-fed babies. Table 1 (Exp. 1) shows the number of episodes of AM oriented towards the left and the right as a function of the voice localization. Data from breast-fed babies indicate that their mouthing was clearly positively *oriented* whereas bottle-fed babies mainly mouthed

---

[1]More details concerning the procedure and data can be found in the previous paper. We will limit it here to those necessary to understand the present report.

[2]We have not included data, nor discussion, about the loudspeaker in front of the baby's chair. Some of the complexities observed with it are too long to expose in a paper like the present one. They don't add important issues nor invalidate the present ones.

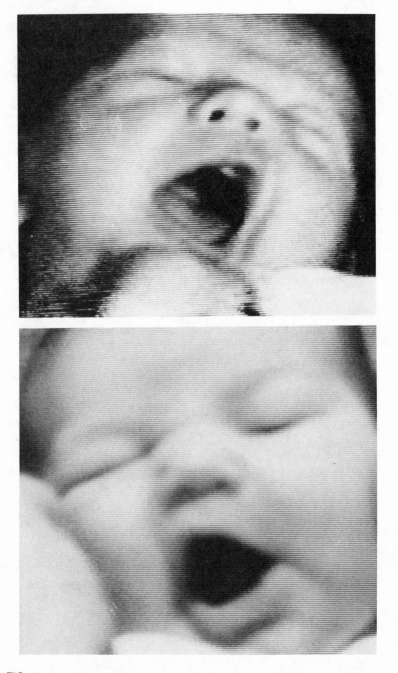

FIG. 1   Two examples of asymmetrical mouthing: towards the right (top) and towards the left (bottom).

TABLE 1

Number of episodes of asymmetrical mouth activity observed as a
function of the voice's spatial location in breast- and bottle-fed
babies in Experiment 1 and 2. In Experiment 3, babies had never been
fed. Data from experimental (voice) and control (silence) groups have
been collapsed in this case.

FEEDING	BREAST-		BOTTLE-		NEVER		
MOUTHING	LEFT	RIGHT	LEFT	RIGHT	LEFT	RIGHT	
LEFT	23	1	41	3			Exp. 1
RIGHT	6	25	28	21			(n = 36)
LEFT	10	1	6	1			Exp. 2
RIGHT	5	8	9	0			(n = 24)
LEFT					15	1	Exp. 3
RIGHT					9	1	(n = 24)

(VOICE LOCATION — left margin label)

towards the left even when the voice came from the right. We have proposed a tentative explanation (Alegria & Noirot, 1978). It postulates that the
babies probably mouthed according to spatial rules established during
feeding. A breast-fed baby, when in his mother's arm (whether it is the left
or the right), will find the nipple of the breast by orienting the mouth
towards the voice location. In the experimental situation he apparently
behaves as if "something to such" will be found in the voice's direction.
For most of bottle-fed babies the situation is quite different because the
mothers take the babies in their left and the bottle in the right. As a consequence the nipple is always located on the left side of the voice. Bottle-fed
babies in the experimental situation could proceed as if "something to
such" will be found at the left of the voice.

These speculations are central to the problem of space elaboration in
newborns. It is suggested that "voices" and "things to such" are in a single
framework where they occupy places defined relatively to each-other. The
feeding situation seems to play an important role in the integration of sensory information. The remainder of this chapter will survey some aspects of
the results obtained in our laboratory aimed to understand the development
of AM. Two experiments have been done following exactly the same procedure as the previous one (Exp. 1). In one of them (Exp. 3) we have tested
babies who had never been fed. They were aged in between 20 min and some
hours. This sample was aimed to inform us about the initial state of AM
and its relations with the voice presence and spatial location. The other experiment (Exp. 2) deals with *babies who had been fed 1, 2, or 3 times.* The
aim was to appreciate how fast the differentiation of AM as a function of
the feeding experiences appears. We also present some data coming from

the following more natural but inevitably more complex situation. The mothers were asked to take the baby in their arms for 1 min. In the experimental group (n = 115) mothers were silent during the first 20 sec, and then, started talking as usually until the end of the minute. In the control group (n = 19) the mother was silent during the whole minute. The sequences were recorded on video tape. For technical reasons we have limited the analysis of the AM to the cases where it was oriented towards the external side of the mother's baby, i.e., towards the left for the babies taken in the left arm and towards the right when taken in the right arm. The mothers were free to take their babies in the way they preferred. This group of babies was aged between 1 and 6 days.

The first question was whether AM exists before any feeding experience, and if so, what its relationships with the voice were. The experiment with never-fed babies (Exp. 3) shows that 25% of them (6/24) produce at least one episode of AM. The voice did not seem to increase AM as was the case with older babies (Exp. 1): Two babies in the control group and four in the experimental group showed at least one episode during the experiment. An important result is that 92% of the episodes of AM observed were directed towards the left (24/26, see Table 1). It seems that, from birth, babies do exhibit some AM, not specifically related to the voice and mainly left-oriented. When compared with the results of the Exp. 1, the present data indicates that both breast- and bottle-fed babies have learned something during their feeding experience.

The experiment involving babies fed 1, 2, or 3 times (Exp. 2) showed that their AM was already systematically related to the voice: 58% of the babies in the experimental group (14/24) and only 25% in the control group (3/12) showed at least one episode of AM. One of the effects of the number of feeding sessions was to increase the voice's power. The AM in babies from experiments 3 (never-fed), 2 (fed 1, 2, or 3 times) and 1 (fed 4 or more times) was 33, 58 and 89% respectively in the experimental groups. No systematic differences related to the number of feeding sessions were observed in the control groups. The corresponding percentages were 17, 25, and 17%. The question now concerns the differentiation observed between breast- and bottle-fed babies in Exp. 1. One of the aims of Exp. 2 was to know whether this differentiation was already present after a few meals. One way to approach the problem consists of looking at frequency of asymmetrical mouthing towards the left relative to the whole AM in breast- and bottle-fed babies. The results were quite clear. In the breast-fed group the percentage of left mouthing was 63%, whereas the corresponding percentage in the bottle-fed group was 94%. A few number of feeding sessions was therefore sufficient to relate AM and voice in a different way in breast- and bottle-fed babies. A second way of looking for the differentiation between feeding groups consists of considering mouth orientation as a function of voice location. The relevant data appears in Table 1. The pattern of results was identical to that obtained in Exp. 1: That is to say that breast-fed babies' AM was *oriented* towards the voice while the bottle-fed group basically show left mouthing.

The last evidence we would like to consider comes from the analysis of records obtained with the babies in their mother's arms. Basically, results were consistent with predictions derived from the previous experiments. The occurrence of the mother's voice increases the AM towards the exterior in babies who had been bottle-fed. Before the introduction of voice, i.e., during the first 20 sec, 18% of the babies in the whole sample showed at least one episode of AM.[3] The presentation of the voice (in the experimental group) changed this percentage into 16% in the control group, 18% in the experimental breast-fed, and 37% in the bottle-fed babies. This results, as well as those obtained in the experiments just described, suggest that the voice enhances the mouth activity directed towards n I ypothetical "object to suck" whose location was defined by reference tc the voice location. Only the bottle-fed babies showed an increase of AM during the talking episode probably because they are the only ones to direct their mouth towards the exterior. Breast-fed babies probably showed an increase of AM towards the interior. Our observations being limited to the exteriorly-oriented activity, it was easy to anticipate that the breast-fed babies would produce results identical to those from the control group.

The AM data produced by the bottle-fed babies in Exp. 1 and 2, as well as those obtained in their mother's arms, were problematic to interpret. Since AM was practically always directed towards the left, it did not fulfill the criterion of an *oriented response* as defined above, i.e. showing a systematic positive (or negative) relation with the spatial coordinates of the stimulus. However, some aspects of the data obtained with the mother-baby pairs allow us to speculate about the *oriented* character of the bottle-fed left-mouthing-activity. Nine out of the 87 bottle-fed babies were spontaneously taken by their mother in the right arm. For this group of babies, the bottle location was at the right side of the voice. Their situation was the opposite to the one usually found in bottle-fed babies. The obvious question was whether the AM of the babies was more frequently directed towards the right than in their peers, fed in the more usual way. The response was clearly positive. Five out of the 9 babies observed showed at least one episode of AM towards the right. This ratio was enormous if we take into account the scarcity of right oriented AM observed in bottle-fed babies in the experiments previously reported. In order to estimate the frequency we considered a group of 46 babies of 1 to 6 days old, all of them bottle-fed and

---

[3]The detailed results for the control, experimental breast- and experimental bottle-fed groups were 11% (2/19), 18% (5/28) and 22% (19/87) respectively.

observed in the experimental situation when presented with the voice for 40 sec (the time as the one used in the mother's arms). Only four out of the 46 showed AM towards the right.[4] The conclusion seems to be that bottle-fed babies really orient their mouths in a direction defined by the voice's location, when it happens to be at the left as well as at the right side of it.

Experimental data concerning spatial-skills development shows that babies from birth discriminate between sounds coming from their right and their left side on the basis of their spatial location. In this chapter we have tried to show that very quickly, experiences related to the feeding situation brings babies to integrate in their spatial framework a new object that seems to occupy a place defined by the *voice location*. The experiments reported indicate that before the first mother-baby feeding interaction, the voice has no power to produce asymmetrical mouthing activity. A few number of meals prove sufficient to relate voice location and mouth orientation. The main argument comes from the fact that breast- and bottle-fed differentiation is already present after less than four meals. The relative facility with which environmental pressures modify the behavior has been considered as an indication of the organisms "preparedness" to integrate information (Seligman, 1970). Learning in fact, seems to be submitted to strong constraints when it implies biologically significant changes in behavior (see Hinde, 1973; for a very clear discussion concerning this point). Our case points out the role played by the mother-baby interactions during feeding in integrating spatial information. The cognitive development and the social interactions are intimately related to each other.

ACKNOWLEDGMENTS

We wish to thank Dr. J. De Paepe, Director of the Clinic C. De Paepe, where this research took place, as well as his colleagues Dr. A. Champenois and J. Fontaine for much help, advice, and understanding. We are also grateful to the whole staff of the maternity department and to the mothers and infants whose participation permitted this work. Many thanks are due to Chris Darwin whose comments on the manuscript were of great help in improving an earlier version. The authors held a grant from the Belgian "Fonds de la Recherche Fondamentale Collective" (contract n° 2.4535.79).

---

[4]This difference was not an artefact of the "mother's arms" as shown by the fact that when comparing the AM towards the left in bottle-fed babies, the proportion displaying this behavior was greater in the experimental situation than in the mother's arms.

REFERENCES

Alegria, J., & Noirot, E. Neonate orientation behaviour towards human voice. *International Journal of Behavioural Development,* 1978, *1,* 291–312.

Bower, T. G. R. *Development in infancy.* Freeman, San Francisco, 1974.

Held, R. (discussion leader). Action contingent development of vision in neonatal animals. In D. Kimble (Ed.). *Experience and capacity. Proceedings of the fourth conference on learning, remembering and forgetting.* The New York Academy of Sciences, 1968, *4,* 31–111.

Hinde, R. A. Constraints on learning: An introduction to the problems. In R. A. Hinde & J. Stevenson-Hinde (Eds.). *Constraints on learning: limitations and predispositions.* Academic Press, New York, 1973.

Millar, W. S. Conditioning and learning in early infancy. In B. Foss (Ed.). New perspectives in child development. Penguin Education, London, 1974.

Muir, D., & Field, J. Newborn infants orient to sounds. *Child Development,* 1979, *50,* 431–436.

Seligman, M. E. P. On the generality of the laws of learning. *Psychological Review,* 1970, *77,* 406–418.

Trevarthen, C. L'action dans l'espace et la perception de l'espace: mecanismes cérébraux de base. In F. Bresson et al. (Eds.), *De l'espace Corporel à l-Espace Ecologique.* Presses Universitaires de France, Paris, 1974.

Turkewitz, G., Birch, H. G., & Cooper, K. K. Responsiveness to simple and complex auditory stimuli in the human newborn. *Developmental Psychobiology,* 1972, *5,* 7–19.

Wertheimer, M. Psychomotor coordination of auditory and visual space at birth. *Science,* 1961, *134,* 1932.

21 Visual Development: From Resolution to Perception

Richard Held
Massachusetts Institute of Technology

We should like to know how infants see and think about their worlds. Do their perceptions of objects and events agree with ours? Can we find evidence that the manner in which they perceive follows the same rules that govern the perceptions of adults? Or, if infant vision differs from that of the adult, then when does it mature into the adult condition? This is of course not a new set of questions, but there have been some new approaches to answering them and new motivation for asking them. In the following discussion I shall give an overview of the research, in particular that of my colleagues and me, done recently in an effort to answer these questions.

The first problem that confronts the researcher interested in the perception of infants is how to find out from them what they see, hear, feel, or otherwise sense. Not only do they not verbalize what we should like to hear, but worse, they cannot be instructed to respond by the examiner's verbalization as do adult listeners. Consequently, we have to resort to strategies much like those familiar from animal experimentation. Infants can be conditioned to respond to stimuli. They can also be habituated to them and then dishabituated in procedures that are described elsewhere in this book. These methods have the advantage of being applicable to almost any stimuli but they require periods of training of varying duration and their success rate is low. More easily applied and less time consuming are those procedures that take advantage of responses of the infant that may be variously described as automatic, reflexive, involuntary, or otherwise not requiring extensive training. The problem with this category of responses is to find those that are specific to the stimuli under examination. Among this category are the physiological responses to stimuli that can be monitored by non-invasive procedures. They include changes in electric potentials from the brain that can be recorded from scalp electrodes, the optokinetic following response, changes in pupillary size, skin resistance change, and others. Finally there are the quasi-voluntary responses such as the looking behavior infants show when presented with visual stimuli localized in space. It is this last mentioned response that we have exploited most and will be the central topic of this chapter.

The looking procedure derives from the old observation that an infant will tend to gaze at bright, solid, configured objects in its environment (Fantz, 1961; Stirnimann, 1944). This tendency can be regarded as adaptive since in general such objects carry more information than less salient objects. To utilize this tendency in order to measure the detection of stimuli they must be presented for testing in such manner that we can expect that they will attract the gaze of the infant if they are detected. For example, if in an otherwise blank field, a spot either brighter or dimmer than the background is presented, we can expect that the infant will gaze at it. We may then vary the luminance (light intensity) of the spot until we find that increment of luminance which attracts the infant's gaze on only half the times it is presented. Since conventionally, the threshold is defined as that stimulus value which elicits a response on 50% of the times it is presented, this increment can then be defined as the incremental threshold for luminance under the conditions of the experiment.

There are of course certain problematic aspects to the interpretation of measurements made with this procedure. Under some circumstances, the infant may detect the stimulus but not gaze at it with the consequence that the calculated threshold increment will be larger than it ought to be. Alternatively, if the infant knows from previous experience when and where the incremental stimulus will appear, it may cast its gaze too often in that direction and the threshold may appear to be lower than it ought to be. Actually, these problems are not restricted to psychophysical measurements taken with infants but are relevant to adult measurements as well. In general, the latter difficulty can be minimized by randomizing conditions of presentation such that the a priori probability of success is established and the observer cannot predict the time and place of the stimulus with any appreciable accuracy. The former difficulty is, however, harder to handle. The very existence of the preferential looking procedure is predicated on the presumed strength of the looking response elicited by presentation of the stimulus. But we do not in general know much about how the strength of that response varies with changes in stimuli. In the absence of that knowledge we must qualify our assertions with statements that we may not be obtaining the best possible discrimination or the lowest threshold. One case in which we have seen the results of a change in strength of looking with levels of the stimulus is discussed below.

Returning to the question of detection, we can ask how to test for other visual properties. Instead of an addition (or subtraction) of the amount of light reflected to the eye from a surface, can we test the limits of spatial resolution? How small a spot can be detected? Actually, a more useful measure of the acuteness of vision consists in finding out how narrow can be the stripes of a set (square wave grating) that is detected when presented against a blank background with the average brightness (luminance) of dark and light stripes equal to that of the background. Obviously, if the mean luminance of the grating is either more or less than that of the background, the brightness difference alone (luminance increment) could account for a preference. If a preference is shown for wide-striped gratings, they can then be varied from wider to thinner (higher spatial frequency[1]) until the percent correct is reduced to threshold level. In fact, this procedure is employed routinely in one laboratory to measure visual acuity (Teller et al., 1974).

The previously discussed cases are examples of detection of stimuli. The following examples deal with discrimination between stimuli. By this we mean that two (or more) detectable stimuli are presented and the tests are designed to decide whether one is preferred over the other in terms of preferential looking behavior. This procedure was developed by Fantz (1961) and has been utilized by many investigators. In our laboratory we have used such a procedure to test visual acuity (Gwiazda et al., 1978, 1980a). A circular region containing a square wave grating of varied frequency is paired with an equal sized blank field of equal space-averaged luminance and presented in a dark room. Both stimulus regions are highly visible. With wide stripes, the infants show a decided preference for looking at the grating as assessed by an observer of the infant. As the stripes are narrowed, the preference drops towards 50% (chance), which indicates no consistent preference. Consequently, a threshold can be defined at some convenient level above 50%, say 75% at which the preference is correct 50% of the time (it is correct by chance alone the remaining 50% of the time). When these procedures are carried out over the first year of life, we have found that grating acuity during the first month is such that only stripes larger than half a degree of visual angle can be discriminated (less than 20/600 in the familiar Snellen notation). In other words, acuity is less than one-thirtieth what it is in the normal adult (Snellen 20/20). The infant's acuity is below the limit of the definition of legal blindness. In terms of perception, this means that the infant of this age does not see fine detail and edges defined by shallow gradients of contrast. Although the infant's acuity starts at a very low level, it improves rapidly so that by one year of age it is at least Snellen 20/50, which is 40% of adult acuity (Gwiazda et al., 1980b).

---

[1]Spatial frequency is defined as the number of cycles (one dark and one light stripe) of a grating per visual degree subtended.

Under the conditions of testing described above, the infant's preference drops to 50% as finer stripes are presented and, as we have recently discovered, if very fine stripes (higher frequency) are presented, the preference will often actually reverse so that the blank field is preferred over the grating (Held et al., 1979). But the preference returns to 50% when the frequency is increased still further. This finding came as a surprise to us and it illustrates that the strength of a looking preference may vary widely. If an infant consistently prefers to look at the blank field over the grating, this preference is as much evidence for discrimination between the two stimuli as is the consistent preference for the grating. While the reversal of preference may be specific to the testing situation we have used, it does indicate that our procedure underestimates acuity by an amount that may approach an octave (half the spatial frequency of the estimate). Moreover, it introduces a cautionary note into the use of the preference procedure.

The above discussed procedure is one of discrimination because the two stimuli (bright circular regions) are both detectable by themselves but differ in the stimulus dimension of interest, namely presence of stripes. The infant's ability to perform this discrimination suggested that even more compounded stimuli might be used. That is to say, the number of definable stimulus dimensions might be further increased without loss of preferential looking produced by a difference along only one of them. These considerations led us to design and carry out further testing of the following kind.

A question that has evoked considerable interest concerns the origin of the oblique effect. Most adult observers show slightly reduced acuity when tested on oblique edges as targets compared with either vertical or horizontal ones. It has been suggested that this effect resulted from habitual viewing of the urban environment with its alleged predominance of vertical and horizontal edges (Annis & Frost, 1973). One way to test this notion is to measure acuities in the oblique and main orientation during early development. If the oblique effect is found before appreciable exposure to the environment said to cause the effect, then we might conclude that the hypothesis is false. In fact, using the procedure described above, we found that acuity for oblique gratings is less than that for main axis gratings (horizontal and vertical) beginning at about six months of age. In an attempt to find a more sensitive method, we devised the following procedure.

The infants were shown two gratings equal in luminance, contrast, and size, but differing in orientation. One grating had its stripes either horizontal or vertical while the other was obliquely oriented (at 45° to the main axes). A series of such paired gratings, varied in spatial frequency through the threshold range and beyond, was shown to the infant. The results showed systematic preferences for the main axis gratings at and near to the threshold frequency beginning in the early weeks of life and extending through the first year (Leehey et al., 1975). When the grating frequency is low (large suprathreshold visible bars), there is no preference for main axis over oblique axis gratings. When the frequency is high (subthreshold bars) there is no preference because the stimuli are not distinguishably different. We interpret the preference near threshold to be a result of the greater visibility of the main axis gratings.

These results show first, that the oblique effect is present in the early weeks and consequently cannot be the result of exposure to an orientationally biased environment. Second, the presence of a varied stimulus dimension (orientation of stripes), which itself evokes no preferential looking, does not interfere with the looking preference for visible edges.

Thus far we have discussed the perception of increments of brightness and of the smallest spatial extents in the frontal plane that can be resolved. But there is no reason to remain restricted to spatial extents in the frontal plane. Of equal importance are differences in the third dimension, corresponding to perceived depth differences. Both detection and discrimination paradigms have been employed in studying infants' responses to depth.

In studying detection, investigators have utilized random dot stereograms (Fox et al., 1980). These consist of two separate views, one presented to each eye by means of a stereoscopic device. Each view consists of a large set of black and white dots having no discernible order in their left-right and up-down sequences. Consequently, only a uniform texture with no salient figure is seen when viewed with either one eye or the other. However, the dots in the two views are correlated in such a way that when both eyes view them, a form appears in a depth plane differing from the background. This form is made to move either right or left within the frame. The infant to whom the display is presented is then observed to see whether he/she will either move eyes and head in the direction of movement, as if entrained by the stimulus, or move then randomly. This response is used as an indicator of detection of the stereo-form and its motion. The results show that sometime during the fourth and fifth months the detection of depth by stereopsis first occurs.

Discrimination of depth has also been demonstrated in a manner not unlike that of grating activity. The infant is presented with two circular regions each having three dark vertical stripes separated by white stripes of equal width. In one region, alternating stripes are made to stand out in depth either in front of or behind the intercalated stripes and whatever part of the background is visible. The other region contains the stripes but no depth difference. Infants very clearly prefer the stimulus that has the appearance of solidity and accordingly prefer to look at the stimulus with depth. When this method is used to study depth discrimination, the results confirm the findings that were revealed by the random dot procedure but allow us to go further and to measure the development of stereoacuity (the finest depth discrimination possible with the stimulus arrangement used).

Once stereopsis has its onset, during the fourth month on average, stereoacuity develops rapidly within the next few weeks. By adjusting the dimensions of the stimuli, we have shown that depth differences as small as three millimeters presented at a distance of 70 centimeters can be discriminated by six months of age (Held et al., 1980). The sudden onset and rapid development of this form of resolution in depth contrasts strongly with the slow growth of grating acuity. It suggests that two different neural substrates are responsible for the two forms of resolution. If one had to speculate, one might assign the growth of grating acuity to the development of the central retina, which is known to be immature at birth, while stereoacuity might more likely result from development of the visual cortex in the cerebrum, which is the first important center in which inputs from the two eyes converge.

Studies of perception and resolution in the infant have proven of great interest from both a theoretical and a practical point of view. Discoveries stemming from animal experiments on the visual nervous system have proceeded apace during the last decade (Lund, 1978). The anatomical structure and function of the cells of this system have been revealed by new methods of marking and of recording their activities. Much of the organization of the system is either present at birth or develops under the influence of endogenous, presumably genetically controlled, growth. However, conditions of stimulation make a significant contribution at least to the maintenance of function of the system. Conditions that produce an imbalance in stimulation of the two eyes during a sensitive period early in the life of the animal have been shown to cause marked changes in neural connections in the visual cortex within the cerebrum, in the physiology of single cells, and in the visually controlled behaviors that this system mediates. Two major types of loss occur: loss of binocular cells—those that respond to stimulation of both eyes—and loss of central connections to an eye that has been deprived of appropriate stimulation as a result of prolonged blurring of the retinal image during the susceptible period. Both changes are accompanied by corresponding deficits in vision as assessed behaviorally.

The new findings in animals have prompted questions concerning human parallels. The most obvious ones are loss of binocular cooperation, as evidenced in stereopsis, and amblyopia, a form of blindness not attributable to causes in the eyeball itself and popularly known as lazy eye. Individuals who have a history of crossed eyes (a form of strabismus) and those who have had one eye occluded as a result of either natural causes or for therapeutic reasons, often are deficient in stereoacuity and not infrequently suffer amblyopia. One wonders just how these syndromes are related to the neurobiological changes observed in the animal studies. We cannot of course perform research requiring techniques that invade the human body, but we can use behavioral measures of resolution to track the course of development, maintenance, and loss of function as it occurs. To that end, we have carried out tests of acuity on a large number of infants and some children who come to an eye clinic because of evidence of ocular problems.

In the course of these tests we have discovered that infants suffering from congenitally crossed eyes, a condition known as esotropia, show the onset of a difference between acuities in the two eyes at an average age of 20 weeks (Jacobson et al., 1981). Tentatively, we suppose that this time is the beginning of a period of susceptibility to developing amblyopia resulting from crossed eyes. The effects of a period of occluding or blurring the vision of one eye are quite clear. The occluded eye declines in acuity (tested without occlusion) while the non-occluded eye shows an increase in acuity (Mohindra et al., 1979). This finding confirms the common clinical practice of occluding a non-amblyopic eye in order to improve vision in the amblyopic one. These results and others demonstrate the plasticity of the infant's and child's visual system. The upper age limit of the period of susceptibility to binocular imbalance is harder to establish. It is variously estimated at between four and eight years of age. We are just beginning to apply the method of measuring stereoacuity to clinical subjects and it is too early to predict the outcome.

While studies of detection and discrimination of stimuli are fundamental to our understanding of perception, they only set the limits to perceptual capabilities. Questions concerning the ubiquitous global organization of vision involved in the perception of objects and events remain unaddressed. The gestalt laws characterize many of these organizational properties. Several investigators have attempted to trace the origins of these capabilities during development (see chapter by Spelke). We believe that an application of the preferential looking procedure may provide a sensitive new test for the operation of these rules of organization and in the following we discuss one example for testing them.

When one object lies in front of another, the edges of the former are continuous and interrupt those of the latter. This condition is of course the familiar occlusion of far objects by near ones. When the edges of such objects are depicted in two dimensions on a flat plane, the appearance nonetheless is one in which the occluded figure is seen in back of and hence behind the occluding figure. The familiar figure–ground phenomenon is a special case. Reversible figure–ground pictures are ones in which the occluder and occluded parts are underdetermined and hence ambiguous.

The question at issue is when do human perceivers first exhibit the operation of rules such as that which prescribes that an occluded figure appears behind the occluder? Can we test the non-verbal infant for this capability? Our observation of the development of stereopsis and measurement of stereoacuity suggests an approach to an answer.

Consider a figure in which a long thin vertical rectangle partially occludes another rectangle B (behind), whose long edges are orthogonal to it (Fig. 1a). A third rectangle F (front) also has long edges orthogonal to those of the first but occludes it. An infant, who has achieved stereopsis, is presented with two such figures (a and b). Since the figures are identical, no preference would be expected. However, stereoptic technique allows us to make the occluding rectangle appear either in front of (F) or behind (B) that which is occluded by means of appropriate binocular disparities. In the former case (as in Fig. 1a), the appearance is consistent with the depth relation prescribed by occlusion while in the latter (Fig. 1b) it is inconsistent.

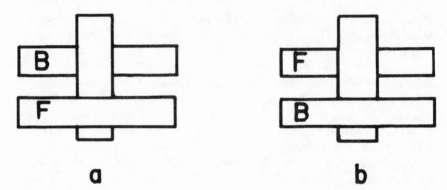

a　　　　　　**b**

FIG. 1　Occlusion figures with stereoptic depth indicated by B (behind) and F (front). Figure 1a has stereopsis cues consistent with occlusion. Figure 1b has stereopsis cues inconsistent with occlusion.

One of the two otherwise identical figures shown to the infant is consistent, the other inconsistent in this fashion. If the infant shows a preference and responds differentially to the consistency-inconsistency difference, we are on the way to a proof that the occlusion principle operates. One further control is needed. We must also show that the depth cues, apart from occlusion, do not yield the observed preference. Procedures of this sort give us a potentially quantifiable approach to higher-order questions of perception that verge on cognition.

ACKNOWLEDGMENTS

This research was supported in part by grants from the National Institutes of Health (No. 5P30–EY02621, NO. 2–RO1–EY01191, and No. 2–RO1–EY02649), an equipment grant from the National Science Foundation (No. BNS-7915097), and a grant from The Spencer Foundation (LTR–DTD–71373).

REFERENCES

Annis, R. C., & Frost, B. Human visual ecology and orientation anisotropies in acuity. *Science,* 1973, *182,* 729–731.

Fantz, R. L. The origin of form perception. *Scientific American,* May, 1961.

Fox, R., Aslin, R. N., Shea, S. L., & Dumais, S. T. Stereopsis in human infants. *Science,* 1980, *207,* 323–324.

Gwiazda, J., Brill, S., Mohindra, I., & Held, R. Infant visual acuity and its meridional variation. *Vision Research,* 1978, *18,* 1151–1157.

Gwiazda, J., Brill, S., Mohindra, I., & Held, R. Preferential looking acuity in infants from two to fifty-eight weeks of age. *Am. J. Optom. & Physiol. Optics, 57,* 428–432, 1980. (b)

Gwiazda, J., Wolfe, J., Brill, S., Mohindra, I., & Held, R. Quick assessment of preferential looking acuity in infants. *Am. J. Optom. & Physiol. Optics, 57,* 420–427, 1980. (a)

Held, R., Birch, E. E., & Gwiazda, J. Stereoacuity of human infants. *Proc. Nat'l Acad. Sci. USA,* 1980, *77,* 5572–5574.

Held, R., Gwiazda, J., Brill, S., Mohindra, I., & Wolfe, J. Infant visual acuity is underestimated because near threshold gratings are not preferentially fixated. *Vision Research,* 1979, *19,* 1377–1379.

Jacobson, S. G., Mohindra, I., & Held, R. Age of onset of amblyopia in infants with esotropia. *Documenta Ophthalmologica,* Proceedings Series, 1981, *30,* 210–216.

Leehey, S. C., Moskowitz-Cook, A., Brill, S., & Held, R. Orientational anisotropy in infant vision. *Science,* 1975, *190,* 900–902.

Lund, R. D. *Development and plasticity of the brain,* New York: Oxford University Press, 1978.

Mohindra, I., Jacobson, S. G., Thomas, J., & Held, R. Development of amblyopia in infants. *Trans. Ophthal. Soc. U.K.,* 1979, *99,* 344–346.

Stirnimann, F. Ueber das Farbenempfinden Neugeborener. *Ann. Paedia.,* 1944, *163,* 1–25.

Teller, D. Y., Morse, R., Borton, R., & Regal, D. Visual acuity for vertical and diagonal stripes in human infants. *Vision Research,* 1974, *14,* 1433–1439.

22 Perceptual Knowledge of Objects in Infancy

Elizabeth S. Spelke
University of Pennsylvania

The visible world is furnished with objects. These may be large or small, rough or smooth, rigid or flexible, and moving or still. Objects are encountered in shapes of limitless variety, arranged on surfaces in infinitely many possible configurations. But as adults, we nearly always perceive each object as unitary, as separate from the surfaces around it, and as persisting over time. Our ability to do this is intriguing, for the boundaries of an object are rarely preserved, in any direct way, in the structure of light at the eye.

Consider the portrait in Fig. 1. Ingres' painting depicts a complex arrangement of adjacent, interlocking, and partly hidden surfaces. The artist did not indicate directly which of these surfaces lie on the same object. For example, he did not show us that Madame Devauçay's left index finger is connected through her ring to her hand, that the arm of her chair is attached, behind her cape, to its back, or even that her cape and chair are distinct. His portrait presents only small fragments of his subject and smaller fragments of her surroundings. Yet we perceive Madame Devauçay, her chair, her clothing, and her jewelry. We carve Ingres' array of pigments into objects, much as we do when we scan dynamic arrays of light from ordinary scenes.

Adults perceive the boundaries of objects in a number of ways. In some cases, we seek to divide visual arrays into the simplest possible units, in accordance with the Gestalt principles of organization (Koffka, 1935; Wertheimer, 1923). Madame Devauçay's shoulder may appear connected to her neck, for example, by virtue of the principles of similarity and good continuation. In other cases, we draw on our knowledge about particular sorts

409

FIG. 1   Madame Devauçay, by Jean Ingres. Courtesy of the Musée de Chantilly, France.

of objects or knowledge about properties of the physical world. Knowledge of hands and jewelry, for example, suggests that Madame Devauçay's diamonds are connected to the band of her ring and separate from her finger; knowledge of the effects of gravity may dictate that each strand of her necklace continues behind her back. But the detailed nature of our ability to perceive objects, and its development, remain unknown.

Studies of young human infants may shed light on this ability and on the knowledge that underlies it. In this chapter, I discuss research on infants' perception of an object as distinct from the surfaces behind it, as separate from any surfaces that touch it, and as continuing behind any surfaces that partly hide it from view. The studies provide evidence that infants perceive the unity and boundaries of objects in a variety of configurations. They perceive objects in some, but not all, of the ways that adults do. The similarities and differences between infants and adults will suggest a general account of the development of object perception.

PERCEPTION OF SUSPENDED OBJECTS

When young infants scan a layout of surfaces, can they ever perceive objects as unitary and persisting? It is hard to imagine a perceptual world without stable units—a world in constant flux. Yet many philosophers and psychologists have proposed that the infant's perceptions begin in such a state. This proposal is extremely difficult to refute, even after decades of experiments. But there is growing evidence that infants perceive the unity and boundaries of objects in the simplest of scenes: scenes in which one object is suspended fully within their view.

The best evidence is provided by studies of reaching (for example, White, Castle, & Held, 1964). At about 4½ months of age, infants begin to reach for suspended objects in visual scenes, and they adapt their reaching to certain spatial properties of the objects. They attempt to reach near objects more often than distant ones, they reach in the direction of an object, and they reach differently if an object is very large than if it is small. Infants even adjust their reaching to an object's pattern of movement. If an object moves at a constant rate into reaching distance, a 4- or 5-month-old infant will attempt to capture it. Careful observations show that the reaching is predictive. Infants aim toward a future position of the object, and they usually succeed in capturing it, despite their limited motor skill. They evidently perceive the object's movement and extrapolate its trajectory (von Hofsten, 1979, 1980; von Hofsten & Lindhagen, 1979). It certainly seems that these infants perceive suspended objects as separately moveable and persisting.

Observations of younger infants are more difficult to interpret. Within the first three months of life, an infant's arms and hands appear to be drawn to objects in the immediate surroundings (Twitchell, 1965). These movements rarely result in contact with an object, but they are adapted to some of an object's spatial properties such as its size (Bruner & Koslowski, 1972) and direction (Bower, Broughton, & Moore, 1970; von Hofsten, 1982a; de Schonen, 1977; Trevarthen, 1974; White et al., 1964). It is not clear, however, if these activities reflect the infant's perception of an object as unitary and bounded. Young infants could extend their arms toward the most interesting region of a visual array, without perceiving that region as a distinct object.

In view of these limitations, it is important to study the development of object perception with additional measures. Wendy Smith Born and I have begun a series of experiments using a surprise measure (Spelke & Born, 1982; Spelke, Born, Mangelsdorf, Richter, & Hrynick, in preparation). We have presented infants with a single object suspended in front of a background surface. Then we have moved the display in different ways, observing the infants' reactions to these movements. We ask whether infants expect, on some level, that an object can move independently of its background but must do so by moving as a whole.

In the first experiment (Spelke & Born, 1982), 3-month-old infants viewed an orange cylinder in front of a flat blue surface (Fig. 2). The object and background were carpeted and differed in texture as well as color. This display was stationary for 30 seconds and then a part of it began to move. In one condition, the object as a whole moved forward and back while the background remained still. In the other condition, the movement broke the object apart: Half the object moved forward in tandem with a neighboring region of the background (see Fig. 2). Infants viewed each of these events twice for 30 seconds at a time. Half the infants saw the stationary (S), object movement (O), and broken movement (B) episodes in the order S-O-S-B-S-O-S-B-S. The rest saw these episodes in the order S-B-S-O-S-B-S-O-S. Infants were videotaped throughout the session.

Born and I reasoned that if infants perceived the object as unitary and separate from the background, they would be surprised or puzzled when the object broke apart and moved together with part of the background. To assess surprise, we depended on the intuitive judgments of an experienced observer. The observer viewed the videotapes and judged whether each infant appeared more puzzled during episodes 2 and 6 or during episodes 4 and 8. Separate observers also recorded the duration of looking to the display during each episode, and they attempted to code the infant's facial expressions and motoric activity. None of the observers knew what event a baby was watching on any given trial.

The infants' apparent reactions of surprise were related significantly to these events. Most infants were judged to be more puzzled during the broken movement episodes than during the object movement episodes. According to the principal observer, the signs of surprise were subtle, they tended to vary from infant to infant, and they consisted more often of changes in motoric activity than of changes in visual attention or facial ex-

FIG. 2 Displays used by Spelke and Born (1982), Experiment 1.

pression. Analyses of the behavioral measures were consistent with these impressions. Infants looked equally long to the two kinds of events, with predominantly neutral expressions. Some infants appeared to stop moving abruptly or to breathe in a more pronounced manner during the broken movement episodes, but no single behavior reliably differentiated between the episodes. The observer's judgments suggested, nevertheless, that the infants perceived the object as unitary and bounded, and that they expected it to persist as a unit when it moved.

What information might infants use to perceive an object's boundaries? This object differed from its background in color and texture and was separated from it in depth. Two further experiments (Spelke & Born, 1982) investigated whether 3-month-old infants group together regions of an array by detecting the colors and textures of surfaces and/or by detecting the spatial arrangement of surfaces.

In the second experiment, the object and background were separated in depth but did not differ in color or texture. Infants were presented with the cylindrical object and the flat background surface, both covered with the orange carpeting. This display was moved as in the first study, infants were videotaped, and the same observer judged their reactions of surprise. The results were clear. A significant majority of the infants was judged to be more surprised during the broken movement events than during the object movement events. Infants apparently can perceive the boundaries of a suspended object by detecting its separation from the background.

In the third experiment, the "object" and "background" differed in color and texture but were not separated in depth. Infants viewed a flat surface consisting of two regions: a region that was similar in projective size and shape to the object in the first study, and a surrounding region that was similar in projective size and shape to the background. These regions were covered with the orange and blue carpeting respectively. The display was moved as in the first study: Either the orange region moved as a whole, or half of it moved with part of the blue region. The same observer judged reactions of surprise. In contrast to the previous experiments, there was no relationship between the observer's judgments and the movement episodes. In fact, slightly more than half the infants were judged to be more surprised by the unitary movement of the orange region than by the movement that broke up the orange and blue regions. The borders of these colored regions evidently were not perceived as the boundaries of an object.

Our studies suggest that infants perceive objects by detecting the spatial arrangement of surfaces in a scene. Young infants do not perceive objects by analyzing the colors and textures of those surfaces. Some observations of reaching support these suggestions. Newborn infants have been reported to extend their arms more often toward a three-dimensional object, separated in depth from its background, than toward a two-dimensional depiction of the object and background (Bower, 1972; Bower, Dunkeld, & Wishart, 1979; DiFranco, Muir, & Dodwell, 1978). This tendency is not observed in all studies (Field, 1976) or with all measures of reaching (DiFranco et al., 1978; Dodwell, Muir, & DiFranco, 1979). Its occurrence under certain conditions, however, may reflect the infant's perception that only the three-dimensional display contains a unitary, bounded object.

PERCEPTION OF PARTLY OCCLUDED OBJECTS

Most of the objects in a scene are not suspended in the air, fully in view. They lie beside or behind other things, forming a complicated arrangement of overlapping surfaces. An adult's perception of objects hardly suffers when things are partly hidden. In the still life in Fig. 3, for example, Chardin has arranged objects so that only one small apple can be seen without

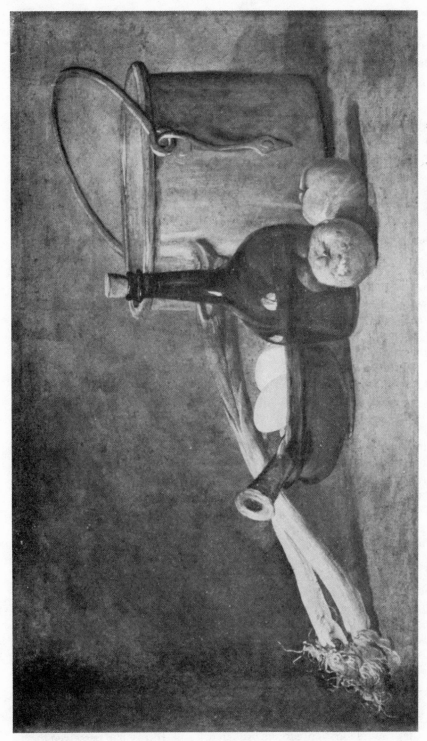

FIG. 3   La Ratisseuse (fragment), by Jean-Baptiste Chardin. From the Kaiser Friedrich Museum, Berlin.

obstructions. Nevertheless, we perceive leeks and eggs, a bottle and a cork, a mortar, a pestle, and more. The pot is seen as a single object with a regular shape, despite the apples that interrupt its base and the bottle that divides its visible surfaces in two. Each of the leeks looks unitary and distinct, although one partly hides the other and both appear in three separated areas on the canvas. In this still life, as in most real scenes, complete objects are perceived despite complex patterns of occlusion.

Do young infants perceive the complete shapes of partly hidden objects? An experiment by Bower (1967) suggests that they do. Following research on adults by Michotte, Thinès, & Crabbé (1964), Bower presented six-week-old infants with a wire triangle whose center was hidden by a cylinder. After the infants learned to suck in the presence of this display, he tested for generalization of sucking to four wire figures. One of these figures was a complete triangle; the others were triangles whose contours were inter-rupted in the region that had formerly been occluded. The infants sucked more frequently in the presence of the complete triangle, as if they had perceived the original triangle to continue behind its occluder in a definite way. Perception of the triangle could follow from the Gestalt principles of good continuation, closure, or good form. In separate experiments, Bower found no evidence that infants perceive two-dimensional patterns in accor-dance with these principles (Bower, 1965, 1966). Nevertheless, he suggested that infants perceived the three-dimensional display in accordance with the principle of good continuation.

Philip Kellman and I designed an experiment to test this suggestion (Kellman & Spelke, 1981). The principal display was a black rod placed behind a tan block that hid its center (Fig. 4). The two ends of this rod were of the same color and texture and were placed in alignment. According to the principles of good continuation and similarity, they should be perceived as parts of one object. Indeed, adults who were shown this display reported that they perceived a single, complete rod. Our experiment investigated whether 4-month-old infants would perceive this as well.

The study used a habituation of looking procedure. Infants in three groups were presented with different rod and block displays on repeated trials, until their looking time had declined to half its original level. The principal group was habituated to the partly occluded rod, one control group was habituated to a non-occluded complete rod, and one control group was habituated to a non-occluded rod with a gap in its center. The block stood behind the rod figures in the control conditions. After habitua-tion, all the infants viewed two test displays: the complete rod and the rod with the gap, with no block present (see Fig. 4). We expected infants in the control groups to look longer to the rod display they had not seen. The critical question concerned the infants who had been habituated to the part-ly occluded rod. If they had perceived the rod to continue behind the block, then they should look more to the broken test rod. If they had perceived the

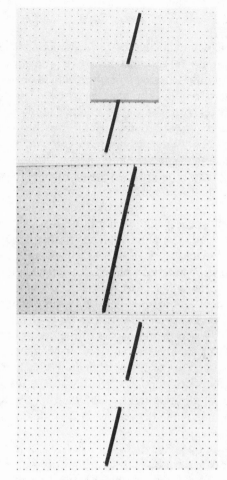

FIG. 4   Principal displays used by Kellman & Spelke (1981), Experiment 1.

rod to end where the block began, then they should look more to the complete test rod.

The infants in the control groups looked markedly longer to whichever rod display was novel. But to our surprise, the infants in the experimental group looked equally to the two test displays. It appeared that they had perceived the partly occluded rod neither as two broken fragments nor as a single connected object.

Kellman and I wondered next whether these infants had seen the partly occluded rod at all: Might infants fail to attend to any object that is partly hidden? Accordingly, our second experiment investigated whether infants perceive the shapes of the visible surfaces of a partly hidden object.

The experiment consisted of two conditions. One group of 4-month-old infants was habituated to the partly occluded rod display used in the first study. A second group was habituated to a rod with a large gap in its center, standing behind the same block. The ends of the rod fragments could be seen above and below the block. After habituation, both groups were presented with the complete rod and the broken rod with the large gap. If infants perceive the visible areas of a partly occluded object, then those who had been habituated to the complete partly hidden rod should have dishabituated to the test rod with the large gap: This display could not have been present during habituation, for the gap was too large to have been covered by the block. For the same reason, infants who had been habituated to the rod with the large visible gap should have dishabituated to the complete test rod. Infants in both groups showed these patterns of dishabituation. Evidently, they had perceived the rod figures as well as the block in the occlusion displays.

These experiments suggest that 4-month-old infants perceive the visible areas of a partly occluded rod, but they do not perceive whether the rod continues behind its occluder. The rod had visible surfaces that were identical in color and texture and were placed in alignment. Infants do not appear to perceive objects by detecting these relationships.

Our next experiment investigated whether infants would perceive partly hidden objects in accordance with the principles of closure and good form. The principal display was patterned on those studied by Michotte and Bower. It consisted of three interconnected black rods in the shape of an equilateral triangle, with a tan block occluding its center. Adult subjects reported seeing a complete triangle behind the block, as had the subjects in Michotte's original studies. Perception of the unity of this triangle was rated as even more compelling than perception of the unity of the rod in the first experiment.

The experiment followed the method of our first study. Three groups of 4-month-old infants were observed. One group was habituated to the triangle partly hidden behind the block, and two control groups were habituated to complete and broken triangles in front of the block. After habituation, all the infants were tested with the complete and broken triangles with no block present. The patterns of dishabituation were the same as in the first experiment. Whereas infants in the control conditions looked longer to the test display they had not seen, infants in the principal condition looked equally to the two test displays. When presented with the partly hidden triangle, these infants evidently had not perceived it either to continue behind the block or to end where the block began. The experiment suggests that infants do not perceive the unity of a partly occluded object, even if its visible ends are similar, are aligned, and can be connected to form a simple, symmetrical figure. Although our finding differs from that of Bower (1967), this conclusion agrees with Bower's conclusions from his studies of perceptual organization of two-dimensional displays (Bower, 1965, 1966).

In our next experiments, we turned to the Gestalt principle of common fate. We investigated whether 4-month-old infants would perceive the unity of a partly hidden object when the object moved as a whole. The infants in this experiment were presented with a partly occluded rod, as in our first study, but now the rod was moved. It moved left and right repeatedly on a horizontal path, though never so far as to bring its center to view. Adults who viewed this display reported that they perceived a single connected object. Their impression of a unitary rod was as strong as their impression of a unitary triangle in the preceding study, and stronger than their impression of the unity of the original stationary rod.

After infants were habituated to the moving rod display, they viewed the complete rod and the rod with a small gap, moving in the same fashion on alternating trials. Subsidiary studies indicated that these displays were of equal intrinsic interest to infants. The subjects in this experiment, however, showed a marked preference for the broken test rod. Habituation to the moving, partly hidden rod generalized to the moving complete rod and not to the moving broken rod. It appeared that the infants had perceived the moving rod as a single unit that continued behind its occluder.

This experiment suggested that infants perceive the unity of a partly hidden object by detecting the movements of its surfaces. This suggestion is supported by the experiments by Bower (1965) on perceptual grouping of two-dimensional displays. Although infants did not group elements in these displays on the basis of their alignment or form, they did group together elements that moved together. Infants may perceive both objects and patterns in accordance with a principle of common fate.

We are beginning to investigate the types of movement that lead infants to perceive unitary objects (Kellman & Spelke, in preparation). In one study, translatory movement in depth was found to be as effective as translatory movement in the frontal plane. Infants who were habituated to a rod moving in depth showed marked dishabituation to a broken test rod. We believe that infants perceive objects by analyzing the movements of surfaces through three-dimensional space. A further study indicated that infants do not perceive the unity of certain rotating objects. Infants were habituated to a rod that rotated in the frontal plane about its midpoint. They subsequently looked equally to rotating complete and broken rods. Infants may perceive a partly hidden object only when its visible parts move so as to carry the object as a whole from one place to another.

In all these studies, infants were presented with a moving object whose surfaces were similar and aligned. A final experiment investigated whether infants would perceive two dissimilar, misaligned surfaces as connected if the surfaces moved in tandem. The principal display appears in Fig. 5. It consisted of a black rod that was partly visible above an occluding block and a red, speckled, irregular polygon that was partly visible below the block. The rod and polygon differed in color, texture, and shape, and neither their contours nor their major axes were aligned. These surfaces moved back and forth together behind the block, as in the first movement study.

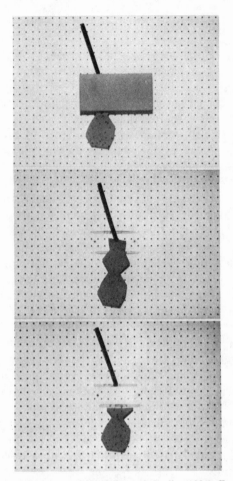

FIG. 5   Principal displays used by Kellman & Spelke (1981), Experiment 5.

When adults were presented with this display, many reported that the moving rod and polygon appeared connected behind the block. The impression that these surfaces were connected was less strong for this display, however, than for the display in which a single rod moved in the same manner.

Infants were habituated to this display and were tested with two fully visible, moving displays: a connected rod and polygon and a rod and polygon separated by a small gap (see Fig. 5). A subsidiary experiment indicated that these test displays were of roughly equal attractiveness to infants. Infants in the principal experiment, however, looked substantially longer to the test display with a gap. Dishabituation to the broken object was as pronounced in this study as in the study with the moving rod. Infants appear to perceive the partly hidden ends of an object as connected when they move together, whether or not their surfaces are similar and their edges are aligned.

In summary, infants can perceive objects by detecting the movements of surfaces through a scene. They perceive the unity of a partly hidden object if its surfaces undergo a common translation, either laterally or in depth. Unlike adults, infants do not perceive the unity of a stationary partly hidden object, even if its edges are aligned, its surfaces are similar, and its shape is regular. In the language of Gestalt psychology, infants appear to follow the principle of common fate, but not the principles of good continuation, similarity, or good form. I am not suggesting that infants fail to detect these gestalt properties. There is evidence, in fact, that all these properties are detectable at an early age (see, for example, Bornstein, Ferdinandsen, & Gross, 1981; Schwartz & Day, 1979). Nevertheless, infants do not appear to use gestalt properties as information about the boundaries of a partly hidden object.

PERCEPTION OF ADJACENT OBJECTS

It is possible that young infants do not perceive the boundaries of any object, partly occluded or fully in view, by analyzing surface colors, textures, and shapes. In that case, infants would perceive certain scenes very differently than adults. Consider again the still life by Chardin (Fig. 3). As adults, we perceive each of the two leeks, two eggs, and two apples as separate from the other, despite the fact that they are touching. This tendency probably depends in part on our knowledge of these objects and in part on the principle of good continuation. The contour of one egg follows a different curve from the contour of the other, and these smooth curves are taken to mark each object's boundaries. We also see the leeks as separate from the adjoining pot and the apples as separate from the bottle. The principles of good continuation and similarity join forces to delineate these boundaries, since the separate objects differ in brightness and texture. If infants do not take account of the alignment and similarity of surfaces, they might not be able to perceive any two adjacent objects as distinct.

There have been no conclusive studies of infants' perception of adjacent objects, but a number of experiments suggest that two such objects are perceived as one. Piaget (1954) observed the efforts of one child to reach for objects that were supported in various ways. At 7 months, the child would reach for objects that were dangled in front of him, perched on an adult's finger tips, or placed on a large surface. Until the age of 9 to 10 months, however, he would not reach for any object that rested stably on a second object. Piaget suggested that two contiguous objects were seen as one unit by the child.

Piaget's most interesting observation suggested an exception to this rule. He placed a matchbox, toward which the child was reaching, upon a book. The child immediately ceased reaching for the matchbox, and his hand came to rest on the book. At this point, the book tilted and the matchbox began to slide over its surface. When the child saw this box in motion, he let go of the book and reached for it directly. Two adjacent objects may be perceived as separate if one moves relative to the other.

According to recent studies, most infants begin reaching for an object on a supporting object at a younger age than the child observed by Piaget. Nevertheless, the pattern of performance that Piaget describes has been substantiated: Young infants reach more readily for a stationary object when it is supported on the finger tips or on an extended surface than when it rests on another object. It has been suggested that the failure to reach for a supported object reflects the perception that the object and support are one unit (Bower, 1979; Wishart, 1979). Alternatively, it has been suggested that this failure reflects the immature control of prehension (Bresson, Maury, Pieraut-le Bonniec, & de Schonen, 1977; Bresson & de Schonen, 1976–1977). After a long series of pilot investigations (Born & Spelke, 1981), we have despaired of deciding between these possibilities with studies of reaching. Reaching and manipulation undergo large changes during infancy, and those developments may mask whatever perceptual changes are also taking place. Accordingly, we have begun to study perception of adjacent objects using two different methods. These experiments are at an early stage, and only tentative conclusions can be offered. They suggest, nevertheless, that infants in the first half-year perceive two adjacent objects as one unit.

One experiment relied on the surprise method already described (Spelke et al., in preparation). Infants were presented with two suspended objects: the large carpeted orange cylinder and a smaller painted yellow box. These objects appeared side by side, with one flat end of the cylinder flush against one side of the box. The display was moved in two ways: The cylinder moved forward alone, or the box and cylinder moved forward together. Infants were videotaped, and their reactions of puzzlement were judged by an observer. If the infants perceived the two objects as separate, they should not have been surprised when one moved independently of the other, and they might have been surprised when the two objects moved together. If the infants perceived the objects as connected, they should have been more surprised by the independent movement of the cylinder.

One group of 6-month-old infants participated in this experiment, and a separate group participated in a replication of the original object-background study using the display in Fig. 2. A significant majority of the infants in the replication study was judged to be more surprised by the movement of half the cylinder with the background than by the movement of the complete cylinder. Six-month-olds appeared as surprised as 3-month-olds when the cylinder broke apart. In the study with adjacent objects, most of the infants were judged more surprised by the movement of the cylinder than by the movement of the two objects in tandem. The observer's judgments were somewhat less consistent in this study, however, than in the previous experiments. It would appear that the infants perceived the adjacent box and cylinder as one unit. Nevertheless, two adjacent objects may not look quite as unitary, to a 6-month-old, as does one object of a single color and a simple shape.

The last experiment focused on perception of adjacent objects by 3-month-old infants (Prather & Spelke, 1982). The experiment made use of a phenomenon recently reported by Starkey (Starkey & Cooper, 1980; Starkey, Spelke, & Gelman, 1980) and by Strauss & Curtis (1980). Infants have been found to become habituated to the number of objects in a display, provided that the number is small. They respond to change and invariance in number irrespective of the particular objects being enumerated, their properties, and their spatial configuration. Prather and I accordingly attempted to habituate infants to displays containing either one or two objects. We hoped to discover whether infants perceive two adjacent objects as one thing or two.

Infants were presented with rectangular solid objects painted a uniform color and covered with glittering bits of paper of a contrasting color. Altogether we presented eight objects in four different colors, each of a different size and shape from all the others. Half the infants were habituated to displays containing one object. The other infants were habituated to displays containing two objects: On each trial, they saw two objects of the same color, with a clear spatial separation between them in the frontal plane. Over the course of the habituation trials, the infants in both groups were presented with six of the eight objects (three of the four colors) in a variety of spatial positions.

After their looking time had declined by half, infants were presented with two objects of the color they had not yet seen, occupying new spatial positions. There were four types of trials. On "one" trials, a single object appeared. On "two" trials, the two objects appeared, separated in the frontal plane. On "adjacent" trials, the two objects appeared side by side with no separation between them. Finally, on "occluded" trials, the two objects were separated in depth, one partly visible behind the other (see Fig. 6).

The results were suggestive. Patterns of looking on the "one" and "two" test trials indicated that most of the infants had not become habituated to the number of objects in the displays. But among the infants who did habituate to number, an interesting pattern of results was obtained. Most of the infants habituated to one object looked longer to the occluded than to the adjacent configuration, whereas most of those habituated to two objects showed the reverse preference. This interaction was significant. The infants appeared to treat the adjacent objects as "one" and the objects separated in depth as "two."

This experiment suggests that infants perceive two objects as distinct when they are separated in depth, even if their projections overlap at the eye. Infants perceive two objects as one unit, however, when they are placed side by side. Studies of adjacent objects give further evidence that infants

FIG. 6   Adjacent and occluded test displays used by Prather & Spelke (1982).

perceive object boundaries by detecting the spatial separations of surfaces and not by analyzing the alignment of surfaces or the shapes of the configurations those surfaces form.

In summary, infants perceive the unity and boundaries of objects under a variety of conditions. They perceive an object as separate from any other object or surface that lies behind it, provided that the object is separated in depth from its background. Infants also perceive the visible ends of a partly occluded object as connected behind the occluder, provided that the ends undergo a common translation. But infants do not perceive the unity and boundaries of objects under other conditions that are effective for adults. They do not seem to perceive two stationary adjacent objects as separate, even if their surfaces differ in color and texture and their edges are not aligned. Moreover, they do not perceive two stationary ends of a partly hidden object as connected, even if the ends are the same in color and texture and are placed in alignment. Finally, perception of suspended objects and of moving, partly occluded objects is not affected by the shapes of these objects or the colors and textures of their surfaces. All these findings can be described in a simple way. Infants appear to perceive objects in accordance with two principles.

PRINCIPLES OF OBJECT PERCEPTION

My account of object perception depends on certain assumptions about the infant's perception of surfaces. First, I assume that infants perceive surfaces at their proper distances and orientations in three-dimensional space. If two surfaces meet at a visible juncture, infants perceive that they are touching. If one surface partly occludes another, infants do not perceive the partly hidden surface to end where the occluding surface begins. If one surface is displaced, infants perceive the three-dimensional path of its movement. These assumptions are supported by a considerable body of research (for reviews, see Gibson & Spelke, 1982; von Hofsten, 1982b).

Second, I assume that infants distinguish between the relatively small surfaces of objects and the larger surfaces that form the background of most visual scenes. They distinguish the surfaces of manipulable objects from extended surfaces such as walls, floors, ceilings, and perhaps tabletops. This assumption is shared by others (Bower, 1979; Bresson & de Schonen, 1976–1977; Piaget, 1954), although the infant's differentiation of object and background surfaces has received little study. Object surfaces and background surfaces may be distinguished on the basis of the size of the region they occupy in the visual field: Infants may perceive an object surface if and only if they view a surface whose edges are contained entirely within the visual field (Bower, 1979; Bresson & de Schonen, 1976–1977). Alternatively, object surfaces and background surfaces might be distinguished on the basis of their real size, perhaps in relation to the size of the hand. These possibilities have not been investigated systematically.

Thus, an infant who faces a visual scene is assumed to perceive a three-dimensional layout of object surfaces and background surfaces, each of which is moving or still. The infant discovers which of the object surfaces lie on the same object by following two principles.

The first will be called the *connected surface principle*. It states that two surfaces pertain to the same object if they touch each other directly or through other object surfaces. Two surfaces otherwise pertain to distinct objects. More precisely, two points on any surfaces in a layout lie on the same object if, and only if, there exists a curve that lies only on object surfaces and that connects them. For example, this principle dictates that two adjacent objects are one unit, since all points on the objects lie on connected object surfaces. If two objects rest on the same background surface and are separated in depth, the principle dictates that they are separate. Any curve that connected points on these objects would necessarily lie partly in the air or on the background. Note that both pairs of objects would send adjacent projections to the eye. The connected surface principle refers to the spatial connectedness of surfaces in a three-dimensional layout, not to the contiguity of their two-dimensional projections.

The second principle will be called the *common movement principle* and is adapted from the Gestalt principle of common fate (Wertheimer, 1923). It states that two surfaces lie on the same object if they undergo a common translation through the layout: a movement that carries the surfaces from one place to another without destroying the connection between them. Two surfaces lie on different objects if one moves relative to the other in a manner that would disrupt any connection between them.

These principles are offered tentatively, for they rest on a narrow set of studies. For example, infants' perception of the boundaries of moving objects has just begun to be studied, and only a few rigid movements have been investigated. Certain non-rigid movements can also carry an object from place to place without destroying its connectivity: Walking movements are a prime example. Presented with lights undergoing the movements of a human walker, adults perceive a unitary, jointed object; a person (Johansson, 1978). We do not know whether infants would also perceive the unity of an object that moved non-rigidly. As this and other possibilities are tested, the common movement principle may need to be reformulated. It seems clear, however, that infants perceive obects by detecting some arrangements and movements of surfaces through a scene.

What is perceived when the connected surface and the common movement principles conflict? We do not know, but I think it likely that separate objects are always perceived in this case. Adults appear to perceive distinct objects whenever spatially separated surfaces move together. A flock of geese is never one object to us, nor is a stream of traffic. And Piaget's observations suggest that infants perceive two separate objects when adjacent surfaces move independently. This, too, is a question for further research.

The connected surface and the common movement principles are the only principles infants follow, I suggest, when they divide visual scenes into objects. In particular, infants do not follow any similarity principle, perceiving as a unit surfaces that are identical in color or texture or shape. Infants also do not follow any form principles, grouping together surfaces so as to create objects with simple shapes and smooth edges. Although infants are sensitive to the colors, textures, and shapes of objects, they do not take account of these properties when they perceive an object's boundaries. In these respects, infants perceive objects differently from adults. When adults are presented with a scene consisting of unfamiliar objects, we tend to divide that scene into units so as to form the simplest, most regular objects that the scene allows. Infants of three and four months do not show this tendency.

DEVELOPING KNOWLEDGE OF OBJECTS

In closing, I consider how the infant's ability to perceive objects might develop. This ability may grow hand in hand with ›ur conceptions of objects and their properties.

Research on object perception in infancy provides some support for a hypothesis raised many years ago by Brunswik (Brunswik, 1956; Brunswik & Kamiya, 1953) and implicitly by others before him (Helmholtz, 1925; Mill, 1865). Brunswik suggested that all the Gestalt principles—all tendencies to perceive objects so as to form simple, regular configurations—are learned. These tendencies reflect acquired knowledge about the likely properties of objects. When he analyzed a variety of photographs of scenes, Brunswik found that nearby regions of a photograph were more likely to lie on the same object than distant regions, and that closed, symmetrical contours were more likely to enclose an object than open or asymmetrical ones. Thus, the properties of proximity, closure, and good form were predictors of object boundaries in these scenes. Brunswik hypothesized that children discover such predictive relationships through a kind of correlational learning, in which the Gestalt properties are assessed against other sources of information about objects. In this way, children learn to perceive in accordance with the Gestalt principles of organization.

One can imagine how learning could lead to the emergence of the principles of similarity, good continuation, and good form. If children initially perceive objects in accordance with the common movement and the connected surface principles, and if they are sensitive to the coloring and shapes of surfaces, then they could discover that the objects they see are likely to be uniformly colored and textured and that each object's color and texture are likely to differ from those of other objects. In addition, children could discover that objects often have smooth edges and simple shapes. Children might come to rely on the color and shape of an object to detect its boundaries as they discover that color and shape provide useful information about those boundaries.

Are the connected surface principle and the common movement principle also learned in a Brunswikian fashion, in the first three months of life? I think not. For if all principles of visual organization were learned, it is not obvious how the process of correlational learning could ever begin. One must have some ability to perceive objects, or one could never assess the validity of new sources of information about them. Moreover, it is likely that the initial ability to perceive objects is expressed through vision: young infants are clearly not adept at perceiving objects with their hands or ears. As the Gestalt psychologists maintained, our ability to learn about visual scenes seems to depend on an unlearned ability to perceive organization in these scenes (Koffka, 1935; Köhler, 1947).

Thus, some principles by which adults perceive objects may reflect our innate perceptual predispositions, whereas other principles may reflect the nature of the objects we have encountered. We might divide visible surfaces into objects by detecting their spatial continuity and their movements regardless of the nature of our visual world. But if we had grown up in a sufficiently different world, we might not carve arrays into units by analyzing their colors, textures, and forms.

These conclusions may pertain only to the development of perception, but I am intrigued by a different possibility. Our ability to perceive objects may be related to our ability to think about them. In particular, the initial principles of object perception may spring from a conception of what an object is.

What do we mean when we call something an object? I think we mean, roughly, that it is a physical entity that exists in some place, that all its parts are spatially interconnected, and that it will tend to maintain its connectedness as it moves. A handful of sand is not an object, for its individual grains are not interconnected. A body of water is not an object, for its unity is easily destroyed by displacing it in certain ways. When we call something an object, however, we do not mean that it is uniformly colored, smoothly contoured, or simply shaped. A twisted, multicolored piece of coral is just as much an object as a perfectly formed shell. The coral would not cease to be an object if its coloring and shape were made even more irregular, but only if it were broken into pieces. Uniformity of color and simplicity of shape are characteristic, but not essential, properties of objects. An object is in essence a coherent body that maintains its coherence as it moves.

These considerations suggest that the adult's perception of objects reflects knowledge of two kinds. The Gestalt form principles and the similarity principle appear to reflect knowledge about the characteristic attributes of common objects. The connected surface principle and the common movement principle appear to reflect knowledge about the essential nature of an object. Knowledge about the characteristic properties of objects may be acquired gradually over infancy and childhood, as children encounter objects and explore them. But knowledge of an object's essential nature may be shared, in part, by the youngest infant. It may first be expressed through the infant's perception of objects in visual scenes.

ACKNOWLEDGMENTS

I thank Wendy Smith Born, Kenneth Cheng, Rochel Gelman, Lila Gleitman, Julian Hochberg, Philip Kellman, Barbara Landau, Ulric Neisser, Penny Prather, John Sabini, and Scott Weinstein for comments and suggestions. Preparation of this manuscript was supported by a grant from the National Institutes of Health (HD-13248).

REFERENCES

Born, W. S., & Spelke, E. S. *Reaching for supported objects by 5- and 6-month-old infants.* Unpublished manuscript, 1981.

Bornstein, M. H., Ferdinandsen, K., & Gross, C. G. Perception of symmetry in infancy. *Developmental Psychology, 1981, 17,* 82–86.

Bower, T. G. R. The determinants of perceptual unity in infancy. *Psychonomic Science, 1965, 3,* 323–324.

Bower, T. G. R. The visual world of infants. *Scientific American, 1966, 215,* 80–92.

Bower, T. G. R. Phenomenal identity and form perception in infants. *Perception and Psychophysics, 1967, 2,* 74–76.

Bower, T. G. R. Object perception in infants. *Perception, 1972, 1,* 15–30.

Bower, T. G. R. *Human development.* San Francisco: Freeman, 1979.

Bower, T. G. R., Broughton, J. M., & Moore, M. K. Demonstration of intention in the reaching behavior of neonate humans. *Nature, 1970, 228,* 679–680.

Bower, T. G. R., Dunkeld, J., & Wishart, J. G. Infant perception of visually presented objects (technical comment). *Science, 1979, 203,* 1137–1138.

Bresson, F., Maury, L., Pieraut-le Bonniec, G., & de Schonen, S. Organization and lateralization of reaching in infants: An instance of asymmetric function in hand collaboration. *Neuropsychologia, 1977, 15,* 311–320.

Bresson, F., & de Schonen, S. A propos de la construction de l'espace et de l'objet: La prise d'un objet sur un support. *Bulletin de Psychologie, 1976–1977, 30,* 3–9.

Bruner, J. S., & Koslowski, B. Visually preadapted constituents of manipulatory action. *Perception, 1972, 1,* 3–14.

Brunswik, E. *Perception and the representative design of psychological experiments.* Berkeley: University of California Press, 1956.

Brunswik, E., & Kamiya, J. Ecological cue-validity of "proximity" and of other Gestalt factors. *American Journal of Psychology, 1953, 66,* 20–32.

DiFranco, D., Muir, D. W., & Dodwell, P. C. Reaching in very young infants. *Perception, 1978, 7,* 385–392.

Dodwell, P. C., Muir, D. W., & DiFranco, D. Infant perception of visually presented objects (technical comment). *Science, 1979, 203,* 1138–1139.

Field, J. Relation of young infants' reaching to stimulus distance and solidity. *Developmental Psychology, 1976, 12,* 444–448.

Gibson, E. J., & Spelke, E. S. The development of perception. In J. H. Flavell, & E. Markman (Eds.), *Cognitive Development.* Vol. III of P. Mussen (Ed.), *Handbook of Child Development.* New York: Wiley, 1982, in press.

von Helmholtz, H. *Handbook of Physiological Optics, Vol. III,* Tr. by J. P. C. Southall. New York: Optical Society of America, 1925.

von Hofsten, C. Development of visually directed reaching: The approach phase. *Journal of Human Movement Studies, 1979, 5,* 160–178.

von Hofsten, C. Predictive reaching for moving objects by human infants. *Journal of Experimental Child Psychology,* 1980, *30,* 369–382.

von Hofsten, C. Visual control of pre–reaching in neonates. *Developmental Psychology,* 1982, in press (a).

von Hofsten, C. Foundations for perceptual development. In L. P. Lipsitt (Ed.), *Advances in Infancy Research, Vol. II.* Norwood, N.J.: Ablex, 1982, in press (b).

von Hofsten, C., & Lindhagen, K. Observations on the development of reaching for moving objects. *Journal of Experimental Child Psychology,* 1979, *28,* 158–173.

Johansson, G. Visual event perception. In R. Held, H. W. Leibowitz, & H. L. Teuber (Eds.), *Handbook of sensory physiology: Perception.* Berlin: Springer-Verlag, 1978.

Kellman, P. J., & Spelke, E. S. *Infant perception of partly occluded objects: Sensitivity to movement and configuration.* Paper presented at the Society for Research in Child Development, Boston, April, 1981.

Koffka, K. *Principles of gestalt psychology.* New York: Harcourt, Brace & World, 1935.

Köhler, W. *Gestalt psychology.* New York: Liveright, 1947.

Michotte, A., Thinès, G., & Crabbé, G. *Les compléments amodaux des structures perceptives.* Louvain, Belgium: Publications Universitaires de Louvain, 1964.

Mill, J. S. *Examination of Sir William Hamilton's philosophy (1865).* Excerpts reprinted in R. Herrnstein, & E. G. Boring (Eds.), *A source book in the history of psychology.* Cambridge, MA: Harvard University Press, 1965.

Piaget, J. *The construction of reality in the child.* New York: Basic Books, 1954.

Prather, P., & Spelke, E. S. *Three-month-olds' perception of adjacent and partly occluded objects.* Paper presented at the International Conference on Infant Studies, Austin, March, 1982.

de Schonen, S. Functional asymmetries in the development of bimanual coordinations in human infants. *Journal of Human Movement Studies,* 1977, *3,* 144–156.

Schwartz, M., & Day, R. H. Visual shape perception in early infancy. *Monographs of the Society for Research in Child Development,* 1979, *44,* Serial No. 182.

Spelke, E. S. & Born, W. S. *Perception of visible objects by three-month-old infants.* Unpublished manuscript, 1982.

Starkey, D. P., & Cooper, R. G. Perception of numbers by infants. *Science,* 1980, *210,* 1033–1034.

Starkey, D. P., Spelke, E. S., & Gelman, R. *Number competence in infants: Sensitivity to numeric invariance and numeric change.* Paper presented at the International Conference on Infant Studies, New Haven, April, 1980.

Strauss, M. S., & Curtis, L. E. *Infant perception of numerosity.* Paper presented at the International Conference on Infant Studies, New Haven, April, 1980.

Trevarthen, C. The psychobiology of speech development. In E. Lenneberg (Ed.), *Language and brain: Developmental aspects. Neurosciences Research Program Bulletin,* 1974, *12,* 570–585.

Twitchell, T. E. The automatic grasping responses of infants. *Neuropsychologia,* 1965, *3,* 247–259.

Wertheimer, M. Principles of perceptual organization, (1923). Tr. by M. Wertheimer, in D. C. Beardslee, & M. Wertheimer (Eds.), *Readings in perception.* Princeton: Van Nostrand, 1958.

White, B. L., Castle, P., & Held, R. Observations on the development of visually-directed reaching. *Child Development,* 1964, *35,* 349–364.

Wishart, J. G. *The development of the object concept in infancy.* Unpublished doctoral dissertation, University of Edinburgh, 1979.

23 On Gaps Undetectable for Language Learners

François Dell
C.N.R.S., Paris

During the first years of their lives, children learning their mother tongue are exposed to a huge number of well-formed sentences, but they are provided with very little "negative" information, i.e., information about what sound sequences are not well-formed (cf. Braine 1971). This fact can help us to gain some insights into the workings of children's language acquisition capacity. In Dell (1981) I discussed some of its implications concerning the way optional phonological rules are acquired.[1] These had to do with the manner in which the language acquisition device (henceforth LAD) evaluates alternative hypotheses concerning the structural description of such rules, and their relative ordering in the grammar. In this article I extend my argument to the acquisition of exceptions and I furthermore suggest that under certain assumptions about the way the LAD stores primary linguistic data, some gaps in these data are undetectable for it.

French has a rule, call it LIQ, by which a word-final liquid optionally drops if preceded by an obstruent and followed by a pause or a consonant, e.g. *faut l'éteindre* "you've got to put it out" can be pronounced [foletẽd], et *éteindre les feux* "to put out the fires" can be pronounced [etẽdr lefö][2] or [etẽdlefö]. The rule applies more frequently in fast and/or relaxed styles of diction, but its application is not compulsory even in the most informal styles.

---

[1] Its implications for general syntax are discussed in Baker (1978; 1979). For general assumptions about language acquisition, I follow Chomsky (1965, esp. 25–47; 1975).

[2] Shwa is inserted by rule EPEN, cf. below. Setting irrelevant details aside, the underlying representation of *éteindre* is /etẽdr/, and more generally, all the words that show up phonetically as [XCC] before a pause have an underlying form /XCC/.

431

Furthermore, even in the most informal styles, not all words meeting the conditions of that rule can undergo it. According to my intuitions as a native speaker, the words *livre* "book," *exemple,*[3] *ministre, arbre* "tree," *souffle* "blow," can for instance lose their final liquid when in the proper environment, whereas *ivre* "intoxicated, wild," *ample* "roomy," *rustre* "poor," *pourpre* "purple," *buffle* "buffalo," cannot. Taking *livre* and *ivre* as representatives of those two classes, one has the following pattern.

(1)   (a)   (b)   (c)   (d)

       [livr]   [liv]   [ivr]   *[iv]

I have not found any set of phonological, morphological and/or syntactic criteria that would enable us to set the two classes apart. Apart from the fact that common words as a rule can undergo LIQ whereas rare words cannot, the ability of words ending in an obstruent-liquid cluster to lose their liquid seems to be a matter of lexical idiosyncrasy.[4] Assume for the time being that items like *ivre* are idiosyncratically marked [− rule LIQ] in the lexicon. Assume furthermore that LIQ is a major rule,[5] i.e. that it belongs to a class of rules for the acquisition of which learners apply the following strategy:

(2)   Given rule R and any lexical item I, assume that the lexical entry of I contains the specification [+ rule R] until you find evidence to the contrary.

Looking at things from the point of view of acquisition, one might ask what process results in a [− rule LIQ] marking getting entered into the lexicon of the language learner.

The evidence pointing to the exceptionality of *ivre* with respect to LIQ is all of the "negative" sort of (1d). Imagine a child exposed to the speech of adults who sometimes say [liv] for *livre* but never say [iv] for *ivre*. She hears forms like (1a, b, c), but she has no way to decide whether the absence of form (1d) from the data is due to its ungrammaticality or whether it simply is an accident. We must conclude, then, that the exceptionality of *ivre* and the like with respect to rule LIQ must have been explicitly pointed out to her in one way or another.

More generally, leaving the particular example of rule LIQ, which is used here only by way of illustration, my point is that mere exposure to a sample, however large, of adult language, does not provide the child with evidence sufficient to enable her to acquire lexical exceptions to a major optional

---

[3]French translations are omitted when transparent.
[4]For some discussion of the distribution of the exceptions to LIQ in the lexicon, cf. Dell (1976).
[5]On the distinction between major and minor rules in phonology, cf. Lightner (1968).

rule. Entering such exception markings into the lexicon necessarily involves some item by item teaching.

In the case of a major optional rule where one knows for a fact that no such teaching is involved, positing [− rule R] markings in the lexicon cannot be an adequate account for the immunity of certain lexical items to the rule. This is in fact the case with LIQ. The unacceptability of pronunciations such as [iv] for *ivre* cannot have been taught by adult corrections of the child's "mistakes" during the preschool period, since, as argued in Braine (1971), these play at best a minor role in language acquisition and since most words of the *ivre* type are first encountered through exposure to written material anyway. Moreover it cannot have been done later on through formal teaching, for from a normative point of view, the operation of LIQ is equally forbidden in all words as "sloppy," "vulgar," and so on. One is then forced to conclude that native speaker's intuitions such as mine as to which words can undergo LIQ and which ones cannot, are not the result of any item by item teaching.[6] Rather, they are the product of an interaction between phonological and stylistic factors that have yet to be worked out (cf. Dell, 1970; 1976).

In the preceding, I stated that the absence of the pronunciation [iv] (for ivre) from the primary linguistic data is not unequivocal evidence as to its ungrammaticality, and it may sound as though this is the only reason why language learners should not be able to infer that ungrammaticality from the data.

But it seems to me that a LAD working under the assumption that LIQ is a major rule cannot even detect the absence of [iv] from the data to begin with.[7] In order to do this, it would have to search through a complete record containing every phonetic variant of all the words it has ever been exposed to since it adopted rule LIQ. But the LAD cannot be keeping such a record as this would imply attributing to it a capability for the storage of primary linguistic data that is otherwise unmotivated. I assume that the LAD records the primary linguistic data it encounters in something like the following way.

Let us view the progression of learning as a succession of grammars $G_1 \ldots G_k$, where for every state i, exposure to a new set of primary

---

[6]In order to avoid that conclusion, one could assume that LIQ is a minor rule, i.e., one for which the LAD uses, instead of strategy (2), the strategy derived from it when one replaces "[+ rule R]" by "[− rule R]". But this assumption is contradicted by the fact that speakers extend the operation of LIQ to words which are uncommon in the speech of other speakers, and which are usually not subject to the rule, if these words become very frequent in their own speech, as, for example, when *engendrer*, "to generate," drops its liquid in the speech of a linguist.

[7]The argument below about the undetectability of certain gaps can be carried over, *mutatis mutandis*, to the gaps discussed in Dell (1981).

linguistic data leads to the replacement of G_i by G_{i+1}. Consider a LAD currently equipped with grammar G_i that encounters some primary linguistic datum d. If d is not accounted for by G_i, I assume that the LAD records it in its memory so as to take it into consideration when looking for a successor to G_i. But if d is accounted for by G_i, I assume that it leaves no trace in the LAD's memory (and hence will have no influence on the choice of G_{i+1}). I assume furthermore that when the LAD adopts a new grammar G_{i+1}, it erases from its memory all the previously recorded data that is accounted for by G_{i+1}. In other words, a piece of primary linguistic data remains stored in the memory of the LAD only as long as the LAD has not reached a grammar accounting for it. Here is another point where the analogy between a language learner and a linguist trying to discover the grammar of a language breaks down. As pointed out in Braine (1971), the linguist has at any moment access to a complete record of all the data she has ever encountered,[8] whereas the child does not.

To summarize, assuming that in some cases the LAD searches through the data for gaps of a specific nature,[9] its limited ability for storing primary linguistic data puts restrictions on the kind of gaps it can detect in principle. It cannot for example perceive gaps resulting from lexical exceptions to major optional rules. It is important to understand that there is no absolute sense in which the absence of X from the data constitutes a "gap." The notion of "a gap in the data" is relative to certain hypotheses entertained by the LAD. For instance, the absence of [iv] from the data constitutes a gap under the assumption that LIQ is a major rule, but it does not under the assumption that it is a minor rule. When the absence of X from the primary linguistic data is what is expected by the LAD, there is no need to bother about how the LAD might go about to detect this absence, as can be seen from the following example.

The grammar of an adult speaker of Tagalog excludes morpheme-final consonant clusters, which implies that the absence of any such consonant cluster from the primary linguistic data has had an effect on the LAD during the period of learning. Given current knowledge about the phonotactics of many languages and about the acquisition of phonology by children, let us speculate that when a LAD starts learning a language, its initial hypothesis is that all forms of that language conform to the strongest possible restrictions on consonant clusters (e.g. they must all fit into a CVCV . . . pattern), and that it subsequently relaxes its restrictions only to the ex-

---

[8]As any linguist keeping fieldwork notes knows, the retrievability of any individual recorded datum decreases very quickly as the global amount of material recorded increases. It is often more efficient for the linguist to elicit new data from her informants, even at the cost of duplicating data already recorded, rather than hunt through the records for it. The language learner is certainly faced with analogous problems.

[9]A debatable assumption.

tent that it is forced to do so by violations encountered in the primary linguistic data, e.g., it will not entertain as a hypothesis a grammar allowing clusters of three consonants unless it has encountered a certain amount of such clusters in the data it was exposed to. In the case of Tagalog, then, the absence of certain data in the primary linguistic data (namely, the non-existence of morpheme-final consonant clusters) has an influence on the LAD's choice of successive grammars because presumably the absence of such data constitutes the "unmarked" case. This absence is already built in, as it were, in the first grammar entertained as a hypothesis by the LAD, and will be inherited by subsequent grammars hypothesized by the LAD in the course of language acquisition.

The theoretical framework developed in Chomsky and Halle (1968) implies that lexical items can be marked as exceptions to major optional rules. Assuming this to be true, I have argued that during language acquisition such exception markings cannot be entered into the lexicon simply as a consequence of the child's being exposed to adult speech, and that some richer experience is needed, of the kind provided by teaching. But what about the truth of our initial assumption? One would like to tighten linguistic theory so as to exclude the very possibility of lexical exceptions to major optional rules.

To show that one cannot exclude such a possibility would require more than just showing that speakers of some language know, as a result of teaching, that certain lexical items are exceptions to a major optional rule. I will now examine an example where this is the case, and yet this knowledge does not reflect the existence of [− rule R] markings in the lexicon. Rather, it results from the interaction of two systems: orthographic competence, and a grammar acquired on the sole basis of experience acquired through exposure to adult speech.

French has a late rule, call it EPEN, which inserts shwa at the end of a word ending in two consonants or more when the following word begins with a consonant,[10] e.g. *film russe* "Russian film" can be pronounced either [filmrys] or [filmərys], and similarly:

(3) a. *veste sale* [vɛst(ə)sal] "dirty jacket"
    b. *carte verte* [kart(ə)vɛrt] "green card"
    c. *l'Egypte gagne* [ležipt(ə)gañ] "Egypt wins"
    d. *insecte marron* [ɛ̃sɛkt(ə)marɔ̃] "brown insect"
    e. *récolte d'orge* [rekɔlt(ə)dɔrz] "barley harvest"
    f. *quetsche mure* [kwɛtš(ə)myr] "ripe damson"

(4) a. *test simple* [tɛst(ə)sɛ̃pl] "simple test"
    b. *short vert* [šɔrt(ə)vɛr] "green shorts"

---

[10]This is only a first approximation. For a more precise formulation, cf. Dell (1980).

c. *concept clef* [kɔ sɛpt(ə)kle] "key concept"
d. *strict minimum* [strikt(ə)minimɔm] "absolute minimum"
e. *trois volts deux* [trwavɔlt(ə)dö] "3.2 Volts"
f. *match nul* [matš(ə)nyl] "a draw"

I call "colloquial" (henceforth CQ) the range of styles of pronunciation used in everyday conversation, and "orthoepic" (henceforth OP) the style of pronunciation that is prescribed for the reading of prose. In CQ all the words of the form *XCC* without exception can undergo EPEN when in the required environment (cf. 3–4). In OP on the other hand, only those *XCC* words which have the letter *e* in the last syllable of their conventional spelling may be pronounced as [XCCə] in that environment. Hence, in OP, the examples in (3) can be pronounced with or without shwa, but pronouncing the examples in (4) with a shwa is considered incorrect, because it would then sound as though the *XCC* words in these examples were spelled with a final letter *e*. The situation is summarized in (5), with the phrases *un pacte défensif* and *l'impact des balles* "the impact of the bullets" (For reasons of space I transcribe only the medial syllables).

(5)   *pacte défensif*   *impact des balles*

	(i)	(ii)	(iii)	(iv)
a. CQ	paktde	paktəde	paktde	paktəde
b. OP	paktde	paktəde	paktde	*paktəde

The contrast between *pacte*-type words and *impact*-type words is relevant only to the description of OP. Apart from the fact that, in a given phonetic and syntactic environment, shwa tends to occur more frequently in OP than in CQ, the only difference between the two styles that is relevant to our discussion is the contrast between (5-bii) and (5-biv). This contrast is the only kind of data that distinguishes between the *pacte*-type words and the *impact*-type words, i.e., were it not for the data of (5-biv), there would be no phonetic reason for a linguist to distinguish the two classes of words.[11]

Words belonging to certain morphological categories or ending in certain consonant clusters are predictably of the *pacte* type,[12] but there remains a sizeable portion of the lexicon where inclusion of a given item in the *impact* class is an idiosyncratic fact to be learned by rote. Following are quasi-minimal pairs exemplifying this for various clusters.

(6) [rk] *cirque* "circus" vs. *arc* "bow"; [lk] *catafalque* vs. *talc;* [rt] *inerte* vs. *yaourt* "yogurt"; [lt] *adulte* vs. *volt;* [rs] *ours* "bear" vs. *corse* "Corsican"; [lm] *calme* "quiet" vs. *film;* [ks] *sexe* vs. *index;*

---

[11]But cf. note 13.

[12]Such is the case for all verbal forms, for the feminine forms of adjectives, and for all words with a final obstruent-liquid cluster: *il filme* "he films," *stricte* "strict, fem.", *entre* "between."

[ld] *solde* vs. *Léopold;* [ps] *gypse* "gypsum" vs. *biceps;* [lf] *golfe* "gulf" vs. *golf.*

In order to account for the data of (5), a linguist might be tempted to write a grammar *A* that would contain rule EPEN and where all the items of the *impact* class would be listed in the lexicon as exceptions to EPEN in OP speech. But since the only data which compell the linguist to posit a class of exceptions to EPEN are "negative" data such as (5-biv), data not available to children, the only way for speakers of French to discover the existence of a class of exceptions to EPEN, and its exact extension, is through conventional spelling, which provides them with the necessary "negative" data.[13]

Consider those preschool children who are exposed to a significant amount of data belonging to OP, and whose grammars are presumably devised so as to account for this type of data as well as CQ. All they can acquire, then, on the basis of the primary linguistic data (5ai-iv; 5bi-iii), is a grammar that is identical to *A*, except that it contains no [− rule EPEN] markings in its lexicon. Call that grammar *B*. This is the same grammar as is acquired by those children who are not exposed to any data from OP.

How, then, should one represent the educated adults' competence as reflected in (5)? The prohibition of (5-biv) is merely a particular case of a very general principle implicit in the conventions that tie the orthoepic pronunciation of French to its spelling system. We can express it roughly as follows.

(7) Every segment that appears in the pronunciation of a French sentence must have a counterpart in the written form of that sentence.[14]

---

[13]For the sake of simplicity of exposition, my label OP includes only the style of pronunciation prescribed for the "correct" reading of prose. There exists besides other non-CQ styles where the *pacte*-type words and words of the *impact*-type contrast. In singing, where shwa is allowed at the end of a line, the line-final *pacte*-type words may be pronounced with or without a final shwa depending on the requirements of the meter, whereas the *impact*-type words should always be pronounced shwaless. This does not change anything in my argument, however, since the materialization of the contrast between the two classes of words in line-final position in singing is again only optional, and my point depends crucially on this optionality.

In classroom recitation of classical verse, all the *e* letters between consonants should be pronounced, regardless of the location of the word boundaries, i.e., the only permissible pronunciations in (5) are (bii) and (biii). Hence data from this style would in principle be a possible source for data permitting the acquisition of the *pacte-impact* contrast. But exposure to the recitation of classical verse plays a negligible role, if any, in the shaping of the pronunciation of pre-school children, for obvious reasons.

[14]A common example of a violation of (7) is the pronunciation [lɔrsəkə] for *lorsque* "when," alongside the "correct" [lɔrskə]. (7) is only a first approximation and should be refined so as to make allowance, for instance for the glottal stops that can appear at the beginning of words that are otherwise vowel-initial, for the yods that are obligatorily inserted between an *l* and a following vowel belonging to the same word (*crier* [krije] "to shout"). But the exact content of (7) is not at issue here. The converse of (7) does not hold, as is well-known. Many letters never have any counterpart in pronunciation.

Whereas (5a) is directly generated by the grammar B, which contains rule EPEN with no lexical exceptions, (5b) is accounted for by the interaction of that grammar B and the conventions of French spelling, to which (7) belongs. One can use (7) as a filter on the output of B. In order to be well-formed in OP, a phonetic representation must be generated by B, and must furthermore meet condition (7).

We have here an example of a situation where formal teaching results in a modification of the language learner's overall competence, and yet his grammar *stricto sensu* remains unaffected.

ACKNOWLEDGMENTS

I thank Ken Safir and Dan Sperber for their comments on a first draft of this chapter.

REFERENCES

Baker, C. L. (1978) *Remarks on complementizers, filters, and learnability.* Paper presented at the Sloan Foundation Workshop on Criteria of Adequacy for a Theory of Language, Stanford University.

Baker, C. L. (1979) Syntactic theory and the projection problem. *Linguistic Inquiry 10*-4: 533–581.

Braine, M. D. S. (1971) On Two Types of Models of the Internalization of Grammars. In D. Slobin (Ed.), *The ontogenesis of grammar,* Academic Press, New York.

Chomsky, N. (1965) *Aspects of the theory of syntax,* MIT Press, Cambridge, Mass.

Chomsky, N. (1975) *Reflections on language.* Pantheon Books, New York.

Chomsky, N., & M. Halle (1968) *The sound pattern of English,* Harper and Row, New York.

Dell, F. (1970) *Les régles phonologiques tardives et la morphologie dérivationnelle du francais,* PhD Dissertation, MIT.

Dell, F. (1976) Schwa précédé d'un groupe obstruante-liquide, *Recherches Linguistiques, 4,* 75–111, University of Paris VIII-Vincennes.

Dell, F. (1981) On the learnability of optional phonological rules. *Linguistic Inquiry, 12*-1, 31–37.

Dell, F. (1980) *Generative phonology and French Phonology,* revised English version of *Les Régles et les Sons,* Hermann, Paris, 1973, translated by C. Cullen, Cambridge University Press.

Lightner, T. (1968) On the use of minor rules in Russian phonology. *Journal of Linguistics, 4,* 69–72.

V COMMENTARY

24 Comments on Chomsky's Chapter, "On the Representation of Form and Function"

Luigi Rizzi
Università della Calabria

I would like to focus on two aspects of the framework outlined in Chomsky's paper: (1) the distinction trace/PRO and, in general, the theory of "missing elements"; (2) the types of evidence on the basis of which the language learner fixes the parameters of Universal Grammar and determines core and marked properties of the particular grammar acquired. I discuss some facts that in my opinion significantly support the relevant aspects of the proposed framework. I then make a shorter remark, much less structured and conclusive, on the properties of Logical Form in configurational and non-configurational languages.

1. Trace/PRO and the theory of "missing elements." If considered in an historical perspective, the distinction between trace and PRO is, among other things, the framework specific characterization of the classical distinction between Raising and Control, or Raising and EQUI NP Deletion. Such a characterization represents a major improvement on the traditional accounts for essentially two reasons. The first is that it is embodied within a sophisticated theory of phonetically null positions, which identifies highly differentiated types of "missing elements," and explains their peculiar behaviors in terms of general principles of binding. Such a theory of missing elements appears to be one of the most fruitful achievements of the recent "Government-Binding" framework, developed by Chomsky in the Pisa Lectures and outlined in the article in discussion.[1] The second reason is that the modular approach consistently developed in this

---

[1]Cfr. Chomsky (1980b), and also Kayne (1980).

framework permits a considerable sharpening of the evidence available, by showing that certain properties or distinctions are required by converging indications originating from independent modules. In this sense, the sub-theory of lexical semantics and θ structure requires that, if the θ Criterion is checked at LF, PRO and trace must be distinct theoretical entities at this level. This conclusion is by no means obvious: It would be inconsistent even with the theory that is the immediate antecedent of the GB framework, i.e., the theory presented in "On Binding" (Chomsky, 1980a), in which trace and PRO are non-distinct at LF. The very minor contribution which I would like to give to this discussion is to show that there are converging indications for a PRO/trace distinction at LF which come from totally independent modules.

The basic observation is one which has been made in the descriptive literature on infinitival complements in Italian: there are environments in which only control structures are permissible, and other environments in which only raising structures are permissible. A striking level of explanatory adequacy is achieved on this partial complementarity by independently motivated principles of the GB theory, if it is assumed that the "missing subject" of a control structure is the pronominal anaphor PRO, the "missing subject" of a raising structure is an empty category (a trace), and this distinction is represented at LF, the level where the relevant principles apply.

A. First of all, control complements can be "moved around" rather freely in Italian. For instance, they can be moved to the focus position of a cleft construction:

   (1) Gianni vuole tornare a casa
      (Gianni wants to come back home)
   (2) E' tornare a casa che Gianni vuole
      (It is to come back home that Gianni wants)

But such a freedom does not exist for a raising complement: Clefting is impossible in this case:[2]

---

[2]This is clearly not a lexical idiosyncrasy: *sembrare* can also take control complements in Italian (with the PRO subject controlled by the matrix experiencer), and in this case clefting is possible again:

   (i) Mi sembra di tornare a casa
      (It seems to me to come back home =
      It seems to me that I am coming back home)
   (ii) E' di tornare a casa che mi sembra
      (it is to come back home that it seems to me)

Moreover (4) cannot simply be excluded via proper binding, i.e. the principle (perhaps itself derived from the general theory of binding) according to which anaphors must be c-command-ed by their antecedents. Clearly, in the case of the cleft construction some subsidiary conven-

(3) Gianni sembra tornare a casa
     (Gianni seems to come back home)

(4) * E' tornare a casa che Gianni sembra
     (It is to come back home that Gianni seems)

B. There are also structural environments in which a raising complement is allowed and a control complement is impossible. In Italian, as in many other languages, both raising and control verbs can take passivized complements:

(5) I colpevoli sembrano essere stati puniti duramente
     (The guilty seem to have been punished heavily)

(6) I colpevoli dichiarano di essere stati puniti duramente
     (The guilty assert "to" have been punished heavily = . . . assert that they have been . . .)

But in Italian there is also another passive construction, sometimes called "impersonal" or "middle" passive, which involves the clitic *si,* interpreted as an unspecified human agent: for example,

(7) I colpevoli si sono puniti duramente
     (The guilty "si" have punished heavily =
     The guilty have been punished heavily by someone)

Now, this construction is possible in the complement of a raising verb, but impossible in the complement of a control verb:[3]

(8) I colpevoli sembrano esser*si* puniti duramente
     (The guilty seem to "si" have punished heavily = (5))

(9) (*)I colpevoli dichiarano di esser*si* puniti duramente
     (The guilty assert "to" "si" have punished heavily = (6))

Why such a double asymmetry between raising and control structures and between ordinary and impersonal passives?

The theory of missing elements outlined by Chomsky in this paper and fully developed in the Pisa Lectures provides a strikingly simple explana-

---

tion is needed to assign the clefted element to the c-domains which its trace belongs to, as far as proper binding and choice of antecedent is concerned. Such a convention is required by the well-formedness and nonambiguous interpretation of such sentences as

(iii) E' di se stesso che Mario dice che Gianni parla sempre
       (It is of himself that Mario says that Gianni talks all the time)

(only acceptable with *Gianni* = antecedent of the reflexive pronoun) See Belletti and Rizzi (1980) for discussion. This convention should also be available for the raising structure which consequently could not be excluded via proper binding.

[3]The asterisk in (9) is parenthesized since this form is acceptable with an irrelevant interpretation, i.e., with *si* interpreted as reflexive or reciprocal pronoun (interpretation obviously available for (8) too). The original descriptive observation on the asymmetry (8)-(9) was made in Aissen and Perlmutter (1976) for Spanish and independently, in Rizzi (1976) for Italian.

tion. This framework contains the following principle constraining the possible occurrence of empty categories (traces):

(10) Empty Category Principle (ECP): "an empty category must be properly governed".

where proper government is, essentially, local c–command by a lexical category.

Moreover, the following theorem concerning PRO is derived from the binding principles:

(11) PRO Theorem: "PRO must be ungoverned"

ECP and the PRO Theorem have been justified on totally independent grounds, but their explanatory power naturally extends to the problems outlined, given very reasonable supplementary assumptions.

First of all, why control complements can be freely moved around, while raising complements must be kept contiguous to their main verbs (observation A.)? Answer: because of ECP: the trace in subject position of a raising complement must be properly governed, and this requirement can be fulfilled if the complement stays in its base position (structure (12)a). If the complement is moved, e.g. to TOP in the cleft construction ((12)b), the trace in subject position is ungoverned, and ECP is thus violated. If a control complement is moved to TOP (as in (12)c) no ill-formedness is produced, since the PRO subject is not an empty category in the relevant sense, and therefore does not fall into the domain of ECP:

(12)a Mario$_i$ sembra (e_i tornare a casa)
   b * E' ($_{S''}$ ($_{TOP}$ (e_i tornare a casa) ($_{S'}$ che Mario$_i$ sembra ____)
   c E' ($_{S''}$ ($_{TOP}$ (*PRO$_i$* tornare a casa) ($_{S'}$ che Mario$_i$ vuole ____)

Let us now turn to the second asymmetry between raising and control (observation B.). It has recently been argued on independent grounds that the clitic *si* found in the impersonal and middle construction is base-generated under the node *infl,* introduced by the base rule

(13) S ⟶ NP infl VP

(see Belletti, 1980, for discussion). Now, it is an ordinary assumption within the GB framework that the abstract inflection introduced via rule (13) structurally governs the subject position. This is motivated, among other things, by the analysis of the PRO Drop Parameter, which we will consider later, and by the ill formedness of

(14) * John$_i$ doesn't know (what PRO$_i$ did)

which is thus ruled out by the PRO theorem. Consider now the S structures of (8) and (9) (i.e., prior to the application, in the phonological component, of the rule which moves clitic pronouns to the right of an untensed verb, a rule which may be conceived of as a sort of analogue of Affix Hopping):

(15)a I colpevoli$_i$ sembrano (e_i *si* VP)
     b * I colpevoli$_i$ dichiarano di (*PRO$_i$ si* VP)

In (15)b PRO is governed by the abstract inflection *si* and the structure is thus ruled out by the PRO theorem, on a par with (14). In (15)a the presence of *si* does not bother, since by definition the PRO theorem does not apply to traces.[4] As for the lack of asymmetry with ordinary passives (i.e., (5) and (6)), it follows from the fact that ordinary passive does not involve per se an abstract inflection in the position introduced by rule (13), so that the PRO option is permissible on a par with the trace option, since the PRO theorem is satisfied.

Since there is ample evidence that ECP and the Binding Principles apply at LF,[5] we conclude that, in order to keep the proposed straightforward explanation we must assume the PRO/trace distinction at LF, thus converging on the requirement of the θ Criterion. Such a convergency in the requirements of analyses of the form and analyses of the interpretation was the original motivation for the raising/EQUI distinction[6], and in fact laid in the background of the very idea of transformational grammar. But the convergency argument seems now much more stringent, given the degree of modular sophistication attained by the theory, with the identification of autonomous and interacting subtheories, each governed by its own principles and properties.

 2. *On the Types of Evidence Available in Language Acquisition.*   The second remark I would like to make concerns certain hypotheses suggested by Chomsky on the role of markedness and core grammar in the study of language acquisition and cross-linguistic variation.

In the described system the acquisition of a particular grammar is abstractly characterized in terms of two basic operations: The language learner assigns specific values to the parameters of UG, thus deriving a core grammar, and adds to it certain marked processes and structures which are not immediately deducible from the principles of UG. Perhaps this distinction is more a matter of exposition and presentation than a principled one: if even the values of the most fundamental parameters are not equally valued, but are ranked in a scale of markedness, as seems not implausible, then the two operations basically reduce to the same. An important question which is raised in Chomsky's discussion is the following: on the basis of which kind of evidence does the language learner discard an unmarked op-

---

[4]The acceptability of (15) requires a minor extention of the notion "minimal governing category", relevant for the theory of binding, which I will not discuss here.

[5]See Chomsky (1980b), Kayne (1979).

[6]Consider for instance the classical analysis of Ruwet, 1972, chapter 2.

tion, and choose a marked one (or, more realistically, discards a less marked option and chooses a more marked one)? This question is briefly addressed in the final part of Chomsky's paper with some remarks that seem to me to deserve detailed consideration. There are basically two types of cases, which I will discuss separately.

I. In the first class of cases, the answer is simple: Positive evidence is sufficient to justify the choice of a marked option. For instance, it follows from Case theory, as is formulated in the GB framework, that case assignment across sentential boundaries is a marked process. Still, in the acquisition of English such a process can be directly acquired on the basis of the positive evidence provided by such sentences as

(16) John believes (Bill to be a nice fellow)

(17) John wants (Bill to go)

Incidentally, this property of the case system provides an interesting answer to an objection sometimes raised against the abstract theory of infinitival complementation argued for by Chomsky. This theory states that the bracketted infinitival verb phrase in sentences like

(18) John wants (to go)

is represented as a full sentence with a PRO subject at the abstract levels of D and S structure. Now, it has been noticed that children acquiring the English grammar master structures like (18) earlier than structures like (17), and this fact has been interpreted as evidence against the sentential analysis of (18). The same conclusion has been drawn from the fact that children acquiring control structures like (19) do not make errors like (20):

(19) John tries to win

(20) * John tries Bill to win

i.e., the non-existence of (20) is not learned via error and correction.

It has been argued (see e.g., Maratsos, 1978) that the later occurrence of (17) w.r.t. (18) and the non-occurrence of errors like (20) are only compatible with a less abstract syntactic analysis of (18) and (19), which directly incorporates their superficial differences from (17) and (20). In this alternative, *to want* would be independently subcategorized for infinitival clauses and for bare infinitival VP complements; *to try* would be only subcategorized for bare infinitival VP's.[7] Within such a "concrete" double subcategorization hypothesis one would expect that the two types of complements of *to want* can arise independently in acquisition, and that the sentential subcategorization for *to try* is discarded, since no evidence justifying it is ever encountered in the course of acquisition. On the contrary, it

---

[7]See Bresnan (1978) for detailed discussion.

is argued, within the more abstract "uniform" hypothesis the discussed facts are unexpected and problematic.

This objection is now answered by Case theory.[8] It follows from this theory that the unmarked situation for the subject position of an infinitival clause is to be un-case marked. Therefore, the case filter will force the choice of a phonetically non-realized subject, which will be PRO or trace, depending on the interacting requirements of lexical and structural properties of the syntactic environment. Therefore, the system predicts that, along this dimension of markedness (18) and (19) represent the core situation. (17) is allowed only via a marked device, i.e., case marking across clausal boundaries. In the rather natural assumption that relative markedness is somehow related to order in acquisition, the appearance of (18) earlier than (17) is directly accounted for. As for (20), the problem is solved by the very plausible assumption that the language learner abandons a core hypothesis only on the basis of evidence contradicting it. Since (20) is not found in the primary linguistic data, the child simply does not consider the marked hypothesis that would permit it. In this way, the discussed interesting observations on acquisition turn out to be perfectly compatible with the principled account of infinitival complementation proposed by Chomsky.

II. Let us now turn to a more complicated and interesting case, in which the choice of a marked option cannot be done on the basis of positive evidence only. The parameter of UG which has been more extensively studied in recent work is the so-called PRO Drop parameter: certain languages (for instance Italian) allow phonetically null subjects in tensed clauses, free subject inversion, WH extraction of the subject across an over complementizer (cfr. (21)a, (22)a, (23)a; other languages do not have these options (e.g. English: cfr. the *b* examples):

(21)a *e* verrà
   b * *e* will come

(22)a *e* verra Gianni
   b * *e* will come Gianni

(23)a *Chi* credi che *e* verrà
   b * *who* do you think that *e* will come

Intuitively speaking, the situation seems to be the following: The subject position of a tensed clause can be basically empty or transformationally vacated in the Italian language type, but not in the English language type. In recent analyses this observation is given a theoretical status by means of a general principle and a related parameter.[9] The general principle is the Emp-

---

[8]See Chomsky (1980a, b), Rouveret and Vergnaud (1980), Vergnaud (1980).

[9]See Taraldsen (1978), Chomsky (1980b) for discussion. In Rizzi (1980) a minor revision is proposed of this analysis, concerning aspects which do not directly affect the present discussion.

ty Category Principle already discussed; the parameter which has been suggested is that in the Italian language type the tensed verbal inflection is a proper governer, while in the English language type it is not. The Italian sentences are thus rescued since the ECP violation is prevented by the properly governing verbal inflection, while the English sentences are ruled out by ECP. In this way, a coherent pattern of cross-linguistic variation is given a theoretical account by localizing a single irreducible difference in the two systems (the different values assigned to the parameter), which interacts with common rules and principles producing wide and systematic differences in the languages characterized.

The question is now: On the basis of which data does the child fix the parameter for different languages? Let us first adopt the common view that no significant negative evidence is available to the language learner (see e.g., Baker, 1979, and the references quoted there). Now, the Italian side of the parameter can be learned from positive data, i.e., by hearing (21)a, (22)a, (23)a, while the English side obviously cannot. Therefore, if one wants to keep the assumption that no negative evidence is available in learning, the English-Italian comparison requires a markedness assumption: The English side of the parameter must represent the unmarked case, that is to say, the hypothesis of lower cost, which is abandoned by the learner only on the basis of contradicting positive evidence. This markedness assumption is somehow problematic since the Italian side of the parameter seems to be by far more frequently attested than the English side across languages (as noticed by Pesetsky, 1979). But one might plausible argue that statistical considerations of this type are not necessarily compelling for markedness, and that in some cases marked options might turn out to be more frequently attested than their unmarked counterparts.

Anyhow, the assumption that no negative evidence is available in learning is harder to maintain in view of more complicated cases. Consider French. French clearly belongs to the English side of the parameter, since it does not allow phonetically null subjects, free subject inversion, wh extraction of the subject (unless rescued by the *que* ⟶ *qui* rule). But French has a highly selective inversion process, the so-called "stylistic inversion," which is found in

(24)a A qui e_i a parlé Jean$_i$?
  b Où e_i est allé Jean$_i$?

This process is only permissible (in a first approximation) when the COMP is filled by a WH pronoun or trace. The most structured analysis of this phenomenon (due to Kayne, 1980) shows that the ECP violation in (24) is rescued by a highly marked process that essentially consists in assigning quantifier status to the postverbal subject, which in general is a non-quantified NP.[10] Even in absence of a full-fledged theory of syntactic

---

[10]See also Kayne and Pollock (1979).

markedness, conceived of as a formal theory of substantive syntactic universals,[11] it is rather clear that any such theory will assign highly marked status to Kayne's device, which consists in imposing to a certain element a behavior that does not correspond to the natural intrinsic properties of its category. The question is then: How does the child learning French come to such a highly marked choice? In particular, why doesn't he interpret such data as (24) as evidence for the plausibly less marked choice that in French too the verbal inflection is a proper governer, thus overextending the full range of the PRO Drop properties to the whole system in acquisition? The obvious lack of such an overgeneralization in the system finally acquired seems to require a weakening of the assumption that no negative evidence is available. But a radical weakening (direct negative evidence *is* available) would not give satisfactory results either: It would lead to the rather implausible conclusion that the highly marked device responsible for the selective inversion process in French is arrived at only when the overgeneralizing hypothesis is discarded via direct negative evidence, i.e., correction on such data as *viendra, *viendra Jean, etc.

A way out of this quasi-paradoxical situation is suggested by Chomsky with a qualification on the kinds of negative evidence possibly available:

> . . . a not unreasonable acquisition system can easily be devised with the operative principle that if certain structures or rules are not exemplified in relatively simple expressions, where they would be expected to be found, then a marked option is selected excluding them in the grammar. In this way, so-called negative evidence might be available to the "language learner", though there is reason to believe that direct negative evidence—e.g. corrections by the speech community—is not a necessary element in acquisition of grammar. [p. 000]

Such an operative principle could be implemented in several ways that I will not discuss here. Anyhow, a clear consequence of it for the case at issue is that if a certain process is found in interrogatives, relatives, etc., but not in simple declaratives, then the process is not overgeneralized from the more complex to the simpler structure; although the overgeneralization can involve a less marked device, the operative principle leads the learner to a more conservative attitude, even at the price of adopting a highly marked device. In this way, the choice of certain marked options can be accounted for without any need of postulating unattested and implausible steps and procedures.[12]

---

[11]Cf. Kean, 1979; see also van Riemsdijk, 1978, chapter 7, where a promising program for the construction of such a theory is discussed.

[12]A possibly interacting factor which is overlooked in the preceding discussion is the actual richness of the concrete verbal morphology. One might argue that the child does not consider the hypothesis that French is a PRO Drop language since its verbal morphology is not rich enough. If this is correct, we would presumably have another dimension of markedness interacting with the one discussed in the text.

3. "Move α" and LF's in Configurational and Nonconfigurational Languages. There is a question which naturally arises in connection with the proposed treatment of the syntax of nonconfigurational languages. In recent work it has been suggested that LF's of familiar languages are syntactic in nature in an interesting sense: i.e., LF's are derived from S structures via "move α," among other things. This seems to be the case at least for the aspects of LF involving the explicit representation of quantifier scope.[13] Now it is suggested in Chomsky's paper that "move α" might be incompatible in principle with nonconfigurational languages. Then, the question that arises is: How does quantification work in these languages. As far as I can see, there are essentially two possible answers, both of wich have non-trivial implications: One is that quantification works differently in these languages, and, in particular, that the level of representation "LF" in Japanese does not involve operator-variable structures. The second possible answer is that nonconfigurational S structures are mapped onto configurational intermediate representations via structure building rules in the syntax of LF; then "move α" can apply on such representations. Both possibilities sound somewhat unnatural; the second is perhaps more in the spirit of the proposal, made in the article, that grammatical functions are defined in terms of pairs of syntactic categories even in nonconfigurational languages, e.g., direct object is defined as (NP,VP) in Japanese even if, in the analysis adopted, there is no category VP in the syntax of Japanese.

There is, of course, also a third possibility which would consist in questioning the hypothesis that nonconfigurational languages are in principle incompatible with "move α." Should we expect that in no case a question or a relative clause is formed in a nonconfigurational language by moving some element to clause initial position? This question is independent from, but related to another one: should we expect that whenever "move α" is found in a grammar it necessarily performs both GF-affecting and non-GF-affecting operations? I am aware that such questions can receive an answer only through careful inspection of the properties of form and interpretation in nonconfigurational languages. But I think it is worthwhile to keep these problems in mind from the very beginning of this new line of inquiry.

REFERENCES

Aissen, J., & D. Perlmutter (1976): Clause reduction in Spanish. In *Proceedings of the II Annual Meeting of the Berkeley Linguistic Society,* University of California, Berkeley.
Baker, C. L. (1979): Syntactic Theory and the Projection Problem. In *Linguistic Inquiry,* 10.

---

[13]See Chomsky (1976), May (1977), Kayne (1979).

Belletti, A. (1980): Morphological passive and PRO Drop: A note on the impersonal construction in Italian. Unpublished manuscript, MIT.

Belletti, A., & L. Rizzi (1980): The Syntax of *ne:* Some Theoretical Implications," paper presented at the IV GLOW Conference, Nijmegen.

Bresnan, J. (1978): A Realistic Transformational Grammar. In Halle, Bresnan, & Miller (Eds.) (1978).

Chomsky, N. (1976): Conditions on Rules of Grammar. In *Linguistic Analysis, 2.*

Chomsky, N. (1980a): On Binding. In *Linguistic Inquiry,* 11.

Chomsky, N. (1980b): *Lectures on government and binding,* Foris Publications, Amsterdam (to appear).

Halle, M., J. Bresnan, & G. A. Miller (Eds.) (1978): *Linguistic Theory and Psychological Reality,* The MIT Press, Cambridge, Mass.

Kayne, R. (1979): Two Remarks on NIC. Paper presented at the IV GLOW Conference, Pisa.

Kayne, R. (1980): ECP Extensions. Manuscript, Université de Paris VIII to appear in *Linguistic Inquiry,* 11.

Kayne, R., & J. Y. Pollock (1978): Stylistic Inversion, Successive Cyclicity, and 'Move NP'. In *Linguistic Inquiry,* 9.

Kean, M. L. (1979): On a Theory of Markedness. Paper presented at the IV GLOW Conference, Pisa.

Maratsos, M. (1978): New Models in Linguistics and Language Acquisition. In Halle, Bresnan, & Miller (Eds.) (1978).

May, R. (1977): The Grammar of Quantification. PhD Dissertation, MIT.

Pesetsky, D. (1979): *COMP-Trace Phenomena, NIC and Doubly-Filled COMP's.* Unpublished paper, MIT.

Rizzi, L. (1976): La Montée du sujet, le *si* impersonnel, et une règle de restructuration dans la syntaxe italienne. In *Recherches Linguistiques,* IV.

Rizzi, L. (1980): Negation, WH Movement, and the PRO Drop Parameter. Paper presented at the V GLOW Conference, Nijmegen.

Rouveret, A., & J.-R. Vergnaud (1980): Specifying the Reference to the Subject: French Causatives and Conditions on Representations in *Linguistic Inquiry,* 11.

Ruwet, N. (1972): *Théorie syntaxique et syntaxe du Français,* Seuil, Paris.

Taraldsen, T. (1978): On the NIC, Vacuous Application, and the *That-Trace* Filter. Unpublished manuscript, MIT.

van Riemsdijk, H. (1978): *A Case Study in Syntactic Markedness,* Foris Publications, Amsterdam.

Vergnaud, J.-R. (1980): Quelques éléments pour une théorie formelle de cas, unpublished paper, Amherst.

25

Comments on Chomsky's Chapter, "On the Representation of Form and Function"

Richard S. Kayne
Université de Paris VIII

I shall focus my comments on the question: What are the building blocks of the principles and rules of universal grammar and particular grammar? One plausible candidate is grammatical relations (subject, object). For example, Chomsky suggests that a verb like 'break' in English "must be specified in the lexicon as an item that assigns a certain θ-role to its object and that (given an object) assigns a certain θ-role to its subject." And later that "in Japanese and many other languages, subjects (whether thematic or not) and only subjects can be antecedents for the reflexive element." Thus grammatical relations might enter into the formulation of rules forming part of the theory of θ-roles and part of the theory of binding.

Let me take the liberty of recasting the θ-rule for 'break' as follows, still using grammatical relations: Assign a certain θ-role to the direct object; if there is no direct object, assign that θ-role to the subject. This brings out the relationship between 'John broke the window' and 'The window broke.' Consider now the effect of this kind of θ-rule on a verb that takes an indirect object in addition to a direct object, e.g. 'show.' The corresponding pair would be 'John showed the child the window' and '*The window showed the child.' The latter is impossible, and, as far as I know, there are no English verbs that enter into such alternations. This is unexpected. Put another way, the formulation of θ-rules in terms of grammatical relations appears to be too powerful.

Concerning Japanese reflexives, there is an example due to Kuno cited by Tonoike (1980, p. 138), in which the antecedent of a reflexive is a non-subject independent topic. Thus it might be possible to characterize Japanese reflexives as requiring a non-object antecedent. But an important

453

question would still remain open: Why does there exist such a restriction on anaphora? Formulating the relevant principles in terms of grammatical relations yields no further understanding, as far as I can see.

I would like to propose, then, that grammatical relations are not among the building blocks from which the principles and rules of grammar are constructed. Instead, I would like to consider the possibility that in the two areas just discussed (thematic relations, reflexives), the correct building blocks are of a rather different sort.

Let a path P (in a (rooted) tree T) be a sequence $\{A_i\}$ $0 \le i \le n$, of distinct nodes such that $\forall$ i, $0 \le i < n$, A_i either immediately dominates or is immediately dominated by A_{i+1}. Let us call P an *unambiguous path* if P meets the following condition: $\forall$ i, $0 \le i < n$, if A_i immediately dominates A_{i+1}, then A_{i+1} is the only node in T (with the possible exception of A_{i-1}) that A_i immediately dominates. (The comparable condition for A_i immediately dominated by A_{i+1} is trivially satisfied by the lack of upward branching in *PS*-trees).

I introduce the following terminology: Let A, B be two nodes in T such that neither dominates the other. Then A *p-dominates* B $\equiv_{def}$ there exists an unambiguous path P from B to A (i.e., with B corresponding to A_0 and A to A_n). The choice of the term 'p-dominates' is meant to emphasize a partial similarity between this relation and the dominance relation (for example, with respect to what we might call 'left-local anti-symmetry': for a, b, c distinct, aRc and bRc $\longrightarrow$ *not (aRb* and *bRa)*. This holds of p-dominance and of dominance (but not of c-command)).

My hypothesis is that p-dominance, i.e., the existence of an unambiguous path in the above sense, is a necessary condition for the antecedent-anaphor relation, as well as for the government relation that Chomsky alluded to. (From this point of view, the theory of government does not underlie the theory of binding; rather both are instantiations of what might be called a theory of p-relations).

From the requirement that an anaphor must be p-dominated by its antecedent, it follows that (in a flat *VP* structure), a (direct) object cannot be the antecedent of anything. On the other hand, a subject can be the antecedent of a *NP* contained in *VP*. Similarly, a topic sister of S is permitted to be an antecedent. In other words, if we think in terms of p-dominance (and if we attribute to Japanese a certain amount of hierarchical structure), the restrictions on Japanese reflexives mentioned above become comprehensible. We may continue to use subject and object (and topic) as convenient terms to pick out certain *NP*'s, but the principles underlying the theory of binding will be built up directly from notions like p-dominance, if this approach is correct.

Since p-dominance has something in common with dominance, it is natural to introduce the notion of 'immediate p-dominance': *A immediately p-dominates* $B \equiv_{\text{def}} A$ *p*-dominates B and there is no C such that A *p*-dominates C and C *p*-dominates B. Furthermore, let us introduce the notion of p^F-dominance, where F is some property (category): A p^F-*dominates* $B \equiv_{\text{def}} A$ *p*-dominates B and A has the property (is a) F.

Combining these two, we get immediate p^F-dominance: A *immediately* p^F-*dominates* $B \equiv_{\text{def}} A$ p^F-dominates B and there exists no C such that A p^F-dominates C and C p^F-dominates B. Informally put, A immediately p^F-dominates B iff A is the 'closest' F that *p*–dominates B.

Set $F = NP$. Then we have 'immediate p^{NP}-dominance,' which can be taken to be one of the building blocks of Chomsky's (1973; 1980) Specified Subject Condition. More precisely, the *basic* case of the SSC can be formulated as follows: An anaphor must have as its antecedent that element α that immediately p^{NP}-dominates it.

Set $F = L = \{$lexical categories + COMP$\}$. Then a first approximation of the definition of government is: An NP is governed by the element α that immediately p^L-dominates it (cf. Chomsky's (in press) minimal c-command).

Thus two of the basic constructions of binding and government theory may be formulable in terms of the building blocks I have proposed. Note in particular that the *SSC* would then need to make no explicit reference to the notion 'subject'; cf. Koster, (1978, chapter 3).

Consider now the rule that determines the assignment of objective (accusative) Case in a language like English, French, or German. It can be formulated as follows: Assign accusative Case to a *NP* that is immediately p^L-dominated by a *V*. Thus accusative Case assignment uses the fact that in, e.g., $(_{VP}$ *V NP*$)$, *V* *p*-dominates *NP*.

But in such a structure, *NP* also *p*-dominates *V*, i.e., here the *p*-dominance relation is symmetric. Might some rule of Case assignment not reverse the orientation imposed on the path between *V* and *NP*, and use the *p*-dominance of *V* by *NP*? What would the result be? A natural formulation of such a rule would be the following: Assign Case X to any element α that immediately p^{NP}-dominates *V*.

Thus in '*NP* (*V NP*)', the object receives Case X. However in '*NP* (*V (PP)*)', the subject will receive Case X. In other words, a natural Case assignment rule based on 'immediate p^F-dominance' as a building block turns out to give exactly the kind of Case distribution found in what are called ergative languages.

If this is correct, then 'ergative type' Case assignment (Case X is usually called 'absolutive') is virtually identical to the more familiar 'objective type.' The only essential difference lies in the choice of orientation of the *V-NP* path. Thinking in terms of grammatical relations made the ergative-type Case marking look unnecessarily mysterious; it was never clear why Case-marking should cut across grammatical relations in just that way.

From this point of view, we can claim to have discovered one of the parameters that the language learner must set (in those instances where the choice of orientation is not determined by universal grammar), namely, the orientation to be imposed on the V-NP paths (a given language might have rules for each orientation).

Immediate p^{NP}-dominance can be used to build up a θ-rule for a verb like 'break': Assign a certain θ-role to that α which immediately p^{NP}-dominates V. This θ-rule, unlike the earlier one defined in terms of grammatical relations, has no natural extension to verbs like 'show,' as desired (in particular, the presence of an indirect object would block the rule from applying; cf. the middle construction in English ('These books don't sell *(to) linguists') which lends itself to a similar analysis, as opposed to passives).

If these suggestions are on the right track, then p-dominance is a more promising building block for the principles of universal and particular grammar than are grammatical relations.

REFERENCES

Chomsky, N. (1973) Conditions on transformations. In S. R. Anderson, & P. Kiparsky (Eds.), *A Festschrift for Morris Halle,* Holt, Rinehart and Winston, New York, 232–286.

Chomsky, N. (1980) On binding. *Linguistic Inquiry, 11,* 1–46.

Chomsky, N. (in press) Markedness and core grammar. In A. Belletti, L. Brandi, G. Nencioni, & L. Rizzi (Eds.), *Theory of Markedness in Generative Grammar* – Proceedings of the III GLOW Conference.

Koster, J. (1978) *Locality principles in syntax.* Foris Publications, Dordrecht.

Tonoike, S. (1980) Intra-Subjectivization. In Y. Otsu, & A. Farmer (Eds.), *Theoretical Issues in Japanese Linguistics (MIT Working Papers in Linguistics, 2,* 137–147.

26

The Meaning of an Experiment Combining Cognitive and Neurobiological Approaches

Jean Requin

When I was told that I would have to talk after Michael Posner, I was afraid I would have nothing to discuss, since I expected to be in complete agreement with him. After reading a preliminary draft of his paper and listening to his talk, I am only partially relieved.

Because of the large amount of information presented by Michael in support of his views, I propose to focus my comments mainly on some aspects of the theory underlying the developing concept of a cognitive neuroscience, somewhat provocatively defined as the "physiology of human cognition."

First of all, I fully agree with Michael when he suggests that the idea of developing a cognitive neuroscience must not be introduced through the classical philosophical problem of body-mind relations, but rather from an empirical point of view. That is to say the question is how can one increase or extend the interface between these two linked levels of explanation: Information processing on the one hand and the underlying brain activity on the other hand, thus extending the well-known metaphor provided by software and hardware in computers. However, one must keep in mind that neuroscientists themselves are sometimes pessimistic about the potential fecundity of such an attempt. I recall only one of the concluding remarks of Eccles in his book with Popper ("The Self and its Brain," 1977) when he wrote: "the problem of the relation between our bodies and our minds, and especially of the link between brain structures and processes on the one hand and mental dispositions on the other is an exceeding difficult one. Without pretending to be able to foresee future developments, both authors of this book think it is improbable that the problem will ever be solved, in the sense we shall really understand this relation. We think that no more can be expected than to make a little progress here or there." While I cannot, of course, adhere to such a discouraging conclusion drawn from a basically dualistic position, I am afraid that Michael's holistic position calling for some kind of integration of independently developed approaches must be moderated, or at least limited in its applicability at the present time, even though I would like to share Michael's enthusiasm.

I understand however the difficulty in resisting the excitement resulting from the fast accumulation in the last few years of a number of new powerful methods for exploring in detail brain activity, especially in awake animals and in human beings; the prospects so opened form, of course, the main justification for proceeding in organizing the extending field of cognitive neuroscience. The logical issue of such an empirical position is, I believe, well-summarized by Mountcastle's idea of "combined experiments" and their ability to "yield a deeper insight into the brain mechanisms that govern behavior," these experiments being based upon the joining of concepts and methods of neurobiology and of psychology in the same experimental strategy. It is striking, of course, that such a strategy is defended by a prominent neuroscientist who, after being deeply engaged in a strictly analytic approach of nervous mechanisms, invoked psychological concepts such as "attention" when he started single-cell recording experiments in awake monkeys. This answers the criticisms that Granit (1973) addressed some years ago against a too analytical approach to neurophysiology of motor system organization that neglects the questions of "what purpose (this organization) serves and how it responds to variations of demand," thus providing merely a body of knowledge that Granit called "an amorphous conglomerate of well-documented facts." However, I believe that the main point is to determine the necessary conditions for these "combined experiments" to be really fruitful. In my opinion, there are two dangers which must be avoided here: The first one is clearly what Michael has called "naive reductionism"—I am not sure it is so naive in fact—which can be expressed in two ways. Its extreme form tends to appear when a new advance in the field of neurobiology encourages neuroscientists to believe that they have found sufficiently sophisticated tools to permit a direct investigation of the cognitive processes that determine complex behaviors. Especially significant here is, for example, the fact that the fascinating tools provided by both the deoxyglucose and the PET (Positron Emission Tomography) techniques that Michael mentioned, were not used at first to explore brain activity related to elementary cognitive processes underlying complex behaviors, but to explore the brain activity during these complex behaviors themselves, often in loosely controlled experimental conditions. I remember that Michael quoted in his latest book (Chronometric explorations of mind, 1978) the appropriate response given by Neisser (1967) when he was explaining that "Psychology should not be viewed as just something to do until electrophysiology comes around to solve the problems.''

There also exists a more subtle form of reductionism exemplified by the use of powerful tools to explore brain activity in animals or humans performing a task chosen on the basis of technical constraints only, and not explicitly designed to solve a precise question in terms of cognitive processes. As I have already noted, some of the single-cell recording experiments conducted initially, with often somewhat disappointing results, were probably sustained by such an attitude. Of course, in such asymmetrical "combined experiments," most often the neuroscientist must call upon psychological concepts to give some ad-hoc behavioral explanation to his experimental findings, an explanation that could hardly be found—perhaps only by chance—since the experiment was generally not designed to verify any defined behavioral hypothesis.

The second danger probably results from what could be called "naive antireductionistic" attitudes. The extreme case derives from the well-admitted idea that cognitive processes on the one hand and brain activity on the other, refer to two different, even separated levels in the organization of biological reality. This extreme attitude leads to the conclusion that not only can one field not be reduced to another, but that even any attempt to find some kind of relationship between the two fields is useless, and even compromising. In a recent paper published in *Trends in Neurosciences,* Sutherland (1979) pointed out such a defensive attitude not in the European, but in the continental psychologists, who tend to avoid "taking part in the new and interdisciplinary enterprises of neuroscience and cognitive science." Of course, this cannot be applied to those who have chosen to work at the boundary of the psychological and neurobiological fields and who regard the future promise of this position to be worth its present discomfort. But here too, a more ambiguous, although complementary, defensive attitude is apparent when psychologists introduce systematically and, therefore, often arbitrarily, neurobiological methods of investigation in experiments not designed and guided by concerns for the underlying brain mechanisms. Such a practice is probably justified only by the concern for adding some kind of "scientificity" to their work. Perhaps the most relevant examples could be found in the trend of "correlation fishing" experiments, especially those in which a differential study of complex human behavior is paired with recordings of various physiological indices, such as evoked potentials autonomic activity changes, pharmacological measures, and so on . . . without any convincing justification for doing so.

In attempting to summarize what should be the necessary condition for developing a psychobiological approach to behavior, or a cognitive neuroscience, I believe that it is useful to take into consideration what Michael Posner said, namely "In the process of developing an experimental psychology of mind, it would be foolish to ignore the hints provided by modern neurophysiology" (Posner, 1978), but also what he did not say and that I propose to include as a complementary guide-line: In the process of developing a neurobiology of cognition, it would be foolish to ignore the hints provided by a century of experimental psychology. This implies that a "combined experiment" must not be an artificial linkage between concepts of one field and methods of the other, or the reverse; it must result, for each specific question, from the statement of some kind of isomorphic relationship, or at least some minimal similarity, between structural and/or functional models proposed by cognitive psychologists on the one hand and neuroscientists on the other. At least it must be sufficient to plan an experimental strategy integrating as far as possible methods of both fields. It is in this sense that I have understood the general suggestion of Michael that "cognitive scientists need to seek model cognitive systems where appropriate experimentation may yield close contact with related neurophysiology," as well as his specific proposal for defining cognitive systems themselves by analogy to neuronal systems, raising, furthermore, the unavoidable question of spatial localization of function. One may suggest, in turn, that such an effort should also be made by neuroscientists, as soon as they are interested in cognitive processes, to pay more attention to, and even to formalize, the logics of brain operations in reference to the purposive behaviors they underly.

It is clear, of course, that at any given time, the application of an integrated cognitive neuroscience approach cannot reach the same level of efficiency for all the subsets in the field. For example, if one goes back to the classification of cognitive systems that Michael proposes, one can suggest that the conditions required to interface closely cognitive psychology and neuroscience certainly exist for the "recognition system," especially considering the connections between serial models of visual information processing and the analysis of the organization of the visual neuronal system initiated for example by Hubel and Wiesel (1962); such conditions have been met too for "arousal and orienting systems," especially concerning the questions of selective attention, orienting and movement control; I am not so convinced, as far as I understand the field, that they are so adequate, at least now, for "comprehending language system," perhaps because of the specific problems raised by the privileged connections of the cognitive approach with the methods ad data provided by neuropsychology and neurology. Finally, one must admit that such a synthetic cognitive neuroscience approach is probably not relevant for many of the problems first stated in cognitive terms. In other words, no benefit could be expected, as far as one can foresee, in connecting them to some hypothetical neurobiological viewpoint.

In conclusion, I shall try to illustrate the strategy of "combined experiments" by an example drawn from my own work, namely the problem of adaptive preparatory adjustments for action that take place on the motor side of behavior, that could be called, in a Posnerian language, covert attentional mechanisms in the processing of motor information.

Very briefly, the general background of this problem is as follows (cf. Requin, 1980). Preparatory adjustments to motor activity refer to the simple idea that the efficiency of the processing systems involved in the successive operations underlying this activity can be improved in advance, as soon as information is given to the subject about what he will have to do. The application of such a notion from the psychobiological approach previously suggested supposes a minimal convergence between conceptions proposed by psychologists and by neurophysiologists concerning the structural and functional organization of motor activity itself. A popular idea in the field of information processing is that motor activity develops through three serial operations, as for example J. Theios suggested in 1975, namely the response determination process, corresponding to the retrieval of the appropriate response to a given stimulus in a S–R code stored in memory, the response program selection process, corresponding to the specification of the program determining the biomechanical properties of the motor response, and the response output process, corresponding to the execution stage of this program. If one turns now to neurophysiological data, especially those provided by single-cell recording experiments, a functional organization of nervous motor structures, which presents some analogy to the serial processing stage model of psychologists, progressively emerges. A privileged axis would be formed by a first stage, starting in the associative cortical areas and ending in the cerebellum, responsible for the action project definition, a second stage, starting in the cerebellum and ending in the precentral motor cortex, where the motor program is selected and built, and a third stage, starting in the motor cortex and ending by motoneuron activation, leading to movement execution. Thus, one can consider that the main condition required for the strategy of "combined experiments" has been realized, namely that the isomorphic relations between structural models of motor organization in both fields is sufficient to state the specific problem of preparation in the same manner: For a given stage of the model, preparatory adjustments evidenced by the adequate paradigms used by psychologists and presetting processes found by neurophysiologists in the expected corresponding structures could be considered as two versions of the same story.

The mechanisms by which the efficiency of each processing stage is modulated according to the environmental demand for movement could thus be studied from either a psychological or neurophysiological point of view. For example, the classical probability effect observed in a choice–RT paradigm is generally interpreted as a modification of the speed in setting up the appropriate search strategy in memory for discovering the correct response, this speed increasing with the probability for the response to be performed. On the other hand, there is now much data from single-cell recording experiments, especially the recent unpublished results of MacKay, showing that at what could be considered the earlier stage in motor organization, for example in the area 7 of the parietal lobe, some units respond not only when a target for a hand pointing movement is presented in the visual field (as previously found, for example by Hyvarinen, & Poranen, 1974), but also when this hand-pointing movement is performed (as shown, for example by Mountcastle, Lynch, Georgopoulos, Sakata, & Acuna, 1975). Furthermore, the activity of these units can be preset by a warning signal. Therefore, it is reasonable to perform experiments where the unitary activity of these sensori-motor structures is investigated in a choice-reaction time paradigm including probability biases between different pointing movements. But, such an experiment has never been done, as is true for a number of similar experiments which could be derived from the simple statement of some kind of isomorphic relationship between information processing models and neuronal functioning models.

Of course, what I am defending through this example is neither the viability of the specific hypotheses proposed, nor, even, the interest of the expected results themselves, but rather the validity of the experimental strategy itself. Finally, I must confess that I had to restrain my tendency to share Michael's optimistic view. It is, I believe, not surprising given the context of a French psychophysiology which has always been rather different from what is currently called psychophysiology in the Anglo-Saxon tradition but looks more, to some extent, to the strong and fast-developing psychobiological stream, now labeled cognitive neuroscience.

REFERENCES

Granit, R. Demand and accomplishment in voluntary movement. In R. B. Stein, K. G. Pearson, R. S. Smith, & J. B. Redford (Eds.), *Control of posture and locomotion*. New York: Plenum Press, 1973.

Hubel, D. H., & Wiesel, T. N. Receptive fields, binocular interaction and functional architecture in the cat's visual cortex. *Journal of Physiology*, 1962, *160*, 106–154.

Hyvarinen, J., & Poranen, A. Function of the parietal associative area 7 as revealed from cellular discharges in alert monkeys. *Brain*, 1974, *97*, 773–792.

Mountcastle, V. B. The world around us: neural command functions for selective attention. *Neural Sciences Research Bulletin*, 1976, *16*, suppl. 2.

Mountcastle, V. B., Lynch, J. C., Georgopoulos, A., Sakata, H., & Acuna, C. Posterior parietal association cortex of the monkey: Command functions for operations within extrapersonal space. *Journal of Neurophysiology*, 1975, *38*, 871–908.

Neisser, U. *Cognitive Psychology*. New York: Appleton Century Crofts, 1967.

Popper, K. R., & Eccles, J. C. *The self and its brain*. Berlin: Springer Verlag, 1977.

Posner, M. I. *Chronometric explorations of mind*. Hillsdale, N.J.: Lawrence Erlbaum Associates, 1978.

Requin, J. Toward a psychobiology of preparation for action. In G. E. Stelmach, & J. Requin (Eds.), *Tutorials in motor behavior*. Amsterdam: North Holland Publishing Company, 1980, 373–398.

Sutherland, N. S. Neuroscience versus cognitive science. *Trends in Neurosciences,* 1979, *2.*

Theios, J. The components of response latency in simple human information processing tasks. In P. Rabbitt, & S. Dornic (Eds.), *Attention and performance V*. London' Academic Press, 1975.

27 Comments on the Chapters by Shepard and Kosslyn

Pierre Jacob

I would like first to make a comment on these two chapters and then throw in a few questions to both authors for further discussion.

My comment has to do with what I think slightly distinguishes the approaches followed by Roger Shepard and by Steve Kosslyn. While both are strongly arguing for and I think convincingly demonstrating the existence of a visual or analogical mode of reasoning, they emphasize different aspects of it. And maybe the differences of emphasis show up in the different kinds of experiments they favor. Steve I think is mostly interested in the process of imagery—the relation between storage of images in long term memory and retrieval of particular images in short term memory. Roger Shepard seems to be after more abstract principles—principles of motions and transformations that preserve the rigid three-dimensional structure of objects: as if he was looking for some abstract characterization of the "competence" underlying the visual or analogical capacity. For him, it seems that this competence has to do with the class of possible abstract motions or transformations. And I was interested to hear Roger Shepard's reference to the "missing (or empty) elements" of generative linguistics. He compared those empty elements to the mental paths created by the mind in perception.

Now, Steve Kosslyn has shown how he was looking for constraints on the class of possible theories of visual thinking or imagery. And in the light of his research, I would like to pursue the following line of investigation. As everybody knows, there has been a lively controversy, generated by the work of both authors, as to the functional (as opposed to epiphenomenal) role of imagery and its reducibility to linguistic or propositional thinking. I wonder whether any experimental work has been done with the purpose of specifying a class of possible images.

So, taking the role of colors in mental images first, one could try to specify the differences between the interpretation of odd pairs of words like "a green cat" or "a red lawn" and images or lack of images. If a subject were instructed to imagine a green cat or a red lawn, what image would he get? Assuming that the propositional instruction receives a semantic interpretation of some kind, one could perhaps get information about the difference of capacity between word understanding and image forming.

Take now the famous impossible tuning-fork that one encounters in the literature. I would suggest the following line of investigation. And I wonder whether it has been pursued. On the one hand, it seems possible to give oneself propositional rules enabling one to reproduce or to copy the impossible tuning-fork, by cutting it into two pieces; a three-dimensional piece and a two-dimensional piece. So one could probably learn propositionally to draw it. But could one "naturally" or spontaneously imagine it? Is it part of the class of natural images falling within the natural image-forming capacity? If one takes mental rotation, say, as a test for what can be a natural image, is it possible to mentally rotate the impossible tuning-fork? Is it possible to discriminate between a rotation and a mirror-image of an item of the impossible tuning-fork? This line of investigation would attempt to map the difference between following propositional instructions or computing along propositional lines, and imagining or computing mental images. I don't know whether both speakers agree on the "holistic" character of visual thinking as opposed to the more analytic computations carried on propositional units.

Alternatively, one could take some odd statement, say a statement that instantiates a violation of the logical principle of contradiction, and see how it correlates with the image-forming capacity. Take the following possible argument. Suppose one says: If one understands the principle of contradiction, then presumably one must understand its negation. At least it is a reasonable assumption that adding a negation sign to a statement does not block the semantic interpretation of the statement. So, consider a particular instance of the principle of contradiction such as "It is not the case that the sky is blue and the sky is not blue." Consider now its negation: "The sky is blue and the sky is not blue." Under our previous assumption, some interpretation of this statement is possible. So a speaker of English must in some sense understand it. Now, what kind of an image could a subject associate with such a statement? That's the kind of investigation I am thinking of. And the general idea would be to try to specify the differences between the semantic interpretation (or processing) of a semantically odd statement, and the formation of mental images. In order to clarify the issue of the irreducibility of analogical reasoning with respect to propositional reasoning, I think that a reflection of this kind about the constraints specifying what is an impossible image could be useful.

Finally a last point to throw into the discussion and again relating to the interface between the two modes (propositional and analogical) of reasoning. I would like to know if the two authors think that a fruitful area might not be provided by recent discussion about the notion of "stereotype" or "prototype." In linguistic and philosophical semantic theory, there has been considerable discussion as to whether the best model for a semantic theory of natural kind terms (terms referring to natural kinds, be they mineral, chemical, physical, or biological) is a decompositional model or a stereotype model. Now, it strikes me that if the decompositional model is on the right track, then imagery plays no role in the semantics of such words. But if the stereotype model is on the right track, then imagery is intimately connected with the semantics of such terms. If the latter is right, then the semantics of words like "gold" or "tiger" involves a set of images, corresponding to a stereotypical chunk of gold or to a stereotypical tiger. Maybe processing such words involves constructing some model, with the properties attributed to mental images. And I wonder how both authors would react to such a suggestion.

28 Perception and Cognitive Properties of the Initial State

Eliane Vurpillot

I am not going to comment specifically on Elizabeth Spelke's or Dick Held's data but to contribute to the discussion by offering a few assumptions relative to cognitive properties of the initial state. These assumptions are not only mine, they were formulated after a series of discussions with André Bullinger from Geneva. Therefore I shall be speaking in both our names.

My discussion will be centered around the problem of what is identity for a very young infant (less than two months). Let me recall first a fundamental distinction between individual and categorial identity. In categorial identity, objects, events, are treated as units, which are perceived separate and different but considered as equivalent according to a criterion. In individual identity, a single object is recognized as being preserved across perceived transformations. In both kinds of identity, some perceived differences are tolerated, others are not. But in one case identity is established between many different samples, many units, whereas in the other case identity is established between successive encounters of a *single* unit.

My first assumption will be that there cannot be individual identity for an infant before the end of its first year but that categorizing begins at birth. My argument is that the notion of individual identity implies at least the permanence of objects. An impressive amount of data provided by numerous researchers demonstrates that existence and permanence of objects—as we adults define them—are not present before the end of the first year. I shall just mention the researches on Piaget's stage IV reviewed by Gratch, (1975) and recent research of Moore and col. (1978) about tracking a mobile object with temporary occlusion by screens.

Thus if we admit that for a young infant there exists no object (defined by a singularity and a permanence) this infant deals with an infinity of sensory patterns that are for him all new patterns. Nevertheless habituation can be obtained with neonates in situations controlled to eliminate an interpretation by fatigue. Steven Friedman (1972), among others, has observed a decrement in visual fixation time during repeated presentations of a checkerboard and recovery of visual response when a new checkerboard, differing in size and number of squares, was presented. This sequence of habituation/deshabituation leads us to contemplate the possibility that a 3-day-old infant can memorize and categorize.

We adults speak about checkerboards, but there is certainly nothing like a checkerboard, not even a visual target for the neonate. Its responses (visual fixations) are function of a sequence of global and indifferentiated events resulting from the temporal contiguity between a biological state, visual, postural and possibly also auditory excitations. Habituation means that the series of events involving the presence of the first checkerboard have acquired some equivalence; the change in visual excitation brought by the appearance of a different checkerboard has changed the whole event. Modification of the global event is the relevant change, *identity* is relative to the global event, not to the number or sizes of squares. In this perspective, a modification of the event can result from a change of posture, or of state, as well as of a change in the visual target. Therefore we can expect at the same time difficulties in obtaining habituation, in front of the same visual target and dishabituation, if we change the posture of the infant from supine to sitting, from asymmetrical body orientation towards left to orientation towards right, for example. Experiments are underway to test these last predictions.

We cannot explain, at least in my opinion, the phenomenon of habituation–dishabituation any more than any form of habit making in neonates if we do not assume that the infant is born with a series of expectations, which constitute the foundations of cognitive activity. So I shall assume that, before any real experience, the infant expects an event to recur and that such an expectation is the root of identity and categorizing activity. If it was not expecting the reproduction of the event it has just been experiencing, why would it be surprised by the occurrence of a different event? But probability for perfectly identical events to recur is not high, so there must exist a process of selection between relevant and irrelevant changes. Such a process might be supported by a high sensitivity of the living organism to regularities.

Modifications in nature are not random, and behavior of living creatures not totally unpredictable. Regularities, present in the infant's environment impose regularities to sensory stimulations. Jimmy Gibson (1950) has made us aware of the various regular transformations undergone by the visual proximal stimulus when a modification occurs in the physical world, and the specificity of such transformations. There are also regularities in the functioning of the living organism and in the processes of exchanges between the organism and its environment. Sensorimotor loops, like orientation reflex for example, biologic functions like digestion, unfold in a precise sequence of steps, the duration of each step not being distributed at random. Respiration, blood circulation function in a rhythmic fashion: All these functionings have regularities and their parameters vary around some optimal values.

We make the assumption that the infant is innately sensitive to regularities and built to look for them, enhance them, and finally impose them. Such ability gives the infant the possibility of extracting invariances from variations.

Let us take an example.

A baby, between 1 to 3 weeks, is awake, alert, supine or seated. A rattle is shaken on its right side. The infant turns its head towards the sound. After a long controversy, many well controlled experiments have demonstrated that such orientation reflex (not a coordination between audition and vision) can be observed at birth.

During this displacement of the head, which can also involve shoulders, three sensory modalities are stimulated: audition, proprioception, and vision. If the eyes are open during the head rotation, the pattern of excitation on the retina undergoes a regular transformation that is modified when the rattle enters the infant's visual field. The three sets of excitations (auditory, postural, visual) vary according to specific *rules* and these variations are *concomitant*. When the infant faces the rattle, the head movement stops and for a period of time a retinal pattern involving the rattle occurs simultaneously with the sound of the rattle and a certain posture of head and body (if we left the body free to move). The simultaneous transformation of visual, auditory and postural excitations, constitute an event. Possibly the final stage is another event.

Through repetitions of these events, the infant becomes more and more sensitive (1) to the multiple regularities produced in the course of the event and (2) to their concomitance, which is a special kind of regularity. If the event were always identical the infant would not make much cognitive progress.

But in real life a situation is rarely reproduced identically. Sometimes the rattle will be shaken nearer sometimes farther from the ears, or on the other side of the head, or another sound than that of a rattle will be produced, or the infant will be held in arms instead of supine, etc. In these cases part of the regularities will be disrupted. First, search disruption will be perceived as the occurrence of another event but some part of the regularities, at least the concomitance between excitations, the sequence of steps of the reflex will remain constant and the infant will progressively come to differentiate between visual regularities and postural regularities and consequently between visual events and postural events. From this time onwards it will become possible for identity between visual events to be maintained despite changes in posture.

We come to a last assumption: the sensitivity to regularities on the one hand, and to their disruption on the other hand is the key to differentiation between sensory modalities, then to extraction of perceptual invariants (constancy, distinction between rigid and non-rigid movements), to the differentiation between action and stimulation self and not self, etc.

REFERENCES

Friedman, S. Habituation and recovery of visual response in the alert human newborn. *Journal of Experimental Child Psychology,* 1972, *13,* 339–349.

Gibson, J. J. *The perception of the visual world.* Boston, Houghton Mifflin, 1950.

Gratch, G. Recent studies based on Piaget's view of object concept development. In L. B. Cohen, & P. Salapatek (Eds.), *Infant perception: From sensation to cognition.* New York, Academic Press, 1975.

Moore, M. K., Burton, R., & Darby, B. Z. Visual tracking in young infants: evidence for identity or object permanence? *Journal of Experimental Child Psychology,* 1978, *25,* 183–198.

Author Index

Numbers in *italics* denote pages with complete bibliographic information.

Subject Index